Bush v. Gore

BUSH v. GORE

Exposing the Hidden Crisis
in American Democracy

Charles L. Zelden

University Press of Kansas

Published by the University Press of Kansas (Lawrence, Kansas 66045), which was organized by the Kansas Board of Regents and is operated and funded by Emporia State University, Fort Hays State University, Kansas State University, Pittsburg State University, the University of Kansas, and Wichita State University

Library of Congress Cataloging-in-Publication Data

Zelden, Charles L., 1963–
 Bush v. Gore : exposing the hidden crisis in American democracy /
Charles L. Zelden.
  p. cm.
 Includes bibliographical references and index.
 ISBN 978-0-7006-1593-3 (cloth : alk. paper)
 1. Bush, George W. (George Walker), 1946– —Trials, litigation, etc. 2.
Gore, Albert, 1948– —Trials, litigation, etc. 3. Contested
elections—United States. 4. Contested elections—Florida. 5.
Presidents—United States—Election—2000. I. Title.
 KF5074.2.Z445 2008
 342.73'07—dc22
                    2008014477

British Library Cataloguing-in-Publication Data is available.

Printed in the United States of America

10 9 8 7 6 5 4 3 2 1

CONTENTS

The Case That Must Be Named

Has *Bush v. Gore* Become the Case That Must Not Be Named? . . .
The ruling that stopped the Florida recount and handed the presidency to
George W. Bush is disappearing down the legal world's version of the memory
hole, the slot where, in George Orwell's "1984," government
workers disposed of politically inconvenient records.
—*Adam Cohen,* New York Times, *August 15, 2006*

Bush v. Gore. Just whisper the name of the case that ended the 2000 presidential election and you are likely to get one of three responses: a yawn of active indifference ("not that again"), teeth-grinding anger at the Supreme Court and the presidency of George W. Bush ("let me tell you. . . ."), or an eye-roll of frustration ("Get over it already, Bush won!").

Two things tie these disparate responses together—their shared disdain for the event and their tendency to treat the case in only the most superficial, dismissive, and unwelcoming ways. The indifferent do not understand what all the furor is about. As far as they are concerned, 2000 was a long time ago and *Bush v. Gore* has about as much meaning to their lives as the French and Indian War or the fall of Rome. The angry cannot get past the Supreme Court having picked a president, one whom they object to and who became president by a means they find illegitimate. To them, *Bush v. Gore* was a disastrous decision best forgotten. The frustrated see *Bush v. Gore* as finished and settled. The Supreme Court did what was necessary to resolve an electoral crisis and Bush became president. In their view, there is no reason to discuss the case or its aftermath.

It was with these attitudes in mind that Adam Cohen of the *New York Times* editorial board declared in August 2006 that *Bush v. Gore* had become "the case that must not be named." In Cohen's words, the ruling that stopped the Florida recount and handed the presidency to George W. Bush had "disappeared down the legal world's version of the memory hole, the slot where, in George Orwell's '1984,' government workers disposed of politically inconvenient records." To prove his claim, Cohen noted how the Supreme Court had not cited *Bush v. Gore* even once since it was decided—nor had the lower federal courts made much reference to the case. Even Justice Antonin Scalia, who loves to hold forth on court precedents, snapped in early 2006 when asked about the case at a forum, "Oh God. Get over it." *Bush v. Gore*, Cohen concluded, had become the "non-person" of Supreme Court decisions.

Even the legal academy has joined this conspiracy of indifference, disregard, and silence. Cohen describes a fall 2005 law school Supreme Court conference featuring a panel on "The Rehnquist Court." To his surprise, not one panelist mentioned *Bush v. Gore*—nor did anyone ask about the case during the question-and-answer period. When Cohen asked a prominent law professor about this strange omission, the professor explained that he had been invited to participate in another Rehnquist retrospective where he was told in advance that *Bush v. Gore* would not be discussed. The same ground rule was probably operating in this panel as well, the professor explained.[1]

Cohen's characterization of *Bush v. Gore* is all too accurate. After a surge of books and articles in 2001 and 2002, writing on the case has dropped off to practically nothing. Except for a handful of legal scholars in the subfield of election law, an occasional mention in popular books on election fraud, and the requisite three to five parenthetical references ("and then there was *Bush v. Gore*") in histories of the Rehnquist Court, it was as if *Bush v. Gore* had never happened.[2] Even those who do write extensively about the case use evocative titles, such as "The Untimely Death of *Bush v. Gore*" and "Please Don't Cite This Case!: The Precedential Value of *Bush v. Gore*."[3] In sum, as far as academia in particular and the nation in general are concerned, *Bush v. Gore* is dead—an ignored remnant of the past best forgotten.

Such willful historical amnesia about a pivotal electoral and constitutional crisis resolved by an unprecedented and controversial Supreme Court decision is a mistake, however. The events of 2000 were, to use Thomas Jefferson's famous description of the controversy over slavery, a "firebell in the night"—a warning that bad things were happening and that, if not faced and responded to, would produce catastrophic results.

Too many writers on *Bush v. Gore* tend to treat the result—the picking of a president of the United States by a five-to-four vote of the justices of the U.S. Supreme Court—as the entire story. By contrast, the central message of the crisis of 2000 and the case of *Bush v. Gore*—lost in the furor over the judicial picking of a president—should be that the United States has a broken electoral system. That electoral system's problems include:

- voting machines that we know are inaccurate, unverifiable, or both, but that we use anyway;
- partisan election officials lacking expert training who consistently use the power of their office legally, but unethically, to give the advantage to their party's candidates—often providing the deciding factor as to who wins in a close election;
- out-of-date, ambiguous, and inconsistent election statutes that not only dif-

fer from state to state, but that administrators and judges often apply differently within the same state;

- a constant tension between the goals of empowering the voter and maintaining the vote's purity and accountability;
- a growing level of knee-jerk partisanship in which each side sees the other
  as "the enemy" and thus makes winning more important than upholding
  the system by which we choose our leaders;
- an increasing willingness to turn to the courts to settle complex electoral
  questions—not only after, but often before, the electoral process has run its
  full course;
- the tendency to resort to such desperate means as outright cheating to win,
  while rationalizing those means as efforts to protect the system from "the
  enemy" who is supposedly bent on subverting it;
- the growing gap between the need for an impartial, nonpartisan, adequately
  funded, and professionally run means of administering our electoral system
  and the partisan, amateur, underfunded means by which we hold elections
  at all levels of government;
- the mismatch between the growing nationalization of American society and
  the continuing local character of our system of holding elections and counting votes (producing widely disparate results in the application of electoral
  procedures).

Of what use is a firebell in the night if no one listens to it? What good is a
democracy if there is no way effectively to determine the will of the people? How
can we call ourselves a democracy—let alone present ourselves to the world as the
exemplar of democracy—while allowing such practices to continue unchecked?
These are the hidden dilemmas and challenges laid bare by *Bush v. Gore*—the ongoing failure of the American electoral system to adequately reflect the collective
will of the American people as expressed through their votes. As historian Alexander Keyssar notes in his book *The Right to Vote*, "a nation certainly could have universal suffrage without being a democracy, [but] a polity cannot be truly
democratic without universal suffrage."[4] And a vital component of any effective
system of universal suffrage worthy of the name is a working electoral system in
which every vote counts—and every citizen who wants to vote is able to cast a
ballot.

Bush v. Gore, if understood correctly, makes clear the need for essential electoral
reforms—reforms which, in the fallout of the postelection meltdown, were not
only essential but achievable. Sadly, our focus on the Supreme Court's picking of
a president has obscured these facts both in the immediate aftermath of the election and the present as well. Continuing to view the events of 2000 through such
a narrow window has been a mistake—and still remains one today. Thus we ignore
this ruling and its lessons at our peril.

And so, like investigators of a catastrophic train wreck or airplane crash or bridge collapse, we must put aside any preconceived notions and concerns and re-examine all of the available evidence of the 2000 electoral and constitutional crisis, considering as many of the factors that contributed to it as we can identify. Further; we must look beyond the obvious explanations and problems (such as who won the presidency and how) while not ignoring them; we must sift through the available arguments and draw out what is useful from each; and most important, we must begin to construct a response to our analysis of the event that will help to prevent the problems that caused it from causing another such calamity.

This book proposes to begin the construction of just such a revised perspective on the events of November and December 2000 and the Supreme Court's ruling in *Bush v. Gore*. It asks readers to put their emotions to one side; to understand that *Bush v. Gore* raises questions beyond the picking of a president; and, most important of all, to look at the crisis of 2000 and *Bush v. Gore* with an open mind. For *Bush v. Gore* is the case that *must* be spoken of—and thought about, and debated, and finally understood in its wider historical context.

Before we go on, a few words on what this book is, and what it is not, are necessary. First, this is not an attempt to write the definitive history of *Bush v. Gore* and the 2000 election. Not until all the participants die and their papers become available to historians can such a history even be contemplated. Rather, this is an effort to place the election and case into its wider historical context and to build from that context a deeper understanding of what was at stake in November and December 2000—of what was possible and what was actually attempted. *Bush v. Gore* was not the first nor even the twentieth case before the federal courts dealing with questions of electoral processes and even electoral outcomes. To view the case outside this context, as many previous commentators have done, or to merely contrast this ruling doctrinally with those that came before it (as other commentators have), is to miss much of its significance as both a historical event and, more importantly, as a virtual firebell in the night warning us of the danger to America's experiment in popular government.

Similarly, this is not a book about electoral reform, at least, per se. The problems and difficulties of our electoral system—and the need for reform—underlay the structure and importance of what follows, but they are not the primary focus of this book. This is first and foremost a work of history. As such, its primary goal lies in exploring and explaining past events. It is the events and lessons of 2000 that concern us here—and the ways that we attended to, or did not attend to, those lessons. How those lessons could be implemented into a reform program today and in the future, though hinted at briefly in the concluding chapters, is a topic left to other books.

Moreover, the book's focus on the broader context of the case does not mean that it ignores or devalues the importance of the election's immediate outcome. One of the most distinctive aspects of this case was the unprecedented nature of five judges picking a president. That fact stated, however, we should not overstate its importance, either. Had the electoral system worked effectively in 2000, the justices never would have had the chance—or the need—to pick anyone. Underlying the Court's role in this case, in other words, is the wider story of democracy in America and its growing fragmentation under the dual influences of social change and political partisanship.

It is in this light, therefore, that I ask you, the reader, to place your personal views of both candidates and the 2000 election's final outcome on hold when reading this book. If we are to truly understand the lessons of 2000 and the wider significance of *Bush v. Gore*, we must be willing to view both events independent of the merits of the candidates and our personal views of their virtues and/or failings. In particular, how we view the long-term effects of George W. Bush's presidency—positive or negative—should not be allowed to interfere with our efforts to understand within its own historical and doctrinal context the constitutional significance of the postelection crisis and the Supreme Court's ruling in *Bush v. Gore*. This is not to say that an outcome that saw George W. Bush take the oath of office was—or is—unimportant. The events of 2000 set the stage for the next eight years of politics in the country. Books have already been written seeking to evaluate the impacts of George W. Bush's presidency, and many more are sure to follow.[5] However, permitting our knowledge of the events following the Supreme Court's December 12 ruling to shape our understanding of these proceedings is not only ahistorical, it effectively hides the many important wider issues raised by this case—issues that quickly moved beyond the candidates or politics to the failings of the electoral process itself. It also permits our emotions to rule our intellect, in the process undercutting our understanding of the events of November and December 2000. As the words of English writer Rebecca West remind us, "To understand is not to forgive. It is only to understand. It's not an end but a beginning. Knowledge is power."[6]

In a related vein, I ask for your patience in dealing with the legal and factual complexities associated with these matters. Election law and procedures can be as complex and opaque as the Talmud or the philosophical arguments of a Jesuit. I have made every effort to cut through the legal jargon and lay out the issues in as straightforward a manner as possible. However, the intricacies of the law often demand a certain level of technical detail to portray accurately the events and the legal reasoning being described. Please have faith that all will be made as clear as possible as the narrative continues to its conclusion.

Another area of likely confusion is the case title or term "*Bush v. Gore*." In this book, "*Bush v. Gore*" is used in two differing, but related ways. On the one hand, it refers directly to the Supreme Court ruling that ended the 2000 presidential election controversy. In this context, the term relates specifically to the doctrinal issues raised in the case—the arguments, precedents, and eventual rulings. On the other hand, the phrase "*Bush v. Gore*" also has come to denote the entire legal and political conflict over who won the Florida vote—for after all, in the end, what occurred in Florida really was a battle between Bush and Gore. Here the term encompasses over forty different litigations (including the final case actually named *Bush v. Gore*) and thirty-six days of political and legal conflict. Ultimately, what ties these two terms together is the fact that the narrower, technical *Bush v. Gore* is actually a subset of the larger, more conceptual use of this term—and that the actions of the Supreme Court in the narrower *Bush v. Gore* can only be understood in the context of the issues raised by the wider conflict. In most instances, the meaning of the term "*Bush v. Gore*" should be obvious by its context.

Lastly, I ask for patience for dealing with the narrative complexities of the 2000 postelection crisis. A lot of action and reaction was crammed into a mere thirty-six days. From multiple court cases being argued in multiple levels and jurisdictions of courts (often on the same day), to the interplay of political events with legal events and the complex chronology mixing vote counting with court cases and the ongoing public relations debate, it is almost impossible to produce a single-strand narrative. Even the best narratives of these events to date—the Washington Post's *Deadlock*, Jeff Toobin's *Too Close to Call*, and Jack Tapper's *Down and Dirty*[7]—are often little more than short snapshots of events (or parts of events) linked together by date as closely as possible. While such an approach makes clear the whirlwind of action taking place, it also makes it difficult to see the internal workings of the litigation process and the conceptual (as opposed to chronological) links between all of the litigations leading up to *Bush v. Gore*—not to mention linking all this to the political events surrounding the court cases. This book therefore discusses each separate event in its totality (or as much as possible), covering the same ground chronologically over and over again to build up a three-dimensional depiction of these events. The drawback to this approach is the potential for confusion as to what was happening when and in relation to what other events. The advantages, however, largely outweigh the disadvantages.

To help the reader with any confusion over the sequence of events, appendix 1, "A Timeline of Events," provides a chronology of significant developments. Chapters 1–3 set the stage, outlining the key events of November and December 2000—the election, the vote counting, and the political infighting—that led to litigation. Chapter 4 deals with the many categories of cases that, for one reason or another, did not end up in the U.S. Supreme Court. Chapter 5 sets out the debate that led to the U.S. Supreme Court's first foray into these matters—the fight over certification deadlines. Chapters 6–8 then discuss the many facets of the election contest litigation that became the second and final case argued before the High Court, *Bush v. Gore*. Finally, chapter 9 breaks down and explains the issues and arguments

raised in the Supreme Court's *Bush v. Gore* ruling, in the process exploring the possible motivations on the part of the individual justices in ruling as they did. Meanwhile, chapter 10 discusses the events and litigations in the years that followed, taking the narrative to the present. Finally, an afterword seeks to provide closure and a summary of the some of the lessons to be learned from this entire set of events. Appendix 2, "A Note on Methodology," concludes the book.

ACKNOWLEDGMENTS

The truism that no book is written alone—no matter what the author's byline says—is very true in this instance. Many individuals and organizations have aided me in the completion of this book. And I am grateful for all of their help and support.

Most of the archival research for this book was completed online. I am grateful to the original posters of court documents for their efforts and to the library staffs of Stanford University, University of Michigan, and Florida State University for hosting and maintaining these useful resources. The same thanks are due to the staffs of the Legal Information Institute at Cornell University, Findlaw.com, and JURIST Legal News and Research at the University of Pittsburgh's School of Law.

I am also grateful for the gracious help I received from the reference librarians and acquisitions staff of the Alvin Sherman Library, Research, and Information Technology Center at Nova Southeastern University (NSU). The paper and electronic resources provided by the library proved invaluable in researching this book.

While Dean Don Rosenblum of the Farquhar College of Arts and Sciences at NSU could not excuse me from my teaching duties, he and the Division of Humanities director Marlisa Santos did work with me to set up a teaching schedule that allowed ample time for writing. I thank them for this flexibility and support.

My colleagues in the Division of Humanities at NSU provided not only moral support but a ready ear, a welcoming shoulder, and a critical perceptiveness as I coped with the stresses associated with writing this book. I am especially thankful to Marlisa Santos, the department staff (Santa Alemonte, Kelly Little, and Rachel Johnson), and to Professors Stephen Levitt, Gary Gershman, Jim Doan, David Kilroy, and Tim Dixon. Tim Dixon also read over each of the chapters and his comments proved most helpful as I revised and polished the book.

Longtime friends Brad and Jenny Cohen, Brian and Luda Cohen, David and Heidi Needleman, Robin Sherman, Connie Killebrew, Sue Danis, David Narrett, Andy Cove, Carol Franko, and Tamsen Valior, all provided much-needed support and encouragement.

Many colleagues from colleges and universities around the nation provided essential assistance during the writing of this book. Tom Mackey of the University of Louisville read the entire manuscript and his comments proved invaluable in revising the book. Brian Dirck, Mel Urofsky, Tim Heubner, Josiah Daniel, Sally Hadden, Carla Spivack, and Felice Batlan all provided much-needed encouragement. Finally, David Koenig of Washington University in St. Louis helped set the stage for my research and writing when, informed of my intent to write a book about *Bush v. Gore*, he responded with outrage against the Court majority and its ruling—some six years after the decision had been handed down. It was at that moment that I understood just how controversial and emotional a topic this case could be for those who had followed its twists and turns throughout November and December 2000.

I would also like to thank the administration and faculty of the Oklahoma City University College of Law for allowing me to present my findings at their school in February of 2007. Their comments, questions, and suggestions proved most helpful in the revising of this manuscript.

Not enough can be said about Mike Briggs and the entire staff at the University Press of Kansas. Their support in the writing, and especially the revising, of this book was beyond estimate. I am especially grateful to the three readers who reviewed the manuscript for the press. Their insightful and well-taken advice on the original drafts of the manuscript made this a much, much better book.

I also want to thank the many students in my classes at NSU in 2006 and 2007. Miraculously, no matter what the topic I was teaching, I could always find a link to *Bush v. Gore*—often more than once. I am grateful for their patience and humor in the face of my obsessive focus on this book and the topics it covers.

This book would not have the form it has today without the training I received from my graduate advisor, Harold M. Hyman. While the process was often frustrating and even painful, whatever skills I possess as a historian originate in his teachings. From the first day as a graduate student—when he told me to pick a topic and start researching and writing about it—to advice given over the last decade and a half, Professor Hyman has provided me with a model of dedication and ability that I have sought to emulate to my benefit.

I would also like to thank my family—my mother Janice, my sister Renee, my wife Lynn, and my daughter Miriam—with as strong a thanks as possible. More than anyone else, they had to put up with the obsessiveness that is my normal writing mode. I know that it was often not easy to be around me as I wrote, and I am indebted to their forbearance and support.

Finally, I would like to dedicate this book to R. B. Bernstein—colleague, friend, brother—who not only provided essential moral and technical support, but read and commented on every word in this book. He also helped argue out with me the most complicated issues raised by the postelection crisis and the multiple litigations it spawned. Without his help, whatever quality this book has achieved would have been vastly diminished. If I could make this paragraph light up like a neon sign I would. Richard's help was that important to the completion of this book. More importantly, Richard's friendship is that important to my life.

Bush v. Gore

CHAPTER ONE
A Vote Too Close to Call

> We thought it would be close. But never in my wildest
> dreams did I ever think it would be this close.
> —*Florida Governor Jeb Bush*

> As the presidential election drama unfolded in Florida last November,
> one thought was foremost in my mind: there but for the grace of God go I.
> Because the truth is, if the presidential margin had been razor thin in Georgia
> and if our election systems had undergone the same microscopic scrutiny
> that Florida endured, we would have fared no better. In many respects,
> we might have fared even worse.
> —*Cathy Cox, Chief Election Official of Georgia*

November 7, 2000. Election Day. As they do every four years, Americans across the nation went to the polls to cast their votes for president. In fire stations and public libraries, in Rotary clubs and city halls, an estimated 100 million Americans participated in the pivotal act of democracy—the simple act of voting.

Throughout the day, tracking polls showed a very close election. As late as 4 p.m. eastern standard time (EST), CNN's senior political analyst, Bill Schneider, informed his colleagues, "It's going to be very close." How close? A dead tie, he responded—48 percent to 48 percent on the national popular vote. He suggested that they get ready for a long night.[1]

That night, the television networks began to report the returns. Using data provided by Voter News Service (VNS), an organization (jointly owned and governed by five networks and the Associated Press [AP]) that had conducted exit polls from sample precincts all day long, as well as from counted returns, the networks began "calling" the election state by state. At first, events seemed to be going according to the usual script. One by one, moving generally westward, the networks called individual states for George W. Bush, the Republican, or Albert Gore Jr., the Democrat. At the bottom of the screen, a running count of the Electoral College vote (whose number is the pivotal one in choosing the new president) showed that the tracking polls were correct: this election was going to be one of the closest races in modern American history.

Most closely watched were the so-called swing states: Ohio, Pennsylvania, Michigan, Missouri, Wisconsin, Washington, and, above all, Florida. These states would determine the election's outcome. In fact, Gore had gambled his entire presidential campaign on a swing-states strategy. Win Pennsylvania, Michigan, and Florida, his strategists promised, and the election was his. By contrast, Bush had to win Ohio, a couple of midwestern states, and Florida. As the night progressed, each candidate had reason to cheer. Gore won Pennsylvania by over 4 percent. Michigan and Wisconsin were also Gore victories. Ohio, on the other hand, went to Bush with a margin of 3.5 percent. So too, Bush took Missouri with a 3.34 percent margin. Bush even won the normally Democratic state of West Virginia and Gore's home state of Tennessee.[2]

And then there was Florida.

In Florida, the count progressed slowly. With only about 4 percent of the vote counted, George Bush had a 6 percent lead. However, VNS tracking polls, which had been closely shadowing the Florida election all day, showed Al Gore with a "substantial" victory margin over Bush of 6 percent. By 7:45 p.m., VNS statisticians were reporting to the networks that they were 99.5 percent sure of a Gore victory in Florida (meaning that they projected only 1 chance in 200 that they were wrong). At 7:48 p.m., NBC became the first network to call Florida for Gore. By 8:02 p.m., all five networks and the AP had placed Florida in the Gore column. It looked like a Gore victory. Even George Bush "got the smell" of defeat as he contemplated leaving his campaign headquarters for the Texas governor's mansion.[3]

Then it happened. At a little after 10 p.m. EST, the networks pulled Florida off the table and placed it in the "too close to call" category. It seemed that the actual returns coming in from Florida did not match the tracking poll's projections. With 24 percent of the precincts reporting statewide, Bush led Gore by 3 percentage points. Worse yet, one of the key VNS statistical estimates—known as CORE 13 (which used a county-by-county reporting system)—had Bush ahead by 7.3 points. While the more general VNS exit-polling data still had Gore winning by between 4 and 10 percentage points, this new information was cause for rethinking who had won Florida. Then, at 9:38 p.m., VNS reported that some of its polling data were wrong. A Florida keypunch operator had erroneously given 98 percent of the Duval County vote to Gore. (Around this time surfaced as well the rumors of tens of thousands of elderly, mostly Jewish voters in Palm Beach County mistakenly voting for third-party candidate Pat Buchanan—a most unlikely choice for this particular group of voters to have made—due to a misleadingly designed "butterfly ballot"). Faced with questionable data, the networks felt it prudent to back off their predictions for Florida.

What exit polls said should have been a straightforward win by a margin of over 10,000 or more votes for Al Gore was suddenly a very close race once again. So events stood for the next few hours. As late as 1:45 a.m., CNN commentator Hal Bruno was still reporting a dead heat. Florida, Bruno noted, "has gotten so close now that there's just absolutely no way of counting it until probably every last vote is in." However, the numbers soon changed. By 2:00 a.m., VNS reports showed Bush ahead with a lead of slightly more than 29,000 votes with 96 percent of the vote counted. Eight minutes later, an erroneous report out of Volusia County gave

Bush an extra 20,000-plus votes for a lead of over 51,000 votes. (A faulty computer memory card in the tabulation machine had *subtracted* more than 16,000 votes from Gore's total and added those votes to Bush's total. In addition, an apparent reporting error in Brevard County reduced Gore's total by an additional 4,000 votes.) By this time, only about 3 percent of the state's precincts remained outstanding. With so few votes remaining to be counted (VNS erroneously estimated that only some 180,000 votes remained uncounted) and given Bush's lead of 51,000 votes, the networks began to alter their stance on Florida. Fox News was the first to jump at 2:15 a.m. NBC gave the race to Bush one minute later, followed in another minute by CNN and CBS, and finally by ABC at 2:20.[4]

Placing Florida in the Bush column was momentous. By this time, the networks had already called most of the other states for either Bush or Gore. Based on their records, they estimated that Gore had 255 electoral votes, while Bush had gained 246. To win the presidency, a candidate needs a minimum of 270 votes out of a total electoral vote of 538. Only three states remained undecided—New Mexico, Oregon, and Florida. Yet it was Florida with its 25 electoral votes that was the key. Neither New Mexico nor Oregon alone had enough electoral votes to assure either candidate victory. Win Florida, on the other hand, and you win the election regardless of the outcome in the other two states; lose Florida and victory out west meant nothing. So by calling Florida for Bush, the networks in essence were declaring George W. Bush the next president of the United States. Soon word came that Vice President Gore—discouraged by the reported returns and feeling that a quick concession was best for the country—had conceded the election to Bush. The long night seemed to have reached an end.[5]

Then it happened—again. As the Florida returns continued to show an unchanging statistical tie, word came down to the networks at 3:40 a.m. that Gore had rescinded his concession. It turned out that over 400,000 votes remained to be counted in Florida. Many of those votes were in Democratic strongholds—Broward, Palm Beach, and Miami-Dade counties. As Nick Baldick, Gore's lead adviser in Florida, informed the Nashville team, given the votes still to be counted, "we're either gonna win by 50 or lose by 100." Anyway you cut it, Baldick concluded, "this thing's still too close" to call. At 2:48 a.m., Volusia County had retracted its vote total, lowering Bush's lead to 39,600. Soon after, a chunk of Palm Beach County's vote arrived, lowering Bush's advantage still further to 11,000. Ten minutes later, it was down to 10,000 votes. By 3:40 a.m., Bush's lead over Gore was a mere 6,060 votes—out of a total vote of some 5.6 million cast statewide. Realizing that with so narrow a margin of victory Florida law called for automatic recounts, the Gore team had decided to wait on results before formally conceding the race. Still the tally narrowed. By 3:57 a.m., the difference between the two candidates was less than 2,000 votes. By this time, the networks accepted their mistake and returned Florida to the "too close to call" column.[6]

By morning, 1,600 votes—a difference of less than .005 percent—separated the candidates. George W. Bush was still on top, but with absentee ballots un-counted and with Florida law requiring an automatic recount where vote tallies were this close, no one could say with certainty who had carried the state, and thus who won the election. As events proved, the election's outcome remained up in the air for the next thirty-six days. In the end, it took a controversial Supreme Court decision to determine the winner in Florida and hence the forty-third President of the United States.

Observers had known for weeks that the 2000 presidential election would be one of the closest presidential campaigns in memory. On October 15, the *New York Times* reported a "presidential race . . . so agonizingly tight" that—in the words of Senator Robert G. Torricelli, Democrat of New Jersey—"any false move could cost one of these guys the presidency of the United States." For months, the two candidates had been leapfrogging each other in the polls. Whereas Bush had shown an early lead in the polls, the difference was narrowing as the campaigning came to a close. On October 21, for instance, an ABC News poll showed Bush with a slight lead of 3 to 4 percent. Three days later, a merging of the major daily tracking polls showed a statistical dead heat (Bush 46 percent, Gore 44 percent, with a mar-gin of error between 3 and 4 percent). This dead heat remained in effect a week later, with Bush and Gore each drawing 45 percent of the "likely vote" according to the *New York Daily News*. On November 6, one day before the election, the polls still showed a statistical dead heat between the candidates in the popular vote.[7]

Similarly, the Electoral College vote was too close to call. In late October, na-tional polling showed George W. Bush safely ahead in Texas, the Deep South, and most of the landlocked West. Vice President Gore knew from the same sources that he had a commanding lead in most of the Northeast and the Pacific Coast states. Yet these results still left eighteen "swing states"—with a combined total of over 200 electoral votes—in which polling numbers were so close that the ultimate winner was anyone's guess. By November, the number of swing states had fallen to a dozen (representing 125 electoral votes) as the industrial Midwest began to show clear preferences, some states for Al Gore (Illinois, Pennsylvania), others for George W. Bush (Ohio, Indiana). What remained were an array of smaller states, each with a handful of electoral votes, and Florida with its 25 votes.

The potential winning combinations were endless. Bush, for instance, could win by taking Florida and Ohio—along with Tennessee, Missouri, and a small state or two such as West Virginia. Gore needed to capture most of the open Mid-west states and either Florida or a combination of smaller states including Arkansas and his home state of Tennessee. Alternately, taking Pennsylvania and Florida took pressure off the Midwest states. "We're going out of our heads trying to work out all the various possibilities, so we can allocate time and money accordingly," noted a Gore strategist on November 4. "It's come down to this: Maine and Nebraska both can divide their electoral votes, and we have people trying to figure out how to capitalize on that anomaly. One electoral vote, two, maybe three" could decide the election.[8]

The election was so close, in fact, that many speculated on the eve of Election Day that one candidate (Bush) could win the popular vote while the other (Gore) would win the electoral vote and thus the presidency. Unwilling to accept this turn of events, even though the existence of side-by-side systems of popular and electoral votes made it an ever-present possibility in presidential elections, the Bush team had prepared to launch a campaign to convince the nation's 538 electors to ignore state-by-state results and instead honor the popular vote by voting for Bush. "The one thing we don't do is roll over," noted a Bush aide to the *New York Daily News*. "We fight." The Gore team was set to fight as well. Asked what would happen if the "what if" scenario came out the other way, a Gore campaign official told the *News*, "Then we'd be doing the same thing Bush is apparently getting ready for. They're just further along in their contingency thinking than we are. But we wouldn't lie down without a fight, either."[9]

Even though neither candidate had to win Florida, capturing the electoral votes of the Sunshine State was the surest way to victory. The electoral math was clear: lose Florida, and you had to win almost all the remaining swing states to top 270 electoral votes; win Florida and you only needed a couple more states to get over the top. Both candidates felt that they had a good chance to win Florida. George W. Bush could not help but be confident. When he looked at Florida, he saw a state whose legislature and congressional delegations were controlled by Republicans, whose voting record in presidential elections since 1954 had leaned mostly Republican, and whose governor was his own brother, Jeb. Gore, on the other hand, saw a state with more registered Democrats than Republicans; one with large concentrations of elderly, Jewish, and minority voters thought likely to vote Democratic; a state with a strong economy for which he could take credit; and, most of all, a state that he and Bill Clinton had won four years earlier.[10]

Actually, both candidates were accurate in their assessments of Florida's political landscape—which should have been a hint of the troubles to come. Florida in 2000 was a microcosm of the nation: diverse, conflicted, and highly partisan. In 1959, Florida was a largely rural state with a population of 2.7 million. By 2000, Florida had 15.9 million residents living mostly in urban areas. In the 1950s Florida was a stereotypical southern state filled with residents who proudly called themselves "southerners" and even "crackers." By 2000, Florida was one of the most diverse states in the Union. Anglos made up the largest segment (65.4 percent) of the population, with Latinos coming in at 16.8 percent and blacks at 14.6 percent. The Anglo population, however, was not the southern mix of earlier times. Steady migration from the North had transformed the ethnic and regional makeup of the state's white population. The same was true of the Latino population, where Cubans no longer were the dominant subgroup. Even the black population split between traditional African Americans and those of Afro-Caribbean origin. Age was also a factor. Nearly one in five Florida residents was 65 years or older—and while these voters had largely voted Republican in past elections, given the long and continuing debates on the future of Medicare and Social Security, how they would vote in November 2000 was impossible to predict. Adding to the complexities, many of the state's residents were immigrants or the children of recent immigrants. For many, this would be the first election in which they were participating.[11]

Politically, Florida split almost evenly between Democrat and Republican—at least in terms of registered voters. Forty-three percent of voters registered as Democrats in 2000, while 39 percent registered as Republicans. An additional 15 percent identified themselves as independents. The large proportion of independent voters combined with the evenly matched parties seemed to put Florida up for grabs. Still, in 2000 Republicans dominated the state's government. While the Clinton-Gore ticket had won the state in 1996, state Republicans soundly defeated state Democrats in that election. For the first time since Reconstruction, Republicans controlled both houses of the state legislature (61 seats out of 120 in the state House of Representatives; 23 out of 40 in the Senate). Two years later, the Republican candidate, Jeb Bush, became governor with 55 percent of the vote. The party also increased its control of the legislature by 12 seats in the House and 2 seats in the Senate. The *Almanac of American Politics* went so far as to describe Florida as "the most Republican of the 10 largest states."

The political value of this advantage had waned by November 2000, however. The Clinton impeachment was unpopular in Florida; three-fifths of Floridians opposed impeachment. Similarly, Jeb Bush's "One Florida" plan to end affirmative action initiatives in education and state hiring practices incensed African American voters—15 percent of whom had voted for the governor in 1998. The result was a reenergized and angry Democratic electorate mobilized for the upcoming campaign.[12]

Florida was, simply put, a political mess. The Florida electorate was made up of equal parts liberals and conservatives, southern rural "crackers" and urban immigrants. Throw in the 15 percent of registered voters who claimed no affiliation, and it was anyone's guess how the state would vote in a close election. Still, both sides needed Florida to win, and each made campaigning in the state a priority.

Thus, even though both candidates already had assured themselves of their party's nomination, both Gore and Bush campaigned hard in the Florida primaries. Bush stressed his tax-cut plans while lambasting Gore on campaign finance reform and smearing him with the taint of the Clinton scandals. "I think he'll say anything to get elected," Bush told a crowd in Plant City. Gore, meanwhile, criticized Bush's tax cuts as too risky, called for campaign reform, and questioned Bush's experience as a leader. Each stressed in his stump speeches the importance of Florida in the impending election.[13]

Tellingly, both the Republican and Democratic conventions gave Florida delegates high-visibility roles. At the Republican convention in Philadelphia, Jeb Bush and his son George P. Bush made memorable speeches. At the Democratic convention in Los Angeles, Florida Democratic leaders Senator Bob Graham and state attorney general Bob Butterworth both spoke. Most prominent of all was insurance commissioner and former U.S. representative Bill Nelson, the Democratic candidate for the U.S. Senate, who spoke during the prized 7 p.m. time slot. Gore even gave Florida the honor of casting the votes that assured his nomination—an honor usually reserved for the candidate's home state.[14]

Gore even chose his vice-presidential running mate—Connecticut senator Joe Lieberman—in part with Florida in mind. Lieberman, an Orthodox Jew, not only appealed to Florida's large Jewish population, but his moral stance against Bill Clinton over the Monica Lewinsky affair reached out to social conservative north Florida, a region that Democrats feared might be susceptible to poaching by Bush.[15]

As the election got closer, the pace of campaigning in Florida intensified. Both candidates spent liberally on advertising. Bush spent $14,471,492 on television ads in Florida alone. Gore spent less—$10,063,322—but this was his second highest total nationwide for spending in a single state. Each candidate also used surrogates to ensure an almost constant presence in Florida. Bush once again depended on family. Former President George H. W. Bush and his wife, Barbara Bush, were frequent visitors to the Sunshine State. Jeb Bush, as both state campaign co-chair and governor, crisscrossed the territory on his brother's behalf. George P. Bush, Jeb's son, worked the Latino and youth vote. Gore, lacking family members with Florida ties, still reached out in the person of running mate Lieberman, who made Florida one of his priority campaign stops. In addition, both candidates made an ever-increasing number of visits to the state. Gore in particular visited the state on a regular basis. Before the first presidential debate, which took place in Boston, Gore chose Florida as the locale where he would prepare himself, to stress the state's importance to his campaign. As a final underlining of the state's strategic importance, both candidates chose to end their campaigns in Florida. On November 6, Bush spoke in Tampa (which he was visiting for the fifth time in two months) and Miami as part of a five-state swing. That same day, Gore ended his campaign with a midnight rally in South Beach.[16]

As Americans awoke on November 8 to find out who had won the election, they discovered to their dismay that there was no definitive outcome. Indeed, both sides were claiming possible victory. The counting was not even done yet. With only some 1,600 votes separating the two candidates, Florida state law mandated automatic recounts. "If the returns for any office reflect that a candidate was defeated or eliminated by one-half of a percent or less of the votes cast for such office," declared the applicable state statute, "the board responsible for certifying the results of the vote on such race or measure shall order a recount of the votes cast with re-spect to such office or measure."[17]

The losing candidate had the option of declining an automatic recount—but Gore was in no mood to decline. Convinced that he had won Florida, Gore wanted recounts. One hitch existed, however. The procedure for recounting votes was the same as that applied in the original vote tallying. As the law specified, "each can-vassing board responsible for conducting a recount shall examine the counters on the machines or the tabulation of the ballots cast in each precinct in which the of-fice or issue appeared on the ballot and determine whether the returns correctly reflect the votes cast." The state achieved this tabulation by rerunning the votes through these same machines. The county boards then compared the two number counts, with the latter count deemed the more accurate. "If there is a discrepancy between the returns and the counters of the machines or the tabulation of the bal-lots cast," the statute declared, "the counters of such machines or the tabulation of the ballots cast shall be presumed correct and such votes shall be canvassed ac-cordingly."[18]

Yet what if simply rerunning the voting machines was not enough? What if the machines themselves were so inaccurate as to invalidate the recount? What if state and local voting procedures excluded large numbers of legitimate voters from the polls? What if there were deeper problems with the Florida vote than could be ex-plained by a close election requiring a perfunctory recount? Simply rerunning the ballots proved nothing if the machines were incapable of providing an accurate count. Unfortunately, such was the case in Florida.

Even before the polls had closed on November 7, angry voters inundated the offices of the supervisors of elections in Miami Dade, Broward, Palm Beach, Vo-lusia, and Duval counties with complaints about the vote. By mid-morning, the volume of complaints and calls for clarification to county elections offices had grown so large that it became impossible to reach these offices by phone.[19] In South Florida, the number of complaints called into local media outlets grew so great that many set up phone banks staffed by local political experts to answer the calls—calls that arrived steadily throughout the night until the phone banks closed at midnight.[20] By week's end, the Florida attorney general's office alone received more than 2,600 complaints and 1,000 letters.[21]

Most visible among the many complaints were objections to the "butterfly bal-lot" in Palm Beach County. In common with other election supervisors across the state, Palm Beach County Supervisor of Elections Theresa LePore faced a problem in setting up the ballot for election 2000. A 1998 revision of the state constitution had made it relatively easy for third-party candidates to get on the Florida ballot. Before 1998, Florida had some of the toughest rules in the country for access to the ballot. In the 1996 presidential election, for example, the state ballot listed only four presidential candidates. Under the new rules, though, Florida law now allowed ten candidates access to the ballot—the most candidates permitted in any state in the union in 2000. The problem was how to fit all of these candidates on the ballot. Traditionally, candidates for the same office were listed on the same page, one office to a page. Yet to do this in 2000, LePore would have to shrink the type on the ballot significantly, making it difficult to read the ballot. Given the large elderly population of Palm Beach County, LePore felt that this response to the problem would create insuperable problems. Instead, LePore and her staff chose to adopt what came to be called the butterfly ballot.

Unlike the traditional ballot, the butterfly ballot used both sides of the page, placing candidates' names in two columns across two facing pages, similar in format to a book or magazine. Candidates' names were staggered. The first candidate listed (in 2000, George W. Bush) was on the top of the left page and had the first hole assigned to him. The second candidate (Pat Buchanan) was placed on the right page and was assigned the second hole. The third candidate (Al Gore) had his name placed directly below the first candidate and was assigned the third hole. And so on down the list for all ten candidates. In each case, an arrow led from the candidate's name to the assigned hole. Unfortunately, the lines separating the candidates seemed to lead directly to the hole above the proper location. Hence, while the butterfly ballot preserved a readable type size, its design proved confusing to voters who were used to the idea that one punched the hole directly to the right of the candidate of their choice. Consequently, where their candidate was the second listed on the left page (as was the case for Gore), many voters punched the second hole (which registered a vote for Buchanan) and not the third (as was required to actually vote for Gore). Add in the extra confusion provided by the dividing lines, and mistakes became inevitable.

The most common mistakes were "overvotes" in which voters selected more than one candidate for the same office. Palm Beach had 4.1 percent of its presidential vote (19,120 ballots) discarded for overvoting. Most involved votes for both Vice President Gore and Reform Party candidate Pat Buchanan. A *Miami Herald* post-election analysis found that "voters in Palm Beach were 100 times more likely than those elsewhere in South Florida to spoil their ballots by picking both Gore and . . . Buchanan" for president. In contrast, only 3,783 ballots (.82 percent of the vote) were thrown out as overvotes in the U.S. Senate race.[22]

Affidavits collected after the election by lawyers for the Democratic Party show that in most cases the overvotes in Palm Beach County were the result of confusion created by the butterfly ballot. Many voters, realizing that they had made a mistake, simply hit the correct hole in the expectation that this vote would be the one counted. Others hit both holes by mistake. In most cases, these "mistakes" were made in Gore strongholds. In precinct 185 in Delray Beach, for instance, Gore received 92 percent of the vote. However, 105 ballots—11.27 percent of the total— were thrown out for overvoting. In precincts 221, 222, and 223—all found in the pro-Gore community of Century Village West in Boca Raton—the Gore vote was 92 percent, yet 359 ballots were banned as overvotes. Precincts with large African

American populations—strong Gore supporters—also had large numbers of ballots disqualified. In the largely black sections of Riviera Beach, for instance, 1,277 ballots had to be declared ineligible due to overvoting. Some newspaper estimates had as much as 15 percent of the African American vote disqualified because voters punched two holes for president.[23]

Perhaps even more startling—and indicative of the sources of the problem with the Palm Beach County vote—were the 3,407 votes for Pat Buchanan in Palm Beach County. Most arose from precincts with mostly elderly Jewish voters. Few, if any, of these voters were Buchanan supporters. Buchanan had not campaigned in Palm Beach County, nor even bought any ads. He did not view the county as a likely source of votes. His organization in the county, according to his sister and campaign manager, Bay Buchanan, was at best "in 'disarray' with little organization, much less a groundswell of support." In the end, even Buchanan himself acknowledged that his votes in Palm Beach County were probably in error.[24]

Duval County had the opposite problem from that afflicting Palm Beach County—but with the same problematical results. Whereas the Palm Beach supervisor had turned to the butterfly ballot to keep all the candidates for president on the same two-page spread, the Duval County supervisor, John Stafford, chose to keep the traditional left-hand-side-only ballot style, in consequence extending the candidate list onto a second page. On the first page, he listed the leading candidates for president, with George W. Bush on top, followed by Al Gore and then Buchanan, and so on. At the bottom of the page, the ballot read in bold font, "Turn page for continued list of candidates for president and vice president." Voters were also reminded to "Vote appropriate pages" when casting ballots for president.

The problem was that a sample ballot published in Jacksonville area papers just two days prior to the election used an earlier draft of the ballot, one in which all the candidates were listed on the same page. Worse yet, the sample ballot instructed voters to "vote all pages." Given that this was the norm in voting before the 2000 election (and in fact was the rule for all other national and statewide offices on the ballot), many voters instinctively voted twice for president. Most did not recognize the names listed on the second page nor did they realize that these too were candidates for president. Adding to the confusion, many Duval County voters—in particular African American voters—were first-time voters. As part of his Florida strategy, Gore had stressed getting out the minority vote. Black civil rights organizations, including the NAACP, and African American community leaders, such as the Rev. Jesse Jackson, had responded with massive grassroots voter registration drives. In a number of instances, members of these drives had told new voters to "vote on every page," reinforcing the message of the published sample ballots.[25] In the end, almost 22,000 Duval County voters—the largest group of whom were pro-Gore African American voters—had their ballots discarded as spoiled overvotes.[26]

In Broward and Miami Dade Counties, overvotes were less of an issue. Jane

Carroll, Broward supervisor of elections, and David Leahy, the Miami-Dade supervisor, had each chosen to go with smaller type fonts, thus listing all the presidential candidates on a single page. Consequently, they did not have the massive overvote problem that plagued Duval and Palm Beach Counties.[27] These counties did have large numbers of "undervotes," however. (So, too, it turned out, did Duval and Palm Beach Counties, a fact hidden, at first glance, by the large overvote problem.) Broken or worn-out voting machines could, and often did, produce inaccurate markings on the ballot—markings that did not register the will of the voter as far as the tabulation machines were concerned. It is here that the so-called chad problem arose. Chads are the little pieces of paper punched out by the stylus when a voter uses a punched paper ballot. Where the voter does not fully punch out the chad, the tabulation machines will often read them as having not entered a vote.

These undervote problems were a direct result of the voting machines employed by these counties. In the 1960s, states across the nation began using IBM-manufactured Votomatic machines to record and count votes. Based on the IBM punch card computer systems commonly in use at that time, the Votomatic machines were inexpensive, light, portable, and fast. Voting "booths" consisted of lightweight tables with a slot for the punch card; a booklet listing the offices and candidates was placed over the card. As the voter turned the pages, he or she would be directed to punch into the hole next to the candidate of his or her choice. In theory, this punching would separate the precut chad from the card, leaving a clear hole on the card for the tabulating machines to read. One hole equaled one vote. Depending on which hole was exposed on the card, a vote would be given to a particular candidate.[28]

But what if the chad had not fully separated from the card? In those cases, the tabulating machines generally refused to count the vote. As Rebecca Mercuri, an expert on electronic voting, notes, "With any marginal card, the card reader says, 'I'm going to throw it out.'"[29] The result is an undervote in which no candidate for this office receives a vote. The problem lies initially with the voting booths. During the voting process, the ballot card rests on a rubber backing, and where the backing is not properly maintained, it begins to harden. This lack of give makes it harder for the stylus to punch a complete hole. The same result can occur where the card is not properly aligned with the rubber backing. "Such misalignment occurs frequently," reports the Miami *Herald*, "and, when it does, voters—unaware of the misalignment—proceed with their voting attempt" unsuccessfully. Similarly, a dull stylus may fail to punch all the way through the cardboard card, leaving a dimple that the card reader cannot read. Still another cause of failure occurs when large numbers of accumulated chads clog up the undersurface of the voting booth so that voters have trouble pressing the stylus fully through the hole.[30]

The use of cheap, third-party machines only exacerbated these problems. Unlike Broward and Miami-Dade, in 25 percent of its precincts, Palm Beach County used the Data-Punch, a cheaper and less reliable clone of the Votomatic. All of the problems found on the Votomatic were magnified on the Data-Punch machines. From too-stiff backings to clogging problems with chads, from out-of-date and battered templates to broken styluses, the Palm Beach machines were worn out, out of date, and highly inaccurate. Tests carried out after the election by *Miami Herald* reporters showed a significantly greater chance of dimpled chads on Data-Punch machines (4.4 percent) than on Votomatic machines (1.6 percent). The result was a three times greater chance of a Palm Beach voter having an undervote in the 2000 election than in other counties across the state. In fact, surveys after the election conducted by the *Miami Herald* found that in the fifteen precincts with the highest number of undervotes, almost all of the machines used were Data-Punch machines (226 out of 242).[31]

Administrative error was another source of machine failure. It was standard procedure in election offices across the state to test the voting machines before the election. For punch card machines, this testing consisted of one poll worker reading the names of the candidates, with another punching the appropriate hole to make sure that everything was aligned right and that the chads were properly detached from the ballot. Where everything worked as required, the testers would write down the serial number of the voting booth on the test ballot, which was then signed and saved for archiving. Those machines failing these tests were supposed to be reported to the county supervisor's office and then taken off line to be replaced by working machines. Unfortunately, this exchange did not occur in key precincts.

The problem was worst in Palm Beach County, where no machines were reported in as having failed Election Day tests. However, an inspection of 462 test ballots showed a failure rate of nearly 21 percent (96 machines that showed at least one major problem, such as hanging or dimpled chads). According to the *Herald* reporters who examined them, some of the test ballots were "completely mangled—not a single proper vote on them." Miami-Dade County had similar problems. In the two precincts with the largest number of undervotes and overvotes countywide, *Herald* reporters found that thirteen of the twenty voting machines used had failed—at least for part of their prevote tests—just minutes before the election began. Yet, despite this failure, these polling booths remained in service throughout the day. The result was a spoilage rate of 13 and 12.8 percent, respectively, for these two precincts. By contrast, in the Miami-Dade precinct with the least spoilage of votes, the machines passed their tests with flying colors.[32]

Voting officials in Florida (and the rest of the country) knew of the potential downsides to employing a punch card voting system. They knew that the machines were not accurate and that, on average, they could expect a near 2 percent failure rate in counting the vote. Broward Supervisor of Elections Jane Carroll, for instance, repeatedly requested money from the county board to replace Broward's inaccurate Votomatic machines. Other county supervisors did not even bother to ask. The money to replace the machines was not available—especially in large urban counties such as Broward and Miami-Dade. Rather, the electoral officials became used to the concept of large numbers of spoiled ballots, viewing the rejection of thousands of ballots as simply "a natural part of elections" rather than as "an ominous warning sign" of failures to come. Besides, most did not believe that alternative voting methods were significantly more accurate.[33]

This view proved to be accurate in Gadsden County (if not elsewhere in the state). Gadsden, a poor, rural county with a heavily African American population, employed optical scanning for its vote. Though optical-scanner systems are generally more accurate than punch card systems, they too can have difficulties if voters do not mark the ballots correctly. Use of the wrong pencil or not completely filling in the circle next to the candidate's name invalidated the vote as an undervote. Fill in too many circles and it was an unacceptable overvote. Ballot design could also add to voter confusion. Optical scan systems, however, can catch and correct these mistakes, so long as the ballots were scanned in the precincts in front of the voter. In these cases, voters could correct incorrect ballots to reflect their intent more accurately and thus enable their votes to be counted. Gadsden County, however, could not afford to place a scanner in every precinct. The primary cost of adopting an optical scanner system lies in the optical reader, not the ballots themselves. Rather, in a money-saving effort, Gadsden counted its votes at a central tabulation center. Consequently, mistakes that could have been—and most likely would have been—corrected at the precinct level had to be discarded in Gadsden County. Thus while Leon County—just across the Ochlockonee River from Gadsden—had only a .18 percent spoilage rate with optical precinct tabulation, Gadsden with its centralized system had 12.4 percent spoilage—the highest rate in the state.[34]

Inaccurate ballots and broken machines were not the only sources of voter dissatisfaction. Another problem undermining the validity of the vote—and one not correctable by the recount—was that of voters who had sought to vote but who had been denied the right to cast a ballot. Among the complaints were: registered voters not being permitted to vote due to incorrect purging from the voter rolls, misspelled names on voter rolls, inability to communicate with local election offices to confirm or deny registration, switching of precincts without prior notification, misinformation at precincts, polling places that closed early or were moved without notice, problems with absentee ballots, and inadequate or nonexistent support for non-English-speaking voters. There were also scattered complaints of police intimidation.[35] It was with this type of disorganization in mind that former president Jimmy Carter remarked, "If we were invited to go into a foreign country to monitor the election, and they had similar election standards and procedures, we would refuse to participate at all."[36]

One of the most troubling aspects of the many procedural failures troubling Election 2000 in Florida was their racial and class overtones. As already noted, the majority of vote spoilage took place in minority-majority poll sites. The U.S. Commission on Civil Rights (USCCR) estimated that "African American voters were nearly 10 times more likely than white voters to have their ballots rejected in the November 2000 election."[37] Likewise, the voter purge lists were not only highly inaccurate (of the 5,762 names on a 1999 purge list for Miami-Dade County, for example, 14.1 percent of those named successfully challenged their inclusion on the list) but racially biased. The USCCR reported after the election, "African Americans in Florida were more likely to find their names on the [purge] list than persons of other races." The commission estimated that, in fact, African Americans made up 65 percent of the names on purge lists while totaling less than 20 percent of the total state population.[38] Similar, though undocumented, complaints were raised by activists who claimed that minority voters were more likely to be wrongfully turned away from the polls when their names were not immediately found on the voter lists, whereas white voters were given the opportunity to sign affidavits and vote.[39]

The high level of minority disenfranchisement called into question the legitimacy of George W. Bush's victory in Florida. Over 150,000 Floridians had their votes for president thrown out uncounted. Countless others had not been able to cast a vote. Given the narrow margin separating Bush from Gore, and given the general trend of minority voters to vote Democratic, the possibility existed that Al Gore had won Florida, if only the votes of all the citizens had been properly counted. Even leaving aside the many voters turned away from the polls (who after all, did not fill out a ballot, and thus could not have their votes counted), the numbers still tantalizingly argued for a potential Gore victory. The only questions were whether Gore was willing to enter into the fray and fight for every possible vote and what, if anything, those disenfranchised by the process could do to get their votes back.

The 2000 presidential election crisis was predicated on a simple but unavoidable reality: in a number of states, but especially in Florida, the contest between George W. Bush and Al Gore was too close to call without including *every single vote*. This closeness caused all the problems. Statistically the election was a tie; and given unavoidable margins of error and technical mistakes, determining *exactly* whom the people of Florida (and hence the nation) had chosen for president was a nearly impossible task. Unfortunately, both practical politics and the Constitution required that one of the candidates be declared a winner. The question was, who would be that winner? More accurately, we had to confront the threshold question: by what standards or means would we determine who the victor was?

No one disagreed that Al Gore received the majority of popular votes nationwide. Yet under the Constitution, the national popular vote is not the final determinant of victory. Article II, Sections 2–4 of the Constitution, as amended by the

Twelfth Amendment, lay out the methods by which the president is chosen. Under these sections, each state is assigned a certain number of electors in the Electoral College, a majority of whose votes are required to win the presidency. And while the *popular* vote within each state determines who gets that state's electoral votes, the magic number for victory is 270 *electoral* votes. On November 8, Al Gore had 266 electoral votes while George W. Bush had 246. With neither candidate holding a clear majority in the Electoral College, whoever won Florida with its 25 electoral votes would be the victor: win Florida and win the presidency; lose Florida, and all was lost.

Yet with the vote in Florida so close, the normal mechanics of determining the winner broke down. Suddenly, errors and inconsistencies that in other elections would have been irrelevant became the key to victory or defeat in this election. These included: outdated voting methods, under-trained and overwhelmed volunteer election officials, and local control of the voting process with its attendant lack of uniform standards as to what was, and was not, a proper vote. Then there were the claims of race-based intimidation and voter fraud, of confusing ballots and outright vote denial. The electoral deadlock of 2000 threw a harsh spotlight on the voting process in Florida, and by association, on that of the nation as a whole. The resulting picture was not a pretty one. Sadly, it only would get worse before it had a chance of getting better.

CHAPTER TWO

Enter the Lawyers

So many litigators have descended on the Sunshine State, a new precedent
may have been set for future elections. Forget one man, one vote.
How about one lawyer, one vote?
—Atlanta Journal and Constitution

In the Old West, men wouldn't venture out without a six-gun
strapped to their hips. Today, we pack lawyers instead.
—Washington Times *on the 2000 Presidential postelection litigation*

Recounts are a normal part of elections. In highly contested elections, close votes
happen often; it is only natural to want to check to make sure that the count was
accurate. In fact, the closer the margin, the harder it is *not* to recount. If recounting
a vote wrests a victory from defeat, who would not seek a recount? It is only human
nature to want to do everything possible to win. The stakes are too high *not* to
check the ballots one more time (and, if necessary, a third or fourth time). The
pressure to refuse to accept defeat is even greater when rumors of electoral fraud
and misconduct come to the fore.

This was the situation in Florida in 2000. When the networks awarded Florida
to Bush by 2:20 a.m., Gore was prepared to admit defeat. At the time, Bush's announced lead in Florida was over 50,000 votes. Calling Governor Bush in Texas,
Gore congratulated the presumptive president-elect on a good race and wished
him well. Gore and his closest advisers then took a limousine to Nashville's War
Memorial, where he planned to give his formal concession speech. The election,
as far as Gore and his aides were concerned, was over. It was time to concede and
let the nation move on without them. Before they reached the War Memorial, however, Gore's campaign manager, William Daley, got a frantic phone call from
Michael Whouley, supervisor of Gore's operations "boiler room." Whouley had
been watching the actual vote counts coming out of Florida, and, with over 99
percent of the vote counted, he saw a virtual tie. His message to Gore was simple:
do not concede anything. "This thing's going to automatic recount," Whouley explained to Daley. With fewer than 2,000 votes now separating the candidates,
Florida law mandated an automatic recount of the statewide vote. Daley responded
with a quiet "oh, shit" and shouted to his aids, "Don't let him [Gore] get out.
Grab him!" Getting on the phone with Florida attorney general (and Gore state
campaign chair) Bob Butterworth, Daley questioned him about the recount

process. "Are you sure we have an automatic recount?" he asked. Yes, Butterworth replied, "I'm the Attorney General, I'm sure."

It was decision time. Gore and his advisers knew that machine recounts almost never change election outcomes. True, vote totals for both candidates would likely adjust as the counting machines reran the ballots, picking up previously missed or miscounted votes. Yet normally these changes tended to balance each other out—the gains for one candidate canceling out the gains for the other. Nor was a hand recount a guaranteed win, either. Unless some clear accident or mistake occurred in the original counting of the votes—say, a tabulation error that reversed the vote totals or a stack of uncounted ballots withheld from the count by some angry election judge—the chances of overturning an election-night vote were slim. Granted, reports of vote irregularities were making the rounds even at this early stage. However, such experienced politicians as campaign manager Daley (whose father was the former Mayor of Chicago, infamous for his electoral manipulations) discounted the reports—after all, claims of this sort circulated after most elections. Unless these reports panned out, the automatic recount was all that Gore could count on at this time.[1] Still, a difference of less than 2,000 votes was tantalizingly close. Only a few votes shifting either way would take Florida and thus make Gore the next President.

Did Gore want to keep on fighting? Not if fighting splintered the electorate and harmed the public's perceptions of the government. However, if he could win the election without destroying the nation in the process, then, yes, he was interested.[2] Why not let the mandated recount take place? Why not fight for all those people who had voted for him in Florida—only to have their votes ignored? Was it fair to these people—not to mention the majority of Americans who had voted for him across the nation—for him to give up now? Anyway, he was so close to winning Florida and with it the presidency. How could he not let matters stabilize, roll the dice, and see what came up?

With this decision, Gore pushed the 2000 presidential election into extra innings. Calling Bush, Gore rescinded his concession: "Circumstances have changed dramatically since I first called you," Gore informed a suddenly confused and increasingly belligerent Bush. "The State of Florida is too close to call." "Are you saying what I think you're saying," Bush demanded. "Let me make sure I understand. You're calling back to retract that concession?" Stung by Bush's sharp tone, Gore retorted, "You don't have to get snippy about it." The situation had changed. Whereas he would step aside if Bush prevailed in Florida, until the vote was fully determined, he felt that both of them should say nothing. "I don't think that we should be going out making statements with the State of Florida in the balance," Gore concluded. "But," a shocked Bush retorted, "my little brother says it's over" in Florida. Well, Gore noted icily, "I don't think that this is something your little brother gets to decide." Staring in amazement at those around him, Bush ended the conversation, telling Gore, "Do what you have to do."[3]

Once this pivotal conversation ended, the two candidates and their closest advisers probably sat in silence and contemplated the long and difficult path that was to follow. Key advisers in both campaigns were familiar with contested elections. Three of Gore's advisers, Timothy Downs, Chris Sautter, and John Hardin Young, were authors of *The Recount Primer*—a forty-three-page self-published pamphlet and the leading treatise on election recounts. Young and Sautter had gained much of their experience by successfully fending off three congressional recounts of Indiana's Eighth House District election in 1984—up to this time the longest and most complex recount in American political history. Indeed, Bush's campaign counsel, Benjamin Ginsberg, had fought on the losing side in that contest.[4]

These and similar experiences had taught each side the keys to victory and defeat in a postelection challenge. Each knew the range of strategic and tactical options available—not only for their own side, but for the other side as well. In fact, this expert knowledge was the problem. Each side understood the difficulties ahead—for both sides. They understood the likely chain of events to follow and appreciated the resources that would be needed to achieve victory. Most important, each side realized that the room for error was negligible, while the potential for error was immense. This fight was not going to be easy for either side.

Recounts are like chess. The moves in a recount contest are all well defined. The range of moves at any point in time is constrained by the limits of the board, the rules of the game, and the potential and actual moves of the other side. As the pieces on the board shift, so too the strategic and tactical options available to each player shift. Each side—if they are talented enough—knows the moves available to the other side. Victory—in recounts as in chess—comes not from surprises, but from thinking through your own and your opponent's moves five or even ten steps ahead. Small errors of judgment—unnoticed at the time, but increasingly noticeable as time passes—are keys to victory or defeat.

In the case of Florida, therefore, each side had a good idea of the other side's likely tactics. Gore had to be the aggressor. He needed votes or he would lose. Ideally, this strategy meant seeking as wide a recount as possible. As *The Recount Primer* notes, "If your candidate is behind, the scope [of the recount] should be as broad as possible, and the rules [applied] should be different from those used election night." Or, to use a favorite football analogy of John Young's, "it's the end of the fourth quarter. When you're behind, a recount is a Hail Mary. The one who is behind has to gather votes." Conversely, as the candidate with the most votes on election night, Bush needed to narrow the recount process as much as possible. His job was to delay the counting process, to throw up roadblocks to any effort to expand the scope or rules of the recount—in other words, to play defense. As the *Primer* explains, "If a candidate is ahead, the scope of the recount should be as narrow as possible, and the rules and procedures [applied] . . . should duplicate the procedures of election night."[5]

Further complicating matters, each of these strategies had to be put into effect within the confines of Florida law and election procedures. Like most states, Florida had statutory and administrative provisions allowing for recounts. And, as in most states, these rules and provisions had their limitations when invoked in a challenge of this scope and significance. In addition to the already mentioned automatic recounts in close races, Florida law allowed for hand recounts on the written petition of a candidate who believed that the vote totals were inaccurate. These petitions had to address the specific canvassing board(s) of the county or counties where the candidate determined these inaccuracies lay. The request had to include "a statement [setting out] . . . the reason the manual recount [was] being requested" and be filed with the "canvassing board prior to the time the canvassing board certified the results for the office being protested or within 72 hours after midnight of the date the election was held, whichever occur[red] later." Upon receipt of the recount petition, the canvassing board then had the option either to refuse the petition or to order a sample manual recount "taken from three precincts (chosen by the challenging petitioner) totaling at least 1 percent of the total vote." Where this sample recount showed a likelihood that "the manual recount indicate[d] an error in the vote tabulation which could [have] affect[ed] the outcome of the election," the board then could order a full hand recount.[6]

This procedure had to be repeated in *every* county where a candidate sought a hand recount. No provisions for statewide recounts existed. (Of course, no prohibitions on statewide recounts existed, either—but a statewide recount would have to be carried out on an *ad hoc* basis, county by county, with each county canvassing board making its own determination whether a recount was necessary).[7] Nor did the statutes provide guidance to local canvassing boards as to when—if at all—they should implement hand recounts. The decision to recount or not recount lay solely within the board's discretion. The expectation was that such matters were of purely local concern, and as such, recount questions should be decided locally. As Joe Sandler, the Democratic Party's chief lawyer, explained to William Daley early on the morning of November 8, "The recount procedures in Florida are designed to resolve contests in sheriff races and county commissioner races. They never contemplated something the size of this."[8] Yet the nation's two leading candidates for president of the United States would have to operate under these rules.

Nor did the difficulties with Florida election law stop here. Section 102 of Title IX of the Florida Code also set forth a number of specific deadlines for the various steps in counting and recounting votes. In fact, three different sections of the code exhorted the canvassing boards "to file the certified returns 'immediately' with the State Department." On the other hand, section 102.112 set a clear seven-day deadline following the election in which to certify the vote totals. Yet what if a county canvassing board missed either of these deadlines? The code provided little guidance to the State Elections Canvassing Commission on what to do with late returns. One section required the commission to ignore all returns "not received by the Department of State by 5 p.m. of the seventh day following an election." Yet the next section allowed the commission to accept late returns at its own discretion. Adding to the confusion, a rule of the Florida Department of State (the state administrative agency charged, among other things, with overseeing elections) expressly *permitted* the inclusion of overseas absentee ballots in the countywide vote totals ten days after the election (so long as the ballots were postmarked by Election Day). Adopted in response to a federal lawsuit, this ten-day window was in direct violation of the state's election code, which required that "all marked absent electors' ballots to be counted must be received by the supervisor by 7 p.m. of the day of election." Yet for years the canvassing boards had counted, and the State Department had accepted, the late absentee ballot returns. So, whereas the code seemed to contemplate a seven-day window in which to certify the state vote, in actual practice, the vote remained uncertified for ten days.[9]

Defining a proper vote posed yet another difficulty under Florida's election laws. Section 101.5614[5] of the Florida election code stated that no vote "shall be declared invalid or void if there is a clear indication of the intent of the voter." In a 1975 decision, the Florida Supreme Court explained the general meaning and reason for this rule.

> The real parties in interest here, not in the legal sense but in realistic terms, are the voters. They are possessed of the ultimate interest and it is they whom we must give primary consideration. . . . Ours is a government of, by and for the people. Our federal and state constitutions guarantee the right of the people to take an active part in the process of that government, which for most of our citizens means participation via the election process. The right to vote is the right to participate; it is also the right to speak, but more importantly the right to be heard. We must tread carefully on that right or we risk the unnecessary and unjustified muting of the public voice.

In practice, as later decisions of the Florida Supreme Court made clear, so long as officials could identify the intent of the voter, votes should be counted regardless of whether technical errors were made by the voter, by election officials, or by the machines used to count votes.[10]

But what constituted the "clear indication of the intent of the voter"? Here Florida law and legal precedents were silent. What the Florida courts did say was that what the county canvassing boards could *not* do was set up rules *per se* outlining a valid vote—that is to say, they could not set out specific rules beforehand as to what was or was not a valid vote. Rather, each ballot had to be examined individually and a determination made based on the totality of the circumstances for each vote.[11] Hence, in theory, whereas one ballot's indented or "pregnant" chad would be enough to constitute the "clear intent" of the voter, in another instance a similar but less obvious indentation would not be clear enough to determine intent. The same rule mandating individual determination of the voter's intent was controlling for "hanging chads" as well.[12]

This legal thicket left the canvassing boards on their own when it came to determining what it meant to show the intent of the voter. While not a totally unreasonable state of affairs—at the time sixteen other states also allowed for manual recounts without setting specific guidelines for counting ballots—this legal context did place an enormous burden on the members of the canvassing boards.[13]

Florida law was not the only source of difficulties facing the two sides. Time complicated matters still further. Gore did not have enough of it, and Bush had too much for his own comfort. Each side realized that, unlike congressional or local races, this recount could not go on indefinitely. Neither knew how long the American public would tolerate not knowing who was president-elect, nor who would receive the blame when their patience ran out. If Gore was going to find votes, he would have to do it quickly. For him, time was the enemy. By contrast, Bush knew that if he could just hold onto his vote lead, eventually he would be the victor. For Bush, delay was a friend.

Finally, each side labored under the burden of fighting a two-front war. In close political contests such as this, there are the technical details and methods of victory, and then there are the public perceptions as to the legitimacy of the process by which victory is gained or lost. Victory in the courts or by legislative intervention means little if the public perceives the process as illegitimate. The eventual winner, after all, has to govern when the dust settles and he is sworn in as president. Although the likelihood of such public disparagement did not limit the range of options and tactics available to either Bush or Gore, that threat did shape the choices they made within those limits—often trumping legal advice in setting strategy.

For now, however, the focus of both sides was waging the recount battle as a legal battle. It was time for the lawyers to enter the game and take control of the fight.

They called the plane *Recount One*. Just two days earlier, it had been vice-presidential candidate Joe Lieberman's campaign plane. The plane even had the Gore/Lieberman logo still painted on its side. Now it was filled with lawyers and advisers sent by Gore to get the recount process in Florida started. *Recount One*'s first stop was Tallahassee, Florida's state capital, where in the early hours of November 8, the plane disgorged a dozen or so lawyers ready to fight the good fight. Then the plane flew on to Jacksonville and Tampa, and so on.

As the day progressed, *Recount One* airlifted lawyers and political operatives to cities across the state. Their objective was to get a clear picture of what had *really* happened in Florida. Rumors of a broken election were everywhere, but which were valid and which were not? Which of the many possible justifications for a hand recount would hold up best in the courts of law and the courts of public opinion? More to the point, which set of circumstances gave Al Gore the best chance to gain votes?

Although state law allowed for a seventy-two-hour window in which to request hand recounts, Friday, November 10, was a state holiday. To get the requests in on time for the county canvassing boards to act over the weekend, the Gore team effectively had less than forty-eight hours to adopt and implement a recount strategy. Given these limits, speed was essential and knowledge was power. Without information, Gore and his team were operating in the dark, and they simply could not afford to make a false move. As *The Recount Primer* notes, "Don't assume anything. When you're behind, you want to gather as much information as you can because you actually are going to make some decisions that are strategic, based on [this] data."[14]

Transporting lawyers and gathering data, however, was only a beginning. The real question was how to use this expertise and knowledge to prove that Gore had won Florida. As reports from the field started to come in, Gore's command team met in Tallahassee. In a rented retail shop in a strip mall, William Daley, Ron Klain, Jack Young, Mitchell Berger, Ben Kuehne, Kendall Coffey, and Chris Sautter sat down with recently arrived Warren Christopher. Christopher, a pillar of the Washington legal establishment and a former secretary of state, had been tagged by Gore to serve as his chief representative in Florida. Gore's command team felt that Christopher, highly respected by both Republicans and Democrats, would bring a level of credibility to the recount process. More to the point, by bringing in a statesman like Christopher to run his Florida operations, Gore was trying to make clear his understanding that this was no longer a political race. Making this point clear to the American public was, in fact, one of Gore's primary objectives throughout the recount phase. He was terrified of being branded a "sore loser" and hence was in favor of any action that negated this view.

By this point, some twenty-eight hours after the polls had closed, events in Florida started to come into focus. They were also starting to look up for Gore. While Florida secretary of state Katherine Harris was rushing the automatic recount process faster than the Gore team expected or wanted, to everyone's surprise the recount had narrowed the margin between Bush and Gore. By mid-afternoon on November 9, fifty-eight of the state's sixty-seven counties had completed their recounts. Most of the additional votes generated by that recount were for Gore. As a result, Gore was now only 403 votes behind Bush—less than half the original margin. By nightfall, Bush's lead was down to 229 votes. A chunk of this gain was the discovery of 1,100 uncounted absentee ballots—478 of which went unexpectedly to Gore—in what was generally a Republican stronghold of Pinellas County. Similar gains came from Republican-friendly Duval County, where Gore added 184 votes and Bush picked up just 16. The greatest gains, however, came from

Democratic strongholds. Palm Beach County, for example, added 751 votes for Gore to just 108 for Bush; Orange County gave Gore 105 extra votes.[15]

This narrowing of the gap between the candidates had a significant effect on Gore's subsequent strategy. Advice was coming in from all sides. A number of Florida lawyers familiar with Florida election law and litigation practices, such as Dexter Douglass, recommended skipping the recount phase and going straight to the contest or challenge phase.[16] This was also the view of David Boies when he joined the Gore team as lead appellate litigator.[17] Unlike recount challenges, which were carried out by the independent county canvassing boards, a contest central-ized the counting process in the hands of one judge. An election contest, the local lawyers and Boies argued, was the only way to assure an accurate and uniform vote count.[18]

Others on the Gore team objected, noting that once the secretary of state cer-tified the vote in Florida, it would seem to the average citizen that the race was over and Gore was the "sore loser" that the Republicans claimed he was. Also, the issue of time loomed ever larger. Could Gore afford to sit still and wait seven or perhaps even ten days for Secretary of State Katherine Harris to certify the election before initiating his appeal? Warren Christopher, for instance, argued that if Gore were "perceived as fighting too long, it [would] damage the country, the party, and Gore's future prospects."[19] Besides, Gore needed only a few hundred votes to win. Maybe a hand recount would be enough.[20]

Another popular approach among the lawyers was to challenge the Palm Beach County butterfly ballot. By the early morning hours of November 9, the fiasco that was the butterfly ballot was well documented. Not only were stories on the soon-to-be-infamous ballot plastered across the news, but the local Democratic Party headquarters in Palm Beach and Broward Counties had begun collecting testimony from angry voters who were sure that theirs was one of the misplaced votes—either as undervotes, overvotes, or "wasted" votes for Buchanan. It was clear that, whatever her intentions, Theresa LePore had done a major disservice to the Democratic Party by adopting the butterfly ballot design. Attorney Ron Klain was shocked at the ineptitude of LePore and her office. "The level of injustice was overwhelming," Klain later recalled. Some at the meeting argued that the butterfly ballot was technically illegal under Florida law—which demanded a particular order to the listing of names and the placement of punch holes. So why not take the whole matter to court? Already (November 9, 2000), angry voters challenging the butterfly ballot had filed five lawsuits in state courts.[21] Why not support one of these cases, or file one of their own?

Taking the matter to court was a tempting solution. With the exception of Young and Sautter, none of Gore's lead lawyers was a recount specialist. They were, however, skilled lawyers, and as such, understood a good lawsuit. Yet for all of its superficial attractiveness as a solution to their problems, the more the Gore lawyers looked at the situation in Palm Beach, the less they liked an outright attack on the butterfly ballot. For one thing, no one on the Gore team welcomed the image of Al Gore running to the courts. Many in the nation already believed that Gore had lost and was willing to do anything to "steal the presidency." At the least, shifting directly to litigation mode undermined Gore's "we're just counting the votes" response to a "sore loser" tag.

On the substantive level, a real question existed as to what, if any, remedies the courts could provide to the Palm Beach County mess. Yes, it was within the realm of the courts' authority to order a revote in Palm Beach County. Some precedents in Florida even existed requiring the rerunning of entire races in response to procedural misconduct. But this contest was not some mayoral race. This contest was an election for the president of the United States. How could a judge order a new election in a single county—especially given the current situation—when this would have been tantamount to leaving the choice of the next president of the United States to a few hundred thousand Palm Beach County voters? What judge would have the hubris to order such a radical step? Few if any, the lawyers concluded.

Another option would have been for the courts to reapportion some of the miscast votes. The idea would be for the courts to recognize that the ballot design had undermined the will of the voter and to redesignate who should get the votes at issue (Bush, Gore, or Buchanan). The court could then either divide the vote in those precincts with problems based on the countywide vote tallies, or alternately, divide up the vote based on testimony by voters who might have miscast their votes. However, neither option had ever been attempted in Florida—nor, for that matter, in a presidential election. Without precedent, it was unlikely that a judge would choose either of these options. When added to the slim chances of a revote, this situation left Gore without a workable remedy for the butterfly ballot mess— and without a remedy, taking the butterfly ballot to the courts did Gore no good.

Of course, Gore and his legal team hoped for help from the courts if they could get it without too much negative fallout. They knew that as the fight to gain votes went on, it would raise questions that only the courts could settle. Properly used, state courts could be a useful, even necessary counterweight to the Republicans' control of the political branches of Florida's government. This was especially true of the Florida Supreme Court, whose past rulings promised an open, even friendly, forum for Gore.[22] For all these reasons, therefore, Gore turned down a direct litigation-based strategy as his principal means of winning the election.

Recount specialists Jack Young and Chris Sautter pushed for a third line of attack—statewide recounts. They understood the difficulties that such an effort would entail. First, it had never been done before. Second, they would have to petition individually sixty-seven separate canvassing boards. And, third, many of the Republican-dominated canvassing boards in the northern and western reaches of the state were likely to turn the requests down. Still, experience showed that the side needing votes had to cast as wide a net as possible. As the *Recount Primer* noted, "If your candidate is behind, the scope [of the recount] should be as broad as possible." One never knew where the necessary votes were going to come from. Undervotes, overvotes—all were possible sources of victory. The more ballots that were counted, the more chances to find votes. As Young explained to the other Gore lawyers, when "you get 2,000 pitches, you get a better chance of having homers."[23]

Not everyone agreed with Young and Sautter's reasoning. More accurately, while they may have agreed with it, they differed on the conclusions they drew from that reasoning. Daley, Christopher, and the others appreciated the logic for a statewide recount, but saw practical, political, and legal reasons not to make the effort. First, state law required that the petitioning party give a "reason" for hand recounts. If there were no discernable problems in a particular county's vote tally, was there any reason for Gore's team to commission a recount? And even assuming they could, would they? A real question existed whether Gore would even get such a recount if he tried. Over half of the county canvassing boards were Republican-dominated. It was unlikely that these commissions would respond favorably to Gore's requests for hand recounts. The press, in turn, might take these refusals as a sign that the momentum was sliding Bush's way—which would only increase the pressure on Gore to accept defeat. Worse yet, as Ron Klain noted, what if the Republican-dominated canvassing boards *did* accept the recount petitions, but then only found votes for Bush? Meanwhile, in those counties where Gore had a chance at gaining votes, the Republicans could delay the votes with court cases and objections to individual ballot rulings. The result would be that Bush would gain more votes while the count for Gore would sit in limbo. Once again, the pressure for Gore to concede would grow exponentially. No, the veteran lawyers concluded, mounting sixty-seven separate fights, county by county, was a recipe for chaos and disaster.[24]

And then Gore, his advisers, and his lawyers faced the thorny questions of time and perception. The Gore lawyers figured that they had a very narrow window to make their case and gain the necessary votes before the nation began to object. They knew that they could justify the recount on the grounds that "every vote should be counted." As Gore explained in a press conference on November 13:

> What is at stake [here] is more important than who wins the presidency. What is at stake is the integrity of our democracy, making sure that the will of the American people is expressed and accurately received. That is why I have believed from the start that while time is important, it is even more important that every vote is counted and counted accurately. Because there's something very special about our process that depends totally on the American people having a chance to express their will without any intervening interference. That's really what is at stake here.

"This is a time to respect every voter and every vote," Gore reiterated two days later. "This is a time to honor the true will of the people." So "let the legal system run its course," requested William Daley in another news conference. "If at the end of the process George Bush is the victor, we will honor and respect those results."[25]

Still, the minute that the American public decided that Gore was a sore loser, the fight would be over. A statewide recount would not only split up the Gore team's resources, it would also take longer to carry out. As one Gore staffer told the *New York Times*, "We had to keep our focus on where our biggest return was, and we couldn't stretch our resources."[26] So even though state-wide recounts might appear to be the answer on paper, the recount efforts would have to focus on those counties most likely to gain Gore the votes he needed—and to do so quickly.[27]

In the end, Gore and his top advisers decided to go with a limited request to recount votes in four counties. Palm Beach and Volusia Counties constituted clear candidates for a recount. Whatever anyone else could argue about the election, it was clear that something had gone wrong with the counting of votes in these two counties. At the urging of Young and Sautter, the Gore team agreed to add Broward and Miami-Dade Counties to the request.[28] Whereas it was not quite as clear that voting irregularities had occurred in these counties, the use of punch-ballot voting combined with the large Gore vote in both made it likely that Gore could pick up some needed votes.

The Gore team would pin their hopes on the administrative recount, try to pick up the necessary few hundred votes for victory, and wait out events. Given the limits set by Florida law, the extreme time constraints, the perceived responses of the Republicans, and the necessity not to anger the American public, the Gore team decided on a limited response as the most efficient and effective option available. Not *the best* perhaps; had they had unlimited time, resources, and maneuvering room, most of the Gore team would have chosen a more aggressive battle plan. It was just the best option that they saw available at the time.

Back in Austin, Bush took his time in organizing his response team for Florida. As the "defender" in this process, he had the luxury of time. He could afford to think his moves out before acting. Of course, he also had the luxury of friendly state government officials already on his side. Not only was brother Jeb Bush governor in Florida, but the state's senior election official, Secretary of State Katherine Harris, was his state campaign's co-chair. Both, in turn, sat on the state canvassing commission, the ultimate certifier of the state vote.[29] More important, each brought to the table knowledge and experience. Jeb had staffed the governor's office with bright and committed Republicans. Most useful in this context was the governor's general counsel, Frank Jimenez, and his staff of lawyers. They knew not only the law in Florida, but the players and the terrain as well. Without having to be told, they knew what moves would be necessary to assure a Republican victory. As deputy general counsel Reg Brown noted, "there was never a moment when Jeb said, 'go do this or that.' It was just instinctive—people knew that's what he'd want them to do or that it was the right thing to do from a Republican perspective."[30] Consequently, while Gore thought tactically from the start, fighting each battle as it came up, the Bush team focused on strategic moves, always subordinating their individual choices to an overall plan for victory.

After talking with Ben Ginsberg, Bush's recount expert, for instance, Jimenez began calling the state's largest law firms. The goal was to sign up as many of the big firms to work for Bush as possible before Gore could get to them. The first call went to Barry Richard of Greenberg Trauig. Though a Democrat, Richards had worked for Jeb and the governor trusted him. More to the point, if Richards worked for Bush, neither he nor any member of his firm could work for Al Gore. Next on the list was Gray, Harris & Robinson. Then came Fowler, White, Gillen, Boggs, Villareal & Banker—a Tallahassee firm specializing in lobbying. The big prize, however, was Holland & Knight. The largest law firm in the state and one of the twenty largest in the world, Holland & Knight has close ties to the Democratic Party. It also has offices in each of Florida's major cities. Its lawyers knew the relevant law and the political lay of the land. Were Holland & Knight to work for Gore, it would sharply curtail the Republicans' strategic and tactical advantages. Jimenez knew that he was unlikely to sign Holland & Knight to the Bush side. For one thing, the firm's managing partner, Bill McBride, was preparing to run against Jeb Bush for governor in 2002. Other lawyers in the firm were too strongly identified with the Democrats ever to work for Bush. However, Jimenez did have hopes of scaring the firm away from Gore. The threats were never actually spoken, yet the implied threat of the governor's displeasure was clear. It was also successful. When Gore's chief legal adviser, Ron Klain, sought to sign up Holland & Knight for Gore, he failed. Holland & Knight was going to sit this one out. As a leading Gore strategist later noted, "the Republicans didn't have to hire the big firms, or tie them up. They scared them shitless. Jeb Bush didn't need to send a note for them to know" the costs of doing business with the Democrats.[31]

Without sending a single outside lawyer to the state, the Bush team had won the first skirmish. In the end, Gore found adequate counsel in Florida (for example, Tallahassee lawyer and political "fixer" Dexter Douglass), building what Klain called Gore's "virtual law firm."[32] However, as a direct result of the Republicans' strategic maneuvers, Bush's campaign deprived Gore not only of the technical legal support that the large Florida firms would have given him but, more important, of the practical support—office space, secretaries, phones, copiers—that they could have brought to the table as well. Hence, while the Bush team organized itself in the Governor's Mansion and in law firms across the state, the Democrats had to bivouac in old campaign offices in strip malls and hotel conference rooms.

Another example of strategic thinking focused on Katherine Harris. The Bush team was worried that Harris might be overwhelmed by the task before her. State law made Harris, as secretary of state, the key Florida official in the recount process. Not only would she be the public face of the state government in these matters, but she was also slated to play an important role in Bush's strategy to gain the White House.

Unfortunately, Harris's experience in such matters was nil. As the *Tampa Tribune* sarcastically put it, the secretary of state's job normally was simply to protect "the state seal, to make sure no one uses it for a cocktail coaster, or a giant Frisbee."[33] Needing to get Harris up to speed—and fully in step with their game plan—the Florida Bush advisers sent Republican insider and Florida lobbyist J. M. "Mac" Stipanovich to Harris's office as a legal adviser. Starting on the Thursday morning after the election and continuing throughout the crisis, Stipanovich would slip into the secretary of state's office and provide advice (and suggestions from the Bush camp) to Harris and her staff. Stipanovich explained his daily routine after the election:

> I would arrive in the morning through the garage and come up on the elevators, and come in through the cabinet-office door, which is downstairs, and then in the evening when I left, you know, sometimes it'd be late, depending on what was going on, I would go the same way. I would go down the elevators and out through the garage and be driven—driven to my car from the garage, just because there were a lot of people out front on the main floor, and, at least in this small pond, knowledge of my presence would have been provocative, because I have a political background.

Did this constitute control by the Bush camp? Stipanovich refused to say. "It's a small town. I know a lot of people and I talk to them all the time," he told the *Washington Post* after the election. "I don't want to be more specific—did you talk to the Bush campaign, did you talk to the governor's office—I don't want to get into that."[34] Yet all denials aside, in almost every instance, when Katherine Harris took a policy stand, her decisions fit the Bush strategy of limiting recounts and pushing for a quick resolution of the whole issue. And there, in the background, was Stipanovich.[35] It was just this sort of strategic Republican steering of the state governmental apparatus controlling the recount—both formal and informal—that led Ron Klain to explain in frustration to Gore, "Sir, you have to understand, this is Guatemala."[36]

Even the organization of its legal team showed the superior organization of the Bush effort. Though Bush did not begin assembling his legal team until a day and a half after Election Day, by Thursday, November 10, he had in place a virtual law firm of over 200 lawyers. Divided into separate divisions with clearly defined objectives, the Bush team organized itself like a corporate law firm. For example, Theodore B. Olson, an eminent Washington, D.C., litigator and a founder of the conservative Federalist Society, headed the federal courts division. Barry Richard, one of Frank Jimenez's first hires, ran the state court division. Kirk Van Thyne, of Baker and Botts in Houston, coordinated the legal research. Bush campaign manager Joe Allbaugh handled the logistics, organizing a full staff of secretaries, couriers, drivers, and even a three-meal-a-day catering service. George J. Terwilliger III served as managing partner, administering the efforts of the various divisions. At the top, serving as senior partners, were Ben Ginsberg and James A. Baker III.[37]

By late Wednesday, Baker, who was Bush's chief Florida spokesperson, had arrived in Tallahassee. Baker was the ultimate Republican insider. A former secretary of the treasury and presidential chief of staff under Ronald Reagan and secretary of state under the first President Bush, Baker was a skilled and experienced political fixer. He also had a long association with the Bush family—despite the failure of George H. W. Bush's reelection campaign in 1992, which Baker had been brought in to run at the last minute, and which had supposedly led to some bad blood between the principals—and was the consensus choice to lead the Bush effort in Florida.[38]

Baker brought with him the outlines of what would become the public Bush strategy on recounts. As far as the Republicans were concerned, the election was over. The vote had been counted—and recounted. Governor Bush had won. Any further discussion of recounts was simply a product of the Democrats' unwillingness to accept the election's outcome. "We will vigorously oppose the Gore campaign's efforts to keep recounting, over and over, until it happens to like the result," Baker noted in a news conference. In support of this position, the Republicans defended the legality of the Palm Beach County butterfly ballot—noting that no one had questioned the ballot before Gore's loss, and that there were "no do-overs in Presidential elections." They also questioned the validity of hand recounts. Hand recounts were less reliable than machine counts, Baker argued. "A manual recount permits the electoral boards in each county in Florida to determine the intent of the voter without setting forth any standards for deciding that intent," Baker insisted. "One electoral board may decide to count votes that are not fully punched; another may not. One electoral board may decide that a stray mark indicated an intent to vote for a particular candidate; another may not." Worse yet, Baker added, the more one counted by hand, the greater the chance for human error to enter the process. "It is precisely for these reasons that over the years our democracy has moved increasingly from hand counting of votes to machine counting," Baker noted. "Machines are neither Republicans nor Democrats, and therefore can be neither consciously nor unconsciously biased." Finally, the Bush team called for a quick resolution of the election dispute "for the good of the country." Baker urged the nation to "step back for a minute and pause and think about what's at stake here. . . . The purpose of our national election is to establish a constitutional government, not unending legal wrangling."[39]

Privately, the Bush advisers worried. Whereas the conviction of Bush's lawyers that he had won the election remained unwavering, they did understand the like-lihood that Gore actually could pick up the necessary few hundred votes with a hand recount. Worse yet, they feared that Gore's "let every vote count" justifica-tion for recounts was gaining traction. Were the public to accept this rational for recounts, any efforts by the Republicans to limit or halt recounts could be seen as partisan grandstanding. Inasmuch as their private strategy was to delay, delay, and delay some more until the time for recounts had passed and all that was left was for the federal courts to settle the matter (or better yet, for Gore to concede), this possibility was a real danger. Luckily, Gore's limited request for recounts in only four mostly Democratic counties allowed the Bush team to spin the issue and to question Gore's sincerity in "counting every vote." But how to delay and limit the recount process without seeming to be obstructionist and thus dismissive of the sanctity of the voting process?[40]

One approach that promised success was for Katherine Harris to use her office to put up procedural roadblocks hindering, or even halting, the hand recounts. Harris could accomplish this goal in two different ways. The first entailed ruling on the legitimacy of hand recounts. As the state's chief election officer, Harris could issue binding interpretations of Florida election law. On November 13, her office did just that. Florida law allowed for recounts where there was an "error in the vote tabulation." But, did this mean *voter* error that led the counting machines to ignore an improperly filled out ballot, or a *machine* error that ignored an other-wise valid ballot? Florida law was silent on this issue. Issuing Advisory Opinion DE 00-11, Harris's subordinate, Division of Elections Director Clayton Roberts, un-surprisingly came down on the side of the more restrictive second option—ma-chine error only. "An 'error in the vote tabulation' means a counting error in which the vote tabulation equipment fails to count properly marked marksense or prop-erly punched punchcard ballots. . . . The inability of voting systems to read im-properly marked marksense or improperly punched punchcard ballot is not a 'error in vote tabulation.'" So, unless the county canvassing boards found evidence of mechanical failure—which they would not—then hand recounts were not called for, Roberts concluded.[41]

The second attempt focused on deadlines for certification. As noted above, state law required county canvassing boards to turn in their certified vote within seven days of the election. Hand recounts, however, are a slow process. None of the four counties chosen by Gore to take part in the recount process were likely to finish their recounting within this seven-day limit. Whereas state law allowed for discre-tion on the part of the state canvassing board in the matter of late ballot results—section 102.112 allows that late "returns *may* be ignored [emphasis added]"—Harris announced that she would hold to the 5 p.m. deadline on the seventh day (No-vember 14) as set by statute, ignoring any late returns. When a state circuit court later ruled that Harris should use her discretion in deciding whether to accept late ballots on a case-by-case basis, Harris announced once again that she would not accept any late returns. Said Stipanovich of these decisions, "Katherine kept turning the screw to bring this election in for a landing."[42]

A third option for the Bush team was to turn to the federal courts for help. Not everyone on the Bush legal team welcomed this recourse. For one thing, there was a real political cost should the public decide that the Bush team was the first to "turn to the courts." Bush and Gore were playing political "chicken" when it came to the public's views of which side was overreaching in its attempt to win the presidency—and the ultimate proof of overreaching was asking the courts to settle the dispute. Americans distrust political candidates who seem to trust the courts more than they do voters. As John Danforth, the widely respected former Republican senator from Missouri, warned Baker on the phone, "Candidates don't sue. You could ruin Governor Bush's career. He's only fifty-four years old, and the decision to file a court case like this one would be a black mark that followed him forever. It would destroy the reputation of everyone on the Bush side."[43]

On a more practical level, many of the Bush lawyers questioned if they could even get the federal courts to hear their case, let alone rule in their favor. The problem was one of jurisdiction. Most election law is state law. To get a case heard by the federal courts, however, one generally needs a question of federal law or constitutional rights. Without such a federal question, the federal courts lack the authority to rule in such matters.

Finding an appropriate federal question proved a difficult task. Michael Carvin and John Manning, both former Justice Department lawyers, for instance, searched for hours on November 10 and 11 to find a legal justification for involving the federal courts. However, every constitutional angle they could come up with—First Amendment violations, due process infringements, equal protection exclusions—seemed to them too weak to have much chance of success. The same held true for claims under Article II of the Constitution. The problem was not in showing a link between these federal rights or laws and the events in Florida, but proving that these violations were so extreme that action from the federal courts was mandated.

The reason that the arguments had to be so strong lay in the federal courts' historic aversion to interfering in election outcomes. Picking who won or who lost an election was not a judicial function. Federal judges call such cases "political question" suits, and since the early nineteenth century federal courts have held that such political questions should be left to the political branches of the federal government to settle. Only where there is some other underlying issue at hand, such as racial discrimination or proof of official malfeasance, do the federal courts even contemplate action. And even here, wherever possible, courts shape the remedies adopted to limit their effects on current elections. Rather, the most common remedy is to accept the current electoral outcome and order reforms to fix the problems for the next election. Associate Justice Felix Frankfurter had a more prosaic name for such suits—one with an implicit warning buried within it: he called voting rights suits "political thickets," with the clear implication that no matter what the outcome, any court that dared to enter was going to be scratched up.[44] If the Bush team were to persuade the federal courts to accept their case, let alone rule in their favor, their constitutional arguments would have to overcome a significant burden.

Favoring a turn to the federal courts were Baker, Terwilliger, and Ginsberg—and ultimately, George W. Bush himself. From day one, Baker believed that the whole matter was destined for the Supreme Court. He was not worried about getting the Supreme Court involved. At some point one side or the other was going to seek a judicial remedy. And once in the courts, Baker felt confident that the mostly conservative justices on the Supreme Court would take on the burden of these matters—especially if the mostly liberal democratic Florida Supreme Court began to rule on these matters as well. In fact, it was a fear of how the Florida Supreme Court would respond to these issues that motivated Baker to seek out the federal courts up front. Given Florida precedents—and what Baker saw as a clear liberal bias on the part of the Florida judges—Baker knew that if he did not get the federal courts involved, Bush was going to lose.[45]

Yet until they could get the federal courts to act, the Bush team had a less elegant—but (they hoped) effective—method for victory. This scheme focused on the deliberate delaying of the recount procedures through reliance on the hypertechnical rules of recounts. In simpler terms, the Republicans could delay the recounts by constantly demanding that the canvassing boards follow the most limiting rules available for defining a valid vote. Even when they lost a given debate, the time taken to argue was time lost to the recount process. Pile up enough arguments and the counting could be slowed to a crawl. A similar approach entailed disrupting the recounts by aggressive group actions outside—and even inside—the counting sites. Produce a loud enough noise, and the recounts once again would be delayed. Raise enough disorder and bother, and the recounts could even be postponed. As noted, although not an elegant remedy, it did offer a significant chance to delay the recounts and thus allow the Bush team's more elegant strategies time to work.

A final option—and a last-ditch one at that—rested with the Florida legislature. Section one of Article II of the U.S. Constitution places the decision on the method of choosing electors in the hands of the state legislatures—"Each State shall appoint, in such Manner as the Legislature thereof may direct. . . ." The Florida legislature, in turn, had placed the choice of presidential electors in the hands of the people of Florida. Section 103.011 of the Florida Code held, "Votes cast for the actual candidates for President and Vice President shall be counted as votes cast for the presidential electors supporting such candidates." This provision meant that the candidate with the most votes automatically received the state's twenty-five electoral votes. However, there was nothing in the U.S. Constitution *requiring* the state legislature to apportion Florida's presidential electors based on the popular vote. If it so chose, the legislature had the theoretical power to reserve to itself—or reclaim for itself—the choice of presidential electors. And while in the normal course of events, no state representative or senator ever would contemplate removing this choice from the people, in Florida in 2000 events were not even close to normal.

Between political wrangling, dueling constitutional interpretations, and what Republicans would see as the interference of the state supreme court in the electoral process, many in the legislature felt that the only way to assure that Florida had a say in the 2000 Electoral College vote was for the legislature itself to certify a group of electors. The plan would have them certify the same electors that would have been chosen had George W. Bush's electoral victory in Florida been allowed to stand unchallenged. While not without its political costs (James Baker worried about the political fallout if the state legislature imposed its will in place of that of the voters), having the state legislature choose electors if all else failed was a plausible last-ditch option—one that only grew in attractiveness in Republicans' minds as events played out and the state supreme court seemed to be "giving" the election to Gore.[46]

Still, this was an option for the future. In the short run, Bush had to find a way to stop the recounts or face the dire possibility that he would lose Florida, and with it, the presidency. With the state legislature as a safety net, the Bush lawyers chose a three-pronged strategy. Katherine Harris would attack the recounts administratively. The Bush lawyers would attack them in the courts. And finally, political operatives on the ground in West Palm Beach, Ft. Lauderdale, and Miami would do everything in their power to disrupt the counting process—and, failing that, to fight for as narrow an interpretation of voter intent as the canvassing boards would allow. Bush would play the waiting game. Time was on his side, and his team would use time as a tool to undermine the Gore recount strategy.

And so the stage was set. Like two chess masters waiting for the start of a match, the Bush and Gore legal teams were ready for battle. They had their pieces (personnel) in place. They had their arguments and strategies ready. They even had their backup plans prepared—just in case. Each side knew what it had to do for victory. And each knew what it had to avoid at all costs to stave off defeat. It was time for the Florida recount controversy to begin in earnest.

CHAPTER THREE

Eye of the Beholder

chad (chăd)—Scraps or bits of paper, such as the perforated edges of paper for tractor feed printers or the tiny rectangles punched out from data cards.
—The Free Dictionary

It's not the voting that's democracy; it's the counting.
—*Tom Stoppard*, Jumpers *(1972), Act 1*

It was the iconic visual of the 2000 election crisis: a middle-aged government official sitting in a crowded room holding a rectangle of cardboard up to the light to see if any light shone through its perforations while others scrunched in close to scrutinize the card as well, arguing quietly. In the background, through tempered glass windows and doors, crowds of partisan supporters loudly cheered their candidate's victories and booed their defeats. Meanwhile, a nation watched, mesmerized by the slow count of the cards. What image better captures the intensity—and surreal nature—of the 2000 presidential recount?

Yet behind the odd and iconic visuals, a serious and potent contest of wills was under way. Until, and unless, the courts ruled on the matter conclusively—or one side simply gave up and surrendered—the key fight over who had won the 2000 presidential election lay in four Florida counties: Palm Beach, Volusia, Broward, and Miami-Dade. Potential victory or defeat rested in the hands—and the decisions—of the twelve members of these four county canvassing boards—and in their hands alone. Most of the members had never participated in a recount before, certainly not in one with the magnitude of this election. None had ever been so clearly in the public's eye as they would be in the days to come. Nor had they ever expected to be so. Yet their decisions on what constituted proof of a voter's "valid intent" could determine who would become the next president of the United States.[1]

Understanding this dynamic, both camps pulled together considerable numbers of "advisers" to argue their cases before the various county canvassing boards. Some were local political bosses, well known to each county's three canvassing board members; others came down from Tallahassee or Austin or Washington. All were committed to getting their interpretation of a proper recount adopted. Tactically, they *had* to get their interpretation of "intent" adopted. Gore's entire strategy required liberal interpretations of proof of voter intent. If the canvassing boards proved unwilling to accept partially removed chads (hanging chads) or indented chads (dimpled or pregnant chads) as proof of intent, then Gore's campaign for the presidency was over. Bush, on the other hand, needed the canvassing boards to stick as closely to the original machine-based standards as possible.[2]

The pressure on the canvassing boards was immense. Whatever route they chose to take—lenient or strict—someone was going to cry foul. Worse yet, uncertainties in Florida election law meant that those objecting would have a legitimate case to make. Lobbying by the two sides only made matters worse. To whom could the board members turn to for advice? Local political advisers—most of whom were Democrats? Representatives from the state canvassing board and the secretary of state's office—Republicans all? Their personal lawyers—many of whom already were signed up to represent one of the candidates? Adding to the confusion, many of the canvassing board members were registered Democrats. Yet, at the same time, some had been appointed to public office by Governor Jeb Bush, whereas others (mostly the four supervisors of elections) viewed themselves as apolitical public servants (or as apolitical as one could be in what were usually elected positions). Even the media was more hindrance than help, as talking heads and editorial boards gave plenty of advice—all of it contradictory. And, to top it all off, Florida's "sunshine" laws, which prohibited secret government meetings, meant that the counting had to take place in a public forum open to the whole world.

The recount process, in other words, was from top to bottom a partisan tug-of-war between ideological and political foes—each of whom worked to achieve the strategic and tactical objectives necessary for victory. This was no neutral search for the truth. Nobody cared who really won. For one thing, there was no "real truth" to be determined—the election was so close, and the margin of error so great, that finding a "real" winner was impossible. The presidential race was a statistical tie—a dead heat—and the contestants were arguing about how to flip the coin to determine the winner. Whoever was eventually declared the winner—and both the Constitution and practical politics required that *someone* be declared the winner—depended on how the votes were counted and recounted.

So, too, the nation as a whole had long since given up on a search for the truth in the 2000 election. By the time officials were recounting ballots by hand, most Americans had already decided who they felt had "won" the election.[3] Most were just waiting for the recounts to confirm their view—or for the recounts to prove that the other side had "stolen" the election. The focus of concern and public dialogue was on results, not process; on winning at all costs, not on finding the actual winner. All one seemed to see on television, read in the op-ed section of local and national papers, and hear in political speeches and in press conference after press conference, was that to lose the recount meant being swindled of a hard-won "victory." That the other side was bent on "stealing the election," and that they had to be stopped. That this was more than an election crisis, it was a crisis of political democracy. The future of the nation was at stake. The result—played out live on television sets across the nation—was chaos and dark comedy.

Then again, why should anyone have expected things to have been any different? The politics of the last years of the twentieth century had been as contentious as those of any period in U.S. history, except perhaps the years leading up to the Civil War. Republicans, committed to a social and political agenda of conservative retrenchment in government and social morals, saw themselves as the dominant political authority in the nation. After twelve years of Republican control of the presidency, many Republicans had come to see that office as theirs to keep. The thought of any Democrat in the White House was anathema. Bill Clinton's victory over George Bush the elder in 1992 was, in this view, more than a crisis, it was a catastrophe, a clear case of unworthy "radicals" trespassing on their rightful preserve.[4] Needless to say, Democrats rejected this view. As they saw things, the Republicans were out of step with American values, and Clinton's victory proved the nation's commitment to Democratic ideals.

In the years that followed, as Congress shifted to Republican control in 1995 (the House for the first time in four decades) and the cultural and social forces underlying this conflict intensified, an increasingly aggressive and bitter tug-of-war developed between the two parties. Each side seemed to view the other as fundamentally illegitimate—as a threat to the nation's well being and prosperity. In consequence, political defeat took on a larger significance—for defeat was a crushing blow not only to one's political career, but to the fate of the nation as well. The result was a political war in which victory was the only option, and any technique or tool that promised such victory was eagerly adopted. In such a political war, the goal was not just to win, but to crush the opposition.[5] The fate of the nation demanded nothing less. The Clinton impeachment was only the most visible and extreme example of this growing polarization between the parties and the escalation that led both sides to adopt combative, scorched-earth rules of politics. The "good old days," when Ronald Reagan had respect for his political opponents in Congress—and they had respect for him—despite their clear ideological differences, were over. In their place had come the politics of distrust and loathing—the politics, in other words, of total war to the death.[6]

This was the context within which the 2000 presidential election had been fought. It was not just a fight over who would be the next president, but rather an all-out war at any cost to determine the shape of American public life in the twenty-first century. The election's intensity and passion carried over to the postelection contest. Underlying the talk of strategies and tactics—of lawsuits and public relations—was a deep undercurrent of fear and anger in both camps. The fear was that they might lose and thus see their dreams for America die; the anger was that the other side might somehow pull the victory out despite the "plain" truth that "our" side had won the election. The recount process, in other words, shows us not only the content of the two-front war between Republicans and Democrats, but makes clear the intensity of feeling that fueled it.

Hand recounting began in Palm Beach County promptly at 9 a.m. on Saturday, November 11. It began with a short lecture by elections supervisor Theresa LePore on past recount procedures. LePore noted that in a 1990 recount—the most recent on record—the canvassing board had adopted a partial separation rule in which any "chad that is hanging or partially punched may be counted as a vote." Those chads with indentations, but no separation, in turn, "should not be counted," explained LePore.

In this election, however, things could not be so simple. Complicating matters were differing standards used by other canvassing boards not only in their contested elections, but also used in earlier Palm Beach County recounts. One such standard was the stricter "three-corner" rule. Under this rule, a chad had to be completely detached on three of four sides to count as a valid vote. Alternately, there was the more liberal "sunshine" rule. This rule accepted as a valid vote any ballot in which a dimpled chad also allowed light to shine through. Even a pinhole of light was deemed as proof of intent under this system. A third rule counted dimpled chads whether the light shown through or not. So long as a ballot consistently bore similar markings for other races—especially if these consistent votes were for a single party—it was deemed acceptable proof of intent.[7]

With four differing yet valid standards of "proof of a voter's intent" before the board, the lawyers for Gore and Bush moved in. In fact, they had been moving in since election night. By Saturday, November 11, they were present in large numbers. As LePore explained in a February 2001 interview, "all of us [the canvassing board] were being lobbied very heavily by both parties to do a manual [recount or], not to do a manual [recount]." The atmosphere, remembers LePore, was "very tense."[8]

Not surprisingly, Benedict P. Kuehne of Miami, Gore's lead lawyer in Palm Beach County, not only pushed hard for the most liberal of the three standards, the indention rule, but the most liberal interpretation of this standard possible. "The Democratic Party wanted every impression, ding, nick, dimple, spit mark [to] count as a vote," recalled the canvassing board chair, Judge Charles Burton. "The Republicans, of course, did not."[9] In the end, the board decided to use the sunshine standard—in practice if not necessarily by formal vote. However, other votes deemed "questionable" by the candidates' observers were to be put aside for later consideration.[10]

The counting process itself was deceptively simple. Tables were set up and ballots from the four sample precincts were held up to the light. Where the chad was clearly missing, the ballot was returned to the pile. Those ballots in which the chads were not clearly removed were set aside for review by the canvassing board. The problems arose with these other ballots. Republican counsel Mark Wallace repeatedly objected to the withheld ballots. As Wallace saw it, the counters were "finding light and glimmers of hope" that did not exist. Democrats responded that Wallace was just delaying in the hope of derailing the recount process. Ballots with loose chads (and thus light showing) were valid votes. Wallace responded by reiterating that the Democrats were seeing light that did not exist.[11]

Between objections and counterobjections, the counting process moved at a snail's pace. By the early afternoon, only one-half of a single precinct had been counted. The vote trend, however, was clearly in favor of Gore. Despite the small numbers of votes examined and ruled upon, Gore had already picked up some fifty new votes. Were this trend to continue, and given the heavily Democratic makeup of the sample precincts this was a real possibility, the 1 percent sample recount *alone* potentially could have swung the election to Gore. Increasingly desperate, Wallace amplified his objections, in the process irritating all three board members.[12]

Wallace did have a point, however. Whether in response to Democratic lobbying or their own Democratic Party backgrounds or just the tedium of examining so many ballots by hand, the board had been slowly adopting an ever-more generous standard for a proper vote. Realizing this fact, the board even decided to reexamine the earliest ballots under a more lenient standard.[13] Shifting standards, however, called the entire recount process into question. Judge Burton in particular was concerned by the shifting criterion being applied by the board. His view of the recount process was that "we ought to be open and we ought to be public and we ought to be consistent." Otherwise, Burton asked, how would the people have any "confidence in the outcome"?[14]

At 5:00 p.m., the board called for a break. As the three board members separated, the lobbyists followed, pushing their agendas. Wallace, for instance, pleaded with Burton to abandon the new lenient standards. He reminded Burton that he was a judge and supposed to be impartial. "Please," he said to Burton, "think about it. Your actions are going to be judged for a long time." Burton, however, just walked away.[15]

Wallace's words were not without effect, however. As noted, Burton was troubled by the board's shift in standards. Wandering into the backrooms of the supervisor of elections offices, Burton turned for advice to Kerey Carpenter, self-proclaimed representative for the state Division of Elections (Carpenter even had a silver "Division of Elections" badge). Throughout the day, Carpenter had provided legal advice to the board members. Burton, for one, viewed Carpenter as the state equivalent of the county attorney—the provider of nonpartisan legal guidance. Turning to Carpenter, he asked if the sunshine standard was legal as applied. Carpenter said no. In her considered opinion, not only was the sunshine standard wrong, but "she did not think the manual recount [itself] was lawful."[16]

In actuality, Carpenter did not work for the Florida Division of Elections. Rather, she was assistant general counsel for Secretary of State Katherine Harris. Harris and the director of the Division of Elections, Clay Roberts (who had given Carpenter her badge), had sent Carpenter to Palm Beach County as their representative. Democrats saw Carpenter as little more than a political hack, an undercover lobbyist in George W. Bush's drive to derail the recount. The truth was not far off this mark. By all indications, Carpenter was authorized to speak for Harris in these matters, and Harris's primary objective was to end the recount process as quickly as possible and thus to certify the Florida vote for George W. Bush.[17]

Whether out of ignorance or incompetence or some personal support for the Republican candidate (it cannot be determined which), Burton chose to ignore these issues and treated Carpenter's advice as not only coming from the state Division of Elections itself but also as totally nonpartisan in its content. Wandering back toward the counting tables after a 25-minute disappearance, Burton told county attorney Leon St. John that he was "a little uncomfortable about" the standards used prior to the break. The whole recount was getting out of hand. They should be following the 1990 standard, he argued, and they were not. "Bring it up," St. John replied.

Reentering the counting room, Burton did just this, informing the board that, in his opinion, the only legal standard for the board to follow in organizing its recount was that used in 1990—the partial separation rule. Unless a chad had clearly been separated from at least two, and preferably more, sides of a ballot, Burton ruled, said ballot should not be counted as a valid vote. Putting the matter to a vote, Burton pushed for the stricter guidelines. "I want to do it, and I want to do it right," Burton explained. Agreeing on the need for some sort of uniform standard, the other two canvassing board members, LePore and County Commissioner Carol Roberts, agreed to the change.[18]

The consequences of this shift in standards were dramatic. At Burton's command, the board went over the previously counted ballots, this time applying the new stricter standard. Whereas previously Gore had gained fifty votes from a mere half-precinct, the new count gave Gore a net gain of only six votes for the same half precinct. In the hours that followed, the Gore team saw continued minor gains under this new standard, as Gore picked up a vote here and there—but not the flood of votes they had hoped for and expected under the older set of standards. Now it was the Democrats who were objecting on a regular basis as ballots that an hour earlier would have been counted were placed on the "no vote" pile. And so the counting continued.[19]

11:05 p.m. Carol Roberts announced that she was holding the last ballot. The results showed that Gore had gained 33 votes to 14 new votes for Bush—a difference of 19 votes. Now came the hard part: deciding if 19 votes out of a 1 percent pool were enough to necessitate a full hand recount.

Commissioner Roberts was in favor of expanding the recount. She reasoned that 19 votes out of 1 percent meant that there could be at least 1,900 votes for Gore in the general ballot population. "If we were to assume that the votes represent 1 percent of the counted ballots," Roberts explained, "and they were not picked up by the machine, then they would represent a total of 1,900 votes that is possible countywide . . . and this would affect the result of the national election, given the importance of the election and the fact that the present margin is approximately 200 votes statewide. . . ."[20]

Judge Burton was unsure if a full recount was necessary, let alone legal. He proposed instead that the board seek legal advice from the state. "This is a situation that I think is new to everyone," Burton said. "I believe we have the authority to ask the secretary of state or Department of Elections [*sic*] for an advisory opinion, and it would be my intent as chair to do that." Earlier in the evening, Burton had raised this very point with Carpenter, who told him repeatedly that the board was acting beyond its authority. Carpenter informed Burton that she could have an advisory opinion by Monday morning if requested. (However, she failed to explain that, once requested, the response from the Division of Elections would be legally binding on the board.)[21]

This left Theresa LePore. Were she to second and then support Burton's motion, the decision on a full recount would have been tabled until Monday when the state's advisory opinion most likely would have ruled against hand recounts. Support Roberts's motion and the recounts would start the next day. By this time, LePore was visibly exhausted, even ill. She had not slept well for over a week and was unsuccessfully fighting off a sinus infection and laryngitis. On top of these ailments, for days she had been vilified by the national press for the butterfly ballot. LePore could not even enter or leave the elections building without a SWAT escort, so violent had the crowds surrounding the building become. So when Judge Burton asked for a second, she automatically said "yes." (LePore later explained that she was seconding both Roberts and Burton's motions, so confused and exhausted had she become by this time.) Her lawyer, Robert Montgomery (who happened to be a Gore supporter), advised LePore that this was not a good idea. "You don't need to ask for any advice," Montgomery whispered into LePore's ear. "It's a nest of vipers up there in Tallahassee. You better identify who you're dealing with." Heeding this advice, LePore withdrew her second.[22]

Roberts, hoping to regain the momentum, called for a vote on her motion to authorize a full recount. Burton stalled. He allowed Mark Wallace to address the board: "It was pandemonium today," noted Wallace. "We vigorously lodge our protest and plead with you not to put the county through [a county wide recount]."[23] Burton then called on Kerey Carpenter to speak to the board. Carpenter informed the board that countywide hand recounts were permissible only where the source of difficulties lay with machine error. "What we found today was not an error of that type," Carpenter explained, "but instead was voter error." In support of this position, Carpenter begged the board to request a formal advisory opinion from the Division of Elections. She could have an opinion from the secretary of state's office on that very point by tomorrow, she promised, if the board would just wait. Burton again moved to request an advisory opinion from the state before coming to a decision on further hand recounts. This time no one seconded his motion.

Roberts once again called the question, demanding a vote. Finally, after over an hour of debate and argument, Judge Burton called for a vote. Roberts voted yes to the motion calling for a recount. Burton voted no. This left the decision up to Theresa LePore. LePore was torn as to her vote. She understood what a hand recount of almost 500,000 votes entailed. On the other hand, she also understood that most people were not going to be satisfied with the election's outcome unless the board recounted all the votes. "Not that I thought it was the right thing to do," LePore explained in a later interview. "I believe I made that clear, when I said that I am voting for it because it seems to be the will of the people, not because I think there is a problem with the tabulating equipment." Still, if the people needed to see the ballots hand counted, then LePore was willing to hand recount the ballots. Besides, she was feeling guilty about the mess her butterfly ballot caused. In either case, LePore voted yes. Palm Beach County would recount—by hand—all 500,000 or so of its ballots.[24]

Like Palm Beach County, Broward County was a Democratic stronghold. In fact, Broward was Florida's most heavily Democratic county. Gore had easily taken the county in the election by a more than 2 to 1 margin (by some 210,000 votes). The county canvassing board was also Democratic by a 2 to 1 margin. (The sole Republican was outgoing Supervisor of Elections Jane Carroll.) In many ways, Broward was Al Gore's great hope for victory. If he was going to find more Democratic votes anywhere, the odds were best in Broward County.[25]

As was the case in Palm Beach County, the Broward canvassing board responded to Gore's request for a hand recount by immediately ordering a 1 percent sample recount to determine if a countywide recount was necessary. The vote to recount was 2 to 1 and split along party lines. Unlike Palm Beach, however, which started counting the very next day, the Broward board delayed the count until Monday, November 13. The delay was largely the result of elections supervisor Jane Carroll's vacation plans. When the Gore request arrived at the canvassing board, Carroll was in North Carolina. She had left Broward the day after the election. She even had to participate in the vote to do a sample hand recount via speakerphone. It would take her two days to get back—hence the delay in getting the sample recounts started.

Once counting started, the process went smoothly. Broward applied a similar standard to the one ultimately adopted by the Palm Beach Board: a two-corner rule that accepted as a valid vote only those ballots in which the chad detached from the card on a minimum of two sides. In contrast to the sequence of events in Palm Beach, though, the Broward board applied this standard throughout the sample recount. As a result, the Broward recount only took the four hours experts said it should.

By the end of the day, Gore had netted only 4 additional votes out of 3,893 ballots counted. Utilizing the two-side rule, few of the undervotes passed muster. There were marks on the cards, true, but they just were not deep and complete enough to be counted. This was a troubling trend for the Democrats, especially given that these ballots were drawn from some of the most Democratic precincts in Broward County (Gore had won by a margin of around 90 percent in each of the three precincts). Given this poor showing, elections supervisor Carroll argued against a countywide recount. Carroll, in fact, was adamant in her opposition to any hand recounts, which she viewed as "setting a bad precedent." It was not the canvassing board's job to decide "whether a voter really intended to vote it. . . . That's the reason that I've not been in favor of this sort of thing before." County Commissioner Suzanne Gunzburger was just as strongly in favor of a full recount. "We should bend over backwards to protect this democracy," she cried. "Whatever we need to do to allow voters to have their voice counted, it is our responsibility as a canvassing board to do so."[26]

This left County Judge Robert Lee. Known as an apolitical jurist, Lee was bothered by the lack of clear guidelines in the law. The problem was not so much that laws did not exist, but that they were unclear as to how they were to be applied in situations such as this one.[27] Lee, however, had in his possession a memorandum from Clay Roberts, director of the Division of Elections. Roberts, a Republican appointee of Secretary of State Katherine Harris, had written the memorandum in response to a request from state GOP chair Al Cardenas. In it, Roberts argued that "an 'error in the vote tabulation' means a counting error in which the vote tabulation system fails to count properly . . . punched punchcard ballots. Such an error could result from incorrect election parameters, or an error in the vote tabulation and reporting software of the voting system. The inability of a voting system to read an improperly . . . punched punchcard ballot," however, was "not 'error in the vote tabulation' and [thus] would not trigger the requirement for the county canvassing board" to undertake a countywide hand recount.[28] Although some questions exist as to Roberts's authority to issue such an opinion (questions asked mostly by Democrats),[29] Lee was persuaded. Lacking any opposing views on the law, Lee voted against extending the hand recount. "The elections results stand," concluded Lee.[30]

Or maybe not, as the case turned out. The Democratic faithful of Broward County were not pleased with the board's decision. Almost immediately, Gore's attorneys and local political bigwigs assailed the two Democratic board members. U.S. Representative Peter Deutsch and Broward County attorney Charles Lichtman started shouting that Clay Roberts's letter was meaningless. County GOP chair Ed Pozzuoli and state senator Jim Scott responded loudly that it was. And so the war of words was on—until Judge Lee, frustrated and tired of all the yelling, ordered all observers out of the room. Even then, the yelling did not abate. Soon it was apparent that the Democrats were not going to accept the board's decision and would take the matter to court (which they did the next morning). Responding to this threat, the Broward board agreed to meet the next morning and reevaluate their decision.

Events seemed to be going more smoothly in Volusia County. The east-central Florida county had a number of advantages when it came to hand-counting votes. For one, they had significantly fewer votes to count. Whereas Broward and Palm Beach Counties together generated almost 1 million votes, Volusia had only 184,019 ballots to count. Volusia also used a Scantron ballot. This type of ballot made identifying voter intent much easier than was the case with the Votomatic machines. Lastly, politics played less of a role than in the other counties. Though the Republicans had a 2 to 1 advantage on the canvassing board, the board's chair, Judge Michael McDermott, was determined to avoid any partisan conflict. When Bush's central Florida finance chair, David Brown, refused to stop arguing in a November 9 meeting, for instance, McDermott had Brown thrown out of the building. McDermott was fed up with the Republicans' obstructionism. The board had a job to do, and it was going to do it.[31]

Given these advantages and the intent of the board to get the job done, the Volusia board decided to forego the sample recounts and begin recounting the countywide vote right away. As county media representative Dave Bryon explained, "This manual recount process had nothing to do with any lack of confidence of the unofficial totals as they stand right now. But [county election officials] felt that because this issue is so, so important to the public, it would be appropriate to take this extraordinary step so that when this process is completed, there will be absolutely no question whatsoever about what [was] the total in Volusia County."[32] And although technical issues delayed the start of actual counting until Monday morning, with twenty-two tables and the efforts of dozens of county employees, the recount would progress swiftly toward completion.[33]

Then there was Miami-Dade. When asked by the Gore team to recount their ballots, the Miami-Dade board chose to set up a meeting to discuss the request four days hence, on Tuesday, November 14. This date was an interesting choice, as November 14 was the day that all the counties were supposed to turn in their vote totals. The board saw little reason to rush, however. Miami-Dade elections supervisor David Leahy knew that there was no way that Florida's largest county could manually recount its ballots in just a few days. At a minimum, it was going to take two weeks to examine and evaluate the almost 600,000 votes countywide. Besides, Leahy was confident that they had plenty of time to do a recount if they wanted. The only truly important date for getting in votes was December 12. This was the congressionally mandated "safe harbor" deadline. Under this rule, state judicial and/or administrative methods of settling election disputes—at least so long as they were completed by this date—were deemed "conclusive, and shall [thus] govern in the counting of the electoral votes as provided in the Constitution." Miss the deadline, however, and Congress was free to challenge the vote-counting methods and totals.[34]

Another reason for Miami-Dade's serenity on the topic of recounts lay in its composition. Unlike the three other canvassing boards, the Miami-Dade Board was not filled with partisan politicians. Leahy was not an elected official. Unique among all of the state's counties, Miami-Dade appointed its supervisor of elections. Leahy had been on the job since 1981 and was, by choice and practice, politically neutral. The board's third member, County Judge Myriam Lehr, was also a registered independent added to the board just before the election when other candidates had to recuse themselves for personal or political reasons. Only the chair, Judge Lawrence D. King, was a party member (Democrat).[35]

Meeting on November 14, the board decided to do a 1 percent sample recount. Carried out over a period of six hours, the recount (which allowed some dimpled chads to count as valid votes where the whole of the ballot showed a pattern of dimpling, but generally applied a hanging chad requirement) only generated a disappointing six additional votes for Gore. Democrats pushed the board to authorize a full recount based on this total, anyway. As former U.S. Attorney and Gore lawyer Kendall Coffey argued, "it's pretty darn plain that if six votes are extrapolated over the entire area of Metro Dade County that's 660 votes." Responding for the Republicans, state representative Miguel De Grandy ridiculed the Democrats' math, arguing that the most Gore could hope for in a total countywide recount was forty votes.

Put to a vote, the Miami-Dade board split 2 to 1 against extending the recount process. Not only did the two nonaligned members accept the Republicans' arguments that six votes were not enough to "establish tabulation error justifying even the most limited [of] recounts," but Leahy was concerned over the amount of work that counting so many votes would generate. "Three precincts took us over six hours" to count, Leahy later explained to reporters. "We have 614 precincts. It would take us over a month if we worked 16 hours a day, seven days a week, to do a manual recount."[36]

So events stood after the first day or so of recounts. Palm Beach was going to do a countywide recount, but had not yet started to count. Broward had decided against doing a full recount, but was planning on reconsidering the issue later. Volusia was recounting all of its ballots and hoped to be done soon. And Miami-Dade County was doing nothing, at least for the moment. Despite the looming deadline of 5:00 p.m., November 14—by which time all vote totals were supposed to be in the hands of the secretary of state's office—the fight over recounting ballots was far from concluded.

At this point, the narrative starts to get confusing. Events begin to tumble one onto another, multiple actions taking place at approximately the same time, each serving as both a cause and an effect of changing events. With the sole exception of Volusia County (which would get its amended vote totals in on time), the decision to count or not to count would be made and rejected again and again and again. Changing events, judicial rulings, and the pressures of political necessity all would intrude on the recount process. The battle over recounts was about to get serious.

The first salvos in the battle to control the recount process came out of Tallahassee. State Attorney General Bob Butterworth—who had served as a state chair for the Gore/Lieberman campaign and was the Democratic equivalent of Katherine Harris, a partisan with official powers—responded to Clay Roberts's advisory opinion against hand recounts. In a six-page opinion filled with citations and references to statute and case law, Butterworth argued that "the Division of Elections opinion [was] . . . clearly at variance with the existing Florida statutes and case law."

First, Butterworth explained, Roberts's opinion blurred "the distinctions that the legislature clearly delineated" between "vote tabulation" and "vote tabulation system." In Section 102.166 of the Florida Code, for instance, the legislature used the terms "vote tabulation system" and "automatic tabulating equipment" when "it intended to refer to the system rather than the vote count." The Division of Elections in its advisory opinion, however, read these two terms as "synonymous," which blurred the "distinctions that the Legislature clearly delineated in section 102.166." To merge the two concepts into a single meaning, Butterworth argued, effectively "nullifie[d] the language of section 102.166(7)"—and did so without "authority or support." This was simply wrong, for it was a "fundamental principle of statutory construction that statutory language [was] not to be assumed to be surplusage; rather a statute [was] to be construed to give meaning to all words and phrases contained within [the] statute." Put another way, if the legislature used two words to describe the proper times to recount votes, then the legislature had in mind two different situations.[37]

A similar argument was available for case law as well. "The division's opinion," wrote Butterworth, "fails to acknowledge the longstanding case law in Florida which . . . held that the intent of the voters as shown by their ballots should be given effect." Many judicial rulings made clear that "the intent of the voter [was] of paramount concern and should be given effect if the voter ha[d] complied with the statutory requirement and that intent may be determined." Consequently, where "the Florida Statutes contemplate that where electronic or electromechanical voting systems are used, no vote is to be declared invalid or void if there is a clear indication of the intent of the voter as determined by the county canvassing board."[38]

How then, Butterworth asked, could this intent be determined if no hand recounts were made? The answer was that it could not be determined. "Rather, I am of the opinion that the term 'error in voter tabulation' encompasses a discrepancy between the number of votes determined by a voter tabulation system and the number of votes determined by a manual count of a sampling of precincts pursuant to section 102.166(4)."[39]

Compared to Roberts's opinion, Butterworth made a much stronger case for his point of view. Although one could logically argue either side as to the "real" meaning of the statutory language in 102.166, Butterworth's case law arguments were clear and well documented. Since the late nineteenth century, the Florida courts had stressed that the primary objective in counting ballots was giving force to the "intent of the voter." Just because the error was the result of the voter's confusion did not invalidate the duty to determine the voter's intent when counting votes.[40]

Butterworth had a problem, however. In the minds of many, he lacked the jurisdiction to issue an opinion on this topic. The attorney general's own Web site seemed to undermine his authority to speak on these matters. According to the Web site, "questions arising under the Florida Election Code should be directed to the Division of Elections in the Department of State." Further down, the page noted: "Attorney General Opinions are not a substitute for the advice and counsel of the attorneys who represent governmental agencies and officials on a day to day basis."[41] Butterworth had argued in his opinion that this was a unique situation demanding exceptional action on his part. "Because the Division of Elections opinion is so clearly at variance with the existing Florida statues and case law, and because of the immediate impact the erroneous opinion could have on the ongoing recount process," Butterworth explained, "I am issuing this advisory opinion."[42] The question was, would simply claiming extraordinary need be justification enough for people to follow his advice?

As if this were not enough, the same night that Bob Butterworth was writing his opposition opinion, Secretary of State Katherine Harris announced that she was set to certify the election on Tuesday (November 14) *regardless* of any hand recounts in the four designated counties. Any votes not in by 5:00 p.m. EST, Harris warned, would not be included in the final state tally. As her press release explained: "The electoral process is a balance between the desire of each individual voter to have his or her intended vote recorded and the right of the public to a clear, final result within a reasonable time." The law, Harris emphasized, "unambiguously states when the process of counting and recounting [of] the votes cast on election must end." The statutorily mandated deadline was 5:00 p.m. on the seventh day following the election. No discretion existed on this matter. "Florida law does not provide any date for return certifications other than tomorrow at 5 PM." The *only* possible exception to this rule was when a natural disaster—"such as Hurricane Andrew"—made compliance with the law physically impossible. "But," Harris advised, "a close election, regardless of the identity of the candidates, [was] not such a circumstance."[43]

Harris's announcement was the equivalent of sticking a metal bar between the spokes of a bicycle wheel and watching the bike seize up and fall to a dead stop. None of the three South Florida counties could meet this deadline. Miami-Dade was not even going to decide on recounts until the morning of November 14. Volusia with its smaller number of ballots might make the deadline (they would in the end, giving Gore an additional ninety-eight votes), but there were no guarantees that they could. Already burdened with deciding whether Roberts's or Butterworth's opinions on the law were controlling, the canvassing boards now faced an impossible deadline.

And on top of all of this, the public relations campaign by both sides moved into high gear, adding to the confusion—and the pressure—faced by the canvassing boards attempting to finish quickly before everything fell apart. On Wednesday, November 15, Gore offered to stop all the political and legal wrangling if the Bush camp would just drop all its legal challenges to his recounts. Should Bush do this, Gore proposed, then he would accept the results of the votes already certified by the state as modified by the overseas absentee ballots and the fresh tallies from the hand recounts in Volusia, Broward, and Palm Beach Counties. Or, Gore said, he would alternately abide by the results of a hand count of the entire state. The choice was Bush's. "We need a resolution that is fair and final," Gore said Wednesday evening with his running mate, Senator Joseph Lieberman, by his side. "We need to move expeditiously to the most complete and accurate count that is possible. And that is why I propose this evening a way to settle this matter with finality and justice in a period of days, not weeks," Gore said. "If this happens, I will abide by the result," promised Gore. "I will take no legal action to challenge the result, and I will not support any legal action to challenge the result. I am also prepared, if Gov. Bush prefers, to include in this recount all the counties in the entire state of Florida," Gore said. "I would also be willing to abide by that result and agree not to take any legal action to challenge that result."

Bush's reply was a definitive "no." What did he have to gain from such an agreement? More to the point, in Bush's own mind, he had already won the election. The votes had been counted and recounted, Bush noted. "In some counties they [had] been counted a third and even a fourth time." There was no need for hand recounts. Hand recounts could only introduce human error. This was not the way to run an election. "Unfortunately," noted Bush with a bit of a sigh, "what the vice president proposed is exactly what he has been proposing all along, continuing with selective hand recounts that are neither fair nor accurate, or compounding the error by extending a flawed process statewide. This means every vote in Florida would be evaluated differently, by different individuals using different judgment and perhaps different local standards and perhaps, no standards at all. This would be neither fair nor accurate, it would be arbitrary and chaotic." Other Republicans were harsher in their criticism of the vice president's proposal. This was just "grandstanding" from Gore, one Bush lawyer complained.[44]

The four county canvassing boards' principal response to these dilemmas was to turn to the Florida courts, seeking legal clarification and extensions of time to file their amended vote totals. We will deal with this process in the next chapter. For our purposes here, it is enough to note how Harris's announcement ratcheted up the tension and pressure (as had Roberts's and Butterworth's advisory opinions and Gore's offer of a "final" state-wide recount). It also intensified the partisan bickering.

As noted in chapter 2, this fight was being fought on two separate but linked battlefields. Whereas the first battlefield dealt with results (hence the move to the courts), the second was all about perception. It was not enough for the canvassing boards just to count the votes; they had to do so in a manner that most Americans would consider legitimate and authoritative. As events would show, as the pressures on the four boards increased, the whole recount process would become so chaotic and even paradoxical that legitimacy was clearly left in the eye of the (partisan) beholder. And what that eye saw, in turn, was directly influenced by the practical results of the recount process.

On the morning of November 14, Judge Lee in Broward County held a copy of Butterworth's opinion in his hands as he reopened the board's consideration of recounts. He also knew that Broward Democrats had filed a lawsuit in state circuit court that morning seeking a writ of mandamus ordering the board to ignore the Division of Elections' advisory opinion and to begin a full hand recount. The motion also asked for an injunction prohibiting the board from certifying the election results until they had recounted all the ballots by hand.[45] Combined, both factors led Judge Lee to rethink his position from the day before. In particular, he found the attorney general's opinion highly persuasive. Lee had only ruled the way he had the previous day in an effort to follow the law. Butterworth's well-reasoned legal interpretation of Florida election law, as Lee described it to the board, gave him an opportunity to change his mind with a clear conscience. "It would be very nice if we could go just by what our hearts feel," Lee explained, "but we are guided by law, not how we feel."[46] Broward was going to recount its ballots. And if the secretary of state wanted to stop them, "then let her go get her mandamus [order] to make us stop."[47]

That next afternoon, Broward began recounting its nearly 600,000 ballots. The going was slow. As it had in the 1 percent sample count, the Broward board chose to apply the two-sided hanging chad standard. And, just as before, the Democrats argued that legitimate votes were being ignored while Republicans objected to almost every claimed vote in a clear effort to delay the process. The Democrats may have had a point about the standard. With 40 percent of the vote counted, Gore had gained only seventy-nine new votes. Given that there were many ballots filled with dimples (the chad punctured through but still attached to the ballot) that remained uncounted under this standard, this was a questionable result.[48]

As the counting went on and on, the board began to have second thoughts about its adopted standard. Even Republican county attorney Edward Dion, who was advising the board, was troubled by what he saw as potentially missed votes.[49] Just a few hours before they started counting, Judge Jorge Labarga in Palm Beach

County had ruled that canvassing boards needed to take a broad approach to the counting process, seeking at all times to empower the voters' intent.[50] On Friday, November 17, Broward Circuit Judge John A. Miller seconded this view, suggesting that the canvassing board look at a voter's clear intent when viewing a ballot.[51] Later that same day, the Florida Supreme Court barred Katherine Harris from certifying the election as it considered the matter carefully—meanwhile explicitly making clear that "it is NOT the intent of this order to stop the counting."[52]

Convinced by these rulings, Dion recommended to the board the adoption of more open standards when, on November 19, Gore's lawyers came with a petition to include dimpled chads in the count. (They also threatened an additional lawsuit if the board refused to change their standards.) Heeding Dion's advice, the board voted unanimously to widen its definition of a valid vote.[53] The board further decided that, rather than recount the over 40 percent of precincts that they had already counted, that they would simply reevaluate the withdrawn undervotes. These ballots had already been set aside as questionable and were thus accessible for easy recounting.[54] And so the counting continued.

Meanwhile, outside the counting room the public relations front was in full force. In the hallways and on the streets, Bush supporters attacked the recount process as unreliable and ridiculous while Gore surrogates defended the process. County GOP chair Ed Pozzuoli was vocal about what he saw as a lack of "standard[s] being followed in Broward."[55] On November 16 he noted how "for the second straight day, Hurricane Chad has hit Broward, wiping away the results of Tuesday's [November 7] election. . . . You will see a result that is unfair," he warned.[56] Republicans were especially angry at the change of standards. Bush spokesperson Ray Sullivan argued that "any semblance of a standard of fairness in the hand-counting process in Broward County has been abandoned" with the new standard. (To which county attorney Dion replied, nonsense. "My only job is to represent the canvassing board. This is an evolving situation. What we believed to be accurate legal advice on Monday is now changed." Besides which, Dion pointed out, he "was a Republican".)[57] The Republicans even began charging that election workers were shaking chads loose, resulting in unearned votes for Gore. GOP officials asked the Broward sheriff's department to collect the chads for possible litigation. (Democrats, in turn, dismissed Republican claims of cheating, noting that these fallen chads could have come from votes for any one of over forty candidates.)[58] Republicans even filed a nuisance lawsuit, which required the three board members to leave the counting room and travel thirty minutes to the county courthouse, only to find that the hearing had been canceled. On the way back, two of the board received calls on their cell phones that the hearing was on again. Turning around, they arrived at the courthouse to find that, once again, there was no hearing. A little digging shows that the second call came from an attorney who worked for a firm supporting Bush's case.[59]

On Sunday, November 19, partisan tensions spilled over onto the board itself, when Jane Carroll abruptly quit her job and flew off to California to visit family for the Thanksgiving holiday. Carroll, who was seventy years old and had been planning her retirement from public office following the November 7 election, claimed exhaustion. "I don't feel well," Carroll said. "I'm not as young as I used to be." Democrats were less forgiving of Carroll's human frailties. County Commissioner Lori Parrish criticized Carroll's leaving. "We're elected to do a job," Parrish said. "You earn a salary. It's your job. This is the president of the United States." Finding a replacement for Carroll was difficult. Normally a replacement would be pulled from the county commission; however, the entire commission was Democratic. Turning to the courts for a judge proved equally difficult. Everyone understood that the Republicans would not stand for an all-Democrat canvassing board. However, finding a qualified Republican judge in Democratic stronghold Broward (at least, one whom the Democrats would accept) was difficult. In the end, Republican Judge Robert Rosenberg was chosen to fill Carroll's slot on the board.[60] And so the counting continued.

On Tuesday, November 21, the Broward board finally got a deadline it could make. In a per curium opinion in which all seven judges agreed, the Florida Supreme Court ruled that manual recounts must be included in the state's final vote tally. To this end, the justices give the three counties still counting until 5 p.m. on Sunday, November 26, to submit their amended results.[61]

It turned out to be just the amount of time the Broward board needed. On Wednesday, November 22, all 609 precincts had had their ballots examined. All that remained were 38,000 absentee ballots and 2,422 undervote ballots to examine. After several thirteen-hour days counting ballots, the end was in sight. Redoubling their efforts, the board worked through Thanksgiving and into the weekend. At 11:52 p.m. on Saturday, November 25, the counting was over. With a unanimous agreement rate of about 81 percent, the three board members had reviewed the ballots and arrived at a total count of 567 additional votes for Al Gore.[62]

Interestingly, Roberts's and Butterworth's opinions (not to mention Harris's decision not to accept late hand recount totals) had very different effects in Palm Beach County. Faced with conflicting legal opinions, the Palm Beach board decided to halt its recounts. Board chair Burton felt that they had to follow the Division of Elections' reading of the law. They had asked for advice. They were now legally bound to follow this advice. "Florida statute 106.232 makes it clear," Burton announced to the media that "the opinion this board received from Clay Roberts, director of division of elections . . . stated a manual recount under the circumstances confronted by this board is not authorized and is binding until such opinion is amended or revoked." "I want to make it clear," Burton concluded, "that I would vote to immediately begin the recount if I had unfettered discretion, I do not."[63]

Carol Roberts was just as adamant that they should listen to Butterworth and get on with the counting. Even the courts were on Butterworth's side. On Monday, the Democrats had brought suit in state court challenging the board's standards in determining voter intent. On Wednesday morning, Judge Jorge Labarga had ruled that the canvassing board did have the authority to manually recount ballots in any way they deemed effective so as properly to determine the voters' intent. Though not totally to the point, this was enough for Roberts. "If we decided yesterday to go forward," she argued, "I believe we should still go forward." What was the worst thing that could happen if they did recount? "Do we go to jail? Because I'm willing to go to jail!"[64]

This division left the issue in the hands of Theresa LePore. Uncertain as to which of the opinions was valid, LePore turned to civil rights attorney Bruce Rogow for advice. LePore had hired Rogow, a law professor at Nova Southeastern University and an experienced appellate litigator, to serve as her counsel during the crisis. Rogow advised that the only safe option for the board was to seek the advice of the Florida Supreme Court. "It's like a real estate deal," Rogow later explained to the press.

> You're buying a piece of property and you give a real estate broker a down payment. Then the deal falls through and you want your money back. The person selling the property wants your down payment because it is your fault the deal fell through. The broker is left in the middle holding the goods and needs someone to tell them what to do. Well, the canvassing board is like the real estate broker stuck in the middle. But the goods they are holding are the votes.

Until the state supreme court clarified matters, Rogow suggested, the counting should remain stopped. Heeding her attorney's advice, LePore agreed to stop the counting. After the state supreme court had spoken, then it would be time to begin recounting ballots again.[65]

Days passed as the litigation process worked its way up the appellate ladder. Finally, on November 16, the Florida Supreme Court ruled unanimously that those counties still conducting manual recounts of ballots could continue. In consequence, Palm Beach did not begin its full recount until November 17—a full five days after the board had ruled that it would perform a hand-recount. Beginning at 7:00 a.m., the plan was to organize twenty-five to thirty teams of counters who would work through to midnight, with work restarting at 7:00 a.m. the next morning. However, lack of bodies meant that only thirteen teams were in place when counting began.[66]

Once again, the count moved slowly forward. Between not enough counters and repeated objections by the Republicans (and counterobjections by the Democrats), the count totals grew at a glacial pace. This was a troubling trend, as the board had only nine days in which to meet the Florida Supreme Court's November 26 deadline. The board, however, pushed on. Once again, their standard of a valid vote required at least two detached sides to the chad. Slowly the undervote pile grew. And so the counting continued.

In the end, the Palm Beach board faced some 10,000 undervote ballots requiring their personal examination. Ultimately, this number proved to be too many to count in the time allowed. By Thanksgiving Day (when the board voted to stop the counting and to spend some time with their families), the number of checked undervote ballots was in the mid-thousands. As late as Saturday night, November 25, after twelve grueling hours of counting, the board had 5,400 ballots yet to count. Even a twenty-four-hour push at the end would not be enough. Palm Beach County was not going to make the deadline.

With only a few hours left to go before the deadline was passed, Judge Burton faxed the secretary of state's office begging an extension. Even an extra hour or two would be enough. Katherine Harris, however, rejected the board's requested extension of two hours outright. Harris also overruled the board's subsequent request to include the partially hand-recounted ballots in the county's vote total. It was over. "Hindsight's 20-20," Burton said of their effort. "I really believed we could make it—and we fell a little short." After weeks of counting and recounting, it was Palm Beach County's original machine tally that Harris certified as accurate.[67]

In Volusia County, the count moved smoothly. Ignoring both Harris and Butterworth, the Volusia board just counted its votes. The board understood that they might not get all of the ballots counted before the 5:00 p.m. deadline on Tuesday, November 14. This was why the board brought suit in a Florida Circuit Court seeking more time to count (more on this case in the next chapter). Yet with hard work and a willingness to take control of the process, the board met the deadline, giving Gore an additional ninety-eight votes on November 14. Judge McDermott would later say that you had to be willing to hurt some feelings to get a job like this done—that you could not "be afraid of being a sonofabitch"—that it was the only way get things done in the midst of chaos. Of course, it also helped that Volusia County employed Scantron ballots. Most of their overvotes and undervotes were simply cases in which the voter had placed an X on the ballot instead of filling in the oval as required. In other cases, after marking the wrong oval, the voter wrote "no" next it and then marked the desired candidate's oval. Some had the voter properly marking the oval but then also writing in the name of the same candidate. In any of these cases, the machines did not register a vote, but the board was easily able to determine the voter's intent.[68]

Miami-Dade County was also less affected by the Roberts-Butterworth debate and the Harris deadline crisis than its two neighbors to the north (though Volusia County was affected even less). They already knew the substance of the debate when they decided on the 14th not to recount. The court decisions in Palm Beach and Broward Counties, however, left some room open for reconsideration. The ongoing fight over Secretary Harris's decision not to accept late vote totals added more pressure. So too did the decisions by the Palm Beach and Broward canvassing boards to recount.

On the morning of the 15th, Miami Democratic Party chair Joe Geller petitioned the board for a hearing on reopening the recounts. After hearing arguments against additional recounts from the Republican county chair and rebuttal arguments from Geller, the board agreed to meet on Friday, November 17, to discuss the issue and vote on the Democrat's motion. This meeting proved highly charged.

In a hearing lasting several hours, the board heard impassioned pleas from both sides for and against restarting recounts. "Events in this case are exploding upon us," argued attorney Kendall Coffey. Broward and Palm Beach Counties were recounting their ballots. "Can we say no because we're too busy? It's too much hassle? Of course not." Democratic attorney Stephen Zack drew a comparison between manual recounts and the instant replay on *Monday Night Football*. If we used instant replay to assure that the right calls were made during a televised sporting event, did the presidency of the United States deserve any less care? "The truth is always better than guessing," Zack concluded. "The truth is all we are seeking. What happened in Dade could very well determine this election." Miami-Dade County had over 10,000 undervote ballots that had never been counted. The voting machines simply could not count them. A hand recount—like slow motion instant replay in football—would fix this problem.

Republicans countered that a hand count was likely to be less accurate, because it opened the process to human error. Bush spokesperson Bob Martinez urged the board not to grant a full recount, saying nothing had changed since the board's earlier vote. "Let me tell you first what I did not hear. . . . What I did not hear was any recitation of facts or law that would justify reconsideration. . . . What I did not hear is any compelling new evidence." The board had reached a reasoned and legal conclusion against recounts on Tuesday, and "nothing has changed since that time. No new facts. No new law. Just more lawyer talk." "You have shown great courage in applying the rule of law, Mr. Leahy, Judge Lehr, Judge King," Martinez concluded. "I respect you. I am not going to push you. But you're being pushed now. What I ask you at this point in time is that you stick to your conviction[s]."[69]

It was about this time that word came down of the Florida Supreme Court order blocking Katherine Harris from certifying the election results at 5:00 p.m. The window was now officially open for manual recounts to be included in the final total. Not that this stopped the debate. If anything, the supreme court's ruling intensified the Republicans' opposition to recounts while sharpening the Democrats' support of the same. "This is turning into chaos," Martinez would later say. "This is not the way to elect a president."[70]

After hearing the impassioned arguments from both sides, and taking note of the state supreme court's order on hand-recounts, the chair, Judge King, called for a vote. He voted first. "I'll vote yes in concurrence with the recount of all ballots in Dade County by hand," exclaimed King. Judge Lehr voted next. "I, too, am going to concur with you, Judge King. I believe the people of Dade County are entitled to have their votes counted. . . . You read the papers, and you listen to the television, and the news—a lot had been happening. And I have taken a lot of what has been happening into consideration." Among those things that were "happening" was the state supreme court's decision to extend the deadline for certified results. While Leahy voted no—his reasons the same as before—Miami-Dade was back in the vote-counting business.[71]

All that was left now was the practical problem of actually hand-counting over 650,000 votes. Leahy, however, had a plan that he felt confident would allow the board to count all the ballots by December 1. (Which, Leahy conceded, was after the state supreme court's new certification deadline, but was the earliest date he could conceive of finishing the vote counting.) First, he would separate out by machine the 10,750 undervotes from the last count. He would then organize twenty-five teams of counters to examine manually the remaining ballots looking for improperly counted votes. In contrast to the other counties, however, Leahy mandated that observers would not have the right to challenge individual ballots. Rather, after the designated counters had collected enough ballots to measure an inch thick, they would hold up the ballots to the observers to show that light passed through the entire stack. The assumption was that a clear path meant valid votes for a particular candidate. Questionable ballots—for example, those ballots in which the chads had successfully been removed but from the wrong box—would be added to the pile of undervotes for examination by the board itself.[72]

Recounting began on Monday morning. On Sunday, elections supervisor Leahy had his staff pull the 10,750 undervotes. While county volunteer workers started to manually check the remaining ballots, the board itself started with the undervotes. In contrast to their rulings in the 1 percent recount on Tuesday, the board counted dimpled ballots as valid votes. "We have accepted [dimples] as a valid vote," Judge King explained. "We err on the side of trying not to disenfranchise any voter." The result of this standard shift helped both candidates gain additional votes. However, the general trend was more to Gore's favor than Bush's.[73]

As with the efforts in Broward and Palm Beach, the recounting went slowly. By the end of the first day, only 67 out of 614 precincts had been fully examined. Despite rules aimed at limiting objections from the candidates' observers, arguments and accusations of cheating or delaying tactics slowed the process down. On the second day of counting, for example, Leahy grumbled when a Republican volunteer, Grant Lally, asked that county worker Ivy Korman be removed from the counting room for being rude. "We are running behind because of interruptions like this," Leahy fumed. Other Republican complaints were that a county worker was handling the ballots "too roughly" and that Democratic observers were chewing gum. (Lally, who raised this objection as well, later explained that he was worried about "sticky" hands.) By day's end, the returns from an additional 32 precincts had been counted—for a total of 99 out of 614. Out of this number, the vice president gained a net of 157 votes. And so the counting continued.[74]

As tense as feelings were getting in the counting room, the tension was even greater outside. In the hallway outside the counting room and on the street, hundreds of Republican supporters stood to protest the recount process. "This thing is rigged!" Republican Congressman David Hobson of Ohio cried. "It is a joke on our democracy." New York Congressman John Sweeney complained, "Miami-Dade has become ground zero for producing a manufactured vote." Inside, GOP supporters and observers, most from out of state, slowed down the recounts by pounding on the glass windows and stomping their feet while yelling "Stop the fraud!" and "Voter fraud!" At one point, when Miami-Dade County spokesperson Mike Villafana stepped out into the hallway, he was trapped against the door by a mob of angry protesters shouting, "Don't hit me, don't hit me." (Interestingly, the only one being hit at the time was Villafana, who was being kicked by protestors out of sight below the bottom edge of the image shown on TV.) Perhaps the scariest incident occurred when county Democratic Party chair Joe Geller was mobbed by dozens of Republicans when he went downstairs to pick up a clearly marked sample ballot. "This guy's got a ballot," yelled house staffer Duane Gibson. "This guy's got a ballot." Yelling "Thief, thief!" and "Arrest Him!" the group chased Geller down to the first floor where county sheriffs led him to safety.[75]

While most of the protestors claimed to be just "average" Americans outraged by what they saw as an improper procedure, in reality the majority of those protesting on the Republican side had ties to the Republican Party and the Bush-Cheney campaign. From premade signs and t-shirts to help with transportation and housing, the protests were organized and directed by skilled political operatives of the Bush recount team. The goal was to disrupt the recount process while making clear their opposition to hand recounts. Hence, when the Florida Supreme Court's ruling setting a final deadline of November 26 for recounts was announced and the board decided to recount only the undervotes, a call from Bush representative Sweeney resulted in a crowd of eighty protesters storming the hallways and chanting "Let us in, let us in!" while banging on the doors and windows and walls.[76]

It is impossible to know exactly what influence loud and disruptive protests had on the board's thinking. However, not being able to leave the counting room for fear of the mob outside their door most likely played a part in shaping the board's response to the Florida Supreme Court's deadline. Leahy argued that there was no way that the board could complete the recount in the time allotted. "The canvassing board cannot work 24 hours a day, which is what would be needed," explained Leahy. The board's first response was to count just the undervotes. "If we, the canvassing board, did approximately three hundred ballots an hour—which is pushing it, but possibly doable—it would take us about thirty-six hours to do that," noted Leahy. He suggested moving the counting upstairs to a smaller room where excess observers (and the press) could view the proceedings only through a window. It was now that the Republicans' protests reached their peak and began disrupting the proceedings so that the board could no longer proceed. A motion was made by King to return to the larger room to allow more observers into the process.

Perhaps this would lessen the chaos? The board agreed and, clearly unable to do its job, adjourned until later in the day.[77]

Reconvening at 1:30 p.m., the board members were shaken by the day's events. They called in counsel from both parties. "The reason and purpose for our meeting here at this hour after we previously had decided that we felt we could reasonably meet the deadline of the Supreme Court of Florida for an expedited yet accurate count has been somewhat changed," explained King. They asked county attorney Robert Ginsburg if an extension to the 5:00 p.m. Sunday deadline was likely. Ginsburg answered no. "I will advise you," said Ginsburg, that "the supreme court opinion in its conclusion specifically negates any kind of petition for rehearing." The deadline is "final." Leahy then moved that they halt all recounts. Even trying to count the 10,750 undervotes might be too much for the board. "I can't sit here and tell you that if we begin the process, it will be concluded," said Leahy. The logistics of separating votes on one floor and counting them on another were just prohibitive. King agreed. "We cannot meet the deadline." Judge Lehr agreed as well. And so the counting in Miami-Dade ended—and with it, so too ended the likelihood that Al Gore would find the necessary votes he needed from the hand recounts to pull ahead of George Bush.[78]

Recounts were not the only source of additional votes following the election. There was also the matter of overseas absentee ballots—most sent in by military personnel stationed overseas. Division of Elections rules allowed the counties ten days following the election to collect and count absentee ballots from abroad. The rules for these ballots were the same as for all absentee ballots—they had to be filled out correctly and signed by both the voter and a witness. So long as they were postmarked by Election Day and sent from a foreign postal service, however, the county boards could include them in their final tally, even if the ballots did not arrive on or before Election Day.

The problem with these ballots arose because many of them were improperly filled out. There was nothing new about this problem. In 1996, Florida counties threw out approximately 40 percent of all overseas absentee ballots. The same would be true in this election. The most common problem was the lack of a postmark. In addition, many lacked the proper signatures (either of the voter or the witness or both). In a few cases, the signature on the ballot did not match the signature on record with the elections office. Others were postmarked after the November 7 election. Finally, a very small number of ballots were invalid because the voter was not properly registered as a voter.[79]

Still, the absolute numbers of invalidated votes were staggering. Broward rejected 304 of 396 (246 of those military ballots). Miami-Dade threw out 209 of 312. Orange County rejected 117 of 147, while Duval County threw out 116 of 618. The state statute, however, was clear in this matter. A 1989 law required the presence of a postmark and signature for a valid vote. "My dad was in the military for 22 years," noted Rick Mullaney, member of the all-Republican Duval County Canvassing Board that threw out 42 military ballots that either were without a postmark or postmarked after November 7. "I'm appreciative of all the efforts [of] the military, but Florida statute is clear. . . . We need to do better, but unless there is a postmark, I don't think we can record the vote." Pat Hollam, elections supervisor in Okaloosa County, was even blunter in his views: "We never accepted them [without postmarks] before, and we didn't accept them this time."[80]

This should have been the end of the debate. However, in this election, little was going the way it was supposed to go. The real problem here was that a majority of the rejected overseas ballots were from serving military personnel who were expected to vote for George Bush. With a separation between the two candidates of fewer than 300 votes, these few votes could be the difference between victory and defeat. The expectation among many was that the "Republican overseas military vote is going to win this for Bush."[81] The result was a reversal of roles for the two parties. Now it was the Republicans who were fighting for an inclusive count and it was the Democrats who were holding the line in defense of the statutory rules.[82]

Katherine Harris, for instance, issued an order that canvassing boards had to "accept otherwise-valid ballots from overseas that were postmarked after Election Day" so long as they were dated and signed by this date—a move that many Democrats charged was nothing more than a blatant attempt to gain "the maximum number of overseas votes counted, valid or not, in the belief that they would benefit Bush."[83] Democrats, on the other had, were under orders to "challenge, and challenge again, hoping to deny Bush the overseas votes."[84] To facilitate this end, Florida attorney Mark Herron even wrote a memo on behalf of the Democratic Party outlining the ways that one could invalidate an overseas absentee ballot.[85]

More than anything else in this postelection process, this role reversal showed the tactical imperatives that drove the postelection contest. When Republicans like Brian Cresta argued that "Al Gore's campaign doesn't believe that every ballot should be counted. They think that only their ballots should be counted," there was validity to this charge. It was, after all, a war for votes, and Gore needed to limit Bush's gains from the absentee ballots almost as much as he needed votes from the hand recounts. "If we had not done this, Bush would have had 700 to 2,000 more votes," one key Gore operative explained. The troops on the ground were even more explicit. Allow in these votes and "we would lose."[86]

Of course, when Democrats charged that the Republicans were hypocrites who were telling lies about their true views, they also had a point. The Republicans were arguing for something that they had been attacking for days in the recount process.[87] As state Democratic Party chair Bob Poe complained to the press: "They use the law when it suits their purposes, and ignore the law when it suits their purposes. There's an amazing, tremendous inconsistency on their part."[88]

Still, the Republicans knew they had an advantage and were going to play it for all it was worth. This was especially the case on the public relations front. Despite knowing how insincere the Republicans' words in praise of counting every vote were—given their actions and positions in the recount process—the absentee-ballot matter put the Democrats on the defensive. Once they got a copy of the Herron memo in their hands, the Bush team attacked. "Last night," said Montana governor Marc Racicot, "we learned how far the vice president's campaign will go to win this election. And I am very sorry to say but the vice president's lawyers have gone to war, in my judgment, against the men and women who serve in our armed forces." From his sickbed (he had the flu), General Norman Schwarzkopf complained to the media (at the request of a Bush staffer): "it is a very sad day in our country when the men and women of the armed forces are serving abroad and facing danger on a daily basis, yet because of some technicality out of their control, they are denied the right to vote for the president of the United States who will be their commander in chief."[89]

Criticisms of this sort were a public relations disaster for the Democrats. Gore was basing his entire effort on his plea to "let every vote count." It was for this reason that Gore had offered to accept (however late) the results of a statewide manual recount. As presented by the Republicans, however, Gore's absentee ballot efforts were a total repudiation of his stated objectives.[90] (Of course, the Democrats could have argued—and many did—that they were opposing *only* those ballots that clearly were invalid under state law, no different in impact than the overvotes that they accepted as invalid, but the damage already had been done.)[91] The situation got even worse for the Democrats when vice-presidential candidate Joe Lieberman and Florida Attorney General Bob Butterworth argued publicly (Lieberman on TV and Butterworth in an advisory opinion issued by his office) that all the challenged ballots should be counted. "If I were there, I would give the benefit of the doubt to ballots coming in from military personnel generally," Lieberman told the TV audience. "Go back and take another look. Because, again, Al Gore and I don't want to ever be part of anything that would put an extra burden on the military personnel abroad who want to vote."[92]

With dissent within their own ranks and Republican cries of hypocrisy heard all over the airwaves, the Democrats backed down. By this time, most canvassing boards had already certified their absentee ballots. However, following the filing of a lawsuit to force the inclusion of military ballots, the Republicans got some of the Republican-dominated canvassing boards to re-inspect their military ballots. The Duval County board, for example, decided to reopen the issue after it was dropped from a Republican lawsuit. Quoting Lieberman's stated position on military ballots, board chairman Rick Mullaney asked Gore's lawyers how they wanted to proceed. Their answer was: the board should do whatever it felt was right. "They were in a box," recalled Mullaney. "Those lawyers were in a difficult position, and their attitude had completely changed." With no real objections, the board decided to reevaluate a number of the disputed ballots. The result was an additional forty-four votes added to Bush's tally. And so began what the Gore team called Bush's "Thanksgiving stuffing" as still other counties reexamined their military ballots as well. Santa Rosa County netted Bush twenty-one more votes after a review of their rejected overseas ballots. Clay County added twelve more votes for Bush. Brevard added eight net votes and Bay and Okaloosa Counties added two net votes each.[93] And so the counting process came to an end.

On November 26, at 5:00 p.m., Florida secretary of state Katherine Harris announced the amended returns and certified the results. With a vote total of 2,912,790 votes, George W. Bush defeated Al Gore (who had 2,912,253 votes) by a mere 537 votes. The election was over. Or was it? Gore had lost his recount gamble. However, after nineteen days of fighting, Gore was still convinced that he had won Florida. In fact, the recount process strengthened his conviction that he was the winner.[94] As went Gore, so went the Democratic Party. "Right now, ladies and gentlemen, we are at a statistical dead heat," declared Democratic Representative Ed Markey in West Palm Beach. "Hold on to your hats." The election was far from over.[95] Other Democrats agreed. Former president Jimmy Carter warned that "this may take time, but it is time well spent. . . . We must not sacrifice accuracy for speed in deciding who has been chosen by the voters."[96] Gore lawyer David Boies noted that thousands of votes remained uncounted. "Until these votes are counted, this election cannot be over," Boies told a news conference. "There are thousands of votes that haven't been counted once."[97]

Back in Washington, D.C., Al Gore entrusted his political future to the Florida courts. He would contest the Florida election totals as permitted under Florida law. And that verdict, whatever it may be, Gore promised, would prove to future generations that "We were indeed a country of laws." Our Constitution "matters more than convenience," Gore said. "So, as provided under Florida law, I have decided to contest this inaccurate and incomplete count, in order to ensure the greatest possible credibility for the outcome." "Two hundred years from now, when future Americans study this presidential election, let them learn that Americans did everything they could to ensure that all citizens who voted had their votes counted," Gore said. "Let them learn that democracy was ultimately placed ahead of partisan politics in resolving a contested election. Let them learn that we were indeed a country of laws."[98]

Republicans, as one would expect, ridiculed this position. The election was over, they cried. "Enough is enough," said New York's Republican governor, George Pataki, who had observed the recount process for the Bush campaign. "The American people understand that the person who carries Florida will be our next president. We've now had a count, a recount, a recount of the recount. Governor Bush has won all three. I think it's time for him to be recognized by the Gore team as our president-elect." Senator Trent Lott of Mississippi agreed with this view, calling on Gore "to end his campaign and concede this election with the honor and dignity the American people expect." The views of the party's rank and file found voice in Todd Emoff, a forty-four-year-old investment adviser from Columbus, Ohio, who drove all night to join other Bush protesters in front of Florida's capitol. "I had to be with people that are on the front lines of preventing this election from being stolen," Emoff said. "Everyone knows we won now. Al Gore's unemployed. He's going to have to get a job!"[99]

George Bush's own response to the Democrat's legal challenge was to expand his lineup of trial lawyers. It was time, he said, to "set the record straight."[100] If Gore wanted a court fight, then he was going to get one. As James Baker pointed out in a news conference, "We've got quite a bit of accumulated years of trial experience behind me here." They were ready and they were confident that the courts, in particular the U.S. Supreme Court, would vindicate their position.[101]

And so the 2000 presidential postelection moved into the courts. In fact, it had already been in the courts for almost two weeks. Mirroring almost every twist and turn in the recount and absentee ballot debate were court cases. Brought by both sides and third parties, lawsuits were a crucial part of the postelection conflict. All claims of not wanting to involve the courts aside, both the Gore and Bush teams depended on the courts as integral to their strategies for victory. It is to these legal struggles that we now must turn.

CHAPTER FOUR
The Battlefield of Litigation

Politics is war conducted by other means. In political warfare you do not fight just to prevail in an argument, but to destroy the enemy's fighting ability. . . .
—*David Horowitz*, The Art of Political War

The boundary between law and politics is hardly an impregnable barrier. It is more like a cell membrane, porous, flexible, and highly permeable. The domains of constitutional law and constitutional politics are continually interpenetrating.
—*Jack M. Balkin*, Yale Law Journal

In retrospect, we should not be surprised that the 2000 presidential election controversy ended up in the courts. Rather, it would have been astonishing had the courts *not* come to play a key role in resolving the crisis. This was, after all, America—the land of the lawsuit—overflowing with more lawyers per capita than any other nation in the world. Granted, our fears of a litigation explosion are usually limited to just that—fears. Still, we are a rights-conscious, lawyer-driven, litigation-focused society.[1] When things fail to go our way, our first thought may well be to take the matter to court. Where other cultures might use mediation or government bureaucracies to settle a dispute, we resort to litigation. We are even more likely to reach for a lawsuit when the underlying dispute is founded on the sorts of technical legal issues that are the judiciary's normal dominion. And election contests are, by their very nature, highly technical legal matters involving essential questions of fundamental constitutional rights.

In other words, the situation in Florida was ripe for litigation. Both candidates had teams of lawyers armed and ready to fight. Each side was convinced that its candidate had "won" Florida, and with it the presidency. Each side was committed to applying every lever it could find to win this fight—including, if necessary, turning to the courts. And everything seemed to be pushing both sides to litigate. For all intents and purposes, Florida election law was ineffectual in the face of the current election crisis. Although the rules were generally clear, the procedures for their application were not. The recount process generated endless numbers of questions of law and fact—questions whose technical and legal content begged for judicial resolution. What was a valid vote? What constituted proof of the "will of the voter"? When under Florida law were hand recounts permissible? When, if ever, were they mandated? Someone would have to answer these and similar questions. Who better than the Florida courts could answer what were essentially legal questions? Like it or not, the state's judiciary would be drawn into the fray. Both sides knew this, and were ready and willing to take their case to the courts.

Nor should we be surprised—though at the time most legal scholars were very surprised—that ultimately the *federal* courts took the central role in settling the dispute. True, as noted previously, the federal courts had a long tradition of avoiding cases posing political questions—in particular, questions associated with electoral outcomes.[2] Election contests are messy. By definition, such disputes speak directly to the divided will of the people. Rarely is there a "right" or "wrong" solution to the dispute. Inevitably, judges have to make choices that "ignore" the will of at least a part of the electorate. The result, no matter how hard the courts work to find a middle ground, usually will be controversial—and often inadequate to solving the problem.[3]

Nor were democratic theory and practical sense the only reasons for federal courts to be wary of electoral messes such as Florida in 2000. Federalism—the concept of split government in which some matters remain under national control and some under state control—also pushed federal courts away from these matters. The Constitution largely leaves the running of elections—state and federal—in the hands of the states. In the question of choosing a president, for example, Article II of the Constitution requires: "Each State shall appoint, in such Manner as the Legislature thereof may direct, a Number of Electors, equal to the whole Number of Senators and Representatives to which the State may be entitled in the Congress."[4] A similarly worded provision in Article I empowers the states to run congressional elections—specifically permitting the states to define the "Times, Places, and Manner" by which members of Congress are elected.[5] Likewise, federal statutes give the states rather than the federal government the power to resolve controversies over the selections of presidential electors.[6]

Still, on deeper examination, the federal courts' intervention in the 2000 electoral crisis was inevitable—or at least highly likely. Although tradition, federalism, and constitutional text all seemed to fix these matters firmly in the realm of the state courts, the federal courts did not necessarily *have* to remain aloof. Since the late nineteenth century, federal courts and Congress had taken turns "constitutionalizing" the voting process as the Supreme Court struggled with the implications of the civil rights amendments and federal statutes enacted under their authority. What had once seemed matters of local concern, these amendments transformed into questions of potential or actual national importance, depending on the facts of the dispute. Actions limiting the franchise or otherwise hindering the voting process, therefore, no longer were *just* political questions affecting political contests; they also were potential violations of fundamental constitutional and civil rights. By necessity, these possibilities forced federal judges to look beyond the obvious political ramifications when hearing voting rights cases. These new constitutional realities required them to understand that whereas voting might be a political question (and hence not a concern of the federal courts), the right to vote itself was constitutional—at least, in extraordinary circumstances placing at risk the integrity of the vote or some other important related constitutional right. Whereas the federal courts could and probably should avoid getting entangled in the former process, the Constitution demanded their involvement in the latter category of issues. In other words, sometimes the issues raised by voting could become so big as to require federal courts to enter the political thicket and get scratched. In these instances, voting disputes were matters of national concern demanding federal intervention.[7]

Such was to be the case with the 2000 presidential election controversy. If the federal courts wanted to get involved, they had a legal justification to do so—at least as long as they were willing to deem events to have moved into the "extraordinary" realm of fundamental constitutional rights. Pushing them in this direction, in turn, was the public's notable confidence in the unelected judiciary's ability to wrestle with painful and complex issues of constitutional law—a confidence significantly lacking when it came to the government's political branches. It may have been a feature of the boilerplate of political rhetoric to denounce activist federal judges, but at the same time those judges commanded greater respect among the electorate than the politicians mouthing that rhetoric could do. This perception helped to spark a similar conviction in the minds and hearts of the federal judiciary themselves. Thus, an agonizing constitutional and legal crisis seemed to cry out for judicial resolution.

Perhaps it is best to view this process in terms of momentum. Once the two candidates had assembled their legal teams and defined their strategies, the move to litigation was predictable. To win, each side needed the recounts to follow a specific pattern—liberal for Gore, conservative for Bush. Any deviation from these patterns required a turn to the courts to get matters "back on track." The result was a blizzard of court cases. By the crisis's end, for instance, Katherine Harris's lawyers—the firm of Steel Hector—alone either defended against or brought forty lawsuits in the state and federal courts (all this in thirty-six days).[8] And once the state courts were involved, it was inevitable that the crisis would find its way into the federal courts. For, as the constitutional and legal issues argued in these courts grew ever more intense, the momentum of the electoral crisis as a legal crisis built up like a train heading downhill. And, as with a fast-moving train, once momentum built up, it was inevitable that the train would keep moving no matter what red lights were flashing demanding that the train stop. At the bottom of the metaphorical hill sat Washington and the U.S. Supreme Court. With gravity and momentum on its side, this train was not going to stop until it hit the bottom of the hill. The questions were going to grow too big, the potential answers too controversial, and the consequences too vital for the U.S. Supreme Court not to get involved.

Thus, when commentators and critics call this "the election that the judges decided," they are correct. In the end, the 2000 presidential election crisis was all about judges striving to find answers to difficult and highly controversial legal and constitutional questions—and to do so in very short periods of time while under enormous pressure and in the face of unprecedented public scrutiny. Yet we must remember that it was not just the U.S. Supreme Court that decided the election. Judges from every level in the Florida and federal court systems would reach decisions that affected the election's outcome—and they did it because it was their job to do so. This is not to say that the decisions they came up with were necessarily good ones—they often were not—nor that these differing judges would arrive at similar conclusions—because they did not—but that the courts had well-defined and vehemently demanded roles to play in this process.

Election 2000 was a pitched battle with legal briefs in place of rifles and bayonets—lawsuits fired across a metaphorical bloody battlefield—and the last team standing would be declared the winner. Each side had come to view the contest as an "all-out war of good versus evil, right versus wrong and playing fair versus playing dirty, with no easy choices." Their legal strategies reflected this view. "How could they be feeling anything but apprehensive and concerned?" asked one official of the Bush camp. "If they have options, then the other side has options. And when you think about what are their options, what are our options, your head just explodes."[9]

But this is getting ahead of the story. On Saturday, November 11, as the Palm Beach County Canvassing Board began its sample hand count to determine if a full countywide recount was necessary, the only litigation under way was a flurry of lawsuits by Palm Beach County residents angry about the butterfly ballot and its perceived damage to their right to vote. Filed in the immediate aftermath of the election, these suits challenged the butterfly ballot as confusing, illegal, and ultimately unconstitutional. Declaring themselves disenfranchised, the plaintiffs called on the courts to declare the election results for president and vice president in Palm Beach County "null and void" and to direct a total or partial revote without the butterfly ballot "on an expedited basis."[10]

By day's end, however, the situation had changed. That morning, just hours after the sample count had begun in Palm Beach County (and almost a day before the Palm Beach County Canvassing Board would vote 2 to 1 in favor of a countywide recount), George W. Bush's lawyers filed motion in the Southern District Court of Florida challenging the hand recounts. In its introduction, the complaint argued that hand recounts were less accurate than machine counts and that "human error and individual subjectivity" was no replacement for "precision machinery in tabulating millions of small marks and fragile hole punches." The complaint also questioned limiting hand recounts to a few select counties. It was bad enough that the counts would be inconsistent, the complaint argued, but what was worse was that this procedure was just recounting the votes for a specific desired result—not to determine who really won. Recounts by hand, "until the results are different," the complaint concluded, "will not further the interests of the voters or of the nation."

Having established the importance of the matter while attacking the questionable usefulness of hand recounts, the complaint next explained the inadequacies of Florida law—inadequacies that demanded federal action. It noted that Florida law granted almost unlimited discretion to local canvassing boards to determine how to conduct the tally of votes. This meant that "one canvassing board may decide to count votes that are not fully punched; another may not." Worse yet, "one canvassing board may decide that a stray mark indicated an intent to vote for a particular candidate; another board may not." Such discretion, the complaint argued, "creates arbitrariness in the implementation of a process that concerns the fundamental right to vote." The complaint contended therefore that the lack of uniform standards in defining a valid ballot was an unconstitutional violation of the Fourteenth Amendment's grant of equal protection.

The next point in the complaint's sights was Gore's decision to limit the recounts to a few select counties. In attacking the discretion left to the county canvassing boards by Florida law, the complaint noted that under the existing statute, "a disappointed candidate in a close election can seek recounts [in] successive favorable jurisdictions until he is satisfied with the results, and thereby arbitrarily deny the force and effect of the votes cast and validly counted (and verified on recount) for the winning candidate." In addition, the potential for selective recounts to limit the political speech of those voters whose votes were not recounted continued so long as the "standardless nature of the recount and contest scheme [granted] government officials . . . [the] arbitrary power and authority to deny the vote and thus thwart political speech." Combined with the potential for vote dilution and political manipulation of selective recounts, the result was again a constitutional violation—in this case of both the First and Fourteenth Amendments.

Given such violations, the Bush team requested a federal injunction ordering an immediate halt to all hand recounts. Failing that, they requested the court to declare unconstitutional those provisions under Florida law that granted to the county canvassing boards total discretion in determining the will of the voter. Failing this, they next demanded that the court declare the butterfly ballot legally valid and further that "any ballot punched or marked for two Presidential candidates [i.e., overvotes] not previously counted cannot now be counted." Ultimately, whichever option the court adopted, the plaintiffs wanted an order forcing the county canvassing boards to certify the vote totals "that have been the subject of two vote counts since November 7, 2000."[11]

Officially, neither Gore nor the Democratic Party was a participant in this case. True, the lawsuit was challenging Gore's recount request, yet it named as defendants only the canvassing board members of the four counties contemplating recounts. The Democrats, however, needed to block this complaint. Were the judge to grant even one of Bush's motions for an injunction, Gore's chances of victory narrowed significantly. Consequently, in a brief largely written by Harvard Law School professor Laurence H. Tribe, and filing as an intervener in the case, the Democrats challenged the logical underpinnings of the Bush argument against manual recounts.

Gore's brief argued that before a federal court can exercise jurisdiction and rule in a matter, the plaintiffs had to establish that (1) "an actual or threatened injury" had in fact occurred and caused an actual harm; (2) that "a causal connection [existed] between the injury and the challenged action of the defendant"; and (3) that the court's favorable ruling to this motion would effectively "redress that injury." Arguing in defense of the state's recount procedures (in particular the validity of hand recounts), the Democrats challenged the adequacy of Bush's complaint in each of these categories. Given the presence of the state procedures for contested elections, the Florida state courts' long-term acceptance of these procedures, the lack of a valid federal question for the district court to rule upon (for these matters were questions of state law only), and the fact that no real harm had yet occurred (at best the plaintiffs had shown the possibility that something might go wrong during a hand recount and even this was just conjecture) they called on the judge to deny the Bush motion for an injunction.[12]

It was now up to Judge Donald Middlebrooks to decide. Ruling on November 13, Middlebrooks declared first that he appreciated the "serious" nature of these arguments. He understood that the dispute's outcome would go a long way toward determining who would be the next president of the United States. He shared with all concerned a "desire for finality" in these matters. Yet he questioned whether his court was the proper forum for achieving this finality. In the end, he determined that it was not.

After summarizing the facts of the case, Judge Middlebrooks explored Florida's election provisions. He found them "reasonable and non-discriminatory" on their face. Florida's manual recount provisions, he noted, were the sort of "'generally-applicable and evenhanded' electoral scheme designed to 'protect the integrity and reliability of the electoral process itself'—the type of state electoral law often upheld in federal legal challenges." True, they allowed a large measure of discretion on the part of the county canvassing boards. However, this discretion was not "wholly standardless." Existing guidelines made clear that "the manual recount provision [was] intended to safeguard the integrity and reliability of the electoral process." This was a good thing. Decentralized recounts with adequate discretion in the hands of election officials secured the system. As he noted, "rather than a sign of weakness or constitutional injury, some solace can be taken in the fact that no one centralized body or person can control the tabulation of an entire statewide or national election. For the more county boards and individuals involved in the electoral regulation process, the less likely it becomes that corruption, bias or error can influence the ultimate result of an election."

Having upheld the validity of Florida's electoral procedures, Judge Middlebrooks then placed oversight of these procedures squarely in the hands of the state courts. Florida's recount provisions were "the type of state electoral law that safely resides within the broad ambit of state control over presidential election procedures." As he read the precedents, the "federal courts [were] not the bosses in state election disputes unless extraordinary circumstances affecting the integrity of the state's electoral process [were] clearly present in a high degree." This he took as a basic statement of federalism, "that federal courts interfere in state elections [only] as a last resort." Such was not the case in Florida. Bush had an adequate forum in the state courts to argue his case. There was no need for the federal courts to get involved. The judge therefore ruled against the injunctions requested and dismissed the complaint.[13]

While Judge Middlebrooks contemplated George W. Bush's request to invalidate hand recounts as a matter of constitutional law, the hand recounts began in Palm Beach, Volusia, and later Broward Counties. As we have seen, it was not long before the limits in Florida's election laws came to the fore as the vote counters faced the many practical and procedural difficulties in holding a major recount for such a nationally important office.

Almost from the start, arguments and complaints as to what was and was not a valid ballot (more precisely, proof of a voter's intent on the ballot making it valid or not) threatened to derail the recount process. Did proof require enough penetration to separate part of the chad from the card, or was partial penetration (in the form of an indentation) enough? If separation was necessary, how much separation? One corner? Three sides? Just a pinprick that allowed light to shine through the chad's perforations? The law was unclear.

Absentee ballots from abroad posed similar concerns. State policy allowed these ballots extra time for delivery before being counted, but left open the question of their acceptance. What if the ballot had been signed and sealed by Election Day, but postmarked the day after? Should this ballot be accepted? Did military ballots have to have a valid postmark for inclusion? Or were military ballots different and thus exempt from this rule? Here too, the law was unclear.

Then there was the question of timing. How much time was available to complete the recounts? What if the boards carrying out the recounts needed more time than state statute allowed? On November 9, Katherine Harris announced that her office would not accept *any* late returns. The statutes said that all returns were due seven days after the election, and seven days it would be. Any revised county totals not in by 5:00 p.m. on November 14 would be excluded from the final totals.[14] In a later memo dated November 13, Clay Roberts on behalf of Harris argued that this was a mandatory requirement, one that left Harris no discretion in the matter.[15] Yet did she really lack discretion? Could the county boards get an extension despite Harris's denials? And if not, were returns based on only partial recounts legally acceptable? One again, the law was unclear.

Even more demanding were questions challenging the validity of hand recounts under Florida law. Were hand recounts allowable under state statutes given the existing conditions? Once again, Harris's office ruled no—hand recounts were permitted *only* where the cause of error was machine-related. Close races and voter-based errors were not legitimate grounds for manual recounts. Conversely, attorney General Bob Butterworth argued that any error in the tabulation of an accurate vote count was grounds for manual recounts. So who was correct? Here too, the law did not say.

The butterfly ballot hinted at yet another dilemma drawing the players to the courts. Given the limitations of the butterfly ballot and—as we shall see—procedural improprieties associated with absentee ballots in Seminole and Martin Counties, was the election as held even valid? The multipage presidential ballot in Duval County raised similar questions. If one could not even trust the ballot one was voting on—or trust the government to register properly those who sent in their forms—how could the election itself be trusted? And if voters were improperly denied the ballot or even the chance to get a ballot, could the election be allowed to stand? Then there were the claims brought by the African American community of voter denial and disenfranchisement—of broken machines, moved precincts, illegal voter purges, and police intimidation. Here was a clear case—if proven true—of serious electoral breakdown. Was this not what the Fourteenth and especially the Fifteenth Amendments had been written to avoid?

These were valid questions, but could a Florida court, or even a federal court, invalidate a presidential election—especially as, given the current state of affairs, the winner of Florida was the winner nationally? In other words, the quandary in these cases was not in noting the problems, but in finding solutions. What remedies could—and would—the courts provide for these cases of vote denial and dilution—again assuming that the contentions of misconduct were proven true?

Finally, there were the issues in contention before Judge Middlebrooks. Could a valid determination of accurate vote totals be contemplated in a legal system that lacked a uniform standard as to what constituted a valid vote? Was it fair that one ballot could be accepted as valid in one county while a similar ballot was denied legitimacy in another county? How could two similarly marked ballots in two different counties be proof and not proof of a voter's intent at the same time? Here the law was not so much unclear as extremely conflicted, each side arguing from its own chosen precedents for or against the local autonomy that produced such variations.

Adding to the confusion, the move to the courts to answer these questions was often less about discovering answers than it was a search for vindication and support for answers already predetermined by the participants. Neither side was shy in arguing its case. Nor were they shy about turning to the courts for help when their views were ignored. Where a canvassing board's answers to a legal, political, or practical question were not to their likings, both sides quickly turned to the courts for clarification and help; so too, when the secretary of state's office issued advisory opinions that challenged one or the other side's efforts. Indeed, the secretary of state's office and the county canvassing boards were just as willing to turn to the courts for help. In fact, just about everyone involved in the dispute—the candidates, their parties, government agents involved in the recounts, and even the people— were predisposed to turn to the courts if it meant support for their specific legal positions or provided answers to their legal quandaries. And, as we shall see, the courts themselves would prove more than willing to take up these issues.

The result was a complex and confusing narrative—only now of overlapping litigations rather than of events, policy decisions, and recount frenzy. By month's end, thirty-four different lawsuits were on the dockets of both the state and federal court systems. December would see the start of an additional six cases with more to follow.[16] November 13 alone saw five suits initiated in the state courts with an additional six complaints filed with the courts on November 14. Each case, in turn, affected the other cases in many ways—and each was affected by the others just the same. It was common for the judge in one case to refer to the ruling of another court in handing down his own judgment. That judgment, in turn, might then modify the impact of the earlier case, necessitating a return to court in that earlier case—or even the filing of an entirely new legal action. And so events continued, with lawsuit following lawsuit after lawsuit.

The narrative that follows in this and the next three chapters, of necessity, will treat each of the categories of legal quandaries described above separately. Any other approach would prove too confusing in our efforts to understand the nature and impact of these litigations.[17] However, we must keep in mind the multistrand nature of the litigation process and the close time frame in which these legal actions took place. Not only does the multistrand time frame mean that most of these issues were argued in the courts simultaneously, but it shows just how intense the processes of arguing and deciding these cases were. No participant had the luxury of an ample period in which to construct his or her legal arguments. Nor did the judges have the opportunity to sit and contemplate their answers. A delay of days or even of hours could change the entire course of events in Florida. As noted, sometimes decisions in one category of lawsuit would completely change the context in which another was being argued or decided. Everyone involved not only had to be willing to move rapidly, but to be flexible and open to multitasking. And although the results of this process lacked the surreal dark comedy of the recounts, they were definitely not the staid actions that we normally associate with judicial proceedings.

November 13 was a difficult day in the Palm Beach County recount. After one and a half days of hand-counting ballots, the board was beginning to lose its cohesion (such as it was). Not only was the board split on the issue of how to carry out the recounts, but they disagreed on whether to continue the recounts at all. In the space of a few hours, the board would decide to tighten its standard of a valid vote to a two-sided separation rule, to initiate a full manual recount of the county's ballots, and to seek advice from the secretary of state's office on the legitimacy of manual recounts. These decisions, in turn, initiated a series of reactions from not only the secretary of state's office, but also the state attorney general's office and the Democratic Party.

In terms of counting votes, the Palm Beach board's decision to tighten their standards for a valid ballot placed the Democrats in a difficult position. They needed these votes. With Gore, the bottom line was always the same—without more votes he lost. So while the Democrats were pleased that the board had agreed to a complete manual recount of the county's votes, they needed the board to return to a more lenient standard of proof of a voter's intent or all their efforts were for naught. It was with this in mind that the Florida Democratic Party sued in Palm Beach County Circuit Court on November 13, seeking "a declaratory judgment holding that the Canvassing Board's present standards for reviewing challenged ballots [was] illegal and in violation of Florida law." Further, they asked for an "injunction ordering the Canvassing Board to review" the disputed ballots "based on the totality of the evidence in the four corners of the punchcard ballot."

The Democrats argued in their complaint that Section 102.166(7) (b) of the *Florida Statutes* prohibited a canvassing board from applying a per se rule that limited a valid vote to only those ballots with "detached chads." The statute called for canvassing board members to review the ballots "based on the totality of the evidence." Predetermining that a ballot without two sides of the chad detached was invalid was not looking at the totality of the ballot. Perhaps the entire ballot was filled with indentations, but had no separation of chads? Could this not stand as proof that the voter was trying to vote but mechanical difficulty with the voting machine or physical infirmity limited the strength of penetration? Such ballots, the Democrats had argued to the canvassing board (and now to the judge) should be taken to show the voter's intent. As Benedict Kuehne, attorney for the Florida Democratic Party, noted to the press, there were several hundred "dimpled" ballots that would have been counted but were excluded by the canvassing board's too-strict standard—enough votes to change the election's outcome.[18]

Responding quickly to the Democrats' complaint, Circuit Judge Jorge Labarga issued a one-page declaratory order early in the afternoon of November 15. In this order, Labarga noted how "the present policy utilized by the local election officials restricts the canvassing board's ability to determine the intent of the voter." This being the case, the judge held that the "Palm Beach Canvassing Commission [*sic*] ha[d] the discretion to utilize whatever methodology it deem[ed] proper to determine the true intention of the voter and [that] it should not be restricted in the task." The board, the judge explained, had "the discretion to consider . . . ballots and accept them or reject them." However, "the present policy of a per se exclusion of any ballot that does not have a partially punched or hanging chad, [was] not in compliance with the law."[19]

Without explaining his legal reasoning or making clear how the board could have full "discretion to consider . . . ballots and accept them or reject them" while at the same time was "not in compliance with the law" when it made just such a determination to reject ballots without a hanging chad, the judge's order was, to say the least, confusing. The Palm Beach canvassing board's response was to do nothing. The two-side standard had been effective in 1990, and they saw no reason why they should not use it now. This was their "methodology . . . to determine the true intention of the voter," and they saw no reason not to stick with it.[20]

Getting desperate (and reading a stronger imperative to count dimpled chads into Judge Labarga's ruling than did the board), the Democrats returned to Judge Labarga's courtroom on November 20 for an emergency hearing to force the board to adopt a more open definition of a valid vote. With the manual recount already under way, time was of the essence. (The Republicans were worried, too. Bush lawyer John Bolton later recalled, "We saw this as the battle of Stalingrad. If we lost here they would just roll over us.")[21] The Democrats needed a more complete examination of the disputed ballots if they were going to get the Palm Beach board to do its job properly (as they saw the job) and help Al Gore regain the votes that he had lost. "Because the manual recount is already underway, and because of the importance that the manual recount be conducted using the correct standard for determining what counts as a vote," their petition argued, "it is critical that this Court address the issues" raised by the original complaint in greater and more concrete detail. The Republicans, needless to say, opposed this request as unnecessary. In defense of this position, they cited the canvassing board's own determination that they already were in compliance with Judge Labarga's original order.[22]

Judge Labarga was willing to provide additional direction. Given the wording of Section 101 of Title IX of the *Florida Statutes*, he explained, it was clear that the "Florida Legislature intended to leave any determination concerning the question of voter intent with the canvassing board." The question before the court, therefore, was "the *standard* that the canvassing board must apply in determining the intention of the voters as it examines ballots without a clearly identifiable puncture through one of the Presidential slots." To determine what this proper standard was, Judge Labarga turned to the Florida Supreme Court's just-issued ruling in *Palm Beach County Canvassing Board v. Katherine Harris* (challenging Harris's certification deadline and discussed in detail in the next chapter). In that decision, the court had stressed that the principal purpose of election laws was to allow officials to "obtain an honest expression of the will or desire of the voter." All other considerations were subordinate to this prime objective so long as "the intention of the voter can be fairly and satisfactorily ascertained."[23]

In practical terms, this holding meant that where a ballot was marked with an indention near or on a chad, that indention should be accepted as proof of intent to vote for the office associated with this chad. As the Florida Supreme Court had ruled in 1917, "where a ballot is so marked as to plainly indicate the voter's choice and intent in placing his marks thereupon, it should be counted as marked unless some positive provision of the law would be thereby violated." The goal was to empower the voter, not defeat them. Given such reasoning, Judge Labarga once again ruled that "the only bright line rule a canvassing board is permitted to have in Florida is that there can be no per se rule excluding any ballot."

The judge, however, did not issue an injunction forcing the canvassing board to accept any one particular standard of intent. The assessment of what constituted proof of a voter's intent remained solely the preserve of the canvassing board— they simply could not judge a ballot without looking it over "in its totality" first.[24] All of this left the Palm Beach recount right back where it started—with the board holding that a two-corner rule was in compliance with the state statutory requirements for counting votes and the Democrats complaining loudly and arguing for a looser standard.

One day after filing their initial complaint with Judge Labarga, the Democrats were back in court again, this time in Broward County. This suit differed slightly from the Palm Beach case in that the Broward Democrats needed not only to force the board members to loosen their standards of a valid vote, but to force them to initiate a countywide recount as well. Their initial motion on November 14, therefore, was for a writ of mandamus (a court order requiring a government official to do his or her job) to force the board to begin counting ballots. When the Broward board voluntarily chose to reopen its manual recounts on the afternoon of November 14, the Democrats returned to court and amended their complaint to challenge the board's two-corner rule for counting valid votes.[25]

As had been the case in Palm Beach County, they requested a declaratory judgment mandating the application of an open and generous definition of a valid ballot. A hearing on this motion took place at 4:30 p.m. on November 17, in Judge John Miller's courtroom. After a short hearing, Judge Miller ruled from the bench in favor of counting dimpled chads as valid votes. He was concerned that the canvassing board could disenfranchise voters if it invalidated ballots with marked but undetached chads, and under Florida law, this was unacceptable. "If I find that the Board isn't counting the pregnant chads and all this other stuff that's supposed to show the totality of the ballot and show the intent of the voter, then I will tell them to do it again," the judge declared to the packed courtroom. The Broward board had argued that their two-corner rule, "under which two corners of a chad must be detached and hanging in order to count as an expression of the voter's intent," was "sound and lawful." Judge Miller disagreed. "I presume that the Broward County Canvassing Board knows what the law is that they're supposed to follow in counting the ballots by hand and knows that under the law they're not supposed to limit that to one or two points in their criteria." It was time for the Broward canvassing board not only to count votes, but also to do so in a proper manner.[26] Pushed by the judge's orders, the Broward board therefore shifted its standards of a valid vote. The result was the discovery of hundreds of additional votes for Al Gore.

The Democratic Party and Al Gore were not the only ones calling for recounts of votes. In Duval County, angry black voters seethed over the large numbers of overvotes caused by that county's use of a multipage presidential ballot. If anything, the number of overvotes from this ballot was greater than those caused by the butterfly ballot. Gore and the Democrats, though, had chosen not to challenge the situation in Duval County for the same reasons that they ultimately would abandon the butterfly ballot—it was unlikely that overvotes would gain Gore the number of votes that he needed to win the elections.[27] Political concerns such as victory or defeat were not a consideration to the African American residents of Duval, however.

Led by U.S. Representative Corrine Brown, six Jacksonville African American politicians (along with Jesse Jackson's Rainbow/PUSH, Inc., and one Duval County voter) brought suit on December 5 in Florida's 2nd Circuit Court contesting the election's outcome based on the failures of the Duval County ballot. "Due to the confusing and misleading illegal form of the ballot employed in Duval County," their complaint read, "thousands of voters were effectively denied their right to vote for their candidate of choice for the presidency and vice-presidency of the United States." This failing was directly attributable to the illegal format of the Duval County ballot, which was in conflict with the sample ballot published by the elections office before the election. This problem was compounded by the ballot's multipage format, which had the effect of luring voters to vote for more than one presidential candidate—invalidating their vote in the process. The complaint also challenged the use of punch card ballots, which caused a large number of undervotes. Finally, the complaint noted the high incidence of ballot failures for African American voters and charged that this pattern of vote denial and failure was a clear case of race-based discrimination in violation of the Fourteenth and Fifteenth Amendments (not to mention the provisions of the Voting Rights Act of 1965).

Their call was for a full reexamination of the Duval County vote. They also requested an injunction prohibiting Secretary of State Harris from certifying the election before the completion of this court ordered recount. Ultimately, they requested that the vote in Duval County be adjusted to reflect more properly the intent of the voters and to name the electors for Al Gore and Joe Lieberman as the proper electors for Florida.[28]

Assigned to Judge Terry P. Lewis, the case sat until December 8, at which time George W. Bush's lawyers asked for a dismissal. They argued that the complaint lacked a valid cause of action. At no time did the plaintiff's complaint argue or show that the irregularities claimed had affected enough votes materially to change the election's outcome, the dismissal petition read. Similarly, the complaint never alleged nor proved, as state statute required, that official misconduct, fraud, or bribery were the cause of the problems complained. Lastly, the Bush lawyers argued that the complaint itself was filed too late. State law required the filing of a contest ten days after the last county canvassing board had certified its vote. This date they argued had been November 14, over two weeks before the plaintiffs had filed their lawsuit.[29]

Five days later, Judge Lewis responded positively to the defense's motion to dismiss. Lewis agreed that the case was ripe for dismissal, but not for the reasons set out by the Republicans. "The problem here is simply one of time," the judge noted. State and federal law both placed a deadline of December 12, "by which time all contests of the election must be resolved." Failing to meet this date meant that the determination of Florida's electoral votes would fall to "legislative bodies." Time had run out to litigate this matter. The judge therefore dismissed the case with prejudice.[30]

Democratic efforts to force looser definitions of a valid vote on the canvassing boards angered Republicans. In fact, the whole litigation process in these matters infuriated Republican supporters of George W. Bush. Republican lawyers passionately criticized the Democrats' efforts to count votes that, as far as they were concerned, were not there. They railed at judicial rulings that seemed to encourage a move away from the clear rules and procedures set out in state statutes. Petitions such as that in Duval County, which Republicans saw as being without substance, infuriated them as a waste of time. Judge Labarga's refusal to say no to the Democrats exasperated them (despite the positive result of the case, as they saw it). Then there was Judge Miller in Broward County. Republicans were so frustrated with Judge Miller's ruling in favor of dimpled chads that they went so far as to demand that the Judge disqualify himself from the proceedings for his clear "pro-Democratic bias."[31]

The verbiage in the public relations battle was just as extreme. Republican operatives before the courts and outside the manual recounts were filled with righteous anger at what they saw as efforts to undermine the electoral process. Al Gore and the Democrats were trying to steal the election by changing the rules until they found enough votes to put Gore in the White House, they complained. A vote was a vote and all their talk of "counting every vote" was nothing more than a smokescreen for electoral larceny by the Democrats. Electoral rules were in place for a reason, not to be ignored when they became inconvenient.[32]

Yet, just two days after losing their case on hand recounts before Judge Miller, with the issue shifting to the counting of overseas absentee ballots, the Republican Party was back in court *defending* the acceptance of technically invalid ballots as "just counting all the votes"—in the process seeking rulings similar in scope and purpose to those that the Democrats won in Palm Beach and Broward Counties. (Of course, the Democrats were just as quickly spouting arguments against these efforts that sounded remarkably similar to those made by the Republicans in counting undervotes.) This was a battle to the death, and both sides were more than willing to use any weapon that promised victory in the form of additional votes. If the cost of this victory was logical inconsistency, then this was the price both sides would have to pay. The stakes were too high not to exploit every legal advantage they could find.

The first overseas absentee ballot suit, filed in Leon County on November 22, pitted the Florida Republican Party against fourteen county canvassing boards.[33] The complaint argued that the Democrats, fearing that military absentee ballots would give the election to George W. Bush, had "embarked upon a campaign to disqualify as many Overseas Military Ballots as possible on spurious grounds." Influenced by these efforts, the defendant canvassing boards had then wrongly rejected ballots for such "failings" as lack of a postmark, smudged postmarks, late postmarks, use of a federal Overseas Military Ballot (in place of a Florida absentee ballot), and lack of a proper signature and handwritten date on the envelopes. Ballots also were invalidated when the signature on the ballot did not exactly match the signature on file with the canvassing boards and where no evidence could be found that the voter was a registered voter.

Republicans questioned the legitimacy and justice of these procedures. "Members of the U.S. Armed Forces who deposited their ballots in the military mail system for delivery are not responsible if their ballots were not postmarked, if the postmark is illegible or smudged, or if military mail delivery procedures resulted in the application of a late postmark," they argued. "Their votes should not be disqualified as a result of subsequent actions not within their control." More to the point, "controlling Florida and Federal law [made] clear that Overseas Military Ballots [did] not need to bear *any* postmark" to be valid.[34] Turning to the Florida Supreme Court for precedent, Bush's lawyers noted that in *Boardman v. Esteva* (1975),[35] the Florida Supreme Court had argued that "there is no magic in the statutory requirements. If they are complied with to the extent that the duly responsible election officials can ascertain that electors whose votes are being canvassed are qualified and registered to vote, and that they do so in a proper manner, then who can be heard to complaint [*sic*] the statute has not been literally and absolutely complied with?" Indeed, the court had noted, "Election laws relating to absentee ballots are to be liberally construed in favor of the absentee voter" and "substantial compliance with the absentee voting laws is all that is required to give legality to the ballot." At the federal level, the plaintiffs pointed to Section 3406(a)(1) of Title 39 of the U.S.

Code, which protected military absentee ballots from any state rule that stood "as an obstacle to the accomplishment and execution of the full purpose of Congress in passing the act." (In this case the purpose was to allow military personnel to vote absentee while in service of their country.) "Any such state law would thus be preempted and inoperative as to Overseas Military Ballots."[36]

It was with these facts in mind that the Republicans requested a declaration that "Overseas Military Ballots are valid and should be counted even if they bear an illegible or smudged postmark, a late postmark or a U.S. postmark, or lack a handwritten date." Further, the complaint requested an injunction "directing the Defendant Canvassing Boards to consider all bona fide Overseas Military Ballots and to promptly transmit the amended totals to the Secretary of State." Valid ballots had been improperly disqualified and justice demanded that these votes be included in the final tally.[37]

Two days later, Judge L. Ralph Smith convened a hearing on the Republicans' motion for a declaratory judgment and injunction, during which he proved highly antagonistic to the Republican position. Smith repeatedly asked Republican counsel to explain how Florida law could demand that absentee ballots "must be received by the supervisor by 7 p.m. the day of the election," when the administrative rules of the Division of Elections allowed up to ten days after the election for overseas absentee ballots to be counted. Should not a state statute supersede an administrative rule, he asked? Even after being told of the 1985 consent agreement with the federal government allowing for the extra time, it was clear that Judge Smith was troubled by this conflict of laws. The judge was equally troubled by the scope of the proposed injunction. Bush lawyer Fred Bartlit argued that all military ballots, even those without a postmark or a signing date, should be counted as valid votes. To this claim the judge asked skeptically, "So you can have an undated ballot received by the supervisor of election after the election has already taken place, and that should be counted?" Most damning, however, was the issue of proof. "Without any proof that any of these canvassing boards have not complied with the law," the judge noted, "the court is very hard-pressed to grant any relief, because the court just doesn't enter orders telling elected officials to comply with the law" without due cause.[38]

Despite these musings, the judge did not issue a ruling on November 24. At the request of Bush's lawyers, Judge Smith agreed to hold judgment until the lawyers could file additional documentation. They then filed a memorandum in support of their motion for emergency injunctive relief later that day.[39] At this point, events overtook the court. As the *New York Times* reported, "even before the case was heard, the publicity had led a number of canvassing boards to reconsider the disqualified ballots." All told, six of the original fourteen county canvassing boards struck deals with the Republicans to reevaluate their ballots in return for being dropped from the suit.[40]

With only eight remaining defendants, Bush's lawyers decided to change tactics, voluntarily withdrawing their motions for relief. Instead (perhaps in the hope of finding a friendlier judge), they announced their plan to pursue "their remaining claims in other forums."[41] That same day they filed separate cases in six county courts with an additional county added the next morning. In addition, the lawyers filed a federal lawsuit with the Northern District Court of Florida in Pensacola against all seven county canvassing boards, raising the same arguments in their complaint that they had made in Judge Smith's courtroom.[42]

As if this were not confusing enough, on December 1, six Florida residents brought suit in state court against the State Elections Canvassing Commission and all those county canvassing boards that had included absentee ballots arriving after November 7. They argued that, as the U.S. Constitution allowed the inclusion of *only* those votes received by Election Day, late absentee ballots should be thrown out (which, as they noted, would have the effect of giving Florida to Al Gore).[43] Four days later, a different group of Florida residents brought similar charges attacking the election based on the inclusion of late overseas absentee ballots to the same court.[44] That afternoon, the secretary of state's office successfully petitioned to have both cases unified and removed to the Northern District Court of Florida, where they were placed on senior judge Maurice Paul's docket.

Judge Paul promptly held hearings and on December 12 issued an order upholding the inclusion of the military absentee ballots. As he saw it, the consent agreement allowing ten days for absentee military ballots was, in essence, a federal court order, enforceable even when in conflict with state laws. More to the point, "the fact that this rule has been in effect, without controversy or attempt by the legislature to overrule it, is a recognition by the legislature that they were subject to the Court's authority as expressed through the administrative rule." In essence, the judge explained, "the lack of challenge . . . reveals a recognition that the administrative code provision was properly enacted by the state executive branch to allow the state to comply with federal law and thus that the Rule should not be read to be in conflict with the statute but instead to be engrafted onto it, to allow the entire voting procedural scheme to comply with federal law."[45]

This still left George W. Bush's Western District federal suit in support of counting the military ballots. Hearings in this suit had commenced in tandem with the other federal cases. On December 8, Judge Lacey A. Collier issued her opinion. The crucial issue here was whether to exclude all the rejected overseas absentee ballots from the final vote tally. In particular, Bush challenged the exclusion of ballots for such reasons as: (1) the signatures on the ballots not matching those closely held by the canvassing board, (2) the lack of a postmark, and/or (3) ballots submitted with a postmark dated after Election Day (if there was no handwritten date on the envelope to suggest that the vote was cast before November 7, 2000).

In each of these and other similar instances, the court was troubled by the denials. In a footnote Judge Collier noted, "The Court is compelled to comment on the reports that absentee votes were rejected because of minor differences in the signature on the envelope and the registration records, including instances where a middle or first initial was used on the ballot rather than the complete name as indicated on the records. Although the Court recognizes a state's interests in preventing fraud and the necessity of vesting a certain degree of discretion with local canvassing boards, such a practice is unacceptable." Later, Judge Collier added, "It is truly an unfortunate circumstance when a citizen of the United States is denied the fundamental right to vote. . . . It is even more unfortunate when a vote cast by a member of the Armed Forces serving abroad is rejected for no legitimate or compelling reason." Still, despite her strong words of condemnation, Judge Collier refused to order the inclusion of undated ballots, nor did she force the canvassing boards to accept ballots without adequate postmarks. However much the judge would have had these boards rule differently, under Florida law the discretion in these matters did rest with the canvassing boards.[46]

In the end, the overseas absentee ballot fight was a clear win for the Bush team. However, this victory only served to counteract Gore's successes in getting at least some of the county canvassing boards to apply a looser standard of voter intent. When the counting was done, Bush had picked up only about 100 additional votes. Of course, given the closeness of the election, every single additional vote could be crucial. Even the handful of absentee votes granted to Bush by the federal bench loomed large in the ultimate outcome of the election. As one overseas absentee voter noted bemusedly, "I know they say that every vote makes a difference, but who would imagine?"[47]

Then there was the butterfly ballot. On November 20, Judge Labarga was seated once again in his packed courtroom. The issue this time, however, was not hanging versus pregnant chads. Judge Labarga was assigned to what had become the lead case challenging the butterfly ballot's constitutionality, *Fladell v. Palm Beach Canvassing Board*. Given the similarities between this case and many of the other butterfly ballot suits, Judge Labarga's ruling in *Fladell* would be controlling for all similar cases filed or to be filed on this topic.

The plaintiffs' complaint began by stressing the importance of the right to vote. They then moved quickly on to note the confusing layout of the butterfly ballot and to point out its significant and negative impact on the election's outcome. Without the butterfly ballot, the complaint noted, Bush would not be ahead in the vote count. More generally, "the foregoing improprieties, irregularities and statutory violations cast doubt on the integrity to the election process. . . ." The plaintiffs therefore requested an injunction from the court invalidating the November 7 election in Palm Beach County and ordering "a revote or partial revote for the office of President and Vice-President of the United States be held in Palm Beach County, Florida . . . on an expedited basis."[48]

The issues raised by this case distressed Judge Labarga. He understood the anger and anguish felt by those whose electoral choices were not registered. Many of those involved had past experiences that made voting a very important act. As the judge noted in his judgment's conclusion, "while some might dismiss such concerns without a second thought, the Court is well aware that the right to vote is as precious as life itself to those who have been victimized by the horror of war, to those whose not-too-distant relatives were prohibited from exercising the right to vote simply because of their race or gender, and to those who have risked it all by venturing across an unforgiving sea in makeshift rafts or boats in order to one day exercise the right to vote." The problems with the butterfly ballot were real and significant. Fully qualified voters had entered the polling station with every intent of casting a vote for president, and yet due to the ballot's faulty design had been denied the fruit of their efforts. Yet, sadly, none of these problems was relevant to the case at hand. "For over two centuries, we have agreed to a constitution and to live by the law. . . . Consequently, this court must follow the mandate of the law." And in this instance, the law did not provide for an adequate and legal remedy for the butterfly ballot's failings.

Although, the judge explained, it was true that Florida law and past judicial precedents give the courts the power to call for new elections, none of these cases had been presidential elections. Presidential elections were unique. They were "the only *national* elections held in our country." Moreover, both the Constitution and federal laws made clear that these elections were to be held on the same day nationwide. Florida law, in turn, codified this understanding in its rules and procedures for running elections. Yet even had the state not done so, congressional intent was paramount when observing the rules for running a presidential election—and Congress wanted the members of the Electoral College chosen on the same day.

With this thought in mind, Judge Labarga was forced to rule that it was "not legally possible" to hold a revote or new election "for Presidential electors in Florida." Congressional rules mandated this limitation, as did state law. Even the courts (both state and federal) made clear in their many rulings on improperly run elections that the available remedy for the butterfly ballot—a partial revote—was legally impermissible. The judge therefore ruled against the plaintiffs' motion for a declaratory judgment.

Before completing his ruling, Labarga took the time to make clear that he did not rule against the plaintiffs' factual concerns surrounding the butterfly ballot in any way. His was a legal ruling on the powers of the courts to provide relief; at no time did the court make any determinations as to the factual validity of the plaintiffs' claims (which, from his side comments in his ruling, he clearly favored).[49]

Unsatisfied with the judge's ruling, Fladell and the other plaintiffs in the butterfly ballot suits appealed to the 4th District Court of Appeals.[50] Realizing that time was running short (if a revote were to occur, it would have to be carried out "prior to the December 12, 2000 deadline" of the safe harbor statute), the plaintiffs petitioned to get their case before the Florida supreme court as quickly as possible. In a ruling handed down on November 27, 2000, the district judges granted this petition, arguing that "delay in the ultimate resolution of this issue may be critical, and resolution of this issue is one of first impression upon which the state supreme court would ultimately decide."[51]

Heeding the district court's judgment about the importance of this case, the Florida Supreme Court immediately took up the case. Only hours after the district court had certified the case as important and needing a quick resolution, the supreme court ordered all briefs and supporting materials on their desks by 5:00 p.m. November 28.[52] Three days later, on December 1, they handed down a short and blunt per curiam opinion in which all seven justices concurred with the results. (A per curiam opinion is a decision of an appeals court as a whole in which no judge is identified as the specific author.)

The opinion opened with a discussion of the basic rule that "a court should not void an election for ballot form defects unless such defects cause the ballot to be in substantial noncompliance with the statutory election requirements." Even more than this, "when considering a petition alleging a violation in the form of the ballot, 'a vital consideration guiding the courts in determining whether an election should be voided is the reluctance to reach a decision that would result in the disfranchisement of the voters. Indeed, as regards defects in ballots, the courts have generally declined to void an election unless such defects clearly operate to prevent that free, fair and open choice.'" As pertained to the Palm Beach County ballot, this basic rule was controlling. "Even accepting appellants' allegations . . . as a matter of law . . . the Palm Beach County ballot does not constitute substantial noncompliance with the statutory requirements mandating the voiding of the election," concluded the justices.[53]

The fight over the butterfly ballot was over. Even though almost every judge who examined the butterfly ballot grasped the frustration and anger of those voters who felt that they had lost or wasted their vote, none was willing to go the extra step and order a remedy for this problem. Judge Labarga and the judges of the 4th District Court felt that constitutional provisions and federal statutes barred them from demanding a revote. The Florida Supreme Court justices questioned whether the harm caused by the butterfly ballot was significant enough to demand such a sweeping and unprecedented remedy. As they saw it, without clear examples of official misconduct, the courts could not even contemplate ordering a new election. Finally, despite its obvious negative impacts, the butterfly ballot did not exhibit a clear case of a government official trying to "steal" the election.[54]

In the end, it was probably inevitable that the butterfly ballot suits would not prevail. The remedies called for were too extreme in their impact. It is never easy for a court to order a new election. Casting aside by judicial order the votes of thousands or tens of thousands of voters seems an ultimate contradiction of democracy. This concern spurred the judges' demand of proof of true misconduct before the courts would even contemplate such a remedy. Further, the ultimate significance of any such result in this case doomed it to failure. A new election in Palm Beach County, no matter how proper its justifications, would leave the effective choice of the next president of the United States in the hands of some 500,000 voters in one county. How could any court put a national election in so few hands?

If official misconduct had not been an issue with the butterfly ballot, it definitely was in a second round of suits brought by individual citizens against the 2000 election's results. The core of the dispute was an absentee ballot controversy brewing in Seminole and Martin Counties. In both cases, plaintiffs questioned the process by which local election officials organized and ran the voting process. Each case featured claims of official misconduct large enough to shift the election's results. Yet at the same time, the misconduct was small enough in numbers, and clear enough in scope (at least in the eyes of the plaintiffs), that providing a remedy would not be difficult—all the courts would have to do would be to throw out the disputed ballots.

The violations in question took place before the November 7 election. In the months leading up to the election, Florida Republicans had initiated a major statewide absentee voter drive. Mass mailings, sent out over the governor's name and with a picture of the state seal in the background (to give it an official look), urged Republicans to vote "from the comfort of their own homes."[55] To facilitate the process, the party contracted with a company to print postcard request forms for an absentee ballot. Preprinted on the card were the voter's name, address, and other required information. All the voter had to do was add his or her social security number, sign the card, and drop it in the mail to the local supervisor of elections.[56]

State laws allowed political parties to print and send to voters prepared requests for absentee voter ballots. However, following a highly corrupt 1997 Miami mayoral race (in which hundreds of absentee ballots were deemed improperly signed, in some cases, by a dead person),[57] the state legislature in 1998 had toughened the rules for absentee ballots. Among the new rules were requirements that only the voter or a family member could fill out the forms (including the application for an absentee ballot). Similarly, the legislature required that the voter include not only his or her name and address but also a social security number *and* his or her voter identification number on the application.[58] This requirement was the source of the problem at issue.

Mistakenly, the GOP's printed postcards omitted the voter identification numbers on over 80 percent of the cards mailed. Without these numbers, the applications were incomplete. Whereas in some counties, such as Orange, the elections office accepted the applications without the required numbers (so long as the remaining information was provided), in Seminole and Martin Counties they did not. At first, the two offices mailed cards to the voters informing them that their applications were incomplete. However, they quickly stopped this practice as the number of incomplete applications became too great; in Seminole County alone there were almost 4,700 rejected applications; Martin County's were closer to 1,500. Contacted by the Florida Republican party leadership, who knew of the problem and were concerned lest potential Republican voters not vote, both supervisors (who were Republicans) agreed to allow the party to "fix" the problem by adding the necessary voter identification number by hand.

In Seminole County, Supervisor Sandra S. Goard allowed Michael Leach, a state field director for the Republican Party, to enter her office and set up shop on a table in the back. Armed with a laptop computer, Leach spent the next three weeks going over the rejected applications and filling in the voter identification numbers of the Republican voters he found.[59] The situation was similar in Martin County. The only real difference was that, rather than fix the problem in house, Martin County Supervisor of Elections Peggy Robbins allowed local Republicans to take the applications out of her office and return them completed.[60] In both cases, the revised applications were approved and absentee ballots sent out to the voters.

There was no doubt that what the election offices did was improper and possibly illegal. It was also highly partisan; when Democrats asked if there was anything that they could do to fix their rejected applications, they were told that nothing could be done.[61] The question was, did the Republicans' modifications invalidate the absentee votes of those absentee voters who, had the changes not been made, would not have received ballots?

Democrats believed that the answer to this question was yes. They viewed the Republicans' actions as nothing less than illegal vote-tampering.[62] Concerned about the potential of these ballots to shape the election's outcome, Democratic Party supporter and local lawyer Henry Jacobs brought suit on November 12 in Seminole County Court alleging that 4,700 voters had their absentee ballot applications altered by Republican workers in violation of state law.[63] He requested that, if the affected voters could not be identified and their votes disqualified, all of the County's 15,215 absentee votes be thrown out as tainted. "Where we have misconduct, wrongdoing sufficient to influence the outcome of an election, then the Florida courts have decided that this is even more important than the individual ballot submitted by an absentee voter," Jacobs said.[64]

The Republicans responded that any mistakes that were made were at worst a "hypertechnicality." As lawyers for Goard noted, it was the applications that were in question, not the ballots themselves. As far as the voters were concerned, they had done nothing wrong. "The plaintiffs make no allegation that any person ever had any inappropriate access to any ballot," argued attorney Jonathan Sjostrom. Meanwhile, "the choice to permit the party to correct its error was not a fraud or a crime." Even more important, as the ballots accurately reflected the views of the voters, there was no impact on the election's outcome. Throwing out ballots in this instance would be "absurd." There was "nothing wrong, nothing felonious," with the election itself. "The Democrats say they want every vote counted,"

Goard's lawyer charged, "but, in this case, they want 15,000 votes uncounted." GOP lawyer Ken Wright was even more disdainful. It would "unconscionable" to throw out 15,000 ballots, he noted to the press, "cast by people who couldn't get to the polls because of age or disability, [just] because of a printer's error."[65]

The case was initially set to be heard in County Judge Debra S. Nelson's Seminole County courtroom. However, following Secretary of State Catherine Harris's certification of the vote on November 26, Republicans motioned for the case to be removed to a Leon County courtroom. In the end, both sides agreed to the move.[66] Jacobs, in turn, refiled his lawsuit to add the secretary of state as a defendant. The charges, however, remained the same. Jacobs once again asked the court to throw out all of the county's absentee ballots, as it was not possible to identify the ballots cast in consequence of the doctored applications. "Absentee voting is a privilege," Jacob's lawyer Gerald Richman noted. "It is not a right. There is precedent for throwing them all out."[67]

Four days later, Democratic voters from Martin County filed suit in the 2nd Circuit Court challenging Martin County's absentee vote. Here too, the charges were that absentee ballot applications were illegally tampered with and that this tampering was done with a partisan purpose. As the complaint noted, when Democratic voters sent in similarly incomplete absentee ballot requests, the Democratic Party was given no notice by which to fix the problem, nor was anything done by the office itself to correct the mistakes. The result was the issuing of "several thousand invalid absentee ballots that thereafter were cast in Martin County" in numbers sufficient to change the outcome of the election. As with the Seminole County case, the plaintiff requested disqualification of these ballots, or if this proved not possible, the disqualification of all of the county's absentee ballots.[68]

At this point, both trials ran in parallel.[69] Circuit Judge Nikki Ann Clark heard the Seminole case, while Circuit Judge Terry P. Lewis handled the Martin County suit. Both cases were very active. Over the next eight days, the two judges heard dozens of motions, held many hearings, and presided over three days of trial proceedings. Both judges denied motions to dismiss each case for lack of adequate grounds and both decided against jury trials (based on another motion from the Republicans).[70] Both even held their trials on the same days (though at different times to allow the lawyers to move between the two cases).[71]

At trial, each judge asked hard questions of the lawyers. Both, for instance, asked Republican lawyers how they could be expected to ignore what appeared to be a clear violation of the law. "Doesn't the statute say the voter must request the application and that the person making the request must provide the information?" asked Judge Lewis. Both also expressed concerns about the proposed remedies in these matters. Judge Clark was especially concerned with the scope of the requested remedy: "What about absentee ballot voters who thought they were voting legally and thought their votes were going to count?" To this end, Judge Clark imposed on the plaintiffs a high standard of proof in arguing their case, informing the lawyers that her analysis of the evidence would focus on "whether the addition or completion of voter-registration identification numbers [was] sufficient to invalidate [the] ballots." Judge Clark further noted she would also decide whether "the irregularity complained of affected the sanctity of the vote" and if "the Democratic and Republican parties were treated differently" enough to also compromise "the integrity of the election."[72]

On December 8, both judges handed down their separate rulings. Reading from a prepared statement for both judges, Court Clerk Terre Cass announced, "Despite irregularities in the requests for absentee ballots, neither the sanctity of the ballots nor the integrity of the elections has been compromised." The election "reflected a full and fair expression of the will of the voters" in Seminole and Martin Counties. This was not to say that there had been no misconduct on the part of election officials. "Without question," wrote Judge Lewis about the Martin County elections office, "there were irregularities relative to the request for absentee ballots." Clearly "the procedure utilized was contrary to [Florida election statutes] . . . and that it offered an opportunity for fraud and created the appearance of partisan favoritism on the part of the Supervisor of Elections." However, given recent Florida Supreme Court rulings on the need to promote the expressed will of the people through their ballots and given also that there was "no evidence of fraud or other irregularities in the actual casting of the ballots, or the counting of the ballots," empowering the will of the voters was the controlling factor.[73]

Judge Clark was equally blunt in her judgments. "While the Supervisor of Elections of Seminole County exercised faulty judgment in first rejecting completely the requests in question, and compounded the problem by allowing third parties to correct the omissions on the forms, no remedy against her is available in this election contest under [Florida election statutes]. Faulty judgment is not illegal unless the Legislature declares it so." And, given that the integrity of the vote was in no way undermined by these actions, and that "the very purpose of election laws is to obtain a correct expression of the intent of the voter," the court had no option but to rule against the plaintiffs.[74]

The plaintiffs in both cases immediately appealed the trial courts' rulings, and the appeals were fast tracked to the Florida Supreme Court. The justices handed down their ruling on December 12. In a per curiam opinion, the seven justices noted, "We find competent, substantial evidence to support the trial court's conclusion that the evidence in this case does not support a finding of fraud, gross negligence, or intentional wrongdoing in connection with any absentee ballots." Yes, there was misconduct on the parts of both supervisors of elections.[75] This was a troubling conclusion. "Nothing can be more essential than for a supervisor of elections to maintain strict compliance with the statutes in order to ensure credibility in the outcome of the election," the court noted. Still, misconduct in question did not rise to the levels necessary to call for court action. The absentee ballots were valid and should remain in the final vote totals from each county.[76]

With the decision by the Florida Supreme Court on the Palm Beach and Semi-nole/Martin County cases, the third-party challenges to the 2000 presidential election in Florida were complete—with one notable exception. Perhaps the most troubling aspect of the election debacle (at least, after the quandary of figuring out who was president) was its racial overtones. Black voters were ten times more likely to have their votes thrown out than other voters were. Blacks were also more likely to have had their names wrongly purged from the voter lists. Responding to this pattern of race-based disenfranchisement, the NAACP brought a class-action suit on January 10, 2001, in the U.S. District Court for the Southern District of Florida. The lawsuit's goal was to force state and local officials to update their voting technology and to reform the procedural failings that had resulted in so many black voters' being denied the fruits of their voting efforts in 2000. The suit also alleged the private company ChoicePoint had knowingly mislabeled innocent voters as felons. (Under Florida law, convicted felons cannot vote.)[77]

After one and a half years of legal wrangling, the case was set to come up for trial in August 2002 before U.S. District Judge Alan Gold. By this time, a number of the defendant counties had entered into consent agreements with the plaintiffs, promising to update their electoral machinery to limit the possibility of additional disenfranchisement of African American voters. So too had ChoicePoint, which agreed to reprocess its voter lists using narrower, more accurate criteria than the state used before the November 2000 elections.

Now, as the date for the trial approached, the two sides began to work on a complete consent agreement. Finally, on September 3, 2002, they announced that an agreement had been worked out to all parties' satisfaction. The two sides built the settlement on the foundation of the newly enacted Florida Election Reform Act of 2001. Terms of the settlement included changes in registration list maintenance, provision of funding for improved voter education and poll worker training, and creation of alternative voting and registration procedures. The agreement also demanded that state officials ensure that elections were administered properly, including the fair distribution of equipment, resources, technology, and staffing at polling places.[78]

Argued in batches, interweaving arguments and rulings until it was difficult to keep track of which case was which, the third party, federal recount challenge, and vote standard lawsuits each trashed the conventional wisdom that litigation was a dignified process at odds with politics. This was politics by other means, a political war fought not by soldiers or political operatives but lawyers in expensive suits. The goal was to win and win at all costs. Further, whereas on the public relations front each side argued a coherent position—Gore in favor of "counting every vote," Bush against "subjective" and "unnecessary" manual recounts—in court each side fielded whatever arguments promised the best chances of victory. In legal terms, each side was presenting *arguments in the alternative*, a technique in which lawyers present conflicting (even contradictory) arguments in an effort to convince a court in support of their clients. And even though this approach might work for the law (as it has for centuries), as politics it was a dangerous and problematic development.

What developed in Florida before the horrified eyes of the nation and the world was the legalization of politics and the politicization of the law. Not only were the methods and attitudes of the law infusing the political process, but those of politics were permeating the legal process—to the benefit of neither realm. The high levels of cynicism combined with the intensity of argument and the shortness of time all conspired to undermine the reasoning and contemplation that was the law's strong suit. Meanwhile, what were essentially political statements of opinion were being imbued with the solidarity and conviction of legal argument. Worse yet, as with the election as a whole, the law's focus was becoming so centered on the outcomes that the procedures that normally shape the legal process were either ignored or overwhelmed. Political discourse, in turn, was so co-opted by the legal language of rules and rights, that compromise, and even rational discourse, was almost impossible.

Perhaps the best example of the merging of politics and law was the linked debates over the legitimacy of hand recounts and the deadlines within which these recounts had to be completed. The ease with which political opinions were given the moral force of law—and legal rulings were affected by the political components of these matters—shaped the outcome of this debate as the courts struggled with the central questions raised by the recount process: what was the ultimate purpose in holding recounts and who got to decide? Was it to pick a winner and thus provide closure and political continuity? Or was it to empower the voters' choices as far as possible? Was getting the election's outcome right as important as being accurate, or was the intent behind the vote of greater significance than technical consistency? And should the decision rest with the legislature or the judiciary?

How the courts answered these and similar questions would go a long way toward shaping the eventual outcome of the Florida election controversy. Tellingly, it would be over these questions that the U.S. Supreme Court would enter the fray and begin to shape the eventual outcome of the dispute. The complexity of these questions requires a careful sorting of the issues in succeeding chapters. The deadline debate is the focus of chapter 5, and the wider debate over the purpose and structuring of our electoral processes takes center stage in chapters 6 and 7.

CHAPTER FIVE
The Ticking of the Clock

There is no magic [in] . . . statutory requirements. If they are complied
with to the extent that . . . electors whose votes are being canvassed are qualified and
registered to vote, and that they do so in a proper manner, then who can be heard to
complain the statute has not been literally and absolutely complied with?
—Boardman v. Esteva, *Florida Supreme Court (1975)*

I am not so naïve (nor do I think our forebears were) as to be unaware that
judges in a real sense "make law." But they make it as judges make it, which is to say,
as though they were finding it—discerning what the law is, rather than decreeing
what it is today changed to, or what it will tomorrow be.
—*Justice Antonin Scalia, concurring,*
James B. Beam Distilling Co. v. Georgia *(1991)*

Of all the postelection lawsuits filed in early to mid-November 2000, none loomed
larger than the challenges filed to oppose Katherine Harris's strict certification
deadline. As noted, on Monday, November 13, the secretary of state's office formally announced that it would strictly enforce the Tuesday 5:00 p.m. certification
deadline: "The electoral process is a balance between the desire of each individual
voter to have his or her intended vote recorded and the right of the public to a
clear, final result within a reasonable time." The law, Harris emphasized, "unambiguously states when the process of counting and recounting the votes cast on
election day must end." The statutorily mandated deadline was 5:00 p.m. on the
seventh day following the election. There was no discretion on this matter:
"Florida law does not provide any date for return certifications other than tomorrow at 5 pm."[1] Nor, Harris announced, would her office accept any partial hand recounts. Either the canvassing boards would have to get their recounts done by 5:00
p.m. Tuesday, or they would have to accept and submit the original machine counts
as their county's vote total.[2]

Entangled with the certification deadline was the broader issue of the legitimacy
of manual recounts. Harris, through her aides Clay Roberts and Kerey Carpenter,
had pushed hard the idea that the *only* legitimate reason to hand recount ballots
was if the machines that were supposed to do the counting had broken. On November 13, Roberts issued Advisory Opinion DE 00-11, arguing that "an 'error in
the vote tabulation' means a counting error in which the vote tabulation equipment
fails to count *properly* marked marksense or *properly* punched punchcard ballots."
In particular, Roberts declared, the "inability of voting systems to read *improperly*

marked marksense or *improperly* punched punchcard ballots [was] not an 'error in vote tabulation' [emphasis added]."[3]

As we have seen, Harris's decision to abide strictly by the letter of the law on certification and recounts was a central part of the Bush team's "push and pull" strategy in the postelection contest. Bush needed the recounts to end as soon as possible to make sure that Gore did not get enough votes to wrest a victory in Florida. The general idea was to limit the time available for the Democrats to finish their recounting "to less than thirty-six hours" and then "freeze the official results in the Republicans' favor."[4] And it was Harris's job to ensure that the time frame available to Gore was as short as legally possible. (On the other hand, when delay or a liberal interpretation of the law was in Bush's favor, such as with the late post-marked overseas absentee ballots discussed in the last chapter, Harris was available to see that Bush's needs were met here, too.) It had been for just such circumstances as these that the Bush team had placed Republican insider and Florida lobbyist J. M. "Mac" Stipanovich in Harris's office to "advise" her on the legalities of her job and help her to "land" the election.

The certification deadline cases, in other words, show clearly the political motivations underlying the legal discourse throughout the postelection cycle. It was not just the Republicans who blended political considerations with electoral law; the Democrats also pursued their version of the calculus of victory. Each side had specific procedures that had to be applied just their way if they were going to win. With Gore, the need was time to recount votes; with Bush, the need was to limit Gore's ability to gain votes. Gore's call for more time was thus as politically motivated as Bush's demands for finality. Bush, however, had the luxury of Republican control of the state electoral infrastructure; all Gore had was the help of the (presumably) friendly canvassing boards and the Florida courts. So while on the surface the disputes in the certification cases were between the county canvassing boards and Katherine Harris, at their core they were really the penultimate act of the 2000 election, as Al Gore fought for the time he needed to keep his victory hopes alive and George W. Bush pushed back as hard as he could to deny Gore that time.

These cases also focused public attention on the ambiguous roles of the judiciary in settling these matters. What part should the courts play in negotiating the complexities of state and federal election laws as applied to the realities of the Florida postelection crisis? Should their response be largely "hands-off"? Did federal law and Article II of the Constitution leave the entire issue in the hands of the state legislature? What if a state's election statutes and legal precedents provided for a judicial role in setting disputed elections? Could the state courts act, harmonizing various state election-law provisions when such provisions came into conflict? Or did federal rules, if they existed, trump even these provisions?

The Florida crisis also raised the perennial debate about judicial interpretation versus judicial lawmaking. What if the courts' answers to these problems required them to make substantial changes in the process of counting votes? Would such changes be making new law or just adapting existing laws to new and unique situations? The questions were nearly endless, and the debates over them proved ever more bitter and persistent.

The certification deadline cases also were important because they forced all sides to deal with one of the central issues raised by the postelection crisis: what was the purpose behind recounting votes? Was it merely an administrative process to ensure that the machinery (mechanical and human) had worked on election night? Or was it an effort to ensure that the will of the voters as expressed by their ballots was properly reflected in the certified vote totals? If the answer was the former, then a strict deadline made sense. If it were the latter, then allowing extra time for recounts was both reasonable and necessary. And whereas the motivations behind their answers might have been strategically set by political need, the content of each side's arguments before the courts would have to deal with these substantive issues directly. If either side could not find strong arguments to support its contentions, their postelection efforts were over.

Finally, the certification deadline cases make clear just how technical and convoluted the issues before the courts could, and would, become. When viewed through a partisan lens the answers may have seemed "obvious," but the frustrating truth was that the laws and precedents that would control in these matters were vague and often self-contradictory. The rulings at every level of the judiciary, from trial through the state and federal supreme courts, would be built on close textual readings of laws and precedents largely written in the eighteenth, nineteenth, and early twentieth centuries. Other provisions, while of more recent vintage, had been constructed to deal with different problems from that faced by the courts in 2000. Yet these legal sources were all the courts had at hand to guide their charting of the proper course in the postelection crisis.

Determining how all these various pieces fit together was an almost impossible task. Yet answers had to be found and applied. As noted more than once, the Constitution and practical politics demanded that someone be declared the winner and sworn in as president on January 20, 2001. But the ironclad need for an answer did not make the process any easier. In fact, the substantive and temporal pressures on the courts, combined with their constant and unyielding nature, ratcheted up the pressures faced by these courts to unprecedented heights, making these thorny issues even harder. Worse still, the electoral puzzle before the judges permitted many "correct" answers. And as we have seen already with some of the other questions of law being debated in 2000, the ultimate outcome of this crisis was largely predicated on *which* answers one adopted to these questions.

Consequently, even though the ultimate conclusion to these particular litigations would prove inconclusive, and it would be other matters that produced the final showdown in *Bush v. Gore*, the lawsuits still helped build the foundation for moving the postcertification process toward completion. We cannot understand the tensions between the Florida and U.S. Supreme Courts in *Bush v. Gore* without first experiencing the frustrations generated by the final certification deadline case, *Bush v. Palm Beach County Canvassing Board.* These cases helped to fix in place the angry climate within which all the parties were operating in December 2000 as the December 12 "safe harbor" deadline loomed, bringing with it the increasing likelihood of an ongoing electoral crisis. For it was at this stage that the "they stole the election" passions of the recounts blended with the rights consciousness of the law—and politics and law were thereby fused into a single process aimed at settling the electoral crisis of 2000—with, as we shall see, troubling results.

Katherine Harris's adamant refusal (formally announced on November 13 but informally made known as early as November 8) to extend certification deadlines put the four canvassing boards recounting votes in an untenable position. The only board that had even a chance of making the Tuesday afternoon deadline was Volusia County, and even they were uncertain that they could finish their counting in time. Palm Beach and Broward Counties, with over 500,000 votes each to count, had no chance at all of finishing. Miami-Dade County was not even set to decide whether to hold manual recounts until the day of the deadline.

This situation left the canvassing boards with a difficult decision. Should they give up counting? If recounts were legally questionable (as Clay Roberts argued) and the deadline was fixed (as Harris maintained), why bother even to start recounting? Had this been the only legal advice available to the canvassing boards, it is likely that they would have stopped counting and put an end to the election. However, Attorney General Bob Butterworth's advisory opinion directly contradicted the views of Clay Roberts on recounts and indirectly challenged Harris on the law's inflexibility toward extended certification deadlines. Unsure which views on the law were correct (and pressured by the Democrats to continue the recounts at all costs), three of the four boards decided to seek advice and guidance from the courts.

The first to act was the Volusia County Canvassing Board. Though it looked likely that the board would complete its manual recounting in time to make the 5:00 p.m. deadline, the canvassing board still decided to file suit in the 2nd Circuit Court in Tallahassee on November 9, challenging the secretary of state's certification deadline. They sought a declaratory judgment setting out their duties under the law and an injunction ordering the acceptance of their ballots after the November 14 deadline (should the law be on their side in this matter). What they were asking for in essence was time to count all the votes. Harris was rushing the process and they not only challenged her right to do so but questioned her justifications for speed.[5]

Sharing these concerns, the Palm Beach board immediately petitioned the court to join the suit. So too did the two candidates and the Democratic Party.[6] In comments made to the press as they sought to intervene, the Democrats seconded Volusia County's contention that Florida law gave "Ms. Harris flexibility" to wait at least until Friday, when the deadline expired for overseas absentee ballots to arrive in Florida, before certifying the vote. "Her plan, I'm afraid, has the look of an effort to produce a particular result in the election rather than to ensure that the voice of all the citizens of the state would be heard," Gore's chief representative in Florida, former secretary of state Warren M. Christopher, argued. "It also looks like a move in the direction of partisan politics and away from the nonpartisan administration of the election laws." The Republicans, in turn, reiterated Harris's assertions that the law demanded a 5:00 p.m. Tuesday deadline. They drew on Judge Middlebrooks's ruling (which even they had to admit had been a defeat for George Bush) to support this position. "The judge essentially ruled that the state law has to be followed," one Republican official noted to the press. "And part of that state law was that the recounts have to be done by 5 p.m. Tuesday, . . . [so] now there's a federal judge who says Florida law has to be followed."[7]

On Monday afternoon, November 13, all parties met in Circuit Judge Terry P. Lewis's courtroom in Tallahassee. During two intense hearings, Lewis questioned both sides closely. He was especially concerned about the practical logistics of carrying out a manual recount. He asked how the large counties, such as Palm Beach, which clearly needed many days to hand count votes, could complete a "manual" recount within such a short time frame. "How do you reconcile this statute that seems to provide a manual count if you can't get done within the time period?" Lewis asked. Bush attorney Barry Richard contended that this was the legislature's decision. "It is not our place to question the wisdom of the Legislature," Richard observed. Democrats disagreed, arguing that there was no reason not to extend the deadline. Gore attorney Dexter Douglass and other Democratic attorneys argued that extending the deadline would do no harm. After all, they noted, state officials would have to revise their final vote totals after receiving absentee ballots from Floridians who were overseas on Saturday. Why not extend the deadline so that all the votes could be properly counted?[8]

Much of the discussion during the heated hearings centered on the conflicting wording of Sections 102.111 and 102.112 of Title IX the *Florida Statutes*. Section 102.111 ordered that "if the county returns are not received by the Department of State by 5 p.m. of the seventh day following an election, all missing counties *shall* be ignored, and the results shown by the returns on file *shall* be certified." Section 102.112, on the other hand, set out that "if the returns are not received by the department by the time specified, such returns *may* be ignored and the results on file at that time *may* be certified by the department [all emphasis added]." The former rule set the deadline in stone, the latter allowed for discretion on the part of the State Elections Canvassing Commission.[9] So which was it, "shall" or "may"?

Republicans argued that it was up to Harris to interpret the law as she saw fit; so long as Harris's interpretation of the law was reasonable, they contended, the judge had no authority to overrule her. "There has been no compelling reason to order the secretary of state to do something by law she is not obligated to do," Barry Richard concluded. And Harris viewed the mandatory wording as controlling in this instance.[10] Democrats disagreed. In her announcement declaring her intention to honor the 5:00 p.m. Tuesday deadline, Harris had mentioned that the *only* possible exception to this rule was when a natural disaster—"such as Hurricane Andrew"—made compliance with the law physically impossible.[11] Clearly exceptions to the rule were possible. As State Senator Ron Klein had noted to reporters, "I don't see anything about Hurricane Andrew in the statutes." Should not a *presidential* election be just as important a reason for an exception?[12] "This is not only a hurricane," Gore attorney Douglass told the Court, "this is a bark-splitting North Florida cyclone with a hurricane tailing on the end of it. It's one that whips across the entire nation. It's a hurricane, cyclone or whatever you want to call it that winds itself all over this country and all over this world. The issue is does Florida stand up for a honest vote? . . . Or are they elections where some bureaucrat writes a letter and says you lose, your vote doesn't count?"[13] Added Douglass: "The only way to get an honest count is a ballot-by-ballot manual recount."[14]

As to the judge's potential ruling, the Republicans urged Judge Lewis to show restraint and not to step into an elections dispute. They argued that neither the counties nor Gore had presented any evidence to suggest why a manual recount was needed. "There's no evidence of fraud or systematic problems," said Barry Richard. "In any election of this magnitude, there's going to be mistakes. But those mistakes will balance themselves out across the state." Richard then repeated the Bush argument that manual recounts gave an unfair advantage to voters living in recount counties where a hand count was not being conducted. "It skews the election to a candidate who has a constituency in those four counties," noted Richard.[15] Dexter Douglass responded for the Democrats that the important thing was to get an honest vote count, not to follow a bureaucratic determination by the secretary of state. "The issue is, does Florida stand up for an honest vote so that people in other countries can say the United States has an honest election?" asked Douglass. Gore was willing to abide by the recount results; should not Governor Bush be willing to do so as well? "My client, Vice President Gore, is prepared to lose this election, based on an honest count," Douglass said. "He is prepared to accept the finality within a reasonable time to allow this recounting to be done in Palm Beach County and the other counties."[16] Democratic lawyer Bruce Rogow, representing the Palm Beach County Canvassing Board, had a simpler response. The hand count was democracy in action. "Is it messy? Does it go on and on in some fashion? Yes, yes it does, but that is democracy."[17]

On November 14, Judge Lewis handed down his ruling. He began by noting that "The plaintiffs insist that the Secretary of State *must* consider the certified results from Volusia and Palm Beach Counties, even if they are filed late, if they are still engaged in the manual recounts of votes. The Secretary of State insists that, absent an Act of God such as a hurricane, any returns not received by the statutory deadline *will not* be counted in the statewide tabulations and certification of the election results." He then made clear that he gave "great deference to the interpretation by the Secretary of the election laws." Still, there was this ambiguity in the law's wording. Consequently, Judge Lewis ruled that the canvassing boards *did* have to turn in their vote tallies by 5:00 p.m.; however this *did not* preclude the boards from filing amended returns later. On this matter, Harris was wrong. State statutes made clear the legislature's intent of assuring both accuracy *and* finality in the counting of votes. Harris's ruling provided for finality, but had the potential of undermining accuracy.

None of this meant, however, that the secretary of state *had* to accept the revised tallies from the hand recounts. Section 102.112 made clear that the secretary *"may"* ignore late returns. Whereas this language meant that she *"[did] not have to"* ignore them, she could also *choose* to do so. The decision was hers to make. Still, warned the judge, "to determine ahead of time that such returns *will* be ignored, . . . unless caused by some Act of God, [was] not the exercise of [Harris's proper] discretion." This was rather, the "abdication of that discretion."[18]

Judge Lewis therefore ruled that the canvassing boards *had* to submit their original returns by 5:00 p.m. (as required by state statute), but could subsequently *request* the right to tender amended returns based on the hand recount results. Secretary Harris, in turn, was required to listen to these requests and, applying her discretion based on the totality of the facts and circumstances, make a decision whether to accept or reject the amended returns. The answer, however, was hers, and hers alone, to make. The judge therefore refused to issue the requested injunction forcing the secretary of state to accept all late returns. (He did, however, note that if she refused to accept them, this was proper grounds for contesting the election's outcome in state court under the state's election contest rules.)[19]

Later in the afternoon, a spokesperson for Secretary Harris announced that Harris expected all sixty-seven counties to comply with her deadline for filing vote totals for certification. This included the four counties within which Gore had requested hand recounts. Harris did allow, however, that if updated totals were submitted later, she would apply "her discretion to consider all the facts and circumstances" and take the updated tallies under advisement.[20] Harris announced further that any canvassing board wishing to amend its results had to submit a request to her office by 2:00 p.m. Wednesday.

On Wednesday night, seven hours after this deadline had passed, Harris went before the press and announced that four county canvassing boards had submitted extension requests.[21] The Broward County board's letter, for instance, made clear that the large voter turnout on Election Day, combined with the normally large size of the county's voting population, had generated an enormous number of ballots to hand count. The very size of the vote, in turn, had created logistical problems requiring the time-consuming moving of ballots before counting could even begin. And, once the counting began, the board had encountered additional delays, such as lawsuits, conflicting opinions from state officials, the Veterans Day holiday, and the state-mandated need to carry out a second machine recount before launching manual counts.[22] Collier County wanted time to count twenty-five absentee ballots that had been overlooked in the initial count. They expressly did not want any hand recounts.[23] Miami-Dade County requested the inclusion of the votes generated from its 1 percent sample recount, completed a mere three hours after the 5:00 p.m. deadline. The board felt it "imperative" that these votes be included in the county's final vote totals.[24] Finally, Palm Beach County stressed the potential of its recounts to affect the outcome of the election. Given the numbers generated by the sample vote recounts, the possibility of changing the election's outcome was real. They also noted how the conflicting opinions from the state elections office and the attorney general's office had led them to halt recounts pending judgment from the courts on the legitimacy of manual recounts. If the courts approved manual recounts, then they would need the extra time to submit their returns.[25]

After naming the four counties seeking an extension, Harris announced that (having considering each request carefully) she had determined that the law did *not* permit her acceptance of revised returns. "As a result of these deliberations, I have decided it is my duty, under Florida law, to exercise my discretion in denying the requested amendments."[26] As her letters to the canvassing boards had noted, Harris was willing to accept modified returns only if: (a) there was proof that voter fraud affected the election's outcome; (b) there had been substantial noncompliance with elections procedures and there was reasonable doubt that the certified returns truly reflected the voter's intentions; and (c) where an Act of God or other extenuating circumstance had made it impossible for the board to complete its vote tally. Voter error, confusing ballots, and the mere potential only that the outcome of an election would have been affected were not acceptable reasons for modifying election returns.[27] Given that no amendments to the received vote totals were necessary, Harris then announced that the state canvassing commission, which she chaired, had already met and certified the results from Tuesday's returns. These were now set. Once the overseas absentee votes were in on Friday, she expected that the commission would quickly certify the results of the presidential election in total.[28]

Democrats responded to this announcement quickly, attacking Harris's decision and demanding a new hearing from Judge Lewis. "It's an outrageous decision," Gore spokesperson Mark Fabiani said. "It's a rash decision and it won't stand." Harris was supposed to use her discretion, Democratic spokesperson Doug Hattaway also noted, adding: "She didn't do that. He [Judge Lewis] asked her to wait, and she didn't do that, either."[29] Their motion to Judge Lewis argued that Harris, "rather than considering all relevant facts and circumstances in taking these actions, . . . [had] directed an unwavering effort to stop the manual counting of ballots." Rather than allowing the canvassing boards simply to submit their reasoning for recounts with their amended results, Harris had "interposed an unprecedented requirement on these Boards to explain, in advance, in writing, why they might need to amend their vote totals." At no time did Harris indicate "what would guide her decision whether to grant such extensions, nor did she indicate when such a decision would be made." Yet a mere seven hours after the boards, with great effort, had submitted their reasons, Harris was announcing to "a well prepared press conference" that she had rejected the ballots. Worse yet, in that short time, she "had already sought and received certification" by the state canvassing commission "in a private and unnoticed meeting in violation of the Florida Sunshine Laws." When, the motion asked, had Secretary Harris taken the time to "consider all relevant facts and circumstances"? Clearly, it concluded, she had not.[30]

Judge Lewis promised to rule on their motion by Friday, November 17; on that day, he denied the Democrats' motion. The Democrats had asserted that Harris had acted "arbitrarily" in denying their petitions for amended returns—but the judge disagreed. Florida law, he ruled, granted the secretary of state "broad discretionary authority to accept or reject late filed returns." His order had merely been issued to ensure that the secretary properly exercised her discretion rather than arbitrarily rejecting such requests out of hand. As far as the judge was concerned, Secretary Harris had done just as he had requested. His order was satisfied.[31]

While Judge Lewis pondered the Democrats' requests to force Secretary Harris to accept late returns, and while Harris was rejecting them nonetheless, the litigation merry-go-round continued unchecked. On November 14, the Palm Beach County Canvassing Board, supported by the Broward County board, petitioned the Florida Supreme Court for an "extraordinary writ"[32] settling the conflict between the secretary of state's and the attorney general's views on the legality of hand recounts.[33]

Were recounts legal? Part of Harris's justification for holding to a strict deadline for certification was the irregularity of the ongoing recounts (at least according to her reading of the relevant statutes). If they were improper, then her response to the extension requests was logical and inevitable. If not, then room existed for arguing against her ruling.

Appreciating the matter's importance, and noting that the Palm Beach board had halted recounts until the court ruled in this matter, the state supreme court issued an interim order. "It appears that the relief sought on the question of whether the Canvassing Board may conduct a manual recount of the votes cast for President and Vice President has been answered in the affirmative by the circuit courts of Leon and Palm Beach County," the seven justices wrote. "At present, this is binding legal authority on this issue and there is no legal impediment to the recounts continuing. Thus, Petitioners are authorized to proceed with the manual recount."[34] The next day, the supreme court joined this case with appeals from Judge

Lewis's initial ruling on the certification deadlines (upholding the November 14 deadline but "permitting" Harris to accept or deny revised returns at her discretion), and on its own volition issued a stay order halting *all* election certification results.[35] Immediately thereafter, the court issued orders setting the procedures for oral argument on the substance of these matters. The justices would hear arguments on the legitimacy of hand recounts and the secretary of state's certification of the election results three days hence, on Monday, November 20.[36]

During the weekend of November 18, the Florida Supreme Court received briefs and other motions from those parties interested in the case—many of them filing more than one version of their briefs as they revised their positions in response to the other side's arguments. The array of parties included not only the two candidates and their political parties, but also the interested county canvassing boards, the state attorney general, and the secretary of state's office.

Gore and the Democratic Party opened their brief by reminding the justices that "manual recounts [were] an essential part of the law of Florida . . . applied on numerous occasions in elections for lower level offices." More to point, this practice reflected "the sound legislative judgment [of the Florida legislature] that manual recounts are the most accurate method of objectively determining voter intent." The question before the court, therefore, was "as fundamental as it [was] straightforward: whether lawfully cast and counted ballots [were] to be included in a vote total that will resolve an issue of paramount national importance—the selection of the President of the United States."

If the secretary of state had her way, Gore's brief observed, lawfully cast and counted ballots would not be included in Florida's final count. "She is seeking to reject some—but oddly, not all—votes that have been tabulated through manual recounts, which are a lawful means for correcting errors in vote tallies, and thereby ascertaining the will of the voters," the brief noted. This stance was both technically and conceptually wrong, Gore and the Democrats insisted. Selectively rejecting manual recounts as part of Florida's vote tally was totally "contrary to the fundamental public policy of this state," noted the brief. As the Florida justices themselves had written, "'the electorate's effecting its will through balloting, not the hypertechnical compliance with statutes, is the object of holding an election.'" Nor were Harris's reasons for rejection legally acceptable. To the extent that Harris rejected these ballots based on "her opinion that such manual recounts [were] available only in cases of machine breakdown, that view [was] wholly unsupported by statute or case law."[37]

On a more technical level, because state law required canvassing boards to count "*all*" ballots showing "evidence of the voter's intent," logic demanded that "manual recounts had to be available under the law to allow such ballots to be counted." Any other reading of the law ran into the well-established doctrine "that if a voter . . . marked a ballot in a manner that cannot be read by a machine, but the voter's intent [could] be discerned from the ballot, that ballot *must* be counted." To allow the secretary to ignore the recounts "for the convenience of a quick certification" violated this rule.[38]

In a second brief, Gore and the Democrats defended the validity and constitutionality of manual recounts. They stressed how common manual recounts were across the country. They noted how, "contrary to Respondents' argument, machine voting was not introduced to eliminate errors from the ballot counting process. It was introduced because it [was] faster and more efficient." Machine votes were potentially very inaccurate. Indeed, the brief continued, "Governor Bush signed into law a Texas statute providing that where both an electronic and manual recount are requested, '[a] manual recount shall be conducted in preference to an electronic recount. . . .'"

In the same way, the brief challenged the idea that manual recounts were unconstitutional. "The claim that voters in some of Florida's counties will suffer vote dilution in violation of the Equal Protection Clause as a result of a manual recount in other counties [was] demonstrably unsound. *All* qualified voters have a constitutionally protected right to have their votes counted, including those whose ballots were erroneously missed in the automated tabulation." Moreover, "the manual recount provisions of the statute [were] applicable to all counties and thus all voters." Contrary to the Republicans' claims, "the vote of a citizen of one county [was] not 'diluted' by a process which ensure[d] that all properly cast votes in another county [were] actually included in the final vote count."[39]

In their brief, George W. Bush's lawyers began on the defensive, noting that "the laws of Florida, enacted by the legislature long before the present extraordinary circumstances confronted the State and Nation, anticipated and resolved the way in which election results in this State [were] determined." The relevant statutes gave the canvassing boards seven days to count, and only seven days. The same statutes required the state canvassing commission to certify the vote immediately following this seven-day period. Given these statutory structures, Secretary Harris's actions throughout the course of events since the election were "perfectly consistent with (indeed, mandated by) the laws of Florida."[40]

The Florida legislature knew that there would be close elections requiring manual recounts. Yet they still worded the statute to require a seven-day deadline on vote counting. They set this deadline presumably knowing "the time pressure they would create." If a county canvassing board felt itself unable to meet the statutory deadline, they simply did not have to carry out a manual recount. Manual recounts were not, in the eyes of the Florida legislature, "a necessary ingredient in determining the will of the people." They were available as a remedy, but not when they got in the way of "the values of finality and uniformity created by an evenhanded deadline."[41]

The Bush lawyers also challenged the legitimacy of the Democrats' claims that without a hand recount the will of the voters would be somehow lost. If equity demanded that the votes in four counties be manually reviewed to be deemed accurate, the brief demanded, what about the other sixty-three counties of Florida? Would not their machine counts be invalid too? Yet the "Petitioners, notwithstanding their devotion to manual recounts in all circumstances, did not request that all Florida counties conduct manual recounts, as was their right. . . . Nor [did] they ask this Court to order a statewide recount." No, the Democrats only asked for recounts in four counties, each of which was heavily Democratic in its voting. If anyone was seeking to skew the results of the election in a partisan manner, charged the brief, it was the Democrats, not the secretary of state.[42]

On more technical legal grounds, the Republican brief challenged the Florida Supreme Court's powers to overturn the secretary of state's rulings on these matters. State and federal laws required that all rules for choosing electors had to be in place *before* the election.[43] This requirement protected the sanctity of the vote. And although the legislature had granted the Secretary of State some limited powers to ignore some late vote totals, nowhere were the Florida courts granted equitable authority "to disregard both the deadline and the Secretary's exercise of reasoned discretion." Should the supreme court chose to act nonetheless, the brief argued that such action would violate the equal protection clause of the Fourteenth Amendment. Similarly, to allow hand recounts to continue as they currently were, without meaningful standards for officials conducting such recounts, would create results so chaotic as to violate the due process and equal protection guarantees of the U.S. Constitution.[44]

The remaining briefs, filed by the interested county canvassing boards, the state attorney general, and the secretary of state's office, generally followed the lead of the two candidates. Harris's brief was notable for its combative and dismissive tone. As far as she was concerned, she had properly followed the law as set out by Florida's statutes. Any misconduct she lay at the feet of the Democrats who, in effect, advocated "the fashioning of a presumably common law right to manually recount votes, the creation of superclasses of voters in three counties whose votes are entitled to special consideration and multiple counts (as opposed to the voters of the other 64 counties), and the creation by this Court of administrative guidelines to determine how a human ought to interpret machine ballots—the ever expanding universe of chad issues." All of these specious claims were set against the backdrop of "felons who were permitted to vote, claimed irregularities in the actual manual counting in the two counties currently underway, and the disenfranchisement of overseas voters."[45]

The attorney general argued that his interpretation of state law—which he had set out in his advisory opinion—was the correct reading of Florida statute. The secretary of state was simply wrong in contending that she lacked authority to grant more time to count votes and that hand recounts were only permissible when the tabulating machines were at fault.[46]

The county canvassing boards, in turn, argued for more time to do their duty under the appropriate state laws. As the brief for the Broward board noted, "the

Secretary of State's interpretation of her statutory discretion to impose temporal deadlines on the submission of certified election results from the Board must yield to the Board's statutorily imposed obligation and authority in authorizing a county-wide manual recount."[47]

On Monday afternoon, in a packed courtroom, and broadcast live to the world via cable and satellite television, the oral arguments began.[48] Chief Justice Charles T. Wells opened the proceedings on a serious note, observing how "the Court is certainly aware of the historic nature of this session and is aware that this is a matter of utmost and vital importance to our nation, our state and our world."[49] The justices had allocated two and one-half hours for argument, each side limited to no more than a single hour. The remaining half hour was made available to the various state agencies and canvassing boards with an interest in the proceedings. Most of the arguments echoed the views expressed in the briefs. The big difference in the hearing was the justices' ability to ask questions and in this way show the direction their concerns were taking them as they contemplated an answer to this legal and constitutional quandary.[50]

Most notable in this regard was Chief Justice Wells, who was particularly concerned about how much time the state had to certify a winner and still have its voice heard when the Electoral College met to pick a president. As the chief justice saw it, the rules laid out a continuum of time, from November 7 to some point in December, after which Florida's votes could be lost. It was this later date that was of concern. Exactly what was the date "in December," asked Chief Justice Wells of the attorney general's lawyer, Paul Hancock, when "Florida's electoral votes would be prejudiced or not counted in the electoral college, if there [was] no certification by the Secretary?" Hancock's answer was the December 12 safe harbor deadline, a date seconded by attorneys for the Broward canvassing board and Al Gore's lawyer, David Boies.

Justice R. Fred Lewis was also concerned with the time issue, but on a more practical level. How, he asked, could one reconcile the time constraints of both a protest recount (done before certification) and a contest recount (done after certification)? Was it even possible that all of this counting could happen within a time frame that allows both to coexist? Would not the court, in adding time for the protests, make it impossible for there to be a contest after certification? Or alternately, would the court in so acting allow a contest to go on so long as to cost Florida her votes in the Electoral College?[51] In response, Boies argued no. He saw no reason why certification could not be held off until the December 12 certification deadline, which would still allow the time between that day and the voting of the Electoral College (six days later) for contests.

Justice Major Harding asked whether there was any current law to guide the court's decision on how to come up with a workable time table. Boies responded that "there is some information in the record, but to be completely candid with the Court I believe there is going to have to be a lot of judgment applied by the court as well." But did not the legislature set such a timeline, countered Harding? "I don't think that's what they have done," Boies replied, adding that the intention of the legislature was not to bring "down the curtain a mere week after the election." Harding pushed even harder. "What is *the* time limit?" To this, finally, Boies had no answer—nor did any of the Democratic lawyers.

Moving to the issue of standards, the justices were uncertain why they had to set the standards for a proper vote—or more accurately, why now and not later, during a contest phase. Boies's response boiled down to one phrase: "in the interest of time." December was fast approaching and there were still many ballots to recount. Without clear guidelines, the voting process was slow and inefficient, Boies explained. Yet what standards would you have us apply, demanded Justice Leander J. Shaw Jr. Boies, with a small smile, pointed to the many precedents provided in Gore's brief—in particular, "for obvious reasons, the statute from Texas, which provided statutory guidelines for defining that."

Justice Barbara Pariente was concerned that selective recounts were unfair to voters who lived in counties where the ballots were tabulated only once. "Any candidate could have requested a recount," Boies countered. Nor would Gore oppose a statewide recount. "We believe the court has the power to order that," Boies said. But, asked Justice Peggy Quince, "Aren't we just adding another layer if we request a statewide recount?" Boies answered yes, but added that the most populous counties are already recounting their ballots, which would simplify the matter if a full recount were initiated.

When Bush's lawyer, Michael Carvin, began his argument, the justices once again raised the issues of time and standards. Was the seven-day deadline only necessary in presidential elections due to the December 12 federal deadline? Would not common sense allow for additional time to get the vote count right were such an external deadline not in place? How were Florida's hand recounts different from those of Governor George W. Bush's home state of Texas? Would Bush object to any manual recounts? Why had this issue not been taken to the legislature to fix the problem? The questions came fast and hard. Carvin, not expecting such hard questioning, tried to maintain his footing. In the end, his arguments came back to the idea that delay was bad: "My point is, as we wait for the Dade and Broward County's returns to come in, there will be no clearer position to know who the true winner is in Florida than we are today, and that is exactly why the legislature said, look, here is what you do. Take all of the returns in, pursuant to a methodology that we have used for decades and certify those results."

By the time Bush's other lawyer, Barry Richard, got up to speak, most of the substantive questions had been asked and answered. Richard therefore stressed to the justices his client's argument that

> what the Appellants are asking this Court to do and, in fact, what the Court must do, in order to arrive at the conclusion that they seek, is read a statute that

says that returns must be filed by a certain date and time, as though it said . . . "must accept late-filed returns," to disregard the statute that says that the secretary of state's opinion as to election matters is binding upon all those officers and agents within the elections system, and to disregard the well established and long-standing doctrines regarding clearly erroneous standards and implied repeal.

Clearly, none of this was either necessary or advantageous, Richard concluded.

The hearing ended with a rebuttal by Gore's lawyer. David Boies wanted "the Court to understand . . . the nature of the other side's argument. They say . . . what they want us to do is have a contest," but in other instances they have repeatedly said that "once the results are certified, then the recount becomes superfluous and ought to stop." Further, they have even held that, "as soon as the results are certified, the Secretary of State can . . . declare who the electors are, and it is their view that, when that declaration of electors has been declared, it [the election] is over with."[52] Clearly, Boies explained, "what this Court . . . has to do, is to reconcile the entire statutory scheme" with reality—"and the statutory scheme, long before there was this election, provided for manual recounts."

With the hearings ended, the justices returned to their chambers and began work on their judgment. Understanding the need for a quick resolution, they completed and announced their per curiam opinion the next day. After summarizing the facts and prior proceedings in the case, the justices began with a statement of their guiding principles in answering the difficult questions raised by these cases. "Twenty-five years ago, this Court commented that the will of the people, not a hyper-technical reliance upon statutory provisions, should be our guiding principle in election cases." In *Boardman v. Esteva* (1975), the court had noted that "the real parties in interest here, not in the legal sense but in realistic terms, are the voters. They are possessed of the ultimate interest and it is they whom we must give primary consideration. . . . Our goal today remains the same as it was a quarter of a century ago, i.e., to reach the result that reflects the will of the voters, whatever that might be. This fundamental principle, and our traditional rules of statutory construction, guide our decision today."[53]

The court first took up the question whether a county canvassing board could legally recount votes when there was no machine error in the original tabulation. The secretary of state had argued no. The court disagreed. Whereas traditionally the Florida courts deferred to the views of the executive branch agencies in their areas of expertise, the justices explained that they did not have to do so when that view was legally wrong. Such was the case with the Division of Elections ruling against manual recounts. Rather, the justices agreed with Attorney General Bob Butterworth's views that "vote tabulation" meant any vote problem, not just those relating to machine error. As the justices explained, "although error cannot be completely eliminated in any tabulation of the ballots, our society has not yet gone so far as to place blind faith in machines. In almost all endeavors, including elections, humans routinely correct the errors of machines. For this very reason Florida law provides a human check on both the malfunction of tabulation equipment and error in failing to accurately count the ballots."[54]

The court next took up the seven-day certification deadline. After surveying the relevant statutes, the court noted the statutory ambiguity between a canvassing board's duty under the recount procedures and the deadlines for the submission of their certified returns. Given this ambiguity, it was hard for the court to agree with the secretary of state's narrow reading of the law: "If the mandatory provision in section 102.111 were given effect, the votes of the county would be ignored for the simple reason that the Board was following the dictates of a different section of the Code." Basic statutory interpretation argued against such a narrow reading of the law. "The Legislature could not have intended to penalize County Canvassing Boards for following the dictates of the Code," concluded the court. And if this was the case, then some flexibility in the certification deadline was obligatory.[55]

Then there were the "shall" and "may" conflicts in the wording of Sections 102.111 and 102.112. Turning to what they saw as the legislative intent in writing the statute, the court noted that generally, where two provisions of a statute conflict, the courts would follow those provisions that were (a) most specific and (b) most recent. Further, the court had to read the statutory provisions as a coherent whole. In each of these categories, it was the more permissive section, 102.112, which allowed that "if the returns are not received by the department by the time specified, such returns *may* be ignored [emphasis added]," that proved the most compelling.[56] Similarly, that absentee overseas ballots were accepted after the seven-day statutory deadline implied strongly that "if a Board fails to meet the deadline, the Secretary [was] not required to ignore the county's returns but rather [was] permitted to ignore the returns within the parameters of this statutory scheme."[57]

In support of these positions, the court turned to "the interplay between our statutory and constitutional law at both the state and federal levels." For example, "the right of suffrage is the preeminent right contained in the Declaration of Rights [of the Florida Constitution], for without this basic freedom all others would be diminished. The importance of this right was acknowledged by the authors of the Constitution, who placed it first in the Declaration." Consequently, any acts of the legislature regulating the electoral process were void if they imposed an "unreasonable or unnecessary" restraint on the right to vote. The court found the implications of this principle clear: "Because election laws are intended to facilitate the right of suffrage, such laws must be liberally construed in favor of the citizens' right to vote. . . . Technical statutory requirements must not be exalted over the substance of this right."[58]

Based on this reading of the constitutional imperatives of the electoral process, the justices held against the secretary of state: "Ignoring the county's returns is a drastic measure and is appropriate only if the returns are submitted to the Department so late that their inclusion will compromise the integrity of the electoral process in either of two ways: (1) by precluding a candidate, elector, or taxpayer from contesting the certification of an election . . . ; or (2) by precluding Florida voters from participating fully in the federal electoral process." In the present case, the justices held that the trial court was correct when it concluded that the county canvassing boards did have to submit their returns by 5:00 p.m. of the seventh day following the election and when it held that the department of state was not required to ignore any subsequent amended returns. Judge Lewis was wrong, however, "in holding that the Secretary acted within her discretion in prematurely rejecting any amended returns that would be the result of ongoing manual recounts."[59]

In conclusion, the court ruled that, due to the "unique circumstances and extraordinary importance of the present case, . . . and because of our reluctance to rewrite the Florida Election Code, we conclude that we must invoke the equitable powers of this Court to fashion a remedy that will allow a fair and expeditious resolution of the questions presented here."[60] To this end, the court ordered that "amended certifications must be filed with the Elections Commission by 5 p.m. on Sunday, November 26, 2000."[61] The Court's prior order permitting recounts would remain in force until this new deadline.[62]

The Florida Supreme Court's ruling brought great cheers from the Democratic side and loud grumbling and complaints from the Republicans. To Gore and his supporters, this was vindication of all their hard work. "We obviously think this is good news," said Senate Minority Leader Tom Daschle's spokesperson Ranit Schmelzer. "Vice President Gore has said all along he wants to see that all Floridians have their votes counted, and the Florida Supreme Court has just said they agree with that." Bob Poe, the Florida Democratic Party chairman, was "thankful the Supreme Court unanimously saw this the same way we did—that the right of the people to have their votes counted and voice heard is paramount to anything." In Broward County, Democratic Canvassing Board member Suzanne Gunzburger shared high-fives with Democratic observers. "The people's voice will count, and it will be a fair decision, made by all the people in the state of Florida, at least in Broward County," she cried.[63]

Some Democrats whispered words of caution, noting that the ruling did not give Gore everything that he had hoped for. While Gore got the time he wanted for recounts, the court's ruling was ambiguous on the issue of standards. The Florida Supreme Court "has confirmed what we thought was the law of Florida—which was that any indication of the intent of the voter—whether it is pricked through, or whether it is completely dislodged or whether it is indented, that is what counts," argued David Boies. However, the court had done this largely by quoting from a 1990 Illinois Supreme Court ruling, not by stating its own rules on the subject.[64] The court, noted Florida Senator Bob Graham, stopped short of setting standards for counting ballots. "Nor did they do what many of us, including myself, would have hoped, and that is that they would have said all the counties should have a manual hand count so all Floridians would be treated equally."[65]

Republicans simply saw a miscarriage of justice. House Majority Leader Richard K. Armey described the decision as "a partisan ruling by a partisan court." Senator Christopher Bond of Missouri was "stunned" by the decision and added that Bush "is being victimized by an opponent who will do anything to win—even after the election is over." James Baker reminded everyone of Justice Harding's question about Florida's electoral laws and standards. He had said, "Is it right to change the rules in the middle of the game?" Baker argued that this was exactly what "the Florida Supreme Court and some Democratic county electoral boards have decided to do. . . . Today, Florida's Supreme Court rewrote the legislature's statutory system, assumed the responsibilities of the executive branch, and side-stepped the opinion of the trial court as the finder of fact." U.S. Representative Joe Scarborough agreed: "Tonight the Florida Supreme Court declared war on the rule of law in Florida. Seven radical Democratic lawyers have chosen to ignore the clear intent of Florida's legislative and executive branches. If it is political war they want, it is political war they should get."[66]

A central component of most Republican complaints was that the Florida Supreme Court was made up of six Democrats and an independent named to the bench by a former Democratic governor. The Florida Supreme Court was not only partisan, so the arguments went, but well known as a liberal, activist court. House Majority Whip Tom DeLay called the ruling "a blatant and extraordinary abuse of judicial power. . . . With this decision, a collection of liberal activists has arbitrarily swept away thoughtfully designed statutes ensuring free and fair elections and replaced them with their own political opinions." State Senator Daniel Webster, a former Speaker of the Florida House of Representatives, argued that the court had totally disregarded the legislature's authority to set policy. "If we allow this to be the final step, our power has been greatly diminished as a Legislature. . . . If you can challenge the technical portions of a statute and say they really don't matter, I think we're in trouble." In a nationally televised statement, George W. Bush seconded this view: "The court has cloaked its ruling in legalist language. [But] make no mistake, the court rewrote the law. . . . It changed the rules and it did so after the election was over." "If the presidency is going to be decided in the courts," Dick Armey proposed angrily, "why stop short of the [U.S.] Supreme Court?"[67]

The U.S. Supreme Court was, in fact, Bush's next option if he wished to continue the legal fight to certify the election. As we have seen, the Republicans had been thinking in terms of a federal solution almost from the beginning. James Baker in particular was convinced that, whatever else happened, in the end it would be the U.S. Supreme Court that would settle the dispute.[68] The Republicans had already brought an unsuccessful action in federal court on the general issue of hand recounts and had hopes that their appeal would end up in the Supreme Court. After all, both Judge Middlebrooks and the 11th Circuit had denied the requested injunctions on the procedural grounds that the state courts had not yet acted. At no time did they rule against the substance of the Republicans' equal protection arguments.[69]

Still, there was real doubt in the Bush camp that the Supreme Court would agree to hear the case. Not only was this a troubling suit involving a political question, a suit involving state not federal laws, but there were legitimate concerns as to Bush's standing even to bring an appeal before the U.S. Supreme Court on these matters. Tradition argued that the justices would seek to avoid the issue given any legitimate excuse to do so. Justice Scalia was known as a stickler on the technical issue of standing to bring suit. Similarly, Chief Justice Rehnquist was known for his adamant refusal to hear matters before a real, final judgment had been handed down in the courts below. With recounts ongoing, such was not the case in Florida. Would these be enough to persuade these two conservative justices to avoid the issue? Justice O'Connor was a former state legislator; perhaps she would refuse to see a reason to intervene in what she would see as a legislative matter. Then again, maybe she would intervene to counteract the poaching of the Florida Supreme Court into legislative realms. And then there were Chief Justice Rehnquist's writings on the Tenth Amendment and his strong New Federalist views that state law matters were beyond the scope of federal court review. Besides, everyone assumed that any formal contest to the election (filed after certification) would produce additional litigation, thus giving the Court an additional chance to intervene later if it so wished.[70]

Given such concerns, the Republicans began laying the foundations for their Plan B and even Plan C options should the recounts go in Gore's favor. As early as Wednesday, November 15, Tom DeLay circulated a memorandum on Congress's role in tallying presidential votes. In it, DeLay focused on the Electoral Count Act of February 3, 1887. Intended to make clear Congress's role in counting electoral votes, the act provided for the "safe harbor" provisions that had so intrigued the Florida Supreme Court. DeLay argued that the act gave Congress the power to reject electors if the members found fault with the methods applied at the state level. Implicit in this argument was the assumption that should the Florida courts "give" the election to Gore, Congress had a remedy to overturn that result under the Electoral Count Act.[71]

Even more explicit were claims made by the Republican-led Florida legislature. As early as November 18, the Republican legislative leadership were talking about "regaining" their powers over the appointment of electors. Newly elected House Speaker Tom Feeney said the court's ruling showed "an extreme lack of respect" for the legislative process and argued that the seven-member panel had potentially brought Florida to the brink of a "constitutional crisis." "The judicial branch has clearly overstepped their powers," Feeney said. "The Florida Legislature intends to uphold the Constitution."[72] Though unspoken at the time, Feeney was referring here to Title 3, Section 2 of the U.S. Code, which read, "Whenever any state has held an election for the purpose of appointing electors, and has failed to make the choice on the day prescribed by law, the electors may be appointed on a subsequent day in such a manner as the legislature thereof may direct."[73] That the legislature could make such a choice was reinforced by an 1892 Supreme Court case, *McPherson v. Blacker*, which noted, "The Constitution does not provide that the appointment of electors shall be by popular vote, nor that the electors shall be voted for upon a general ticket, nor that the majority of those who exercise the elective franchise can alone choose the electors. It recognizes that the people act through their representatives in the legislature, and leaves it to the legislature exclusively to define the method of effecting the object."[74]

Feeney and the Florida Republican legislators were serious about their threat to pick their own electors should the judicial process turn against Bush. On November 27, they commissioned a special, joint-legislative committee to explore the legislature's options in these matters.[75] The committee, in turn, recommended applying Title 3, Section 2 of the U.S. Code and having the Florida legislature name electors if necessary. The next day (December 6), both houses of the Florida legislature passed (on a strictly partisan vote) a "Joint Proclamation" calling for a special session to explore the appointment of electors should normal methods of picking electors not "produce a final, constitutional choice of electors."[76]

These were plans for the future, however. In the short run, Bush's primary response to the Florida ruling focused on the U.S. Supreme Court. Not everyone on the Bush legal team worried about the Court taking up the case. Bush's chief federal litigator, Theodore Olson, was confident that the Court would hear the case. So, too, were many Republican lawyers who had clerked for the more conservative justices. They knew the personalities involved and insisted that any appeal to the Supreme Court on these matters would be heard. The justices read the papers. They knew the importance of these matters. Trust us, they argued, *this* is a case that the justices will want a piece of.[77]

Acting quickly, the Bush team finished a petition for a writ of certiorari seeking a review of the Florida case before the U.S. Supreme Court less than twenty-four hours after the Florida Supreme Court's ruling in *Palm Beach County Canvassing Board v. Harris* (renamed in this petition *Bush v. Palm Beach County Canvassing Board* since it was Bush that was bringing the appeal and not Secretary of State Harris). "In plain contravention of the requirements of the Constitution of the United States and federal law, the state supreme court has embarked on an *ad hoc*, standardless, and lawless exercise of judicial power, which appears designed to thwart the will of the electorate as well as the considered judgments of Florida's executive and legislative branches," argued the petition. "Because the selection of presidential electors is governed directly by the Constitution and congressional enactments, as well as by state law, the court's decision involves issues of the utmost *federal* importance."[78]

In support of this position, the Republicans raised three constitutional contentions, each attacking the Florida court's ruling. (1) That "post-election judicial limitations on the discretion [of] . . . state executive officials to certify election results," and/or "judicially created standards for the determination of controversies concerning the appointment of presidential electors" after the election, "violate[d] the Due Process Clause or 3 U.S.C. §5 (which requires that a State resolve controversies relating to the appointment of electors under 'laws enacted prior to' election day)." (2) That the state court's decision was "inconsistent with Article II, Section 1 of the Constitution, which provides that electors shall be appointed by each State 'in such Manner as the Legislature thereof may direct.'" (3) That "the use of arbitrary, standardless, and selective manual recounts . . . threaten to overturn the results of the election for President of the United States" in violation of "the Equal Protection or Due Process Clauses, or the First Amendment."[79]

Gore's response to the petition for certiorari, not surprisingly, challenged Bush's contentions point by point. In particular, Gore objected to Bush's bald declaration of a federal question important enough to demand review by the U.S. Supreme Court. Basic and fundamental principles of federalism argued strongly *against* accepting Bush's invitation to interfere with Florida's electoral process, counseled the brief. "The authority of the States to establish principles and procedures for selecting their electors is fundamental to state sovereignty," the brief explained. "By expressly providing for state discretion, the Framers constitutionalized each State's right to organize and administer elections in the manner that best reflected the will of its respective citizenry, thereby reinforcing the decentralized nature of American Government." The Florida legislature, in turn, had created a clear set of rules and procedures for running its elections, procedures that the Florida Supreme Court was applying in its ruling. There simply was nothing unusual or exceptional in Florida's election statutes or the Florida Supreme Court's interpretation of those statutes. Many states had similar provisions. So where was the federal question? Bush's certiorari petition was nothing more than "a bald attempt to federalize a state law dispute over whether a manual recount is authorized and appropriate." Gore's brief thus ended with a call on the justices to rebuff Bush's efforts and to leave this matter where it belonged, in the state court's hands.[80]

Three days later, on November 24—to the great joy of Republicans, the dejection of Democrats, and the outright confusion of legal scholars across the nation who were confident that this case would never be brought up for argument under the rules of federalism—the High Court accepted the certiorari petition and set the matter down for oral argument on December 1. In their grant of certiorari, the justices agreed to hear arguments on Bush's first two contentions: (1) that the Florida Supreme Court's ruling violated the requirement that a state resolve its election controversies under "laws enacted prior to" Election Day, and (2) that in doing this, the Florida Supreme Court co-opted the constitutionally established role of the legislature to pick the means by which presidential electors were chosen. In addition, the Court added its own query for argument: "What would be the consequences of this Court's finding that the decision of the Supreme Court of Florida does not comply with 3 U.S.C. Sec. 5?"[81]

The brief on the merits of the case filed by Bush's lawyers responded to these queries by first attacking the Florida Supreme Court's ruling as a clear change in the manner by which Florida chose her presidential electors—a change adopted after Election Day. This change, the brief argued, was a violation of Section 5 of Title 3 of the U.S. Code. "Responding to a presidential election crisis much like that unfolding in Florida during the past three weeks, Congress enacted a statutory scheme to implement the constitutional mechanism of the Electoral College, 3 U.S.C. §§1–15," noted the brief. "One of those statutes, §5, provide[d] that state-court resolutions of controversies regarding the appointment of presidential electors shall be conclusive only if they [were] made pursuant to 'laws enacted prior to' election day."[82] By resorting to its "equitable powers" to prescribe "new standards and deadlines, suspend mandatory enforcement mechanisms, and curtail the discretion conferred on the state executive by the legislature," the Florida Supreme Court had created "a clear departure from the legal requirements established before election day, and announce[d] new rules governing the resolution of election disputes."[83]

As for issue two, the Bush brief held that the Florida Supreme Court, "by arrogating to itself the authority to make new rules applicable to this election contest, also violated Article II of the Constitution, which invests the authority to regulate the manner of appointing presidential electors in state legislatures." Article II, the brief explained, established "a federally mandated separation of powers between the state legislature and other branches of state government in the context of choosing presidential electors." Significantly, "the Framers deliberately chose to invest the power to determine the manner of choosing electors in this particular branch of state government, thereby excluding the exercise of such power by the other branches." Nor had the Florida legislature ever "granted to the state supreme court the authority to determine the manner of choosing electors." In fact, it was the executive branch to which the legislature had turned for the supervision and administration of elections. The court below had "no authority under the federal Constitution to announce new rules for this presidential election. Its attempt at judicial legislation was unconstitutional, and its actions patently" beyond its powers to enact, "and the court's decision [was] thus void."[84]

Finally, responding to the justices' query on consequences, Bush's brief was optimistic and concise. "The resulting consequences are two-fold," it argued.

"First, the executive officials in Florida would be able to discharge all of their duties, including their duties imposed by federal law, under the rules in place on election day. Second, Congress would be able to give conclusive effect to the official certification of the Elections Canvassing Commission regarding the appointment of Florida's electors. . . ." Vacating the Florida court's decision "would thus allow the Electoral College process to reach a lawful, final, and conclusive resolution of the presidential election."[85]

Gore and the Democrats began their brief on the merits with a direct attack on the legitimacy of Bush's case—and on the U.S. Supreme Court's jurisdiction to hear these matters. "This dispute over the Florida Supreme Court's interpretation of the Florida Election Code is a state-law case that, despite its undoubted importance, does not belong in federal court," it read. "The process legislatively adopted by Florida for resolving disputes regarding the appointment of electors include state judicial review." Principles of federalism, in turn, "counsel strongly against interference by this Court, or any federal court, in that process." Furthermore, "the federal claims purportedly presented by petitioner were insubstantial." The Florida Supreme Court had not usurped the role of the Florida legislature—far from it: "The Florida court [rather] played a familiar and quintessentially judicial role: it interpreted Florida law us[ing] traditional rules of statutory construction to resolve [statutory] ambiguities."[86]

In consequence, continued the Gore brief, the first two claims brought by Bush and the Republicans were irrelevant to the case at hand. Properly understood, "Section 5 merely offer[ed] the States a safe harbor with respect to a hypothetical controversy that ha[d] not yet arisen—a dispute over electors that might arise before Congress when the electoral votes [were] counted." There could be no judicial remedy for failure to comply with Section 5.[87]

In this same manner, the Gore brief insisted, the Florida Supreme Court ruling was not in conflict with Article II, Section 1 of the U.S. Constitution, which provided that "Each State shall appoint" electors "in such Manner as the Legislature thereof may direct." Properly understood, this provision "neither displace[d] the state judiciary nor forbid it from undertaking statutory interpretation pursuant to state law. [For], where a state legislature ha[d] enacted an election code (as Florida ha[d]), nothing in Article II, §1, cl. 2 prevent[ed] the state courts from playing whatever interpretive role state law grants to them."[88] As the brief made clear, "the institutional mechanism of judicial review to decide disputes about electors was in place in Florida long before the day fixed for the appointment of electors." And, as such, "the Florida Supreme Court acted well within its statutory jurisdiction in this case."[89]

Along with the primary players in this suit (while the Palm Beach County canvassing board was technically the named respondent in this case, there was little doubt that this was primarily a contest between Bush and Gore), a number of parties filed briefs with the Court. Some were formal participants, such as Katherine

Harris and the Florida attorney general Bob Butterworth.[90] Others were outside observers who filed amicus curiae (friend of the Court) briefs with the Court. The American Civil Liberties Union, for example, presented a brief that supported Al Gore's contentions, while the American Civil Rights Union supported Bush.[91]

All of these third-party briefs echoed to varying extents the arguments of the candidates and their parties.[92] One of the more interesting amicus briefs was that of the Senate and House of the Florida legislature, which had filed a brief "in support of neither party." While obviously less than truthful as to the legislature's objectives—the legislature's actions before filing this brief demonstrated its preference for a Bush victory—the brief raised an interesting argument that "the Legislature itself, and not the courts, [was] the arbiter of when a failure to make such a choice has occurred." Further, it held that these matters were "not justiciable . . . a political matter to be decided in the first instance by the State Legislature . . . and then by Congress." A ruling of nonjusticiability, argued the Florida legislature, "would avoid involving this Court in a political dispute best resolved by the political process. It is neither surprising nor inappropriate that the law should lodge that authority in the State Legislatures and Congress. What is at stake here is after all a political determination of who shall be the next President. The issue to be determined is uniquely political."[93]

No doubt read in haste by the justices and their clerks,[94] these briefs along with the trial documents from below were what the justices had before them when they heard oral arguments on December 1.[95] As with the Florida Supreme Court hearings, these proceedings gave the justices a chance to challenge the parties with questions—in essence, giving the lawyers their best shot at convincing the justices as to the validity of their position. And despite the shortness of time, the justices were ready to argue.

Bush's lawyer, Theodore Olson, was up first. Starting with the traditional "May it please the Court," Olson had not gotten far into his prepared comments when he was interrupted by the justices. At issue was Bush's argument (set out in his brief) that Title 3, Section 5's "safe harbor" provisions created a presumption of intent great enough that *any* efforts on the part of the state courts that potentially threatened this safe harbor were, in effect, substantive changes in the methods of picking a presidential elector.[96]

Justice O'Connor, for one, was skeptical. "Isn't Section 5 sort of a safe-harbor provision for states," she asked, designed to help *Congress* settle challenges to Electoral College votes? "I just don't quite understand how it would be independently enforceable?" Justice Kennedy wondered how Section 5 was any different from a "grant-in-aid" package, a legislative bribe to do something that Congress wanted from the states, but not an enforceable order to act. "What they did was . . . [say] if you run a clean shop down there, we'll give you a bonus, and if you don't, well, you take your chances with everybody else." Kennedy later asked Olson to help him find "a federal issue" for the Court to rule on. Maybe the Florida court had misinterpreted Section 5 in some way? If not, why was this issue even before the Court? Justice O'Conner seconded this request. She noted that "if it were purely a matter of state law, I suppose we normally would leave it alone, where the state supreme court found it. And so you probably have to persuade us there is some issue of federal law here. Otherwise, why are we acting?" Chief Justice Rehnquist was equally troubled by the Bush claim of a special imperative in Section 5. "Do you think that Congress when it passed 3 U.S. Code, intended that there would be any judicial involvement?" he asked. "I mean, it seems to me it can just as easily be read as a direction to Congress, saying what we are going to do when these electoral votes are presented to us for counting." Justice Souter agreed. "Why should the Court, why should the federal judiciary, be interfering in what seems to be a very carefully thought-out scheme for determining what happens if you are right" and the state judiciary had overstepped its bounds? Even Justice Scalia wondered why these election provisions were any different from a "scheme that says states can get highway funds if . . . they hold their highway speeds to a certain level." If highway provisions were subjected to judicial interpretation, why not the election provisions?[97]

Olson, doing his best to keep up with the fast and forceful questions, returned repeatedly to the chaos of the 1876 presidential election and argued that Congress had seen the need for something more than just a set of rules designed to shape congressional reactions to an electoral controversy. Congress saw the need to provide a benefit not just to the states (in the form of a presumption of legitimacy) but also "to provide the benefit to the United States of the states accepting that implicit proposal." And that benefit was an orderly election for president. "That is to say that if the rules are complied with, if disputes are resolved according to the rules that are set forth, then not only will the electors chosen by the voters in that state be given conclusive effect at the time they are counted by Congress, but [that] we will not have the controversy, dispute and chaos that's been taking place in Florida."

Moving on, three justices then challenged Olson on the argument that the Florida Supreme Court had "changed the laws." Justice Stevens asked, was it "not arguable, . . . that all [the Florida justices] did was fill gaps that had not been addressed before?" Justice Breyer wondered if the state court had simply not been carrying out the traditional judicial role of determining if a state official had reasonably exercised her discretion under the law. Justice Ginsburg took this argument even further, questioning Olson on what she believed was the "key piece of the Florida legislation." Was not the Florida court merely settling a conflict between two provisions (the seven-day certification deadline and the recount provisions) of the statute? Yes, their reading on the law might be argued against, Ginsburg noted, but it also could be agreed with, too. So why should the Court adopt a different view of the law from that adopted by the Florida court? Was it not the norm for the Court to "read a state court decision . . . in the light most favorable to the integrity of the state supreme court[?]" After all, she explained, "if

there are two possible readings, one that would impute to that court injudicial behavior, lack of integrity, indeed dishonesty, and the other one that would read the
opinion to say we think this court is attempting to construe the state law—it may
have been wrong, we might have interpreted it differently, but we are not the ar-
biters, they are." That Olson was proposing the former reading bothered Ginsburg. "I do not know of any case where we have impugned a state supreme court
the way you are doing in this case. I mean, in case after case we have said we owe
the highest respect to what the state says, state supreme court says, is the state's
law," concluded the justice.

Near the end of Olson's time, Justice Scalia opened a line of questioning that
could have permitted Olson to argue that, in basing its actions on the Florida constitution and not state statute, the Florida justices had violated the dictates of
McPherson v. Blacker (which, noted Scalia, held that "the Constitution . . . recognizes that the people act through their representatives in the legislature, and leaves
it to the legislature exclusively to define the method of effecting the object").
McPherson, after all, seemed to grant exclusive authority to the legislature in these
matters unchecked by state constitutional provisions. Consequently, if the Florida
judgment was founded on state constitutional imperatives, and not statutory interpretations, then in this instance it was improperly applied.[98] Olson, however,
missed the hint in Justice Scalia's questions, and just continued to argue that the
Florida court had "changed the rules."

If Olson missed the point, the other justices did not. When Gore's lawyer, Laurence H. Tribe, came before the bench (following the rather inconclusive questioning of Harris's and Butterworth's lawyers), the justices quickly dealt with such
issues as Gore's contention that Section 5 presented a question for Congress to answer, not the Court. They then moved to the issue of *McPherson v. Blacker* and the
foundations of the Florida Supreme Court's rulings on recounts and certification
deadlines.

During a heated exchange on the issue of federal jurisdiction in these matters,
Tribe argued that "it seems to me that the Federal question, which is really what
brings us here, can only arise if 3 U.S.C. Section 5 is something other than what Mr.
Olson called the indemnification of the state." The chief justice disagreed. "It can
also arise under the section of the Constitution that was construed in *Blacker*," he
noted. "That's quite independent of 3 U.S.C. §5." In fact, the chief justice saw the
Florida court's use of the Florida constitution as ample grounds not only for federal
jurisdiction, but to reverse that court's ruling. "It seems to me a Federal question
arises if the Florida Supreme Court in its opinion rather clearly says that we are
using the Florida Constitution to reach the result we reach in construing the statute.
I think *Blacker* is a strong argument they can't do that." When Tribe tried to argue
that the Florida court had not done this, but rather was just referring to their state's
constitution, Rehnquist jumped in again, "Well, you know, if the Supreme Court
of Florida simply said in its opinion, look, these sections of the statute conflict,

we've got to under our judicial principles resolve it one way or the other, but—but it doesn't say that. It goes on to say, look, in the light of the Florida Constitution and the general rights conferred there, we are construing it this way." In fact, Rehnquist continued, "I don't think that the Florida Supreme Court used the Florida Constitution as a tool of interpretation of this statute. I read the Florida court's opinion as quite clearly saying, having determined what the legislative intent was, we find that our state constitution trumps that legislative intent. I don't think there is any other way to read it, and that is, that is a real problem."

Responding to the chief justice's contentions, Justice Souter challenged this reading of the law and the Florida Supreme Court's actions. In its place he proposed an alternate reading of the Florida court's proceedings. "Isn't there another way of looking at what the Florida court did[?]" he asked Tribe—that perhaps the only way to "apply the statute" effectively was to determine under "interpretative criterion, that where there is any discretion for interpretation, an unconstitutional result should be avoided"? And given this point, would it also not be logical that "the only way to avoid an unconstitutional meaning of the statute so far as Florida law was concerned was to get into this constitutional concern about preserving the franchise, and that because the legislature intended one standard to cover both Federal and state recounts, it therefore is valid to consider the state constitution in order to derive a general meaning that will apply to a Federal, as well as a state election. Can you look at it that way?"

Justice Breyer had his own alternate explanation. He noted that under the law, no state court could say, "our Constitution selects the electors." But what if "the Court had said, look, we reach our result based on the canons we found in Blackstone. Now, nobody is going to say they said Blackstone is selecting the electors, right. . . . Now, I suppose they said, we reached this decision based on the values found in the Constitution. That would be like Blackstone."

Justice Stevens extended this argument further, pointing out that the Florida court had relied on "four things" in reaching their decision—"the Florida Constitution, earlier Florida decisions construing statutes, an Illinois case, and a Federal case. Not just their constitution." Indeed, Stevens noted, "didn't they say that the date of the 7th cannot stand, not because of the constitution alone but because there are other provisions in the statute that cannot be accommodated with sections—with the 7 date?"

This was an argument that Justice Ginsburg found informative. Responding to Justice Stevens's comment on the inability of the statute to be accommodated with the seven-day certification deadline, she noted, "they said that twice, and I think that's critical if you add to that that we read a decision of a state court in the light most favorable to that court and not in the light least favorable. I suppose there would be a possibility for this Court to remand for clarification, but if there's two readings, one that's questionable, one that isn't, all of our decisions suggest that we read the one. . . ."

Justice Scalia, on the other hand, joined Chief Justice Rehnquist in expressing strong reservations about the sources of the Florida Supreme Court's ruling. He noted how the reference to the state constitution was made in a "separate section of the opinion, . . . that [was] entitled *the right to vote*." It came, in turn, directly "after the legislative intent section and it says categorically, to the extent the legislature may enact laws, they are invalid." Scalia suggested that "perhaps the reason that the Court did it is that however expansive the doctrine of constitutional doubt is, there is no way that can make December 7 mean anything except December 7. I mean, they were almost constrained to use the constitution to override . . . the firm deadline . . . that was explicitly set forth in the Constitution."

Scalia was adamant in his views that the Florida court had used the state constitution exclusively. "I would feel much better about the resolution if you could give me one sentence in the opinion that supports the second of these supposed alternative readings, that supports the proposition that the Florida Supreme Court was using the constitutional right to vote provisions as an interpretive tool to determine what the statute meant. I can't find a single sentence for that." When Tribe tried to argue that "the entire structure of that part of the opinion, as Justice Stevens points out, would be incoherent if the constitution was decisive," Justice Scalia disagreed. "You would bother with it because having decided very clearly what the statute requires and finding no way to get around the firm dates set, you say the reason it's bad is because of the state constitution. That's how it's written."

Before adjourning, the Court granted Olson a few minutes for rebuttal. Responding to the justice's questions and comments on *McPherson* and the sources of the Florida Supreme Court's rulings, Olson stressed how difficult it was "to read the Florida Supreme Court decision as saying anything else other than the Florida Constitution in their view, . . . is trumping everything else." As *McPherson* pointed out, this was not acceptable construction under Article II of the Constitution. The power to shape the naming of presidential electors lay exclusively with the legislature. "The Florida Supreme Court radically changed the legislative scheme because it thought it could do so under the Florida Constitution. By doing so, it acted inconsistently with Article II of the Constitution, and inconsistently with Section 5 of Title III, and it has brought about precisely the circumstances that Section 5 of Section 3, Title III, was designed to avoid."

With these words, Olson ended the oral argument. Now it was up to the justices to determine the sources of judicial action. This was not going to be an easy decision. As the questions over *McPherson* had pointed out, the justices were split as to their readings of the Florida Supreme Court's legal foundations for changing the certification deadlines. Also problematic were their differing attitudes toward the role of judicial interpretation versus judicial activism (both between the two courts and between members of the Supreme Court itself). And while most of the justices generally seemed to agree that Bush's argument that the Florida court had somehow "changed the rules after the election" by their ruling was weak, even here there was room for some dispute (Scalia and the chief justice, for instance, were clearly leaning in this direction).

Three days later, on December 4, the Court issued its opinion. In a per curiam ruling, the justices began the body of their opinion by conceding how, "as a general rule, this Court defers to a state court's interpretation of a state statute." However, "in the case of a law enacted by a state legislature applicable not only to elections to state offices, but also to the selection of Presidential electors," the rules were different. Here, "the legislature [was] not acting solely under the authority given it by the people of the State, but [also] by virtue of a direct grant of authority made under Art. II, §1, cl. 2, of the United States Constitution." And, as the Court had ruled in 1892, this difference was controlling. Article II, Section 1 granted the power to choose electors to "each State . . . in such manner as the legislature thereof may direct." This wording meant that the decision on how to pick presidential electors rested solely with the legislature regardless of any other state authority, including the state constitution. In practical terms, this meant that *in this unique instance*, when the office being elected was that of president, state statute trumped state constitutional provisions. The *only* controlling rules for picking the president were those enacted by the state legislature. (Or, at least, so a number of the justices had seemed to read this statute in the oral arguments.)

It was the potential of the Florida court's ruling to contravene these provisions that troubled the justices. "There are expressions in the opinion of the Supreme Court of Florida," their opinion noted, "that may be read to indicate that [the Florida court] construed the Florida Election Code without regard to the extent to which the Florida Constitution could, consistent with Art. II, §1, cl. 2, circumscribe the legislative power." Given such statements of the Florida court as "to the extent that the Legislature may enact laws regulating the electoral process, those laws are valid only if they impose no 'unreasonable or unnecessary' restraints on the right of suffrage guaranteed by the state constitution," the justices saw evidence that the Florida Supreme Court might be depending on the Florida constitution in ruling against the secretary of state's certification deadline decisions, and not just state statutory provisions. Were this the case, then their actions potentially would be invalid.

The justices also were concerned with the Florida court's ruling given the limits of 3 U.S.C. §5 and the safe harbor provisions. As they viewed the ruling, it too had the potential to produce troubling constitutional repercussions. Since all agreed that the Florida legislature intended for the state to meet the safe harbor requirements, any action that might jeopardize this acceptance by extending the settlement of all contests beyond the six days limit had the potential to be a change that Congress would deem violated the safe harbor requirements. "Since §5 contains a principle of federal law that would assure finality of the State's determination if made pursuant to a state law in effect before the election, a legislative wish to take advantage of the 'safe harbor' would counsel against any construction of the Election Code that Congress might deem to be a change in the law."[99]

Yet despite these troubling concerns, the justices were unwilling to overturn the Florida ruling—or, alternately, were unable to come to enough of a consensus to do so. In fact, given the clear splits between the more conservative and liberal justices expressed in the oral arguments, that they issued a unanimous but unsigned per curiam opinion most likely meant that they had, in essence, decided not to decide. The justices could have done so by dismissing the case as a political question, as being not yet ripe for judgment, or as a moot matter (as no harm had befallen Bush by these rulings) no longer requiring judicial remedies. These approaches, however, would have ended the matter and left the Florida Supreme Court's ruling standing as the final say in these matters. In this instance, rather, they chose to return the case to the lower court based on the doctrine that while "state courts [ought to] be left free and unfettered by us in interpreting their state constitutions. . . . it is equally important that ambiguous or obscure adjudications by state courts do not stand as barriers to a determination by this Court of the validity under the federal constitution of state action."[100]

The Court, in other words, chose to be confused as to the Florida court's motivations for their ruling since they could not agree on a more affirmative response to the issues raised by the case. And they probably chose this particular approach to not deciding because at least some of the justices were convinced that the Florida Supreme Court had overstepped its proper bounds (while others, no doubt, were convinced of the alternative). The Court therefore vacated the ruling and remanded the case to Florida with directions to eliminate "the obscurities and ambiguities from the opinion."[101] That the justices vacated the ruling provides a hint of how at least three or four of the justices' views were developing. Had there been five, the Court would have reversed. Had there been fewer, the Court would most likely have taken a different approach to not deciding the substance of the case. Even though vacating the judgment did not imply that the ruling below was totally wrong, it did hint loudly that many on the Supreme Court were troubled by the original state court ruling.[102]

When on December 4 the Florida Supreme Court received the directive from the U.S. Supreme Court to eliminate "the obscurities and ambiguities from the[ir] opinion," the seven Florida justices sat on the matter, not responding to the U.S. Supreme Court for a full seven days. During this period, Al Gore would lose his challenge bid in the circuit court, win a reversal before the Florida Supreme Court (which restarted the recounts), and then face an appeal before the U.S. Supreme Court (accompanied by a stay motion that halted the recounts once again).

We do not know why the Florida justices took so long to respond to the U.S. Supreme Court. Perhaps the reason for the delay was their involvement in the other complex and fast-moving events leading to the U.S. Supreme Court case of *Bush v. Gore.* What we do know is that, when they finally did respond on December

11, their revised judgment was almost exactly the same in scope and result as their original opinion. Other than remove all mention of the Florida constitution as a potential source of authority and adding specific references to 3 U.S.C. §5, the two opinions were very similar.

Whereas before they based their ruling limiting Secretary of State Harris's discretion largely on the state constitution's mandate to empower the voters, now they declared that the interpretation came from statutory provisions: "Our examination of that issue has been limited to a determination of legislative intent as informed by the traditional sources and rules of construction we have long accepted as relevant in determining such intent. Not surprisingly, we have identified the right of Florida's citizens to vote and to have elections determined by the will of Florida's voters as important policy concerns of the Florida Legislature in enacting Florida's election code."[103] While not quite the same as waving a red flag before a bull, the Florida Supreme Court opinion on remand displayed a certain stubborn testiness toward the justices of the U.S. Supreme Court. Convinced that they had done their job correctly and in particular had properly interpreted the law as applied to the certification deadline, the Florida justices refused to change the scope or focus of their ruling. They had to have known that this would not go over well with some, perhaps even a majority, of the justices in Washington.[104] They had to have known that their refusal to accept the hints so plainly buried in the remand order (hints suggesting that the court take the concerns of the Florida legislature, which was solidly pro-Bush, more readily into account in reworking their judgment) would cause problems. Most of all, they had to have known that sending this opinion back to the U.S. Supreme Court just as the even more contentious appeal of their ruling on judicial recounts was reaching the justices would not make matters any less contentious. Still, this is what they did.

Though not yet fully explored by either court, a clear difference of opinion about the judiciary's role in electoral recounts was coming to the fore in these competing rulings. Whereas the U.S. Supreme Court wanted a more careful reading of statutes and a recognition of the special conditions associated with a presidential election, the Florida Supreme Court was still emphasizing the need to empower the voters. Just what these differences would mean in terms of the election's final conclusion would have to wait for the next round of litigations, however.

Justice Oliver Wendell Holmes Jr. famously warned, "Great cases, like hard cases, make bad law."[105] This may or may not be true. However, one thing that is always true is that cases that are both great and hard generally make for hard decisions. And if it was nothing else, the issue of extending the certification deadline was a hard case. At its root, the issue in *Bush v. Palm Beach County Canvassing Board* was the scope of the judicial function as applied to election contests. Was the Florida Supreme Court just interpreting conflicting laws, as they proposed? Or was the court interposing its views in place of those of the legislature—in effect changing the rules by judicial fiat? At a deeper level, this question merges into the broader issue of the purpose of running an election. Was it merely an administrative process to assure that the machinery (mechanical and human) worked on election night? Or, was it an effort to ensure that the will of the voters as expressed by their ballots was properly reflected in the certified vote totals? If the answer were the former, then a strict deadline made sense. If it were the latter, then allowing extra time for recounts was both reasonable and necessary.

Tellingly, different judges kept coming up with different answers to these questions. The reason, in large part, was that there was no one correct answer. The judicial function is not as straightforward as most of us like to believe. It is almost never as easy as linking A to B. Usually, it is more like trying to link A to Z by way of G but without hitting E, M, and W (and, if you hit B, you then cannot land on J, and so on). Even on such technical matters as statutory interpretation, where one might assume that a court's job is specific and restricted, there are various different methodologies available to guide judicial action. Judges could look exclusively at the wording of the statute. If a deadline is set, then that deadline should be followed—even if, as is often the case, this rule comes into conflict with another section of the act. The court merely follows the sections that most closely relate to the issue under contention. Conversely, a second method starts with a general understanding of the legislature's intent in passing the law. Is it to empower the voter? Is it to stress statutory rules as a source of stability and uniformity? Once the court determines the overriding goal of the legislation, it can interpret the specific provisions in light of this goal. Where the statutory provisions seem at odds with the goal, the assumption is that the legislature would not have intended this difference, and therefore, that the intent of the law has to be different—even where fixing the discrepancy might require taking actions that seemingly ignore the plain wording of the act.[106]

In the end, it all comes down to choosing from the many available options. And, needless to say, which option a judge chooses to follow generally determines the result of his or her efforts. There is nothing wrong with this. Legal interpretation at its best is still a human endeavor. Different judges viewing the law from different perspectives will make different decisions, even getting to the same result by widely and wildly different lines of reasoning. Rules of precedent and endorsed legal interpretation limit the range of difference but cannot eliminate it. The thing to keep in mind is that these differing options are all generally legitimate.[107]

We need to separate our understanding of the process from that of the results. When the Florida Supreme Court interpreted the legislature's intent toward voting, it was acting in a legitimate manner. It was doing its job. The court was not trying to "steal" the election, nor was it seeking to "replace" the legislature. It was, as the Florida justices said, just doing its job as it had on many other occasions. Legitimate, however, does not necessarily mean right. The result of the justices' ruling could have been wrong. So, too, their chosen methodology could have been wrong. Perhaps a different reading of the statutes would produce a more just, or fair, or technically advisable, answer. Perhaps they missed some key point, or ignored some key factor. This is why we have the appellate process, to allow for a second or third look at these choices. This is also how law professors earn their living, pointing out how judges were wrong or right in their readings of the law. We can disagree with the Florida court's views, in other words, without having to demonize the court itself.

Similarly, when the U.S. Supreme Court began to hint that the Florida court had misread the statutory process and thus had overstepped the bounds of its authority, they too were correct in their actions. Even when the justices seemingly plucked a somewhat unique legal reading (Justice Scalia's reading of Article II, Section 1 of the Constitution) out of nowhere, this was proper. It was different from the Florida court's reading of the law. In fact, Justice Scalia's reading of the law was potentially antithetical to the Florida court's views. Yet just because one court's views differ from the other court's reading of the law, this does not mean necessarily that one court was doing its job and the other was not.

To reiterate, we have to separate our understanding of the process by which the courts operate from the results of that process. Unfortunately, in 2000, nobody was being careful to distinguish process from result: not the litigants, not the political parties, not the lawyers, not even the justices themselves. The politicization of the law had so ratcheted up the tensions that emotion was getting in the way of reason, and partisan affiliations were shaping behavior more than was good for the judicial process. This had been the case in the deadline certification cases, and it would be the case—only magnified—as the courts struggled with Al Gore's formal challenge to the 2000 Florida vote count. Though few recognized it at the time, the crisis was moving toward its endgame.

CHAPTER SIX

Ballots before the Bench

It's important [to know who really won the election]. It's important now, and it's important as a precedent for the future. If this had ended up that whoever controlled the election machinery could win by changing the rules as to how votes could be counted, it would have been a poor lesson in democracy.
—*David Boies,* Courting Justice *(2004)*

There is more to the right to vote than the right to mark a piece of paper and drop it in a box or the right to pull a lever in a voting booth. The right to vote includes the right to have the ballot counted. . . .
—*Justice William O. Douglass, dissenting,* South v. Peters, *339 U.S. 276, 279*

Given the high drama and conflict of the events that were to follow, the formal certification of Florida's presidential vote at 5:00 p.m. on November 26, 2000, should have been a huge event—a powerful upheaval affecting the whole postelection crisis with the impact of a category 5 hurricane. At the time, however, certification and the subsequent election contest by Al Gore were but two in a series of ongoing events and proceedings, any one of whose resolution was capable of putting an end to the postelection dispute. In fact, in the two weeks following Katherine Harris's certification of the Florida vote, seven major litigations were being argued simultaneously; any one could have changed the postelection dynamic by giving Al Gore the votes he needed to win Florida (or alternately, by invalidating the recount process and thus ending the election).[1]

Today we know that ultimately the contest litigation ended the 2000 presidential election. But, at the time, it was just one more hurdle for Gore to overcome as he struggled to find enough votes to win the presidency—and one more attack for George W. Bush to defend against. Despite the change from protest to contest, this was still a two-front war, fought in court and over the public airwaves. This fight still pitted Bush, working to maintain a slim lead in votes, against Gore, fighting tooth and nail to overtake it. Certification intensified these conditions, but did not radically transform them. The postelection crisis had become entangled in a Gordian knot of interlocking litigations, and the protest phase seemed but another strand adding to the confusion.

Still, on a technical level, a postcertification protest was a completely different course of action from what had come before. The certification of the Florida presidential vote formally shifted the postelection contest into an entirely new realm. Up until then, the dispute had been firmly fixed in the realm of administrative politics and process. Though the courts were involved, they were acting as umpires of what was still technically a political procedure. Certification brought the politics to an end—at least on the surface. Gone was the decentralized counting that epitomized the protest phase. In its place were the (presumably) uniform procedures of the courts. The courts would now set the standards. It was they who would determine which, if any, ballots needed recounting. And they would oversee the final tallying of who won Florida's electoral votes as well.

But more than just a practical difference is present at this juncture. Gore's decision to contest the election also shifted the conceptual focus. Unlike the other cases growing out of the 2000 election, the contest litigation had the potential to encompass *all* aspects of the postelection crisis—from disputed absentee ballots to questions of timing and ballot design, from race-based disenfranchisement to vote-counting standards and the equal protection implications of differing vote-tabulation methods. Gore was claiming that something was fundamentally wrong with the election; that the intent of the voters in the polling booth was not reflected in the final totals certified by Florida's secretary of state. Consequently, everything was on the table in the contest phase.

For tactical reasons, Gore chose to limit the scope of his contest. The primary focus continued to be on undervotes from the mostly Democratic South Florida counties of Palm Beach and Miami-Dade (Broward, by finishing its recount before the certification deadline, no longer was involved). Bush also would try to limit the courts' scope for action—in fact, more so than Gore—by repeatedly defining the contest phase so narrowly that any attempt to use these provisions to change the election's outcomes was virtually impossible. As subsequent events were to show, however, the Florida courts were not bound by the litigants' attempts to limit the scope of review of the election. As defined by Florida statute, election contests were *de novo* reviews—a fresh look at the topic, with all prior perspectives put aside and all potential remedies available to the courts.

Of course, nothing obliged the courts to adopt a wide-ranging review. The contest phase offered probabilities, not certainties. And yet, within those probabilities rested the central questions raised by the entire postelection crisis: What was the purpose of holding an election? Was the overriding purpose behind voting the empowerment of the voter, or was it producing as clean and uncorrupted a vote as possible? To what extent did errors in the election process undermine either of these objectives? And what were the best methods to achieve any of these ends?

The contest litigation also brought front and center the tension between state and federal law, and with it the inconsistencies within federalism generated by such tensions. Were presidential elections a state or federal matter? If federal rules were superior to state rules, as the Constitution declares, at what point did federal rules stop trumping normal state procedures? After all, the Constitution left it to the states to organize and run elections, so at some point there had to be a transfer of constitutional authority. Conversely, when did state control of election law become subordinate to federal legal imperatives? Where, in other words, was the balance point between these two legislative realms? The questions and uncertainties were nearly endless.

Finally, the contest once again reemphasized the difficulties plaguing the judiciary in settling these matters. Florida law, federal law, and even the U.S. Constitution all set out specific procedures for settling contested elections, only no one seemed to want these procedures to be used—or no one could agree on which procedures should be used and when and how. Yes, the state courts had a place in electoral contests—at least in Florida—but what exactly was this place and how should it be used in this instance? What about the federal courts? Were they or were they not legitimate players in this debate? The Constitution seemed to leave such matters to state laws and procedures. Yet the election in question was a federal election with federal rules affecting its ultimate organization and even outcome. At what point, therefore, did a state matter become a federal question? And why were the courts even involved at all? Should not this matter be best left to the legislative bodies that supervise elections? After all, both the original Article II and the amended version in the Twelfth Amendment left it to Congress to pick the president when there was no clear winner in the Electoral College. Why not just let Congress clean up the mess, as the Constitution provided?

Merely having a role in the process, in other words, did not make the contours of that role clear or settled. In fact, one of the central arguments in the contest litigation was the proper role of the judiciary in settling a disputed election. By this point, the electoral and political issues were well known and firm. What was now at play was the choice of remedies available to end the conflict and the linked task of establishing who legitimately got to pick the remedies that would be applied. Not only were the disputed ballots before the bench for adjudication, but the judiciary's specific roles in these matters were on trial as well. And the winner in this two-sided disagreement got the chance to shape how we picked the forty-third president of the United States.

On the morning of Monday, November 27, 2000, Dexter Douglass, joined by many of Gore's other lawyers, walked into the Leon County Circuit Court building and formally filed Al Gore's contest challenging the certified totals for the 2000 presidential election. As far as Gore was concerned, "the vote totals reported in the Election Canvassing Commission's certification of November 26, 2000 were wrong. They included illegal votes and [did] not include legal votes that were improperly rejected." Combined, these errors were in numbers "more than sufficient to place in doubt, indeed to change, the result of the election."[2]

The refusal of the State Elections Canvassing Commission to accept the completed but late recount from Palm Beach County (a net gain of 215 votes for Gore) combined with its refusal to include the partial 20 percent recount from Miami-

Dade County (a net gain of 160 votes for Gore) denied 375 voters the fruits of their vote, the complaint argued. More to the point, it also deprived Vice President Gore of these votes. These were valid votes approved by the county canvassing boards. Yet the secretary of state had refused to include these valid votes in the final tally. This mistake needed correcting. Meanwhile, the secretary of state had accepted improperly counted ballots from the Nassau County board which, contrary to state law, had sent in the original machine count for inclusion rather than the mandated machine *re*count (all to a net gain of 50 votes for Bush).[3] Corrected, these mistakes shrank the gap between candidates to a mere 112 votes. With a starting difference of only 537 votes separating Gore from Bush, this was a significant reduction.

Nor were these the only votes excluded in the final tally. The complaint directed the court's attention to the potentially valid votes left uncounted by the Palm Beach County board's refusal to accept about 4,000 ballots—many with indented chads—as valid votes. "If discernable indentions on such ballots were counted as votes," noted the brief, "Al Gore . . . would [have] received more than 800 additional net votes." Then there were the roughly 10,000 uncounted ballots in Miami-Dade County. These ballots had never been counted—ignored by both machines that could not read them and canvassing board officials who refused to examine them. Were they counted in the same manner as the 20 percent partial recount completed by the Miami board (but not included in the final tally), the result could be a gain of about 600 additional votes for Gore.[4]

The complaint estimated that a corrected vote tally should place Al Gore ahead of George W. Bush by almost 1,200 votes. Clearly something was fundamentally wrong with the certified totals. Worse yet, the complaint documented the improper and often illegal ways in which these votes had been excluded from the final tally. Most troubling was the Miami-Dade experience, where "a near riot" by Republican supporters of George W. Bush so disrupted the vote counting process that (quoting from the *New York Times*) "when the ruckus was over, the protesters had what they had wanted: a unanimous vote by the board to call off the hand counting."[5] In Nassau County, the Republican-dominated canvassing board met without the notice required by law and decided to amend their returns to reflect not the mandated machine recounts (which had given Gore an additional fifty votes) but the original unofficial election night returns. The board acted, the complaint noted, in contravention of Section 102.141(4), which mandated that where a difference existed between machine counts, the latter recount would "be presumed correct" and certified as the proper vote tally.[6] Worse yet, taking part in the decision to change the vote tally was an improperly selected substitute board member, sitting in for an unavailable member.[7] All remaining errors were laid directly at the feet of either the secretary of state and the state canvassing commission for refusing to accept the additional votes generated in the recount process in both Palm Beach and Miami-Dade Counties (whether partial in number or delivered soon after the certification deadline), or the individual county canvassing boards for failing to abide by court-ordered recount provisions.[8]

Gore's prayer for relief mirrored his individual objections. It requested that the 10,750 uncounted Miami-Dade ballots be transported to Tallahassee for the court to count and ultimately add to the final certified vote tally. Gore also sought the same treatment for 892 "pregnant chad" ballots from Palm Beach County. His complaint further called for the Nassau County tally to be revised to reflect the machine recount totals, and demanded that all hand-recounted ballots, whether partial (Miami-Dade) or late (Palm Beach), be included in the final total. Finally, the complaint called for all uncounted ballots to be judged by a "totality of the circumstances" standard for determining the intent of the voter. In particular, it argued that a clearly marked indented chad had to be viewed as legitimate proof of a voter's intent. The complaint then ended with a request that the November 26 certification be thrown out and that the state canvassing commission be required to await all court-ordered recounts before naming the winning presidential electors (which, the complaint made clear, should be pledged to Al Gore).[9]

Gore's filing with the circuit court was no surprise. His lawyers already had announced, in the aftermath of the Florida Supreme Court's refusal on November 23 to force the Miami-Dade Canvassing Board to finish counting disputed ballots, that Gore would contest the election no matter what outcome the certification process produced. "We want a full, fair and accurate count, and the only way left to do that is to file a contest," noted Gore campaign spokesperson Jenny Backus. Ron Klain had seconded this view, remarking how "'we believe we stand on both strong political and legal ground for fighting beyond Sunday." Other Gore advisors echoed these points, observing that "Gore had been prepared to give up if the votes had been hand counted in all three counties—Palm Beach, Broward and Miami-Dade—but that the shutdown in Miami and Bush's aggressive efforts to pick up votes elsewhere have given Democrats, they believe[d], political standing to press their case well beyond tomorrow, if necessary."[10]

Work on Gore's contest effort had actually begun on November 17. Following Judge Lewis's denial of their motion for an order to force an extended certification deadline on Katherine Harris, Gore's lawyers began preparing for what they now saw as an inevitable election contest. Concerned with the shortness of time, and not totally convinced that the protest recounts would gain enough votes for Gore anyhow, they also started preparing their contest complaint and accompanying briefs for the appeal that was sure to follow. The Bush team was also preparing to defend against an election contest (or alternately, to file one should the recounts gain Gore enough votes to overtake Bush). In fact, whereas both sides were focused on the issues before them in the overseas absentee ballot, the Seminole and Martin County absentee ballot, and the certification deadline cases (all argued in the last two weeks of November), in the back of their minds, both sides were clearly preparing for a full-out election contest as well.[11]

This was time that both sides needed, especially the Gore team. One of the more interesting—and tactically challenging—aspects of Gore's contest filing was the range of choices available to him in shaping the scope and form of his contest. The number of potential irregularities to challenge were legion. The butterfly ballot? The race-based vote dilution and even denial in Duval and Miami-Dade Counties? Miami-Dade's refusal to finish their hand recounts? Perhaps the Republicans' "Thanksgiving stuffing" of overseas absentee ballots? Or maybe Palm Beach's unwillingness to accept indented chads as proof of a voter's intent? Each had the potential to win the election for Gore if successfully argued before the courts. Yet which to choose?

David Boies argued for a streamlined contest—and prevailed. The goal was to get the South Florida ballots counted—and counted in as permissive a manner as possible. Combine the Palm Beach County recount with the partial recount in Miami-Dade and correct the mistake in Nassau County, Boies reasoned, and the vote difference was a mere 100 votes. Ease up on the standard used to determine valid voter intent, and the election was Gore's. As Boies later told the press, "we focused on the absolutely easiest, cleanest contest points. Until we were really able to be sure we could get those issues done, there was a reluctance to try and take on Seminole County, or Martin County or any of the other places."[12]

Yet none of this was obvious. What if the courts proved unwilling to recount the overlooked ballots in Palm Beach and Miami-Dade Counties? Perhaps adding the absentee ballot controversies might be necessary. Or an attack on the "Thanksgiving stuffing" might be needed. If recounts were a chess game, then this was speed chess near the end of a game, when the moves were few, the pressures great, and a single mistake, no matter how small, could lose the whole match. While Boies's reasoning was probably accurate, no one knew this for sure.

A similar troublesome choice arose over which judge should hear the case. Given the strong connections between the contest and the ongoing certification and absentee-ballot suits, Gore easily could have asked that this matter be assigned to a judge already hearing a "related matter." This approach most likely would have placed the case before Judge Terry Lewis, who had just refused to push Katherine Harris on the issue of certification deadlines, but whom both Douglass and Boies still saw as a "fair" judge with an open mind on the issues. Asking for Judge Lewis, however, carried a serious political cost. The perception would have been that they were "judge shopping," seeking a friendly judge to hear their contest complaint. Combined with the ongoing Republican charges that Gore was only recounting votes in Democrat-friendly South Florida, the impact on the public relations front could have been devastating. Consequently, the Gore lawyers opted instead for a new judge to hear the case.[13]

This too was a risky proposition. Seeking a new judge left the matter up to the computer program that randomly assigned cases to judges. If the Gore team got lucky, the case might land on Judge Nikki Clark's or Judge L. Ralph "Bubba"

Smith's dockets. There was an equal chance that it would end up before Judge Lewis or Chief Judge George S. Reynolds. Not only were all four perceived as more likely to be sympathetic to Gore's contest claims, but they all were known to work fast.[14] On the other hand, if they were unlucky, the case would go before Judge N. Sanders Sauls. Sauls, in Dexter Douglass's experienced view, had "certainly voted for Bush" and was unlikely to put aside his political preferences in hearing the case. Douglass saw him as "arrogant," "lazy" and "a redneck." Even a friend of Sauls described him to David Boies as "self-important," "relaxed," and "conservative, with the social attitudes that most people in this part of the country used to have and quite a few still do." Worse yet, he was "slow."[15] Douglass, however, figured the odds against their drawing Sauls were in their favor.[16]

Douglass was wrong. The computer gave Sauls the case. Appalled, Douglass and Boies immediately asked Judge Sauls to transfer the case to another judge with more experience in these election cases. Sauls refused. They could then have asked the judge to recuse himself (give up the case because of a perceived or real conflict of interest). However, in the interest of time, they chose not to act. Douglass and Boies figured that if Sauls would not transfer the case, he was unlikely to recuse himself. And arguing the matter would take up precious time that Gore did not have to waste. They also worried, again, about the perception of "judge shopping." With Harris's certification of the vote, the pressure on Al Gore to concede was growing. While Democrats were still standing behind the Vice President's ongoing challenge (for the moment at least), Republicans were loud in their demands that the whole mess be ended. Meanwhile, a CNN/*USA Today*/Gallup poll showed that almost six in ten Americans felt that Gore should concede the election. A *Washington Post*/ABC poll seconded this view. It also showed that a small but significant proportion of Gore's supporters—about one in four—wanted him to give up. Gore was losing the public relations war and could not afford to hand his opponents any additional ammunition.[17]

Time and the presence of Judge Sauls also shaped Gore's litigation approach. Figuring that their chances of winning in Judge Sauls's courtroom were small, Boies and Douglass decided to play to lose—but to lose as fast as possible. A defeat at trial was not the worst result for Gore; it was defeat (or even victory) in a *slow* trial that was the worst possible scenario. The objective was to get the case into the hands of the Florida Supreme Court with enough time left to count ballots and swing the election to Gore. To this end, Boies and Douglass requested that Judge Sauls expedite his proceedings and also order the delivery of the disputed Palm Beach and Miami-Dade ballots into the court's keeping. Ideally, they hoped that Judge Sauls would allow these ballots to be counted while the contest trial was under way. If the judge ruled against the contest, the revised numbers need never be applied. However, if he ruled in favor of Gore's contest, then significant time would have been saved. As Boies explained to the judge, "here the witnesses are primarily the ballots. The issue is whether particular ballots do or do not express the voter's intent."[18]

Boies and Douglass knew that they were unlikely to get everything they wanted from Judge Sauls. They wanted to win, but if they did not, their motions still put pressure on Sauls to move the case along. They were also building a case for the Florida Supreme Court. The Gore team knew that if they could show that Judge Sauls was totally antithetical to their case (so that they could not get a fair hearing in his court), their chances of convincing the Florida Supreme Court to act improved dramatically. Moreover, they predicated their efforts to get the disputed ballots to Tallahassee on their belief that once the ballots were on the ground, it would be difficult for the Florida justices not to have them counted.[19]

Republicans, not surprisingly, objected strongly to each of Gore's proposals. Their strategy was to delay the litigation and run out the clock. As far as they were concerned, Bush had won the election and the recounts and Gore was simply a sore loser who did not know when to give up. "Counsel is trying to put the cart before the horse," Bush lawyer Barry Richard told the Judge. "I would suggest to Your Honor that the first thing we need to do is schedule a hearing for Your Honor to determine whether or not the canvassing boards . . . abused their discretion in some fashion. If they didn't, there is nothing more to do." The issue before the court was not the ballots, but the procedures of the canvassing boards. Only when board members acted in an improper manner was a contest recount even called for. Absent such malfeasance, there was nothing for the court to do but deny the motion for a contest recount. Anyhow, Richard continued, the Republicans needed more time to view discovery and to depose witnesses. Their list of potential witnesses was ninety-seven names long. "I would urge Your Honor that the hearing ought not to begin on Friday [December 1], which is not sufficient time. We need to get witnesses here, we need to get documents here . . . and [to do all] that [the trial] needs to start next week."[20]

Despite the strong objections from the Republicans, Judge Sauls ordered expedited hearings. The trial was set for December 2, only a week after Gore's initial complaint. Sauls also ordered the transport of the disputed ballots north to Tallahassee. He did not, however, grant Gore his motion to begin counting the ballots immediately. He would enter them into the record as evidence, but nothing more.[21]

On the whole, Boies and Douglass were satisfied with this outcome. As Boies later noted in his autobiography, "on the positive side, the contested ballots were on their way to Tallahassee; Sauls had said that the contest hearing would be held on Saturday; and Bush's lawyers had taken some potentially helpful positions." (In seeking to exclude the disputed ballots from the proceedings, Bush's lawyers had argued *in favor* of discretion by the canvassing boards as to how they counted votes. This position in Boies's view strengthened Gore's chances in defending the South Florida recounts, each of which had been carried out using different standards of proof of a voter's intent.) "On the negative side, we had drawn Sanders Sauls; he had refused to transfer the case; and he had refused to rule on when, if ever, he would review the ballots."[22]

Next came the contest hearing before Judge Sauls.[23] Once again, the expectation that Sauls would rule against them shaped the Gore legal team's litigation strategy. For a while, Boies toyed with the idea of calling no witnesses at all. Although this would lessen their chances of victory, it would save considerable time for the inevitable appeal(s) to follow. However, Boies knew that they needed to enter two solid facts into the record for when the ballots were actually counted. First, they had to show that punch-ballot machines were inaccurate; next, they had to show that manual recounts were accurate. To this end, Boies called only two witnesses.[24] The first was Kimball Brace of Election Data Services. An expert on voting technology, Brace argued that punch-ballot machines were vulnerable to tabulation error due to misread ballots. For example, Brace noted, as punch-ballot machines were used, buildup of chads in the disposal box could so stiffen the backing beneath the paper ballot that chads would not be fully separated from the ballot. Such ballots would not be read by the tabulating machines. The results, Brace concluded, could be significant. Next was Nicholas Hengartner, a statistician from Yale, who argued that the rate of undervotes in punch-ballot machines was greater than that found in Scantron machines—in fact, almost 500 percent greater. Hengartner concluded that this difference was statistically significant.[25]

Despite their threat to call ninety-seven or more witnesses, the Republicans responded to Gore's abbreviated argument with only a handful of their own witnesses. Faced with what Bush attorney Phil Beck viewed as the "ridiculously dismal quality of the expert witnesses" called by Boies, the Republican lawyers realized that they did not have to call out their whole arsenal of witnesses to prove their case.[26] They started with Judge Charles Burton from Palm Beach, who discussed the Palm Beach County canvassing board's efforts to count votes. (Burton, in fact, so impressed Judge Sauls with his hard work and effort that Sauls excused him from the witness box with a salute, calling Burton a "great American.") Burton was followed by Bush's statistical expert, Laurentius Marais. Marais, an experienced expert witness with many trial testimonies under his belt, argued that we simply could not know—at least, not with statistical assurance—that most of the undervotes would go to Gore. The greatest likelihood was that these votes were random in their impact. The last significant witness was John Ahmann, a California rancher and engineer who had helped design punch card machines in the 1970s. Ahmann's primary task was to counter Kimball Brace's argument on chad buildup causing undervotes.[27]

On the whole, these and other similar witnesses did well on direct examination. However, on cross-examination, both Bush's and Gore's key experts proved to have feet of clay. A barrage of questions from Bush attorney Beck showed Kimball Brace to be less than fully knowledgeable of the many small details of the Florida voting machines and their specific failures on November 7.[28] Similarly, statistician Nicholas Hengartner was shown not to have done his homework. Hengartner had argued that chads on the left side of a ballot were more likely to fail due to their greater use (ballots generally moved from left to right columns in recording votes, so the left side column was always in use). He used as his example a 1998 race in which more votes were cast in the Florida governor's race than in the U.S. Senate race. The Senate race, Hengartner argued, was on the left, the gubernatorial was further to the right. Yet when Phil Beck pulled out a copy of the 1998 ballot in which both races were on the same column, Hengartner had to admit that he had never examined the 1998 ballot; rather, he was basing his testimony on information provided him by the Gore team.[29]

When it was the Democrats' turn to cross-examine Bush's witnesses, the same pattern repeated. The focus here was John Ahmann and his claim that punch-ballot machines worked fine. Gore attorney Steve Zack knew that Ahmann had filed for several patents to "improve" upon the IBM punch card system. In particular, in the early 1980s, Ahmann had applied for a patent covering an improved stylus. As part of his patent petition, Ahmann had argued that punch card machines could produce "potentially unreadable votes" when styluses were unable to penetrate the paper ballot fully due to chad buildup and other causes. This was exactly Gore's point. Shaken by this revelation, Ahmann began to agree with almost everything that Zack asked. He even agreed that hand recounts were both necessary and more accurate than machine counts.[30]

In the end, it is hard to know how much impact all of this conflicting testimony had on Judge Sauls's decision. Boies's and Douglass's hopes of even a partial victory were low. The trial had done nothing to lessen their negative views of Judge Sauls. The Republican lawyers, on the other hand, were more optimistic. Still, they were cautious in their optimism—the stakes were too high for anything less than caution and care. As the trial ended on Sunday night, Judge Sauls promised a ruling the next morning. He would miss that self-imposed deadline by a few hours, but at 4:30 p.m. Monday, he reconvened his court and read his judgment.

Speaking from the bench, Sauls slowly made clear his total refusal to accept a single one of Gore's arguments, ruling repeatedly against the need for further recounts. Florida law, Sauls noted, required that "in order to contest election results under Section 102.168 . . . the Plaintiff must show that, but for the irregularity, or inaccuracy claimed, the result of the election would have been different, and he or she would have been the winner. It [was] not enough to show a reasonable *possibility* that election results could have been altered by such irregularities, or inaccuracies, rather, a reasonable *probability* that the results of the election would have been changed must be shown [emphasis added]." Gore had failed to meet this legal burden. "The Court . . . concludes the evidence does not establish any illegality, dishonesty, gross negligence, improper influence, coercion, or fraud in the balloting and counting processes." That there was some question of the accuracy of the vote totals in some counties was irrelevant under the law. "These balloting and counting problems cannot support or effect any recounting necessity . . . absent the establishment of a reasonable probability that the *statewide* election result would be different, which has not been established in this case [emphasis added]." Put another way, although the vote might not have been totally accurate, it was close enough in the current situation (and based on the current evidence before the court) to count.[31]

Not surprised at the scope or the negative outcome of Judge Sauls's reasoning, Boies, Douglass, and the other Gore lawyers already had prepared their response. Before Judge Sauls had even completed reading his judgment (which took no more than eighteen minutes), the Gore team delivered their notice of appeal to the First District Court. That court quickly certified the appeal and sent it up to the Florida Supreme Court. The Florida justices, in turn, accepted the case and set a twenty-four-hour deadline for briefs (noon, December 6, 2000) with oral argument scheduled for the morning of December 7.

For Gore, the stakes could not be higher. With his recent losses on absentee ballots (both military and tainted), this was looking to be his last chance. Should the Florida Supreme Court rule against him, the election was over. Wishing to make things as easy as possible for the Florida justices, and perhaps concerned as well about the U.S. Supreme Court's remand of *Bush v. Palm Beach Canvassing Board* and its strong hint to abide by the clear wording of state statutes in organizing any recount, Gore's lawyers based his appeal's argument squarely on a direct reading of the words of Section 102.168.

The brief pointed out four major errors by Judge Sauls. First, when the judge had held that "in an election contest, the court cannot review *only* the contested ballots, but must review *all* ballots cast, or *no* ballots at all," he was in error. There was not "a single Florida case in which a court has held that it was required to review any ballots other than those contested by the plaintiff in the contest action."[32] Second, the brief objected to Judge Sauls's ruling that "the county canvassing boards' decisions had to be reviewed for 'a clear abuse of discretion.'" Not only was this reading of the statute "contrary to consistent precedents in this and other states that the review of contested ballots [was] a matter of law for the court's *de novo* review," it contradicted the statute's clear wording, which nowhere imposed such a limitation.[33] Third, the brief noted how "the trial court held that the plaintiff must establish a 'reasonable probability that the results of the election would have been changed' before it could look at the contested ballots." Once again, this was "contrary to the express standard" of state statute—in this case, of "§102.168(3)(c), requiring only that the inclusion or exclusion of the contested votes 'will change *or place in doubt* the result of the election.'"[34] Finally, the brief raised the specter of 3 U.S.C. §5. In an ironic turn of events, it argued that whereas "the Circuit Court's separate legal rulings [were] erroneous on their own terms," when "viewed together they [also] effect[ed] a breathtaking change in that remedy, creating a cause of action dramatically different—and far, far narrower—than the one enacted by the Florida Legislature." Judge Sauls's "novel, and unjustifiably cramped, rewriting of Section 102.168 . . . constitute[d] just the sort of free-form judicial decision making that defendants have warned of [in other cases], intruding on the State Legislature's authority to fashion the rules governing the selection of Presidential electors in violation of Article II." If Florida were not to lose its safe harbor, Judge Sauls's reworking of the rules had to be overturned.[35]

Given such errors, and given the shortness of time remaining to complete these proceedings before the December 12 deadline, the Gore brief concluded with a plea for the Florida Supreme Court to retain control over this matter, either ordering and supervising recounts itself or remanding the counting to the lower court with specific orders as to which ballots to recount and how to recount them. In particular, the brief asked that the court "specify the standard to be applied in the review of those ballots" in order to "eliminate any uncertainty regarding the process of reviewing the ballots." Their preferred standard, needless to say, was the more liberal interpretation of Judge Lebarga and other judges in states across the nation, which held that "a failure to count indented ballots as votes . . . improperly disregard voter intent." However, at this point, they would take almost any standard so long as the recounts were carried out.[36]

Filed almost simultaneously with Gore's brief, George W. Bush's brief echoed Judge Sauls's arguments step by step. "To prevail under Florida law," it noted, "an election contestant must conclusively demonstrate that county canvassing boards abused their duly conferred discretion, and that either illegal votes were counted or legal votes were not counted in sufficient numbers to overturn the results of the election. This is an imposing burden, and one that Appellants . . . never met." In fact, when given the chance by the judge to argue their case at trial and thus convince him that they had met this burden, the plaintiffs had proffered only two expert witnesses. "Beyond those two experts, Appellants offered the court below nothing to support their case."

Moving to the legal issues raised by the case, the brief noted that "the Circuit Court made five independent findings, each of which, standing alone, [was] sufficient to support the verdict." First, there was the legal basis for ordering a recount—a basis that Gore had failed to establish. Put simply, a candidate was not entitled to a recount merely by asking. Contests were for reviewing procedural failures, not for repeating the whole counting process anew. Next, the brief noted how the Circuit Court had found that "there [was] no credible statistical evidence, and no other competent substantial evidence to establish by a preponderance of a reasonable probability that the results of the statewide election . . . would be different" from that held by the county canvassing boards. This was a "factual finding, based on direct assessments of the credibility of Appellants' witnesses." As such it should be fully honored on appeal. Third, as to the question of discretion and the actions of the county canvassing boards, the brief noted that the circuit court had "found that none of the county canvassing boards had abused their discretion." Given that "this finding . . . [was] likewise not clearly erroneous," the appeals court should abide by the decision of the trial court judge who had heard all of the evidence direct. Fourth, on the issue of partial recounts, Judge Sauls had ruled that "there was no authority in Florida law for a partial manual recount" nor any provision . . . that "permit[ted]—let alone require[d]—the local canvassing boards to certify or the Elections Canvassing Commission to accept such partial returns." Once again, the brief asked the justices to honor the trial judge's prerogatives in reading the law this way. Finally, the brief defended Judge Sauls's reading of 3 U.S.C. §5. Were ballots in one county to be "reviewed under a standard different than that applied in other counties," the judge had held, "significant disparities could arise among in the impact of individual votes creating a situation that would violate federal constitutional standards."

In the end, Bush's brief was a call to the Florida justices simply to honor the decisions made by Judge Sauls. Gore had not proven the factual basis of his case—far from it. At every step, the Bush team argued, Gore sought court action "without demonstrating the substantial factual or legal predicate necessary to overturn a certified election." So Judge Sauls had ruled and so too the record showed. "These heavily fact-laden determinations were made by a trial court that heard all the witnesses, weighed all the evidence, and was in the best position to resolve these factual disputes," the brief concluded. "This Court should not second-guess its judgment."[37]

Closely observed, the two briefs showed a remarkable role reversal between the two sides. Now it was Al Gore who was arguing for a strict reading of statute, with Bush asking the courts to apply the "statutory scheme" in its totality, parsing the statute's words in light of good public policy choices. In large part, this switch was the result of circumstance. This time, the statutory language was on Gore's side. Section 102.168, Subsection 3, listed five categories of grounds for contesting an election. Whereas the first grounds for a contest was the "misconduct, fraud, or corruption . . . of any election official or . . . member of the canvassing board," other subsections included such grounds as "receipt of . . . illegal votes or rejection of . . . legal votes sufficient to . . . place in doubt the result of the election," the "ineligibility of the successful candidate for the nomination or office in dispute," and/or "any other cause or allegation which, if sustained, would show . . . that the outcome of the election . . . was contrary to the result declared by the canvassing board or election board."[38] Taken together, these grounds for action argued strongly that the legislature intended to allow contests in almost every instance when a candidate might have a reason to object to an election outcome (excepting only, of course, legitimately losing the vote). This scope for contests allowed Gore the luxury of pointing to the statutes and only the statutes as his justification for action; conversely, it forced Bush to argue that good public policy demanded a more nuanced reading of the legislature's words.[39]

The two briefs also show a remarkable lack of concern with the constitutional implications of these matters. Bush's earlier briefs to the Florida Supreme Court, for example in *Bush v. Palm Beach County Canvassing Board*, had stressed the equal protection, due process, and Article II implications of extending the certification deadline. And, of course, his federal court filings were totally based on equal protection, due process, and Article II arguments. But here, with the exception of its last section, Bush's brief was strangely quiet on these matters. And even that last section's mention of equal protection, due process, and 3 U.S.C. §5 was just that— a mere mention with almost no complaint or argument.[40] Similarly, with the exception of Gore's effort to apply 3 U.S.C. §5 as a defense for wider-ranging judicial review of the election, he too seemed unconcerned with the Constitution's provisions on these matters.[41]

It is hard to say why, exactly, each side minimized the federal constitutional implications of these matters. One explanation might be the short time in which they had to produce these briefs (approximately twenty-four hours). Another might be their focus on the Florida Supreme Court, which to date had shown little concern for or interest in the federal legal foundations of these matters. For Gore, the most likely explanation was that, because Bush had not raised these issues, there was no need to spend time arguing against something not yet on the table, given all that was already on the table. With Bush, however, this lack of constitutional argument was surprising. Judge Sauls had even raised an equal protection argument in his ruling, questioning the validity of partial recounts. The judge had argued that for a recount to be fair, it would have to include "all of the counties in this state with respect to the particular alleged irregularities or inaccuracies in the balloting or counting processes alleged to have occurred."[42] Translated, this meant that any challenge based on the irregularities of a punch card ballot needed to involve recounts of all the counties that used this method of counting, not just two or three of them. One can see why Gore would ignore this passage. While he was not averse to wider recounts, this was a direct attack on Gore's focused recount strategy. Moreover, applying this lack as a justification for *not* recounting was a death blow to Gore's chances to win the presidency. But for Bush to ignore it was, as noted, surprising.

So the arguments stood as the two sides met before the Florida Supreme Court for oral argument on the morning of December 7. Tensions were high in the crowded courtroom as the seven justices sat and began the hour-long proceeding. With serious looks on their faces, the justices had come ready to work. "I could feel an intensity between the attorneys and the justices," noted Matt Butler, an intervener in the case, who observed the proceedings. "I mean I could feel the heat-of-the-grill session."[43] Only days had passed since the U.S. Supreme Court had rebuked their efforts in *Bush v. Palm Beach County Canvassing Board*, and in the eyes of some, the Florida justices were chastened by that experience.[44] At the least, this was not going to be the same friendly forum that had voted unanimously for Al Gore seventeen days earlier.

This was clear from the start. Almost before David Boies could conclude his "May it please the Court" introduction, Chief Justice Charles Wells was pressuring him on the reach of 3 U.S.C. §5. In particular, Wells was concerned with the impact of *McPherson v. Blacker*: "You know when the case was here previously in the protest part of the proceeding, no counsel for any party in briefs or in argument raised with this court the U.S. Supreme Court [case] of *McPherson v. Blacker*, seemingly because counsel did not believe that it was important for our consideration." The same was true for the current round of briefs. Yet, "that case was forcefully argued to the U.S. Supreme Court and the U.S. Supreme Court has now called that case to this court's attention in the opinion that came out this Monday." So, Wells wondered, how important was this case in this instance? Did not *McPherson* preclude judicial review in this matter? When Boies responded that all the Florida Supreme Court was doing in this instance was "reviewing, and reviewing in an ordinary judicial interpretation way, [as set forth by] the statutes of this state," the chief justice pushed back again: "But why isn't this like sovereign immunity, where courts only have such power to resolve disputes and claims that [are] expressly given to it by the legislature? .... Why isn't this analogous to that?" Boies's only response was to repeat his view that the court was doing nothing unique here, that it was merely using its powers—granted to it by the legislature—to ensure that the law was being followed properly. After all, explained Boies, "whenever the legislature passes a law, what the legislature is doing is passing a law that [it knows was] . . . going to be interpreted by the courts. . . . This is a situation in which you have a statute that the legislature has passed that provides very specific remedies. And we think that those remedies are the remedies that this court has the jurisdiction to enforce, both in terms of appellate review and under its original mandamus authority."

Still clearly unconvinced, the chief justice shifted his questioning. Even granting that it had the authority to do so, he asked, why should the court get involved in this case at this time? "What you're asking this court to do is to have the courts of this state get involved in any instance in which someone comes in and merely alleges that there needs to be a count, because there were legal votes left out. . . . Someone [could] say they lost by 130,000 votes in Dade County, and we'd have to have the court count those votes." Where was the value in this, the chief justice asked. Boies vigorously disagreed. This was not the case of a loser coming in and just saying, "I want a recount." Gore had named specific instances in which votes that could be counted were not counted. "This [was] a situation in which the evidence [was] clear and undisputed, that there [were] voter errors and machine errors that create[d] this undervote in punch card equipment. In fact, the court [below] found . . . that this [problem] had been known to county officials for many years. So this [was] not a situation in which you simply have somebody coming in and saying, 'We lost, and we want to have another chance at it.'" As such, concluded Boies, they were not asking the court to produce a ruling that would open the floodgates to hundreds of unworthy election contests.

Speaking next, Justice Peggy Quince wondered why Gore was limiting his recount efforts to a handful of counties. Boies replied, "when you have a very close election, you have to have a manual review of those [specific] ballots [under contention] in order to have an accurate tally." Unsatisfied with this answer, Justice Barbara Pariente took up the question. "Why wouldn't that apply to all the other counties, at least the punch card counties," which had their own undervotes problems? "Those votes also [hadn't] been counted. If we're looking for accuracy, which . . . has been the statement from day one, then why isn't the request made" to count these votes? In other words, asked the justice, "is there something different about Dade, Broward and Palm Beach and their use of the punch card than the 17 other counties that also use punch cards?" Boies responded by pointing to the wording of the statute and the Florida courts' interpretation of that statute, both of which allowed for partial recounts. The decision was in the hands of the losing candidate, Boies explained. Dade, Broward, and Palm Beach were where Gore saw the greatest problems, hence it was where "a manual recount was requested and that's where ballots were contested." Other recounts were possible, true. After all, Gore had called for a statewide recount, but Bush had refused the offer. But, though wider recounts were possible, they were not mandatory under current Florida law.

Justice Leander Shaw's questions shifted the topic to Judge Sauls's ruling and the range of review allowed to the supreme court. Judge Sauls had made certain findings. "For instance," Shaw noted, Sauls "[found] that there was no credible statistical evidence . . . to establish by a preponderance of a reasonable probability that the results of a statewide election in the state of Florida would have been different." Was this not a finding of fact beyond the court's powers of review?[45] When Boies tried to argue that it was a mix of both, and hence within the court's purview, Shaw was skeptical. "But when you put on experts and the judge listens to these experts and then he makes a determination based upon that," he asked, "normally isn't that a question of fact?"

When Barry Richard came before the bench, the questions were just as pointed. However, with a few exceptions, the justices asking the questions were different from those grilling Boies. First, Chief Justice Wells asked once again his question about *McPherson v. Blacker*. Richard's response stressed the importance of *McPherson*. "I think that what *McPherson v. Blacker* tells us," argued Richard, "is . . . that this court does not have the ability . . . to disregard the statutory scheme and fashion a remedy based upon extraordinary equitable powers of the court set forth in the constitution"—at least when it came to choosing "presidential electors." So, countered the chief justice, does this mean "we have the right to review the action of the circuit court?" Of course, replied Richard. "This [case] is nothing more than a garden-variety appeal from a final judgment by a lower court that reviewed after an entire, full evidentiary hearing." Still, warned Richard, given the limits imposed by *McPherson*, the explicit provisions adopted by the legislature limited this review. The court could review to ensure that the traditional rules were followed, but it could not impose new rules in the guise of review.

Justice Harry Lee Anstead wondered if it was not "highly unusual for a trial court to admit into evidence certain documents that one party claims will be controlling, with reference to the claim they bring to the court, and yet never examine those documents before making their decision." Was this not what had happened with Judge Sauls? When Richard tried to waffle on the issue, Anstead pushed harder. "The trial court either did or did not admit the ballots into evidence. Did the trial court admit those into evidence?" When Richard was forced to admit that "my recollection is that the trial court did," the justice responded, "Did the trial court examine those documents?" Finally, Richard had no choice but to admit that the answer was no.

Justice Pariente kept the pressure on Richard. "Then what does Subsection 8 mean, the subsection [to 102.168] that was specifically added in 1999," she asked. "You've told us we've got to follow this statute." And that statute read in part that "'the circuit court is to do whatever is necessary to ensure,' which is rather unusual language to use in a statute, 'to ensure that each allegation in the complaint is investigated, examined or checked.'" If it did not mean that "the circuit court [was] to look at the very ballots that have been brought to the court for investigation, what does that section mean in the context of this litigation?" Richard's response repeated the argument that "the application of Section 168 does not change the necessity to show an abuse of discretion when it arrives at the court. . . . This court gave the plaintiffs the opportunity to have a trial to prove their case, and it was an absolute failure in the record of this case to establish an abuse of discretion by any of the challenged canvassing boards."

Once again the questioning shifted back to Justice Pariente, who pushed Richard on the statutory wording over the remedies in a contest and the likelihood of a changed outcome. "You keep on using the language that there should be a reasonable probability of a change, and you've said that, again, we've got to stick to the statute. My reading of the statute says 'sufficient to change or place in doubt the results of the election.' 'Place in doubt' is a different standard than 'a reasonable probability of different result.' Do you agree with that?" When Richard tried to answer the question without providing a substantive answer, the justice deepened her question: "So your position is that, in the contest, . . . that it is not the role of the judiciary in a contest to evaluate undervotes?" Richard responded that "it is not the role of the judiciary to do so when a canvassing board has already done so and has made a reasonable decision." Unwilling to accept this answer, Justice Pariente pushed even harder at Richard's logic. "Where in the statute is that standard that you have to show that a mistake was made through no fault of the voter? It seems to me that we've gotten off of what the standard is for showing the rejection of votes. And it seems to me that the statute, Subsection 3, says that rejection of votes which may put in doubt the result of the election [is enough to justify a contest recount]." Under this reading, the standard of proof was not "that I am going to win," but rather that the outcome "is in doubt that I did not win." Isn't that a different standard, Pariente asked. Richard's answer, once again, was no.

The hearing ended with a second round of questions for David Boies on the issue of timing and the ability of the courts to finish a recount before the December 12 "safe harbor" deadline intervened. Both Justices Pariente and Anstead were concerned with the closeness of these deadlines. "We're now here on December the 7, with December the 12 . . . fast approaching," said Justice Anstead. If Gore got his way, a significant number of ballots remained to be counted. "How can we resolve an issue like that at this late date?" Boies, however, was confident that the ballots could be counted in time, if the ballots were counted quickly enough. Boies reminded the court that they had been trying to get these ballots counted for "for many weeks." The key was getting started as soon as possible. With this exchange, the proceedings came to an end.[46]

In the turmoil of speculation and political spin that followed the seventy-minute session, a couple of basic points became clear. First, this was a court under intense pressure. Journalists described the justices' demeanors as "curt, often standoffish." Their questioning, in turn, "showed little patience for either side."[47] The *New York Daily News* called the questioning a "grilling" and an "inquisition."[48] Clearly the U.S. Supreme Court's remand had had an effect on at least some of the justices' thinking; so too perhaps, the likelihood that this ruling could determine the next president of the United States. Second, this was not the unanimous court it had been less than two weeks prior. The questioning patterns—which justice asked which questions of which lawyer—showed unmistakable splits among the justices. Chief Justice Wells, along with Justices Shaw and Harding, clearly had troubles with Gore's arguments for overturning Judge Sauls's ruling. Just as clearly, Justices Pariente, Anstead, and Lewis were troubled by aspects of that same ruling, doubting at the least parts of its logic and/or conclusions. Of course, Justices Quince and Pariente had shown concerns over the issue of limited recounts, so how these concerns would translate into votes for or against the lower court ruling remained an open question.

It did not take long for the justices to answer this question. The next morning, the Florida Supreme Court issued its ruling—a 4 to 3 judgment in favor of Al Gore and the counting of votes under the contest provisions.[49] The majority agreed with most of Gore's complaints against Judge Sauls's ruling. They agreed that the trial court had erred—"as a matter of law"—by not including "the 215 net votes for Gore identified by the Palm Beach County Canvassing Board" as well as the "168 net votes for Gore identified by the partial recount by the Miami-Dade County Canvassing Board." Similarly, in terms of "the approximately 9000 additional Miami-Dade ballots placed in evidence, which have never been examined manually," the majority once again sided with Gore. These ballots should be recounted.

On the other hand, the majority found "no error in the trial court's findings, . . . concerning the Nassau County Canvassing Board and the additional 3300 votes in Palm Beach County that the Canvassing Board did not find to be legal votes." The canvassing boards had made a decision, and without proof of fraud or malfeasance on the part of the board's members, there was no reason for the courts to second-guess these decisions.[50] These votes stood as certified.

The majority could have finished their decision at this point: give Bush back his 50 votes from Nassau County, allow the circuit court to review the 9,000 Miami-Dade votes, and call it a day. However, in a sign of just how extensive a contest proceeding could become, the majority was unsatisfied with the limited nature of Gore's recount requests. They agreed with Judge Sauls "that it [was] absolutely essential in this proceeding and to any final decision, that a manual recount be conducted for all legal votes in this State, not only in Miami-Dade County, but in all Florida counties where there was an undervote."[51] Consequently, the justices in the majority widened Gore's request to recount ballots from just Miami-Dade into a statewide recount.[52]

Understanding the radical step that they were taking, and no doubt worried by the recent remand from the U.S. Supreme Court, the majority went to great lengths to explain and justify their order. "When an election contest is filed under section 102.168, *Florida Statutes* (2000)," they explained, "the contest statute charges trial courts to fashion such orders as he or she deems necessary to ensure that each allegation in the complaint is *investigated, examined, or checked*, to prevent or correct any alleged wrong, and to provide any relief appropriate under such circumstances [emphasis added by the court]." This principle was controlling in this instance. "Through this statute, the Legislature has granted trial courts broad authority to resolve election disputes and fashion appropriate relief. In turn, this Court, consistent with legislative policy, has pointed [in its prior decisions] to the 'will of the voters' as the primary guiding principle to be utilized by trial courts in resolving election contests." It did not matter if the election was for county commissioner or president of the United States. *Florida Statutes* (2000) provided "that the focus of any manual examination of a ballot shall be to determine the voter's intent." The justices were merely following the "clear message" in this legislative provision that "every citizen's vote be counted whenever possible."[53]

The majority next addressed Judge Sauls's contention that "in order to contest election results," the plaintiff must "show a reasonable probability that the results of the election would have been changed." This reading of statute law, the majority held, was incorrect. In particular, it overlooked "the specific and material changes to the statute which the Legislature [had] made in 1999." These changes, the majority argued, controlled the proper reading of the statute. In particular, the new version of the law "now explicitly include[d] . . . the receipt of a number of illegal votes or rejection of a number of legal votes sufficient to change *or place in doubt* the result of the election [emphasis supplied by the court]." In practical terms, this meant that while the old version of the statute had required a "reasonable probability" of change in order for the courts to act in a contest, the newer version did not. Gore, in turn, had shown "the existence of some 9,000 'under votes'" in an election contest decided by a margin measured in the hundreds. This was enough to meet his burden of proof in demanding a recount.[54]

Next was the question of vote standards. The standard in Florida, set by statute and case law, was "the intent of the voter," noted the majority. Repeatedly, the Florida courts had held that "so long as the voter's intent may be discerned from the ballot, the vote constitutes a 'legal vote' that should be counted."[55] The question raised here was, did a machine or hand recount's rejection of a ballot keep the circuit court from reviewing these ballots during a contest? The majority's answer was yes. Whereas the courts had power under the law to review such matters *de novo*, "when a manual count of ballots has been conducted by the Canvassing Board pursuant to section 102.166" and there was no evidence of malfeasance or mistake on the canvassing board's part, "the circuit court in a contest proceeding does not have the obligation *de novo* to simply repeat an otherwise-proper manual count of the ballots." As regarded the 3,300 disputed ballots from Palm Beach County, if Judge Sauls was satisfied with the canvassing board's work, then the supreme court would be, too.[56]

The issue was different, however, when a canvassing board simply refused to recount ballots. Once they decided to recount, the Miami-Dade Canvassing Board had a "mandatory obligation to recount all of the ballots in the county." Deciding to stop was not the same as ruling against the ballots in terms of proof of a voter's intent. Further, the circuit court had the power to review this decision. "The focus of the trial court's inquiry in an election contest authorized by the Legislature pursuant to the express statutory provisions of section 102.168 [was] not by appellate review to determine whether the Board properly or improperly failed to complete the manual recount. Rather, as expressly set out in section 102.168, the court's responsibility [was] to determine whether 'legal votes' were rejected sufficient to change or place in doubt the results of the election." By not examining the disputed ballots, Judge Sauls had denied Gore the "very evidence that [he had] relied on to establish [his] ultimate entitlement to relief." This was improper, a Catch–22 that was not necessary and in fact conflicted with existing precedent on the issue of contest recounts.[57]

In concluding their judgment, the majority noted that "in close elections the necessity for counting all legal votes becomes critical." True, the "need for accuracy must be weighed against the need for finality"—especially in the case of "presidential elections where there [was] an outside deadline established by federal law." None of this, however, freed the courts from their "legislative mandate" to do "everything required by law to ensure that legal votes that have not been counted are included in the final election results." Ultimately, the faith of the voting public in the "political process" itself was at stake in assuring "an accurate vote count." Given that it was only "by examining the contested ballots, which are evidence in the election contest," that "a meaningful and final determination in this election contest [could] be made," the majority saw their duty clearly. They recognized that time was short.[58] But their duty to act, under statutory authority, was clear.

Accordingly, the majority reversed the final judgment of the trial court and remanded the case to the circuit court "to immediately tabulate by hand the approximate 9,000 Miami–Dade ballots, which the counting machine registered as non-votes, but which have never been manually reviewed, and for other relief that may thereafter appear appropriate." The supreme court also directed the circuit court "to enter such orders as are necessary to add any legal votes to the total statewide certifications" and/or necessary "to ensure the inclusion of the additional legal votes for Gore in Palm Beach County and the 168 additional legal votes from Miami–Dade County." Finally, as time was short, they ordered the circuit court judge to take all actions necessary to organize and finish the statewide undervote recounts on or before December 12.[59]

All in all, this was both a sweeping ruling and a closely reasoned one. Right or wrong, the majority had set out a clear justification for recounts and ordered the circuit judge to take all actions necessary to do the job quickly. In practical terms, this meant organizing state and local officials (judges, clerks, and canvassing board members) into enough vote-counting teams to count ballots quickly and (presumably) effectively. Unfortunately, when it came to the one thing that would have helped most in carrying out a speedy recount, the majority remained silent. Despite Gore's request for the justices to name a uniform standard for a valid vote, the majority refused to name a single practical standard. Once again, they merely quoted from state statute and held that, "in tabulating the ballots and in making a determination of what is a 'legal' vote, the standards to be employed is that established by the Legislature in our Election Code which is that the vote shall be counted as a 'legal' vote if there is 'clear indication of the intent of the voter.'"[60]

Then there were the dissents. As strong as the majority had tried to make their argument, Chief Justice Wells, along with Justices Shaw and Harding, were not convinced. They objected to both the logic and the outcome of the majority's ruling. Justice Harding, for instance, dissented because he agreed with Judge Sauls's "ultimate conclusion in this case, namely that the Appellants failed to carry their requisite burden of proof and thus are not entitled to relief." Granted, Harding agreed with the majority that Sauls had misinterpreted his powers to review the actions of the county canvassing boards.[61] Similarly, Harding felt that Judge Sauls had overstated the need for a "reasonable probability that the results of the election would have been changed" before a court could act. This too was a misreading of the relevant statutes. But in the end none of this mattered:

While I disagree with Judge Sauls on the standards applicable to this election contest, . . . I believe that Judge Sauls properly concluded that there was no authority to include the Palm Beach County returns filed after the explicit deadline established by this Court. I conclude that the application of the erroneous standards is not determinative in this case. I agree with Judge Sauls that the Appellants [Gore] have not carried their burden of showing that the number of legal votes rejected by the canvassing boards is sufficient to change or place in doubt the result of this *statewide* election. That failure of proof controls the outcome here.[62]

Harding also was deeply troubled by Gore's failure to seek a statewide recount. To allow Gore to win a statewide election based on partial recounts in hand-picked counties was improper. To allow such procedures, Justice Harding explained, "would disenfranchise tens of thousands of other Florida voters," and potentially run afoul of the Fifth and Fourteenth Amendments to the U.S. Constitution.[63] Yet even if, by some quirk of fate, the statutes allowed for partial recounts, it would not matter. In Justice Harding's mind, there was no adequate remedy available under the law "sufficient to warrant relief." In its prior opinion on certification deadlines, the court and all of the parties had agreed "that election controversies and contests must be finally and conclusively determined by December 12, 2000." This date was soon upon us, Justice Harding noted. To provide an adequate remedy would mean organizing and carrying out "a statewide recount of more than 170,000 'no-vote' ballots by December 12." This simply was not possible.[64]

In the end, Justice Harding was "concerned that the majority [was] departing from the essential requirements of the law by providing a remedy which [was] impossible to achieve and which will ultimately lead to chaos." In ordering Judge Sauls to organize a statewide recount, "the majority permits a remedy which was not prayed for, which [was] based upon a premise for which there is no evidence, and which presents Judge Sauls with directions to order entities (i.e., local canvassing boards) to conduct recounts when they have not been served, have not been named as parties, but, most importantly, have not had the opportunity to be heard." The only likely result of such an effort was chaos. "The uncertainty of the outcome of this election will be greater under the remedy afforded by the majority than the uncertainty that now exists," concluded Harding. Time had simply run out. The game was over. Or, as Vince Lombardi once put it, "'We didn't lose the game, we just ran out of time.'"[65]

Chief Justice Wells's dissent built on Justice Harding's arguments. Wells disagreed with Harding on his "conclusions with regard to error by Judge Sauls and his conclusions as to the separateness of section 102.166 and 102.168, Florida Statutes," but otherwise shared Harding's views on the law and the dangers associated with the majority's ruling. In fact, most of the chief justice's dissent focused on how risky and wrong extending the recounts could be. Although Wells did not question "the good faith or honorable intentions of my colleagues in the majority," he could not "more strongly disagree with their decision to reverse the trial court and prolong this judicial process."

> My succinct conclusion is that the majority's decision to return this case to the circuit court for a count of the under-votes from either Miami-Dade County or all counties has no foundation in the law of Florida as it existed on November 7, 2000, or at any time until the issuance of this opinion. The majority returns the case to the circuit court for this partial recount of under-votes on the basis of unknown or, at best, ambiguous standards with authority to obtain help from others, the credentials, qualifications, and objectivity of whom are totally un-known. That is but a first glance at the imponderable problems the majority creates. Importantly to me, I have a deep and abiding concern that the prolong-ing of judicial process in this counting contest propels this country and this state into an unprecedented and unnecessary constitutional crisis. I have to con-clude that there is a real and present likelihood that this constitutional crisis will do substantial damage to our country, our state, and to this Court as an in-stitution.[66]

Historically, continued Chief Justice Wells, the Florida Supreme Court did not involve itself in election matters unless there had been "substantial allegations of fraud and then only upon a high threshold because of the chill that a hovering ju-dicial involvement can put on elections." Judge Sauls, in turn, "after an evidentiary hearing, . . . expressly found no dishonesty, gross negligence, improper influence, coercion, or fraud in the balloting and counting processes based upon the evidence presented." To intervene in this case, as the majority proposed, meant lowering the threshold for judicial action beyond the requirement of "a substantial noncom-pliance with election laws." This was a very dangerous proposition.[67]

And then there was the problem of standards. Wells wrote, "Directing the trial court to conduct a manual recount of the ballots violate[d] article II, section 1, clause 2 of the United States Constitution, in that neither this Court nor the circuit court ha[d] the authority to create the standards by which it will count the under-voted ballots." Yet even if this power did rest with the courts, the majority had de-clined to name adequate standards for a valid recount. How could the trial judge count votes if neither he nor anyone else knew "whether to count or not count bal-lots on the criteria used by the canvassing boards, . . . or to do so on the basis of standards divined by Judge Sauls[?]" And even if he did hand down an answer, how could anyone trust the results of the manual recounts? "It only stands to rea-son that many times a reading of a ballot by a human will be subjective, and the in-tent gleaned from that ballot is only in the mind of the beholder. This subjective counting is only compounded where no standards exist or, as in this statewide contest, where there are no statewide standards for determining voter intent by the various canvassing boards, individual judges, or multiple unknown counters who will eventually count these ballots."[68]

The majority's ruling, in a word, was a mess. "I must regrettably conclude that the majority ignores the magnitude of its decision," argued Chief Justice Wells. They waved their hands and said count, but the majority had failed to make provision for carrying out a valid statewide count in the time remaining. "This Court's responsibility must be to balance the contest allegations against the rights of all Florida voters who are not involved in election contests to have their votes counted in the electoral college. To me, it is inescapable that there is no practical way for the contest to continue for the good of this country and state." The case had "reached the point where finality must take precedence over continued judicial process. . . . 'The margin of error in this election [was] far greater than the margin of victory, no matter who wins.' Further judicial process will not change this self-evident fact and will only result in confusion and disorder."[69]

The gap between the majority justices and the Chief Justice could not have been greater. (Justices Shaw and Major stood somewhere in the middle.) The problem was not just that they disagreed about the level of malfeasance necessary to justify a contest recount (the majority stressed the potential for errors to change the outcome, the Chief Justice demanded that there had to be some recognizable sort of fraud, gross negligence, or coercion in the ballot counting), but that each differed on the fundamental objective behind counting votes. To the majority, the possibility that legitimate votes might not be counted was an injustice that the court was duty bound to prevent. The purpose of holding an election was empowering the voters' choices. Chief Justice Wells, on the other hand, viewed elections as a process shaped by rules and laws. The rules, in turn, did not allow the sort of last-minute rush to count that the majority called for. To attempt such an effort was not only improper, it was undermining the very foundations of the electoral system. The only result could be chaos and disorder.[70]

Any potential for confusion and disorder aside, it was the majority's ruling that had the force of law. While George W. Bush set about appealing this ruling to the U.S. Supreme Court, the case returned to Judge Sauls's courtroom. Reading the majority's judgment as a rebuke (which in large part it was), Judge Sauls withdrew from the case and Judge Terry Lewis was appointed to organize and supervise the recounts.

Judge Lewis came ready to act. At 8:00 p.m. that night, he opened a hearing to set the statewide recount procedures. Boies asked for immediate action. "The Court meant immediately when it said immediately," Boies told the Judge. "Hours make a difference here." Phil Beck for Bush asked for an adjournment until the next morning at which time he proposed to "educate" the Judge on the intricacies of the standards to be applied in counting votes. "We have a wealth of evidence on that," Beck told the Judge. But it was going to take time to cover it all. Not willing to wait until the next day to act, Judge Lewis asked Beck to explain to him immediately what standard the court should apply. He already had the judges lined up to begin counting the Miami-Dade ballots, so what standard should they be applying? After hemming and hawing, Beck came back with the customary "intent of the voter" standard. Pushed by the judge to come up with a more specific standard, Beck refused to answer. The "intent of the voter" was all they had. Any more specific standard would be a change in the rules after Election Day and hence would put the safe harbor deadline at risk.[71]

Clearly seeing the delaying trend of the Republicans' arguments, Judge Lewis was unwilling to wait. (He also clearly understood the Catch–22 implicit in the Republicans' arguments, where a lack of standards undermined the counting process, but any judicial definition of the standards constituted a new rule after the election, which invalidated the safe harbor provisions.) After a short meeting with his fellow judges, Lewis returned to the hearing and announced that the recounts would begin at 8:00 a.m. the next morning. The court itself would count the Miami-Dade undervotes (which constituted the largest batch of undervote ballots). The remaining disputed ballots would be recounted by the applicable county canvassing boards under the supervision of the court (in the form of circuit court judges from around the state and with Judge Lewis available around the clock to settle disputes or answer questions). Although observers from both parties were allowed, no objections were permitted. Rather, they were to note any discrepancies and bring them up at a later hearing before his court. The standard of a proper vote, in turn, was that provided by the Florida Supreme Court: the "clear intent of the voter," based on the "totality of the ballot." Judge Lewis, however, stressed to all the "clear" part of that phrase. When discussing the recounts with his fellow judges earlier, for example, he announced that "if you've got some question about it, it's probably not a clear intent. I've got my Johnnie Cochran sound bite for you. 'If in doubt, throw it out.'" This would be the standard applied. Finally, all counting was to be completed by 2:00 p.m. Sunday, December 9.[72]

That night, both camps frantically worked to get enough volunteer observers to man all sixty-four of the counties ordered to recount undervotes. Throughout the night, training sessions sought to explain the process to the observers, preparing them for the job. At 9:00 a.m. Saturday morning, the counting began. As we might guess, there were some bumps along the way. In Collier County, the local canvassing board needed five hours to decide how to count forty absentee ballots. In Duvall County, the all-Republican County Canvassing Board had trouble separating the undervote ballots from the rest. In the end, it took a computer expert from Miami to get things up and running again. In Clay County, officials were having trouble finding counting teams. In Bradford County, officials did not have the computer software necessary to cull the undervoted ballots from the remainder. Observing the recount effort, the elections supervisor from Pinellas County noted exhaustedly, "Damn, we need a better process."[73] Meanwhile, back in Texas, the

Bush advisers watched the recounts and shook their heads at the disorganization and lack of uniformity in identifying a valid vote.[74]

Yet for all the worries about disorder and chaos, the hard-working court and election officials buckled down and got the system to work. In Tallahassee, the Miami-Dade ballots—the ones that elections supervisor David Leahy argued would take days and even weeks to count—were being counted at a fast clip. Without the infighting that had characterized the protest recounts, the process moved along quickly. In fact, although some counties were experiencing delays and problems, by day's end in nine of the largest counties the counting was done, and in four more, they were on the verge of completing their recounting. Though other counties were behind schedule, it still seemed as if Judge Lewis's 2:00 p.m. Sunday deadline would be met.[75] And then, as had so often been the case in this crisis, the unexpected happened.

2:40 p.m., Saturday, December 9. Seemingly out of the blue, CNN announced that George W. Bush's request to the U.S. Supreme Court for an order halting the vote counting—which he had filed immediately following the Florida Supreme Court's ruling on Friday—had been granted. They reported as well that the Court had treated the petition as a motion for review and that the case was now set for oral argument on Monday, December 11, 2000, at 11 a.m. Twenty minutes later, the chief judge of the 2nd Circuit Court in Tallahassee, George Reynolds III, distributed a press announcement confirming the order and issued instructions to halt all recounts. The case—renamed *Bush v. Gore*—was going to the U.S. Supreme Court. The recounts were being sent to limbo.

As word of the Supreme Court's stay order spread, so too did speculation as to how the justices would rule. Most insiders were cautious in their views. As the *Washington Post* reported, "After the mind-numbing series of twists and turns over the past 32 days, no one on either side of the battle was ready to make any bold predictions about what might happen at the Supreme Court next week—given the reality that a shift of one justice could give the advantage to Gore—or when the battle might end."[76] There was little doubt that emotions were high. The Florida Supreme Court's majority in *Gore v. Harris* was yet another challenge to the conservative views of at least five justices on the U.S. Supreme Court. These conservative jurists were likely to view it as an implicit denial of their Court's reasoning in remanding *Bush v. Palm Beach County Canvassing Board* to the Florida Supreme Court. Yet just how the entire Court viewed this case was unclear. Gore argued in a brief opposing the stay order that the Florida Supreme Court's majority had taken "to heart" concerns raised the previous week by the U.S. Supreme Court and had "carefully avoided" relying on anything other than Florida statutes or cases in its Friday ruling. "There is no federal question and no basis for reversal," Gore's lawyers asserted.[77] Yet would a majority of the justices view it this way?

Interestingly, the stay order itself provided some hints as to the justices' think-ing—and also of the conflicts to come. The Court's decision to stay the recounts was not unanimous. Four justices—Stevens, Souter, Ginsburg, and Breyer—took the rare step of appending a dissent to the stay order expressing their objections to this decision. "To stop the counting of legal votes, the majority today departs from three venerable rules of judicial restraint that have guided the Court through-out its history," noted Justice Stevens for the dissenters. Traditionally, the Court respected the rulings of a state court on matters of state law. Similarly, the Court's general policy was to avoid interference "on questions whose resolution [was] com-mitted at least in large measure to another branch of the Federal Government." The same held true for "federal constitutional questions that were not fairly pre-sented to the court, [and] whose judgment [was] being reviewed." Here "we have prudently declined to express an opinion." In doing each of these things, the dis-senting justices argued, "the majority has acted unwisely." Stays should be imple-mented only where "an applicant [made] a substantial showing of a likelihood of irreparable harm." Such was not the case in this instance. "Counting every legally cast vote cannot constitute irreparable harm," Stevens stated. "On the other hand, there is a danger that a stay may cause irreparable harm to the respondents—and, more importantly, the public at large—because of the risk that "the entry of the stay would be tantamount to a decision on the merits in favor of the applicants." There was no proof that Florida law had been violated. In fact, the state's "intent of the voter" standard was not only a coherent rule with a long line of supporting precedents, but "as a more fundamental matter, the Florida court's ruling reflects the basic principle, inherent in our Constitution and our democracy, that every legal vote should be counted."

On the other hand, troubled by the dissenting opinion, Justice Scalia went to the even more unusual step of defending the stay—actually holding up the issuing of the stay by an hour to set out his views. In a less than accurate statement, Scalia noted that he refused to discuss the merits of the case, but added that "it suffices to say that the issuance of the stay suggests that a majority of the Court, while not deciding the issues presented, believe that the petitioner has a substantial proba-bility of success."[78] In other words, a majority of the justices were clearly in line with Bush's legal reasoning in this matter, and the argument to follow was Bush's to lose. In terms of irreparable harm, Scalia disagreed with Stevens's argument that counting legal votes cannot cause harm. The problem was not with counting legal votes, but that the votes being counted in Florida were yet to be proven legal votes. "The counting of votes that are of questionable legality does in my view threaten irreparable harm to petitioner, and to the country, by casting a cloud upon what he claims to be the legitimacy of his election." The lack of a uniform standard for determining a valid vote in Florida—one that would not allow for each county to apply its own standard of "intent"—raised serious questions as to the legality of the undervotes being counted. And every hand recount "degraded" the accuracy of the ballots for future counting. "Count first, and rule upon legality afterwards, [was] not a recipe for producing election results that have the public acceptance democratic stability requires," concluded Scalia. Better first to determine if the votes in question were valid votes, and only then, if this were the case, count them out.[79]

With such clear splits already showing between the justices, the hearings and opinion writing to follow promised fireworks. This was going to be a case far different from *Bush v. Palm Beach County Canvassing Board*. In that case, the Court's ruling had largely avoided the case's merits—though most likely that avoidance reflected deep differences between the justices on the issues. Yet no one believed that the Court would—or even could—evade the issues here. With deadlines looming, this was likely to be the ultimate case in these matters. One way or the other, the Court would have to form a majority and rule on the substance of George W. Bush's complaints. But just what that majority would look like, and what the content of their opinion or opinions would be, remained uncertain. Only time—and the efforts of two skilled lawyers, nine justices, and a small army of law clerks— would tell.

CHAPTER SEVEN
"A Florida Hurricane Heading to Washington"

This was not a footnote of history—this was history. This was living
history and I was there witnessing the Constitution and the
constitutional process working.

—*U.S. Rep. John Baldacci (D-ME) on the oral arguments in* Bush v. Gore

Think of it as a Florida hurricane heading to Washington.

—*Reporter James V. Grimaldi of the* Washington Post, *on the move
from Tallahassee to Washington in* Bush v. Gore

Argument before the U.S. Supreme Court is never easy. Along with the inevitable
case of nerves that comes from arguing before the nation's highest court, there is
the real problem of figuring out how to convince the justices that your position is
the right one. As Justice Sandra Day O'Connor noted in a TV interview, the
Supreme Court "does not take the easy cases."[1] And difficult cases make for hard
arguments (not to mention, hard decisions for the justices). Even where the legitimacy of your cause seems obvious to you, it may not seem so to the justices. Worse
yet, you cannot always depend on such familiar supports as precedent when arguing before the High Court. Unlike other courts, the Supreme Court has the power
to ignore precedent and reverse even long-standing legal doctrine. The justices' job
is to interpret the Constitution's meaning *in practice*, and where they feel that past
practices are wrong, they are duty-bound to act.[2] Then again, like most judges,
Supreme Court justices do not *like* to overturn precedent. Given a choice, they almost always will leave existing precedents, existing landmarks of legal and constitutional interpretation, intact.

With *Bush v. Gore* these customary difficulties were magnified by both the high
stakes the case posed and the strict time constraints that looming deadlines created.
Normally lawyers could take weeks to construct their arguments to the Supreme
Court and enjoy even more time following the filing of their briefs to prepare for
oral argument; now the lawyers had one day to prepare. The same held true for the
Court. Typically, justices have the summer to decide whether to accept a case for
argument, followed by days or even weeks to prepare for oral argument and months
in which to decide the case and draft their opinions.[3] Not so with *Bush v. Gore*.

Time was short for all concerned. Briefs were due within a single day, limited
by court order to just fifty pages each. Oral argument was extended beyond the

normal one-hour time frame to ninety minutes, but time to prepare for this argument was, once again, about a day. The lawyers had no time to prepare for oral argument by consulting with outside colleagues on specific doctrinal issues or by practicing their presentations before moot-court panels (mock panels in which other lawyers play the justices and pepper the arguing attorney with the sorts of questions that they likely will face before the real justices). There was barely enough time for the lawyers to talk through their arguments with the rest of their legal teams—including the very lawyers writing the briefs they were going to have to defend before the Court. They would have to go to the Court cold, hoping that the justices did not ask any questions for which they had no answers.[4]

The justices were working with an even tighter timeline than the lawyers appearing before them. Following oral argument, the justices only had one day before the "safe harbor" date of December 12 passed in which to decide the case and produce a majority opinion that could garner the votes of at least five justices. This time frame included not only deliberations and voting to decide the case, but writing and rewriting the opinion to satisfy the concerns of the majority justices (while simultaneously answering the complaints or criticisms of any dissenters).[5] In the end, the Court would act quicker than it had ever done before, announcing its decision a mere thirty-six hours after oral argument. (*Bush v. Gore* thus became the fastest case ever decided by the Supreme Court, faster even than the Court's 1971 decision of *New York Times v. United States* [the Pentagon Papers case], its 1974 ruling in *U.S. v. Nixon*, or its first decision growing out of the 2000 election, *Bush v. Palm Beach County Canvassing Board*.)[6]

Missing from this case, in other words, was the deliberative nature of the typical Supreme Court litigation. Supreme Court decision making is normally a thoughtful, methodical process. Whereas the justices vote soon after the oral arguments, establishing the majority and minority sides in a case, only in the writing of the opinion does the actual structure of the ruling develop. (Indeed in some cases, the writing of the opinions may even cause justices to switch sides, making a majority opinion a dissent and vice versa.)[7] And it is this structure—comprising justifications and definitions, exceptions and limits, explanations for action and inaction—that constitutes the substance of the Court's decision. It is here that we see not only how the Court voted, but why they voted and to what effect (both on the case at hand and on the law in general). Getting the wording right, in other words, is essential for the Court to be effective as an interpreter of the law. Yet getting the wording right often takes time—time that the justices did not have in this case.[8]

Worse yet, this was clearly a divided Court. The stay order, for instance, showed that the justices were split on the issues. But split in what ways? And on what issues? Justice Scalia clearly was leaning toward Bush's views on the impermissibility of judicial intervention by the Florida Supreme Court—and observers knew that when Scalia chose a side, it was usually safe to include Chief Justice Rehnquist and Justice Thomas on that side as well. The four liberal/moderate justices, on the other hand, were clearly unconvinced by these arguments, as expressed by their dissent to the stay. But unconvinced in what ways? Was it the granting of certiorari that they found objectionable, or just the stay order? Did they have objections to the substance of Bush's arguments? Their dissent to the stay order, though implying all three, was unclear. Then there were the two remaining justices, Kennedy and O'Connor. If traditional patterns held true, they were the swing votes that would decide the case. Both, in turn, had signed off on the stay order, yet were their reasons for halting the recounts and taking the case on appeal the same as that of the conservative troika of Rehnquist, Scalia, and Thomas? And if not, how did they differ? The possibilities were legion.

These splits posed a significant problem—and opportunity—for the lawyers on both sides. Each team of lawyers understood that they had to construct a five-member majority if they were going to win. As the late Justice William J. Brennan Jr. used to say, "The first rule of the Supreme Court is that you have to be able to count to five."[9] Despite the setting, with all nine justices sitting side-by-side, unified in their common focus on the case, experienced Supreme Court lawyers know that they are arguing not to a single Court, but rather to nine different, opinionated individuals. Like putting together a puzzle, lawyers arguing before the Court need to keep in mind at all times each justice's perspectives and biases and figure out how to fit these pieces together to form a coherent argument that will win five votes.[10] The lawyer who best guesses how the pieces can fit together is usually the winner.

To their advantage, both sides could draw on some of the best and most experienced appellate legal talent in the nation. On December 11, as the final oral arguments of the 2000 election marathon were getting under way, the *New York Observer* noted how

> over the past month, we have seen some of the best lawyering in the country, if not the world. Ted Olson and Laurence Tribe each argued clearly and persuasively before the U.S. Supreme Court on Friday, Dec. 1. David Boies in Florida . . . displayed his impressive analytical and rhetorical skills. The Bush lawyers, Barry Richard and Philip Beck, kept their case in the Florida Circuit Court simple and made proper and effective use of the tactic of delay. It's a time for lawyers to be proud.[11]

The two lawyers arguing before the Supreme Court that day, David Boies and Ted Olson, had stellar reputations. Choosing to argue that "there was no federal question" posed by the case, Gore selected Boies as his lead counsel, hoping to benefit from his experience in arguing Florida law, rather than picking Professor Laurence Tribe, who had argued for Gore in the first Supreme Court case. (Tribe, however, still helped write the vice president's brief.)[12] In 1999, the *National Law Journal* named Boies Lawyer of the Year for his handling of the *U.S. v. Microsoft* litigation. *Time* magazine granted Boies the same title for 2000.[13] Dexter Douglass, with more than four decades of experience as a lawyer, considered Boies as "the best. . . . I've met very few people in my 46 years of law that are as talented at getting to the essence of a case and stating it so that everyone understands it," he said. "And he has incredible concentration."[14] Olson, in turn, was not only well respected—he also was one of the most experienced Supreme Court litigators available, having argued thirteen cases before the justices. Daniel Troy, a former clerk for Judge Robert H. Bork and a constitutional lawyer and an associate scholar at the American Enterprise Institute, described Olson as "one of the leading—if not the leading—Republican constitutional and appellate lawyers in the country." He was, in fact, a respected leader among conservative lawyers, a founder of the conservative Federalist Society, and head of a law firm filled with former law clerks from all five of the more conservative justices.[15]

Both sides also were intimately familiar with the facts and legal arguments in these matters. For weeks, they had being doing little else than argue the constitutional and practical underpinnings of Florida election law. There was nothing new in their arguments to the Supreme Court. Both sides had their best arguments laid out in front of them, and they would win or lose on the strength of these factual and legal positions.

Still, this was not going to be an easy case for anyone involved. The justices' ruling, whatever it turned out to be, almost certainly would determine who won the presidency (either directly or indirectly). Taking control of the case was a lot like grabbing a live hand grenade and hoping that you could get rid of it before it went off. No matter what you did, the result was still going to be an explosion in your general vicinity. By taking this appeal, the justices were jumping head-first into Justice Frankfurter's political thicket. Worse yet, they were doing so at full speed—and without a full consensus as to the need or advisability of taking this leap. Deliberation had been replaced by haste and massive exertion substituted for careful reasoning. No matter what the decision, the result would be explosive in its legal, political, and popular impact. How the Court responded to this challenge—its ruling, the number of justices in the majority, the outcome's effect on the election—would go a long way in determining just how explosive an impact their ruling would have.

By the time the nine justices received the briefs from each side (along with an additional thirteen briefs filed by interested third parties), they already were well informed as to the issues this case raised. For one thing, many unresolved questions from *Bush v. Palm Beach County Canvassing Board* carried over into this lawsuit—in particular, the proper role of the state judiciary in interpreting the statutory and constitutional rules controlling elections. Further, each justice had been watching the ongoing events in Florida. In this they were no different from the rest of the nation, glued to their television sets as the litigation process in Florida unfolded, their views of events shaped as much by the public relations battle as by the often hidden substance of these events.[16] Finally, and most important, the filings over the issuing of the stay presaged the arguments each side would make in their briefs.

Bush, for instance, set out three main arguments in his petition for a stay. The first questioned "whether the Florida Supreme Court erred in establishing new standards for resolving presidential election contests that conflict with legislative enactments and thereby violate[d] Article II, Section 1, Clause 2 of the United States Constitution, which provides that electors shall be appointed by each State 'in such Manner as the Legislature thereof may direct.'" Number two drew on 3 U.S.C. §5 and asked whether the judicially created standards of the Florida Supreme Court threatened "to overturn the certified results of the election" by changing the rules of the election after Election Day. Finally, question three asked "whether the use of arbitrary, standardless and selective manual recounts, . . . including post-election judicially created selective and capricious recount procedures, that var[ied] both across counties and within counties in the State of Florida violate[d] the Equal Protection or Due Process Clauses of the Fourteenth Amendment."[17]

Bush's brief on the merits, filed on December 9, repeated these contentions and expanded them into a detailed and multifaceted attack on the Florida Supreme Court's rulings on these questions. For instance, after summarizing the judicial rulings below, the brief contended that "the new standards, procedures, and timetables established by the Florida Supreme Court for the selection of Florida's presidential electors [were] in conflict with the Florida Legislature's detailed plan for the resolution of election disputes." Article II of the Constitution, the brief noted, placed control of the electoral process exclusively with the legislature. The Florida legislature, in turn, had crafted a "statutory scheme to govern the appointment of presidential electors"—a scheme that at no time "authorized judicial revision of the legislative structure it so meticulously conceived." Yet the Florida Supreme Court ignored this established scheme in crafting its ruling. In effect, the Florida Supreme Court had "substituted its judgment for that of the legislature in violation of Article II." This substitution could only be seen as a direct violation of Article II, Section 1, clause 2 of the Constitution, argued the brief—"a usurpation of constitutionally delegated power" as set out by "the Framers' plan."[18]

Among the many judicial usurpations of legislative intent, the brief explained, were "the elimination of the Secretary of State's authority to maintain uniformity in application of the election laws; disregard for the statutory provisions that require manual recounts to include 'all' ballots; the substitution of courts for canvassing boards in determining ballot validity; and the imposition of *de novo* judicial review by courts of canvassing boards' certified judgments." If one could ask a court to do all these things merely by bringing a contest action under section 102.168, asked the brief, why would anyone ever bother with the canvassing boards under section 102.166? No, absent explicit instruction from the legislature, each of these acts was a clear, illegal usurpation of the legislature's authority.[19]

Yet even assuming for argument's sake that the Florida Supreme Court had the authority to rule in these matters, continued the brief—that the contest statute actually applied to presidential elections and thus granted them the authority to review and "refine" such statutory procedures—the content of the Florida Supreme Court's ruling so totally disregarded the plain language of those statutes as to effect the same negative, and unconstitutional, results. The Florida election statutes did not allow for *de novo* review, nor did they allow for partial recounts. They especially did not ignore the certified vote totals established by the county canvassing boards and the state canvassing commission. What was being "contested" in these matters was "the certification" itself. The deadline for filing a contest action, noted the brief, ran from "the date the last county canvassing board . . . certifie[d] the results of the election being contested," and it further held that in any such action, "the proper party defendant" was the canvassing board. Such language was controlling in these matters. "It would be hard to find," noted the brief, "language that more clearly indicate[d] the legislature's intent to provide for judicial review of the certification decision, as opposed to a *de novo* examination of each purportedly disputed ballot without regard to the certified judgment of the body whose statutory duty [was] to count the votes." Yet the Florida Supreme Court in its ruling completely ignored this clear legislative intent and imposed its own, unsubstantiated election procedures. "The resulting, judicially promulgated election scheme," argued the brief, thus not only flew "in the face of the specific language of the contest statute," but effectively "rendered all but irrelevant the detailed statutory provisions addressing when and how canvassing boards may conduct manual or other recounts." The consequence, once again, was "nothing less than the evisceration of the internal coherence of the legislature's design."[20] And with this evisceration, the demands of Article II were, once again, disregarded to the point of requiring a reversal by the U.S. Supreme Court.[21]

As for the Florida justices' defense of their action, of course the Florida Supreme Court majority had argued in its defense that they were merely "interpreting" existing state statute; this was nothing more than misdirection on their part, however. "Repeatedly," the Florida Supreme Court ruling made reference to its earlier, subsequently vacated, November 21 decision—a decision that based that court's authority to act on the Florida constitution, not on the election statutes. This was the source of the majority's claims for jurisdiction in these matters. Yet, as the U.S. Supreme Court had noted in its remand, "state constitutions cannot alter Article II's direct and exclusive grant of authority to legislatures." The only legitimate source of judicial action in these matters was state statute. This power was exclusive of any state constitutional provisions.[22] To argue, as Gore did, that the legislature somehow had "intended its statutory scheme to be 'supplemented' with appellate review provisions it chose *not* to include in the statute itself" was disingenuous. The Florida legislature had never delegated to the state supreme court the power to act as a court of equity in these matters. Hence, the brief concluded, "the Florida Supreme Court did not have jurisdiction or authority to decide this case." In fact, the brief noted as an aside, if any court had the authority to rule on this matter, it was the circuit court, the only court named by the Florida legislature to review election matters. And that court had ruled *against* Gore's contest.[23]

Turning to 3 U.S.C. §5, Bush's brief once again stressed the ways that the Florida Supreme Court's ruling had improperly changed the rules for conducting an election—in this instance, notably *after* the election itself was held. At issue here once again were the safe harbor provisions of 3 U.S.C. §5. Section 5, explained the brief, was a compact between the states and Congress intended to ensure that, by enacting laws before Election Day, states could resolve potential controversies or contests concerning presidential electors without the need for Congress to intervene actively in a presidential election. Indeed, "Congress [had] enacted §5 precisely to avoid a repetition of the near-cataclysmic result of its effort to resolve the presidential election of 1876." The Florida legislature, in turn, "in accordance with its exclusive authority vested by Article II," had "sought to obtain for the State of Florida and its voters the protections that §5 affords." Unfortunately, the Florida Supreme Court, despite the warnings by the U.S. Supreme Court that "it [was] not free to disregard the Florida Legislature's decision to secure for the citizens of Florida the benefits of §5," had done just that with its ruling.

Among the court-ordered deviations from or reversals of state statute were: (1) that existing laws did not authorize the Florida Supreme Court to order a statewide manual recount, which it had done; (2) that these laws provided for recounts by canvassing boards only rather than by the courts (and thus these bodies were rendered "superfluous" by the court's expansive interpretation of the contest statute); and (3) that they did not allow for recounts of only the undervoted ballots, as the court's orders did. Other deviations included (4) allowing courts rather than canvassing boards to determine the validity of a ballot along with (5) the circumstances under which manual recounts should or should not be conducted. Similarly, did these statutes allow (6) "dimpled" ballots to be counted as votes, (7) the courts to review some ballots *de novo* while not reviewing others at all, and/or (8) the courts to count votes after the seven-day deadline for certification? The answer, the brief noted, was no. Combining all these points, the brief concluded, it was hard to find a single aspect of the state statutes that the Florida Supreme Court's orders did not contravene.[24]

Bush's brief ended with its equal protection and due process arguments. Unlike the other two contentions, these arguments had never been argued before the U.S. Supreme Court with regard to these matters. Bush had raised them in his first Supreme Court petition for certiorari, but the justices had explicitly refused to consider them—presumably as being irrelevant to the issues raised by *Bush v. Palm*

Beach County Canvassing Board, but also perhaps because they did not know how to handle them were they argued.[25] Bush's other attempts to apply an equal protection/due process spin to these matters had also failed to gain any real traction with the lower-court judges who heard the arguments (Judge Middlebrooks in *Siegel v. LePore*, the judges of the 11th Circuit Court of Appeals in *Touchston v. McDermott*).[26] Recall that even Bush's own lawyers were concerned over the weakness of these arguments, noting that similar procedures to those under attack in Florida could be found in most of the other states. The Florida procedures even had the presumption of legitimacy provided by long use. Adding to the complexities, the scope of an equal protection or due process ruling in these matters was massive—potentially affecting the entire nation—which made the chance that the justices would adopt them all the more unlikely. Still, these arguments lay at the center of Bush's objections to the entire recount process—the irrationality and subjectivity of hand recounts—and, if five justices could be persuaded to listen and agree, these arguments could be the source of victory.

It was with this prospect in mind that Bush's lawyers argued that "the Florida Supreme Court's decision [was] a recipe for electoral chaos. The court below ha[d] not only condoned a regime of arbitrary, selective and standardless manual recounts, but . . . created a new series of unequal after-the-fact standards. This unfair, new process cannot be squared with the Constitution," the brief concluded. The Equal Protection Clause "prohibit[ed] government officials from implementing an electoral system that [gave] the votes of similarly situated voters different effect based on the happenstance of the county or district in which those voters live[d]." Yet this was exactly what the Florida vote counting system—especially as modified by the Florida Supreme Court—was doing. "The new electoral system created by the Florida Supreme Court [was] not facially neutral, but even if it were, the disparate treatment of voters based on the counties or geographic regions in which they live[d] would nonetheless violate the Constitution."[27] As the Supreme Court itself had noted in the redistricting case of *Reynolds v. Sims*, "diluting the weight of votes because of place of residence impairs basic constitutional rights under the Fourteenth Amendment just as much as invidious discriminations based upon factors such as race or economic status."[28]

As to due process, the Bush brief argued that "the Florida Supreme Court's radical departure from preexisting Florida law, and its failure to provide and apply clear and consistent guidelines to govern the manual recounts, also violate[d] the Due Process Clause." As previously noted in the brief, "the Florida Supreme Court ha[d] deviated substantially from the election law and practices in place prior to election day by ordering that the manual recount occur under circumstances and standards that [had] never before existed in Florida law, including fundamentally changing the meaning and legal consequences of certification of election results." Such an action clearly constituted a change in the rules in place when the election was held—"a plain violation of the Due Process Clause." So, too, was Florida's failure to "ensure that meaningful guidelines [were] established for determining whether and how to conduct such a recount, rather than leaving such crucial decisions to the unbridled discretion and arbitrary decisionmaking of local election officials."[29] Nor were additional recounts the answer to these problems. Simply carrying out additional "manual recounts, by another varying and inconsistent set of arbitrary 'standards,' . . . will simply compound the unfair and standardless methods that have been the hallmark of the Florida recount." No, once the rules had been set, they should stay set. Anything less than this simple rule threatened to violate the Due Process Clause.[30]

In conclusion, the Bush brief noted that no matter how one viewed the postelection process in Florida—either via statute or the Constitution, by practical standards or theoretical—the entire Florida recount mess demanded action from the Court. Any one of the three contentions laid out in the brief, Bush's lawyers insisted, was ground for reversal. Indeed, each of these contentions offered multiple grounds for reversal. In this, Bush was adopting the time-honored strategy of argument in the alternative. In essence, he was asking the justices to view each of these arguments—as well as their many sub-arguments—as separate issues, any one of which was adequate to prove Bush's case. In this way, all Bush had to do was win just one of his primary contentions—or even part of one—and he would prevail.

Faced with Bush's multilayered litigation strategy in which any one of Bush's arguments could be grounds for total victory, Gore's brief by necessity mirrored Bush's, question for question, argument for argument. Given Justice Scalia's ominous hints that Bush had already "won" the votes of five of the Court's members, Gore's lawyers had a lot of ground to cover if they were to draw at least one additional justice to his side. To do all this, Gore's attorneys adopted three related lines of argument. First, they sought to undermine the justices' strict reading of the *McPherson* case and of Article II's supposed "absolute" grant of authority to the state legislature in these matters, by arguing the implicit expandability of this grant and its inevitable inclusion of preexisting state constitutional imperatives. Second, they repeatedly cast Bush's objections to the Florida Supreme Court rulings as nothing more than a disagreement with that court's interpretation of state law, as opposed to a fundamentally different reading of that law. Finally, they warned the Court in no uncertain terms that any finding of an equal protection or due process violation in this matter would inevitably undermine election laws and procedures all across the country, setting off a constitutional crisis of untold proportions.[31]

The Gore team began their brief by reminding the Court of the big picture. At issue in this case were "fundamental questions about the legitimacy of political power in our democracy." Specifically, this case asked whether the "President of the United States himself, will be chosen by ascertaining the actual outcome of the popular vote in Florida," or instead "be chosen without counting all the ballots lawfully cast in that state." The Florida Supreme Court had determined—"in a way that would be unremarkable but for the stakes in this election"—that it was necessary to examine ballots that might have been "wrongfully excluded from the certified vote tally" so that the actual winner could be determined. Bush had questioned this effort, arguing that federal law and the Constitution precluded such a search for certainty. Gore challenged this latter reading of the law and the Constitution. And thus the crucial underlying question in this case was made clear. Did "any provision of federal law legitimately foreclose the Florida Supreme Court from interpreting, applying, and enforcing the statutes enacted by the Florida Legislature to determine all election contests and ascertain the actual outcome of the popular vote in any such election?"

Gore's answer to this question, needless to say, was no. The laws in question, and the Florida courts' interpretation of these laws, were unexceptional—similar in scope and form to those found in states across the nation. Most states had statutes expressly providing for "judicial determination" of any contest to determine the rightful winner of an election. Given this, how could the Florida Supreme Court's faithful application of Florida's "own state-law process for determining the rightful winner of its electoral votes in this Presidential election" demand anything less than the full support of the U.S. Supreme Court?[32]

Also at issue in this case, the Gore brief noted, was the necessity for federal judicial action. In his stay petition and subsequent brief, Bush had proposed that the "counting of [the] votes" may "cast . . . a cloud upon [his] claims to . . . the legitimacy of this election." It was on these grounds that Bush justified his request for judicial action. However, such was not the case in actual fact. Counting votes was not the problem. Rather, it was intervention by the U.S. Supreme Court that ran "an impermissible risk of tainting the result of the election in Florida—and thereby the nation." For years "this Court" had championed the fundamental right of all who were qualified to cast their votes "and to have their votes counted."[33] Granting Bush's "request that this Court intervene in a state electoral process to ensure that votes [were] not counted" turned this standard "on its head." Like it or not, the votes were going to be counted. "The only question [was] whether these votes [would] be counted before the Electoral College [met] to select the next President, or whether this Court will instead relegate them to be counted only by scholars and researchers under Florida's sunshine laws, after the next President [was] elected." Gore's preference was to count now and not later. "Nothing in federal law, the United States Constitution, or the opinions of this Court compel it to choose the second course over the first," the brief declared.[34]

Turning to the substance of Bush's contentions, Gore's brief challenged Bush's "primary argument to this Court, that the mere assertion of appellate jurisdiction by the Florida Supreme Court violated Article II"—an assertion that, the brief noted, was "flatly contrary to petitioners' position in the Florida courts." This claim misread the article and its objectives. In fact, such a reading proposed "a radical new proposition in the name of Article II: that the highest appellate court of the state may not exercise its ordinary appellate jurisdiction over decisions of lower state courts where its jurisdiction [was] granted by the state constitution rather than in legislation dealing specifically with presidential elections." Article II, Section 1, clause 2, explained the brief, "presuppose[d] the existence of authority in each state to structure the internal processes and organization of each of its governmental branches; judicial review and interpretation of Florida's election statutes [was] a necessary legislative assumption" for Article II to make any sense. Logic and experience demanded such a reading.[35] So too did a close reading of *McPherson v. Blacker.* The only real source for the theory of legislative exclusivity in these matters was a single passage in *McPherson v. Blacker,* and that passage itself was dictum. Moreover, two other passages in *McPherson* made clear that once a state legislature passed laws establishing the manner of appointing electors, "the state courts may interpret those laws precisely as they would any other state legislative enactment."[36] After all, the Florida legislature itself had "drafted, proposed, and approved . . . the very provisions of its constitution that provide for appellate jurisdiction" in these matters.[37]

Yet, even supposing such a theoretical reading did not provide enough proof of intent, statutory authority for appellate review existed as well. In 1999, the Florida legislature had "re-enacted the [State's] contest statute . . . against the settled background rule that decisions of circuit courts in contest actions [were] subject to appellate review." By that time, it was settled doctrine under Florida law that "legislative provisions granting jurisdiction to the Circuit Court, *without any express limitations,* [were] always taken to include appellate review [emphasis added]." Hence, when the statute referred to the "circuit courts" in Section 102.168, "the Legislature necessarily intended to encompass the ordinary accouterments of appellate review of circuit court decisions."[38]

This reading of the statutory history was reinforced by the current Florida legislature's own actions in filing an amicus brief "in the Palm Beach County matter." As part of that case, the legislature's brief "expressly" recognized the jurisdiction of the state's supreme court to review lower-court rulings involving the presidential election. ("Florida has in place an election code for the resolution of disputes and a court system, *including a Supreme Court,* with the usual judicial powers of such courts.") Hence, the Gore brief noted, "the statute itself supplie[d] the necessary authority for review here."[39]

The Gore brief next responded to another Article II argument proposed by Bush—namely that "when a state legislature exercise[d] its 'plenary authority' under Article II, it must write specific rules to govern only that unique exercise of authority." Gore disagreed. At no time did Article II require "that all the provisions bearing on the selection of presidential electors be located exclusively in a separate statute devoted solely to that end." All that was required was that the legislature determine the process by which presidential elections would be carried out. It specifically did not "require that the legislature must act by enacting a bill into law, as opposed to other means of direction." To demand such an exclusive process was "both unjustified and unrealistic." Rather, when "a legislature decide[d] to hold an election to select Presidential electors, it typically assume[d] that all of the laws, rules, and regulations contained in the state election code [would] be applicable." This was both the norm nationwide and the rule in Florida.[40]

Defending the Florida Supreme Court's actual rulings, Gore's brief noted how "Petitioners . . . impugn[ed] the Florida Supreme Court in general terms, arguing that it violated Article II when it 'substituted its judgment for that of the legislature' and 'rewr[ote] th[e] statutory scheme' governing the appointment of presidential electors in various respects." This, once again, was an improper reading of the facts. Unlike the earlier Supreme Court case of *Bush v. Palm Beach County Canvassing Board*, "the Florida Supreme Court's opinion [in *Harris v. Gore*] ma[d]e clear that it did not rely upon the Florida Constitution . . . in construing the election law." Instead, the "court based its interpretation on entirely conventional tools of statutory construction, including statutory text, traditional canons, and relevant precedents." In other words, "it engaged in altogether routine statutory interpretation."

Finally, the Gore brief reminded the justices that "the process of statutory construction . . . [involved] determining how to resolve issues that [were] not conclusively determined by the language of the statute." As such, adaptations to the specific reach of the statute were inevitable as the courts extended the statute to cover new or unique situations. Consequently, when Bush took the position that "if an issue [was] not explicitly and unambiguously addressed in the language of the statute or in a prior decision that [was] precisely on point, then the court ha[d] usurped the Legislature's constitutionally delegated power," he misread the entire purpose and meaning of judicial review. More to the point, "nothing in Article II so limits the courts' authority. Indeed, the fact that the provisions for election contests in Section 102.168 appl[ied] broadly to all elections confirm[ed] the Legislature's intent that the courts [were] to exercise their usual role as neutral umpires who interpret[ed] the law to resolve disputes."

Taking up the safe harbor provisions of 3 U.S.C. §5, Gore's brief began by noting how "Section 5 constituted *only* a safe harbor from a challenge in Congress to a state's slate of electors [emphasis added]." Section 5 was an internal rule by which the Houses of Congress determined "which electors for President of the United States from a particular State will be entitled to have their votes counted if more than one return purporting to contain the electoral votes of that State [was] received by the President of the Senate." That was all it did. So long as the rules applied were set in place by Election Day, the safe harbor provisions were irrelevant to these proceedings. And irrelevant they were, "because the decision below did not constitute a change in Florida law."

In fact, despite Bush's insistence that the Florida Supreme Court was over-stepping its bounds and making new law with its rulings, a close view of that court's actions painted a very different picture. First and foremost, "the decision below [was] in all respects entirely [consistent] with longstanding Florida election law." None of the doctrines applied to these matters was new or unique; rather, all grew out of long-existing, oft-used judicial precedents.[41] Second, whereas the "petitioners assert[ed] that the decision below conflict[ed] with a 1992 Florida appellate decision describing the discretion of a canvassing board to hold a manual recount in a protest proceeding," in reality, the cited decision went the other way. *Gore v. Harris* was a contest case; at issue in the 1992 case was a protest. The difference was significant. Whereas county canvassing boards had significant discretion and authority to act in a protest recount, they were peripheral players in contests.[42] Finally, "Petitioners allege[d] that the Florida Supreme Court changed the law by adopting a statewide standard requiring that 'dimpled' ballots" be included in "recount proceedings." This argument as a whole was "disingenuous." For one thing, in *Gore v. Harris*, Bush had argued how "in a contest of a statewide election, a statewide recount [was] required by the Equal Protection Clause of the U.S. Constitution and Florida Statute Section 102.168." More to the point, Bush neglected to reconcile the contention that statewide recounts were a change in the law "with [his] due process and equal protection theories that the [Florida Supreme] court's decision [was] unconstitutional because it supposedly fail[ed] to adopt standards for determining voter intent." In essence, Bush was arguing that statewide recounts were necessary, but that any attempt to adopt a uniform rule to count those votes was a change in the law and thus impermissible.

Taken together, Bush's safe harbor arguments demanding that "courts faced with an election controversy may not provide an 'answer . . . created after Election Day'" distorted the "normal application of state election laws," especially "given the necessarily retroactive nature of [all] judicial decisionmaking." Worse yet, application of this "theory would require constant federal judicial superintendence over state procedures and state court rulings in Presidential elections. Federal judges would be called on to examine supposed inconsistencies between different rulings in a never-ending search for what law really [was] 'new' and what law [was] 'old.'" Considered as a whole, "the range of settled practices that would be drawn into question by petitioners' argument, or that would draw the availability of the 3 U.S.C. §5 in question, [was] little short of staggering." Clearly, none of this was what Congress had in mind when it adopted the use of the safe harbor provision.

The Gore brief concluded by confronting Bush's equal protection and due process arguments. Gore's brief held firm that the Florida Supreme Court's ruling contained or caused no violations of the Equal Protection Clause. Bush had based his argument on two supposed errors by the Florida court. First, that it had "erred by ordering a statewide manual count of undervotes, thereby supposedly discriminating against those whose votes were counted by automated means." Second, that "the inclusion for a manual recount of approximately 9000 undervotes from Miami-Dade County caused some votes to be counted twice and others to be counted using standards different from those applied to other Miami-Dade County votes." Neither allegation, explained the brief, had merit.

For one thing, Gore questioned Bush's right even to raise such arguments before the U.S. Supreme Court. For an appellant argument to be deemed appropriate for inclusion in an appeal, the petitioner needed to have "preserved the error" in the lower court proceedings. This means that they needed to have challenged the issue in the court below before they could argue it before the higher court. As far as Gore's brief was concerned, Bush had failed to preserve the error as related to equal protection and due process. "It is important to appreciate the narrowness of the Fourteenth Amendment claim raised by petitioners before the Florida Supreme Court," noted the brief. Bush had "argued (in only one throwaway line, no less) that 'the application of counting standards in different counties as well as the occurrence of manual recounts in only selected counties or selective portions of counties violates the equal protection and due process clauses of the U.S. Constitution.'" That was it: one line, an afterthought. Should this throwaway argument be grounds for further appellate review? Gore argued no.

As to the substance of Bush's Fourteenth Amendment arguments, Gore's brief noted that they rested "principally on the assertion that, if the manual count proceed[ed], similar ballots [would] be treated dissimilarly in different parts of the State." Leaving aside that Bush had had his own chances to contest any recount he felt was improperly carried out, Gore questioned the legal foundations of this argument. "The court below was quite insistent that the counting of ballots must be governed by a *single* uniform standard: the intent of the voter must control," the brief read. Where was the unequal treatment? Of course, Gore conceded, so long as a vote count was "conducted by humans," there was the undeniable possibility "of inconsistency in the treatment of individual ballots." However, this was the case "whenever the application of any legal standard (*e.g.*, negligence, public forum) [was] at issue." In fact, the potential for inconsistency was present "in *every* one of the many jurisdictions that provide for manual recounts; it [was] true whenever States provide[d] for variation in the methods of voting from county to county (*e.g.*, optical scanners as opposed to less reliable punch card ballots), which [was] now the case in *every* State; and it was true *everywhere* prior to the introduction of mechanical voting machines, when all ballots were counted by hand." Bush's equal protection theory, in other words, was so broad that, should it be applied, "all of these practices violate[d] the Fourteenth Amendment." Of course, Bush could have meant "to say that all votes must be tabulated under a fixed and mechanical standard (*e.g.*, the 'two-corner chad rule')"; however, this "approach would render unconstitutional the laws of [those] States that hinge[d] the meaning of the ballot on the intent of the voter." Worse yet, it would also "mean that the Constitution require[d] the disenfranchisement of many voters whose intent [was] clearly discernible."

Turning to Bush's specific equal protection complaints, Gore's brief stressed how the Florida Supreme Court's order to review the approximately 9,000 uncounted Miami-Dade ballots "was consistent with established state law for handling contest actions" and as such, raised "no substantial federal questions." If anything, it was "the exclusion of these ballots, not their inclusion, that . . . raise[d] questions of unequal treatment." All the Florida Supreme Court had done was "place the voters whose votes were not tabulated by the machine on the same footing as those whose votes were so tabulated." Thus, in the end, "all voters [were] treated equally: ballots that reflect[ed] their intent [were] counted." What did it matter if that intent was "captured by a machine tabulation or one performed by election officials?"

The same arguments held sway as to the statewide manual recount of undervotes. Here the brief noted only that the court-mandated recount was, in fact, statewide. In this, the Florida Supreme Court was simply agreeing with Bush's argument that Florida statutes "require[d] a counting of the legal votes contained within the undervotes in *all counties* where the undervote has not been subjected to a manual tabulation." So where was the quandary? More to the point, under this system, all undervotes were treated in exactly the same way by the Florida Supreme Court's order—all undervotes were to be hand-counted under an "intent of the voter" standard. Hence, once again, where was the equal protection violation?[43]

As for the validity of the voter intent standard, the use of a voter intent standard was, in fact, well established in Florida law. Not only was it written into law by the legislature—many "Florida canvassing boards and courts [had] long implemented that standard, and vote totals certified in this and many previous elections reflect[ed] countless ballots manually recounted under this same standard." Indeed, "the Secretary of State's November 14 certification included numerous manually counted votes for petitioners, including vote totals from heavily Republican counties." Bush's contention that a voter intent standard somehow violated the Fourteenth Amendment was thus, at root, nothing less than an attack on hand recounts of any sort, uncalled for and unnecessary. "Manual counting and recounting of ballots under the intent of the voter standard ha[d] been the *rule*, not the exception, in this country for generations—indeed, for most of the period since its founding," explained the Gore brief.[44]

If Bush had complaints about the "treatment of particular ballots . . . in particular locations," Florida procedures offered an available, "perfectly suitable" remedy. Bush could present his complaints "to the circuit court . . . on appeal." But rather than "invoke that traditional remedy," Bush was demanding that "the Court abruptly end the counting altogether and *toss out lawfully cast ballots that have been, and are now being, counted.*" This was "an absurd and unprecedented response to an asserted flaw in the process for tabulating votes, and one that surely [was] not required by the U.S. Constitution." If there was anything to Bush's equal protection claims, "the remedy [was] not to end the counting of votes," but rather "to articulate the proper standards and—as required by state law—to have the counting go forward under that standard."[45]

Bush's due process arguments also lacked merit, the Gore brief maintained. For one thing, although Bush claimed many cases of different counting standards in different counties, he failed to substantiate them with facts and documentation. All he could offer was "unconfirmed rumors and untested accusations." Meanwhile, the actual recount process in Florida had proceeded in an "orderly and uniform fashion" up to the Supreme Court's stay order. Far from undermining the viability of the electoral process, "Florida's manual recount system act[ed] as an important check on the ballot counting process that promote[d], not Erode[d], public trust in the electoral system"—conducted "in full public view by counting teams made up of representatives from different political parties, with the supervision of a three-member canvassing board that include[d] a sitting county judge and review by the Florida judiciary." What more could Bush demand from an electoral system? In point of fact, adopting Bush's arguments "would have the unthinkable consequences of (i) overturning the settled 'intent of the voter' standard; (ii) invalidating the entire election in Florida, . . . and (iii) calling into question numerous other results nationwide in a host of local, state, and national elections."

To the extent that Bush's due process claims rested on a claim that the Florida Supreme Court somehow had changed the rules retroactively, "that argument . . . fail[ed] for reasons already discussed . . . [namely] the law enunciated in the Florida Supreme Court's opinion [was] the law as it existed on election day and long before it." Yet even if this were not the case, rulings by a state supreme court were not normally invalidated simply for being retroactive in their impact. Such rulings also had to be "arbitrary and irrational." Bush, in turn, had failed to show this necessary component in regards to the Florida Supreme Court's ruling.

Ironically, concluded the brief, "the only due process right even arguably implicated by this case [was] the right of voters to have their ballots counted, a consideration that strongly support[ed] the state supreme court's decision," not attacked it.[46] In the end, all that Bush could legitimately do was claim that, "in their view, the Florida Supreme Court got Florida law wrong." However, a "'mere error of state law' was not a denial of due process." To hold that the Florida justices' ruling somehow violated due process did "violence both to principles of federalism and to the independence of the judiciary throughout the United States." It invited an onslaught of cases by losing parties in state courts "alleging that the decisions in their cases constituted an unconstitutional departure from 'preexisting law.'" And it undermined "the authority of the judiciary to decide the meaning of law, by holding that apparently routine judicial acts of statutory construction long thought to involve only questions of state law in fact amount[ed] to illegitimate and unconstitutional usurpations of the legislative role."[47]

December 11, 2000. 11:00 a.m. The U.S. Supreme Court. The final public act of the 2000 presidential postelection controversy opened with Chief Justice Rehnquist praising all sides in the case for "their exemplary briefing under very trying circumstances." With the arguments laid out before them, the justices were set to grill the lawyers. As had been the case when these parties had last argued before the High Court, the justices came to the hearings with specific questions in mind. Most dealt with the issue of federal jurisdiction and the practical difficulties associated with recounting votes. In fact, despite Gore's attempt to stress the centrality of Florida law in these matters, from the start of questioning it was clear that it was federal law and practical vote counting, and not the details of Florida law, that were on the justices' minds.

First up was Ted Olson for George W. Bush.[48] Olson began by summarizing what had become the Bush mantra on court-ordered recounts: the state supreme court had overstepped its authority by changing "statutory deadlines, severely limit[ing] the discretion of the state's chief election officer, chang[ing] the meaning of words such as 'shall' and 'may' into 'shall not' and 'may not,' and authoriz[ing] extensive standardless and unequal manual ballot recounts in selected Florida counties." Worse yet, their most recent ruling had "issued a new, wholesale postelection revision of Florida's election law." Yet before he could get out much more than this introductory summary, in fact, a mere fifty-four seconds into his prepared argument, the questioning began.

Justice Kennedy was concerned with the Court's jurisdiction. "Can you begin by telling us our federal jurisdiction," he asked. "Where's the federal question here?" Olson pointed to Article II of the Constitution and to 3 U.S.C. §5. Kennedy wanted more. "It seems to me essential to the republican theory of government that the Constitutions of the United States and the states are the basic charter. And to say that the Legislature of the state is unmoored from its own Constitution and it can't use its courts and it can't use its executive agency . . . seems to me a holding which has grave implications for our republican theory of government." Choosing to focus on the second half of Kennedy's question, rather than the more troubling first clause, Olson agreed that a state could, if the legislature chose to do so, use both the executive and judicial branches in supervising parts of the state's electoral process. For example, Olson noted, the state election code required "the secretary of state to assure uniformity and consistency in the application and enforcement of the election law." Then there were the contest provisions that vested authority in the circuit courts of Florida. Asked by Justice O'Connor if the use of the circuit court did not impute an appellate authority to the state supreme court, Olson demurred. The legislature's grant was to the trial courts. They could have granted appellate power in these matters to the state supreme court, but chose not to do so.

Justice Kennedy remained unsatisfied with Olson's answers. He was particularly troubled by Olson's suggestion that the Florida Supreme Court had no jurisdiction over the case simply because it had founded its jurisdiction on the state constitution. This attempt to "unmoor" the legislature from the state constitution struck him as potentially dangerous.[49] Justice O'Connor seconded this point. She preferred to think that Article II "created a presumption that the scheme the legislature has set out will be followed, even by judicial review in election matters," but that it did not create a question of federal enforcement that somehow barred "judicial review here in Florida."

Faced with such strong objections from two justices whom he viewed as being on Bush's side, Olson began to back away from his strict reading of Article II and 3 U.S.C. §5. "It may not be the most powerful argument we bring to this court," Olson admitted, to which Justice Kennedy responded, "I think that's right." Olson responded quietly that "it would have been perfectly logical . . . especially in the context of a presidential election, to stop this process at the circuit court and not provide layers of appeal because, given the time deadlines, especially in the context of this election the way it's played out, there is not time for an appellate. . . ." At this point, Olson stopped and stood quietly. Finally, after being pressed by Justice O'Connor, Olson retreated: "I think that the argument we presented and amplified in our briefs is a good argument. It's a solid argument. It is consistent with the way the code is set up, and it's particularly consistent with the timetable that's available in presidential election."

Justice Ginsburg addressed the judicial review issue from a different angle. Pointing to Bush's use of *McPherson v. Blacker* to justify an exclusive grant of authority to the state legislature in picking presidential electors—and the affiliated argument that this grant prohibited any appellate review of these rules and procedures—Ginsburg noted, "Two things strike me about that case; one is, if you're right on your jurisdiction theory, then should not this court have vacated, instead of affirmed, the decision of the Michigan Supreme Court in that case [*McPherson*]? Because the Michigan Legislature didn't confer upon the Michigan Supreme Court in that case any special authority of judicial review?" After all, "there was a decision by the court reviewing, which we affirmed. Under your jurisdiction theory, as I see it, there was no role for the Michigan Supreme Court to play because Article II, Section 1, gives the authority exclusively to the Legislature and the Legislature had not provided for judicial review specially for that measure."

Olson agreed with Justice Ginsburg that *McPherson* was "not the most clearly written opinion." However, he explained, "I think that . . . the relationship of the Legislature to the Constitution in that case and the way that power was exercised . . . can be reconciled with what we're urging the court today, that a wholesale revision and abandonment of the legislative authority can't be turned over, especially *sub silencio*, by a legislature simply because there is a constitution." What the Florida Supreme Court had done was to effectuate a "major, major revision," and this was clearly not acceptable under any reading of Article II.

This declaration brought Justice Stevens into the discussion. "But Mr. Olson," he asked, "isn't that one of the issues in the case, as to whether it was a major revision? Your opponents disagree. And I know you rely very heavily on the dissenting opinion in the Florida supreme court. But which opinion do we normally look to for issues of state law?" Caught out by the question (the correct answer was the majority justices, not the dissenters), Olson fell back on Bush's list of judicial usurpations, among them, that "after the decision of Dec. 8, . . . [the state's] manual recount provisions became mandatory instead of discretionary, . . . pursuant to *ad hoc*, judicially established procedures rather than the procedures that are articulated quite carefully in the statute." Justice Souter now pressed Olson on this point. "Well, aren't *ad hoc*, judicially created procedures the point of subsection 8 of 168? I mean, once we get into the contest phase, subsection 8 gives, at least to the Circuit Court, leaving aside the question of appellate jurisdiction, about as broad a grant to fashion orders as I can imagine going into a statute." Olson acknowledged that Subsection 8 was written broadly, but contended that the larger "statutory framework" precluded such action. To interpret Section 168 to permit the Florida court's action meant violating other parts of the act, including Section 166, that had vested recount authority in elections officials, not the courts. In fact, reading the statutes "the way the Florida Supreme Court did . . . [leaves] the entire process . . . tilted on its head." Justice Souter was not convinced, replying, "You've convinced us, certainly, that there is a disagreement about how it should be construed. But I don't quite see where you cross the line into saying that this had simply become a nonjudicial act. It may or may not be good statutory construction, but I don't see it as a nonjudicial act."

Trapped by this question, Olson shifted his argument to 3 U.S.C. §5 and its "timetable" for action. "We submit that [the Florida Supreme Court] had incorrectly interpreted and construed federal law in [allowing for a statewide recount], because what they have inevitably done [by their ruling] is provide a process whereby it is virtually impossible, if not completely impossible, . . . to have these issues . . . and the controversies resolved in time for that federal statutory deadline." In fact, as Olson had just explained, the Florida justices had "wrenched [the §5 timetables] completely out of the election code, which the Legislature very carefully crafted to fit together and work in an interrelated fashion." Still unconvinced, Souter asked Olson, "Well, if your concern was with impossibility, why didn't you let the process run instead of asking for a stay?" Olson's answer pointed once again to Article II and 3 U.S.C. §5: "I believe that there's a very firm basis for saying that that process already had violated Article II of the Constitution. It was also already throwing in jeopardy compliance with Section 5 of Title 3 because the laws had been changed in a number of different respects." Timetables, Olson noted, "are important."

Confused that Olson had not yet raised any equal protection or due process defenses, and perhaps viewing equal protection as a grounds for action by the Court, Justice Kennedy queried: "I thought your point was that the process is being conducted in violation of the Equal Protection Clause, because it's standardless." This brought Justice Breyer into the discussion. Breyer had hopes of finding a middle-ground consensus in equal protection, one that could garner five or more votes and yet still allow for the vote counting in Florida to continue. In a time-honored practice among the justices, Breyer proposed a compromise to his fellow justices in the form of a question to Olson. Noting how Bush had complained about the Florida court's "intent of the voter" standard and its lack of any uniform standards, Breyer asked Olson to advise the Court what a "fair" standard might be.[50] As one might expect, Olson was understandably hesitant to articulate a standard lest the justices adopt it as a "cure" to the equal protection problem, but Justice Breyer repeatedly insisted on an answer. Finally, Olson answered that, at a minimum, "penetration of the ballot card would be required." Justice O'Connor then wondered if a good starting place for uniformity might be what "the secretary of state decreed for uniformity." Olson quickly agreed that she would be a good source of authority for setting a uniform standard, but that "she had not set one." But could she have set one, asked Justice Kennedy, especially during the contest phase? While admitting he had not thought out the §5 implications of this, Olson agreed that the secretary of state could act even in the contest period.

Intrigued by this answer, Justice Souter piped in. What if "this were remanded to the Leon County Circuit Court and the judge of that court addressed the secretary of state, like it either is or could be made a party, and said, 'Please tell us what the standard ought to be. We will be advised by your opinion.' That would be feasible, wouldn't it?" Olson responded that that would be a "feasible" outcome. After a short interlude in which Justice Breyer pushed Olson to define a "fair standard" and Justice Ginsburg questioned Olson's refusal to accept the circuit judge's powers to fashion a remedy—for which she "couldn't imagine a greater conferral of authority by the Legislature to the circuit judge"—Justice Souter returned to his earlier point. "Is it your position that if any official, judicial or executive, at this point were to purport to lay down a statewide standard which went to a lower level, a more specific level than intent of the voter, and said, for example, 'Count dimpled chads or don't count dimpled chad[s].' In your judgment would that be a violation of Article II?" To the surprise of many, Olson seemed willing to accept the theoretical possibility of a court-ordered statewide uniform standard. "I don't think it would be a violation of Article II provided that [dimpled chads were not counted]," Olson replied.

Olson immediately realized his mistake and backtracked, noting, "If we went from the standard that existed before, the dimpled chads that hadn't been a standard anywhere in Florida—if that change was made, we would strongly urge that that would be a violation of Article II. It would be a complete change." Still, the concession had been made. At this point, Justice Scalia jumped into the argument, "almost," as a writer for the *New York Times* put it, "as if to make sure that Mr. Olson did not make any unnecessary concession on that Bush side."[51] "Mr. Olson," the justice asked, "it is also a part of your case, is it not, that insofar as that language you just quoted is concerned, the power of the circuit judge to prevent or correct any alleged wrong, [may be true, but] . . . that there is no wrong when a machine does not count those ballots that it's not supposed to count?" And further, continued Scalia, was it not also true that "when the voters are instructed to detach the chads entirely, and the machine, as predicted, does not count those chads, where those instructions are not followed, there isn't any wrong." A grateful Olson responded: "That's absolutely correct, Justice Scalia."

With this exchange, Olson reserved the rest of his time and passed the podium to Joseph Klock, arguing for Katherine Harris and the state canvassing commission. After a few words on the issue of time constraints—which Klock argued were federal in nature and which the Florida legislature had clearly shown a desire to abide by—Justice Souter asked Klock, "if there were to be a uniform standard laid down . . . by the Leon County Circuit Court, or in any other valid way, in your judgment, what should the substantive standard be?" Klock's response was to hold firm to the "instructions" given to all voters, namely, that to count a ballot must have a fully removed chad. Yes, Justice Breyer replied, but we are not asking what Florida law requires now, but what standard would suffice under an equal protection perspective. Klock refused to take the bait. The only standard he would accept was the fully removed chad. People need to follow the instructions, he insisted. "The only problem that we have here," concluded Klock, "is created by people who did not follow instructions." But, asked Justice Stevens, what if there was machine error involved in uncounted ballots? Would it not then be acceptable for a court to use the "intent of the voter" standard, which the legislature had expressly chosen, at least in the context of damaged or defective ballots? Klock's answer, made through a round of laughter as he misnamed both Justice Stevens (naming him Justice Brennan, who had died in 1997) and Souter (calling him Justice Breyer) was that "there could be problems under [that statutory standard]." In any event, it "was designed for a very limited situation where there was a problem with the mechanism of voting." At this point, before Justice Stevens had the chance to push further, Klock's time was up.[52]

Now it was David Boies's turn. Gore's lead attorney did not even have Olson's fifty-four seconds free of questions in which to frame his arguments. Just five seconds into Boies's time, Justice Kennedy raised, once again, the issue of jurisdiction. "The Supreme Court of Florida," Justice Kennedy noted, "said that it . . . was cognizant . . . of 3 U.S.C. Section 5.. . . when the [Florida] Supreme Court used that word, I assume it used it in a legal sense. 'Cognizance' means to take jurisdiction of, to take authoritative notice. Why doesn't that constitute an acceptance by the [Florida] Supreme Court of the proposition that 3 U.S.C. Section 5 must be interpreted in this case?" Boies disagreed with this reading of the Florida court's wording. As he saw it, "cognizant" in this instance meant that the Florida justices were simply "taking into account the [Florida Legislature's] desire to get the election over in time so that everyone would have the advantage of a safe harbor." This was not interpreting the law, nor even applying it (both grounds for federal review), Boies explained, but simply noting the consequences of not abiding by the law's mandates. Apparently searching for a more definite basis for the Court's jurisdiction, Kennedy pressed further: "it seems to me that if the Florida court, and presumably the Florida Legislature have acted with reference to 3 U.S.C. §5 that it presents now a federal question for us to determine whether or not there is or is not a new law by reason of the . . . two Florida Supreme Court decisions." Boies still disagreed. He acknowledged that the Florida court "desired" to fit within Section 5, especially its "deadline," but he did not concede that the Florida court had "interpreted" the federal statute. "I think it [the Florida Supreme Court's ruling] does not reflect a desire to change the law or in any way affect what the substantive law is."

Still unsatisfied with the answers he was receiving, Justice Kennedy tried a different tack. What if the Florida legislature had shortened the contest phase by nineteen days. Would this not constitute "a new law under Section 5 . . . under our preclearance jurisprudence?" Further, could we not assume that if "the Legislature would run contrary to the new law prohibition in the statute" by such actions, "wouldn't the Supreme Court do" so as well "if it [did] exactly the same thing?" Not quite the same, Boies responded. The state supreme court "wasn't passing a new law, it was interpreting the existing law." Are you trying to say, asked Kennedy somewhat sarcastically, that "if the Legislature does it, it's a new law, and when the Supreme Court does it, it isn't?" No responded Boies.

What I'm saying, Your Honor, is that if the Supreme Court had rewritten the law the way you hypothesized the Legislature rewrote the law, it might very well be a difference. [However], . . . the Florida Supreme Court did not rewrite the law. . . . What the Florida Supreme Court said is we have to look at what is the criteria by which you decide whether you may ignore and will ignore these returns? And what the Florida Supreme Court said is we're going to interpret that exactly the way we've interpreted it for 25 years.

Granted, the Court might legitimately find such a "change," Boies argued, if it concluded that the Florida court's interpretation was "either a sham or . . . so misguided that it is simply untenable in any sense." Otherwise, Boies said, the standard ought to be the one the Court had "generally applied in giving deference to state supreme court decisions," and the Florida court was certainly worthy of that deference.

This last statement brought Justice O'Connor into the discussion. O'Connor, a former state legislator from Arizona, was deeply troubled by what she saw as disrespect on the part of the Florida Supreme Court for the state legislature. But was this court due any deference, she asked, especially "in light of Article II"? "I'm not so sure," O'Connor continued. "Does that not mean that a court has to, in interpreting a legislative act, give special deference to the legislature's choices insofar as a presidential election is concerned? I would think that is a tenable view, anyway, and especially in light also of the concerns about Section 5." Boies was willing to consent to the general point. "I think the court needs to take into account the fact that the Legislature does have this plenary power. I think when the Florida Supreme Court does that, if it does so within the normal ambit of judicial interpretation, that is a subject for Florida's Supreme Court to take." O'Connor was not satisfied with this answer. She wondered if Boies's standard did not sufficiently account for the special role conferred on state legislatures by Article II. "You are responding as though there were no special burden to show some deference to legislative choices in this one context, not when courts review laws generally for general elections, but in the context of selection of presidential electors. . . . Isn't there a big red flag up there, [saying] 'Watch out'?" Stated as such, this was a hard proposition with which to argue, and Boies did not even try. Asked if he thought that the Florida Supreme Court had acted properly in regard to the legislature's special role in selecting presidential electors, Boies simply answered yes.

Boies's candor in this matter brought an unexpected, and informative, response from Justice O'Connor, one hinting strongly as to how she viewed the entire crisis. In response to Boies's agreement that the court had acted properly, O'Connor responded: "That's, I think, a concern that we have. And I did not find, really, a response by the Florida Supreme Court to this court's remand in the case a week ago. It just seemed to kind of bypass it and assume that all those changes and deadlines were just fine and they'd go ahead and adhere to them. And I found that troublesome."

This statement of pique, in turn, initiated a round of dialogue between Boies and Justice Scalia on the Florida Supreme Court's failure to abide by the Court's rule vacating the extension of the certification deadline. The Florida court had "contravened our vacating of their prior order" by ordering the "certification" of the votes identified by the Palm Beach and Miami-Dade boards, Scalia complained. Boies agreed that changes had been ordered, but held that this was normal in a contest. "The contest procedure is a procedure to contest the certification. What you're doing is you're saying this certification is wrong, change it. That's what every contest proceeding is. And what the Florida Supreme Court was saying after this trial is, yes, you proved that this certification is missing 215 votes." In fact, Boies continued, "that is what happens every time there is a successful contest."

At this point, the hearing could have denigrated into a debate on the details of the Florida recount, as both Justice Scalia and Breyer—along with Chief Justice Rehnquist—asked ever-more-detailed questions about the "extra" votes from South Florida included in the certified totals by the Florida court's ruling. Justice Kennedy, however, brought the key issues (as he saw them) back into focus by asking Boies: "Do you think that in the contest phase, there must be a uniform standard for counting the ballots?" Boies responded yes, and that standard was "whether or not the intent of the voter is reflected by the ballot." "That's very general," a clearly dissatisfied Kennedy retorted.

> It runs throughout the law. Even a dog knows the difference in being stumbled over and being kicked. We know it. Now, in this case, what we're concerned with is an intent that focuses on this little piece of paper called a ballot. And you would say that from the standpoint of the equal protection clause [that] . . . each county [could] give their own interpretation to what intent means, so long as they are in good faith and with some reasonable basis finding intent? . . . Could that vary from county to county?

Answering immediately, and perhaps not fully thinking his answer through, Boies replied: "I think it can vary from individual to individual." The answer was apparently so abrupt that Justice Kennedy asked another version of the same question: "so that even in one county [it] can vary from table to table on counting these ballots?" Boies set about explaining what he meant. Some variations were inevitable "on the margin." Any effort to interpret intent, "whether it is in the criminal law, in administrative practice, [or] whether it is in local government," would produce some variations. Granted, Boies explained in response to Kennedy's continuing pressing, ballot-counting was "susceptible of a more specific standard" of intent. Yet, in every state that had attempted to adopt more specific standards of intent, such as Texas, they still were forced by necessity to adopt a "catch-all" provision that allowed for the inclusion of ballots in which "anything else that clearly specifies the intent of the voter" was present.

Justice Souter reentered the discussion, expressing discomfort with Boies's answers.

> I think what's bothering Justice Kennedy, and it's bothering a lot of us here, is we seem to have a situation here in which there is a subcategory of ballots in which, we're assuming for the sake of argument since we know no better, there is no genuinely subjective indication beyond what can be viewed as either a dimple or a hanging chad. And there is a general rule being applied in a given county that an objective intent, or an intent on an objective standard, will be inferred. And that objective rule varies, we're told, from county to county. Why shouldn't there be one objective rule for all counties, and if there isn't, why isn't it an equal protection violation?

When Boies tried to argue that the counties in Florida were not actually applying different "objective standards" to the same physical characteristics, Souter asked if "we [were to] assume as a fact that there may be variations, wouldn't those variations, from county to county, on objective standards, be an equal protection violation?" Boies's answer to this was no. "I think there are a lot of times in the law in which there can be those variations, from jury to jury, from public official to public official," Boies responded. Yes, returned Souter,

> but in jury to jury cases, we assume that there is not an overall objective standard that answers all questions definitively. We are assuming that there is detail that cannot be captured by an objective rule. The assumption of this question, and I think it's behind what's bothering Justice Kennedy, Justice Breyer, me, and others, is we're assuming there's a category in which there just is . . . no subjective appeal. All we have are certain physical characteristics. Those physical characteristics, we are told, are being treated differently from county to county. In that case, where there is no subjective counterindication, isn't it a denial of equal protection to allow that variation?

Boies's answer, once again, was that the counties were not using differing "objective standards." But what if they were? Souter pressed: "We can't send this thing back for more fact-finding. If we respond to this issue and we believe that the issue is at least sufficiently raised to require a response, we've got to make the assumption, I think, at this stage, that there may be such variation, and I think we would have a responsibility to tell the Florida courts what to do about it. On that assumption, what would you tell them to do about it?"

This was a question that Boies could not avoid. It was also a dangerous question for Gore. If he stuck with the "intent of the voter" standard, he stood a good chance of losing the majority of the Court on the equal protection issue. Souter was supposed to be one of the justices on "Gore's side." He had opposed the stay, after all. If Souter was uncomfortable with the intent standard on equal protection grounds, then Gore's chances of winning were slim. On the other hand, should he agree with the justice and accept that there could be a uniform objective standard applied in Florida, Boies stood a good chance of opening the door to the justices calling the election on account of Article II's prohibition of judicially created rules—or at the least, ordering a remand with instructions to impose a uniform standard could eat up the remaining time before the December 12 safe harbor deadline.

Standing quietly and thinking, Boies finally admitted to the Court, "I think that's a very hard question." Standing silent once again, still searching for some answer that did not doom Gore's chances, Boies paused so long that finally Justice Scalia injected humorously to a round of laughter, "You'd tell them to count every vote. You'd tell them to count every vote, Mr. Boies, wouldn't you?" Grinning slightly, Boies agreed, "I would tell them to count every vote." But, he injected, over the start of a question from Justice Stevens, "I think I would say that if you're looking for a standard—and I say that not because of the particular aspects of this election—the Texas standard, if you wanted to specify something that was specific, gives you a pretty good standard." Stevens's question, which he completed after

Boies stopped talking, attempted to reinforce Boies's position. "Does not the procedure that is in place there contemplate that the uniformity will be achieved by having the final results all reviewed by the same judge?" he asked. A grateful Boies agreed. "Yes. That's what I was going to say, Your Honor, that what you have here is you have a series of decisions that people get a right to object to. This is all going through a process. The people are there, they submit written objections, and then that's going to be reviewed by a court."

Boies's answer satisfied Stevens, but not an angry Scalia. "Well, that causes me some problems that pertain not just to the equal protection aspect of this, but to the rationality of the Supreme Court's opinion," Justice Scalia noted. On the one hand, the Florida Supreme Court opinion says "that there was to be *de novo* review by the circuit judge in Leon County. But on the other hand, it said that he had to accept the counts that had come out of Palm Beach and Broward counties." Given the different standards from these two counties, "how can you at one and the same time say it's a *de novo* standard as to what is the intent of the voter, and on the other hand say you have to accept, give some deference to, quite differing standards by two different counties? That's just not rational." On the defensive, Boies tried to explain away the seeming inconsistency. In so doing, he admitted that some Palm Beach voters had wrongly placed their ballots on top of the election pamphlet, resulting in votes that indented the number instead of the chad. This, in turn, produced another angry retort from Justice O'Connor: "Well, why isn't the standard the one that voters are instructed to follow, for goodness sakes? I mean, it couldn't be clearer. I mean, why don't we go to that standard?"

Following another round of discussion on lawmaking versus law interpretation, Boies's last question was a friendly one, one last effort by Justice Souter to propose a compromise ruling that would not simply reverse the lower court's ruling and end the election. "Mr. Boies, let's assume that at the end of the day, the Leon County Florida judge gets a series of counts from different counties, and those counties have used different standards in making their counts. At that point, in your judgment, is it a violation of the Constitution for the Leon County judge to say, 'I don't care if there are different standards, as long as they purported to follow intent of the voter, that's good enough'?" Welcoming the question, Boies used it as a means to summarize Gore's primary points. First, Boies noted,

I think that the answer that they did it differently—different people interpreting the general standard differently—would not raise a problem even in the absence of judicial review of that. Second, even if that would have raised a constitutional problem, I think the judicial review that provides the standardization would solve that problem. . . . [Finally], any differences as to how this standard is interpreted have a lot less significance in terms of what votes are counted or not counted than simply the differences in machines that exist throughout the counties of Florida.

Like it or not, Boies sought to make clear, the evidence showed that votes were being treated differently from county to county long before the recounts. If anything, the differences in the hand recounting were "resulting in far fewer differences among counties than simply the differences in the machines" that they used originally to count the vote.

Sitting down, Boies was replaced at the lectern by Ted Olson, who had five minutes remaining to his time. Olson wanted to remind the Court that, based on the record, there were significant differences in vote counting from county to county in Florida. Yet before Olson could review the equal protection violations that this situation created, Justice Ginsburg demanded his attention. "How can you have one standard when there are so many varieties of ballots?" she asked. This question forced Olson to admit that "the standard should be that similarly situated voters and similarly situated ballots ought to be evaluated by . . . comparable standards." So you would "have to have several standards?" Ginsburg asked. "Well, you. . . ." sputtered Olson. "County by county, would it be?" asked the justice quietly, her point having been made.

Olson tried to rebound, arguing that in this case the counties were counting ballots from the same punch card machines differently. However, before he could cover much of his argument, Justice Ginsburg took him in a slightly different direction: "Mr. Olson, do I understand that your argument on the equal protection branch would render academic what was your main argument that's troublesome; that is, that we must say the Florida Supreme Court was so misguided in its application of its own law, that we reject that, and we, the Supreme Court of the United States, decide what the Florida law is?"

When Olson attempted to argue that "virtually every aspect of Florida's election code has been changed as a result of these two decisions," Justice Ginsburg noted in response: "But the Florida Supreme Court told us that it hasn't been changed. And just looking at one of the cases that you cite frequently, the O'Brien against Skinner case, this court said, 'Well, maybe we would have decided the New York law differently, but the highest court of the state has concluded otherwise.' It is not our function to construe a state statute contrary to the construction given it by the highest court of the state."

With almost no time left, Olson ended on a strong note, answering, "The only thing that I can say in response to that is . . . what this court said one week ago today, that as a general rule, the court defers to a state court's interpretation of a state statute, but not where the Legislature is acting under authority . . . granted to it by the Constitution of the United States."

With these last few words, Chief Justice Rehnquist announced that time was up and adjourned the hearing. The briefing was over. The oral arguments were over. Even the public relations war was irrelevant at this moment. The issue was now in the justices' hands. Until they announced their ruling, all anyone could do was wait. And although there was some speculation that the Court would announce an almost immediate ruling, as the day passed without word from the Court, most court watchers felt that the earliest the Court was now likely to act was December 12—but there was no official deadline; the justices could take as long as they needed.

Meanwhile, in Texas, George W. Bush was "keeping [his] emotions in check" as he waited for the justices to decide his fate. "Cautiously optimistic" about victory, Bush did not even bother listening to the tape-delayed broadcast of the oral arguments, choosing instead to work out in the University of Texas gym. As Bush explained to reporters, he was "feeling pretty calm about it." More publicly confident of victory than their candidate, Bush's aides were already hard at work planning Bush's assumption of power. The plan was for Bush to appear on national television—after waiting for what one adviser described as a "decent but short interval" for a concession speech by Vice President Gore—and deliver a speech filled with talk of reunifying the country. Drafts of the text were already written and being circulated. Then, within a day or two, Bush would begin announcing his choices for top White House aide and cabinet positions.

The mood of the Gore camp was decidedly different. On Fox's *News Sunday* program, David Boies admitted, "If somehow Florida is told, 'Don't count the votes that were cast,' I think that's the end of the road in terms of contesting the election." House Minority Leader Dick Gephardt of Missouri agreed that Gore most likely would concede if the Court ruled against him. "I believe he [Gore] will, and I think George Bush would do the same thing if it were the other way around," Gephardt concluded. Even Gore's vice-presidential running mate, Joe Lieberman, acknowledged, "If the Supreme Court rules in Governor Bush's favor, that's probably the end of it." Still, all was not gloom among the Gore forces. In a sign of optimism, Ron Klain traveled back to Tallahassee to get ready for the recounts to resume. "I think this case is going to be remanded to the Florida Supreme Court, and I'm going back to work on a remand brief," Klain said just before boarding his plane.[53]

Like the faithful keeping watch at the Vatican for the white smoke signaling the naming of a new pope, the American people waited for the high priests of American law to hand down their decision. Despite intense speculation, no one knew how the Court would rule. Could the justices find a middle ground and provide closure to the election without increasing political turmoil? Or was the Court destined to anger one-half of the nation no matter how it ruled? Some hopefully insisted that the Court could find a middle way. Pointing to the questions asked by Justices Breyer and Souter on equal protection, and on the viability of continuing the recounts, they suggested that this might be a means to draw Justices Kennedy or O'Connor or both into a compromise ruling.

Most Supreme Court observers, though, were less than optimistic that the

Court would be effective in settling this matter with minimal controversy. "There's an incredibly great risk that the Supreme Court is going to get sucked into the political warfare" in the nation's capital, said Professor Heather Gerken of Harvard Law School. Charles Umbanhower, a constitutional law professor at St. Olaf College in Minnesota, agreed. If the split over issuing the stay endured after the oral arguments, Umbanhower noted, finding common legal ground to issue a unanimous or nearly unanimous opinion would be very unlikely. This put the nine justices at risk of partisan attacks on their credibility. "When you do something very unusual like that, you want to be united," Umbanhower said. "When you see this, the Supreme Court looks like partisan hacks." Only time would tell which, if either, of these expectations were met. And so the nation waited.[54]

CHAPTER EIGHT

Headfirst into the Political Thicket

> If the courts jump in the middle of a mud fight, they're going to
> get mud on them. But sometimes they cannot avoid it.
> —*Senator Jeff Sessions [R-AL], December 12, 2000*

> Everyone wants to believe courts make decisions without political
> considerations, but there's nothing more political than an election.
> —*Senator John Ashcroft [R-MO], December 12, 2000*

If the image of an election judge sitting in a chair looking up to the light through a punch card ballot was the most surreal image of the 2000 postelection crisis, then the second most surreal image had to be the sight of news staffers running down the steps of the Supreme Court clutching in their hands copies the Court's *Bush v. Gore* opinion for waiting reporters. What could better symbolize the rushed nature of the entire proceeding than the sight of familiar faces from TV running harder and faster than they had for years, to report the news—only to then have to summarize a complex, multifaceted set of opinions running more than forty pages in length without having taken the time to read it first?

Ever since the end of oral arguments the news networks had been showing pictures of the Supreme Court building, all the while speculating what might be going on within and grousing quietly about the long wait. On ABC's *World News Tonight*, anchor Peter Jennings asked a correspondent outside the Supreme Court why the ruling was taking so long, "or has it really been a long time?" he asked. "It's only been one day," correspondent Jackie Judd pointed out. She added, "There are lights on in the building behind me." At CNN, Roger Cossack spoke honestly, but defied conventional TV wisdom, when he said, "I just think my job, and all of our jobs, is just to sit here and wait and see what the verdict is." Meanwhile, on the twenty-four-hour news channels, which had more time to fill, cameras showed seating charts of the justices while former Supreme Court clerks talked about what was "likely" going on inside the building. Their correspondents, in turn, with no real news to report, started their updates with "I would assume" and "I would imagine."

Finally, at 9:45 p.m., on the night of December 12, MSNBC anchor Brian Williams announced with his hand to his ear, "We're having this baby tonight." CNN and Fox News made similar announcements a few seconds later, though in wording slightly less vivid than Williams's. By 10:00 p.m. the word was out. The Supreme Court had handed down its ruling. First on the air with a copy of the opinion was MSNBC's reporter Bob Kur. Kur, however, spent much of his on-air time fumbling through the opinion's pages trying to find something—anything— that would summarize the Court's judgment. At one point, pushed by Williams in the studio, Kur snapped back, asking for time, complaining of the length and complexity of the ruling. Soon MSNBC tossed its coverage to its sister network NBC, which had Pete Williams and Dan Abrams breaking down the ruling methodically, section by section, tag teaming each other as one spoke while the other read ahead. (At one point, standing in the freezing cold, Abrams took off his gloves the better to turn the pages of the opinion.) Even then, NBC anchor Tom Brokaw's summary of "what we know" began, "It's been a rather chaotic 32 minutes." As late as midnight, MSNBC's Brian Williams still sounded slightly tentative as he introduced "reaction to what we think we have just seen unfold here tonight."

The picture at the other networks was just as confused. On CBS, Bob Schieffer complained, "I do not understand what the Supreme Court means for the Florida court to do. I don't understand what they see as the remedy to all this," as he read through the ruling. "We are in the midst of trying to sort this out and clarify exactly what the court has done," ABC's Peter Jennings admitted. "It is, quite frankly, not particularly easy." At CNN, Roger Cossack, out in the cold with his copy of the ruling, held his ground when asked to interpret too broadly. We just did not know, he stated. One key source of confusion was that the majority opinion formally remanded the case to the Florida Supreme Court, despite the ruling's declaration that the time for recounts had run out, leaving at least the theoretical possibility that the maneuvering might drag on. On ABC, this confusion led Jennings to observe, "A lot of people are sitting at home saying, 'Who's winning, Bush or Gore?'" To which ABC political analyst George Stephanopoulos responded, "I believe, from everything I've heard, Bush," only to have reporter Jack Ford warn, "You could still have a fight here over which slate is going to be in."

For nearly an hour, the nation was treated to the spectacle of correspondents from all the networks shivering in the cold outside the marble temple of the law, reading passages from the opinion, pondering questions aloud, and fumbling their way to the conclusion that George W. Bush had all but won the presidency. Well, maybe he won. It *looked* like Bush had won. At least, we *think* he did. But there were six separate opinions to read—a per curiam for the Court, a concurrence by Chief Justice Rehnquist, and four dissenting opinions. And then there was the question of who voted for what. The per curiam, for example, implied a seven-to-two victory for Bush, but two of the seven wrote dissents—so were they or were they not in the majority? Then there was a concurrence from Chief Justice Rehnquist (joined by Scalia and Thomas) that sounded nothing like the per curiam opinion. Who knew what the Court was saying?

Finally, as reporters and legal analysts had time to read the opinion front to back, it began to sink in that this was essentially a five-to-four ruling against Al Gore. The election was over. "It's an all-out victory for the Bush team, no matter why," reported NBC's Dan Abrams. "This election is over," said ABC's Jack Ford. "I make no claim to being a legal expert," noted CNN's Jeff Greenfield, "but it sure sounds to me that the court left no room for the Florida Supreme Court to construct a recount." NBC's Tim Russert declared, "It does appear this election has come to an end," noting how "it's extremely difficult to accept defeat, no doubt about it. But Al Gore will accept this verdict from the Supreme Court."[1]

And so, much as it had all begun back on Election Night, the 2000 postelection nightmare ground to a halt in a flurry of confused and confusing television news coverage. Once again, the talking heads spoke, only to have the facts trip them up once they had the time to evaluate the evidence before them. Once again, the nation sat and wondered who had really won the presidency. Once again, we waited for finality.

And yet it may be unfair to blame it all on the media. If their coverage of the Supreme Court's ruling was confused, they had reason to be confused. The Supreme Court's judgment in *Bush v. Gore* was not the Court at its best. Filled with internal contradictions, self-serving posturing by the justices, and biting dissents, the ruling was not a simple or easy read. Facing the opportunity—and pressing need—to present a unified face to the world (and with it, to provide closure to an electoral train wreck), the justices proved unwilling—or unable—to find the middle ground of consensus. Instead, the ruling cobbled together a majority of sorts—finding seven votes for this and five votes for that—but never found a true, clear, coherent message to announce. The sad truth was that this was a matter in which almost none of the justices actually agreed with one another very much. Even the seven-member and five-member majorities, when broken down, would prove less solid than one would like in a matter of such national importance. No, if we were still confused as to what this all meant, the blame, such as it was, rested with the justices themselves and their answer(s) to the 2000 postelection constitutional crisis.

There is an art to writing a Supreme Court opinion. Judicial opinions have a specific structure and a purpose that combine to dictate what goes into an opinion—and what is left out. Opinions are written to achieve very specific goals. They must lay out in detail the unique situation underlying the legal dispute; they must set forth the key legal and constitutional questions raised by the case and then answer these questions; finally, they must explain why the justices ruled as they did and make clear the ruling's scope and extent.

On the surface this description might suggest that opinion-writing is a relatively straightforward task. The complexities of the law, however, combined with the need to use an opinion as a means to shape future cases, often make writing a coherent opinion difficult. In a real sense, a justice writing a Supreme Court opinion has multiple constituencies whom he or she must satisfy with his or her words.

There are the litigants in the case, whose primary focus is winning and losing. Then there are the lower-court judges whence the case originated who need to be informed of their errors (if any). Other lower-court judges hearing similar cases, and in need of a clear precedent as to the law's or Constitution's meaning in this particular context, make up a third group. Finally, there is the wider community of Americans for whom a Supreme Court ruling can act as an important means of education about the workings of our constitutional system of government—all the more so if, as in *Bush v. Gore*, they perceive that they have a personal stake in the outcome of the case.

Meeting the needs of each of these constituencies can be difficult. It is not that the answers differ from group to group—the Court's ruling is the Court's ruling. However, the specific details and explanations needed to make clear the Court's actions and reasoning do differ, depending on the audience. Hence, a Supreme Court opinion must be both detailed enough to meet the needs of lawyers and judges seeking precedential guidance on what can often be highly technical issues, and at the same time sweeping enough to convey the overall meaning of the Court's ruling to nonlawyers. Add in that cases before the Supreme Court are rarely straightforward (if they were, lower courts would have already provided satisfactory answers), and the extent of difficulty in writing an opinion becomes clearer.

With *Bush v. Gore*, these standard difficulties were magnified by the case's high status and consequences (the naming of a president), which not only generated intense divisions between the justices but were tearing the nation apart. This was also, we need to remember, a novel situation for the justices. Never before had the Court been in the position of picking a president. Barring doing nothing, an unlikely result as they themselves had chosen to hear the case, the Court's opinion was going to name the next president—and the justices knew this. Finally, there were the complexities of fixing a broken electoral system. What they said about that question could shape the future of democracy for generations to come. It had to be terrifying for them as they were pulled into the gravity well of the 2000 post-election crisis. It must have drained all the air out of the room, leaving the justices breathless, fixated on the size of the challenge they had taken up.

At the least, the dispute's scope combined with its complexities made the job of forming a coherent majority message difficult. It also guaranteed that those in the minority would write stinging dissents. Yet the job of the Supreme Court is to produce order out of chaos and direction out of confusion. The Court had to find some way of settling these matters. And, as noted in chapter 7, they had to do this quickly. There was no time to sit on the case and wait until a more unifying answer could be worked out. The Court would have to go with its first impressions and find a way to explain them for the rest of us. And, some thirty-six hours after the end of oral argument, this is exactly what they did.

Reading the Court's opinion in *Bush v. Gore*, the first thing we notice is that the opinion is, once again, a per curiam. As noted, per curiam opinions are unsigned—

written by one or more justices but presented as merely being "from the Court." Justices turn to the per curiam for numerous reasons. Often the Court issues a per curiam when the justices wish to express a result that enjoyed full and total institutional support of all nine justices. Other times, the justices use a per curiam opinion when a case is so lacking in complexity that it is not worth the time of any member of the Court to draft and sign his or her own opinion for the Court. Per curiam opinions also can provide cover in politically sensitive cases, shielding the writing justice within the protecting arms of the whole Court. Finally, a per curiam—especially when there is dissent among the nine—can be a means to express the barest bones of consensus among the justices.[2]

In terms of *Bush v. Gore*, the per curiam also could have been the result of the Court's strict time constraints. With little time to write, the opinion probably took form in different chambers and later was cobbled together to form a whole. In point of fact, what evidence exists suggests that most of the per curiam was written by Justices Kennedy and O'Connor working in tandem. The per curiam also served as a means to agreement, permitting the members of the Court's majority to reach a rough accord on their basic proposition that the Florida recount was flawed and unconstitutional, expressed in the per curiam, while leaving them free to write separate concurring and dissenting opinions detailing their personal views in greater detail. Of course, the per curiam also spared any one justice from having to sign his or her name to an opinion that, due to severe time constraints, was less fully coherent than its author or authors might have wished. So too, it provided protection from the ruling's politically explosive impact. Most of all, the per curiam gave the Court's ruling an air of consensus that actually did not exist, while simultaneously implying that the Court's ruling was of modest scope and supporting the assertion that the Court was only reluctantly entering the fray to fulfill its constitutional role.[3]

Whatever the actual mix of reasons for adopting the per curiam, the result was an unsigned opinion that attempted to project an air of consensus. It began with a detailed summary of the legal arguments and rulings that had preceded this case. Part A then discussed the electoral calamity that had brought this case before them. In response to this failure, the per curiam noted as an aside how the "closeness of this election, and the multitude of legal challenges which have followed in its wake, have brought into sharp focus a common, if heretofore unnoticed, phenomenon." Namely, that despite the best efforts of election officials nationwide, "statistics reveal[ed] that an estimated 2% of ballots cast [did] not register a vote for President for whatever reason, including deliberately choosing no candidate at all or some voter error, such as voting for two candidates or insufficiently marking a ballot." Troubled by this statistic, the justices in the majority noted, "This case has shown that punch card balloting machines can produce an unfortunate number of ballots which are not punched in a clean, complete way by the voter." And, more important, they suggested that "after the current counting, it is likely legislative bodies nationwide will examine ways to improve the mechanisms and machinery for voting."[4]

With this concern perfunctorily expressed and safely out of the way, the per curiam returned to a point raised in its introductory discussion of the case's prior proceedings. In that section, the justices noted, "The petition [from Bush] present[ed] the following questions: whether the Florida Supreme Court established new standards for resolving Presidential election contests, thereby violating Art. II, §1, cl. 2, of the United States Constitution and failing to comply with 3 U. S. C. §5, and whether the use of standardless manual recounts violate[d] the Equal Protection and Due Process Clauses."

As to the first issue raised, the potential violations of Article II and 3 U.S.C. §5, the majority opinion saw little conflict upon which it had to rule. In fact, other than drawing on these laws as a foundation for grounding their ruling on the third issue—equal protection—the per curiam ignored these matters entirely. Rather, it was the potential violation of equal protection that motivated judicial action in these matters.

The majority began, ironically, by noting how "the individual citizen" had "no federal constitutional right to vote for electors for the President of the United States *unless* and *until* the state legislature [chose] a statewide election as the means to implement its power to appoint members of the Electoral College [emphasis added]." With this fundamental constitutional tenet understood, "the State legislature's power to select the manner for appointing electors [was] plenary" could not be denied. If it so chose, the state legislature had the power and the right to "select the electors itself." However, "history . . . now favored the voter," in the choice of "Presidential electors." This extension of right was key in this matter. "When the state legislature vests the right to vote for President in its people," explained the per curiam, "the right to vote as the legislature has prescribed [was] fundamental; and one source of its fundamental nature lies in the equal weight accorded to each vote and the equal dignity owed to each voter."[5] In fact, "the right to vote [was] protected in more than the initial allocation of the franchise." Equal protection applied as well "to the manner of its exercise." As the per curiam made clear, "having once granted the right to vote on equal terms, the State may not, by later arbitrary and disparate treatment, value one person's vote over that of another." Once granted, in other words, a citizen's right to vote for presidential electors was subject to the full protection of the law, including the equal protection clause of the Fourteenth Amendment.[6]

The majority now turned back to Florida and the 2000 election. As the per curiam acknowledged, "there [was] no difference between the two sides of the present controversy on these basic propositions. Respondents [said] that the very purpose of vindicating the right to vote justifies the recount procedures now at issue." The petitioners argued otherwise. The ballots in question were undeniably difficult to read as to how they were voted. "The question before us," therefore, was "whether the recount procedures the Florida Supreme Court ha[d] adopted [were] consistent with its obligation to avoid arbitrary and disparate treatment of the members of its electorate."

The Florida Supreme Court had ruled that voter inclusion was the primary objective in constructing remedies to the problems associated with the 2000 election. Recall that in *Gore v. Harris*, they had argued that so long as the voter's intent may be discerned from the ballot, [said] vote constitutes a 'legal vote' that should be counted." Voter empowerment, therefore, was the supreme objective in determining judicial action in these matters, "notwithstanding" such other legitimate concerns as "time constraints" or the need to produce a clear winner. "We must do everything required by law to ensure that legal votes that have not been counted are included in the final election results."[7]

The U.S. Supreme Court's majority in *Bush v. Gore* saw things differently. Although empowering voters was a laudable goal, seven of the nine justices held, a lack of concrete and uniform standards as to what was and was not a proper vote raised serious constitutional problems.[8] The Florida court's application of the "intent of the voter" as the primary ingredient of a proper vote, for instance, was "unobjectionable as an abstract proposition and a starting principle." However, "in the absence of specific standards to ensure its equal application," this standard was functionally meaningless. "The formulation of uniform rules to determine intent based on these recurring circumstances [was] practicable and, we conclude, necessary," noted the per curiam.[9]

Sadly, such had not been the case in Florida. The oral argument had made clear that "the standards for accepting or rejecting contested ballots might vary not only from county to county but indeed within a single county from one recount team to another." The trial record from below offered even more examples of unequal treatment of votes. Trial testimony from the circuit court, for example, "revealed that . . . Palm Beach County . . . began the process with a 1990 guideline which precluded counting completely attached chads, switched to a rule that considered a vote to be legal if any light could be seen through a chad, changed back to the 1990 rule, and then abandoned any pretense of a *per se* rule, only to have a court order that the county consider dimpled chads legal." This, noted the per curiam, "[was] not a process with sufficient guarantees of equal treatment."[10] The Florida Supreme Court's order, in turn, had improperly "ratified this uneven treatment."

As the per curiam justices presented the matter, the Florida court mandated that the recount totals from two counties, Miami-Dade and Palm Beach, be included in the certified total. The court also appeared to hold *sub silentio* that the recount totals from Broward County, which were not completed until after the original November 14 certification by the secretary of state, were to be considered part of the new certified vote totals even though the county certification was not contested by Vice President Gore. Yet each of the counties used varying standards to determine what was a legal vote. Broward County used a more forgiving standard than

Palm Beach County and uncovered almost three times as many new votes, a result markedly disproportionate to the difference in population between the counties. Worse yet, "the recounts in these three counties" included not only undervotes but extended to all the ballots, including overvotes. "The distinction," noted the per curiam, "ha[d] real consequences." At oral argument, "respondents estimated there [were] as many as 110,000 overvotes statewide." This meant that a "citizen whose ballot was not read by a machine because he failed to vote for a candidate in a way readable by a machine may still have [had] his vote counted in a manual recount," while "the citizen who mark[ed] two candidates in a way discernable by the machine [would] not have [had] the same opportunity to have his vote count, even if a manual examination of the ballot would reveal the requisite indicia of intent." Where was the equal treatment in this? Even more troubling to the majority justices was the situation with Miami-Dade County, which included a partial recount in the final totals, ignoring potentially overlooked votes in the remaining 60 percent of ballots not recounted. "The Florida Supreme Court's decision," concluded the majority, "thus gives no assurance that the recounts included in a final certification must be complete."[11]

As if this was not bad enough, the Florida Supreme Court's own recount procedures were, if anything, just as bad and perhaps worse. The rules issued from the circuit court (under orders from the Florida Supreme Court) "did not specify who would recount the ballots." This omission forced "the county canvassing boards . . . to pull together *ad hoc* teams comprised of judges from various Circuits who had no previous training in handling and interpreting ballots." Such procedures were constitutionally unacceptable, "inconsistent with the minimum procedures necessary to protect the fundamental right of each voter in the special instance of a statewide recount under the authority of a single state judicial officer."[12] When a court ordered a statewide remedy, "there must be at least some assurance that the rudimentary requirements of equal treatment and fundamental fairness [were] satisfied."[13]

Granted, as the per curiam justices had argued earlier in their opinion, "in some cases the general command to ascertain intent is not susceptible to much further refinement." In this instance, however, "the question is not whether to believe a witness but how to interpret the marks or holes or scratches on an inanimate object, a piece of cardboard or paper which, it is said, might not have registered as a vote during the machine count. The factfinder confronts a thing, not a person. The search for intent can be confined by specific rules designed to ensure uniform treatment."

The deficiency of such uniform rules in Florida, the justices concluded, meant that the "recount mechanisms implemented in response to the decisions of the Florida Supreme Court [did] not satisfy the minimum requirement for non-arbitrary treatment of voters necessary to secure the fundamental right." Such had been the reason behind the Court's stay order. Lacking necessary procedural "safeguards," the contest provisions were simply "not well calculated to sustain the confidence that all citizens must have in the outcome of elections." And as such, they were in direct violation of the equal protection clause of the Constitution.[14]

This left the matter of the appropriate remedy for these violations. It was here that the per curiam majority entered dangerous ground. With little foundation in the rest of the opinion, the per curiam simply stated that the time for recounts had run out. "Upon due consideration of the difficulties identified to this point, it is obvious that the recount cannot be conducted in compliance with the requirements of equal protection and due process without substantial additional work. It would require not only the adoption (after opportunity for argument) of adequate statewide standards for determining what is a legal vote, and practicable procedures to implement them, but also orderly judicial review of any disputed matters that might arise."[15]

Recounting votes in a constitutional matter would take time—something the presidential election process could not afford to spare. As the majority explained, the Florida supreme court had emphasized in its earlier decisions the Florida legislature's intention to have its electors "'participate fully in the federal electoral process,' as provided [for by federal laws requiring] that any controversy or contest that is designed to lead to a conclusive selection of electors be completed by December 12." Unfortunately, noted the per curiam, "that date [was] upon us, and there [was] no recount procedure in place under the State Supreme Court's order that comports with minimal constitutional standards." Given these facts, and "because it [was] evident that any recount seeking to meet the December 12 date [would] be unconstitutional for the reasons we have discussed," the per curiam "reverse[d] the judgment of the Supreme Court of Florida ordering a recount to proceed."

The election was over; George W. Bush was the winner. But was this the right call? Should he have been declared the winner—at least, just yet? Despite the confident words of the per curiam, it did not automatically follow from the adjudged equal protection violations that the recounts *had* to end. All seven justices in the majority agreed that a proper recount demanded more detailed standards. But that was all they agreed upon. As the per curiam noted (in as positive a manner as possible), "seven Justices of the Court agree that there are constitutional problems with the recount ordered by the Florida Supreme Court that demand a remedy" and that "the only disagreement [was] as to the remedy." Of course, as the remedy was a crucial element of the issues before the Court, this was an optimistic reading of the situation. In the normal course of events, a ruling such as *Bush v. Gore* customarily would be followed by an order remanding the matter to the lower court for "further proceedings not inconsistent with this opinion." In fact, two members of the per curiam "majority," Justices Stephen Breyer and David H. Souter, argued strongly for just such a remand—and hence they ultimately joined Justices John Paul Stevens and Ruth Bader Ginsburg in dissent. Justice Breyer, in his dissenting opinion, felt that the Court should "remand this case with instructions that . . .

would permit the Florida Supreme Court to require recounting all undercounted votes in Florida, . . . in accordance with a single-uniform substandard"—even if this meant counting votes past the "safe harbor" deadline. Justice Souter, in turn, found "no justification for denying the State the opportunity to try to count all disputed ballots." Give the Florida courts a chance "to do their best to get that job done," he concluded. The remaining five members of the majority, however, ignored these concerns. Indeed, they explicitly denounced Justice Breyer's proposed solution as a violation of the Florida election code. The vote counting was over. The election was over.[16]

With its bombshell dropped, the per curiam ended with an intriguing attempt to minimize the Court's central role in this matter—despite the revolutionary potential of its opinion. In identifying equal protection as a fundamental entitlement guaranteeing a voter's right to have their vote counted in a manner that "avoids arbitrary and disparate treatment," the majority had enunciated a new equal protection principle, one whose long-term implications for voting in America could be explosive. With voting procedures differing not only between states but within most states, the potential to revolutionize how we voted in this country was enormous and intriguing. Yet, the five justices in the per curiam majority seemed anxious to limit this principle almost as soon as they stated it.

Most explicit in this regard was the majority's earlier statement limiting the scope of its ruling to the current case alone. "Our consideration," wrote the majority, was "limited to the present circumstances, for the problem of equal protection in election processes generally presents many complexities."[17] The majority was and remained silent as to why the ruling could so effectively overcome the many complexities of the 2000 postelection debacle while not being fit for application to future cases.

The conclusion offered a more subtle, and encompassing, distancing effort as well. In one of the most striking paragraphs of the opinion, the Court effectively asserted a limitation on its own judicial role: "None are more conscious of the vital limits on judicial authority than are the members of this Court, and none stand more in admiration of the Constitution's design to leave the selection of the President to the people, through their legislatures, and to the political sphere. When contending parties invoke the process of the courts, however, it becomes our unsought responsibility to resolve the federal and constitutional issues the judicial system has been forced to confront."[18]

As with the equal protection right that the per curiam majority both created and then confined, this statement seems both to assert and to reject judicial power in these matters. As legal scholar Laura Krugman Ray explains:

The first sentence embraces judicial restraint and disavows a judicial role in selecting the president. The second sentence then rejects that restraint because the Court, against its will, has been dragged into the case by the litigants. The

Court is presented as a passive entity, accepting the "unsought responsibility" that "the judicial system has been forced to confront," with no mention of the Court's affirmative role in staying the recount and granting *certiorari* or of the position taken by one party—the Gore campaign—against Court intervention.

The Court's opinion thus pictures the five justices of the per curiam majority as reluctant decision makers, "forced to resolve this case but unwilling to extend their unsought authority beyond the minimum required to perform that task."[19]

Yet just how powerless was the Court in these matters? This question was much more contentious than we might think. Clearly the dissenting justices disagreed with their colleagues' depiction of the Court's role in this matter. Interestingly, so too did Chief Justice Rehnquist in his concurrence (joined, as he so often was, by Justices Scalia and Thomas). If the per curiam opinion aimed at soft-selling the Court's powers—and authority—to act in these matters, Rehnquist's concurrence celebrated them.[20]

As far as the chief justice was concerned, "We deal here not with an ordinary election, but with an election for the President of the United States," and this made all the difference in the world. True, the chief justice explained,

in most cases, comity and respect for federalism compel us to defer to the decisions of state courts on issues of state law. That practice reflects our understanding that the decisions of state courts are definitive pronouncements of the will of the States as sovereigns. Of course, in ordinary cases, the distribution of powers among the branches of a State's government raises no questions of federal constitutional law, subject to the requirement that the government be republican in character. . . . But there are a few exceptional cases in which the Constitution imposes a duty or confers a power on a particular branch of a State's government. This is one of them.

Article II, section 1, clause 2 placed authority over presidential elections in the hands of the state legislatures. As *McPherson v. Blacker* made clear, the Constitution "convey[ed] the broadest power of determination . . . to the legislature exclusively to define the method" of appointment of presidential electors. Any "significant departure from the legislative scheme for appointing Presidential electors [thus] present[ed] a federal constitutional question." The Florida Supreme Court's own reading of 3 U.S.C. §5, in turn, made clear the Florida legislature's intent to take advantage of the safe harbor provisions. Given that "§5 contain[ed] a principle of federal law that would assure finality of the State's determination if made pursuant to a state law in effect before the election, a legislative wish to take advantage of the 'safe harbor' would counsel against any construction of the Election Code that Congress might deem to be a change in the law." Hence, if the Court was going "to respect the legislature's Article II powers, . . . we must ensure that post-election state-court actions [did] not frustrate the legislative desire to attain the 'safe harbor' provided by §5."[21]

In Florida, the legislature chose "to hold statewide elections to appoint the State's 25 electors." Further, it placed authority to run this process in the hands of the secretary of state and the circuit courts. Granted, "isolated sections of the code may well admit of more than one interpretation, but the general coherence of the legislative scheme may not be altered by judicial interpretation so as to wholly change the statutorily provided apportionment of responsibility among these various bodies." In any election but a presidential election, "the Florida Supreme Court can give as little or as much deference to Florida's executives as it chooses, so far as Article II is concerned, and this Court will have no cause to question the court's actions. But, with respect to a Presidential election, the court must be both mindful of the legislature's role under Article II in choosing the manner of appointing electors and deferential to those bodies expressly empowered by the legislature to carry out its constitutional mandate."

Generally the federal courts "defer to state courts on the interpretation of state law." However, noted Rehnquist, there were "areas in which the Constitution require[d] this Court to undertake an independent, if still deferential, analysis of state law." This was one of those instances. As Rehnquist, Scalia, and Thomas read the situation, the Florida Supreme Court's interpretation of Florida election laws "impermissibly distorted them beyond what a fair reading required, in violation of Article II."[22]

The chief justice then surveyed the Florida legislature's election statutes, making clear in the process "the detailed, if not perfectly crafted, statutory scheme" created by the legislature "for the appointment of Presidential electors by direct election." He ended his statutory summary with a bald statement that "in Presidential elections, the contest period necessarily terminates on the date set by 3 U.S.C. §5 for concluding the State's 'final determination' of election controversies."

Next, the chief justice set forth a laundry list of the ways that the Florida Supreme Court had contravened these rules beyond what a fair reading required, in the process changing the election rules postelection. Among the rules changed: the Florida supreme court's order extending the challenge stage (which necessarily shorted the time available for the contest phase); the overruling of the secretary of state's authority to determine whether to accept late returns in the state's certified tally; the ruling that "all late vote tallies arriving during the contest period should be automatically included in the certification regardless of the certification deadline (even the certification deadline established by *Harris I*), thus virtually eliminating both the deadline and the secretary's discretion to disregard recounts that violate it"; and finally, "the court's interpretation of 'legal vote,' and hence its decision to order a contest-period recount," both of which "plainly departed from the legislative scheme."

All these actions changed the legislative scheme for running elections, charged

Rehnquist. None was constitutionally adequate. As the Court had noted in its "remand of the earlier [Florida election] case, in a Presidential election the clearly expressed intent of the legislature must prevail." And nowhere in the record was there a basis for reading the Florida statutes as requiring the various changes proposed by the Florida Supreme Court. "The scope and nature of the remedy ordered by the Florida Supreme Court" thus jeopardized "the 'legislative wish' to take advantage of the safe harbor provided by 3 U.S.C. §5." December 12, 2000, the chief justice patiently explained, was "the last date for a final determination of the Florida electors that will satisfy §5. Yet in the late afternoon of December 8th—four days before this deadline—the Supreme Court of Florida ordered recounts of tens of thousands of so-called 'undervotes' spread through 64 of the State's 67 counties." This was not the act of a thoughtful court honoring the wishes of the legislature. Far from it.

The Florida court justified this act as a search for an "elusive—perhaps delusive—certainty as to the exact count of 6 million votes." But why? "No one claim[ed] that these ballots [had] not previously been tabulated; they were initially read by voting machines at the time of the election, and thereafter reread by virtue of Florida's automatic recount provision. No one claims there was any fraud in the election." Surely when the "Florida Legislature empowered the courts of the State to grant 'appropriate' relief, it must have meant relief that would have become final by the cutoff date of 3 U.S.C. §5." As a practical matter, there was no way that the recounts could be completed in the time remaining. Legal challenges and appeals of this latest round of recounts were inevitable. So even though the ballots might be counted in time, the process still would continue long past the safe harbor date. No matter how hard or fast the Florida courts were willing to work (and the chief justice did note that the Florida Supreme Court had "heard and decided the appeals in the present case with great promptness"), the federal deadlines for the presidential election simply [did] not permit even such a shortened process." As such, he respectfully submitted (quoting from Florida chief justice Wells's dissent in *Gore v. Harris*) that this recount "cannot be completed without taking Florida's presidential electors outside the safe harbor provision, creating the very real possibility of disenfranchising those nearly 6 million voters who are able to correctly cast their ballots on election day."

Given all this—the judicial overreach and the legislative imperatives, especially when taken "in addition to those given in the *per curiam*"—the chief justice saw no choice but to reverse. When it came to presidential elections, the Constitution, along with the appropriate federal statutes, created a unique and controlling set of procedures that had to be followed. The Florida Supreme Court chose not to follow them. This left the Court with little choice but to act to correct the situation. The Court's constitutional responsibilities were clear in this matter. The Florida court had overstepped its authority, the recounts were invalid, and Bush was the winner in Florida.[23]

If Chief Justice Rehnquist and his silent partners felt that the per curiam opinion did not go far enough in stressing the Court's duty to act as it did, the four dissenting justices found the majority's views and actions hard to swallow. While they did not all agree on the matter of equal protection, all four held firm that the majority had overstepped its authority in taking up this case and then in halting the recounts. They not only disagreed with the five-member majority; they disagreed so much that they were particularly harsh in their objections.

Consider Justice Breyer. As noted, Breyer complained that the majority was implementing the wrong remedy. "Of course, the selection of the President is of fundamental national importance," Breyer wrote. "But that importance is political, not legal." The federal legal questions presented by this case, "with one exception," were "insubstantial." For this reason alone, "this Court should resist the temptation unnecessarily to resolve tangential legal disputes, where doing so threatens to determine the outcome of the election." The Constitution and federal statutes themselves, he explained, made "clear that restraint [was] appropriate. They set forth a road map of how to resolve disputes about electors, even after an election as close as this one. That road map fores[aw] resolution of electoral disputes by *state* courts." Tellingly, "it nowhere provide[d] for involvement by the United States Supreme Court. To the contrary, the Twelfth Amendment commit[ed] to Congress the authority and responsibility to count electoral votes."

However awkward or difficult it may be for Congress to resolve difficult electoral disputes, "Congress, being a political body, expresse[d] the people's will far more accurately than does an unelected Court. And the people's will is what elections are about." Those who "caution[ed] judicial restraint in resolving political disputes have described the quintessential case for that restraint as a case marked, among other things, by the 'strangeness of the issue,' its 'intractability to principled resolution,' its 'sheer momentousness, . . . which tends to unbalance judicial judgment,' and 'the inner vulnerability, the self-doubt of an institution which is electorally irresponsible and has no earth to draw strength from.'" Those characteristics, noted Breyer, marked this case.[24]

As Breyer saw it, "The Court was wrong to take this case. It was wrong to grant a stay. It should now vacate that stay and permit the Florida Supreme Court to decide whether the recount should resume." Not only were the benefits of halting the recounts tainted by its questionable constitutionality, he explained, but the costs of the Court's acting were simply too great. In this highly politicized matter, "the appearance of a split decision runs the risk of undermining the public's confidence in the Court itself."

> That confidence is a public treasure. It has been built slowly over many years, some of which were marked by a Civil War and the tragedy of segregation. It is a vitally necessary ingredient of any successful effort to protect basic liberty and, indeed, the rule of law itself. We run no risk of returning to the days when a President (responding to this Court's efforts to protect the Cherokee Indians)

might have said, "John Marshall has made his decision; now let him enforce it!" But we do risk a self-inflicted wound—a wound that may harm not just the Court, but the Nation.

"I fear that in order to bring this agonizingly long election process to a definitive conclusion," wrote Breyer, "we have not adequately attended to that necessary 'check upon our own exercise of power,' 'our own sense of self-restraint.'"[25] Justice Brandeis once said of the Court, "The most important thing we do is not doing." What it does today, Breyer concluded, "the Court should have left undone. I would repair the damage done as best we now can, by permitting the Florida recount to continue under uniform standards."[26]

The only area where Breyer was in general agreement with the majority was on the equal protection implications. The majority concluded "that the Equal Protection Clause require[d] that a manual recount be governed not only by the uniform general standard of the 'clear intent of the voter,' but also by uniform subsidiary standards (for example, a uniform determination whether indented, but not perforated, 'undervotes' should count)." This view Breyer could accept. He understood that, "in light of our previous remand, the Florida Supreme Court may have been reluctant to adopt a more specific standard than that provided for by the legislature for fear of exceeding its authority under Article II." However, given that "the use of different standards could favor one or the other of the candidates," and that "time was, and is, too short to permit the lower courts to iron out significant differences through ordinary judicial review, and since the relevant distinction was embodied in the order of the State's highest court," Breyer agreed that, "in these very special circumstances, basic principles of fairness may well have counseled the adoption of a uniform standard to address the problem."[27]

Now Breyer returned to his fundamental point: there was "no justification for the majority's remedy, which [was] simply to reverse the lower court and halt the recount entirely." A more "appropriate remedy" would have been "to remand this case with instructions that, even at this late date, would permit the Florida Supreme Court to require recounting *all* undercounted votes in Florida, including those from Broward, Volusia, Palm Beach, and Miami-Dade Counties, whether or not previously recounted prior to the end of the protest period, and to do so in accordance with a single-uniform substandard."

The majority's justification of stopping the recount, based entirely on the ground that there was no more time, was in error. The majority had reached this conclusion "in the absence of *any* record evidence that the recount could not have been completed in the time allowed by the Florida Supreme Court," explained Breyer. In point of fact, "the majority finds facts outside of the record on matters that state courts [were] in a far better position to address." Of course, it was "too late for any such recount to take place by December 12, the date by which election disputes must be decided if a State is to take advantage of the safe harbor provisions of 3 U.S.C. §5." But what about December 18, when the electors [were] scheduled to meet?" Whether there was enough time to conduct a recount before this date was "a matter for the state courts to determine." Whether, "under Florida law, Florida could or could not take further action is obviously a matter for Florida courts, not this Court, to decide."

"By halting the manual recount, and thus ensuring that the uncounted legal votes will not be counted under any standard," concluded Breyer, "this Court [had] craft[ed] a remedy out of proportion to the asserted harm. And that remedy harm[ed] the very fairness interests the Court [was] attempting to protect." In a system that allowed counties "to use different types of voting systems, voters already arrive[d] at the polls with an unequal chance that their votes will be counted." How could the fact that this resulted "from [the] counties' selection of different voting machines rather than a court order make the outcome any more fair?" Clearly it did not. Nor did Breyer "understand why the Florida Supreme Court's recount order, which help[ed] to redress this inequity, must be entirely prohibited based on a deficiency that could easily [have been] remedied." Recount the votes, do it correctly, and end this crisis on a proper footing. With this Justice Breyer concluded his "respectful dissent."[28]

Justice Souter was even more blunt in his conclusions about the majority's proposed remedies: "If this Court had allowed the State to follow the course indicated by the opinions of its own Supreme Court, it is entirely possible that there would ultimately have been no issue requiring our review, and political tension could have worked itself out in the Congress following the procedure provided in 3 U.S.C. §15." Sadly, it had not. And having wrongly taken up the case, the "resolution by the majority" was producing "another erroneous decision."[29]

Souter found himself in substantial agreement with the other dissenting justices. Most of their complaints were his. He therefore intended his dissent as a means of showing just how "straightforward the issues" before the Court really were. First, explained Souter, the 3 U.S.C. §5 issue was not a serious matter. §5 merely set up "certain conditions for treating a State's certification of Presidential electors as conclusive in the event that a dispute over recognizing those electors must be resolved in the Congress under 3 U.S.C. §15." That was it. No state was ever "required to conform to §5 if it [could not] do that (for whatever reason)." The "sanction for failing to satisfy the conditions of §5" was simply the "loss of what has been called its 'safe harbor.'" And even that determination was "to be made, if made anywhere, in the Congress."

The same lack of significance attended the issue of judicial "lawmaking." Bush's argument, as Souter understood the contention, was that "the interpretation of §102.168 was so unreasonable as to transcend the accepted bounds of statutory interpretation, to the point of being a nonjudicial act and producing new law untethered to the legislative act in question." This reasoning made little sense, Souter concluded. Appellate courts interpret the law. It is what they do. As Souter read the Florida statutes, "none of the state court's interpretations [were] unreasonable to the point of displacing" the election statutes. Granted, "other interpretations were of course possible, and some might have been better than those adopted by the Florida court's majority," but "the majority view . . . [was] in each instance within the bounds of reasonable interpretation." In sum, concluded Justice Souter, "the interpretations by the Florida court raise[d] no substantial question under Article II. That court engaged in permissible construction in determining that Gore had instituted a contest authorized by the state statute, and it proceeded to direct the trial judge to deal with that contest in the exercise of the discretionary powers generously conferred by Fla. Stat. §102.168(8) (2000)."[30]

It was only when the issue switched to equal protection that Souter found "a meritorious argument for relief." True, it was an issue that "might well have been dealt with adequately by the Florida courts if the state proceedings had not been interrupted, and if not . . . it could have been considered by the Congress in any electoral vote dispute." But, as "the course of state proceedings [were] interrupted, [and] time [was] short," Souter felt that it was only "sensible for the Court to address it." He continued:

It is true that the Equal Protection Clause does not forbid the use of a variety of voting mechanisms within a jurisdiction, even though different mechanisms will have different levels of effectiveness in recording voters' intentions; local variety can be justified by concerns about cost, the potential value of innovation, and so on. But evidence in the record here suggests that a different order of disparity obtains under rules for determining a voter's intent that have been applied (and could continue to be applied) to identical types of ballots used in identical brands of machines and exhibiting identical physical characteristics (such as "hanging" or "dimpled" chads).

Souter saw "no legitimate state interest served by these differing treatments of the expressions of voters' fundamental rights." The differences appeared "wholly arbitrary" to him. Hence, on these grounds, Bush had a case to make.

The problem, Souter continued, lay in deciding what to do about this untenable situation. Souter himself believed that the best option would be to "remand the case to the courts of Florida with instructions to establish uniform standards for evaluating the several types of ballots that have prompted differing treatments, to be applied within and among counties when passing on such identical ballots in any further recounting (or successive recounting) that the courts might order." Unlike the majority, Souter saw "no warrant for this Court to assume that Florida could not possibly comply with this requirement before the date set for the meeting of electors, December 18." To recount these votes manually "would be a tall order, but before this Court stayed the effort to do that the courts of Florida were ready to do their best to get that job done." There was simply "no justification for denying the State the opportunity to try to count all disputed ballots now." With this pointed reproof, Souter ended his dissent.[31]

Unlike his two colleagues in dissent, Justice John Paul Stevens objected to the majority's entire opinion. He complained that "the Constitution assigns to the States the primary responsibility for determining the manner of selecting the Presidential electors." Hence, "when questions about the meaning of state laws, including election laws," arose in the past, it was the Court's "settled practice to accept the opinions of the highest courts of the States as providing the final answers." This was decidedly not the case here.

The federal questions raised by this case, noted Stevens, were "not substantial." Article II provided that "'each *State* shall appoint, in such Manner as the Legislature *thereof* may direct, a Number of Electors.' It [did] not create state legislatures out of whole cloth, but rather [took] them as they [came]—as creatures born of, and constrained by, their state constitutions." Lest the point be lost, a deeper reading into *McPherson v. Blacker* made clear that "'what [was] forbidden or required to be done by a State' in the Article II context '[was] forbidden or required of the legislative power under state constitutions as they exist.' In the same vein, we also observed that 'the [State's] legislative power [was] the supreme authority except as limited by the constitution of the State.'" Article V of the Florida constitution, in turn, subjected the legislative power to judicial review, and "nothing in Article II of the Federal Constitution free[d] the state legislature from the constraints in the state constitution that created it." Moreover, when the Florida legislature chose to employ a "unitary code" for all elections in the state, they placed themselves under the authority of the Supreme Court in such matters as those before the Court. "The Florida Supreme Court's exercise of appellate jurisdiction therefore was wholly consistent with, and indeed contemplated by, the grant of authority in Article II."

Stevens was even more dismissive of 3 U.S.C. §5. "It hardly needs stating," he noted, "that Congress, pursuant to 3 U.S.C. §5, did not impose any affirmative duties upon the States that their governmental branches could 'violate.' Rather, §5 provides a safe harbor for States to select electors in contested elections 'by judicial or other methods' established by laws prior to the election day." More to the point, "Section 5, like Article II, assume[d] the involvement of the state judiciary in interpreting state election laws and resolving election disputes under those laws." Not the federal courts, Stevens insisted—rather, the state. "Neither §5 nor Article II grants federal judges any special authority to substitute their views for those of the state judiciary on matters of state law," he declared.

The per curiam opinion's equal protection arguments did not convince Justice Stevens. The petitioners, Stevens argued, were wrong when they argued that the "intent of the voter" standard violated the Constitution's equal protection clause. In the past, the Court had "found such a violation when individual votes within the same State were weighted unequally" (for example, in *Reynolds v. Sims*), but the Court had "never before called into question the substantive standard by which a State determine[d] that a vote has been legally cast." There was good reason for this. There were simply no good reasons "to think that the guidance provided to the factfinders, . . . by the 'intent of the voter' standard [was] any less sufficient—or [would] lead to results any less uniform—than, for example, the 'beyond a reasonable doubt' standard employed everyday by ordinary citizens in courtrooms across this country."[32]

Admittedly, the use of "differing substandards for determining voter intent in different counties employing similar voting systems [might] raise serious concerns." However, noted Stevens, "those concerns [were] alleviated—if not eliminated—by the fact that a single impartial magistrate [would] ultimately adjudicate all objections arising from the recount process." Government needed "a little play in its joints," Stevens reminded the Court, or "the machinery of government would not work." It was for this reason that the Court had held in *Bain Peanut Co. of Tex. v. Pinson* (1931) that, "as a general matter . . . 'the interpretation of constitutional principles must not be too literal.'" Were it otherwise, then Florida's election methods might "run afoul of equal protection." But then, so too might "the similar decisions of the vast majority of state legislatures to delegate to local authorities certain decisions with respect to voting systems and ballot design."[33]

Yet even had this been the case, and Florida election procedures violated the equal protection guarantees, Stevens still would not have supported the majority. His reasons: their proposed remedy. The decision to stop the vote counting—even after acknowledging that "once a state legislature determines to select electors through a popular vote, the right to have one's vote counted is of constitutional stature," and further that "Florida law holds that all ballots that reveal the intent of the voter constitute valid votes"—was wrong. "Under their own reasoning, the appropriate course of action would [have been] to remand to allow more specific procedures for implementing the legislature's uniform general standard to be established." But no, "in the interest of finality, . . . the majority effectively order[ed] the disenfranchisement of an unknown number of voters whose ballots reveal[ed] their intent—and [were] therefore legal votes under state law—but were for some reason rejected by ballot-counting machines." Worse yet, it did so under deadlines created by a faulty reading of 3 U.S.C. §5. After all, in 1960 Hawaii "appointed two slates of electors and Congress chose to count the one appointed on January 4, 1961, well after the Title 3 deadlines." There was simply nothing in the law to prevent the court, "even if it properly found an equal protection violation, from ordering relief appropriate to remedy that violation without depriving Florida voters of their right to have their votes counted." As Stevens noted, turning the majority's own words against them, "'a desire for speed [was] not a general excuse for ignoring equal protection guarantees.'"[34]

Finally, Stevens derided the majority's attack on the Florida Supreme Court. At no time did the Florida justices "make any substantive change in Florida electoral law." Rather, that court's decisions all were "rooted in long-established precedent and were consistent with the relevant statutory provisions, taken as a whole." After all, what did the Florida court actually do except to "decided the case before it in light of the legislature's intent to leave no legally cast vote uncounted?" And in so doing so, all the court did was rely "on the sufficiency of the general 'intent of the voter' standard articulated by the state legislature, coupled with a procedure for ultimate review by an impartial judge, to resolve the concern about disparate evaluations of contested ballots." Was this not what judges were supposed to do? "If we assume—as I do—that the members of that court and the judges who would have carried out its mandate are impartial, its decision does not even raise a colorable federal question."

Underlying the entire assault on the Florida election procedures, Justice Stevens argued, was "an unstated lack of confidence in the impartiality and capacity of the state judges who would make the critical decisions if the vote count were to proceed." This was a troubling view, one "only lend[ing] credence to the most cynical appraisal of the work of judges throughout the land." Time one day will "heal the wound to that confidence that will be inflicted by today's decision," Justice Stevens concluded. Yet, "one thing, . . . [was] certain. Although we may never know with complete certainty the identity of the winner of this year's Presidential election, the identity of the loser [was] perfectly clear. It [was] the Nation's confidence in the judge as an impartial guardian of the rule of law."[35]

Perhaps the angriest of the dissenters was Justice Ruth Bader Ginsburg. She began her dissent with a thorough challenge to the chief justice's concurrence. "THE CHIEF JUSTICE acknowledges that provisions of Florida's Election Code 'may well admit of more than one interpretation,'" wrote Ginsburg, "but instead of respecting the state high court's province to say what the State's Election Code means, THE CHIEF JUSTICE maintain[ed] that Florida's Supreme Court ha[d] veered so far from the ordinary practice of judicial review that what it did cannot properly be called judging." This was plainly wrong. "My colleagues have offered a reasonable construction of Florida's law," she insisted, one that "coincide[d] with the view of one of Florida's seven Supreme Court justices." Would it not make more sense to follow this reading of the situation?

Granted, Ginsburg continued, "I might join THE CHIEF JUSTICE were it my commission to interpret Florida law. But disagreement with the Florida court's interpretation of its own State's law does not warrant the conclusion that the justices of that court have legislated." There was no cause in this instance "to believe that the members of Florida's high court have done less than 'their mortal best to discharge their oath of office,' . . . and no cause to upset their reasoned interpretation of Florida law." In fact, "the Supreme Court more than occasionally affirms statutory and even constitutional interpretation with which it disagrees." More to the point, it was not uncommon for the Court to "let stand state-court interpretations of *federal* law with which we might disagree." For example, "in the habeas context, the Court adheres to the view that there is 'no intrinsic reason why the fact that a man is a federal judge should make him more competent, or conscientious, or learned with respect to [federal law] than his neighbor in the state courthouse.'"

No doubt, admitted Justice Ginsburg, there were cases "in which the proper application of federal law may hinge on interpretations of state law." And "unavoidably, this Court must sometimes examine state law in order to protect federal rights." But in each of these instances, "we have dealt with such cases ever mindful of the full measure of respect we owe to interpretations of state law by a State's highest court." Where was this respect here? The Court needed to remember that "in deferring to state courts on matters of state law, we appropriately recognize that this Court acts as an 'outside[r]' lacking the common exposure to local law which comes from sitting in the jurisdiction.'"[36]

This same argument held with Rehnquist's Article II dismissal of judicial review. "THE CHIEF JUSTICE says that Article II, by providing that state legislatures shall direct the manner of appointing electors, authorizes federal superintendence over the relationship between state courts and state legislatures, and licenses a departure from the usual deference we give to state court interpretations of state law." This was a mistaken reading of the law, Justice Ginsburg maintained. "The Framers of our Constitution, . . . understood that in a republican government, the judiciary would construe the legislature's enactments." Article IV, §4 of the Constitution guaranteed to every state a "Republican Form of Government." How, then, could Article II "be read to invite this Court to disrupt a State's republican regime?" Yet this was exactly what Chief Justice Rehnquist proposed. "By holding that Article II requires[d] our revision of a state court's construction of state laws in order to protect one organ of the State from another, THE CHIEF JUSTICE contradict[ed] the basic principle that a State may organize itself as it sees fit."[37]

"The extraordinary setting of this case has obscured the ordinary principle that dictates its proper resolution: Federal courts defer to state high courts' interpretations of their state's own law," noted Ginsburg. This principle was the foundation upon which federalism was built, and to which all agreed. The five justices in the majority normally were among the strongest supporters of state authority under federalism. This role reversal frustrated Justice Ginsburg. "THE CHIEF JUSTICE's solicitude for the Florida Legislature comes at the expense of the more fundamental solicitude we owe to the legislature's sovereign [the State and its people]. . . . Were the other members of this Court as mindful as they generally are of our system of dual sovereignty, they would affirm the judgment of the Florida Supreme Court."[38]

Justice Ginsburg then agreed with Justice Stevens that Bush had not "presented a substantial equal protection claim." Ideally, she explained, "perfection would be the appropriate standard for judging the recount. But we live in an imperfect world, one in which thousands of votes have not been counted. I cannot agree that the recount adopted by the Florida court, flawed as it may be, would yield a result any less fair or precise than the certification that preceded that recount." Yet even if there were an equal protection violation, Ginsburg was adamant that the majority's remedy was simply wrong. The majority's concern with the December 12 deadline was misplaced:

> Time is short in part because of the Court's entry of a stay on December 9, several hours after an able circuit judge in Leon County had begun to superintend the recount process. More fundamentally, the Court's reluctance to let the recount go forward—despite its suggestion that "the search for intent can be confined by specific rules designed to ensure uniform treatment," . . . ultimately turns on its own judgment about the practical realities of implementing a recount, not the judgment of those much closer to the process.

Further, "the December 12 'deadline' for bringing Florida's electoral votes into 3 U.S.C. §5's safe harbor lack[ed] the significance the Court assign[ed] it. Were that date to pass, Florida would still be entitled to deliver electoral votes Congress *must* count unless both Houses find that the votes 'ha[d] not been . . . regularly given.'" The majority assumes that time will not permit "orderly judicial review of any disputed matters that might arise," but where was their proof? "No one has doubted the good faith and diligence with which Florida election officials, attorneys for all sides of this controversy, and the courts of law have performed their duties," Ginsburg noted. In particular, "the Florida Supreme Court ha[d] produced two substantial opinions within 29 hours of oral argument." Yet, the majority had adopted a conclusion that was "a prophecy the Court's own judgment will not allow to be tested." Such untested prophecies, Ginsburg concluded, "should not decide the Presidency of the United States." Lacking all respect for the majority's logic, and perhaps distrusting their motives, Justice Ginsburg broke tradition and ended her views bluntly: "I dissent."[39]

It was late in the evening of December 12, 2000. David Boies sat in his New York home reading a downloaded copy of the Supreme Court's just-announced decision in *Bush v. Gore*. On the speakerphone were Al Gore and Joe Lieberman. Both waited tensely for Boies to scan the ruling and tease out the bottom-line message as to who had won the case (and, by implication, the election). The multiple opinions and overlapping dissents made finding a coherent central ruling difficult, Boies recalls. Still, it did not take him long to find this central message—"it was over" he announced to the two candidates. Gore had lost.[40]

This result did not surprise Boies. Even before he traveled to Washington to argue before the Supreme Court, Boies had held deep-seated concerns over Gore's chances of winning—especially given the five-to-four stay order halting the Florida recounts. As he recalled in his autobiography, "the chance that the five-justice majority would take this unique step to protect Bush's 'legitimacy' and then decide the case for Gore seemed remote." After all, with the safe harbor deadline just around the corner, the justices would have looked exceedingly "foolish" for having "unnecessarily deprived Gore and the voters of Florida the safe harbor advantage," only to then rule in Gore's favor.[41]

What did surprise Boies was the Court's declared and undeclared reasons for action—in particular their arguments that Florida's election procedures violated the Equal Protection Clause and that this violation justified immediately ending the recount process.[42] The majority's actions troubled Boies. As he explained in his autobiography, the majority in *Bush v. Gore* had "abandoned virtually every rule the Court ordinarily follows in deciding cases." It "decided issues that had not been fully and fairly litigated in the court from which the appeal was taken"; it disregarded "a state supreme court's interpretation of state law"; and it intervened "before the Florida process had been completed and a record fully developed." Worse yet, continued Boies, "the majority's equal protection decision was contrary to principles used to construe the Equal Protection Clause in prior cases, particularly in opinions in which Chief Justice Rehnquist and Justices Scalia and Thomas joined." The ruling seemed like made-up law, applied for the singular purpose of ruling against Gore and only for that purpose. Boies had faith that, in the end, the Supreme Court would shrug off the effects of this failed ruling and regain the nation's faith in its actions. But he was deeply troubled by the Court's fall from grace none the less.[43]

Whereas Boies's negative response to the majority's per curiam opinion was probably inevitable given whom he represented, Boies's troubled and even bemused response to the per curiam opinion's content hinted of the difficulties to come. Explosive in its content and results alike, the Supreme Court's decision in *Bush v. Gore* seemed destined to provoke an unending controversy about what it meant and what significance it would have for the constitutional dimension of voting rights. Clearly, despite the best effort of the per curiam opinion to claim otherwise, this was not a unified court, nor even a unified majority. To be sure, seven justices agreed that there were serious equal protection issues associated with Florida's electoral machinery (and by implication, that of the rest of the states as well). But that is all they agreed on. Tellingly, Chief Justice Rehnquist (writing for himself and Justices Scalia and Thomas) never discussed equal protection in his concurrence—merely stating that they "had joined" with the per curiam opinion.[44] In fact, reports from the Supreme Court suggested that Rehnquist's concurrence originally had been intended to be a majority opinion. Rehnquist, however, could not convince either O'Connor or Kennedy to accept his legalist Article II argument for reversing the Florida supreme court, and so most likely signed the per curiam—along with Scalia and Thomas—as the best ruling he was apt to get, while recrafting his original draft as a concurring opinion.[45] Even the two dissenting justices who had joined the per curiam in part, Breyer and Souter, had different readings of equal protection. Breyer accepted that the lack of a uniform standard "implicate[d] principles of fundamental fairness." This was a much wider reading of the issue than Souter's; he merely viewed Bush's arguments as "a meritorious argument for relief." Both justices agreed, however, that the per curiam opinion's remedy was excessive and uncalled for, a factor that ultimately drove them to dissent.

How then should we interpret the Court's *Bush v. Gore* ruling? The very complexities that made *Bush v. Gore* so difficult a case for the justices to decide also make it a difficult set of opinions to analyze and interpret. Yet without interpretation, *Bush v. Gore* remains an enigma. Was it, as Boies's immediate critique seemed to argue, merely the act of five partisan justices so blatantly concerned with the presidential election's outcome that they would do anything, argue anything, to see their chosen candidate named president? Did the per curiam majority even mean what it said about the equal protection violations supposedly endemic in Florida's electoral machinery? Was there any doctrinal validity to the Court's equal protection logic, or was it just a convenient fiction on the basis of which it could justify ending the 2000 election with George W. Bush the winner? Was this, in other words, nothing more than a judicial power-grab by conservative Republican justices (overturning, so the argument went, the equally partisan power-grab of the liberal Democratic justices of the Florida Supreme Court)?

Or were other, less self-serving reasons motivating the justices' actions? Were the Court's reasons for taking the case based on the majority justices' attempt to end the election as quickly as they could for the good of the nation? Were there real problems in the Florida vote that demanded action on the part of the U.S. Supreme Court? Was the Court's equal protection logic, despite the variations in perspective among the justices holding this view, a fair reading of the situation— one the justices could support in general terms?

It is to these and similar questions that we must turn in the next chapter. For only by understanding exactly what the Court did and did not do, and by grasping some of the reasons for their actions (or failures to act), can we fully understand the meaning and import of *Bush v. Gore* and the entire 2000 presidential postelection controversy.

CHAPTER NINE
A Self-Inflicted Wound?

> In this highly politicized matter, the appearance of a split decision runs the risk of undermining the public's confidence in the Court itself. . . . We run no risk of returning to the days when a President (responding to this Court's efforts to protect the Cherokee Indians) might have said, "John Marshall has made his decision; now let him enforce it!" But we do risk a self-inflicted wound— a wound that may harm not just the Court, but the Nation.
>
> —*Justice Stephen Breyer, dissenting,* Bush v. Gore

> Time will one day heal the wound to that confidence that will be inflicted by today's decision. One thing, however, is certain. Although we may never know with complete certainty the identity of the winner of this year's Presidential election, the identity of the loser is perfectly clear. It is the Nation's confidence in the judge as an impartial guardian of the rule of law.
>
> —*Justice John Paul Stevens, dissenting,* Bush v. Gore

> We deal here not with an ordinary election, but with an election for the President of the United States. . . . In most cases, comity and respect for federalism compel us to defer to the decisions of state courts on issues of state law. That practice reflects our understanding that the decisions of state courts are definitive pronouncements of the will of the States as sovereigns. . . . But there are a few exceptional cases in which the Constitution imposes a duty or confers a power on a particular branch of a State's government. This is one of them.
>
> —*Chief Justice William H. Rehnquist, concurring,* Bush v. Gore

> Oh, God. Get over it.
>
> —*Justice Antonin Scalia, in response to a question over the Court's ruling in* Bush v. Gore

Any analysis of the Supreme Court's ruling in *Bush v. Gore* has to start by asking why the Court took the case in the first place. After all, the justices had a choice. They did not *have* to take the case. They could have left it in the hands of the Florida Supreme Court. They could have allowed the recounts to continue and, should Florida prove unable to settle on a single slate of electors by December 18, 2000, to permit the constitutionally dictated procedures for contested elections to proceed unchecked. This would have left the final choices in the hands of Congress as outlined in the Twelfth Amendment and regulated by 3 U.S.C. §1–21. Under these procedures, when no clear victor emerges from the Electoral College, it is up to the House of Representatives, each state voting as a single entity, to choose the

President by majority vote. When the problem is multiple slates of electors claiming to represent a single state (as had happened in the Hayes-Tilden election in 1876 and was also likely to happen in this election should Gore win the court-ordered recount), federal law leaves it to both houses of Congress to vote as to which is the "proper" slate of electors.[1] If they agree on the proper slate, this ends the controversy. If they disagree, then the slate certified by the governor of the state will be ruled the valid choice of the state.[2] Similar procedures exist for settling election contests initiated by members of Congress challenging the accuracy or legitimacy of a particular state's vote totals. Here too, both houses of Congress have the job of determining the validity of the complaint.[3] In either case, by law these sessions are not to last more than two hours, and no member of either house is allowed to speak for more than five minutes. Further, while these separate sessions are under way, "No votes or papers from any other State shall be acted upon until the objections previously made . . . shall have been finally disposed of." Finally, both houses must concur for an objection to be sustained. If either the House or the Senate does not accept the objection, then the objection fails and the electoral votes are counted as offered.[4]

In other words, legitimate, workable procedures were on hand for resolving the 2000 controversy. True, they were not the most organized or clear procedures. And, equally true, they had not been applied to a presidential election in many years (and in some instances, such as with §5, had never been fully used at all). But they were in place and available. They were, in fact, the constitutionally sanctioned methods for resolving electoral controversies in place before the election was held.[5] Yet despite all of this, five justices chose not to wait for these measures to come into play. They did not wait for the political and constitutional remedies to fail before stepping in and acting. Instead, they assumed direct authority over the matter, not once but twice; and in the second case, they acted unilaterally to call an end to the entire postelection dispute process—in effect naming the new president by a five-to-four vote.

Why did they choose to act when they did not have to do so? They must have known that this would be a controversial act. They must have known that their actions would be second-guessed—and even third-guessed—by everyone; that their motives and methodologies would be mistrusted by at least half of the nation, no matter which way they ruled. All they had to do was to open a newspaper or watch television to form an idea of the controversy that was sure to follow any Supreme Court ruling. So why shoulder the burden, why risk the political heat?

One of the more common explanations proposed by legal scholars and political pundits to explain the Court's decision to act—and to rule in Bush's favor as they ultimately did—argues that the justices in the majority were motivated by personal political preferences; that their primary aim was to assure—at all costs—that George W. Bush became the forty-third president of the United States.[6] The Court's stay order and grant of certiorari, given this line of reasoning, thus constituted little more than a power grab—a blatant, partisan, self-serving effort to gain control of the case so that the justices could end the recounts; the final ruling was therefore simply a scheme by the justices to name Bush president and ensure a conservative Republican ascendancy over all three branches of the federal government.[7]

An alternate explanation for the justices' actions takes the other extreme: the decision to accept the case was a purely legal and constitutional choice demanded by the complex legal issues raised by the election, or by the blatantly partisan and illegal actions of the Florida Supreme Court in ordering a last-minute statewide recount, or both. The U.S. Supreme Court's ruling therefore was based on sound constitutional and jurisprudential grounds—either fundamentally as a matter of constitutional interpretation, or as a corrective to the excesses of the Florida justices, or, once again, both.[8] A variant on this reading, put forth by many conservative commentators, agreed that the Court did the constitutionally proper thing both in taking the case and in ruling in favor of Bush, but questioned the legality of the majority's equal protection argument as a rationalization of these actions. For these court observers, the real constitutional justification for action rested in Chief Justice Rehnquist's concurrence.[9] Yet another alternate reading of events placed the blame for the Court's actions *solely* on the Florida Supreme Court's irresponsible behavior. Faced with a runaway court, the justices had no choice but to act, and act decisively, goes the argument.[10]

Building on these other views, a fourth variant of the argument that "the Court was right to act" holds that the justices rightly took control of the election because of the growing likelihood of major constitutional or political turmoil were these matters left to the political branches to solve. As presented here, the majority's doctrinal logic—right or wrong—was largely irrelevant to the appropriateness of the Court's decision to act.[11] The Court acted because the costs of their *not* acting were too great. They had to act. As presented by those holding this view, therefore, the justices in the majority were suitably concerned about the chaos arising from the postelection crisis (caused in large part by the improper and even unconstitutional activism of the Florida Supreme Court) and properly distrusted the ability of the political branches of government (mostly Congress) to minimize the ongoing and intensifying chaos.[12]

Finally, between these two extremes—the court as political shill or as constitutional/political savior—lay a third explanation of the Court's actions, one proposed by law professor Larry Kramer, then of New York University School of Law. This view placed the blame for action on the justices' egos—they had simply fallen into the constitutional trap of believing that they, and they alone, could fix the problems posed by the 2000 postelection controversy.[13] Faced with a political crisis that no one wanted and with no practical end in sight and confident of their power to shape the constitutional process, the majority justices simply decided to take on the "burden" of settling the crisis because they knew that they could. Or put more bluntly, "the Court stepped in so aggressively, because, like the Taney Court [in *Dred Scott*], these justices, too, had deluded themselves into believing that only they could save us from ourselves"—even if doing so required them "to bend the law."[14]

The listing of all the various, highly nuanced explanations for the Supreme Court's decision to take the case—and for the ruling that followed—could go on indefinitely. For our purposes, though, it is enough to note that most of these proposals are, in point of fact, plausible explanations for the Court's actions. Likely all played at least some small part in shaping the Court's motivations and decisions. After all, the justices were human, and like most of us, acted most likely based on multiple—and occasionally self-contradictory—rationales.[15] But which was the most powerful motivation? Which of these explanations *best* describes the Court's mindset and thus best explains its decision to take the case and, having done so, to end the election by its own fiat?

A closer look at the Court's options as it took up these matters provides some insight into these questions. Take, for example, the widely held partisan/political motivation thesis. If the primary goal of the Court's majority was to see George W. Bush elected president, then logically this goal would have meant that *in their own minds* the only way for Bush to have won would have been with the Court's help—or, at the least, that without the Court's ruling, there would have been significant chance that Bush could have, and perhaps would have, lost. But did Bush need the Court's help? Consider what would have happened had the justices *not* acted and thus allowed the Florida recounts to progress toward completion.

First of all, George W. Bush might have won the recount. Tabulations carried out by various newspapers after the postelection crisis showed that if the Florida Supreme Court's order to count undervotes had been followed strictly, George W. Bush would have prevailed. Indeed, Bush actually would have gained votes, increasing his lead by around 500 votes.[16] Thus, not only would there have been no ongoing political crisis, but Bush's legitimacy as president would have been strengthened.[17] We should note, however, that this pro-Bush outcome changes when we include the overvotes along with the undervotes in the recounting. In that scenario, Al Gore would come out the victor by as few as 60 or as many as 171 votes—depending on the standards used to determine the will of the voter.[18] Of course, this shift to Gore could have occurred only if Judge Terry Lewis (or the Florida Supreme Court) issued an additional order to include overvotes in the statewide recounting process. This was not an impossible scenario, in point of fact. In memos written at the time and in after-the-fact interviews, Judge Lewis explains that feedback from the counties *may* have led him to order all votes counted.[19] So the potential for a Gore win via the recounts existed. However, given the shortness of time, it would have been difficult for Judge Lewis to order the counting of around 150,000 overvotes and to have expected the recounts to end in a timely fashion—for unlike a majority of the undervotes, these overvote ballots were not necessarily separated out and ready for counting.[20] It could have taken days to separate and then hand count the overvote ballots—days Florida lacked if it were to get its electoral votes in on time. So unless everyone suddenly accepted that Florida had weeks in which to figure out its electoral votes,[21] the odds were good that when the dust had settled, Bush still would have had more acknowledged votes than Gore.

Suppose instead that Judge Lewis *had* ordered a full recount and thus that Gore came out on top—and that all of this was done within the limited time available before the electoral vote was to be taken (December 18). What then? Most likely, the Florida courts would have immediately issued an order to the secretary of state's office to revise its certified totals and to certify Al Gore's electors. Yet this would not have been the end of the story. Leaving aside for now the possibility that Katherine Harris might have refused to comply with this order (or that Jeb Bush might have refused to legitimate this new total with his signature and seal of office), there was still the Florida legislature's threat to name and certify its own slate of electors. This threat was real.

As noted in earlier chapters, by early December the Republican-dominated state legislature had already approved a joint committee report arguing that the legislature had the authority to name electors "if necessary."[22] In fact, on December 6, both houses of the Florida Legislature passed a "Joint Proclamation" calling for a special session to explore the appointment of electors should normal methods of picking electors not "produce a final, constitutional choice of electors."[23] Among the options considered by the legislature's committee: a bill allowing the legislature to pick Bush electors if no choice was made by December 12; a measure certifying earlier machine-count tallies favoring Bush; and/or a concurrent resolution calling on Al Gore to stop contesting the election results. "It would be irresponsible for us to go home and say, 'Sorry, your vote doesn't count,'" explained Florida House Majority Leader Mike Fasano of these plans.[24]

One day later, on December 7, Senate President John McKay and Speaker of the House Tom Feeney announced that, subject to the joint proclamation, "the Legislature would choose the electors, as permitted by the U.S. Constitution, if the court disputes were continuing and there was not yet 'finality' on December 12."[25] The plan they outlined called for a special session of the legislature to meet beginning on Monday, December 11, with the respective House and Senate ethics committees meeting immediately to discuss a proposed joint resolution picking a slate of electors. Were there no resolution of the crisis by the next day, the House then would vote to choose a new slate of electors. On Wednesday, December 13, with the existing process in default, the Senate would take action, making the Bush slate official. "If we find a way to do our duty without bringing this session to a close with a final vote, then I would be the most pleased man in Florida," noted Feeney. However, if push came to shove, Feeney cautioned, the Legislature would act.[26]

When, just hours into the planning of the December 11 special session, the

Florida Supreme Court announced its statewide recount order, the stage was set for a confrontation. House Speaker Feeney was "terribly saddened" by the court's decision, he announced in a written statement. "However," Feeney continued, "it validates my view that it is an absolute obligation of the Florida Legislature to act to preserve election law as it existed prior to this election and to protect the legitimate participation of Florida in the selection of the next president." The Constitution, Feeney explained, demanded nothing less. Senate President McKay was equally committed. "This court's decision confirms the wisdom of convening a special session of the legislature to protect Florida's 25 electoral votes," McKay said. "It's more obvious now than ever that finality—which means conclusion of all lawsuits without further challenges—cannot be reached by December 12." McKay, who had been cautious in his calls for legislative action, reminded his colleagues not to mistake caution for timidity. "While some will say our actions over the next few days will be a partisan exercise, I say it is not," he said. "I feel that I am here performing my constitutional duty. Nothing more, nothing less." Even the U.S. Supreme Court's stay order on the evening of December 9 did not slow down their commitment to action. So long as there was a chance for the December 12 "safe harbor" to be violated, the Republican legislators were set to act.[27]

Events then moved according to plan. On Monday, the ethics committees reviewed the matter while the rules committees agreed to change the existing rules to allow both houses to issue a "concurrent resolution" selecting a slate of electors (this would relieve Jeb Bush of the burden of signing the act for it to become official). By late afternoon on Tuesday, the House had voted in George W. Bush's electors as the state's official slate to the Electoral College. It was at this point that the U.S. Supreme Court made the whole matter largely moot by issuing its ruling in *Bush v. Gore*. But what if the Court had not issued a ruling? What if it had not even halted the recounts? Most likely, the Senate would have voted the next day to confirm the House's naming of Bush's electors as official. In point of fact, even with the U S. Supreme Court's ruling promising an end to the election, some Republican state senators still proposed voting in the Bush electors, just in case. "There has been no concession by the vice president, and there are still some other legal challenges out in the state," State Senator Charles Bronson announced. "Until all those cases are settled and do not have any potential for an overturn, I think to be safe we have to reaffirm the slate of 25 electors already certified."[28]

This action would have placed the legislature's slate of pro–Bush electors in direct competition with the court-sanctioned pro–Gore electors. On December 18, both sets of electors would have arrived in Tallahassee and voted. And with more than one slate of electors voting on December 18, the issue of which slate properly represented Florida would have fallen to Congress to decide. At this point, things become both technical and speculative. As noted above, 3 U.S.C. §15 sets out the congressional procedures for determining which slate of electors is legitimate. Under §15 rules, both the House and the Senate would choose which slate it viewed as lawful. Should both houses agree on a slate, the crisis would be over, and the counting of electoral votes could progress toward completion. However, given that the Republicans only controlled one house of the 107th Congress,[29] this strongly suggests—at least if everyone voted along partisan lines as expected[30]— that the vote would have been split, with the House voting for the Republican slate and the Senate the Democratic one.

So what would have been the impact if both houses chose a different slate of electors for Florida? Ultimately, not much. The likely outcome, had the two houses split, still would have given Bush the win. §15 provides that where the two houses of Congress disagree, the slate certified over the governor's signature would prevail.[31] Note that the Bush slate (which presumably would have been identical to the state legislature's slate) already had been certified and signed off on by both Katherine Harris and Jeb Bush on November 26. And although it is true that the Florida Supreme Court might have ordered the governor to sign the new, pro-Gore slate of electors, it is also just as likely that Jeb Bush and the entire state electoral machinery would have refused—or at the minimum delayed—complying with the Court's orders.[32] This would have left only one slate with the required signatures on January 3 when Congress met to count the electoral votes, thus effectively mandating the acceptance of the pro-Bush electors.

Or, alternately, had Jeb Bush followed a theoretical order from the Florida courts and signed a certificate for the Gore electors, this would have left Congress with two sets of certified electors. At this point, the two houses of Congress would have had to choose which set of certified votes was the proper one. One model for settling such a difference, first applied in 1876, would have been for a special commission to be formed, one with equal numbers from the House, the Senate, and the Supreme Court.[33] While presumably 3 U.S.C. §15 precluded the sort of "electoral commission plan" adopted to settle the 1876 race, there was wiggle room for Congress to adopt a commission remedy if it so wished. A number of the statutory provisions outlined in Title 3—including parts of §15—were "rule-making provisions of law," which meant that either the Senate or the House could alter these rules unilaterally for use within its own body. And, needless to say, if both Houses agreed on a change, then the rules could be changed generally.[34]

So while the appointment of an electoral commission to settle the issues was unlikely, had it chosen to act, Congress had the power to create one. Yet even here, politics played into Bush's hands. In almost every possible scenario, the Republicans would have had a majority on this commission. For example, with the Senate evenly split, bipartisan logic might have dictated that half of the Senate's members to the commission would be Democrats and half Republican.[35] However, given the solid majority the Republicans held in the House and the ultimate five-to-four split on the U.S. Supreme Court (which presumably would have translated to a three-to-two vote for Bush from the justices on the commission), the Republicans likely would have controlled the commission's vote and approved Bush's electoral slate by a vote of ten to five. In fact, even had the Senate ignored bipartisanship and chosen all five of its members from the Democratic side of the aisle, Bush still would have had the advantage (8–7) given the majority support he had on the Supreme Court.[36]

Another model available to Congress for settling disputes between contesting slates of electors—also unlikely, but within the realm of possibility—came from the first federal election in 1789. In that election, New York, which at that time permitted its legislature to choose the state's electors, "was unable to pass an election act in time to choose its allotted 8 Electors." One house of the legislature preferred a Federalist slate, while the other favored an Anti-Federalist slate. In the weeks that followed, the legislature continued to deadlock on its choice. Finally, with no cast "electoral votes on 4 February"—the official meeting date of the Electoral College—Congress ignored New York's electoral votes and reworked the number of votes necessary for a candidate to receive a majority.[37] This precedent was, in fact, Al Gore's best chance to win in Congress. Without Florida's electoral votes, Bush trailed Gore by twenty-one votes. And if Congress set aside Florida's twenty-five electoral votes and recalculated the majority required for victory, Al Gore had enough Electoral College votes for a majority win.

This scenario was highly unlikely, however. For one thing, in this instance, Congress was dealing with too many votes, not a lack of them. Not having any votes from a single state limits Congress's options in ways that having to choose between two conflicting slates of electors does not. Further, no politician wants to be known for throwing out the votes of an entire state. It might have been constitutional and legal, but it was too undemocratic to work politically. Also, and far more important than constitutional theory in this case, why would a Republican House permit such a turn of events to deny their party's candidate the presidency? Here, too, the practical odds favored Bush.

Even if the Democrats had raised constitutional objections to this choice of electors—by whatever method or methods adopted—a step that federal rules permitted after the vote was tabulated, so long as a member of each of the two houses of Congress endorsed the objection, the rules were still in George W. Bush's favor. As noted, it would have taken a vote by both houses of Congress to disallow a certified slate of electors. A split vote would have changed nothing. Given that we have just hypothesized that the House would vote for Bush, the likelihood of a consensus against Bush's electors would have been quite small. The result, therefore, once again would have put George W. Bush in the White House.

All of this leads us back to the partisanship explanation for the Court's actions. If the primary objective of the majority justices were to ensure a Bush victory, they reasonably could have achieved this result by *doing nothing*. The advantages—both technical and political—lay with Bush. If everything ran smoothly, Bush would be the winner. In fact, even if things ran awkwardly, Bush still had the advantage. True, allowing this to happen would have taken faith in the political process on the justices' parts, not to mention some skill in reading the likely chain of events in Florida and Congress if they had allowed the recounts to continue unchecked, but each of the justices had the requisite skill and the potential for such faith. Following the election returns in major political contests was, in fact, a long-time favorite pastime of the justices. As a former legislator, Sandra Day O'Connor was especially skilled in predicting political outcomes. Counting the potential votes in Congress was therefore likely to be well within their abilities.[38] As to their faith in Congress's ability to settle the matter effectively, there is more room for dispute. As is discussed in more detail below, many of the justices had serious reservations when it came to Congress. The justices also may well have wondered if having Congress pick the president was a good thing for the nation. Might such a process not weaken the president, whoever he was, in effect dangerously subordinating the executive to the legislative branch? Was following the constitutionally prescribed remedy in this matter the best approach to solving this crisis?

Still, as defenders and interpreters of the Constitution, the justices were supposed to know the rules that shaped these events and have faith in the Constitution's provisions. Unless one is willing to vilify the majority justices completely, it is hard to argue that their taking up the case was *solely* motivated by partisan political motivations. At minimum, something else had to have been motivating the majority justices.[39]

This is not to say that the justices' personal political views had *nothing* to do with the Court's ruling. There is little doubt that the justices were as wrapped up in the postelection crisis as the rest of us.[40] They were human, after all. To expect the justices to have ignored their own preferences in this matter would be asking for more than the average judge was capable of giving.[41] On the other hand, all nine of the justices were experienced jurists, skilled in the art of constitutional decision making. To have followed their partisan preferences blatantly—as if they were politicians voting the party line—would have violated their oath of office. As the late Justice Brennan noted in a 1988 interview, the justices never treat cases "as fungible goods," their votes for sale to the highest bidder or fit for horse-trading among the justices. This is not how the Court works.[42] So when Justice Thomas argued, as he did soon after the Court's ruling in *Bush v. Gore*, "I have yet to hear any discussion, in nine years, of partisan politics" on the Court, and that "we have no axes to grind," he was being neither deceitful nor insincere—he merely was stating a surface reality. The justices do not "politick" like elected politicians. The "rules of the political world" are not part of the currency of the Court.[43] But this idea does not mean that the justices were unaware of politics or that their own personal views on political matters had no effect on their actions. The existence of personal political views among the justices has a much more subtle influence on their actions than the term "politicking" communicates. It is more a matter of perception than of persuasion.[44] But it is an influence nonetheless.

In any case, barring explicit evidence to the contrary, accusing the justices of bad faith is a questionable approach to understanding the events of November and December 2000—especially when, as we shall see, other alternative explanations are available. If only in their own minds, the justices had to have had some other reasons—and, more important, justifications—for action.

This leads us to the alternative explanation for judicial action—constitutional necessity. Both versions of this argument (supporting either the per curiam's or the concurrence's reasoning) hold that the U.S. Supreme Court acted properly in response to fundamental legal and constitutional imperatives—and therefore was legitimately drawn into action to defend the Constitution's specific dictates and in response to the clear misconduct of the Florida Supreme Court in ignoring those dictates. The law, so the argument goes, was clear when it came to the procedures appropriate to a presidential election. Article II of the Constitution and Title III of the U.S. Code set out the parameters and standards for running a presidential election—in particular, making clear the superior authority of the state legislatures in organizing presidential elections—as well as setting benchmark dates for completion of the electoral process. Meanwhile, the Equal Protection and Due Process Clauses set out the fundamental requirements for a proper, constitutionally run election. By ignoring or misapplying either (or, in the minds of some, both) of these constitutionally required provisions, the Florida Supreme Court had broken the law. What choice did the U.S. Supreme Court have but to act, and act decisively, as it ultimately did?

This is not the place to discuss the rightness or wrongness of the majority's doctrinal reasoning. For one thing, such a discussion calls for too much of a value judgment, one depending too much on "the eye of the beholder" in constructing an answer to be useful. Any answer we could arrive at would depend too much on who was constructing the answer—and on that person's candidate in the 2000 election. And although none of these considerations lessens the intrinsic importance of answering this question nor demeans the answers proposed by many to it, such answers provide little insight into the wider questions surrounding the Court's actions and legal reasoning.[45] More important for our purposes, such a discussion offers little in the way of insight into the motivations shaping this ruling. Just noting that the justices were correct in their doctrinal reasoning tells us little about how they arrived at these ideas or makes clear why they adopted them (as opposed to other, potentially correct doctrinal or practical options).

One aspect of the "the court was right/wrong" argument does offer a window into these matters: the majority's deep-seated opposition to the Florida Supreme Court's legal reasoning—a legal reasoning that the Court's majority totally disavowed. By comparing these two contrasting approaches to counting votes, we can apply a slightly less personal standard to determine if the justices in the majority had grounds to feel "forced to act."[46] For by evaluating the extent to which the individual justices felt troubled—or should have felt troubled—by the Florida justices' actions, we begin to see grounds for legitimately opposing the Florida court's rulings; and the greater the doctrinal difficulty they legitimately faced in this opposition, the greater their grounds for action—even extreme action. Or put another way, to the extent that we can show that the Florida supreme court's reasoning was flawed—or could be viewed as flawed—then the greater the justification that the U.S. Supreme Court justices may have felt in opposing this view with their own (right or wrong) answers. And the greater the (perceived) flaws, the deeper the need for more intense and explicit answers—even answers as radical as ending the election based solely on judicial fiat.

Our discussion here begins with noting, once again, the completely opposite readings of the law of elections by each set of jurists.[47] When faced with conflicting statutory provisions in Florida's election law, for example, a majority of the Florida justices emphasized voter inclusion as the primary objective in constructing their rulings. Drawing both on statutory law and Florida's constitution, they ruled, "This Court has repeatedly held . . . that so long as the voter's intent may be discerned from the ballot, [said] vote constitutes a 'legal vote' that should be counted." They ruled this way, the Florida justices explained, not only because this was the standard imposed by Florida statute, but because it was "only by examining the contested ballots" that "a meaningful and final determination in this election contest [could] be made." Voter empowerment was the supreme objective in determining judicial action in these matters, "notwithstanding" such other legitimate concerns as "time constraints" or the need to produce a clear winner. "We must do everything required by law to ensure that legal votes that have not been counted are included in the final election results," noted the Florida justices. The result of such reasoning was the Florida justices' decision to call for statewide recounts, even four days before the safe harbor deadline.[48]

The majority of the U.S. justices, as evidenced by the per curiam opinion and concurrence, saw things differently. Even though empowering voters was a laudable goal in the abstract, a lack of concrete and uniform standards as to what was and was not a proper vote raised serious constitutional problems. The Florida justices' objective in applying the "intent of the voter" as the primary ingredient of a proper vote was "unobjectionable as an abstract proposition and a starting principle." However, "in the absence of specific standards to ensure its equal application," this standard was functionally meaningless. "When a court orders a statewide remedy, there must be at least some assurance that the rudimentary requirements of equal treatment and fundamental fairness are satisfied," the majority noted. Granted, "in some cases the general command to ascertain intent is not susceptible to much further refinement." In this instance, however, "the question is not whether to believe a witness but how to interpret the marks or holes or scratches on an inanimate object, a piece of cardboard or paper which, it is said, might not have registered as a vote during the machine count. The factfinder confronts a thing, not a person. The search for intent can be confined by specific rules designed to ensure uniform treatment."

The deficiency of such uniform rules in Florida, the U.S. justices concluded, meant that the "recount mechanisms implemented in response to the decisions of the Florida Supreme Court [did] not satisfy the minimum requirement for non-arbitrary treatment of voters necessary to secure the fundamental right." Lacking necessary procedural "safeguards," the contest provisions simply were "not well calculated to sustain the confidence that all citizens must have in the outcome of elections." And as such, they were in direct violation of the equal protection clause of the Constitution.[49]

Chief Justice Rehnquist's reading of the law was even simpler: Article II of the Constitution and 3 U.S.C. §5 created federally enforceable standards for the operation of presidential elections. By ignoring these provisions—the supremacy of the legislature, its statutory provisions for running the election and the safe harbor provisions of §5, among other rules—the Florida justices had violated the law. The Florida justices' "elusive—perhaps delusive—[search for] certainty as to the exact count of 6 million votes," was laudable, Rehnquist wrote, but as implemented by that court, was not legal. The rules were in place for a reason, to provide certainty in an inherently uncertain process. Empowering the voter was therefore a fine goal, the concurrence implied, but not at the expense of the law itself.[50]

The chief justice's antipathy to the Florida justices went deeper than a mere difference of opinion as to the law's dictates, however. In making his case for action, Rehnquist attacked the Florida justices, comparing their actions to those of some of the worst and most blatant cases of judicial misconduct in recent American history—the state courts of the South during the civil rights movement of the 1950s and 1960s. For example, in arguing that although normally the U.S. Supreme Court deferred "to state courts on the interpretation of state law," in instances of egregious behavior on the part of state courts—such as was the case here—the Court would apply its own "independent, if still deferential, analysis of state law," Rehnquist cited as his example *NAACP v. Alabama ex rel. Patterson* (1958). At issue in that case were efforts by Alabama officials to undermine the NAACP in its efforts to combat segregation by the application of ever-changing procedural rules, all directly aimed at the NAACP's civil rights efforts. Rehnquist also cited 1964's *Bouie v. City of Columbia*, in which the U.S. Supreme Court reversed the South Carolina Supreme Court's interpretation of the state's trespass law, which was being used as a weapon against sit-in civil rights demonstrators. Relying upon its earlier *NAACP* holding, the justices in *Bouie* had concluded that "the South Carolina Supreme Court's interpretation of a state penal statute had impermissibly broadened the scope of that statute beyond what a fair reading provided, in violation of due process." Rehnquist argued that this was exactly the situation in Florida—both as to the level of misconduct by the Florida justices and the appropriate remedy. "What we would do in the present case is precisely parallel: Hold that the Florida Supreme Court's interpretation of the Florida election laws impermissibly distorted them beyond what a fair reading required, in violation of Article II."[51]

Which approach was right? More specifically, was one approach so correct a reading of the law and the Constitution that the other view must, by definition, be incorrect and hence, justification for action against it? Sadly for those desiring an easy answer or absolute clarity, the answer is no—neither view was so correct or incorrect as to destroy the validity of the other. At root, the differences between these two groups of jurists focused on their individual determinations of the primary objective shaping the regulation of the voting process: empowering voters versus protecting the integrity and equality of the voting process. Both are perfectly legitimate objectives. Both, to one extent or another, are necessary for the smooth operation of the electoral process. An election that excludes widely, or that denies the votes of legitimate voters, is by definition undemocratic; yet one that allows widespread fraud to shape its outcome and that, as a result, the electorate comes to distrust, is undemocratic as well.[52]

But was there something in the Florida justices' specific reading of the law that could have justified total opposition? Were the Florida justices somehow violating the fundamental functions or duties of an appellate court, as Chief Justice Rehnquist's concurrence suggests? Or were they perhaps ignoring existing precedents that they should have followed?

Here, too, the answer must be no. There is no way to argue objectively that the Florida justices' choices were so extreme as to be fundamentally illegitimate. The Florida courts had been interpreting the law to empower the voter for decades. The precedent "that so long as the voter's intent may be discerned from the ballot, [said] vote constitutes a 'legal vote' that should be counted," came from a 1975 case. In fact, the doctrine of empowering the voter went back in Florida law to 1917's *Darby v. State*. Since then, there had been many instances in which the Florida courts had upheld this precedent. The most recent pronouncement was, in fact, only two years old in 2000—1998's *Beckstrom* case.[53] Meanwhile, Florida's election statutes (in particular section 101.5614) held that "no vote shall be declared invalid or void if there is a clear indication of the intent of the voter."[54] In ruling as they did, therefore, the Florida justices had solid doctrinal grounds on which to base their actions.

The Florida justices could also make a strong case for the legitimacy of their actions as nothing more than statutory interpretation. Faced with ambiguity, the seven Florida justices made choices between conflicting statutes. Often their choices drew heavily on one statutory provision instead of another. But this is what statutory interpretation by the courts is all about. And, as the Florida justices had made clear in their reply to the U.S. Supreme Court's remand in *Palm Beach County Canvassing Board v. Harris*, "legislative intent—as always—[was] the polestar" guiding the Florida courts in their efforts to interpret the state's electoral statutes properly. "Where the language of the Code [was] clear and amenable to a reasonable and logical interpretation," the Florida justices explained, "courts [were] without power to diverge from the intent of the Legislature as expressed in the plain language of the Code." However, such was not the case with Florida's election laws. "Chapter 102 [was] unclear and in conflict [with other rules] in several respects." Given this fact, and "in light of these ambiguities, the Court" properly resorted "to traditional rules of statutory construction to determine legislative intent," the Florida justices argued.[55] Granted that these decisions were clearly in conflict with the current legislature's views on the subject—not to mention, as it turned out, with the views of five of the U.S. justices—but there was nothing technically illegitimate in the Florida justices' self-identified interpretative approach.

What then of the subjective realm? Did the U.S. justices at least have grounds to *perceive* fault and failure—perceptions of legal breakdowns great enough to *demand* action? Clearly seven U.S. justices saw problems with how Florida ran its elections, and five of them showed clear discomfort with the Florida justices' approach in enforcing these procedures. But was this discomfort enough *by itself* to demand action? Once again, we can only speculate. However, by examining the majority U.S. justices' individual judicial philosophies and voting tendencies, along with their expressed views of the ongoing events in Florida (where known), a partial picture of how they might have viewed the situation does emerge. And, in this case, the answer is yes, such grounds for action could have, and most likely did, exist in the minds of the five-member majority.

Consider Justice Antonin Scalia. Since his appointment to the Court in 1986, Scalia had adopted a text-based jurisprudence in shaping his individual rulings. As he explained in 1994's *Callins v. Collins*, when deciding cases, judges should be governed only by the "text and tradition of the Constitution," and not by their own "intellectual, moral, and personal perceptions."[56] The Constitution was not a living document, and judges were not free to interpret the law as they wished. Such was the path to disaster. As Scalia made clear in a 1989 lecture, the "main danger in judicial interpretation of the Constitution—or, for that matter, in judicial interpretation of any law—is that the judges will mistake their own predilections for the law." Subjectivism in constitutional or statutory interpretation was inappropriate, Scalia explained, because such judicial actions violated "the very principle that legitimizes judicial review," namely the idea that the Constitution was, in point of fact, an "enactment that has a fixed meaning ascertainable through the usual devices familiar to those learned in the law." Put another way, for judicial review to work, the Constitution had to provide a stable set of rules and principles by which to judge the actual meaning of the law. For "if the Constitution were not that sort of a 'law,' but a novel invitation to apply current societal values," asked Scalia, "what reason would there be to believe that the invitation was addressed to the courts rather than to the legislature?"[57] Consequently, as Scalia argued in another lecture at the University of Chicago that same year, when the text of the Constitution or of a statute embodied a rule, judges should simply apply that rule as the law.[58]

It is not hard to see how Scalia could have been angered by the Florida justices' actions. Although no doubt Scalia would have agreed that there was enough ambiguity within Florida's electoral statutes to justify judicial review, the Florida justices' attempt to apply an overarching "empower the voter" standard in interpreting these ambiguities would have run head-on into Scalia's text-based, originalist jurisprudence. "Empowering the voter" is a relatively vague standard by which to judge between conflicting statutory wordings. It lends itself, at a minimum, to claims of "judicial lawmaking." Scalia would have been much more comfortable, no doubt, with a narrower, text-based justification for the Florida justices' specific interpretative choices—a clearly stated rule that judges could easily follow. At the least, such a text-based, originalist approach would have lessened the potential for the Florida justices to impose their own personal values on the decision-making process—an objective near and dear to Scalia's jurisprudential philosophy. As Scalia noted in 1989, "it displays more judicial restraint to [base decisions on general rules] than to announce that, 'on balance,' we think the law was violated here—leaving ourselves free to say in the next case that, 'on balance,' it was not."[59]

The Florida justices, however, never wavered in their views. Even those justices who dissented in *Gore v. Harris* did so largely on the practical grounds of a lack of time and not in opposition to the "empower the voter" approach of the majority.[60] It was perhaps with this in mind that Scalia wrote in his concurrence to the stay order: "It suffices to say that the issuance of the stay suggests that a majority of the Court, while not deciding the issues presented, believe that the petitioner has a substantial probability of success."[61] The Florida justices had interpreted the law improperly. As such, their decisions should not be allowed to stand. And if the decision was wrong, so too were the recounts implemented under this ruling. If nothing else, these views underscore Scalia's ultimate vote against the Florida justices' legal logic.

Like Scalia, Justice Clarence Thomas is an originalist. However, where Scalia bases his originalism on text-based analysis, Thomas bases his on history. Thomas's opinions are often filled with references to the Framers' intentions. He sees these intentions as "compelling directives that dictate the outcomes and reasoning in cases." In particular, he sees them as limiting the ability of judges to "impose their own values and policy preferences upon the law."[62] As Thomas explained in *Lewis v. Casey* (1996), "it is a bedrock principle of judicial restraint that a right be lodged firmly in the text or tradition of a specific constitutional provision before we will recognize it as fundamental. Strict adherence to this approach is essential if we are to fulfill our constitutionally assigned role of giving full effect to the mandate of the Framers without infusing the constitutional fabric with our own political views."[63] For, as he explained in a 1996 lecture at the University of Kansas,

if judges and judicial decisions are nothing but the expressions of the preferences and agendas of different groups in society, then the law is nothing more than Force and Will, rather than reason and judgment. If I or any other judge allow our decisions to be guided by popular sentiment and group rights and demands, then the Constitution will be nothing but a malleable, transparent barrier to majoritarian desires. If the rule of law is so easily manipulated, then there are no courts at all, only legislatures, and no Constitution or law at all, only opinion polls.[64]

Thomas's originalist views of the Constitution and the judicial decision-making process thus rest on two bedrock assumptions. First, though he "may concede that original intent is not clear with respect to certain constitutional provisions, he [had] . . . great confidence in his ability to 'know' the Framers' intentions for most issues."[65] Consequently, whereas others have found significant inconsistencies in his application of originalism, Thomas does not. More to the point, this is a standard that Thomas expects other courts to abide by.[66] Second, and perhaps more significant, he believes that the great evil that originalism protects against is judicial activism. Judges should not impose their own personal views upon the law or the Constitution. To Thomas, it is a benchmark of the law that "a judge does not look to his or her sex or racial, social or religious background when deciding a case. It is exactly these factors that a judge must push to one side in order to render a fair, reasoned judgment on the meaning of the law . . . otherwise he is not a judge, but a legislator."[67] And although here too many have argued that imposing his own personal views is exactly what Justice Thomas generally does in his rulings, once again Justice Thomas sees no inconsistencies or improprieties in his actions.[68]

Applied to *Bush v. Gore*, these views similarly portray a justice likely to be uncomfortable with the instrumentalist approach of the Florida justices. As Justice Thomas noted in his 1997 speech, "it is important for us to remember that as judges we cannot use ambiguity as a license to project our modern theories and preconceptions upon the Constitution. Rather, we must strive to operate, even in those areas of ambiguity or unclarity, with principles and with rules. . . . Simply because it is hard to find an answer does not mean that there are no answers. Just because it is tough to discern a principle does not mean that we should seek no principles at all. Just because it is hard to discern the legislature's intent is no reason for judges to substitute their policy preferences."[69]

Hence, when Bush in his briefs argued that the Florida justices "altered the 'manner' of appointing electors," choosing in the process "to substitute a scheme of [their] own devise" from that set out by the Florida legislature, these arguments likely found fertile ground in the judicial philosophy of Justice Thomas. This was judging as lawmaking. This was confusing the distinct roles of legislature and court. And, most of all, this was a case of four judges taking advantage of ambiguous statutes to impose their will in place of that of a democratically elected legislature. Or, at least, such views as these would have been consistent with Thomas's self-identified judicial philosophy.

When we turn to Chief Justice William Rehnquist, the picture gets murkier. On the one hand, Rehnquist was a conservative jurist with strong views as to the proper reach of the law and the judiciary's role in limiting this reach. He agreed with both Scalia and Thomas that the job of the courts did not include superseding or replacing the legislative branch of government. So long as Congress did not impinge on the constitutional structure of government or improperly limit individual rights, Rehnquist held, the courts should refrain from acting. In fact, Rehnquist saw great dangers in uncontrolled judicial action. It was with this viewpoint in mind that Rehnquist argued that judges should bind themselves and their rulings closely to the specific intentions of lawmakers.[70]

On the other hand, in practice the chief justice could be unpredictable in giving effect to this philosophy. Rehnquist was a pragmatist and grew more so with each passing year. He often was more concerned with jurisprudential outcomes than with methodologies. In particular, Rehnquist had strong views on the need for a strict separation of powers within the federal government, on federalism's demand of a more balanced power relationship between the federal government and the states, and on the innate ability of the federal courts to provide leadership in these and similar matters.[71] Tellingly, in his nomination hearings for the chief justiceship in 1986, Rehnquist quoted from Justice Oliver Wendell Holmes Jr. that "where the legislature was dealing with its own citizens, it was not part of the judicial function to thwart public opinion *except in extreme cases* [emphasis added]."[72] The key is that when it came to issues of federalism and separation of powers, Rehnquist saw more grounds for federal judicial action.

With regard to his actions in *Bush v. Gore*, Rehnquist's strict adherence to constitutional statutory construction could explain the general tenor of his concurrence. Article II and §5 set out what Rehnquist argued were clear guidelines for presidential elections. The Florida legislature, in turn, had passed statutes in an effort to abide by these guidelines. In ignoring these provisions, the Florida justices had acted improperly and needed correction. This was, by definition, an example of judges imposing their own views in place of that of the legislature—and in this particular instance, the Constitution of the United States. True, many have argued that the chief justice's reading of Article II and §5 was strained and even mistaken—in particular criticizing his argument that together these two provisions created a strong and determinative federal question, one controlling the running of presidential elections and further that §5 created a mandatory deadline given that the Florida legislature had written this date into its election statutes.[73] Still, there is little doubt that this reading of the law served to limit what Rehnquist likely saw as a court overreaching the bounds of proper judicial action.

What this does not explain is why he felt so angry at the Florida justices and so driven to act as a result. Rehnquist was supposed to be the defender of state-centered federalism. For years he had led a neo-federalism revolution, chipping away at Congress's freedom to impose whatever limits it wanted on the states. Why suddenly change views? Part of the answer, no doubt, comes from the other half of Rehnquist's judicial personality; his willingness to focus on results may have led him to see in Article II and §5 a stronger federal question than might have been the case. In other words, it is possible that, as many have claimed, Chief Justice Rehnquist simply wanted George W. Bush to win. But how to explain the anger and force of emotion behind the chief justice's actions?

This question, in fact, defines where things get murky in regard to Rehnquist and his reading of the law. From the outside, there seems to be nothing to justify Rehnquist's intensity of feeling. Nor does his wanting Bush to win explain his anger, either. Rehnquist still could have worked for a Bush victory without being so clearly angry at the Florida justices and their legal reasoning. Something else had to have been operating in the chief justice's mind; some other factor had to be shaping his actions, at least in part. That something most likely was Rehnquist's perception of constitutional and political crisis—a crisis that he saw originating in the Florida justices' liberal reading of the Florida electoral statutes. In fact, the chief justice's unique reading of Article II and §5—one that seemingly challenged his own views on federalism—also may have been the result of his concerns over political and constitutional crisis. After all, one way to hold off a crisis is to find strict and controlling constitutional provisions that mandate a solution based in law and not in partisan politics. If his reading of the law was strained, therefore, perhaps it was because Rehnquist was straining to save the nation from a horrible crisis.[74]

Finally, we turn to Justices Sandra Day O'Connor and Anthony Kennedy. Both already were seen, as the U.S. justices heard oral arguments in *Bush v. Gore*, as the swing votes on the Court—conservatives who occasionally voted a more moderate line. Both were viewed in particular as the key swing votes in *Bush v. Gore*.[75] Gore's lawyers, in particular, felt (wrongly as it turned out) that they had a chance to convince one, or even both, of these justices to vote in favor of the ongoing recounts. They held this hope as a direct result of the two justices' unique judicial philosophies and styles.

Consider Justice O'Connor. Law professor Craig Joyce, editor of O'Connor's *The Majesty of the Law: Reflections of a Supreme Court Justice* (2003), notes how, "along the way" to writing her 680 opinions for the Court, "there would be no abstract doctrinalism, no rigid interpretive methodologies, no one-size-fits-all rules or slogans. Instead, Justice O'Connor's jurisprudence would be grounded by her special concern for practical problem solving deeply rooted in faithful adherence to the Constitution and the laws as she read them." O'Connor, Joyce notes, "is, above all, a real person who understands real people and has made a life—and, indeed, a jurisprudence—of serving them." More to the point, "Justice O'Connor's style of problem solving, both in Arizona government before 1981 and on the federal bench thereafter, mirrored the style that real people adopt intuitively in solving problems in their everyday lives: they recognize that different problems often require different approaches." Her method of decision making was thus applied "case-by-case," and "required deliberation by incrementalism."[76]

This case-by-case style did not mean that O'Connor lacked guiding principles. O'Connor had many deeply seated principles and beliefs, but these principles were encased in the factual context of the case and, on the whole, were personal rather than ideological. Thus, one of her strongest values was the idea that people should take responsibility for their own lives. In her autobiography, *Lazy B: Growing Up on a Cattle Ranch in the American Southwest*, O'Connor tells a story in which she was driving two hours on her father's ranch to deliver lunch to the workers. On the way, her jeep had a flat tire. Always capable, O'Connor used stones to prop up the jeep and changed the tire. As a consequence, she arrived with lunch for the workers an hour late. Yet when she arrived home, rather than being praised for fixing the flat, she was quietly chided for not getting the lunch to them on time. O'Connor, in retrospect, realized that she should have started earlier. "Only one thing was expected: an on-time lunch. No excuses accepted."[77] On a more technical level, O'Connor also exhibited a strong respect for precedent and an abiding commitment to the principle of stare decisis ("the decision of the court stands").[78] On the other hand, O'Connor's opinions also "frequently justif[ied] exceptions within rules, arriv[ing] at limited, context-specific solutions," when her reading of the facts demanded such a result.[79] The result was a justice whose rulings, though based on sound doctrine and precedents, often were rooted just as much as (if not more) in her personal gut-reaction to the case at hand as in doctrinal or ideological sources.

And when it came to *Bush v. Gore*, O'Connor's gut was most likely very upset. O'Connor believed in individual self-reliance and responsibility, both factors sadly missing in the whole postelection crisis. She preferred to follow precedents and she expected other courts to do the same. She distrusted sweeping doctrinal approaches to settling a case and she worried over judicial overreach. When combined with her generally conservative political leanings, it soon becomes apparent how O'Connor could have found the events in Florida very troubling, in particular the actions of the Florida justices. As O'Connor noted in a recent interview with ABC News reporter Jan Crawford Greenburg, the Florida justices, in her view, were "off on a trip of [their] own."[80] How could the Supreme Court not take up this matter? At the same time, we also can see how she might have been unconvinced by the highly technical reasoning proposed by Chief Justice Rehnquist for overturning the Florida justices' decision—hence her adoption of the equal protection arguments of the per curiam opinion.

In contrast to O'Connor, Justice Kennedy was more clearly a doctrinaire conservative. Kennedy was a central player in the Rehnquist Court's redefinition of federalism, helping to invalidate a number of congressional statutes as inconsistent with the limits of federalism. Kennedy was also a reliable member of the conservative majority's attacks on race-based affirmative action programs. Kennedy's conservatism, however, was built upon a strong core of moderate beliefs and values. As constitutional historian Mark Tushnet explains, Kennedy's "conservatism centered on a moderate libertarian streak, about which he himself was somewhat conflicted, complemented by a vague optimism about the good sense of the American people." This libertarian streak led Kennedy to distrust government intrusions into an individual's life. Thus, Kennedy voted with the liberal bloc on issues of abortion and gay rights. At the same time, his trust in the good sense of the people often led Kennedy to uphold the judgments of the people's representatives in government. Kennedy, in other words, understood that what libertarianism said government should not do, democracy argued that it should be allowed to do—and vice versa. Adding to the confusion, Kennedy had a strong belief in the limits of judicial power. Rooted in both practicality and democratic theory, Kennedy believed that "if judges went too far, the political system would slap them down."[81] Then again, when it came to himself, Kennedy has a deep-seated faith in his ability and duty to "impose order on a disordered reality."[82]

Trying to pull all these pieces together into a coherent jurisprudential philosophy proved difficult, if not impossible, for Kennedy. Despite strongly held personal beliefs, Kennedy's judicial logic was often confused. In fact, according to Court insiders, Kennedy himself often seemed confused as he pondered the issues raised by a case. At the least, Kennedy is known for needing time to deliberate on his opinions. At the most, he often seems simply lost as he tries to find a coherent rationale for his actions. Kennedy's dilemma is best expressed by the oxymoron "moderate conservative." If one is moderate, one is by definition not a conservative. Politically, however, Kennedy was exactly that, a conservative. Yet personally, he was a moderate. Ultimately, Kennedy's judicial decision-making style has been shaped by his need to find a middle ground between his conservative values and his moderate sensibilities. And if, as many have complained, his opinions are full of pompous and self-pitying descriptions of how hard the case before the Court was, his rhetoric is only a reflection of his internal conflict.[83]

The overall effect of Kennedy's jurisprudential—and perhaps personal—confusion was that Kennedy was open to viewing cases in isolation, ruling as much from the gut as from the head. Hence his conservative views opened him to accepting the Bush petition for certiorari ("A no-brainer!" Kennedy noted to Jan Crawford Greenburg. "A state court deciding a federal constitutional issue about the presidential election? Of course you take the case").[84] Meanwhile, the political and legal complexities of the case likely fed Kennedy's tendency to seek the middle ground—both doctrinally and practically—in his final vote and opinion. In this tendency, he resembled Justice O'Connor, though for very different reasons.[85]

Given these descriptions of O'Connor and Kennedy, it is clear why Gore's lawyers felt that they had a chance of winning over either or both of the swing votes. Both justices were committed to viewing each case as a totality, and both (though again for different reasons) tended to prefer limited rulings. It also be-

comes clear why the consensus among legal scholars is that the per curiam opinion's use of equal protection as justification for action—and the Court's decision
to limit this remedy to this case alone—lay with these two justices. Word from the
Court was that neither O'Connor nor Kennedy was willing to adopt Chief Justice
Rehnquist's Article II reasoning for ending the election—which, again according
to rumor, Rehnquist originally presented to his colleagues as his proposed majority
opinion. Presumably, both justices had difficulty in accepting the federal-question
aspects of Rehnquist's argument—especially after the Florida justices came back
with their reply to the Supreme Court's remand in *Bush v. Palm Beach County
Canvassing Board*, arguing that their actions were fully based on Florida statutes
and not the Florida constitution.[86] Combined with these justices' ad hoc approach
to judging, the result shifted the Court toward an equal protection remedy.

We now return to the matter of subjective justifications for action. Although
the Court may have lacked clear and adequate objective grounds for attacking the
Florida justices for their actions, given what we have seen of the majority justices'
judicial philosophies, we should not find it surprising that, on a subjective level,
the majority felt justified in challenging the Florida justices' legal and constitutional reasoning. What the Florida justices were doing was simply too much at
odds with the doctrinal and practical values of the five majority justices to allow
such a ruling to stand. But was this difference alone enough of an explanation for
the majority's intense commitment to overturning the Florida justices' ruling and
ending the election? Recall that the issue here was not whether the U.S. justices had
sufficient grounds for overturning the Florida justices, but whether there were
enough grounds within that state court's ruling to demand *immediate* and *extreme*
action—even at the cost of the Court's own prestige and legitimacy in future cases.
Legitimacy and prestige were exactly what the decision to halt the election cost the
Court. True, just how much prestige the Court would lose, and for how long, remained unknown. But anyone with a modicum of experience in such matters must
have known that the justices were dipping deeply into their capital of good will
and respect, and doing so when the practical benefits of this expense—at least
when based on the wrongness of the Florida justices—were questionable.

It is at this point that the constitutional-justification argument begins to break
down. Did they have legal justification to act? Yes—especially if we view the electoral process as Scalia and Thomas did. But did these grounds demand an *immediate* end to the election? Here the answer is at best a maybe, and most likely a no.
Take for example the Court's ultimate five-to-four split. One of the more interesting aspects of the Supreme Court's ruling in *Bush v. Gore* was how easily the vote
could have been seven-to-two. Based on their dissents, it is likely that all that would
have been needed to bring Justices Breyer and Souter into the majority was a decision to limit the Court's remedy to a simple remand—most likely one with specific instructions as to how the Florida justices were to correct their errors. In fact,
as many commentators have noted, Justices Breyer and Souter both joined the

majority on the issue of equal protection, not only out of a shared reading of the law but also for the tactical reason of trying to shift O'Connor or Kennedy (or both) to the "liberal" side on the issue of ending the recount. One source close to Justice Souter, for example, noted, "David can count, and he knew he was going to lose. So he set about to find a way to make the result palatable and legitimate to the American people, even if he disagreed with the result."[87] Reports from the Court note that Justice Breyer actually walked into Justice Kennedy's chambers (in what turns out to be an uncommon occurrence in the modern Court, if not as much between the two justices) to try to convince Kennedy to change his views on ending the recounts. *Vanity Fair* even reports that, for a time, Kennedy did change his views, only to shift back toward ending the election immediately.[88] After the election, Justice Souter reportedly complained to a group of prep-school students that if only he had had "one more day—one more day," he could have won over Kennedy.[89] Time, however, as always in this case, was the enemy and Souter never got his extra day. And what could have been a wider seven-to-two (or alternately a liberal-based six-to-three) majority under the equal protection banner never formed. Five of the justices felt impelled to end the election immediately despite driving Breyer and Souter into dissent and thus weakening the majority's moral and constitutional authority.[90]

So where in the Florida justices' ruling could this sense of overriding necessity be found? In his concurrence to the stay order, Justice Scalia suggested that the threat of undermining the confidence of the American public in the electoral process—should votes be counted illegally and then have to be overturned—provided such a justification. But this is all. Nowhere in the per curiam opinion does the majority explain how or why the Florida justices' specific ruling *alone* posed such a threat that immediately ending the election was required. To be sure, that ruling might have been constitutionally suspect; and we could argue that the Florida justices were egregious in ignoring federal constitutional provisions. But did this alone justify ending the election at such cost to the Court's reputation?

Similarly, we could argue that Chief Justice Rehnquist's Article II and §5 arguments provided such justification based on the lack of time before the safe harbor deadline. But this argument's intensity rested not on the doctrinal wrongness of the Florida justices—which the chief justice did perceive and which led him to call for the overturning of the Florida ruling—but on the practical issue of the lack of time. Had more time existed, there would have been no grounds under the chief justice's concurrence for ending the election right there and then. A remand with strongly worded instructions to apply the rules as outlined by Article II and §5 properly would have been constitutionally adequate to remedy the wrong (and, incidentally, to elect George W. Bush president). It was only the lateness of the date by reference to the safe harbor deadline that gave the Florida justices' constitutional misreading of Article II and §5 its urgency in Rehnquist's eyes. As the chief justice noted in concluding his concurrence, "the federal deadlines for the

Presidential election simply do not permit even such a shortened process [of vote counting]." Hence, given "the legislative intent identified by the Florida Supreme Court to bring Florida within the 'safe harbor' provision of 3 U.S.C. §5, the remedy prescribed by the Supreme Court of Florida" simply could not "be deemed . . . 'appropriate.'"[91]

So, even though the majority's perceptions of the Florida justices' rulings could explain why the U.S. justices acted, and acted in favor of George W. Bush, it does not adequately explain the intensity and immediacy of this felt need. The political costs of acting were so high, and the constitutional benefits of such immediate action (at least, on a doctrinal or institutional level) so few, that the disproportionate nature of the majority's remedy does not make any sense in this context. Overturning the Florida justices was one thing, but what of unilaterally ending the election? That step seems excessive, too sweeping an act to be justified *solely* on the grounds of the Florida justices' constitutional misconduct.

Partisan political preference could explain this need, and perhaps even justify the remedy adopted, but as we have already seen, partisanship alone was not enough to explain the majority's actions, either. The practical needs of partisanship (that is, ending the election to assure Bush's victory) simply were not great enough to command such actions. Bush was most likely going to win no matter what actions the Court took. Something more had to be going on to explain this factor. There had to be some other concern that drove the U.S. justices to battle on this subject.

It is here that our remaining two categories of explanation—political crisis and judicial ego—come into play. Though in different ways, both explanations are rooted in the intensity of the moment when the Court handed down its decision in *Bush v. Gore*. Put simply, no matter if the political and constitutional crisis posed by the postelection controversy was real or perceived, the need to act to forestall a catastrophe—and their overriding belief in their ability to do just this—explains the majority's drive to act quickly and with massive force (especially when this drive led to results that the majority justices were apt to approve anyway).

Let's start with the perception of a political crisis. Both before and after *Bush v. Gore*, the self-satisfied refrain from legal commentators that dominated the airwaves and print media was that "the constitutional system was working as planned, after all, there were no tanks in the streets or riots over the election's outcome."[92] Yet behind the façade of calm and reason, the general tone of the coverage of the postelection crisis was frenzied and even panicked. Editorialists, commentators, and even reporters talked wildly of "constitutional train wrecks" and political "chaos," of "stolen elections," and "coups d'etat"—of a nation on the brink of something cataclysmic.

Often the commentary took the form of a negative threat—that we were not yet in a constitutional crisis, but if things continued as they were, all bets were off.[93] On November 22, for example, U.S. Representative Billy Tauzin, a Republican from Chackbay, Louisiana, warned how the nation "is on the brink now of a constitutional crisis" as rapid-fire events such as the decision to halt vote counting in Miami-Dade County added more chaos to the disorderly process of counting Florida's critical votes for president of the United States.[94] On December 1, Democratic vice-presidential hopeful Joseph Lieberman argued that the Florida legislature's special session to select its own presidential electors could throw the country into a "constitutional crisis."[95] Eight days later still, Charles O. Jones, an emeritus professor of political science at the University of Wisconsin, warned, "I don't know whether this is a constitutional crisis, but it is totally unknown territory. We are seeking to test a set of processes that are creaky from disuse, and nobody knows how they work or where the oil can is."[96]

At other times, the depiction of a crisis was immediate. As early as November 8, the political historian Sean Wilentz of Princeton University commented, "We're in a constitutional crisis and it's anybody's guess as to how it's going to be resolved. Unless there can be absolute certainty that the result in Florida was not only fair and accurate, but also untainted, then we've got a problem. The question is how legitimate will the vote in Florida be?"[97] Roughly three weeks later, on December 8, Chief Justice Wells of the Florida Supreme Court warned in his dissent how it was his court's decision to order presidential election recounts that "propels the country into an unprecedented and unnecessary constitutional crisis . . . I have to conclude that there is a real and present likelihood that this constitutional crisis will do substantial damage to our country, our state, and to this court as an institution."[98] That same day, James A. Baker III, Bush's lead spokesperson in Florida, reiterated the "constitutional crisis" language of Wells's dissent in a press conference.[99] The following day Frank Keating, the Republican governor of Oklahoma, in what would became a standard Republican speaking point, seconded Wells's and Baker's views. "This court has given us a calamity . . . tragic and unfortunate," said Keating, "it has the marks of a constitutional crisis. It's messy, nasty and regrettable."[100]

Whereas both Democrats and Republicans were guilty of such hyperbole, the majority of comments on the themes of "constitutional crisis" and especially "they're stealing the election" seemed to come from the political right. One reason for this tendency was no doubt tactical, as it had always been Bush's strategy to limit the recount process—and scaring people with talk of a "constitutional crisis" furthered this end. But mostly Republicans warned of a crisis because they either truly perceived that one existed or feared that such was soon to be the case. Thus, as Dwight Kiel of the University of Central Florida notes, "*The Weekly Standard* and the *Wall Street Journal* accused Gore of a coup d'etat and of impeachable offenses because of the litigation he began in Florida" out of political frustration that was thirty years in the building.[101] Meanwhile, the *National Review* blamed Al Gore for what it boldly described as "a constitutional crisis." As the editors wrote:

This is a constitutional crisis. Al Gore has forced it. The supreme court of Florida has nurtured it, and it's doubtful that the Supreme Court can quell it. How is it a crisis? Well, . . . a court in Florida has arrogated to itself the power to pick the president based upon principles found in their magic box of nice and fair things to do. It has refused to address the concerns of the U.S. Supreme Court. In turn, the U.S. Supreme Court has been forced into paying down its reserve of credibility in order to fix the problem. The validity of national elections has been placed in doubt. The idea that courts are more legitimate political organs than elected politicians has been pounded deeper into our political consciousness. Indeed, Joe Lieberman expressly declared that if either legislature— Florida's or Congress—dare *follow* the Constitution then we would be in a constitutional crisis. Considering what liberals think a real constitutional crisis looks like, them's fighting words.[102]

Jonathan Schell of the *Nation* put it even more simply. The Republicans were "manufacturing a crisis" with their intemperate comments. Implicit in their comments was the threat that if Bush didn't get his way in Florida, the Republican Party was prepared to turn what so far has been a legal battle in one state into a true constitutional crisis.[103] And so the "debate" and "commentary" proceeded throughout the five weeks following the November 7 election.

For their part, the justices were most likely following the unfolding events in Florida through the media. According to *Vanity Fair*'s article "The Path to Florida," everyone in the Court, from justices to clerks, was keeping an eye on the growing crisis in Florida—though many doubted that the matter would ever get before the Court. Also, the fact that much of this argument appeared in the conservative press made it more likely that the conservative justices who ultimately made up the Court's majority in *Bush v. Gore* would have seen and discussed these views. In any event, all one had to do was turn on a television news program—any television news program—and the idea that bad or questionable or disorganized things were happening down in Florida was hard to avoid. All one had to do was watch the card counting in Broward or Palm Beach Counties, or the "riots" taking place just outside the Miami-Dade vote counting, to acquire this view.

We cannot know how much this pubic relations–influenced coverage affected the views of the individual justices. However, in the case of Justice O'Connor, there is plausible evidence that her views of the Florida recount and the actions of the Florida Supreme Court were shaped—at least in part—by the public relations battle between Bush and Gore. Take, for example, her comments during oral argument. First, she attacked the Florida justices for their activist ways (echoing arguments from the Bush camp throughout the postelection crisis): "That's, I think, a concern that we have. And I did not find, really, a response by the Florida Supreme Court to this court's remand in the case a week ago. It just seemed to kind of bypass it and assume that all those changes and deadlines were just fine and they'd go ahead and adhere to them. And I found that troublesome." Later, as the conversation switched to the standards used to determine proof of a vote, she asked in a frustrated tone: "Well, why isn't the standard the one that voters are instructed to follow, for goodness sakes? I mean, it couldn't be clearer. I mean, why don't we go to that standard?" Here, too, O'Connor's question tapped into the Republican public relations campaign, which had been placing the blame for all electoral problems on inattentive voters. (It also likely grew out of her own belief in individual self-reliance.) Also telling were the views of some of her law clerks. According to *Vanity Fair*, "at a dinner on November 29, attended by clerks from several chambers, an O'Connor clerk said that O'Connor was determined to overturn the Florida decision and was merely looking for the grounds. O'Connor was known to decide cases on gut feelings and facts rather than grand theories, then stick doggedly with whatever she decided. In this instance, one clerk recalls, 'she thought the Florida court was trying to steal the election and that they had to stop it.'" And, in point of fact, the night before the Supreme Court convened to hear oral argument in *Bush v. Gore*, O'Connor sent a sealed memo to all her colleagues' chambers "stating that she, too, felt the Florida Supreme Court had improperly usurped the state legislature's power."[104] Even six years after the fact, O'Connor still argues that the Florida justices were "off on a trip of [their] own" and needed controlling.[105]

There were, in fact, valid grounds for actual concern on the justices' part—if not necessarily those being pushed against the Florida justices by conservative commentators. Think about the past electoral emergencies that formed the set of contingencies informing the justices' approach to this case. The controversial elections of 1800, 1824, and 1876—and even the all-but-forgotten problems plaguing New York's participation in the presidential election of 1789—each pointed out just how difficult resolving such issues could be. Each of the remedies in these cases, though they worked, did so awkwardly and with serious political and even constitutional ramifications after the fact.

The 1789 election went smoothly, but only because George Washington was the unanimous pick of everyone for president. Had there not been a consensus candidate, imagine what would have followed as the House of Representatives sought to pick a president without the votes of the second most populous state in the Union—a state, meanwhile, that would have had representatives in the House and would have had a say in the final decision as to who became president.[106]

With the election of 1800 (in which the House picked the president only on the thirty-sixth ballot, as no candidate had received a majority of the electoral votes), the political tensions grew so great before Thomas Jefferson was finally named president, that Congress immediately passed and sent out to the states for ratification a Twelfth Amendment, one aimed at forestalling the sorts of problems that arose in 1800.[107]

In the election of 1824, the House's resolution of an election in which none of the four principal candidates had received a majority of electoral votes was plagued by charges and the appearance, if not the reality, of corruption. The "corrupt bargain" by which House Speaker Henry Clay threw his support to Secretary of State John Quincy Adams and then became President Adams's secretary of state (then the stepping-stone to the presidency) so infuriated Adams's and Clay's Democratic opponents that they rendered Adams's presidency a failure. Andrew Jackson, who won a plurality of electoral votes in 1824, easily defeated Adams in 1828 and Clay in 1832.[108]

Finally, the electoral commission plan adopted in 1876 was viewed by most at that time and after as a crude political process, one whose outcome, in the minds of some, had been "fixed" to assure Rutherford B. Hayes the presidency. Most of those who participated on the commission ended up with tarnished reputations. This was especially the case for the deciding vote, Justice Joseph P. Bradley, who— as Chief Justice Rehnquist explained in his 2004 book, *Centennial Crisis: The Disputed Election of 1876*—was "singled out for special opprobrium." And although Rehnquist attempted to restore Bradley's reputation in his book by stressing the need for the justices to act, the general lesson taken from the 1876 election emphasized just how ugly a contested election of this sort could become.[109]

The justices' personal observations of Congress also engendered a similar lack of faith when it came to that body casting the deciding vote. Recall that the most recent political and constitutional crisis in Congress had been the impeachment of William Jefferson Clinton. With the exception of Chief Justice Rehnquist, almost no one associated with the impeachment and trial of President Clinton came away with their good reputations intact. Clinton was proven a liar. He did have "sexual relations" with Monica Lewinsky and we now knew all about it. Special Prosecutor Kenneth Starr's report took on tones of an inquisition—ferreting out numerous and often irrelevant (but always scandalous and often prurient) details in an effort to find grounds (any grounds) for indicting Clinton. The House Republican leadership was proven both inept and highly partisan in its views by the crisis. Even those who objected to Clinton's actions had trouble viewing the House leadership's actions as little more than a biased effort to "get" a popular president whom they despised and resented in large part for his successes. As to their "prosecution" of Clinton in the Senate—which ultimately failed to convict Clinton—time and again the effort seemed to fade into the realm of political farce. Nor did the Democrats come off looking good. Their defenses of Clinton often seemed more like partisan attacks on the Republicans for overreaching than an effort to bring reason and logic to the mess.[110]

The key element was the partisan tone of every aspect of the impeachment and trial. A Republican majority in Congress was attacking a Democratic president on relatively thin constitutional grounds (though, in their defense, they were correct that he did lie under oath, which technically was breaking the law). The Democrats, in turn, fought back tooth and nail against what they viewed as an unfair and blatantly partisan attack on their leadership—an attack that was, they argued, brought under spurious and constitutionally insufficient grounds. The nation, meanwhile, split on the issue and chose sides. The result was controlled chaos. Even though the impeachment and trial did proceed according to the procedures set forth in the Constitution, the partisan tone of this process tainted every aspect of the proceedings. Worse yet, in the end, nothing seemed to come of the whole affair. The Republicans believed that Clinton had slipped the bonds of justice, and the Democrats cheered that the rule of law had been upheld. Yet had the situation been reversed, the positions of the two parties would have switched too. No one was happy. Everyone was angry with the other side. And the result, in the eyes of many at the time and since, was a damaged political and constitutional realm.[111]

And this was largely the same Congress to which the Constitution assigned the final say in the 2000 presidential election. The nation was already at odds over the split between Al Gore and George W. Bush. The public discourse was already heavy with partisan rhetorical attacks by each side on the other side's motives. Representatives and senators from both parties already had been drawn into the fray as talking heads in the public relations war. It did not take much imagination to extend this war of words onto the floor of Congress as it argued over who should be the next president—nor to extend this war of words beyond Congress to workplaces and street corners across America. This was not a pretty picture, especially to justices who worried about the chaotic impact of the postelection crisis. There had to have been some doubt in the majority's mind as to Congress's fitness to handle this crisis in a properly refined and constitutionally adequate manner.

In fact, had they reasoned this way, the justices would not have been alone in such crisis thinking. "That was my worst nightmare," admitted Senator Richard J. Durbin, Democrat of Illinois, to the *New York Times* following the Court's *Bush v. Gore* ruling. "As disappointing as this is, if it had gone to Congress, it would have tainted the Congressional session and the relationship with the president for a long, long time." Senator Harry Reid, Democrat of Nevada, seconded this view: "It would have been brutal." In fact, in the aftermath of the Supreme Court's ruling ending the election, many lawmakers on both sides of the aisle told *Times* reporters how fortunate it was that Congress would play no part in awarding either man the presidency of the United States: "Impeachment, they said, was vitriolic enough. But picking a president along party lines, something that most likely would have resulted in deadlock, with the House choosing Mr. Bush and the Senate choosing Mr. Gore, would have poisoned the political landscape for a long time." Or as Senator Reid puts it, "No matter what the Supreme Court does, I hope this isn't determined by politicians like me."[112]

Although such concerns as these did not demand hijacking the decision from Congress, they did reinforce the perception of crisis and make the adoption of other justifications for action easier. Congress was untrustworthy—not to mention actively afraid of taking on this matter; meanwhile, the potential for an ongoing political war was great enough to threaten the well-being of the nation. What good reasons were there for the Court *not* to act? Where was the negative in the Court's ending matters sooner instead of later? That the ultimate result of acting was also in line with the majority's desired practical outcome only made its adoption all the easier.

Still another possible factor in the majority's crisis thinking might have been simple practical expediency. Better to lance the boil quickly and get the illness over with. Here too, history provided a model for action. Following the Court's 1974 ruling in *U.S. v. Nixon*, Justice Louis Powell wrote to historian Gerald Gunther of Stanford Law School, "I was influenced, perhaps decisively, by a personal conviction that the country was undergoing a prolonged agony which already had diverted attention from pressing domestic problems and, at least arguably, weakened our capacity to influence the dangerous course of international events." The time had come, Powell's letter implied, for quick and decisive action to end the crisis and thus to allow the nation to move on to other matters.[113]

Alternately, the decision to halt the recounts could have been an attempt to fend off future litigation. Once the issue of the Florida vote got into Congress, the potential for constitutional conundrums—and hence for constitutional litigation—was enormous. What were the legitimate grounds upon which to challenge a state's Electoral College votes? Could one house of Congress force the other to act when it chose not to? Did the Florida legislature have the right and power to name its own slate of electors? What about the Florida Supreme Court? As had been the case with *U.S. v. Nixon* and the Watergate crisis in the 1970s, the constitutional stakes would have been so high, and so partisan, as to demand Supreme Court intervention—hence the likelihood that the whole dispute might be returned to the Court repeatedly if they did not bring matters to an immediate close. If nothing else, ending the vote counting precluded this scenario from happening.

These linked objectives may, in fact, have been the primary motivation shaping Chief Justice Rehnquist's response to *Bush v. Gore*. A few weeks after the Court's ruling, Rehnquist gave a lecture to the John Carroll Society, a Catholic service organization, suggesting that sometimes, for the good of the nation, members of the Court may have to become involved in political matters to prevent a national crisis. Discussing the disputed 1876 election, Rehnquist argued that the Court's involvement in that matter was vindicated by the results. "Hayes was a better president than some of his detractors predicted, and the nation as a whole settled down to a more normal existence. . . . The political processes of the country had worked," concluded Rehnquist, though "admittedly in a rather unusual way, to avoid a serious crisis." Rehnquist acknowledged the inevitable awkwardness created when Supreme Court justices assumed such a role. The costs to the reputations of the individual justices who served on the 1876 electoral commission were significant. "There are obviously very good reasons for members of the Court to say 'no' when asked," Rehnquist concluded. "The argument on the other side," Rehnquist continued, "is that there is a national crisis, and only you can avert it. It may be very hard to say 'no.'"[114]

Applied to his actions in *Bush v. Gore*, this speech "helps explain what was in Rehnquist's mind about why he took jurisdiction under such questionable circumstances," argues historian Michael Les Benedict of Ohio State University. "He's making a rather clear statement of what he thought the primary job of our governmental process was" in the Hayes-Tilden conflict. "That was to make sure the conflict is resolved peacefully, with no violence."[115] Despite the cost to their own personal reputations, the five justices on the 1876 electoral commission were simply doing their job—defending the smooth working of our constitutional system of government. Perhaps in Rehnquist's mind he was simply doing the same in *Bush v. Gore*.

We do not have such explicit statements of intent on record from the four other justices in the majority. However, we do have the wording of the per curiam opinion itself. The Court did not seek its conclusive role in this matter, the per curiam notes in its concluding passage. The members of the majority understood the "vital limits on judicial authority . . . and none [stood] more in admiration of the Constitution's design to leave the selection of the President to the people, through their legislatures, and to the political sphere" then they did.[116] The majority's preference, this passage implies, would have been to leave the matter in the hands of the state courts or even Congress. But such was not to be the case. The normal processes of choosing the president had fallen apart. "Counting somebody else's dimpled chad and not counting my dimpled chad is not giving equal protection of the law," argued Justice Scalia in a recent speech.[117] The Florida recount process had overstepped the bounds of legitimate action, and the Florida justices had facilitated this failure. The rules for running a presidential election had been cast aside. Hence, when Vice President Al Gore's legal team involved the courts in the election by asking a state court to order a recount, as Justice Kennedy has argued, the die was cast to force action on the Court.[118] "When contending parties invoke the process of the courts," Kennedy explained, "it becomes our unsought responsibility to resolve the federal and constitutional issues the judicial system has been forced to confront."[119]

Viewed in this light, the Court's actions in *Bush v. Gore* take on an almost self-sacrificing air. Not to act, despite the institutional costs to the Court, would have been abandoning their ultimate jobs as justices. Though they did not put it into these terms, implicit in their statements was an understanding that theirs was a job of constitutional triage, making the hard decisions to assure the constitutional well-being of the nation. That their acts might be unpopular or even seen as partisan was simply the cost of doing their job. The smooth working of the American constitutional system of government demanded nothing less from them.

Granted, as Justice O'Connor recently noted, the justices probably could have done a better job with the opinion if they had not been rushed. "I don't think what emerged in the last opinion was the court's best effort," O'Connor admitted. "It was operating under a very short time frame, to say the least. Given more time, I think we probably would've done better."[120] But they did not have this time. Everything associated with *Bush v. Gore* was compressed by the shortness of time—the arguments, the deliberations, the writing, and the final judgment. In fact, given the time constraints under which they operated, the justices' actions in ending the 2000 presidential election can be seen as the equivalent of battlefield surgery— fast, crude, and aimed at the bottom line of keeping the patient alive and working. Assuring a pretty scar was not an option here; foreclosing further trauma to the patient was. If only in their own heads, the justices of the majority were saving the nation from what they viewed as a much worse fate—the ongoing partisan dispute over the next president of the United States.

The justices' sense of urgency should remind us that this was, in fact, a *presidential* election. The significance of choosing the president overlay everything that the justices did. The presidency is the only governmental office voted on by the entire electorate, even though diluted by voting for electors who then vote for president. Representatives are chosen by their districts, and senators by their states. But the president is chosen by all voting Americans. The nation could afford to take time in determining who had won a House or Senate race, but not a presidential contest. This singularity explains why everyone involved was so concerned with deadlines. The possibility that we would not have a president-elect to swear into office on January 20, 2001, was terrifying. It was not that anyone was saying that this was going to happen. But the fear of just such a turn of events underlay the perceptions of many, if not most, Americans. Would it not be more efficient to solve the problem now rather than later—especially when you could be sure that immediate action would assure a winner, whereas trusting Congress to decide only promised but did not guarantee such a result?

That this was a presidential election may also explain another curious aspect of the Court's actions. Traditionally, the Rehnquist Court had very strict procedural rules for bringing a case before them. In an interview soon after the final decision was made, law professor Suzzana Sherry notes how the Rehnquist Court normally had very strict rules demanding, for instance, that all issues had to be fully argued out in the lower courts before the justices would take action and that petitioners had to have full standing before bringing a suit before the Court.[121] The rule about standing is especially important in this context in that we can legitimately argue that, under a strict reading of the rules of standing, George W. Bush did not have the right to bring his suit before the Supreme Court. If the problem was that Florida's votes were being improperly counted under an equal protection standard, then the injured party in all this was the Florida voter—not the candidates. It was the voters' rights that were being abridged, their votes that were being improperly counted. Only if one assumed that Bush had already won the election and that the recounts were going to improperly "take" the election away from him, did Bush acquire full standing.

The point here is not that the justices somehow broke the rules in George W. Bush's favor in an effort to get him elected. The point is that *no one* ever raised the issue of Bush's standing to bring suit before the Court. To anyone who has explored the arcane legal subject known as "the law of federal courts," such an omission is astonishing—but so it turned out. The Gore attorneys never raised the standing issue in either of their briefs or during oral arguments before the Court; nor did any of the amicus briefs filed by interested third parties. Even the lower federal court judges who heard this matter totally ignored the issue of standing. And while one can take this silence as proof that Bush had standing, that no one on the Democrats' side even tried to keep Bush out of federal court with this argument is amazing. Perhaps it's an argument that only law professors could love—but, then again, it might have worked and thus permitted the recounts to carry on unchecked.

That no one raised even the possibility that Bush lacked standing probably has to do with the dispute at the case's core being a presidential election. The outcome of this case mattered too much to be settled on such technical grounds as a candidate's standing to bring suit. It seems almost obscene for the holder of the most powerful office in the world to be determined based on such narrow grounds. And this is the point. That this was a presidential election focused everyone on the outcome of the dispute to the exclusion of all other considerations—including the process by which the winner was determined. Like a mouse whose eyes were locked with a cobra's hypnotic gaze, we had all been mesmerized by the outcome of this important event. Not just the people and the partisans, nor just the media and the pundits, but the very judges ruling on this matter too—all were hypnotized by the glittering prize of the presidency and the urgent need to decide who had won it.[122]

Finally, we must not ignore ego in our analysis. Even if the perception of crisis among the justices was not as deep as that held by Chief Justice Rehnquist, it must have proven nearly impossible for the five justices in the majority to have stood by and not done anything as important constitutional matters were being settled. Whether intended or not, the rulings of the Florida state courts called into question basic issues of constitutional rights, responsibilities, and policymaking. These were issues near and dear to any Supreme Court justice's heart. They were also issues of great import to the nation. So even though tradition said stay out, ego and a concern for the shape of the law made it hard for the justices not to take on the fight. It was not that the justices felt that they could do it better than the Florida bench—though no doubt, given the amount of self-confidence it takes to be a Supreme Court justice, they did think this way—but that the issues in play and the consequences in sight had grown so large that no one of the intellectual power of a Supreme Court justice was likely to sit out this crisis willingly. Add the fear of ongoing constitutional crisis, their personal concerns with the Florida justices' jurisprudence, and their own political preferences, and the justices' well-developed egos provide a final component to understanding the Supreme Court's decision to act decisively to end the 2000 presidential election.

When all these factors are taken together, the most viable conclusion we can draw is that the justices took the case of *Bush v. Gore*, stopping the recounts and raising the specter of judicial overreach in the picking of the president, out of a mix of personal ego, political preference, and ultimately a sense of duty—all aimed at ending what they perceived to be a crisis so great that they felt almost forced to act. None of the other prominent explanations—not the Supreme Court as partisan hacks out to elect George W. Bush at all costs or as constitutional saviors protecting us from a runaway Florida Supreme Court—are adequate to explain the Court's rulings on their own.

But what of the ruling itself? Those who objected to the Court's decision not only questioned the majority justices' motivations, they also dismissed the justices' use of equal protection as lacking precedent and conflicting the Rehnquist Court's earlier rulings. To quote Cass Sunstein of the University of Chicago Law School, the per curiam decision was without "precedent or history," a ruling that seemed both "ad hoc and unprincipled" and most of all logically and doctrinally incomplete. "The system that the Court let stand seemed at least as problematic, from the standpoint of equal protection," noted Sunstein, "as the system that the Court held invalid."[123]

More to the point, there were—and still are—good reasons to question the validity of the Court's adoption of equal protection. Election law expert Richard Hasen notes three such reasons. First, "the Court's language explicitly limiting its holding to the facts of this case [was] extraordinary," limiting as it did the precedential value of equal protection almost as soon as it applied this doctrine to end the recounts. Second, "the Court itself did not take its holding seriously." The Court recognized that voting was a "fundamental right" and that "the State may not, by later arbitrary and disparate treatment, value one person's vote over that of another," yet "nonetheless, the Court held that the Florida Legislature's interest . . . in taking advantage of the 'safe harbor' provisions of federal law for counting the state's electoral votes trumped the rights of all Florida voters to have valid votes counted." If the right to have one's vote counted is fundamental, how could the state's wish to meet a deadline supersede this right? Lastly, the use of "the Equal Protection Clause to create new federal oversight of the minutiae of state and local elections" was clearly at odds with the majority's ideology and past actions. As Hasen notes, "no Rehnquist Court opinion had ever relied upon *Reynolds* or *Harper* to expand oversight of the electoral process or to expand the franchise."[124]

To these points we can add the insight of Pamela Karlan of Stanford University Law School: that, "in the end, the decision to stop the recount had virtually nothing to do with equal protection." The per curiam opinion, notes Karlan, vindicated no identifiable voter's interests. The form of equality it created was empty: it treated all voters whose ballots had not already been tabulated the same, by denying *any* of them the ability to have his ballot counted. And its remedy perpetuated other forms of inequality that were far more severe: between voters whose ballots were counted by the machine count and voters whose ballots were not, and even between voters in counties that performed timely manual recounts (like Volusia and Broward) and voters in other counties.

Where was the equal protection in this? In fact, "[e]ven if there had been an equal protection problem with aspects of the procedure ordered by the Florida Supreme Court, that would not have justified the remedy the U.S. Supreme Court ordered. To stop the recount," Karlan concludes, "the *per curiam* essentially smuggled in through the back door the Article II rationale advanced explicitly by Chief Justice Rehnquist's concurrence: any constitutionally acceptable recount would require disregarding the Florida Legislature's presumed interest in obtaining the safe-harbor benefits of the Electoral Count Act."[125]

Taken together, such analyses of the majority's use of equal protection were and still are devastating. Given such fundamental weaknesses of argument and intent, it is no wonder that many scholars concluded that equal protection was merely a public relations ploy, a convenient doctrinal cover for a decision reached for other, more nefarious reasons. As Karlan put it, by ruling as it did, the Court seemed to be "trying to wrap its decision in the mantle of its most popularly and jurisprudentially successful intervention into the political process: the one-person, one-vote cases."[126]

Amidst all the tumult and argument, the attacks on and defenses of the majority's use of equal protection to end the election, a few commentators have pointed out the other side of the Court's use of equal protection: that if the justices really meant what they said in the per curiam opinion, *Bush v. Gore* was one of the most radical and liberal rulings in the Supreme Court's history. Granted, most of those taking this position do so exactly in this spirit of doubt—*if* the Supreme Court meant what it said, then it is something special and exciting, *if not*, then it is nothing but a heap of wasted words applied to an illegitimate end. But what possibilities arise if this actually proves to be a valid use of equal protection.[127]

What would the world of equal protection look like had the justices not limited *Bush v. Gore*'s legal effect to the facts of the specific case? The idea that equal protection of the laws required that voters in a given state all had to have their votes treated equally would mean that equal protection would bar local or regional variations in ways that citizens could cast their votes, that the votes would be counted, or that recounts would be conducted. At a minimum it would require each state to adopt a uniform statewide standard for conducting elections. It takes little creativity to see that in a national election such as an election for president of the United States, such an equal protection command would require national uniformity in the administration of elections, with no room for local, regional, or even state rules capable of manipulation and abuse. It is not hard to imagine what the late Thurgood Marshall, in his capacity as longtime leader of the NAACP Legal Defense and Education Fund, would have thought of such an understanding of equal protection as applied to voting.[128]

In other words, hidden within the mess that was the Supreme Court's *Bush v. Gore* opinion was an ideal picture of effective voting equality carrying with it the promise of future reform toward that equality. But was this a valid promise? Leaving all legal technicalities aside, could we take the Supreme Court at its word? Or was it simply an act of misdirection aimed at hiding a deeper, darker purpose, as so many have claimed? Did the justices even believe what they wrote? Did they even see the reformist logic imbedded within equal protection, and if so, why did they abandon it so quickly? Does it matter that the majority formally ignored reform? Was it constitutionally advantageous, or even proper, to apply an equal protection rationale in circumstances such as these?

We can distill the many questions raised by the Court's use of equal protection into the following queries.[129] Why did the majority justices adopt equal protection and what did this adoption mean to them? Was this a valid application of equal protection to settling the election dispute? Or was it a fraudulent smokescreen? And if the latter, does this negative judicial intent preclude the use of the majority's logic in other voting rights matters? Moreover, were the Supreme Court's actions without "precedent or history," as Cass Sunstein and others argued? Or, to paraphrase William Shakespeare, was there method in their seeming madness?

So why did the justices use an equal protection argument to justify their actions? Once again our answers must come from the realm of reasoned speculation. Based on what we know happened in the Court on those hectic days in December, it is most likely that the adoption of equal protection was largely tactical in nature. It came down to a matter of votes. Whereas Chief Justice Rehnquist's solution to the problem—that the Florida justices had run afoul of Article II of the Constitution and Section 5 of Title III of the U.S. Code—was internally coherent, it was not persuasive enough to garner the necessary five votes to form a majority. Justices O'Connor and Kennedy agreed with Rehnquist on the issue of ending the recounts—as their votes would show—but doubted the validity of his Article II rationale for action.[130] The Florida justices were overstepping their bounds of authority and needed correcting; yet neither O'Connor nor Kennedy was comfortable with Rehnquist's hyper-technical justifications for action. Perhaps they saw it—as many later commentators did—as too contrived. Yet whatever the reason, if Article II or §5 did not justify ending the recounts, what else did? It was here that equal protection entered the picture.

During the oral arguments, Justice Kennedy already was toying with equal protection as an alternative rationale for action. He began the proceedings by asking about the federal jurisdiction in this case. "Where's the federal question here?" he asked. Theodore Olson pointed to Article II and 3 U.S.C. §5, but Kennedy was not convinced. (When Olson admitted that this "may not be the most powerful argument we bring to this court," Kennedy responded, "I think that's right.") So if neither Article II nor §5 justified federal action, what did? Perhaps the Equal Protection Clause of the Constitution's Fourteenth Amendment did. Tellingly, it was Kennedy who brought equal protection into the discussion at oral argument. "I thought your point was that the process is being conducted in violation of the Equal Protection Clause, because it's standardless," Kennedy said to Olson. His comment set off a round of discussion on equal protection and the Florida recounts, during which a few justices (in particular Kennedy, Breyer, and especially Souter) toyed with the idea of a response based on equal protection. And although it is true that, having once raised the issue, Kennedy sat back and listened to other justices ask questions about equal protection, his questions show his willingness at least to consider an equal protection remedy to the Florida postelection crisis. Beyond this, however, we cannot go, based on the available evidence.[131]

The evidence is even thinner, in fact almost nonexistent, as to Justice O'Connor's views on equal protection. None of her questions in oral argument touched on equal protection matters, nor did she have an expansive voting record when it came to extending equal protection remedies to voting rights matters.[132] What O'Connor did have, however, was a reputation as an experienced majority-builder. Building on her position as a "swing vote," O'Connor was so skilled at forging a five-vote majority that many publications have described the Rehnquist Court as the "O'Connor Court" (in much the same way that many name the late Warren and early Burger Courts the "Brennan Court").[133] So although we cannot say with certainty how she felt about equal protection in this context, she would have been aware of equal protection's potential as a compromise remedy, one capable of garnering five votes while still justifying ending the recounts (which, as we have noted before, was a major objective for O'Connor).

Meanwhile, Justices Breyer and Souter, each of whom opposed the idea of ending the Florida recounts, found intriguing the idea that a decision based on equal protection might prove a common ground on which to castigate the Florida justices (which five of the justices clearly felt was necessary) while still allowing recounts to continue (which they wanted). Allowing the recounts to continue, in fact, was Breyer and Souter's primary objective at this time. They could read the Court's likely voting patterns. They knew that a reversal in part, with a strongly worded remand to fix the problem and restart the recounts, was the best they could hope for from this Court. As noted previously, one source close to Justice Souter described him as saying, "he knew he was going to lose. So he set about to find a way to make the result palatable and legitimate to the American people, even if he disagreed with the result."[134] Equal protection was a means to this end.

Of all the justices, Breyer may have been the justice most comfortable with equal protection in all of its expansive contexts. In his book *Active Liberty: Inter-*

preting Our Democratic Constitution, Breyer sets forth a justification for the justices to look at cases in light of how their decisions will promote what he calls "active liberty": the Constitution's aim of promoting participation by citizens in the processes of government. His approach emphasizes "the document's underlying values" and looks broadly at a law's purpose and consequences rather than relying on a rigid overarching theory of judicial interpretation. For, as Breyer explains, judicial approaches that cling strictly to the Constitution's text have "a tendency to undermine the Constitution's efforts to create a framework for democratic government—a government that, while protecting basic individual liberties, permits citizens to govern themselves, and to govern themselves effectively."[135]

With Souter, equal protection seems much more likely to have been a tactical response to an undesirable situation. This does not mean that he necessarily objected to the reformist impacts of an equal protection justification—we do not know one way or the other—but we can surmise that his primary focus was on getting recounts restarted, and equal protection offered the best way available to achieve this end. As he noted in his dissenting opinion, while this was an issue that "might well have been dealt with adequately by the Florida courts if the state proceedings had not been interrupted, and if not . . . it could have been considered by the Congress in any electoral vote dispute," given that "the course of state proceedings [was] interrupted, [and] time [was] short," it was only "sensible for the Court to address it." Florida's system of counting votes was "wholly arbitrary." Souter thus saw "no legitimate state interest served by these differing treatments of the expressions of voters' fundamental rights."[136]

This leaves the three other justices who voted for equal protection: Rehnquist, Scalia, and Thomas. Given their past voting records, not to mention their judicial philosophies already described, it is hard to picture them embracing equal protection in these matters. In fact, given their conservative views, it is hard to picture them embracing any of the more liberal aspects of equal protection in voting. That the chief justice issued a concurring opinion offering a different rationale for action implies that he (and Scalia and Thomas, who joined his concurrence) did not find equal protection fully convincing. In fact, the wording of the concurrence and the general tenor of Rehnquist's and Scalia's questions in the oral argument imply that they viewed these arguments as stronger than the per curiam opinion's equal protection reasoning. Reports in the media after the ruling also suggest that Scalia held nothing but disdain for the per curiam opinion's reasoning. The opinion's equal protection logic, according to Scalia, was mediocre and flaccid. "Like we used to say in Brooklyn," he supposedly told a colleague, "it's a piece of shit." (Scalia, it should be noted, has denied disparaging the majority opinion. On the other hand, he has never publicly supported its equal protection logic postdecision, either.)[137] As for Justice Thomas, we do not know how he felt about these issues beyond noting that he joined both the per curiam opinion and the concurrence. As was his norm, Thomas gave no hints of his true feelings, asking no questions on oral argument. However, as a strict constructionist, Thomas probably was uncomfortable with the expansive nature of equal protection applied to anything, let alone as important a topic as voting.

If all of this is true, why did these three justices join the per curiam? Once again, the simplest answer has its roots in the realm of strategy and tactics. They joined the majority because, had they not done so, they might have found themselves in the minority on the key question of ending the election. Rehnquist, Scalia, and Thomas must have taken seriously the threat posed by Justices Breyer and Souter's compromise efforts. We know from the statements of law clerks that all three put pressure on Justice Kennedy to hold firm on the recount issue.[138] All that they needed was for one of the two swing votes to accept a restructured recount process and the crisis was off and running again. Standing firm on their convictions, in other words, would leave the court with a three-two-four split—and the room for compromise was mostly going to be on the other side of the ideological spectrum, with Justices Breyer and Souter. All it would have taken were small shifts on the part of the swing votes and dissenting justices to create a new and different majority, one that would have remanded the case on equal protection grounds with orders to fix the problem and resume the recounting. By joining the per curiam majority, therefore, Rehnquist, Scalia, and Thomas averted what they would have deemed a nightmarish scenario and were thus in a position to put pressure on the swing justices to keep the ruling narrow and to end the recounts once and for all.

This line of reasoning brings us back to the Court's decisions to end the recounts and then to limit its ruling to the case at hand. This was the true dividing point on the Court. Had the majority been willing to accept a revised recount procedure—most likely in the form of a remand with instructions—the final vote easily could have been seven to two. But this did not happen. For the five who ultimately voted for the per curiam opinion, ending the postelection crisis was too important an objective to allow the recounts to continue—even at the cost of unanimity on the Court.

Tactical thinking also probably played an important role in shaping the per curiam's final form. If ending the recounts was so important an objective to O'Connor and Kennedy—and given the final outcome, it must have been—then the justices signing the per curiam opinion most likely inserted the limiting statement as a means to hold the votes of the more conservative justices. Given that the likely objections of Rehnquist, Scalia, and Thomas to equal protection rested largely on its expansive potential to reshape politics (the primary danger in any use of equal protection, a trend that the conservative justices had been fighting for years), then limiting their ruling to this case alone allowed the majority to conciliate the conservative trio by undercutting or even destroying this potential. As such, the limiting statement must have made it easier for Rehnquist, Scalia, and Thomas to join the per curiam opinion. Even if they did not fully agree with the opinion's equal protection logic, there was little harm in joining their names to it if the only case it affected was this one.

On the other hand, tactics were unlikely to be the only reasons that O'Connor (and to a lesser extent) Kennedy were drawn to limit the per curiam opinion's reach. Whereas generating a five-vote majority played some role in their thinking, limiting the opinion to its specific facts also fit comfortably within their preferred jurisprudential styles. As discussed above, both O'Connor and Kennedy favored ad hoc approaches to the law. Each appreciated the complexities of real life and understood the unique aspects of any case. O'Connor's jurisprudence, in particular, was grounded in her special concern for practical problem solving and thus worked best when focused on the distinctive aspects of an individual case. From this perspective, the second part of the per curiam opinion's limiting statement, as to how "the problem of equal protection in election processes generally presents many complexities," is suggestive. In many ways, this statement simply declared one of the fundamental tenets of O'Connor's jurisprudence—that complex cases raised complex issues that often needed to be handled on an individual basis. Meanwhile, Kennedy's style was more an outgrowth of his personality. As a conservative-moderate at heart, Kennedy often saw the political and legal complexities of a case, and this understanding often drove him to seek a middle ground—both doctrinally and practically—in his rulings. Moreover, Kennedy's judicial philosophy centered on the power and duty of courts "to impose order on a disordered reality; . . . to bring rationality to an existence that can be irrational and chaotic."[139] Given the complexities and high emotions in this case, limiting the ruling had to have seemed to Kennedy both a constructive and a calming action.

Additional, substantive reasons existed for limiting the opinion's reach as well. Looked at as a whole, the entire postelection crisis can be seen as a unique event, unlikely to be repeated. After all, the last time we came this close to this sort of crisis was 1876. (There were threats in the multicandidate elections of 1912, 1924, 1948, 1968, and 1992, but none of these threats came close to materializing.) More important, on a doctrinal level this case was, if not unique, based on a very narrow set of circumstances. This was a presidential election, after all, which placed the entire matter under the authority of Article II and 3 U.S.C. §5. Both, in turn, imposed specific requirements for presidential elections—and only presidential elections. Elections had to be held on the same day nationwide; all votes were supposed to be certified and electors chosen in time for the Electoral College to vote; §5 imposed the safe harbor deadline. So even though the states had the duty of running presidential elections, they were hemmed in by federal constitutional and statutory constraints—none of which existed for other federal offices (other than the date for holding the election). Had this been a House or Senate race, there would have been little or no reason to panic. It even would have been possible to restage the whole election, a remedy forbidden in the case of presidential elections by their very nature. So when the per curiam opinion invokes "complexities" associated with equal protection and presidential elections, it had reason to do so. It was a complicated matter.

Finally, it is also possible that the five justices did not want the opinion to include an expansive statement on voting and equality. Equal protection is the morphine of constitutional remedies. In small and measured quantities it is a wonder drug, but used too liberally it can cause enormous harm. Where does one draw the line on unequal treatment? Do left-handed people have a legitimate claim for accommodation in a world in which most tools are designed for the right-handed? Should government regulate the size of everyone's home or car or whatever because yours is bigger than mine? The answer, of course, is no. These are private matters of mundane significance. Yet they also can be seen as clear examples of unfair treatment. At root, the justifications for enforcing an equal protection remedy in these instances is little different from those employed in actual equal protection cases—unfair treatment that is bad or dangerous or improper and deserves correcting. In fact, in almost every instance in which the Court applied an equal protection analysis to enhance voting rights, there was a lone justice or two protesting about the dangers of equal protection on just these grounds.

It is for these reasons that the justices generally impose stringent guidelines such as "strict scrutiny" for the use of equal protection remedies. Use equal protection too often and it becomes a habit. Before long, every problem seems susceptible to an equal protection remedy. After all, it's easy to use and its effects are immediate and effective, so why not use it? Furthermore, even though the justices' effort to limit the per curiam opinion to the case at hand provided a clear barrier to any likely expansion of its equal protection logic, it did not prohibit a future Court from opening this door and applying an equal protection remedy in other voting rights problems. In this light, the per curiam opinions attempt to limit the ruling can be seen as a warning beacon to future Courts to be very careful in using equal protection for such purposes.

Valid as these reasons were, in the end the majority's use of equal protection most likely had its primary roots in a series of tactical and strategic calculations, as we have seen. Perceiving a crisis that their egos and their personal ideological and political perspectives told them that only they could solve, the justices turned to equal protection as the best (and perhaps only) means of forming a majority to achieve these ends. That this was a change from *this* Court's normal attitude toward equal protection was clear. However, when placed in its historical and doctrinal context, the choice by the majority justices to apply equal protection in a voting rights/election context was a legitimate, and surprisingly common, choice. Even a quick survey of past landmark voting rights cases—*Smith v. Allwright, Baker v. Carr, Reynolds v. Sims*—shows a clear pattern in each case of applying equal protection concepts in constructing a workable remedy to voting rights problems—often in the face of intense criticism from dissenting justices that such an expansion was little more than judicial hubris and overreach. When faced with the many factual, doctrinal, and constitutional complexities raised by a voting rights dispute, the Court has regularly reached for equal protection as the best—and often only—means available to cut the Gordian knot and provide a practical solution to the problems before them.[140] Although it was true that the facts of *Bush v. Gore* did differ from those of the earlier cases in many ways (they dealt with issues of access to the polls while *Bush v. Gore* focused on the counting of votes), the general pattern of applying an equal protection remedy to a voting rights problem—and in the process expanding the range of equal protection guarantees into uncharted realms—remained a workable and legitimate option for the Court.

Consider the odd fact that two of the strongest proponents of equal protection—Souter and Breyer—were in the *dissent*. Granted, as argued above, they had probably originally turned to equal protection as a means to establish a compromise. When it became clear that their plan had failed and the majority would go the other way, however, they refused to change their votes with regards to the equal protection arguments of the per curiam opinion. Had equal protection been nothing more than an illegitimate tool by which to form a majority (as many have argued), would Souter and Breyer have stuck with it after their strategy had failed? The answer most likely is no. Justices Breyer and Souter are thoughtful and intelligent men. That they stuck with equal protection shows that in their minds at the least, the invocation of equal protection was legitimate in this context.

The point here is that, whereas the Court did not have to dig so deeply into its tool bag of constitutional remedies to seize on equal protection as the basis for its ruling, its choice to do so was legitimate, especially in the context of voting rights. That Rehnquist, Scalia, and Thomas—each of whom were known as opponents to the use of equal protection remedies—joined in this decision might call into question their motivations for actions, but not the legitimacy of the remedy chosen.

Viewed analytically and with a careful focus on context, the motivations behind the Supreme Court's decision to take *Bush v. Gore* and its subsequent ruling halting all recounts and declaring the election for George W. Bush prove to be highly complex and multifaceted. In a sense, almost all of the many commentators analyzing this case are correct in their explanations of judicial action; and all are equally wrong. By attacking or defending the Court's actions, these commentators have missed the human process by which the justices perceived and responded to the issues. It is always easier to do what is right when what is right reflects one's wants and beliefs. And our beliefs shape our views of right and wrong, as do our more formal ideological views and values. But these were not the only factors in play.

To focus only on beliefs or wants or ideals or abstract principles misses the interrelated nature of these views. It is likely that all of the factors discussed above had some impact in the justices' thinking and motivations. Still, some views can have a greater impact than others in shaping behavior, in particular judicial behavior. Such was the case here. In the end, it is likely that the justices took the case mostly out of a sense of duty—a sense built both on their own personal preferences and on their jurisprudential values, but a sense of duty nonetheless. Whether through an objective or a subjective lens, the justices saw a crisis that needed solving. With confidence in their own abilities, and with a distrust of the skill and ability of the other branches of government to solve this problem, they acted. That it would come with a cost to the Court as an institution they both understood and accepted. That their own motivations might be challenged was also a price they were willing to pay. Whether this was the right decision for the nation—either doctrinally or politically—would remain for future generations to decide. But whatever the motivations or perspectives, one fact holds true: that when given the chance, five justices of the U.S. Supreme Court chose to act, and to act decisively to end the 2000 election controversy.

Unfortunately, when the topic moves to their chosen method of ending this controversy, equal protection, the majority proved much less decisive. Not only was equal protection likely chosen merely as a means to an end—forming a majority willing to end the recounts—but the Court went to great lengths to limit the doctrine's impact on future disputes and controversies. At a time when the nation needed a clear and practical vision of the necessity of running a clean and effective election, the majority blinked; faced with a chance to expand the reach of federal law and constitutional rights better to assure a valid result in elections, the five members of the *Bush v. Gore* majority declined to act beyond the minimum necessary to end the 2000 presidential election standoff.

Finally, despite the many problems exposed by Florida's electoral nightmare, the justices chose to limit their actions to the immediate issue at hand. And with this decision, a unique opportunity to catalyze the fixing of what was broken—to take advantage of the short window of time that a major constitutional crisis creates in which effective reforms are even possible—was wasted, even perhaps lost. Had the justices issued a clear call to the nation to reexamine its voting systems and take steps to repair them to avoid a repeat of the 2000 Florida debacle, they would have invested the Court's reputation in a worthy cause and would have done the nation lasting good.

In many ways the Florida electoral crisis was unique to the Sunshine State, but at the same time a recognizable variant could have happened in any of the other forty-nine states of the Union. This fact chilled the blood of electoral officials in every state, but it was obscured by the almost obsessive focus at every level of the nation on deciding who would be president on January 20, 2001. That serious reforms of our electoral processes and procedures were necessary should have been apparent to everyone. Even so, deprived of the stimulus that a strong reform statement from the Supreme Court could have provided, the political reaction to the 2000 presidential election crisis would be short-lived and inadequate. Lacking the "kick in the pants" that only a constitutionally guaranteed right such as equal protection—especially when bolstered by a call from a unanimous Supreme Court—could have provided to the reform process, partisan politicians mouthed platitudes and ignored the underlying need for reform. Thus, what could have—and should have—become a national crusade for a better democratic process instead slipped back into business as usual—legislative initiatives bogged down by a mix of partisan politics, political inertia, and questionable reform choices. The result not only failed to fix what was wrong in 2000, it actually permitted things to get worse. It is to these subsequent events that we now turn.

CHAPTER TEN
The Unlearned Lessons of 2000

The United States was thus fortunate to avoid another protracted post-election fight in 2004. Despite all the litigation and legislative activity devoted to election reform in the preceding four years, serious flaws in the infrastructure of American democracy remained. The only reason that these flaws did not lead to another contested election is because the margin of victory exceeded the margin of litigation.
—*Daniel P. Tokaji, "Early Returns on Election Reform,"*
George Washington Law Review

It appears the country has learned the wrong lessons from *Bush v. Gore.* Election administration has become more, not less, partisan. Public confidence in election administration, especially among African-Americans, is at troubling and embarrassingly low levels. Elections more frequently result in litigation than before 2000. . . . The result is likely to be further contentiousness and growing voter distrust of the system by which we cast and count votes for the foreseeable future.
—*Rick Hasen, "The Untimely Death of* Bush v. Gore*"*

The word now is, if someone gives you a provisional ballot, turn around and run.
—*Bess McElroy, African American vote organizer, Miami*

With the swearing-in on January 20, 2001, of George W. Bush as the forty-third President of the United States, the nation's postelection nightmare finally seemed to be at an end. The Supreme Court had spoken and the president had been chosen. Like the result or not, the emergency was over. Bush's inauguration provided a capstone to the entire episode, an opportunity to move on and put all the turmoil and controversy behind us—or so argued the victorious Republicans.[1] In his inaugural address, Bush stressed the theme of moving on, observing how "this peaceful transfer of authority is rare in history, yet common in our country. With a simple oath, we affirm old traditions and make new beginnings." Bush thanked "President Clinton for his service to our nation," and "Vice President Gore for a contest conducted with spirit and ended with grace." But it was now time to focus on the future, to live by a set of ideals that would make progress on the public agenda possible: civility, courage, compassion, and character. "America, at its best, matches a commitment to principle with a concern for civility," he said. "A civil society demands from each of us good will and respect, fair dealing and forgiveness." Bush therefore challenged both elected officials and ordinary citizens to take up the task of bringing the country together. As for himself, Bush offered "my solemn pledge: I will work to build a single nation of justice and opportunity."[2]

Others echoed the president's sentiments. In an op-ed article for the *Washington Post*, E. J. Dionne Jr. noted how "get over it" had become "a Republican battle cry, a demand that the circumstances of George W. Bush's ascension to the White House be forgotten in the interests of a successful Bush presidency—oh, yes, and 'for the good of the country.'" In the House, Speaker Dennis Hastert (R-IL) counseled that "we need[ed] to get over" the bitterness and anger created by the close presidential race and the five-week recount fight in Florida. It was time to get to work on the people's business. In the Senate, Majority Leader Trent Lott (R-MS) called on his colleagues to put the election results aside and quickly approve President Bush's cabinet appointments, lest "a major opportunity that we have here now to work together for a positive agenda for the American people" be lost. As for the people, Susan J. Barnard of Rensselaer, New York, spoke for many when she wrote a letter to the *Times Union* of Albany: "I don't believe that the state of Florida has destroyed democracy, weakened our judicial system or the faith of our citizens in our great country. The U.S. Supreme Court decision, although disappointing, did not ruin democracy, our judicial system or overall faith in the system. The system works. . . . I believe the country will recover, if it hasn't already. I, for one, was glad to see closure on this one. The election is decided, and it's time to move on into the new millennium."[3]

True, many remained angry. The level of anger among Democratic political activists and partisans aimed at the Supreme Court for its decision in *Bush v. Gore* was immense and vocal.[4] Many called into question the majority justices' integrity. Some commentators even went so far as to call their actions little more than a judicial coup.[5] Yet tellingly, few directly challenged the presidency of George W. Bush. They might question its legitimacy, but few were calling for a new election or the removal of Bush from his office. Most congressional Democrats, in fact, expressed a willingness to work with President Bush—if only, once again, for the good of the country.[6] Their anger at the Supreme Court, in turn, never directly challenged the institution itself. Most rather echoed in sadness or frustration Justice Breyer's depiction of the ruling as a self-inflicted wound.[7]

Within the academy, the debate over the Supreme Court's ruling was loud and highly divisive. In a review of editorial responses by academics published in the country's top twenty newspapers by circulation, Professor David Cole of Georgetown University Law Center found "in the week following the decision, . . . eighteen unsigned editorials critical of the decision and only six praising it. Signed op-eds in the same newspapers were also overwhelmingly critical, with twenty-six critical . . . and only eight defending the decision." More important, Cole found that law review commentary—which he describes as "a rough guide for the academy's assessment of the decision"—was almost entirely negative. "Of seventy-eight articles that have discussed *Bush v. Gore* between 2001 and 2004," notes Cole, "thirty-five criticized the decision, and only eleven defended it."[8]

Yet for all the verbal fireworks, few people were listening to the political backbiting and even fewer to the academic debate. Opinion polls showed that the public was making a clear "distinction between whether Bush won the election legitimately and whether they accept[ed] him as their legitimate president." From mid-December to mid-January, two ABC News–*Washington Post* polls showed only a slim majority of Americans ("55 percent and 58 percent, respectively") believing that Bush had been legitimately elected." Four Gallup-CNN-*USA Today* polls (carried out between December 15, 2000, and July 2001) showed similar results. Yet when the question shifted to "whether [respondents] would accept or [had] accepted George W. Bush as the legitimate president," in seven separate polls spread out over a six month period, "more than 75 percent said they did."[9]

Most people simply wanted to get on with their lives. Al Gore conceded the election (giving what many considered his best speech ever), grew a beard, and entered the academy as a guest professor.[10] The media shifted its focus from the recounts to other news. The lawyers went back to their private practices—though some Republican lawyers such as Theodore Olson were appointed to government jobs (in Olson's case, solicitor general). Most law professors turned back to their classrooms and other issues of academic interest.[11] The politicians, in turn, got on with the job of being a politician—seeking power and trying to influence how we ran the country.

Still, for all that everyone seemed to be moving on, one clear point arose out of the slowly dissipating debate: the taint of the 2000 postelection crisis was far from gone. With the exception of some of the more prominent lawyers on both sides, few of those participating in the whole controversy saw their reputations enhanced. And while the Supreme Court's reputation would probably survive the controversy, at least depending on how they ruled in the years to come,[12] George W. Bush had yet to fully escape the consequences of his twisted path to the presidency. Many viewed Bush as a weakened—even hamstrung—president destined to serve only a single term in office.[13] Most commentators (including even those who approved of the results of *Bush v. Gore*) were convinced that the next election would be a referendum on the 2000 election and the court order ending it.[14] The generally torpid pace of the Bush Administration's first months in office seemed to give credence to this view. Although Bush got most of his nominees for cabinet positions approved and his proposed tax cuts enacted, by the summer of 2001 his administration seemed rudderless and in search of a focus.[15]

Then came September 11, 2001, and the terrorist attacks on the World Trade Center and the Pentagon. Although the oft spoken claim that 9/11 changed the world was probably an overstatement, one clear casualty of the 9/11 attacks was the ongoing nature of the 2000 election controversy. The emotions generated by this event did not disappear overnight, but they were quickly subordinated to the need for national unity and the rising anger at those who would attack the nation. Dick Morris, the former political adviser to President Bill Clinton, noted after the surprising Republican victory in the 2002 midterm elections, "Still at war, shaken by 9/11, apprehensive about Iraq's and North Korea's pursuit of nuclear weapons, Americans turned to their president and gave him the thumping affirmation he did not get in the 2000 election."[16] Jack Pitney, a political scientist at Claremont McKenna College went even further in 2003, noting that "Among the general electorate, ordinary people who don't follow politics too much, Florida 2000 is already part of history. You may as well be talking about the Punic Wars."[17]

Yet, tellingly, interest in the "lessons of 2000" was waning *before* the 9/11 attack. So much of the focus in 2000 had been on the horserace to choose the president that, once a winner was declared, many felt that the "problem" was solved. Those opposing the ruling might have disagreed with the answer and hoped for the chance to "right what was wrongly done," but the wider issues posed by these events were soon ignored or forgotten. By limiting their ruling to the case at hand, the justices had leached the wider equal protection implications of the 2000 election not only from their rulings but also from the public mind. Lacking the impetus that an active Supreme Court call for reform could have provided, most Americans disregarded the wider issues posed by the 2000 election.[18]

The one exception to this pattern was the issue of voting technology. Because of persistent memories of hanging chads, Americans agreed that outdated voting technology had to go. Here Congress and the states would act. Outdated voting machines, however, were just the tip of the iceberg when it came to America's voting problems. A close look at Florida and the other forty-nine states showed a wide range of technical and practical electoral failures in 2000.[19] From mistake-prone voter-roll purges to inadequately trained precinct workers, from complex and confusing registration rules to partisan control of the vote-counting process, the American voting system was old, creaky, and in need of serious reform.

Updating the American electoral system as a whole, however, was not on the nation's agenda. To be sure, the various legislative, executive, and independent reports issued in the aftermath of the 2000 election did propose sweeping changes—but these calls were largely ignored when it came time to write the laws. As we shall see, the reform effort that did take place focused principally on voting machines, ballot design, and the need for uniform registration databases and voter ID requirements to combat voter fraud. Some further changes, calling for provisional voting and voter education, also were put into effect. But that is where the reform effort ran out of steam. As time passed, the true lesson of 2000—that we had a broken electoral *system*, and not just broken voting *machines*—was ignored and then forgotten. The reforms that took place were often inadequate. When deeper and more substantive reforms were called for, these calls were ignored, modified into irrelevancy, or trapped in a bureaucratic tangle never to see the light of day. What had seemed such a logical proposition—that electoral reform was essential to the well-being of American democracy—disappeared into a morass of partisanship and indifference.

Ironically, the only people ones who seemed to take the lessons of 2000 to heart were those who saw in them the opportunity for partisan political gain. Florida had highlighted the substantial power that local and state officials had to shape an election's outcome—and to do so without breaking the law. Selective voter purges, unequal distribution of voting machines based on class or party criteria, and partisan administrative rulings from state election officials were but three of many perfectly legal actions available to those controlling a state's electoral machinery to shape the outcome of voting. Other options included the continued decentralization of electoral processes and procedures, allowing local officials a free hand in manipulating who could and could not vote, and the implementation of partisan "reforms" such as ID requirements and felony disenfranchisement rules—reforms whose major impact was to exclude unwanted voters from the polls. In a real sense, this was the flipside of gerrymandering of electoral districts to give one party an advantage in winning legislative seats. By selectively shaping the way that we organized and counted votes, and in many cases by limiting who could vote or how we vote in an election, government officials were engaged in what could be called "administrative" gerrymandering. In both cases, the end result was a "controlled," even arguably "fixed" election, in which outcomes were largely predetermined based on who got access to the polls and then how the votes were counted.[20]

The painful truth was that in the years and elections following Florida's electoral train wreck, the electoral system's flaws remained largely uncorrected. Tens of thousands, perhaps even hundreds of thousands, of Americans continued to face effective disenfranchisement—either explicitly by outright vote denial or implicitly by vote dilution via rigged election rules and procedures or uncounted ballots due to inaccurate voting machines or both. Those electoral reforms that were adopted, in turn, proved inadequate to the task of reform; worse yet, in some instances, as with electronic voting and voter ID requirements, these so-called reforms actually created new electoral problems—with even worse results in terms of voter confidence and electoral effectiveness.[21] The fire bell had rung in the night, but as its peals faded in the distance, its message of impending crisis diminished and died. And although future elections would point out the need for remembering the lessons of 2000, the underlying structural flaws that had caused Florida's electoral breakdown remain largely unchecked and open to another collapse as the nation faces the presidential election in 2008.

The first state to attempt electoral reform after the crisis of 2000 was Florida. Two days after the Supreme Court's ruling in *Bush v. Gore*, Governor Jeb Bush issued Executive Order Number 00-349, creating a Select Task Force on Election Procedures, Standards and Technology. Its stated mission was to review how Florida ran its elections and to make recommendations for improvements. Its underlying purpose was to determine what had gone wrong in the 2000 election and to recommend how to fix the system so that Florida never again was placed in such an embarrassing position.[22]

On March 1, 2001, the task force issued its report, a scathing critique of how Florida ran its elections.[23] Passed on to the Florida legislature, each house took up the issue of election reform and began working on legislation. By May 5, they had a finished package ready for the governor to sign. The Florida Election Reform Act of 2001 was a multilayered effort that largely tracked the path proposed by the Governor's nonpartisan task force. Its objectives were (1) improving ballot accuracy and understandability, (2) maximizing voter participation, (3) minimizing voter mistakes and maximizing accuracy, (4) assuring technical compliance with all election law requirements, and (5) revising statutes to make them more consistent, logical, and adequate to their assigned tasks. Among the specific reforms adopted were provisions to:

- Eliminate all punch card ballots and tabulating machines.
- Budget $24 million over a two-year period so the counties could buy optical scanner voting systems.
- Allow provisional ballots for people who were not on voting lists but claimed they were properly registered. (In such instances, elections workers would set aside the ballots and later verify the voters' status, only counting the provisional ballots filled out by valid voters.)
- Budget $6 million for enhanced voter and poll worker education.
- Budget $2 million for a statewide centralized voter database to assure the inclusion of all legitimately registered voters (and the exclusion of those who were not properly registered to vote).
- Extend certification deadlines to seven days after the primary election and eleven days after the general election and formally reject all late-filed returns.
- Require an automatic machine recount if the margin of victory in any race was one-half of 1 percent or less; and a manual recount of overvotes and undervotes if the margin of victory was one-quarter of 1 percent or less.
- Direct the secretary of state to draft rules for manual reviews that took into account voter intent and set a uniform standard on judging oddly marked ballots.
- Require a voters' bill of rights to be posted at each precinct.[24]

Useful as all of these reforms were, the legislature chose not to adopt some of the more radical reforms proposed by the task force where these recommendations impinged on partisan political priorities—choices that, in retrospect, did not bode well for the future of electoral reform. Most notable was the legislature's decision to ignore the task force's suggestion to make the office of county supervisor of elections a nonpartisan appointive post; the same held true for the task force's recommendation that members of county canvassing boards and the state canvassing commission be barred from active participation in political campaigns. Political partisanship thus remained central to the staffing of Florida's electoral machinery.

More subtle, but no less important, was the act's provisions for a statewide voter database. Although the state had budgeted $2 million for a statewide voter database ($1 million less than the task force had recommended), it still left the control of that database in the hands of county elections offices. While efforts were made to ensure that the statewide database was accurate, it was—as the taskforce had found—little more than an out-of-date compendium of the individual county databases. With little money budgeted to updating the *county* database management, errors still were likely to enter the statewide database—errors that once again could result in thousands of Floridians improperly losing their right to vote as a result of clerical errors (and thousands more improperly voting).[25]

Still, compared to other states, Florida was a "poster child" for election reform.[26] At least Florida was acting—and acting forcefully—even if some issues were ignored and many of the reforms still needed to be implemented (not to mention formally funded). According to a report issued by the Election Reform Information Project (ERIP), a nonprofit think tank based in Washington, D.C., in most other states "only a fraction" of proposed election reform bills (estimated at 1,793 proposed as of October 2001) "had been signed into law" by year's end. In most states, plans to overhaul elections were effectively in limbo—"on hold as state lawmakers facing an economic downturn and shrinking budget coffers await[ed] congressional assurances of federal funds to bankroll costly upgrades of voting machines or registration systems."[27]

The only exceptions to this pattern of inactivity were laws phasing out punch card voting systems or upgrading vote counting and recount standards for retained punch ballot systems. The shape of these reforms varied from state to state. Georgia, for instance, replaced its punch ballot system with electronic voting machines, while Minnesota chose Scantron voting. Maryland, Texas, Indiana, California, and North Carolina all abandoned their punch ballot machines but had no clear plans for choosing successor systems.[28] At the other extreme, Ohio, Tennessee, and Virginia retained their punch ballot machines (at least for the immediate future) but passed "bills that defined a vote on a punch card ballot as one in which two or more corners of the chad, . . . [were] broken or separated from the card." The standards, however, once again varied by the state. Tennessee's law "allowe[d] for local election boards to take voter intent into account in those instances." Ohio's and Virginia's did not. Nevada defined a vote "as one in which at least one corner of the chad [was] detached or [where] light [could] be seen through the card."[29]

And these were the states that acted. According to a Princeton Survey poll conducted for the ERIP in late 2001, as of January 2002 "only 14 percent of the state election officials [felt] the Florida furor . . . had a major impact on their plans for the 2002 election. Fifty-eight percent . . . [said] the controversy . . . had a minor impact, and 28 percent [said] it . . . had no impact." In the end, the ERIP polls showed, "nine of ten American voters" were still going to "cast their ballots on the same voting technology in 2002 as they faced in 2000."[30]

The remaining state legislation merely picked at the edges of electoral problems.[31] All told, a January 2002 ERIP report noted, only "about a quarter of state and local election officials (25%) [experienced] major changes in the election laws in their state since 2000, with a somewhat smaller number (18%) reporting other major changes in regulations and procedures." Of this latter number, the reported reforms sorted into 20 percent for laws that made absentee balloting easier, 18 percent for improvements in voter registration procedures, 15 percent for the creation of a central voter registry, and 12 percent for the elimination of punch card ballots.[32]

Underlying this legislation (and nonlegislation) was the question of cost. Most election officials agreed that the majority of reforms, such as they were, would be in place for the 2004 election.[33] The real question was how the states would pay for all of these new voting machines and databases. Even those states that had plans to replace old voting technology had serious problems in deciding who (state or counties) would pay the millions the new machines required. In January 2002, ERIP reported that most election officials viewed money as "the biggest obstacle they face in trying to improve election operations. Fully 54 percent" of polled officials said "that not enough money available [was] the principal reason that they [had] not been able to improve operations since 2000. Eleven percent [said] that there was not enough time to make the improvements and 10 percent [said] that laws or regulations stood in the way."[34]

The simplest answer to the states' funding quandary was for the federal government to pay. The problem, after all, had arisen in a federal election. More to the point, the problems faced were national in scope. Recognizing this fact, a number of national studies were commissioned to search out national solutions. Reports came from professional associations of election officials, such as the National Association of Election Officials' Election Center, from state government groups such as the National Conference of State Legislatures (NCSL), and from academic/public interest groups such as the Caltech/MIT Voting Project, the Election Reform Information Project, and the Constitution Election Reform Initiative, a coalition of sixty organizations working on the issue of election reform. Most prominent was the National Commission on Election Reform organized by the Miller Center for Public Affairs at the University of Virginia and the Century Foundation, and co-chaired by former presidents Gerald R. Ford and Jimmy Carter.[35]

Not surprisingly, given their varying backgrounds, memberships, and practical objectives, no two reports came up with the same conclusions or recommendations. The election-official-dominated Election Center, for instance, rejected the idea that the American election system was in crisis; the more political Carter/Ford National Commission on Election Reform disagreed strongly with this view. The CalTech/MIT Voting Project focused on voting technology whereas the National Conference of State Legislatures report, *Voting in America*, emphasized state legislation. Still, on certain key issues, consensus reigned. Among the areas of agreement were the need for:

- Federal funding for technology upgrades;
- Improvements in the voting system standards;
- Expansion of data collection and dissemination;
- Statewide, networked voter registration systems;
- The broader use of provisional ballots;
- Actions to facilitate voting by military and overseas citizens;
- Actions to ensure equal voting opportunity and accessibility;
- Improvements in voter education; and
- The adoption by states of specific criteria for what is and is not a valid vote.[36]

Forging a consensus among reform groups was one thing; getting the federal government to act was a very different thing. Even with such comprehensive reports and studies available to show the problems, and despite plenty of testimony on the subject, Congress soon found itself deadlocked on the issue of election reform. All agreed on the need for reform, but disagreed sharply on the form that such reforms should take. The result was a legislative stalemate that lasted until well into 2002, almost two years after the Florida election crisis had shown the pressing need for change.

To be sure, Congress did not stand still during this interval. In March, June, and July of 2001 the Senate Committee on Rules and Administration held hearings on election reform.[37] However, little came of them—at least initially. The problem was not with the rules committee's willingness to act. Under the leadership of its chair, Christopher Dodd (D-CT), in August 2001 the committee reported a sweeping reform bill that would have increased federal funding and oversight responsibilities to unprecedented levels.[38] The bill would have given the states and localities "millions of dollars to purchase new equipment, train poll workers and bankroll voter education efforts." Yet notably, the committee approved the bill without a single Republican vote. Republican members did not even show up for the markup— "an act of protest, they said, against the absence of any voter fraud provisions in the legislation."[39]

The Republican protest over voter ID requirements made clear the roots of legislative deadlock. Republicans had been complaining of voter fraud since before the 2000 election.[40] Voter fraud (as opposed to election fraud, which involves official forms of electoral misconduct) occurs when voters cheat at the polls—for example, by voting more than once in a single election, voting in the wrong precinct, or voting under someone else's name. The Republicans saw such fraud as a major problem, one that needed immediate and significant action. Committee member Christopher Bond (R-MO), for instance, explained his opposition to the Democratic majority's bill as a direct response to that bill's failure to protect against voter fraud. "We must make it easier to vote while making it harder to cheat," he said after one of the hearings. Or, as Bond later put it: we needed such rules to "combat problems of votes being cast on behalf of dead people and dogs." Bond "had witnessed first-hand the chaos and distrust voter fraud causes in his home state during elections in St. Louis." Indeed, Bond's staff had "produced a two-inch thick tome filled with evidence of phony registrations that included, in one case, a dead dog who cast a ballot," proving the widespread existence of voter fraud. Yet nothing in the majority bill took action to defend against such wrongdoings. "Without safeguarding against fraud," Bond argued, "the entire country would be as scandal-ridden as St. Louis [in 2000]."[41] Voter fraud and other acts that undermined the trustworthiness of the electoral process *had* to be at the forefront of any electoral reform, Republicans argued. Leaving these problems unattended, as the Dodd bill did, could only lead the election system to collapse.

Democrats viewed voter fraud as irrelevant. As they saw it, the primary problem with voting in this country was the effective disenfranchisement of legitimate voters—most of whom were poor, undereducated, and minority. "It is un-American and wrong to have an election system where certain classes of voters—racial minorities, language minorities, the blind and disabled—are disenfranchised at significantly higher rates than voters not [in] those classes. And until we can say as one Nation that the differences in their disenfranchisement are insignificant, then our work as a Congress and a country is unfinished," argued Senator Dodd in the July hearing.[42] The objective in electoral reform, argued Democrats, should be to open up the electoral process to all Americans. Dodd's bill sought to do just this.[43]

Underlying this debate over voting fraud—was it real or not, a major problem or not—was one of the dirty little secrets of partisan politics: rules that acted to limit voter fraud had the inevitable effect of lowering the voting rates of minority and poor voters, most of whom generally voted for the Democratic Party. Conversely, reforms that sought to increase voter access to the polls generally increased the participation of these same mostly Democratic voters, but at the cost of an increased opportunity for voter fraud. Republicans therefore benefited by strict fraud rules, while Democrats benefited when voters had easier and more open access to the polls.[44] Ultimately, this issue proved the most difficult to solve. While not taking anything away from the honesty of each side's position, both had a partisan inducement in arguing the position that they did.

In terms of formal legislative action, this partisan split took the form of a debate over federal- versus state-centered reforms. The Democrats, with their goal of expanding access to the polls to groups on the margins of society, "favored an increased federal role in elections—especially if states want federal money to correct ills in their election systems." Centralizing larger parts of election administration in the federal government, the Democrats argued, would ensure the uniform application of rules aimed at increasing voter access to the polls. The Republicans, by contrast, "believe[d] that the federal government should invest in the nation's voting systems, but favor[ed] matching block grants that would allow state and local governments to use the money how they see fit, without any federal government requirements."[45]

The result of all this arguing was an ongoing legislative deadlock in Congress. Along with Dodd's bill, S. 565 (and its companion bill, H.R. 1170 sponsored by Representative John Conyers), there were proposed bills from Senator John McCain (R-AZ) (S. 368), Representative Jim Barcia (D-MI) (H. R. 2275), Representative Karen McCarthy (D-MO) (H. R. 2398), and Senators Mitch McConnell (R-KY), Charles Schumer (D-NY), Robert Torricelli (D-NJ), and Sam Brownback (R-KS) (S. 953).[46] Ultimately, none of the proposed bills garnered enough support for passage in either house. The partisan splits between the two parties was too great to bridge.

Recognizing the deadlock for what it was—an impasse demanding compromise if it were to be overcome—the House and Senate leadership in electoral reform, Senators Dodd and McConnell, Representatives Bob Ney (R-OH) and Steny Hoyer (D-MD), began extensive negotiations for a compromise. Consensus proved hard to reach, however. For over a year, the two sides sniped at each other about election reform, neither side willing to give in. Still, over time, pressure for action got each side to budge a little. The result, after months of intense negotiations, was a compromise bill combining aspects of each party's preferences. The Democrats got federal involvement in setting standards and the Republicans got a voter ID requirement to fight voter fraud.[47]

Signed into law by President Bush on October 29, the Help America Vote Act of 2002 (HAVA) authorized $3.8 billion in spending for election reform over a three-year period (although Congress still had to approve spending that money). Specific reforms covered a wide range of issues, including providing money to those states with punch card and lever voting systems to upgrade their voting machines should they wish to do so and creating the Election Assistance Commission (EAC) to supervise parts of the act's provisions. Other provisions called for voting systems allowing voters the chance to review and change their votes before the votes are cast; for the states to adopt uniform standards "that define what constitutes a vote and what will be counted as a vote for each category of voting system used"; and for the states to post sample ballots, voting instructions, information about voting rights, and other information at all poll sites. Most notable, however, were the mandates for provisional balloting and the requirements that each state establish a statewide voter database and some form of voter ID requirement to combat voter fraud.[48]

The presence of these last provisions did not bode well for the act's long-term success. After years of wrangling, the law merely combined each side's chosen election reforms into one package—despite the inherent contradictions between expanding access to the ballot and simultaneously increasing protections from voter fraud. As election law scholar Daniel P. Tokaji put it, "Faced with the tension between access and integrity, Congress effectively punted. HAVA provided money and imposed very general standards, while leaving most of the details of election administration to the states and counties."[49]

Nor was this the only problem with HAVA. Its enactment did not guarantee that Congress or the president would come up with the money promised. Without adequate money, those reforms that did take place would be slow and largely inadequate.[50] Worse yet, the act did not contain provisions to tamp down the partisanship among election officials that had been so central to the Florida debacle. Lastly, by making many of the law's mandates voluntary, or at least dependent on a state's acceptance of federal money, there was no guarantee that every state would participate in the process of electoral reform. HAVA was only a start. Alone, it was little more than a bandage over a bleeding wound. Further action from both the states and the national governments would be needed to avoid a future repeat of the electoral collapse of 2000—and the lack of clear mandates for future reform did not bode well for this result. Still, limited or not, with a few minor adjustments HAVA would be the primary vehicle for election reform for the foreseeable future.

The first real test of the newly reformed state electoral systems would be the 2004 presidential election. The reform process was not far enough along in 2002 to get much of a test. The one exception to this pattern was Florida. Embarrassed by what had occurred in 2000, Florida politicians had pushed electoral reform hard, and by 2002 had in place most of their ambitious reform package. Florida's experiences in 2002 thus provided a window into what likely would happen nationwide in 2004. Unfortunately that picture was not comforting, as recurring procedural and technological problems called into question the effectiveness of millions of dollars of reform in Florida, and hence of the plausibility of the reform process nationwide.

Once again, the problems centered in the fifteen large counties that had used punch card voting machines in 2000—only now they all were using variations of the largely untested, highly expensive touch-screen Direct Recording Electronic (DRE) voting machines. Leading the way into troubled waters once again were Miami–Dade and Broward Counties. Both had invested in what local officials saw as the most modern voting equipment available: a prototype DRE known as the iVotronic sold by Nebraska-based Election Systems & Software (ES&S). Sight unseen, Dade County spent $24.5 million for 7,000 touch-screen machines; Broward spent $17.2 million on its machines. Other counties bought similar technologies, though mostly from competing companies such as Diebold Election Systems, Inc.[51]

The first big test of these new machines was the September 10, 2002, gubernatorial primary. The results proved less than promising. In fact, in Miami-Dade
and Broward they were downright disastrous. In Miami-Dade, for instance, polls
did not open on time due to poll workers' inability to activate the machines; in
other precincts machines failed to print out a "zero" tape (showing that no votes
had been cast before the polls opened); meanwhile, other machines failed to print
results tapes at poll closing. There were also "reports of voters pressing the button
for one candidate and the name of the other candidate appearing."[52] Broward
County had similar problems as polls opened late and closed early, inexperienced
poll workers made mistakes with the new voting machines, the county elections office failed to send out every absentee ballot requested, and uncounted votes were
discovered after initial results were sent to the state.[53]

Facing a general election only forty-five days away, leaders in both counties went
into crisis mode as they sought to avert a potential catastrophe. In Broward, the
county board forced Supervisor of Elections Miriam Oliphant to turn over control
of the general election to them or face losing her job. "This is very much akin to disaster management," County Administrator Roger Desjarlais explained. "No one
can guarantee a 100 percent error-free election, but we will do at least as well as the
other 65 counties did. People will be able to vote and have their vote counted."[54]
Miami-Dade turned to its county police department to organize, supervise, and
run the November 5, 2002, general election; it also had county employees replace
the traditional volunteer poll workers—all at a cost of $7,995,000 or 380 percent
over budget.[55] Costly though such efforts were, the results proved positive as both
counties made it through the general election with minimal problems.[56]

Nationwide the situation with the new machines was much less ominous. Kay
J. Maxwell, president of the League of Women Voters of the United States, reported that her group had only "found 'scattered problems' throughout the country, including overcapacity crowds resulting in long waits, confusion caused by
recent changes in polling place sites, and not enough voting machines." True, in
Georgia, "where the entire state is using touch-screen machines for the first time,"
several voters complained that "the machines were malfunctioning and that their
votes for one party were being recorded as votes for the other." The problems,
however, were "fixed almost as fast as they were reported," and voting went on
with few other delays.[57]

Episodes such as these, especially Florida's problems with DRE machines, worried election officials across the country as they contemplated the upcoming 2004
election. Not only would this be the real test of election reform, but because this
was a presidential election, the number of voters would be larger and the potential
costs of an electoral meltdown that much greater as well. Also troubling—at least
to those in the know—was the actual status of electoral reform across the nation.
Despite the passage of HAVA and various state reform initiatives, many states were
not as ready as they wanted to be.

The problems, once again, were organizational and fiscal. It took over a year for the Election Assistance Commission to organize itself after its formation in February 2003. Given that HAVA was written so that no funds could be distributed until the commission was in place and certifying that state reform efforts were meeting the benchmarks required for matching federal funds, the result was that many reform efforts fell behind schedule. Adding to the fiscal problems, President Bush's 2005 fiscal year budget fell $600 million short of the funds promised by HAVA. Yet even where funds were distributed, the roughly $4,000 per machine provided by HAVA for upgrades often failed to cover the machine's actual cost. Add the effects of an economic downturn (which tightened state budgets already hurting for revenue), the complexities and costs of real electoral reform, and the inevitable partisan gamesmanship in the state legislatures, and the result was an effectively stalled reform process.[58] Still, compared to 2002 and especially 2000, the states were much more prepared for the complexities of running a modern election—or so they hoped.

Actually, hope was an accurate description of where the nation was in electoral reform on the eve of the 2004 election—as in, cross your fingers and hope for a good outcome. In the two years since the midterm elections, reports had emerged that the touch-screen DRE machines were not as effective as advertised. In June of 2003, a Miami-Dade County technology specialist named Orlando Suarez reported findings from a review that he had performed on the audit log and vote image files from a precinct in the May 20, 2003, run-off election in North Miami. To his dismay, Suarez found that the event log and vote image files were deeply flawed and had, in fact, malfunctioned to the point of being unusable: "In my humble opinion (and based on my over 30 years of experience in the IT field)," Suarez had written, "I believe that there is/are a serious 'bug' in the program(s) that generate these reports making the reports unusable for the purpose that we were considering (audit an election, recount and [sic] election and if necessary, use these reports to certify an election)." Given that these audit logs and vote image files were the justification that state officials gave why the state did not need a paper backup system for these machines—Secretary of State Glenda E. Hood described these backups as "a means by which all votes can be ascertained," and hence as all that was necessary if a recount was needed—this was a troubling revelation.[59]

Even more troubling was the state officials' response to Suarez's report. At first denying knowledge of the Suarez report, at least before an article in the *Daily Business Review* of South Florida on May 13, 2004, revealed it,[60] Secretary of State Hood responded with an administrative rule that barred review by county supervisors of elections of these selfsame ballot images generated by the DRE machines. Out of sight, out of mind, seemed to be Hood's answer to Suarez's report. Hood even proposed a change to the state's manual recount statute to impose the same limit (it was defeated in the legislature).[61]

About the same time as the Suarez report from Florida was surfacing, other reports challenging the safety and accuracy of DRE machines arose as well. One of the most troubling was a report from computer scientists from Princeton and Rice Universities that criticized DRE voting machines because the machines' coding was allegedly easy for insiders to tamper with. Among the worst flaws found was the ease with which someone could "program their own smartcards to simulate the behavior of valid smartcards used in the election. With such homebrew cards, a voter can cast multiple ballots without leaving any trace. A voter can also perform actions that normally require administrative privileges, including viewing partial results and terminating the election early. Similar undesirable modifications could be made by malevolent poll workers (or janitorial staff) with access to the voting terminals before the start of an election."[62]

Diebold, the maker of the DRE machine analyzed in the report, disagreed strongly with its results. They argued that the report was technically flawed. The machine in question was an old one, they insisted, and the software being hacked was also out of date. As a press release noted, "in the study, a prior version of Diebold's touch screen software was analyzed while it was running on a device on which it was never intended to run, on an operating system for which it was not designed, and with minimal knowledge of the overall structures and processes in which the terminal software is embedded."[63]

Despite Diebold's defense of its machines, attacks on the safety of DRE-type voting machines continued. Not long after the Princeton/Rice study was released, Maryland governor Robert Ehrlich suspended the state's contract with Diebold pending a scientific review of the safety and reliability of DRE machines.[64] A subsequent report from the Science Applications International Corporation (SAIC) for the state essentially supported the Princeton/Rice findings. As used in Maryland, the Diebold machines "had serious security flaws." Overall, the report concluded, this voting system, "as implemented in policy, procedure, and technology," was "at high risk of compromise."[65] Yet, damning as this report seemed, the ban on Diebold DRE machines did not last long. In September, the governor's office reported that the "faulty software underpinning a touch-screen voting system used in past US elections has been revamped substantially and will be used by Maryland voters in the next US elections."[66]

Over the next year, concerns over the potential vulnerability of DRE machines to hacking and error spread.[67] By July 2004 they had grown enough that the *Nation* was asking (or perhaps declaring) "How They Could Steal the Election This Time." The article noted that "the potential for fraud and error" in the upcoming election was "daunting." Altogether, "nearly 100 million votes will be counted in computers provided and programmed by . . . [four] private corporations." This included machines produced by Diebold Inc., whose chief executive officer reportedly invited Bush supporters to a fund-raiser, saying, "I am committed to helping Ohio deliver its electoral votes to the president next year."[68] Significantly, 36 million of these machines were paperless DRE models for which no manual recount was possible and the "voting-system source codes" were "kept strictly secret by contract with the local jurisdictions and states using the machines." Between the lack of a paper trail and proprietary operating code, this made it "next to impossible for a candidate to examine the source code used to tabulate his or her own contest." We simply had to trust that the machines were accurate.

It was the lack of a paper trail in DRE machines that raised the biggest worries. In the Senate Senators Bob Graham (D-FL) and Hillary Clinton (D-NY) co-sponsored a bill to require paper trails on DRE machines by November 2004, but few had any expectations for its passage in time for the election. In 2003, Representative Rush Holt (D-NJ) introduced a House bill requiring a paper trail on DRE machines. Yet despite having 149 co-sponsors, including a few prominent Republicans, nothing came of it.[69] Between financial woes, time constraints, and the partisan political infighting, everyone was forced to accept that this would be a "come as you are" election—in other words, cross your fingers and hope.

Meanwhile, state and local officials across the nation defended the DRE machines, announcing their confidence in the machines' trustworthiness.[70] "I'm not saying it couldn't happen," Pasco County (FL) elections supervisor Kurt Browning noted for many, "but the chances are so much less likely than in the early days of punch cards because the standards and regulations are there." Requiring a voter-verifiable receipt, Browning continued, was "an unnecessary use of tax money." On the national scene, the League of Women Voters, having considered "expert opinions from all sides of the debate," concluded that it "seem[ed] extreme" to suggest "that DRE machines [were] inherently subject to fraud unless there is an individual paper record of each vote." The league echoed many county elections supervisors, noting that "DREs are not an election system unto themselves; they are simply an instrument within a complex election system. The key is to design an overall system that builds in multiple checks making it improbable that the system will be tampered with."[71]

And so the pressure built. As Election Day got closer, the nation seemed to be gearing itself up for another major electoral meltdown. Would 2004 be worse than 2000?

November 2, 2004. Election Day. With great trepidation Americans went to the polls to vote. To their surprise, in most voting precincts across the country things went well, even very well. Despite all the talk of "hacked" DRE systems and voting machine meltdowns, the next day's newspapers announced that "electronic-voting machines, attacked for months by critics as unreliable and insecure, appeared to perform generally well on November 2." For all the worries about how the machines would work, few complaints were heard about DRE machines that would not work or that registered a vote inaccurately or added phantom votes.[72] This did not mean, however, that there were not problems with the 2004 vote. In fact, in some ways the 2004 vote was even more troubled than the 2000 vote had been.[73] It's just that the problems were not the ones that everyone expected.

With the focus on the machinery of voting, everyone forgot one key lesson of 2000: that how one organizes and runs an election can have an impact on the outcome as big as, if not bigger than, the machines voted upon. By the time voters got to the polls on November 2, much of the damage had already been done. Under the surface, and generally out of sight, election officials in several key swing states had quietly taken steps to unbalance the scales in favor of their party and candidates. Inaccurate and partisan voter purges, gerrymandered precinct boundaries, partisan rulings from government officials over the application of election rules, and the selective and unequal division of available voting machines all skewed the results toward a predetermined end. And whereas none of this administrative gerrymandering guaranteed a victory, in a close election it could—and in this case most likely did—tip the difference toward one side against the other. Besides which, win or lose, the end result was the effective disenfranchisement of hundreds of thousands of American citizens—all drawn, it should be noted, from the pool of citizens who were actually willing to vote on Election Day.

The story once again begins in Florida where, in early 2004, the state was set to carry out its biannual purge of illegal voters from the election rolls. In particular, the focus of this purge was on removing the names of Florida's felons. As in 2000, under Florida law felons were barred from voting unless they had their civil rights restored by the state—a time-consuming, complex process. In early May 2004, the secretary of state's office sent county election supervisors a "scrub list" of 48,000 "potential felons" and asked county election offices to begin to remove those on the list from the voting rolls. As in 2000, the list had been generated by a private company, in this case Accenture, Inc., from data supplied from the state's unified voter database (at a cost of $1.8 million). Along with the list came instructions from Secretary of State Hood not to distribute copies of the list to anyone, but especially not to the media. Responding to this ban, CNN, several local and national newspapers, civil rights groups, and Senator Bill Nelson (D-FL) sued and won a court order granting them access to the lists.[74] It was at this point that chaos ensued.

Having attained an advance look at the purge list, the *Miami Herald* reported on July 2 that "more than 2,100 Florida voters—many of them black Democrats—could be wrongly barred from voting in November because Tallahassee elections officials included them on a list of felons potentially ineligible to vote." It turned out that each of these former felons had had "their rights to vote . . . formally restored through the state's clemency process" but had not had their names removed from the list.[75] Five days later, on July 11, the *Sarasota Herald-Tribune* reported that "out of the nearly 48,000 names on the list, only 61 were Hispanic."[76] Given that many Florida Hispanics voted Republican and most Florida blacks voted Democratic, many saw in this statistic proof of a conspiracy to "fix" the election. At the least, the echoes of 2000's flawed voter purge resonated with such individuals.[77]

At first state officials defended the list. "I can tell you with the utmost certainty that it was unintentional and unforeseen," responded Hood spokesperson Nicole de Lara. When this did not work, they denied responsibility for the purges. In a press conference, "Hood repeatedly stressed that county elections officials—not her office—are ultimately responsible for screening voters and protecting their rights."[78]

Local election officials, already burdened with trying to set up for the November 2 election, objected loudly to this announcement. Ion Sancho, elections supervisor for Leon County, asked, "Why is the state doing this now? Within three minutes we identified an individual who should not be on the list. Right off the bat." Sancho noted how he had "never [before] seen such an incompetent program implemented by the DOE." Kay Clem, from Indian River County, asked, "How do you make somebody prove on election day that they're not a felon?"[79] Broward County Supervisor of Elections Brenda Snipes focused her scorn on the extra cost. With 6,500 names to process from the list in Broward alone, she had to hire two new employees just to manage felon removals. And even then she estimated it would take her staff months to verify the names on the list.[80]

In the end, such complaints proved effective. Under pressure, on July 10 state officials finally agreed to withdraw the purge list. Given the widespread perception that the list was tilted to help the Republicans, Governor Bush felt he had little choice but to pull the list. "It was the right thing to do," Bush explained. "The perception of all this begins to become reality. . . . " Despite withdrawing the list, Bush continued to defend his administration's actions. The omission of Hispanics was simply an "oversight and a mistake," Bush noted. As for the "swirl of conspiracy theories" being bandied about over the list, the governor chalked them up to "'political process' and to Democrats' hopes of turning out voters 'for their own cause.'"[81]

The state's recall of the list did not end the controversy. State law continued to demand that felons be barred from the ballot box. County election officials were still required by state law to verify names of suspected felons, to send registered letters notifying them they were being dropped from rolls, and to advertise names in a local newspaper if they did not respond. More to the point, they were still supposed to drop the names of anyone who did not respond to the letters sent from the election rolls—whether proof existed that the removal was legitimate or not. Moreover, it was up to each individual county supervisor to decide to use the list or not, regardless of decisions by the secretary of state and division of elections. And whereas supervisors in the big counties such as Broward, Palm Beach, and Miami-Dade promised not to use the list and to verify every name before purging felons from the voter rolls, silence from the supervisors in the other counties raised questions whether the discredited list still would be followed.[82]

In point of fact, "supervisors in 14 counties—including Brevard and counties in North Florida such as Gulf and Wakulla—[had already] sent out letters informing voters they were included on the list" before the state's withdrawal of the purge list. Since "voters who fail[ed] to respond to county supervisors" were supposed to be purged from the rolls, the potential for excluding legitimate voters was a reality, not just theory. The state division of elections was finally forced into the embarrassing position of telling the county supervisors to ignore the state list and that "even if voters fail to respond to the election supervisors' letters, they should remain on the voting rolls." Embarrassing or not, this was too little and too late to placate angry members of the African American community and frustrated Democrats.[83]

Florida seemed to be destined for a debacle as she stumbled toward the November 2 election. In August, Governor Bush was roundly criticized for his "streamlining" of the process by which felons applied for executive clemency to restore their civil rights. While his original plan to cut the forms for requesting a hearing from twelve pages to one was widely praised, in July he announced that to further "streamline the process" he was doing away with the one-page form. Now it would be up to the felon to contact the state directly—"by letter, e-mail or phone"—to request a clemency hearing. As the *Pensacola News-Journal* noted in an editorial, this did not "streamline" anything—if anything it made "it harder to get rights restored."[84]

August also saw the state defend its revision in 2003 of the Election Reform Act of 2001 to limit provisional voting to a voter's precinct only. Challenged by the AFL-CIO and other groups, Hood and her office defended the provisional ballot limitations as legal in both state and federal courts. Ultimately, they proved victorious, with U.S. District Judge Robert Hinkle ruling that "Florida law has long required voting at the proper polling place, and nothing in HAVA invalidates that approach." Yet legal or not, the result was thousands of invalidated provisional ballots, many of them once again from poor and minority voters.[85]

Finally, in October, complaints centered on Secretary Hood's advice to county supervisors that registration forms had to be filled out completely. This included checking a "yes" box after the question, "Are you a U.S. citizen?" even though, over the required signature appeared an oath including the following key phrases: "I am a U.S. citizen. I am a legal resident of Florida. All information on this form is true. I understand that if it is not true, I can be convicted of a felony of the third degree and fined up to $5,000 and/or imprisoned up to five years." This decision was widely seen as another example of the Republican Hood's bias toward excluding voters from the polls (on the assumption that poor and minority voters—who generally voted Democratic—were more likely to make such mistakes). Ultimately, rulings of this sort cost Hood her job.[86]

Yet, bad as things looked to be in Florida, Election 2004 went relatively smoothly in the Sunshine State. It was in another swing state, Ohio, that the electoral process broke down and made very clear just how little the nation had learned the lessons of 2000—and just how much it needed them.[87]

Weeks before Election Day 2004, word had been coming from Ohio of administrative rulings that changed voting procedures and had the potential to exclude large numbers of (mostly Democratic) minority voters. The source of many of these reports was Republican J. Kenneth Blackwell, Ohio's secretary of state and chief elections official.[88] Throughout September and October, Blackwell issued a number of administrative rulings that had the potential cumulative effect of excluding tens and even hundreds of thousands of voters from the polls—or so charged the Democrats. Republicans disagreed, noting accurately that Blackwell's administrative rulings were perfectly legal and well within his authority. Democrats countered that although such justifications were factually correct, they did not contradict the exclusionary effect of Blackwell's actions. To this charge, Republicans were largely silent.[89]

Blackwell's first ruling, which came on September 7, focused on registration forms printed on lightweight paper. His directive demanded that county boards of elections reject voter registration forms not "printed on white, uncoated paper of not less than 80 lb. text weight."[90] While on the surface there was nothing controversial about Blackwell's ruling, the timing of its initial publication less than one month before Ohio's voter registration deadline expired raised serious concerns. Many election officials feared that a change in procedures so close to the registration cut-off date would cause widespread confusion and chaos and result in fewer voters being registered. "It will create more confusion than the paper's worth," Jan Clair, director of the Lake County Board of Elections and a Republican, said. "It's the weight of the vote I'm concerned about on Nov. 2—that's the important thing."[91] Steve Harsman, deputy director of the Montgomery County board, worried that given their backlog of application forms, there was a strong possibility that many voters who already had sent in a form (he estimated as many as 800) might not have their applications reprocessed in time before the registration deadline. With over 4,000 registration forms in backlog and more coming in every day, there was not enough time to process them all, given the delay a second registration would entail. He also questioned the need for the ruling. "There is just no reason to use 80-pound paper," Harsman complained.[92]

Blackwell disagreed with such negative conclusions. As Blackwell spokesperson Carlo LoParo explained, the requirement was adopted for practical reasons. Most registration forms were mailed to county elections offices and hence they had to be thick enough to survive mechanical sorters at the U.S. Post Office. "Our directive stands and it is specifically in place to protect new registrants to make sure the forms are not destroyed," LoParo said.[93]

Blackwell's defenses did little to slow down the growing criticism of his actions. On September 24, The *Dayton Daily News* noted that the Federal Elections Assistance Agency had on its Web page a registration form for voters to download, print, fill out, and submit by U.S. mail. In a reversal of his overall position, Blackwell had ruled that these federal forms had to be accepted by Ohio boards regardless of what type of paper it was printed on.[94] More embarrassing was a September 30 report in the *Columbus Dispatch* that Blackwell's own office was using 70-pound paper for its registration forms.[95]

Ultimately, Blackwell was forced to retreat in the face of heavy criticism and threats of litigation. On September 29, he revised his rule on paper weight, explaining that election boards could and should register voters providing all otherwise valid forms (no matter what the weight of the paper) and then send voters who used too light a paper the proper card to fill out for the "permanent record."[96] His revision, however, did little to quiet the waters. Blackwell never withdrew his first directive. His September 30 ruling, Blackwell maintained, was merely a "clarification" of his earlier order, rather than a new position. And though it was a relatively reasonable and even necessary revision of his original ruling, it was also (to quote the *New York Times*) "worded so inartfully that it could create confusion."[97] In fact, it did result in continued confusion. The Delaware County Board of Elections, for instance, even after Blackwell's new ruling, continued to post a notice on its Web site declaring that it could not accept its own voter registration forms (they were printed on the wrong paper) and directing voters to request a new one by calling a specific phone number.[98]

It is impossible to exactly tell how many potential voters could not vote as a result of Blackwell's initial ruling on registration forms. Anecdotal evidence suggests that "delays in processing new voter registrations kept many from being added to the rolls."[99] Statistical analysis conducted by the nonpartisan Greater Cleveland Voter Coalition suggested, "16,000 voters in and around the city were disenfranchised because of data-entry errors by election officials, and another 15,000 lost the right to vote due to largely inconsequential omissions on their registration cards." Statewide, the study concluded, "a total of 72,000 voters were disenfranchised through avoidable registration errors—one percent of all voters in an election decided by barely two percent."[100] Just how many of these voters were excluded due to Blackwell's paper weight order is unclear, however.

Magnifying the problems caused by the debate over the weight of paper, Ohio already was facing a registration tidal wave in 2004. On September 26, the Associated Press reported that "in Ohio's largest counties, election boards [were] getting nearly double the number of registration cards submitted in 2000." The scramble to register voters was "only expected to intensify . . . as the Oct. 4 registration deadline near[ed]." Despite hiring extra staff members and extending working hours, or both, to process cards, election boards across the state kept falling behind. Some boards were processing cards 24 hours a day and it still was not enough.[101] Most of these new voters, in turn, were Democrats. A *New York Times* study in Ohio showed that the Democrats had "registered 250 percent more people in the first half of 2004 than they did in the same period in 2000."[102]

The collision of large numbers of new, mostly Democratic voters with administrative confusion and delay was a troubling, and potentially volatile, combination. With voter lists in disorder, many of these new voters would have to vote provisionally. Indeed, surveys in two Ohio counties commissioned by the Democratic National Committee after the election showed that a large percentage of voters casting provisional ballots did so "in large part because election officials fail[ed] to process voter registrations and changes in registration occurring shortly before the election."[103] Any delays in processing registration cards, therefore, were more likely to affect Democratic voters than Republican. And although most of these voters likely would be allowed to cast provisional ballots, this was not necessarily a clear improvement. Provisional ballots raised their own troubling issues—issues made more complex by Secretary Blackwell's second administrative directive on voting.

Announced on September 17, Blackwell's second major directive restricted the ability of voters to use provisional ballots. The new rule held that provisional voting was allowed only in the precinct where a voter lived. Voters who arrived at the wrong precinct to vote (for example, a precinct that they used to live in but had recently moved away from or one out of which they had been shifted by redrawn precinct boundaries) were to be denied a provisional ballot, instead given instructions on how to find their proper voting place. (The directive did allow such voters to update an address change at their new precinct on Election Day, had they not already done so, and then to cast a provisional ballot *at that precinct*, but only at that precinct.) Where voters were improperly allowed to fill out a provisional ballot in the incorrect precinct (on the mistaken belief that they were in the correct precinct), their votes would not be counted.[104]

In his defense, Blackwell's order was in line with a 1980 state law; however, the directive was a reversal from elections past during which many Ohio county election boards had regularly ignored the law and given provisional ballots to all legitimate voters who showed up "in the wrong precinct, just to give everyone an opportunity to vote."[105] Blackwell justified this zero-tolerance application of state law as required under the provisions of 2002's HAVA. The federal act stipulated that voters whose names did not appear in the poll books had to be allowed to vote provisionally, but before doing so, had to sign "affidavits certifying that they [were] in the correct jurisdiction." Blackwell's ruling, which narrowed this general "jurisdiction" requirement down to a specific precinct prerequisite, was admittedly a strict, narrow reading of the HAVA requirements. Yet it was also a perfectly legal and even justifiable reading of the law.[106]

Democrats charged, however, that in the Election Day confusion voters might be unable to locate their correct precincts. The large numbers of new registrations had necessitated the shifting of precinct lines, transferring many voters to new and unfamiliar polling places. Worse yet, Democrats complained, the ruling was biased against poor, mostly Democratic voters. Lower-income people "moved frequently and were more likely to go to the wrong precincts," state and local party officials complained. The result would be widespread disenfranchisement that predominantly affected Democratic voters. So although the ruling might have been legal, it was decidedly biased in favor of Blackwell's own party.[107]

Steve Harsman, deputy director of the Montgomery County board of elections, estimated that had his county followed Blackwell's rules in 2000, 840 registered voters in Montgomery County alone would have had their votes denied for voting in the "wrong precinct."[108] Ohio governor Bob Taft believed that the new rules could affect over 100,000 voters in the November election.[109] Kay Maxwell, of the League of Women Voters, admitted while visiting in Ohio that neither she nor anyone else knew how many votes would be lost this way, but argued that "any single voter who is disfranchised is one too many."[110]

Democrats questioned Blackwell's motivations for changing the rules so close to the election. "For him to come out with that decision so close to Election Day . . . I'm suspect of his motivations," Franklin County Board of Elections chairman William Anthony said. Other Democratic leaders did more than question Blackwell's rationale for action. State Democratic Party chairman Denny White charged that Ohio had a "secretary of state now that's purposely trying to take your right away from your vote and my vote of being counted. That's what this is all about. . . . He's elected to see that people can vote, not to stop people from voting. That's what Blackwell is trying to do."[111] Sean Grayson, attorney for the Ohio Voter Protection Project, a coalition of voting-rights groups, agreed with this view (though with less expressed anger), complaining that "the intent behind HAVA was to liberalize the process," but that under Blackwell, "it seems to me Ohio is going in the opposite direction."[112]

Blackwell's response to all the complaints was that he was just doing his job. His spokesperson, Carlo LoParo, explained that his ruling was a legal and not political decision. Besides, noted LoParo, "28 [other] states [had] the same or more restrictive requirements on where so-called 'provisional ballots' may be cast"—and in a number of cases the courts had already upheld such rulings as legal.[113] Blackwell himself argued that it was "foolish" to think he wanted to suppress anybody's vote. "The last time I checked I was African-American and proud of it and secondly I came from very modest means," he said. "I think it is an insult to suggest that because you're a minority or because you're lower income you cannot comply with a reasonable law which requires mutual responsibility on the part of elected officials and voters to make sure voters vote in the precinct where they live."[114]

Fearful of the effect that so many new voters would have on the smooth operation of the electoral system—in particular the possibility that many of these first-time voters would have to vote provisionally, would do so in the wrong precinct, and thus have their votes disqualified—Democrats brought suit in federal court on September 27 challenging Blackwell's order. They argued that Blackwell's actions had one principal objective: the purposeful exclusion of poor and minority voters from the November election. They further contended that Ohio's rules for provisional voting did not comply with federal law (in particular HAVA, which mandated provisional ballots), and that poll workers should not be put in the position of determining a voter's eligibility.[115]

Seventeen days later, U.S. District Judge James G. Carr ruled in favor of the Democrats' suit. "Unless Ohio's election officials receive accurate guidance on how to implement HAVA, the risk is great, indeed certain, that persons entitled to vote provisionally will not be given that opportunity," Carr wrote in his thirty-seven-page ruling. For "once they are wrongly turned away from the polls, they cannot return or regain their 'voice in the election of those who make the laws under which, as good citizens, we must live.'" Carr held that Blackwell was wrong to define "jurisdiction" as "precinct," not "county." The "correct precinct" rule, Carr declared, conflicted with HAVA's provisions requiring that all voters who asked for a provisional ballot not only should get one but should have it counted—even if they were in the wrong precinct. As for Blackwell's argument that allowing people to vote provisionally anywhere they wished would result in electoral chaos, Judge Carr disagreed, calling such arguments "speculative at best" and noting how such ballots had to be verified before they were counted. Further, any risk of problems was far outweighed by the need to protect a voter's right to vote. The Judge then issued an order allowing provisional balloting within counties regardless of residence and precinct location.[116]

In response, Blackwell vowed open defiance. He decried Carr as just a "left-wing judge," vowing that "I am not going to sit by while a federal judge tries to legislate from the bench. I'm going to fight this 'til the last dog dies. If, in fact, this has to go to the Supreme Court, we will take it to the Supreme Court." More substantively, Blackwell called the ruling "a misinterpretation" of HAVA and immediately filed notice for an expedited appeal with the 6th Circuit Court of Appeals.[117]

Nine days later, the 6th Circuit handed down its own ruling on provisional ballots under HAVA. In a complete dismissal of Judge Carr's reasoning, the appellate judges upheld Blackwell's reading of HAVA as permitting "precinct only" provisional balloting. "At bottom," wrote the three-judge panel in a per curiam opinion,

this is a case of statutory interpretation. Does the Help America Vote Act require that all states count votes (at least for most federal elections) cast by provisional ballot as legal votes, even if cast in a precinct in which the voter does not reside, so long as they are cast within a "jurisdiction" that may be as large as a city or county of millions of citizens? We hold that neither the statutory text or structure, the legislative history, nor the understanding, until now, of those concerned with voting procedures compels or even permits that conclusion. Thus, . . . we hold that ballots cast in a precinct where the voter does not reside and which would be invalid under state law for that reason are not required by HAVA to be considered legal votes.

"To hold otherwise," the judges explained, "would interpret Congress's reasonably clear procedural language to mean that political parties would now be authorized to marshal their supporters at the last minute from shopping centers, office buildings, or factories, and urge them to vote at whatever polling place happened to be handy, all in an effort to turn out every last vote regardless of state law and historical practice." This was wrong. "We do not believe that Congress quietly worked such a revolution in America's voting procedures, and we will not order it." The panel thus reversed Judge Carr's order and required compliance with Blackwell's decree on provisional voting.[118] The result, as Robert F. Kennedy Jr. explains, "left hundreds of thousands of voters in predominantly Democratic counties to navigate the state's bewildering array of 11,366 precincts, most of whose boundaries had been redrawn just prior to the election," on their own with only the questionable help of overworked and harried precinct workers.[119]

As troubling as Blackwell's preelection actions were to Democrats, they paled in comparison to the direct action taken by the Republican Party itself. Worried by the success of Democratic voter-registration drives ("up 250 percent, compared to only twenty-five percent in Republican areas"),[120] the Republicans began an all-out campaign to challenge voters likely to vote Democratic. Their objective was to exclude as many of these new voters from the polls as possible, and the scope of this effort was extensive.

The Republican campaign began with voter purges early in the year. In Ohio's largest cities, in the course of "scrubbing" the voter rolls, county officials selectively purged voters "from the voting rolls on the basis that they failed to vote in the previous election." (Ohio law did not require such purges, but rather allowed county election boards the option of carrying them out. Most large Ohio cities, however, controlled by Republican county officials, chose to scrub.)[121] Noticeably, most of the removed voters were urban dwellers likely to vote Democratic. Meanwhile, "other voters who had not voted in several elections [and who were presumably Republicans]" were not equally "purged."[122]

As the election got closer, the preferred methods of removing unwanted voters from the voter rolls became more explicit and partisan. In October, GOP representatives filed 35,000 challenges to individual voters' eligibility, almost all in Democratic precincts. They acted under the cover of a longstanding Ohio law that allowed a party to challenge directly a voter's eligibility if the challenger had "a reasonable doubt that the person [was] a citizen, [was] at least 18, or [was] a legal resident of the state or the county where he shows up to vote."[123] To do this, however, they needed to generate proof of their contentions. This was accomplished by an illegal technique known as "caging." Caging occurs when one party sends registered letters to newly registered members of the other party (or those thought likely to vote for the other party) in the hope that they will not accept the letter so that it can be returned "undelivered." The returned letter then becomes the proof that the voter is not a resident of the precinct in which he or she wishes to vote and should be removed from the voter rolls.[124] By the time they filed their 35,000 challenges, Republican operatives had been engaged throughout the summer and early fall in caging poor and minority neighborhoods across the state.[125] It was these names that made up the 35,000-voter challenge list.[126]

Democrats objected loudly to these exclusionary efforts. They pointed out the partisan and racial bias implicit in the Republican challenges. They noted the use of caging to gain such evidence and pointed out the logical limits to this method of proof: for example, that many of those who were being targeted as nonresident were in fact, "homeless, serving abroad, or simply did not want to sign for something concerning the Republican Party." Democrats also pointed out the illegality of caging as an election practice. In the past, Republican caging tactics had been so problematic that in 1982, and again in 1987, federal court decrees barred the party from targeting minority voters for challenges at the polls. Yet, here they were once again applying the same tactics.[127]

Responding to these tactics, Democrats brought suit in the Southern District of Ohio challenging the 35,000-name purge list. That court, in turn, found these activities to be a violation of the Due Process Clauses of the Constitution. In particular, Judge Susan J. Dlott noted, "the timing and manner in which Defendants intend to send notice may discourage Plaintiff Voters from exercising that fundamental right by leading them to believe that they are not eligible to vote." She therefore issued an injunction barring any hearings or other actions against those named on the Republicans' challenge list.[128]

Undeterred, the Republicans shifted their tactics to Election Day challenges. Acting quickly, the Republican Party lined up additional official poll watchers for thirty of Ohio's eighty-eight counties, the vast majority of which were in minority and urban areas.[129] The problem here was not in the presence of party-specific poll watchers making challenges. Like the Republicans, the Democrats had their own poll watchers present and ready to challenge "inappropriate" voters. Rather, the issue was the scope of the Republican effort. Whereas the Democrats had registered only a single watcher per polling site, the Republican Party was registering "one challenger for each precinct" in the affected counties (in a statewide practice, there often were multiple precincts in a single polling place). Further, the Republican decision to up the number of poll watchers came "*four days after the deadline* for partisan challengers to register with their county boards of elections." In an administrative ruling just days before the election, Blackwell had changed his standing orders on poll watchers (which originally had limited the parties to one per polling place) to allow the Republicans to add extra poll watchers. Democrats, on the other hand, were caught flat-footed and could not add more poll watchers before the revised poll watcher registration deadline was passed.[130]

Once again, the Democrats turned to the courts for relief. In one state and two federal court proceedings, the Democrats argued for injunctions to halt what they saw as an unnecessary and clearly partisan act by the Republicans. In all three cases, the trial judges agreed with the Democrats, ruling that the challenge procedures adopted by Blackwell were both problematic and tantamount to voter disenfranchisement. As Judge John R. Adams of the Northern District of Ohio declared, "the Court cannot and must not turn a blind eye to the substantial likelihood that significant harm will result not only to voters, but also to the voting process itself, if appointed challengers are permitted at the polls on November 2. . . . While this harm arguably is speculative, should it occur to any significant extent, the integrity of the election may be irreparably harmed."[131]

Despite the consensus of the three trial courts that heard these suits, the precinct-level challengers were in place and ready to act on Election Day following an appeal by Republicans to the 6th Circuit. That court ruled that "neither district court relied upon racial discrimination as a basis for finding a likelihood of success on the merits. Instead, the courts below found a likelihood that the right to vote would be unconstitutionally burdened by having challengers present at the polling place, and that the presence of such challengers was not a sufficiently narrowly tailored way to accomplish legitimate government interests." After all, "challengers may only *initiate* an inquiry process by precinct judges, judges who are of the majority party of the precinct." These judges would decide the fate of the challenged voter. The lower court orders, however, never addressed the "likelihood of success of plaintiffs' challenges to the procedure that will be used by precinct judges once a challenge has been made." True, "longer lines may of course result from delays and confusion when one side in a political controversy employs a statutorily prescribed polling place procedure more vigorously than in previous elections. But such a possibility does not amount to the severe burden upon the right to vote that requires that the statutory authority for the procedure be declared unconstitutional."[132] In the end, the panel concluded, "the public interest weighs against the granting of the preliminary injunction. There is a strong public interest in allowing every registered voter to vote freely. There is also a strong public interest in permitting legitimate statutory processes to operate to preclude voting by those who are not entitled to vote. Finally, there is a strong public interest in smooth and effective administration of the voting laws that militates against changing the rules in the hours immediately preceding the election."[133]

Election Day brought even more examples of administrative gerrymandering by Ohio's Republican government officials. As expected, provisional balloting proved to be a mess, as 155,428 voters filed provisional ballots.[134] In Pepper Pike, Ohio, Mark Cohn, a local lawyer, ran into exactly the problem that Democrats had repeatedly warned against. When he arrived to vote at his usual place, his name was not on the registered-voter list for his precinct. He cast a provisional ballot, only to learn later that his name had been mistakenly included on the list for a different precinct. Even so, despite the clerical mistake that placed him on a different precinct list, he was informed that his vote was still invalidated because he did not cast his provisional ballot in the "right precinct." Only after Cohn filed suit in federal court did the election board agree to discard his provisional ballot and let him vote again.[135] In Toledo, Alexandra Hernandez described in later hearings her experiences with "a young African American woman who had come out" of a polling place "nearly in tears. She was a new voter," Hernandez explained, "very first registered, very excited to vote, and she . . . had been bounced around to three different polling places, and this one had just turned her down again."[136]

Stories of this sort were common across the state. Reporters from the *Washington Post* found scores of longtime voters who had had their names dropped from the voter rolls. Forced to vote provisionally, they wondered if their votes would count. "I'm 52, and I've voted in every single election," Kathy Janoski of Columbus told the *Post* reporters. "They kept telling me, 'You must be mistaken about your precinct.' I told them this is where I've always voted. I felt like I'd been scrubbed off the rolls."[137] Frustratingly, many rejected provisional ballots such as Janoski's were filled out in precincts housed *in the same polling place* as the correct precincts—the poll workers, overworked and undertrained, simply did not direct the provisional voter to the correct table in the same building.[138]

The numbers of lost votes was significant. In Cuyahoga County, the Greater Cleveland Voter Registration Coalition (GCVRC) registered about 10,000 voters, yet found on Election Day that 3.5 percent of those applications either were not entered into the voter databases or were entered incorrectly. These problems effectively disenfranchised these applicants (even if they were able to vote provisionally, these ballots would not have been counted).[139] In a study carried out after the election, the GCVRC estimated that, "based on the findings of our studies of both Board of Elections (BOE) and voter entry errors in about 9,600 applications for registration or change of address, we project that nearly 7,000 Cuyahoga County voters were probably disqualified and about 12,500 voters were put at varying degrees of risk of disqualification." They further estimated that "over 900 provisional ballots may have been wrongfully rejected because of database problems alone." Overall, the study "estimate[d] that 2 out of every 5 provisional ballots that were rejected should have been accepted as legitimate." Simple factors, such as changing one's residence, exposed "voters to a 6% chance of being disenfranchised." Race and ethnicity also had an impact. "In fact, with respect to just provisional ballots," the report concluded, "we found a two-fold increase in rejection rate in predominantly African-American compared to predominantly Caucasian precincts."[140]

Still another provisional ballot problem had to do with the number of available ballots. According to People for the American Way, many Ohio precincts ran out of provisional ballots. Once these ballots were gone, no more provisional balloting was permitted.[141] Other problems included precincts that lacked provisional ballot booklets; confusing provisional ballot designs that led many voters to fail to fill out their ballots completely; and poll workers who had no training on how to administer provisional ballots. In one case, paperwork for dealing with provisional voters was "missing" for most of the day, only to "mysteriously" reappear near the end of the day. As a result, poll workers and Democratic poll watchers could not direct voters to their correct precincts. Instead, such voters were forced to vote provisionally and hope that they were in the correct precinct.[142]

Absentee voters who returned their ballots by mail faced problems as well. In Cuyahoga and Franklin Counties, hearings held by Representative John Conyers (D-MI) after the election uncovered instances of absentee ballots where the arrows did not align with the correct punch hole. While John Kerry's name was listed third among presidential candidates, the proper slot to punch was the fourth slot. The third slot was George W. Bush's. This inconsistency led many to speculate that some voters had voted for a candidate other than their intended choice.[143] In Hamilton County, a large number of absentee ballots omitted John Kerry's name when "workers accidentally removed Kerry when removing Ralph Nader's name from the ballots." And although election officials did attempt to correct this mistake, an unknown number of ballots had already been sent out before the problem was discovered.[144]

Ohio voters even experienced some of Florida's woes from the 2000 election. In the rush to get ready for the election, many Ohio counties decided to hold off upgrading to electronic voting machines. This meant that hundreds of thousands of Ohioans were still voting on punch card ballot machines.[145] And these machines worked as well in Ohio as they had in Florida in 2000—which is to say, not well at all. Estimates varied, but it was likely that Ohio had just under 100,000 "spoiled" ballots in 2004.[146]

Finally there were the long lines facing would-be voters. Voting machine placement issues had perhaps the most visible and longest-lasting impact on the election's outcome. According to a *Washington Post* investigation, "in Columbus, Cincinnati and Toledo, and on college campuses, election officials allocated far too few voting machines to busy precincts, with the result that voters stood on line as long as 10 hours—many leaving without voting." At Kenyon College, northeast of Columbus in central Ohio, "students were forced to stand in line for eleven hours before being allowed to vote, with the last voters casting their ballots after three in the morning."[147] Carolyn M. Sherman, a poll worker in an inner-city Columbus precinct, reported waits of up to eight hours to vote, as 1,500 voters found just three machines available to them.[148] The human costs of such practices could be seen in the experience of Sarah Locke, 54, of Columbus. Her precinct, "a church in the predominantly black southeast [side of town] . . . was jammed. Old women leaned heavily on walkers, and some people walked out complaining that bosses would not excuse their lateness," Locke noted. Meanwhile, in the suburbs, voting machines were plentiful and lines were short.[149]

The primary cause of this discrepancy between urban and suburban precincts was the significant lack of voting machines in busy inner-city precincts. One report showed that "at seven of eight polling places in Franklin County," all in the heavily populated city of Columbus, "there were only three voting machines per location." This was a notable change from the 2004 primary, when "there had been five machines at these locations." A *New York Times* investigation confirmed this discrepancy, noting that, just before the election, Franklin County election officials had reduced the number of voting machines assigned to downtown precincts and added them to the suburbs. They reassigned these machines by applying "a formula based not on the number of registered voters, but on past turnout in each precinct and on the number of so-called active voters—a smaller universe." In the Columbus area, "the result was that suburban precincts that supported Mr. Bush tended to have more machines per registered voter than center city precincts that supported Mr. Kerry."[150] Making matters worse, these same election officials in Columbus had limited themselves to only 2,866 machines, even though their own analysis showed that the county needed 5,000 machines for a smooth election—hence the shift of machines around the county.[151] Adding to the chaos, 77 machines broke down during the course of the day; meanwhile, in a warehouse sat some 81 voting machines that were never placed in any precinct on Election Day.[152]

All told, one in every four Ohio citizens who registered to vote in 2004 faced some kind of problem on Election Day, from showing up at the polls only to discover that they were not listed on the rolls to unlawful identification requirements to long voting lines. Most of these, in turn, were Democratic voters. The DNC report concluded that "not providing a sufficient number of voting machines in each precinct was associated with roughly a *two to three percent reduction in voter turnout* presumably due to delays that deterred many people from voting [emphasis added]."[153] The vast majority of these lost votes, in turn, resulted from administrative decisions by Ohio's election officials, decisions that not only uniformly lowered the number of valid votes in Ohio, but concentrated these votes in minority, poor, and Democratic-leaning precincts—and all of this without ever once breaking the law.

With the end of the 2004 election, the debate on America's election problems largely went dormant once again. The Democrats held their hearings and wrote their reports, citizens in Ohio brought lawsuits, and the Web was filled with conspiracy theories, but with the exception of the Web's conspiracy theorists, few were listening, and fewer still were believing.[154] Kerry, seeing that the number of votes he was likely to gain from the provisional ballots would not overcome George W. Bush's lead in Ohio, quickly conceded the election.[155] When a recount was pushed by third-party candidates, the result was what Kerry had expected: whereas he gained some votes, they were not enough to overcome Bush's more than 100,000-vote victory margin in Ohio.[156] So long as a recount did not include lost *potential* votes (that is, votes that were not cast, but that could have been cast under different rules), Kerry's chances of victory in Ohio were slim to none.

Without a wild recount fight to put at the center of the story, most of the news media declared the election a success and moved on. When liberal commentators and columnists raised questions about the Ohio vote, the mainstream press either ignored these issues or ridiculed them.[157] When the various independent and Democratic reports surfaced showing the many problems undermining the validity of the Ohio vote, they too were largely ignored. As far as the mainstream media was concerned, the 2004 election had gone off with almost no problems.[158]

By 2005 the national dialogue on voting once again focused on the issues of voter IDs, felon franchise, and especially the safety of electronic voting.[159] Throughout 2005, newspaper reports abounded raising questions about the safety of direct electronic voting. DRE machines had their supporters, but most specialists preferred "hand-counted and optically scanned ballots." Such machines, argued Justin Moore, a voting machine specialist at Duke University, offered "something e-voting does not: a paper trail. That's the best way to make sure all the votes get counted." After all, "in the perfect crime, the question is always, 'What do you do with the body?' In electronic voting, there's no body," warned Moore.[160]

In June 2005, Leon County's elections chief, Ion Sancho, gave reason to question all forms of electronic voting when he announced that he had given two computer hackers access to his optical-scan voting machines (in which voters cast fill-in-the-blank ballots) to see if they could break the system's security. By attacking different parts of the system, in particular by getting access to the guts of the machines that tabulated the votes, the hackers bypassed the security codes, allowing them to make losing candidates win or to add or subtract voters—all without leaving a trace. Informed of this test and its worrisome results, acting Florida secretary of state David Mann, whose office still oversees the state elections department, saw no reason to worry: "I'm confident in the certification procedures that we went through with this department. When used within the context of a normal election and the security procedures that all supervisors follow . . . we're confident that that equipment operates correctly and gives accurate results."[161]

Despite such denials of problems with electronic voting, the drive to demand a paper trail to complement electronic voting grew stronger and stronger. Electronic voting was here to stay; the question was how to make it safe. In June 2005 North Carolina began to examine "possible changes to the state's voting machines, including a requirement that all machines produce a paper record." That same month, the *New York Times* noted how "grass-roots reformers [were] in the middle of a two-day lobbying blitz on Capitol Hill in support of a House bill that would require that electronic voting machines in federal elections produce voter-verifiable paper records." The *Times* supported this effort, calling for "every member of Congress who cares about American democracy" to "get behind [this] bill."[162]

With each passing month, the call for security in voting grew louder. And although some states had laws mandating paper trails on the statute books, in many other states officials seemed unwilling to accept the need. Maryland governor Robert Ehrlich, for instance, noted in February 2006 that he had lost all "confidence in the state's ability to conduct fair and accurate elections." His reasons were "concerns over electronic voting machines and a new early voting law passed by Democrats over his veto." Yet the next day, "the state's top elections official declared her confidence in Maryland's voting machines. . . . Changing systems seven months before the primary election," she argued, "would be a 'catastrophe' and a waste of money."[163] In Ohio, "a three-month review of Diebold electronic voting machines used in Cuyahoga County during the May [2006] primary concluded that the votes recorded electronically and on paper receipts did not always match. The election system, [noted the report] 'in its entirety, exhibit[ed] shortcomings with extremely serious consequences, especially in the event of a close election.'" One week later, "Cuyahoga County election officials and Diebold" announced that they had "resolved vote discrepancies identified in an independent study of the company's electronic touch-screen machines—thus proving that the system is accurate."[164]

Then came the 2006 election, and with it proof that all the fears had been justified. Once again the problem arose in Florida. As previously noted, some of Florida's largest counties used the fully electronic DRE voting machines, all certified as "safe" by state election officials, and all lacking a certifiable paper trail.[165] This number included Sarasota County, where in the 2006 race between Republican Vern Buchanan and Democrat Christine Jennings for the thirteenth House district of Florida (ironically, Katherine Harris's seat from 2003 to 2007), 18,000 ballots out of 237,861 cast were left empty for this race—a 14 percent undervote rate, or 1 out of every 8 votes cast. With a vote difference of only 373 votes separating the two candidates, the inability to recount ballots physically meant that any improper undervotes (undervotes in which the voter intended to vote but the machine did not record a vote) were forever lost. Asked to comment on the large numbers of undervotes, Sarasota County elections supervisor Kathy Dent defended her staff and the machines, arguing that the thousands of voters must have simply decided not to vote for either candidate in a race marked by mudslinging or simply missed the race on the screen. "My machines have recorded accurately for 40 elections," Dent said.[166]

In the days and weeks that followed, Jennings and Buchanan fought over the recount procedures. Machine recounts confirmed the original numbers; "hand" recounts and audits showed that the machines were not broken. Jennings contended that a software problem caused 18,000 people in Sarasota County to fail to cast a ballot. Buchanan and Sarasota election officials disagreed. In the end, Buchanan was declared the winner, but Jennings refused to give up. Filing suit in state court to get access to the voting machine's software, Jennings also petitioned Congress to overturn the election's results. Her argument was that the lack of a paper trail made the state "recount" invalid, and thus called the election's outcome into question. The state's response—as well as Buchanan's—was that everything was fine, and that once again, any problems (even 18,000 undervotes) had to be the result of voter choice or error.[167]

And so the circle turned and Florida found itself right back where it had started from in 2000—voting machines that could not be trusted and public officials who did not seem to care (or cared, but did not know how to fix the problems). Still, as the 2008 presidential election approaches, some good things seemed to be emerging from Florida's ongoing electoral mess. In late February 2007, Republican governor Charlie Crist announced his support for replacing all of Florida's DRE machines with precinct-tabulated Scantron-type, optical read machines. Crist even placed more than $20 million in his budget to pay for these machines.[168] Then in April, Crist announced a new plan to grant nonviolent felons their civil rights automatically following the end of their sentences. While not a perfect solution (the ACLU, for example, objected to the plan as not going far enough), the result of this action potentially re-enfranchised hundreds of thousands of Florida voters.[169] Even Leon County elections supervisor Ion Sancho's warnings over the vulnerability of Scantron voting machines were finally being heeded. In late July 2007 the Florida secretary of state's office announced that they had confirmed Sancho's 2005 tests and would decertify such machines unless their maker, Diebold, Inc., fixed the problem.[170]

Across the country, similar reforms were being proposed—and, in an increasing number of cases, adopted—by state governments frustrated with ongoing electoral problems. In March 2007, Iowa passed a law that allowed for registration at the polls on Election Day. That same month, North Carolina adopted the same practice. Other states, such as Colorado, Hawaii, Idaho, and Indiana, passed legislation allowing for more voting by mail. Rhode Island adopted a provisional ballot rule and required two separate mailings to voters reminding them to bring ID to the polls. Maine put its efforts into instituting an administrative complaint procedure, a new computer-based voter registration application system, and finally an entire set of new voting standards with a uniform definition of what constitutes a vote. In Maryland, both houses of the state legislature approved submitting a constitutional amendment to the voters in 2008 that would make Maryland the sixteenth state to let voters cast ballots in person before Election Day.[171]

As for paperless DRE machines, states across the nation joined Florida in decertifying them as a matter of course as the 2008 elections loomed ever closer. In August 2007 California decertified DRE machines in response to a report outlining several fundamental security flaws in their operation. Not long after this, New Jersey found itself having to implement a paper trail component to its voting machines in response to a court order. In Ohio, Democratic secretary of state Jennifer Brunner issued a report on December 14 that argued the electronic voting machines used in Ohio contained critical security failures that could jeopardize the integrity of state elections. She called for legislation to force the counties still using these machines to quickly move to a paper-based optical balloting system. Responding to this call, Cuyahoga County officials would decide in January 2008 to switch from DREs to centrally counted optical ballots in time for the March 4 primaries. Meanwhile, as 2007 came to a close, Colorado's secretary of state, Mike

Coffman, a Republican, "decertified the state's electronic voting machines, after the alarming finding that one model could be disabled with a magnet and others were scandalously inaccurate."[172]

Thus our narrative reaches to the present on a seeming high note, with the sad story of America's recent voting tribulations apparently on track to be getting less sad, less dire, and ever more optimistic. Across the nation, reform groups and pundits seem hopeful—even confident—that the growing trends in voting technology and government oversight promised an end to the nightmare. It had been a long and difficult journey from 2000, but with every passing election our ability to use electronic voting equipment grows apace. Backed by a paper trail, voting machines are defended as offering a perfect mix of speed (the electronic part) and accuracy (the paper trails). Soon, argue election officials, electoral meltdowns would be a thing of the past. At the least, the tendency of a voting problem to become a political and constitutional crisis should be at an end.[173]

There is just one problem: nowhere in this happy narrative is there any sign of action being taken to defend against the many types of administrative gerrymandering. Both in 2000 and 2004, the failure of voting machines to do their job was noticeable—even splashy. The same was true for 2006 in Sarasota. But this was not the whole story. Beneath the surface there lay a deadly threat, one that, if not solved, challenges the future of American democracy. This threat is the willful manipulation of election procedures and rules for partisan political gain—that is to say, administrative gerrymandering.

As evidence of this ongoing problem, we merely need cite the Republican Party's focus on voter fraud as a justification for widespread voter exclusions via voter ID requirements and voter-list purges (procedures that, as we have seen, disproportionately exclude Democratic voters).[174] Despite repeated studies that argued that little if any credible evidence existed for voter fraud, and even less for the electoral impact of such fraud, Republicans continue to sound warnings about voter fraud. As of January 2008, twenty-five states had some sort of voter ID rules. In most, ID rules were passed by Republican-dominated legislatures and signed into law either by Republican governors or Democratic governors under extreme political pressure. Seven states—each Republican dominated—required that voters produce a picture ID to vote, and one state, Indiana, limited this photo ID to government issued documents.[175] In late 2007 Florida even tightened its voter ID laws to exclude employer IDs or buyer club IDs as acceptable forms of identification at the polls, making Florida's rules the second strictest in the nation after Indiana's—a change quickly approved in early January 2008 for full implementation by the Bush Department of Justice.[176] Even when confronted with the growing pile of new studies on the irrelevancy of voter fraud as a national problem, Republicans refuse to believe—and, where possible, have revised or distorted such reports to fit their preconceptions.[177] There is even some evidence to suggest that the controversial firing of eight U.S. Attorneys in early 2007 was rooted in the unwillingness of these Justice Department officials to press voter fraud cases aggressively enough to suit the needs of Republican party officials.[178] Evidence also shows that the Bush Administration's standard of "aggressive enough" was so aggressive that, in one instance, it led to the filing of a case in which the government's arguments were so weak that a federal district court in Missouri ruled against the Department of Justice;[179] in another instance, it led to the wrongful conviction and incarceration of a low-level Wisconsin government official for a fraud she not only did not commit, but which a panel of the 7th Circuit Court of Appeals found no credible proof of ever having happened.[180]

And this is just one category of administrative gerrymandering. Inaccurate voter rolls, partisan placement of voting machines, and the 1001 ways that election officials could exclude voters merely by being inefficient in processing registration forms or being too literal in the enforcement of registration rules, are equally as capable of having as significant an impact on an election's outcome as paperless electronic voting machines or voter ID laws. The greatest threats to democracy and a clean election, in other words, lie not in machines, but in the perfectly legal, and yet procedurally devastating, actions of government officials who place partisanship above nation, power above service, and most of all, results above process. As law professor and elections expert Spencer Overton explains,

> contrary to conventional perception, American democracy is not an organic, grassroots phenomenon that mirrors society's preferences. In reality, the will of the people is channeled by a predetermined matrix of thousands of election regulations and practices that most people accept as natural: the location of election-district boundaries, voter-registration deadlines, and the number of voting machines at a busy polling place. This structure of election rules, practices and decisions filter out certain citizens from voting and organizes the electorate. There is no "right" to vote outside of terms, conditions, hurdles and boundaries set out by [this] matrix.

How we set up and administer this matrix of rules and procedures shapes who can vote, how they vote, and even who wins and loses. Control this matrix and you control our democratic processes. And, as Overton explains, although there is no "grand conspiracy" distorting the shape and scope of our electoral matrix, so long as partisan government officials are allowed to shape its form, the result will be a circumscribed electorate and manipulated electoral procedures.[181] More to the point, so long as the potential for those in power to shape and reshape the process by which we vote is left unattended, any electoral reforms we attempt—such as paper trails or more effective provisional ballots—will be short-lived and ineffective.

AFTERWORD

The Process Matters

The lasting tragedy of this election will not be found in declaring that one
man stole the presidency from another. The lasting tragedy will be found among
American families who will add 21st-century stories to the long historic narrative of
how, despite their best efforts, they were denied the chance to vote.
—Boston Globe *editorial, December 4, 2000*

The never-ending presidential election has been a national civics lesson,
informing Americans about the inner workings of our political processes. . . . But the
lesson has . . . been a disillusioning one, stripping a veil of innocence from our eyes.
—*Alexander Keyssar, Kennedy School of Public Policy, Harvard University*

Recently, law professor and election law specialist Richard Hasen has argued that
Bush v. Gore is dead. In his view, the reform potential of that case—which many
election law scholars had seen buried within that decision's equal protection holding—had proven both short-lived and largely illusionary. Whatever good it could
have done was dead and gone.[1] Others, such as Orin Kerr, question whether there
ever was a reform potential in *Bush v. Gore*.[2] Clearly, as chapter 10's venture into
the post-2000 electoral landscape has shown, there are very good reasons for giving
Bush v. Gore its last rites as a reform platform.

But did it have to be this way? Did reform have to fail? Are we doomed to an
eternity of political machinations and electoral breakdowns? No one can say for
sure. Questions such as these can be answered only in the realms of future history
and counterfactual history—which, unlike the reasoned speculation and analysis
applied in earlier chapters, are essentially speculations without foundation. As the
historian Harold Hyman once remarked, counterfactual history is a dish best
served with a cold beer and good friends open to a game of "what if." Future history, needless to say, is squarely fixed within the realm of science fiction.

Still, in closing this history of the 2000 presidential election and *Bush v. Gore*,
we can say a few things that might shed light on these questions—points that take
into account the "what-ifs" of history and allow us to ponder the lessons of the past
for the future without entering too far into the realm of speculation unanchored
by historical context.

First, the Supreme Court *never* gave *Bush v. Gore* the support it deserved as a
mechanism for electoral reform. By limiting the reach of the case, by focusing
on who became president while underselling the equal protection logic of their
per curiam opinion, the majority justices deprived the case of its precedential

and educative value. In doing so, any reform potential in *Bush v. Gore* was crippled at its birth.

It did not have to be this way. Imagine what might have happened had the majority added to its per curiam ruling a statement like this:

> Our consideration in this matter is limited to the present circumstances, for the problem of equal protection in election processes generally presents many complexities. However, recognizing the importance of an effective, safe, and trustworthy electoral system, we call upon Congress and the states to respond to this problem, guided by our ruling as to the equal protection rights of all Americans to an effective and uniform vote, and so to find the uniform standards that would protect a citizen's right to an equal vote. Just what shape such a reform of electoral procedures shall take, we leave to the political branches of government, for they are most capable of determining such matters.

With such a call to arms fixed squarely on the national political agenda, it would have been much harder for the political branches to play politics with this subject. They would have had a mandate grounded in the Constitution itself to update our elective system. And it would have been a mandate backed by an unspoken threat: fix this yourself, or we will fix it for you.

Such was the threat behind *Brown v. Board of Education* and many other civil rights landmark cases. Fix this yourself, or we will do it for you. And when the South refused to heed the offer of self-directed reform, and the threat that underlay it in *Brown*, the Court acted, ordering integration in *Green v. County School Board of New Kent County* (1968).[3] And whereas *Brown* arguably was a failure in this regard—many have asserted that the case is an example of how powerless the Court really is to initiate social or political change[4]—the point is that, with the ideal and threat of a constitutional mandate before the American people, the people and their elected representatives acted. What matter if the final mechanisms of change were legislative or judicial? What matter that it took over a generation for even partial integration to become the reality in American schools? The point is, the Supreme Court educated "We the People" about the Constitution's requirements and we learned. *Brown* changed the way that we looked at the world, and with it, the policy choices of Americans for over two generations.

For a model closer to our focus in this book, voting rights, consider *Oregon v. Mitchell*. In this 1970 case, the Supreme Court ruled that, under the Constitution as it then existed, the federal government could not lower the voting age to eighteen across the nation by simple statute. The Court did, however, make clear that there was nothing keeping the nation from amending the Constitution to achieve this end. The result, in just three months, was the Twenty-Sixth Amendment. The Supreme Court spoke and we heard. And with a gentle push from the justices, the entire American political landscape was transformed.[5]

Of course, even with such a mandate, the realities of partisan politics might have undermined reform. It is important not to underestimate the difficulties of reform. What I am saying is not that action on the part of the Supreme Court guaranteed reform. Rather, the *lack* of such support significantly, perhaps fatally, undermined whatever chance there was of serious electoral reform following the 2000 election. At a time when we needed a call to arms from the world's loudest trumpet, all we got was a muted whisper. This was the tragedy of *Bush v. Gore.* That at a time when real reform was possible—in that narrowest of windows created by the electoral meltdown in Florida—the Supreme Court failed to seize the opportunity to make something good come out of the mess. We needed them not merely to fix the crisis but to address the problems that caused this crisis so that it never happened again— at the least to lend their weight to a demand that others fix the problem. This, however, was a task that the justices in the majority declined to undertake—perhaps because they never even considered it.

Such was the opportunity lost that lay at the heart of *Bush v. Gore*. And, nearly eight years later, American democracy still stands at the brink of failure because of this lost opportunity. Democracy is hard. It takes hard work. It takes commitment to, and faith in, the wisdom of one's fellow citizens. It takes institutions, mechanisms, and procedures all aimed at integrating the public will into the process of governance. Most of all, it takes a willingness to trust the methods of popular government—to accept that the process is always more important than the results.

In 2000 we showed just how much we lacked this faith—in the process and procedures of running elections and in the wisdom of our fellow citizens. Even worse, we may have showed just how little we understand the necessities of democracy in the first place. We should understand—but either we don't or we choose not to see—that at root democracy means accepting the outcome of the electoral process no matter how unpalatable we may find the results. We must also accept that other policy choices can be as valid as the ones we would support; and in doing so, we must accept the duty of running as clean and nonpartisan an election as possible.

Yet for such faith to exist, there has to be trust. Trust in the process by which we pick our leaders and shape our public realm. Trust in the institutions of our government. Trust in the people who lead us. For without these kinds of trust, there is only competition. Without trust, the road to excessive partisanship and electoral breakdown is as wide as an interstate highway—and it's all going the wrong way.

In a democracy, this trust can only be built on the foundation of a working and effective electoral system. When our electoral processes are weak or misunderstood, our democracy is equally weak and misunderstood. When excess partisanship and selfishness rule the day, democracy crumbles. When hate and fear outweigh civic duty and pride, democracy is dead. It would be so easy for us to lose the core of our democracy—to keep the forms without the substance. For what good are elections if they change nothing? What good is voting, if the voters feel that they have no say in the shaping of our public realm? As Robert F. Kennedy Jr. warns in regard to the 2004 election, "nothing less is at stake here than the entire idea of a government by the people."[6]

Democracy demands that we accept the legitimacy of our electoral system even as we struggle to make that system worthy of trust. This has been, in fact, the task of all Americans since the nation's founding. As historian Charles Sydnor observed about democratic practices in George Washington's Virginia,

> It is worth recalling that this generation of Virginians did not delay doing essential tasks until they could reshape and perfect the political instruments at hand. They were not ignorant of some of the defects and crudities of their political processes; but they never lost sight of large public issue while they tinkered with the machine. They were wise enough to know that it could never be perfected to such a point that it would automatically turn out a good product. Rather they regarded it as nothing more than an instrument that men could use, or fail to use, to accomplish good purposes. To them, democracy was not like a snug house, purchased in full with a heavy payment of sacrifice at the moment of its establishment, and then to be enjoyed in effortless comfort every after. Their concept of self-government included the idea that it was a burden, valuable but heavy, which must be borne constantly. Carrying this burden was to them more important than refining the forms of political processes; for they knew that if they or their successors ever laid down the burden, or in wariness permitted it to be taken from their shoulders by more willing but less worthy men, self-government would come to an end. They knew no way for democracy to work except for men of good will to labor incessantly at the job of making it work.[7]

The 2000 election, as Jefferson would have put it, was a true firebell in the night. It warned of the threats attacking our democratic institutions—threats that lay not in foreign foes or technological breakdowns, but in our own flawed sense of civic pride, our self-satisfied belief that our electoral system, like the Constitution itself, was "a machine that would go of itself,"[8] and most of all, our overarching partisan emotions, hopes, and dreams. It warned of our old and creaky electoral system's potential for collapse and failure—but only if we allow this failure to happen.

The reform opportunity created by the 2000 electoral train wreck has passed. But the lessons of that constitutional and electoral ruin have not been lost—just ignored. There is no good reason why we cannot take up the cause and fight to save democracy by reforming our electoral system—by facing the dangers of administrative gerrymandering head on. *Bush v. Gore* might be dead as an engine of reform, but the lessons it carries about the need for a more uniform and national electoral system, one in which the "wiggle room" of partisan government officials is taken away, must not be lost. Democracy is dead only if we let it die.

But our time to act is shrinking. In the wake of *Bush v. Gore*, I talked to high school students in Broward County, and their cynicism about and outright disdain for electoral politics is terrifying. They represent the next generation of voters, and yet they just shrug their shoulders and walk away. They feel disenfranchised. To them, voting is a rigged game, one in which those with power get what they want, no matter what the rest of us think or feel. They see no reason to participate in our democratic processes. To the extent that they feel this way, democracy already may be dead in this country. The question we now face is whether we can revive American democracy before it is beyond saving. And the longer we wait, the harder it will be to fix what is broken. The time to act—to do the "essential tasks" of democracy despite the ongoing "defects and crudities of [our] political processes"—is now.[9]

A Timeline of Events for the 2000 Presidential Election and Postelection Crisis

Tuesday, November 7, 2000

- Election Day. At 7:48 p.m., NBC names Al Gore the winner in Florida. The other three networks soon follow suit. At 10 p.m., CBS is the first network to retract the call, placing Florida in the "too close to call" column. The other networks soon follow suit.

Wednesday, November 8, 2000

- At 2:00 a.m., Fox News declares Bush the winner in Florida. By 2:20 a.m., all other networks follow suit. 3:00 a.m., Al Gore phones George W. Bush and concedes election. Approximately forty-five minutes later, after getting word that Bush's lead in Florida is shrinking and there will be an automatic recount, Gore rescinds concession. 3:57 a.m., networks once again place Florida in the "too close to call" column.

- Noting how the presidential vote for each candidate differed by less than .005 percent (just over 1,600 votes), Florida secretary of state Katherine Harris announces an automatic recount required under Florida law.

- Automatic recounts start in all sixty-seven Florida counties. By day's end, Bush's lead has shrunk to approximately 400 votes.

- First lawsuit is filed in Florida by Palm Beach County voters alleging voter confusion over the county's butterfly ballot. Plaintiffs seek to set aside all presidential votes in the county and order a new countywide election. Defendants include the Palm Beach County Canvassing Board, Bush, Cheney, Gore, and Lieberman. (*Fladell v. Palm Beach County Canvassing Board*)

- NAACP President Kweisi Mfume notifies Attorney General Janet Reno of the reported irregularities and minority vote dilution African American voters in Florida may have encountered on Election Day. He asks Reno to investigate the charges.

- Gore sends plane filled with lawyers and political advisors (*Recount One*) to Florida to get the recount process started. Gore also asks former U.S. secretary of state Warren Christopher to act as his lead spokesperson in Florida.

- Florida governor's general counsel, Frank Jimenez, begins calling major Florida law firms on behalf of George W. Bush, hiring such notable attorneys as Barry Richard for the Republican side. Jimenez's efforts would also result in Florida's largest firm, Holland & Knight, refusing to serve as counsel for Al Gore, despite the firm's strong ties to the Democratic Party.

Thursday, November 9, 2000
- Mandatory recounts continue. Bush's lead shrinks to 229 votes.
- Gore officially requests hand recounts in four heavily Democratic counties: Palm Beach, Miami-Dade, Broward, and Volusia.
- Palm Beach County voters file more voter lawsuits challenging the constitutionality of the butterfly ballot and the presidential vote. Other suits directly attack the actions of the Florida Election Canvassing Commission. These actions include:
    Rogers v. Election Canvassing Commission of Florida
    Horowitz v. LePore
    Elkin v. LePore
    Gibbs v. Palm Beach County Canvassing Board

Friday, November 10, 2000
- Florida governor Jeb Bush recuses himself from the recount process and withdraws from the state canvassing commission.
- The Democratic and Republican Parties attempt to show distance from the controversy. George W. Bush tells reporters he is making "low key" preparations for the White House in the midst of recount litigation.
- Gore lawyers ask Florida state election officials to ignore the deadline of 5 p.m. November 14 and not certify the results until hand recounts are done.
- Bush sends former U.S. secretary of state James A. Baker III to act as his lead spokesperson in Florida. Other hires include Theodore Olson to head the federal litigation team and Barry Richard for state litigation. By this time, over 200 lawyers work on the Republican side.

Saturday, November 11, 2000
- The Bush campaign files a federal lawsuit in Miami seeking declaratory and injunctive relief to halt all manual recounts. (*Siegel, et al., v. Lepore, et al.*)
- Duval County officials announce that about 26,000 ballots were thrown out because they were marked for more than one presidential candidate (i.e., overvotes).
- A 1 percent sample hand recount begins in Palm Beach County. Throughout day, standards as to what constituted a valid ballot are changed and changed again. 11:05 p.m., last ballot is examined. The results showed that Gore had gained thirty-three votes to fourteen new votes for Bush—a difference of nineteen votes. The board debates whether to institute a countywide recount.

Sunday, November 12, 2000
- 2:00 a.m., Palm Beach County Canvassing Board votes to institute a recount of all of the county's 460,000 ballots.
- Volusia County Canvassing Board members meet at 9:00 a.m. to begin a manual recount of all of the county's 184,018 ballots. Technical difficulties delay the actual start of counting until the next morning, however.
- Additional suit filed against the Palm Beach County butterfly ballot (*Elkin v. LePore*)

Monday, November 13, 2000
- Florida secretary of state Katherine Harris, a Republican and vice chair of the Bush Florida campaign, says all counties must complete recounts by 5 p.m. the next day. No exceptions allowed.
- The Volusia County Canvassing Board sues Secretary of State Katherine Harris to halt her just-announced 5:00 p.m. vote certification and recount deadline. They want to gain time so they can continue their recount of presidential ballots and include the hand-counted votes that Harris seeks to prohibit. Lawyers for Palm Beach County and Gore campaign quickly join the suit. Bush lawyers just as quickly join Florida to block any extension. (*McDermott v. Harris;* see also *Gore v. Election Canvassing Commission of Florida*)
- U.S. District Court Judge Donald Middlebrooks, holding that Florida's vote-counting process appeared to be neutral without any necessity for federal intervention, denies the Bush campaign's request for injunctive relief to halt a manual recount of Florida voters' ballots. Middlebrooks concludes, "The body of law is pretty pervasive that the federal courts ought to stay out of state elections." (*Siegel v. LePore*)
- Palm Beach County Canvassing Board seeks advisory opinions from the Division of Elections, which is supervised by the secretary of state, and from the Florida attorney general to determine if it should proceed with a hand count.
- Democrats challenge the Palm Beach County Canvassing Board's strict standards of proof of a voter's intent, which by this date does not include indented chads as a valid vote, in Palm Beach County Circuit Court. (*Democratic Party v. Palm Beach County Canvassing Board*)
- Director of the state Division of Elections, Clay Roberts, issues an advisory opinion (AO 0011) arguing that "an 'error in the vote tabulation' means a counting error in which the vote tabulation system fails to count properly . . . punched punchcard ballots. Such an error could result from incorrect election parameters, or an error in the vote tabulation and reporting software of the voting system. The inability of a voting systems to read an improperly . . . punched punchcard ballot," however, was "not 'error in the vote tabulation' and [thus] would not trigger the requirement for the county canvassing board" to undertake a countywide hand recount.
- A hand recount of 4,000 ballots in Broward County finds no major problems. The county canvassing board rejects full recount, in part based on state Division of Elections director Clay Robert's memorandum. Democrats vow to appeal.
- Additional suits filed against the Palm Beach County butterfly ballot.
  Gottfried v. LePore
  The 'People' (Boswell) v. Jeb Bush

Tuesday, November 14, 2000
- Florida attorney general Bob Butterworth issues an advisory opinion (AO 00-65) contradicting Clay Roberts's views on legality of hand recounts. Butterworth concludes that "I am of the opinion that the term 'error in voter tabulation' encompasses a discrepancy between the number of votes determined by a voter tabulation system and the number of votes determined by a manual count of a sampling of precincts pursuant to section 102.166(4)."

- Leon County Circuit Court Judge Terry Lewis upholds Harris's 5:00 p.m. deadline but cautions that he will allow supplemental or corrected presidential vote totals after the deadline and that Harris may or may not use them under her "proper exercise of discretion."
- The Palm Beach County Canvassing Board decides to continue manual recounts of presidential votes, even though Judge Lewis upholds Harris's previously announced 5:00 p.m. deadline for counties to report ballot counts to the state.
- In response to the conflicting advisory opinions of the Division of Elections and the Florida attorney general's office, Palm Beach County asks the Florida Supreme Court if it should proceed with the hand count. Supreme Court accepts case and announces that "it appears that the relief sought on the question of whether the Canvassing Board may conduct a manual recount of the votes cast for President and Vice President has been answered in the affirmative by the Circuit Courts of Leon and Palm Beach County. At present, this is binding legal authority on this issue and there is no legal impediment to the recounts continuing. Thus, Petitioners are authorized to proceed with the manual recount." (*Palm Beach County Canvassing Board v. Harris*).
- Volusia County turns in its recounted ballot totals before the 5:00 p.m. deadline. These numbers are included in the state's certification numbers later that day.
- Bush appeals Judge Middlebrooks's ruling to the 11th Circuit Court of Appeals in Atlanta. (*Siegel v. LePore*)
- Democrats file a motion for a writ of mandamus to force the Broward County Canvassing Board to start countywide recounts and a motion for an injunction to challenge on standards being used to determine proof of voter intent. Later that day, Broward Circuit Judge John Miller allows the county to go ahead with a manual recount of all ballots cast throughout the county and stresses the "totality of the circumstances" requirement of state law in determining the "intent of the voter." (*Democratic Party v. Broward County Canvassing Board*).
- Miami-Dade County election officials initiate hand count of a sample of precincts, later deciding against a full recount.
- At 4:30 p.m., Palm Beach decides to submit its machine-counted results to the state and to proceed with a manual recount of all ballots Wednesday.
- At 5 p.m., the deadline arrives for counties to certify and report their election returns to the secretary of state's office.
- At 7:37 p.m., Katherine Harris issues vote totals as of 5 p.m. Bush holds a 300-vote margin. Harris says she will comply with Judge Lewis's order to "consider late returns." She gives those counties seeking to amend their vote totals until 2:00 p.m. Wednesday to explain, in writing, why they want to add hand recounts after the 5:00 p.m. deadline.
- David Boies joins the Gore campaign's legal team.
- Additional suits filed against the Palm Beach County butterfly ballot:
    Haitian American . . . (HABIL) v. PBC Canvassing Board
    Adrien v. Dept. of Elections
    Crum v. PBC Canvassing Board
    Lichtman v. Jeb Bush
    Rhodes v. Harris

Wednesday, November 15, 2000
- Florida secretary of state Katherine Harris sues in an effort to stop manual recounts and, failing that, to consolidate the various pending lawsuits. (*Harris v. Circuit Judges of the 11th, 15th & 17th Judicial Circuits of Florida*)
- Broward County officials change their mind and begin counting nearly 600,000 ballots by hand.
- In Palm Beach County, Circuit Judge Jorge Labarga rules that county election officials cannot discard ballots with "dimpled chads," ballots indented but not perforated. (*Democratic Party v. Palm Beach County Canvassing Board*)
- By 2:00 p.m., Katherine Harris receives letters from the three counties still hand-counting ballots, explaining their reasons for delay and outlining what amended returns they seek to make.
- The Florida Supreme Court denies Katherine Harris's request to halt recounts and to consolidate all election-related litigation. (*Harris v. Circuit Judges of the 11th, 15th & 17th Judicial Circuits of Florida*)
- Around 6:00 p.m., Gore proposes completion of hand counts in Dade, Broward, and Palm Beach counties and asks that those results and the overseas absentees ballots be added to the election tally. If that is done, he vows, he will not challenge the results in court. He also suggests a manual recount of all sixty-seven Florida counties and proposes that he and Bush meet. Later that night, Bush refuses this offer. "The outcome of this election," he says, "will not be the result of deals or efforts to mold public opinion."
- At 9:14 p.m., Katherine Harris announces that she has reviewed letters from the hand-counting counties and found their reasons for delay insufficient. She will not accept results of any hand recounts when it is time to certify the Florida vote on November 18.

Thursday, November 16, 2000
- Gore lawyers ask Judge Lewis to require Katherine Harris to include ballots being hand-counted after the Tuesday deadline. Harris acted arbitrarily, the lawyers argue, when she refused to include them. Judge Lewis holds a hearing on whether Harris violated his order when she said the hand-counted ballots would not be included in the final tally. (*McDermott v. Harris*)
- The Florida Supreme Court allows hand recounts to continue. (*Palm Beach County Canvassing Board v. Harris*)
- Florida voter Calvin Fox attacks Katherine Harris for trying to halt recounts (questioning her qualifications and ethics) in the Leon County Circuit Court. (*Fox v. Harris*)

Friday, November 17, 2000
- Amid disputes, hand counting resumes in Palm Beach and Broward Counties.
- In Palm Beach County, Judge Labarga holds hearings over whether, if he determines the "butterfly" ballot is illegal, he could actually call for a revote. (*Fladell v. Palm Beach County Canvassing Board*)
- Judge Terry Lewis denies the Gore campaign's emergency motion to compel Secretary of State Harris to comply with and enforce the court's earlier injunction. He

argues that Florida law gives Harris "broad discretionary authority to accept or reject late-filed returns." (*McDermott v. Harris*)

- The Gore campaign immediately appeals Judge Lewis's ruling to the Florida Supreme Court. That court schedules oral argument at a court hearing at 2:00 p.m. EST on Monday, November 20. At the same time, the Supreme Court unanimously rules that Harris may not certify a winner in the state's presidential election until "further order of this court." (*McDermott v. Harris* consolidated into *Palm Beach County Canvassing Board v. Harris*)
- Later that day, the Florida Supreme Court prohibits Katherine Harris from certifying the vote and says pointedly "it is NOT the intent of this order to stop the counting."
- The 11th Circuit Court of Appeals rejects the Bush campaign's appeal for an emergency injunction. The court does not, however, rule on the substance of Bush's appeal. (*Siegel v. LePore*)
- Florida election officials begin counting the state's more than 2,500 overseas ballots, with counties facing a noon Saturday deadline to report their new totals. More than 1,100 of the ballots are reportedly thrown out, and Republicans complain that Democrats are making a coordinated challenge, particularly against ballots from military personnel.
- In the Leon County Circuit Court, Florida voter Matt Butler attacks hand recounts as disenfranchising voters in those counties in which no hand-recounting is being done. (*Butler v. Harris*)
- Additional suits against the Palm Beach County butterfly ballot:
  Green v. LePore
  Katz v. Election Canvassing Commission

Saturday, November 18, 2000
- All parties in the Florida Supreme Court appeal file briefs and prepare for oral argument. (*Palm Beach County Canvassing Board v. Harris*)
- With all of the state's sixty-seven counties reporting their overseas ballot results, Bush's overall lead in the state rises to 930 votes as Bush picks up 1,380 votes from the overseas ballots to Gore's 750.

Monday, November 20, 2000
- Miami-Dade County begins its (short-lived) manual recount. Broward and Palm Beach Counties continue theirs.
- The Florida Supreme Court listens to the parties' arguments on appeal. (*Palm Beach County Canvassing Board v. Harris*)
- Circuit Judge Labarga in Palm Beach County rules that "it is not legally possible to have a revote or a new election for presidential electors in Florida" based upon voter confusion with, and constitutional challenges to, the butterfly ballot. (*Fladell v. Palm Beach County Canvassing Board*)
- Democratic state attorney general Robert Butterworth says that overseas ballots, running roughly 2 to 1 for Bush, should count even if they bear no postmark.
- Jane Carroll, Broward County's sole Republican election supervisor resigns. "It's like having Election Day for 10 days in a row," she says. "I need to get out of here."

- Final suit brought against the Palm Beach County butterfly ballot (*Judicial Watch v. LePore*)

Tuesday, November 21, 2000
- Another day of counting in Miami-Dade, Palm Beach, and Broward (where Circuit Court Judge Robert Rosenberg replaces Jane Carroll on the canvassing board).
- The PR war over overseas absentee ballots rages on. The Republicans deputize World War II veteran Bob Dole and Gulf War veteran General Norman Schwarzkopf to demand inclusion. The Democrats' military man is Senator Bob Kerrey, a Vietnam vet.
- Bush attorneys file a supplemental legal brief with Florida's Supreme Court, arguing that the justices are "without power" to figure out which ballots should or should not be tallied. (*Palm Beach County Canvassing Board v. Harris*)
- At 9:45 p.m., the Florida Supreme Court renders a unanimous decision, ordering that manual recounts must be added to the final certified count of presidential votes by Florida voters. The court holds that a Florida law providing that the secretary of state "shall" ignore late returns conflicts with another statute that says the secretary "may" ignore returns. It finds that "an accurate vote count is one of the essential foundations of our democracy." The court makes clear that it wants to protect voters: "to allow the Secretary to summarily disenfranchise innocent electors in an effort to punish dilatory Board members, as she proposes . . . misses the constitutional mark." The justices give the three counties until 5:00 p.m. on Sunday, November 26—or alternately, 9:00 a.m. Monday, November 27, if the secretary of state's office is closed—to send in the amended results. (*Palm Beach County Canvassing Board v. Harris*)
- The secretary of state's office announces that it will be open on Sunday to receive amended returns up to 5:00 p.m.

Wednesday, November 22, 2000
- Bush petitions the U.S. Supreme Court, seeking to have the decision of the Florida Supreme Court in *Palm Beach County Canvassing Board v. Harris* overruled. Bush accuses the Florida court of "a lawless exercise of judicial power." (*Bush v. Palm Beach County Canvassing Board*)
- The Bush Campaign brings an action in Leon County Circuit Court to ensure counting of hundreds of overseas military ballots previously rejected on technicalities. (*Bush v. Bay County Canvassing Board, et al.*)
- Palm Beach opts to examine "dimpled" ballots. This decision is later reversed.
- As Sunday's counting deadline looms, Miami-Dade election officials abruptly halt their recount, saying they cannot count all 600,000 ballots in time. For a time they propose to recount only 10,750 "undervotes"—ballots missing a presidential choice. However, due to disruptions from protesters and election supervisor David Leahy's opinion that they could not meet the Sunday deadline even counting only the undervotes, the board halts all recounts. This decision costs Gore a 157-vote gain.

Thursday, November 23, 2000

- In an effort to meet the 5:00 p.m. Sunday deadline, Broward County election officials forgo or delay their Thanksgiving dinners to count ballots. Palm Beach County election officials do not, halting the counting process for the day.
- Democrats seek an order to get the Miami-Dade Canvassing Board to restart the recounts. The Florida Supreme Court refuses to issue the order. (*Gore v. Miami-Dade Canvassing Commission*)
- The Gore Campaign announces that, as permitted under Florida law, it would contest the election in Miami-Dade County whatever the results of the final certification tally.
- Vice President Gore and the Florida Democratic Party file their own petition, opposing Bush's request for the Supreme Court to hear the case, arguing there is no federal question at issue for the Court to decide. Gore's lawyers call Bush's request a "bald attempt to federalize a state court dispute." (*Bush v. Palm Beach County Canvassing Board*)

Friday, November 24, 2000

- Broward County, where Gore has already picked up 245 votes so far, begins recording dimpled chads, following Palm Beach's lead (when Palm Beach County switches away from accepting dimpled chads, the Broward board continues to accept dimpled ballots).
- In a historic decision, the U.S. Supreme Court grants certiorari and decides to hear Bush's appeal of the Florida Supreme Court's November 21 decision. The Court declines, however, to hear Bush's appeal of denials by the 11th Circuit and the U.S. District Court in Miami to issue a temporary restraining order and injunction prohibiting any state-ordered manual recount of presidential ballots. Oral arguments are set for December 1 at 10 a.m. (*Bush v. Palm Beach County Canvassing Board*)
- Attorneys in consolidated class action cases for Florida voters challenging the election results and the constitutionality of the butterfly ballots file emergency appeals to the Florida Supreme Court, arguing that trial courts have the legal authority to order new presidential elections in Florida. (*Fladell v. Palm Beach County Canvassing Board*)

Sunday, November 26, 2000

- Palm Beach needs more time to count fewer than 2,000 questionable ballots and faxes a request to Secretary of State Harris's office for an extension to 9:00 a.m. Monday, instead of 5:00 p.m. Sunday. Harris says no. Palm Beach submits its partial recount numbers before the deadline. The board keeps counting and submits its complete recount tally two hours after the 5:00 p.m. deadline.
- Broward County finishes its recount late on November 25 and submits its revised numbers by the 5:00 p.m. deadline. The revised count gave Gore 567 additional votes.
- After Leon County Circuit Court Judge L. Ralph Smith Jr. expresses skepticism about Bush's arguments on overseas absentee ballots, the campaign voluntarily withdraws its suit claiming that the fourteen Florida counties named in it were al-

ready in "substantial agreement" with the Bush position and so it was not necessary to proceed. (*Bush v. Bay County Canvassing Board et al.*)

- Bush's lawyers file separate lawsuits against six county canvassing boards regarding overseas absentee ballots. These boards were Okaloosa, Walton, Hillsborough, Polk, Orange, Pasco, and Collier.
- Florida secretary of state Harris certifies George W. Bush as the Florida voters' choice for president, rejecting Palm Beach County Canvassing Board amended partial recounts. The tally shows Bush ahead by 537 votes: 2,912,790 to 2,912,253.
- Gore announces that he will head to court the following day to contest the certification.

Monday, November 27, 2000

- Gore and Lieberman commence a new lawsuit by filing a complaint and a request for an emergency hearing, contesting the secretary of state's recount, in a Leon County Circuit Court. Gore challenges the vote totals in three counties and asks Judge Sander Sauls to order a hand count of some 13,000 ballots in Palm Beach and Miami-Dade Counties that showed no votes for president during prior machine recounts. Simultaneously, the Gore legal team files an emergency motion to accelerate the contest proceedings. (*Gore v. Harris*)
- Seminole County voter Harry Jacobs challenges allegedly unlawful assistance given by county election officials to Republican workers in adding missing information to absentee ballot applications. He seeks to toss out all 15,000 absentee ballots in the Bush stronghold of Seminole County, claiming that county officials improperly allowed GOP operatives to add missing voter ID numbers on 2,100 Republican absentee ballot applications. (*Jacobs v. Seminole County Canvassing Board*)
- CNN makes a special application to broadcast ad televise oral arguments of the *Bush v. Palm Beach County Canvassing Board* litigation.

Tuesday, November 28, 2000

- Bush, Gore, the Florida secretary of state, and the Palm Beach County Canvassing Board file legal briefs with the Court outlining their respective arguments to the U.S. Supreme Court. (*Bush v. Palm Beach County Canvassing Board*)
- Judge Sauls orders the parties to file "proffers" from witnesses in support of their arguments and sets oral argument for December 2. (*Gore v. Harris*)

Wednesday, November 29, 2000

- Judge Sauls orders that 1.16 million Florida voter ballots from Miami-Dade and Palm Beach Counties be sent to Tallahassee, Florida, for a possible recount. He refuses, however, to begin an immediate recount. (*Gore v. Harris*)
- Gore asks the Florida Supreme Court to order an immediate recount of 14,000 disputed ballots in Palm Beach and Miami-Dade. (*Gore v. Harris*)
- Harry Jacobs's complaint against the Seminole County Canvassing Board is transferred from its Seminole County Court to Leon County Circuit Court Judge Nikki Clark's courtroom. Trial is set for December 6. (*Jacobs v. Seminole County Canvassing Board*)

- The NAACP says that it intends to litigate in Florida on behalf of minority voters who contend that voting irregularities plagued African American voters in the state. They're charging that voters were unlawfully turned away from polls by sheriff's deputies, improperly stricken from voter rolls, or turned away by other means.

Thursday, November 30, 2000
- All parties to the U.S. Supreme Court litigation file reply briefs to oppose the arguments of the other parties. (*Bush v. Palm Beach County Canvassing Board*)
- Judge Clark rejects a Republican request that she recuse herself from a suit brought by Democrat Harry Jacobs. (*Jacobs v. Seminole County Canvassing Board*)
- The Florida legislature considers holding a special session to name a new slate of Florida's twenty-five presidential electors for the electoral college.

Friday, December 1, 2000
- The U.S. Supreme Court hears oral arguments from all parties in the case of *Bush v. Palm Beach County Canvassing Board.*
- Democratic voters file suit to throw out 9,773 votes in Martin County, two-thirds of which went to Bush. GOP officials there, like their counterparts in Seminole County, were allowed to add voter ID numbers to some Republican applications for absentee ballots. The case is assigned to Judge Terry Lewis who sets a trial for December 6, the same date as the Seminole County case. (*Taylor v. Martin County Canvassing Board*)
- The Florida Supreme Court dismisses Gore's petition to immediately start recounting more than 12,000 undervotes from Miami-Dade and Palm Beach Counties. (*Gore v. Harris*)
- The Florida Supreme Court rules that Palm Beach County's "butterfly" ballot was legal. (*Fladell v. Palm Beach County Canvassing Board*)
- A federal appeals court says it will hear a case brought by Florida voters and the Bush campaign challenging the constitutionality of selected hand recounts. It schedules a hearing for December 5.
- Republican John McKay, president of the Florida Senate, hedges on calling a special session to pick the state's electors. He opts to mull the matter over the weekend.

Saturday, December 2, 2000
- Judge Sauls holds a trial to consider Gore's request for a hand count for the 14,000 contested ballots. Gore lawyer David Boies calls only two witnesses. (*Gore v. Harris*)

Sunday, December 3, 2000
- Gore's election contest trial continues. Gore lawyer Stephen Zack scores a point when he gets John Ahmann, one of the designers of the punch-card machine, to admit that chads can clog it badly. But when Gore expert witness Nicholas Hengartner is cross-examined, he concedes that a partial Miami-Dade recount was inconclusive because only Democratic precincts were surveyed. (*Gore v. Harris*)

Monday, December 4, 2000
- The U.S. Supreme Court sets aside the Florida ruling, reasoning that there was considerable uncertainty as to the grounds for the Florida Supreme Court's decision. (*Bush v. Palm Beach County Canvassing Board*)
- In Florida, Gore's plea for a recount of the undervote is rejected by Judge Sauls. Sauls declares from the bench that there is "no credible statistical evidence and no other competent substantial evidence" to establish a reasonable probability that Gore might win if granted a hand recount of the undervotes. Immediately after the ruling, Gore's legal team filed a notice of appeal asking Florida's 1st District Court of Appeal to certify the case to the Florida Supreme Court. (*Gore v. Harris*)
- The Bush Campaign sued the Hillsborough County Canvassing Board for rejecting overseas undated and unpostmarked absentee ballots (including military ballots). (*Bush v. Hillsborough County Canvassing Board*)

Tuesday, December 5, 2000
- The U.S. Court of Appeals for the 11th Circuit listens to oral arguments on Bush's plea to stop the manual recounts. The request for an injunction had been rejected by the U.S. District Court. (*Siegel v. LePore*, argued in conjunction with *Touchston v. McDermott*)
- Florida Supreme Court will hear Gore's appeal of Judge Sauls's ruling on Thursday, December 7. (*Gore v. Harris*)
- Judge Nikki Clark denies a motion by the Bush camp to dismiss the Seminole County lawsuit. (*Jacobs v. Seminole County Canvassing Board*)
- Democratic voters file a suit involving the counting of absentee ballots that were not received by Election Day, as Florida statute allegedly requires. The case was later removed to the U.S. District Court (Northern District of Florida), where it was joined with *Harris v. Florida Elections Canvassing Commission*. (*Medina v. Florida Election Canvassing Commission*)
- Duval County voters and the Rev. Jesse Jackson's Rainbow Coalition bring suit against the members of the Duval County Canvassing Board, alleging that due to the form of the ballot used in Duval County, many voters were effectively denied their right to vote. (*Brown et al. v. Stafford*)

Wednesday, December 6, 2000
- The U.S. Court of Appeals for the 11th Circuit affirms the lower court decision and denies Bush's request for an injunction to stop the recounts. (*Siegel v. LePore*, argued in conjunction with *Touchston v. McDermott*)
- Gore lawyers file a brief with the Florida Supreme Court, arguing that Sauls erred in not looking at the disputed ballots. (*Gore v. Harris*)
- Judge Nikki Clark begins a two-day trial of a Seminole County suit. (*Jacobs v. Seminole County Canvassing Board*)
- Circuit Judge Terry Lewis begins a two-day trial on a similar suit filed in Martin County. (*Taylor v. Martin County Canvassing Board*)
- Florida Senate president John McKay and House Speaker Tom Feeney announce a special session of the Florida legislature. It will convene Friday, they say, to

consider designating its own slate of electors should the results of the Florida vote remain tied up in the courts.

Thursday, December 7, 2000
• The Florida Supreme Court hears arguments from both Gore and Bush's lawyers in the appeal of Judge Sauls's ruling.

Friday, December 8, 2000
• The Florida Supreme Court overturns Judge Sauls's decision that rejected Gore's plea for a recount of the undervote in certain Florida counties by a 4–3 majority. On its own motion, the majority rules that ballots for which there was no vote for president must be recounted in all sixty-seven Florida counties that have not already carried out a hand count. The ruling also adds 383 Miami and Palm Beach votes to Gore's total from previous recounts. The added votes narrow Bush's statewide lead from 537 votes to just 154. Perhaps 45,000 undervotes statewide will have to be counted. A recount of the undervotes is ordered to begin immediately. (*Gore v. Harris*)
• Judge Sauls recuses himself from the case, which is assigned to Judge Terry Lewis, who directs that Florida counties complete their manual recounts by Sunday at 2:00 p.m. (*Gore v. Harris*)
• Bush's legal team announces it will appeal the decision to the U.S. Supreme Court. (*Gore v. Harris*)
• Judges Lewis and Clark reject the efforts of Democratic voters to throw out 25,000 absentee ballots in Seminole and Martin Counties. (*Jacobs v. Seminole County Canvassing Board* and *Taylor v. Martin County Canvassing Board*)
• Federal Judge Lacey Collier refuses to order the inclusion of undated ballots, but says that rejection of ballots for lack of a postmark only is contrary to federal law. (*Bush v. Hillsborough County Canvassing Board*)

Saturday, December 9, 2000
• The U.S. Supreme Court stays the Florida recount. Oral arguments are scheduled for Monday, December 11th. In a concurring opinion, Justice Scalia writes that "the counting of votes that are of questionable legality does in my view threaten irreparable harm to [George Bush], and to the country, by casting a cloud upon what he claims to be the legitimacy of his election. Count first, and rule upon legality afterwards, is not a recipe for producing election results that have the public acceptance democratic stability requires." In dissent, Justice Stevens argues that "to stop the counting of legal votes, the majority today departs from three venerable rules of judicial restraint that have guided the Court throughout its history." Traditionally, the Court respected the rulings of a state court on matters of state law. Similarly, the Court's general policy was to avoid interference "on questions whose resolution [was] committed at least in large measure to another branch of the Federal Government." The same held true for "federal constitutional questions that were not fairly presented to the court, [and] whose judgment [was] being reviewed." Here "we have prudently declined to express an opinion." In ruling as it did, "the majority has acted unwisely." (*Bush v. Gore*)

Sunday, December 10, 2000
- Briefs are submitted to U.S. Supreme Court prior to oral argument. (*Bush v. Gore*)

Monday, December 11, 2000
- The U.S. Supreme Court convenes to hear oral arguments on whether the Florida Supreme Court overstepped its bounds in ordering a statewide recount of undervotes. (*Bush v. Gore*)
- Florida Supreme Court replies to U.S. Supreme Court's remand in *Bush v. Palm Beach County Canvassing Board*.
- A committee of the Florida House votes 5–2 to approve a resolution to name presidential electors for George W. Bush. A half-hour later, a Florida Senate committee approves a similar resolution by a 4–3 vote.

Tuesday, December 12, 2000
- The Florida Supreme Court upholds lower court rulings in the absentee-ballot application cases in Seminole and Martin Counties. (*Jacobs v. Seminole County Canvassing Board* and *Taylor v. Martin County Canvassing Board*)
- The U.S. Supreme Court reverses the Florida Supreme Court with a 7–2 decision. In the per curiam section of its opinion, the Court holds that differing vote-counting standards from county to county and the lack of a single judicial officer to oversee the recount violated the Equal Protection Clause of the Constitution. The majority opinion effectively precludes Gore from attempting to seek any other recounts on the grounds that a recount could not be completed by December 12, in time to certify a conclusive slate of electors. Several justices issue bitter dissents. "One thing . . . is certain," Justice John Paul Stevens argues. "Although we may never know with complete certainty the identity of the winner of this year's presidential election, the identity of the loser is perfectly clear. It is the nation's confidence in the judge as an impartial guardian of the rule of law." Justice Stephen G. Breyer adds that "in this highly politicized matter, the appearance of a split decision runs the risk of undermining the public's confidence in the court itself." (*Bush v. Gore*)

Wednesday, December 13, 2000
- Challenge to Duval County ballot form is dismissed with prejudice for lack of available time in which to provide remedy. (*Brown et al. v. Stafford*)

Friday, December 22, 2000
- The Florida Supreme Court issues an opinion on remand from the U.S. Supreme Court, writing: "Accordingly, pursuant to the direction of the United States Supreme Court, we hold appellants can be afforded no relief."

Saturday, January 20, 2001
- George W. Bush is sworn in as 43rd president of the United States.

APPENDIX 2
A Note on Methodology

Compared to the other branches of the federal government, the federal courts are an enigma. This is especially true of the Supreme Court. On the one hand, the Supreme Court is the most public of government institutions, publishing a detailed explanation of every judicial ruling it issues. Yet what goes on in the back rooms of the Supreme Court remains largely a mystery—not just to the average American, but to scholars of the law as well. The conferences in which all key decisions are made—whether to take a case, how to decide it, or who writes the decision—are completely private. No one but the nine justices are even allowed in the conference room. No clerks. No note takers. No photographers. And definitely, no reporters or historians. Nor are the justices very open about their tasks outside of the conference room. The Court does not hold press conferences and rarely allows reporters into the justices' chambers to "chat." In fact, the press generally lacks any access to the justices. Their job is to report on the Court's rulings, and little more. Interviews by the justices, when they occur, are few and far between, and their content strictly defined prior to the interview. Similarly, when the justices leave the Court building and travel to speak at various universities and other public forums, they almost never discuss actual cases. They might talk of their own personal life story or discuss their views on the law in general terms, but how they or their colleagues voted in a particular case, or what they think of a particular past ruling, is a forbidden topic. So too when justices write a book, as many have done; generally these books are historical in nature, or a private nonjudicial memoir, or else a very theoretical discussion of the law and/or the Court in general. What they are not are exposés of the Court's internal workings and politics.[1]

The Court's staff is generally just as reluctant as the justices to talk about what they know. It is an extreme honor to be a Supreme Court clerk. Those who are accepted into these positions are rightfully proud of their status as insiders. Most choose to follow the lead of the Justices and say little of the Court's workings to outsiders.[2] Where former law clerks do speak up publicly, either in an article or book that they themselves wrote or in an interview with a journalist, it is generally seen as a breach of trust. Many demean those who break ranks as liars or ideologues, implying that the tale bearer had an ax to grind and that their information could not therefore be trusted. The result, by and large, is a code of silence, a general refusal by most former clerks to talk about what they know or even think they know.[3]

It is only when a justice dies and his or her papers are made available to scholars that we begin to see fully the internal workings of the Court. Tell-all memoranda, conference notes, multiple drafts of opinions and/or dissents that were never published, letters written and received, each document gives insight as to how the Court dealt with a particular case or series of cases—the internal debates, the shifting alliances over wording and argument, the positions taken in conference. With enough of these sorts of documents, historians can generally reconstruct the events surrounding the Supreme Court's handling of a particular case or cases. If the documents are especially rich, as is often the case, we can even outline the individual roles played by the justices in shaping the Court's rulings. At the least, we can show the evolution of an idea—from oral argument to initial judgment to final draft ruling—and make clear most of the motivations and antecedents behind the Court's actions.

Unfortunately, when it comes to *Bush v. Gore*, we do not yet have access to these sorts of papers and other documents. For one thing, only one of the nine justices sitting in 2000, Chief Justice William Rehnquist, has died—and his papers are not yet available for study. There is also no guarantee, given the quick pace of the Court's actions in this case, that his papers will have the sort of rich documentation that often can be found in judges' papers. It may be that much of the "negotiations" over the content of the Court's per curiam ruling—the wording and scope of argument, the explanations and exclusions—were verbal, not written. As such, the chief justice's files in this case might be quite thin of content. There is also the possibility of selective pruning by the chief justice and/or his heirs. Many former justices removed and/or destroyed portions of their papers before allowing the public access. Justice Hugo Black, for instance, on his death bed begged his family to burn large parts of his papers so that no one could gain access to them and second guess either himself or the rest of the Court. Abe Fortas also destroyed some of his own "historical relics," documents he "supposed history would do without!"[4] It is possible that the chief justice might have demanded similar edits of his papers prior to their being made available to the public. Then again, maybe not, we simply do not know.[5] Finally, there is no guarantee that Rehnquist's files—or any one justice's, in fact—are totally accurate. Perhaps the memoranda or copies of draft edits contain errors of fact or timing? Maybe they are self-serving, painting the justice in a good light while denigrating a fellow justice with whom the first justice disagrees. Without papers from multiple justices, we are often left making guesses in the dark as to what really happened during the Court's deliberations.[6]

All of which is a long way of explaining the delicate and often tentative nature of Supreme Court analysis posed by a recent case such as *Bush v. Gore*. While we can say with certainty what the Court said in its opinion (and sometimes what the Court did not say), any honest analysis of the justices' motivations and expectations must reside in the realm of hypothesis. We simply do not have enough of the facts before us to speak with certainty. Still, all is not lost for those seeking to understand the underlying framework of the Supreme Court's *Bush v. Gore* ruling. While the complete picture of what went on in the Supreme Court from December 9 to December 12 remains hidden, many parts of the puzzle have snuck out. For one thing, much of what led up to the Supreme Court's two rulings is already in the public record. State judges have spoken on the record and many of the supporting materials from the Florida and lower federal courts are available online.[7] The lawyers have also spoken, summarizing events and presenting their interpretations of court action.[8] In terms of the Supreme Court itself, we have commentary by law clerks who have broken the code of silence and given their views of events to reporters.[9] Even some of the justices have spoken out on the topic, their parenthetical comments on the case often expressing more of their attitudes toward these matters than they perhaps intended.[10] Also useful are the comments from experienced court watchers—lawyers, journalists, legal scholars, former clerks—whose experienced eye often brings up details that might otherwise have been lost in the clutter of events.[11] Finally, one can place the events in a wider historical context. While this might not identify the exact thoughts going through the justices' heads as they asked questions or ruled on matters, it can narrow the range of possibilities (if only based on their past actions and experiences).[12]

The methodology applied to analyze the Supreme Court's actions and inactions in this book build on this mix of often tentative information. As such, its analytical results can best be described as reasoned speculation—otherwise known as careful, fact-based guessing. By placing what we know to be fact into its historical and doctrinal context, we can evaluate, if not the actual, specific motivations and actions of individual players, then at least the range of options that they were most likely to have adopted. We can further rate the likelihood that one option would be chosen ahead of another based on past patterns of choice and evaluate how near or far from their individual norms were the justices' rulings in *Bush v. Gore*. We can also make reasoned guesses as to who wrote what and hypothesize about some of the editing debates that must have gone into the writing of these judgments. Most of all, we can—after the passage of time has lessened some of the emotions surrounding this case—see exactly what it was that the justices said and did not say. But this is all that we can do. A more complete understanding of what went on in those hectic days in December 2000 will have to wait until the participants pass on and their papers become available.

Still, while not the complete picture of events and motivations possible with access to judicial papers, a careful and nuanced—if speculative—analysis is both achievable and useful. For in carrying out such an endeavor, as this book attempts to do, we begin to understand what was at issue before the Court and the nation in December 2000, what were the constraints on the process within and without the Court during those hectic days, and lastly what were the actual effects of this case—both in the short and longer terms.[13]

Even if our conclusions based on these insights have to be tempered by the limits of our resources, the result is still a deeper understanding of the topic than we would have had were we to have waited until all the available data was at our fingertips. We just have to keep in mind that future data might force us to revise our views when the judicial papers become available a generation from now.

NOTES

Preface

1. Adam Cohen, "Has *Bush v. Gore* Become the Case That Must Not Be Named?" *New York Times*, August 15, 2006.

2. See for example Mark Tushnet, *A Court Divided: The Rehnquist Court and the Future of Constitutional Law* (New York: W. W. Norton, 2005), which includes only 9 out of a total of 461 pages in which *Bush v. Gore* is even mentioned once.

3. Richard L. Hasen, "The Untimely Death of *Bush v. Gore*," *Stanford Law Review* 60 (2007), http://ssrn.com/abstract=976701; Chad Flanders, "Please Don't Cite This Case!: The Precedential Value of *Bush v. Gore*," 116 *Yale L.J. Pocket* part 141 (2006), http://thepocketpart.org/2006/11/07/flanders.html. Titles such as these show that even among those who take the case seriously, they still see it in largely negative terms—if only for the case's failure to produce the change many hoped to find within it. At the same time, there are other articles with more positive titles such as Daniel H. Lowenstein, "The Meaning of *Bush v. Gore*," 68 *Ohio Sate Law Journal* no. 4 (2007), http://papers.ssrn.com/sol3/papers.cfm? abstract_id=976960, and Edward B. Foley, "The Future of *Bush v. Gore*," 68 *Ohio Sate Law Journal* no. 4 (2007), http://moritzlaw.osu.edu/lawjournal/issues/volume68/number4/foley.pdf. Thus, my comments above trace a prevailing trend rather than including all scholarly writing on *Bush v. Gore*.

4. Alexander Keyssar, *The Right to Vote: The Contested History of Democracy in the United States* (New York: Basic Books, 2000), xvi.

5. See for example, John W. Dean, *Worse Than Watergate: The Secret Presidency of George W. Bush* (New York: Little, Brown, 2004); Michael Isikoff and David Corn, *Hubris: The Inside Story of Spin, Scandal, and the Selling of the Iraq War* (New York: Three Rivers Press, 2007).

6. The actual quote is by Victoria Glendinning paraphrasing Rebecca West on Anthony Trollope. Victoria Glendinning, *Anthony Trollope* (New York: Knopf, 1993), xxiii.

7. Washington Post, *Deadlock: The Inside Story of America's Closest Election* (New York: PublicAffairs, 2001); Jack Tapper, *Down and Dirty: The Plot to Steal the Presidency* (Boston: Little, Brown, 2001); Jeffrey Toobin, *Too Close to Call: The Thirty-Six-Day Battle to Decide the 2000 Election* (New York: Random House, 2001). Alternately, more technical works such as Richard A. Posner, *Breaking the Deadlock: The 2000 Election, the Constitution, and the Courts* (Princeton, NJ: Princeton University Press, 2001) and Howard Gillman, *The Votes That Counted: How the Court Decided the 2000 Presidential Election* (Chicago: University of Chicago Press, 2001) do present a clearer narrative of the cases, but at a cost of losing the vibrancy of the political events that presaged and shaped the litigation filed with the Florida and U.S. Supreme Courts.

1. A Vote Too Close to Call

1. Jeff Greenfield, *"Oh Waiter! One Order of Crow!" Inside the Strangest Presidential Election Finish in American History* (New York: G. P. Putnam's, 2001), 5.

2. Federal Election Commission, "2000 Presidential General Election Results," http://www.fec.gov/pubrec/2000presgeresults.htm; "President Results Summary for All

States," *CNN*, http://www.cnn.com/ELECTION/2000/results/index.president.html. See also Washington Post, *Deadlock: The Inside Story of America's Closest Election* (New York: PublicAffairs, 2001), 10–11; Diana Owen, "Media Mayhem: Performance of the Press in Election 2000," in Larry J. Sabato, *Overtime: The Election 2000 Thriller* (New York: Longman, 2002), 123–156.

3. Washington Post, *Deadlock*, 19.

4. Joan Konner, James Risser, and Ben Wattenberg, "Television's Performance on Election Night 2000: A Report for CNN" (January 29, 2001): 8–18, http://i.cnn.net/cnn/2001/ALLPOLITICS/stories/02/02/cnn.report/cnn.pdf; Linda Mason, Kathleen Frankovic, and Kathleen Hall Jamieson, "CBS News Coverage of Election Night 2000: Investigation, Analysis, Recommendations" (January 2001): 16–25, http://www.cbsnews.com/htdocs/c2k/pdf/REPFINAL.pdf; Washington Post, *Deadlock*, 19–50; Jack Tapper, *Down and Dirty: The Plot to Steal the Presidency* (Boston: Little, Brown, 2001), 31.

5. Interestingly, neither of the candidates' "boiler room" teams of analysts accepted the networks' projections. Gore's team especially distrusted the numbers—the actual count was just too close for them comfortably to call the election, particularly against their candidate. However, in the immediate minutes following the networks' announcements, communication between Gore and his team of analysts (housed in a separate hotel down the road from Gore's "official" campaign headquarters in downtown Nashville) broke down. It was in those few minutes that Gore "conceded" the election—only to retract his concession when contact was renewed with his advisers. *Deadlock*, 246.

6. Konner, Risser, and Wattenberg, *Television's Performance on Election Night 2000*, 8–18; Mason, Frankovic, and Jamieson, *CBS News Coverage of Election Night 2000*, 16–25; *Deadlock*, 19–50; Tapper, *Down and Dirty*, 31.

7. "The 2000 Campaign: The Strategies: No Room for Error in the Final Weeks before the Vote," *New York Times (NYT)*, October 15, 2000, 1; "New Polls Show Bush Edging Out Gore," *Albany Times Union*, October 21, 2000, A1; "The 2000 Campaign: The Polls: Candidates Play Leapfrog, in Very Small Hops, Surveys Show," *NYT*, October 24, 2000, A27; "Close Call," *New York Daily News*, October 29, 2000, 43; "Twists and Turns on the Road to the White House: This Contest Is Anybody's Guess," *New York Daily News*, November 5, 2000, 16.

8. "An Accounting of How 18 'Swing States' May Determine Who Wins the Presidency," *Buffalo News*, October 29, 2000, A8; "The 2000 Campaign: The Game Plan: Dozen States Seem Too Close to Call in the Final Days," *NYT*, November 5, 2000, 1.

9. Michael Kramer, "Bush Set to Fight an Electoral College Loss," *New York Daily News*, November 1, 2000, 6. See also Deborah Orin, "We Might Not Know Winner 'Til New Year," *New York Post*, November 2, 2000, 6.

10. Martin Merzer et al., *The Miami Herald Report: Democracy Held Hostage* (New York: Saint Martin's, 2001), 16; Tom Fielder, "Introduction: The Encore of Key Largo," in Sabato, *Overtime*, 1–2.

11. U.S. Census Bureau, "State and County Quick Facts: Florida," http://quickfacts.census.gov/qfd/states/12000.html; Raymond A. Mohl and Gary R. Mormino, "The Big Change in the Sunshine State: A Social History of Modern Florida," in Michael Gannon, ed., *The New History of Florida* (Gainesville: University Press of Florida, 1996), 391–417; Fielder, "Encore of Key Largo," 1–14.

12. Mireya Navarro, "Bright Hopes for Florida Republicans: With Election of Jeb Bush, State GOP Has Come a Long Way," *NYT*, November 8, 1998, 18; "Florida Controversies Plague Bushes," *Tampa Tribune*, March 13, 2000, 1; Steven C. Tauber and William E. Hulbary,

"Florida: Too Close to Call," in Robert P. Steed and Laurence W. Moreland, eds., *The 2000 Presidential Election in the South: Partisanship and Southern Party Systems in the 21st Century* (Westport, CT: Praeger, 2002), 149–152 (*Almanac of American Politics* quote on page 150); Lance deHaven-Smith, *The Battle for Florida: An Annotated Compendium of Materials from the 2000 Presidential Election* (Gainesville: University Press of Florida, 2005), 195–209.

13. "An Early Start on November Vote," *St. Petersburg Times (SPT)*, March 13, 2000, 1A; "Florida Has Candidates' Attention," *Tampa Tribune*, March 13, 2000, 1.

14. "Florida Gets Top Spot in Nomination Roll Call," *SPT*, August 20, 2000, A10.

15. Tauber and Hulbary, "Florida: Too Close to Call," 153; Fielder, "Encore of Key Largo," 7.

16. Tauber and Hulbary, "Florida: Too Close to Call," 154–155; "Bush Circles Florida for Last Time" *Tampa Tribune*, November 6, 2000, 1; "Last Words, Final Push," *Miami Herald*, November 6, 2000, 1A; "Now, the Final Push toward Election Day: Bush Calls on Voters in West Palm Beach, Miami on Sunday. Gore Is Due in Miami Beach Tonight," *South Florida Sun-Sentinel (SFSS)*, November 6, 2000, 1A.

17. *Florida Statutes* (2000), Title IX, Section 102.141(4).

18. Ibid. On Gore's views regarding his "victory" in Florida, see *Deadlock*, 21.

19. For example, the U.S. Commission on Civil Rights (USCCR) heard from Maria DeSoto, a poll worker in Palm Beach County, who "testified that she used her personal cellular phone to call the supervisor of elections office all day, but was only able to get through two or three times over the course of 12 hours." USCCR, *Voting Irregularities in Florida during the 2000 Presidential Election* (Washington, DC: GPO, 2001), chapter 2, at note 10.

20. This account is based on the author's personal experiences as one of the many phone bank operators. See also Fielder, "Encore of Key Largo," 8–11.

21. Robert A. Butterworth, Florida attorney general, testimony before the U.S. Commission on Civil Rights, Tallahassee, Florida, January 12, 2001, verified transcript, 193–194 (quoted in USCCR, *Voting Irregularities in Florida*, chapter 1, at note 2).

22. Merzer, *Miami Herald Report*, 32–50.

23. "Ballot-Punching Stories Raise Storm of Confusion," *SFSS*, November 10, 2000, 1A; "19,120 Ballots Invalidated," *SFSS*, November 9, 2000, 1A.

24. Jonathan Wand et al., "The Butterfly Did It: The Aberrant Vote for Buchanan in Palm Beach County, Florida," *American Political Science Review* 95 (December 2001): 793–794; "Canvassers Poll Voters on Butterfly Ballot," Cox News Service (November 9, 2000); "19,120 Ballots Invalidated," *SFSS*, November 9, 2000, 1A.

25. As part of this campaign, local black leaders had adopted the slogan, "Vote for Gore and Brown." The Brown in question was African American Congresswoman Corrine Brown. Unfortunately, on the second presidential ballot page was the Libertarian Party candidate, Harry Browne. Combined with the vote every page recommendation, the sight of the name Browne on an open page led many first time voters to mark this box erroneously. Fielder, "Encore of Key Largo," 8–9.

26. Merzer, *Miami Herald Report*, 37–38; USCCR, *Voting Irregularities in Florida*, chapter 8, at notes 71 and 72.

27. Overvotes could still occur on the Votomatic machines used in these counties. Nothing precluded a voter from punching more than one hole for a particular race. However, the confusion at the heart of the overvote problem in Duval and Palm Beach Counties was absent in Broward and Miami-Dade Counties.

28. For a clear description of the workings and nonworkings of the IBM Votomatic, see Merzer, *Miami Herald Report*, 51–71.

29. Quoted in Frederick E. Allen, "Behind the Cutting Edge," *American Heritage* 52 (April 2001): 39.

30. Merzer, *Miami Herald Report*, 51–71.

31. Ibid., 66, 79–80.

32. Ibid., 80–83. See also USCCR, *Voting Irregularities in Florida*, chapter 1, at notes 65–72.

33. Ibid.

34. USCCR, *Voting Irregularities in Florida*, chapter 8, at notes 15–20.

35. See ibid., chapter 2; Merzer, *Miami Herald Report*, chapters 5 and 6.

36. Jingle Davis, "U.S. Voting Standards Fall Far Short, Carter Says; Nonpartisan Panel Opens Hearings on Ways to Improve Accuracy and Fairness," *Atlanta Journal-Constitution*, March 27, 2001, 1.

37. USCCR, *Voting Irregularities in Florida*, chapter 9, at note 5.

38. Ibid., chapter 1, at notes 75–81; chapter 5, at notes 1–18. See also John Lantigua, "How the GOP Gamed the System in Florida," *Nation* (April 30, 2001), http://www.thenation.com/doc/20010430/lantigua, which describes the efforts to limit minority voting via voting list purges and similar means.

39. USCCR, *Voting Irregularities in Florida*, chapter 1, at notes 75–81; chapter 2, at notes 4–26. See also Dewey M. Clayton, "A Funny Thing Happened on the Way to the Voting Precinct: A Brief History of Disenfranchisement in America," *Black Scholar* 34 (Fall 2004): 42–52; Revathi I. Hines, "The Silent Voices: 2000 Presidential Election and the Minority Vote in Florida," *Western Journal of Black Studies* 26 (Summer 2002): 71–74.

2. Enter the Lawyers

1. The following narrative is drawn from Washington Post, *Deadlock: The Inside Story of America's Closest Election* (New York: PublicAffairs, 2001), 42–82; Jake Tapper, *Down and Dirty: The Plot to Steal the Presidency* (Boston: Little, Brown, 2001), 23–60; Jeffrey Toobin, *Too Close to Call: The Thirty-Six-Day Battle to Decide the 2000 Election* (New York: Random House, 2001), 10–122.

2. This view of Gore's motivations is drawn from W. Dexter Douglass, "A Look Back—One Lawyer's View," *Florida Journal of Law and Public Policy* 13 (Fall 2001): 21. This view was seconded by David Boies, *Courting Justice: From NY Yankees v. Major League Baseball to Bush v. Gore, 1997–2000* (New York: Miramax, 2004), 403.

3. Washington Post, *Deadlock*, 48–49. An alternate description of the wording of this telephone call has Gore saying, "with all due respect to your little brother, he is not the final arbiter of who wins Florida" (ibid.). Still another wording has Gore saying "your *little brother* doesn't get to make that call" (Tapper, *Down and Dirty*, 37). See also Toobin, *Too Close to Call*, 25.

4. Washington Post, *Deadlock*, 51–54; Tapper, *Down and Dirty*, 43–48; Toobin, *Too Close to Call*, 27–28.

5. Quoted in Washington Post, *Deadlock*, 53. See generally Timothy Downs, Chris Sautter, and John Hardin Young, *The Recount Primer* (August 1994), 5–6.

6. *Florida Statutes* (2000), Title IX, Section 102.166. See also Lynne Rambo, "The Lawyers' Role in Selecting the President: A Complete Legal History of the 2000 Election," *Texas Wesleyan Law Review* 8 (Spring 2002): 105–385.

7. An alternate option was to seek an order from the governor requesting recounts in

each county, which was unlikely to happen so long as George W. Bush was ahead in the vote count.

8. Quoted in *Deadlock*, 56. See also Rambo, "Lawyers' Role in Selecting the President"; Tapper, *Down and Dirty*, 61.

9. *Florida Statutes* (2000), Title IX, Sections 102.111–112. Rambo, "Lawyers' Role in Selecting the President," 115–117. On the absentee ballot deadline exception, see *US v. Florida*, case no. TCA-80-1055, N.D. Florida, August 20, 1984.

10. *Boardman v. Esteva*, 323 So 2d 263 (1975). The other cases were *State Ex Rel. Chappell v. Martinez*, 536 So 2d 1007 (1988), which held that voter disenfranchisement is improper when the intent of a voter is ascertainable, and *Beckstrom v. Volusia County Canvassing Board*, 707 So 2d 720 (1998), which ruled that courts should not frustrate the clear will of the voter where this intent can be determined. Lance deHaven-Smith, *The Battle for Florida: An Annotated Compendium of Materials from the 2000 Presidential Election* (Gainesville: University Press of Florida, 2005), 37.

11. As Palm Beach County circuit judge Jorge Labarga noted in *Florida Democratic Party v. Palm Beach County Canvassing Board* (CL00-11078 AB), 15th Judicial Circuit Court of Florida, November 22, 2000, "the only bright line rule a canvassing board is permitted to have in Florida" under Florida law and precedents "is that there can be no per se rule excluding any ballots."

12. Ibid. See also discussion of Judge Labarga's ruling in chapter 4.

13. These states were California, Indiana, Kentucky, Massachusetts, Minnesota, Missouri, Montana, Nebraska, Nevada, New Jersey, Oklahoma, Pennsylvania, Rhode Island, South Dakota, Washington, and West Virginia. See generally Abner Green, *Understanding the 2000 Election: A Guide to the Legal Battles That Decided the Presidency* (New York: New York University Press, 2001), 33–35.

14. Washington Post, *Deadlock*, 51–55 (quote on 54); Tapper, *Down and Dirty*, 56–69. See also Toobin, *Too Close to Call*, 29, describing Young's personal advice to Gore: "You have to gather the information. You have to get on the ground, look at the machines, look at the tally sheets, talk to the people who were there on election day. Recounts only succeed if you find out what happened."

15. David Royse, "Bush Holds Narrow Margin in Florida Recount," *AP Wire* (November 9, 2000); David Royse, "Bush Holds Slim Lead With 1 County Yet To Report," *AP Wire* (November 9, 2000); Pat Leisner, "Gore Gains More Than 400 Votes in Pinellas County Recounts," *AP Wire* (November 9, 2000); Tim Nickens, Diane Rado, and Thomas C. Tobin, "Gap Closes; Tensions Rise," *St. Petersburg Times (SPT)*, November 10, 2000, 1A; Carl Hulse, "America Holds Its Breath For Florida Recount," *Lakeland Ledger*, November 9, 2000, A13.

16. Florida law has two distinct phases for an election contest. The first (set out in Title IX, Section 102.166 of the *Florida Statutes*) is the "recount" phase, an administrative process carried out by the individual county canvassing board to look for errors in the counting of the ballots. The second is called the "challenge" or "contest" phase (set out in Title IX, Section 102.168), and it takes place only after the state vote has been certified by the State Canvassing Board. Challenges are a legal process in which the losing candidate challenges the legitimacy of the election process (asserting, for example, that the vote was not fairly done, mistakes were made in counting the vote, or the certified vote did not truly reflect the will of the voters). Challenges, if held, are done under the authority of a single judge (for statewide offices, sitting in Leon County—location of the state capital in

Tallahassee, otherwise in the county of the challenged office in question) and can involve as many or as few ballots as the judge deems necessary. See generally Rambo, "Lawyers' Role in Selecting the President," 113–125; Washington Post, *Deadlock*, 157.

17. Boies, *Courting Justice*, 365.

18. Washington Post, *Deadlock*, 157.

19. Quoted in Boies, *Courting Justice*, 366.

20. Douglass, "A Look Back—One Lawyer's View," 15–16. Ironically, as events turned out, Gore would probably have had more time to count votes had he listened to this advice and moved as quickly as possible into the contest stage. This, however, is noticeable only in retrospect. See Boies, *Courting Justice*, 366–367, for his views on this issue. See also Washington Post, *Deadlock*, 157.

21. Quoted in Washington Post, *Deadlock*, 70–71. The state court suits would later be consolidated into the case *Fladell v. Palm Beach County Canvassing Board* (Florida 15th Judicial Circuit, CL 00-10965 AN). The initial state cases are *Horowitz v. LePore* (Florida 15th Judicial Circuit, CL 00-10970 AG), *Elkin v. LePore* (Florida 15th Judicial Circuit, CL 00-10988 AE), *Rogers v. Election Canvassing Commission of Florida* (Florida 15th Judicial Circuit, CL 00-10992 AF), and *Gibbs v. Palm Beach County Canvassing Board* (Florida 15th Judicial Circuit, CL 00-110000 AH). Angry voters would file an additional ten complaints against the butterfly ballot with the Palm Beach County Circuit Courts in the week that followed. See Appendix I, "Timeline of Events," for a listing of all relevant cases.

22. Six of the Florida justices were Democrats while the seventh was an independent appointed by a Democratic governor. The Florida Supreme Court was also known as an activist court willing to impose its will on controversial topics. In particular, past precedents from this court had stressed a "count every vote possible" logic that served Gore's strategic needs.

23. Quoted in Washington Post, *Deadlock*, 53–54.

24. Washington Post, *Deadlock*, 77–79; Toobin, *Too Close to Call*, 34–39, 103; Tapper, *Down and Dirty*, 64–71.

25. John Commins, "Experts: Bush, Gore Shouldn't Interfere; Let Vote-Counting Process Take Its Course, Political Observers Say," *Chattanooga Times Free Press*, November 10, 2000, A4; *The American Presidency Project*, "Text: Vice President Gore on the Recount" (November 10, 2000), http://www.presidency.ucsb.edu/showflorida2000.php?fileid=gore11–13; *The American Presidency Project*, "Text: Vice President Gore's Offer" (November 15, 2000), http://www.presidency.ucsb.edu/showflorida2000.php?fileid=gore11–15. See also *The American Presidency Project*, "Text: Gore Campaign Chairman William Daley" (November 9, 2000), http://www.presidency.ucsb.edu/showflorida2000.php?fileid=daley11–09.

26. Kevin Sack, "The 43rd President: After the Vote—A Special Report: In Desperate Florida Fight, Gore's Hard Strategic Calls," *New York Times (NYT)*, December 15, 2000, A1. See also John Hardin Young, "Promoting and Protecting the Vote after *Bush v. Gore*: An Essay," www.fcsl.edu/centers/strategic_governance/election2000/promoting-protecting.pdf, where he notes that "Time was a factor," and how given this limit of time, Bush's lead was "an important legal factor (as well as a psychological one that may explain why Gore's key strategists rejected a statewide recount in favor of a recount in heavily Democratic counties)." See also Mark Danner, *The Road to Illegitimacy* (Hoboken, NJ: Melville House, 2004), 44–45, and Boies, *Courting Justice*, 376.

27. Gore's chief political operative in Florida, Michael Whouley, for instance, doubted that there were many additional Gore votes in the other Florida counties (Boies, *Courting*

Justice, 376). Of course, recounts by the media after the crisis was over showed that Gore would have needed the extra votes found in these other counties to win. See generally Martin Merzer et al., *The Miami Herald Report: Democracy Held Hostage* (New York: Saint Martin's, 2001).

28. According to Boies, *Courting Justice*, 376, Michael Whouley also pushed for the inclusion of Broward and Miami-Dade Counties.

29. On November 10, Jeb Bush recused himself from the recount process and withdrew from the state canvassing commission. Florida's Democratic agricultural commissioner, Bob Crawford—who had supported Jeb's campaign for governor two years earlier—was appointed to take Bush's place. The other commission member was Florida Division of Elections Director (and Republican) Clay Roberts.

30. Washington Post, *Deadlock*, 58.

31. Ibid., 61–63 (quote on 62); Toobin, *Too Close to Call*, 33; Tapper, *Down and Dirty*, 47; Robert Zelnick, *Winning Florida: How the Bush Team Fought the Battle* (Palo Alto, CA: Hoover Institution, 2001), 7. See also deHaven-Smith, *Battle for Florida*, 16. deHaven-Smith also notes that Jimenez and his staff right away began looking for ways to prevent a recount legally.

32. Toobin, *Too Close to Call*, 34.

33. Daniel Ruth, "Election Night in a Banana Republic," *Tampa Tribune*, November 10, 2000, 2.

34. David Margolick, Evgenia Peretz, and Michael Shnayerson, "The Path to Florida," *Vanity Fair* (October 2003), http://makethemaccountable.com/articles/ The_Path_To_ Florida.htm; Washington Post, *Deadlock*, 85.

35. Said Stipanovich after the election, "as far as I was concerned, it was a war to the knife." His job, in turn, was "to bring [this election] in for a landing with George Bush at the controls." Interview of Mac Stipanovich, in Julian M. Pleasants, *Hanging Chads: The Inside Story of the 2000 Presidential Recount in Florida* (New York: Palgrave Macmillan, 2004): 155, 158. In a private interview with attorney Steve Bickerstaff, Stipanovich also proved much more willing to admit to his influence in shaping Harris's actions on Bush's behalf. See Steve Bickerstaff, "Post-Election Legal Strategy in Florida: The Anatomy of Defeat and Victory," *Loyola University of Chicago Law Journal* 34 (Fall 2002): 180.

36. Tapper, *Down and Dirty*, 77–78; Washington Post, *Deadlock*, 71, 81. David Boies also recalls Klain responding to Katherine Harris's refusal to extend certification deadlines in much the same words: "This *is* Guatemala. If this were happening anywhere else in the world, the United States and the United Nations would be trying to send in observers and considering sanctions." Boies, *Courting Justice*, 374.

37. Washington Post, *Deadlock*, 79–80; Zelnick, *Winning Florida*, 15–16.

38. Zelnick, *Winning Florida*, 5–6; Tapper, *Down and Dirty*, 49–51; Toobin, *Too Close to Call*, 40–42; Washington Post, *Deadlock*, 72–73.

39. Tim Nickens et al., "Countering the Recount," *SPT*, November 11, 2000, 1A; "No-Win Situation for Next President," Cox News Wire, November 10, 2000; David Firestone and Michael Cooper, "Bush Sues to Halt Hand Recount in Florida," *NYT*, November 12, 2000, 1. A full transcript of Baker's comments can be found at *The American Presidency Project*, "Transcript: James A. Baker III on Fla. Recount" (November 10, 2000), http:// www.presidency.ucsb.edu/showflorida2000.php?fileid=baker11-10. The "no do-over" comment was made by George Terwilliger, quoted in Washington Post, *Deadlock*, 80.

40. Toobin, *Too Close to Call*, 50–51.

41. L. Clayton Roberts to Al Cardenas, "Advisory Opinion DE 00-11," November 13,

2000 [reprinted in Joint Appendix, Motion for Writ of Certiorari, *Bush v. Palm Beach County Canvassing Board*, JA 52]. See also Zelnick, *Winning Florida*, 28; Bickerstaff, "Post-Election Legal Strategy in Florida," 180–181; Toobin, *Too Close to Call*, 71–76; Washington Post, *Deadlock*, 98–99. It should be noted that Democratic state attorney general Bob Butterworth also attempted to shape the outcome of the hand recount process by issuing his own opinion—in this case in favor of hand recounts. "Because the Division of Elections opinion is so clearly at variance with the existing Florida statutes and case law, and because of the immediate impact this erroneous opinion could have on the ongoing recount process, I am issuing this advisory opinion," wrote Butterworth. "Advisory Opinion 00-65," Office of the Florida Attorney General, November 14, 2000 [reprinted in Joint Appendix, Motion for Writ of Certiorari, *Bush v. Palm Beach County Canvassing Board*, JA 40–46].

42. Zelnick, *Winning Florida*, 30–32; Bickerstaff, "Post-Election Legal Strategy in Florida,"182–183; Toobin, *Too Close to Call*, 109–119; Washington Post, *Deadlock*, 103–105.

43. Quoted in Toobin, *Too Close to Call*, 49.

44. *Colgrove v. Green*, 328 U.S. 549, 552 (1946).

45. See David E. Sanger, "Contesting the Vote: The Texas Governor; Bush's Aides Say an End Is in Sight," *NYT*, December 11, 2000, A1.

46. Zelnick, *Winning Florida*, 53–54. A similar option entailed Congress. As early as Wednesday, November 15, Majority Whip Tom DeLay of Texas circulated a memorandum on Congress's role in tallying presidential votes, focusing on the Electoral Count Act of February 3, 1887. DeLay argued that the act gave to Congress the power to reject electors if the members found fault with the methods applied at the state level. Implicit in this point was the assumption that should the Florida Courts "give" the election to Gore, the Congress had a remedy to overturn this result under the Electoral Count Act. See generally text of 3 U.S.C. §5 and Lynne Rambo, "The Lawyers' Role in Selecting the President: A Complete Legal History," *Texas Wesleyan Law Review* 8 (Spring 2002): 199–200.

3. Eye of the Beholder

1. By state law, county canvassing boards consisted of "the supervisor of elections; a county court judge, who shall act as chair; and the chair of the board of county commissioners." *Florida Statutes* (2000), Title IX, Section 102.141.

2. Don Van Natta Jr. and David Barstow, "Election Officials Focus of Lobbying from Both Camps," *New York Times (NYT)*, November 18, 2000, A1.

3. See for instance, Keating Holland, "Poll: Americans Evenly Divided over Florida Election Dispute," *CNN Online*, November 20, 2000, http://archives.cnn.com/2000/ALLPOLITICS/stories/11/20/cnn.poll/index.html.

4. Marshall Wittmann, an analyst at the conservative Hudson Institute, noted during the postelection conflict in 2000 that "there would have been a conservative ascendancy had not it been for the venality of the Clinton-Gore team. From the 1994 election to the government shutdown, through impeachment, to this point, it has been a seamless web, tied back to the 1992 Clinton campaign and Gennifer Flowers and draft-dodging—and Gore is viewed as the person spinning that web." Thomas B. Edsall, "Rage Sharpens Conservative Rhetoric; Gore Accused of Trying to Mount Coup," *Washington Post*, November 22, 2000, A19.

5. Isaiah Berlin, "Political Ideas in the Twentieth Century," in *Four Essays on Liberty* (Oxford: Oxford University Press, 1970).

6. Gary C. Jacobson, *A Divider, Not a Uniter: George W. Bush and the American People* (New York: Pearson Education, 2007), 61, notes: "Both the heated rhetoric . . . and clear partisan split loudly echoed the struggle over Clinton's impeachment. And as with impeachment, partisan divisions were not confined to politicians and activists. Although ordinary voters were more bemused by than passionately involved in the postelection events in Florida, they too divided strongly along party lines in responding to questions about them." Generally, see ibid., 19–46, 60–67, and Gary C. Jacobson, "A House and Senate Divided: The Clinton Legacy and the Congressional Elections of 2000," *Political Science Quarterly* 116 (Spring 2001): 7–8.

7. Washington Post, *Deadlock: The Inside Story of America's Closest Election* (New York: PublicAffairs, 2001), 87–88; Jeffrey Toobin, *Too Close to Call: The Thirty-Six-Day Battle to Decide the 2000 Election* (New York: Random House, 2001), 77–79; Martin Merzer et al., *The Miami Herald Report: Democracy Held Hostage* (New York: Saint Martin's, 2001), 175–176.

8. "Theresa LePore Interview," February 23, 2001, in Julian M. Pleasants, ed., *Hanging Chads: The Inside Story of the 2000 Presidential Recount in Florida* (New York: Palgrave Macmillan, 2004), 79, 80. See Van Natta and Barstow, "Election Officials Focus of Lobbying," *NYT*, November 18, 2000, A1.

9. "Judge Charles Burton Interview," April 5, 2001, in Pleasants, *Hanging Chads*, 64.

10. Washington Post, *Deadlock*, 88; Don Van Natta Jr. and Rick Bragg, "2 Camps Clash Vote by Vote, Scrap by Scrap," *NYT*, November 12, 2000, 1; Don Van Natta Jr. and Rick Bragg, "Scrutiny and Disagreements Accompany Hand Recount," *NYT*, November 13, 2000, A20.

11. Washington Post, *Deadlock*, 87–88; Toobin, *Too Close to Call*, 81–85; Jack Tapper, *Down and Dirty: The Plot to Steal the Presidency* (Boston: Little, Brown, 2001), 109, 115–117. See also Van Natta and Bragg, "2 Camps Clash Vote by Vote," 33.

12. Toobin, *Too Close to Call*, 85; David Boies, *Courting Justice: From NY Yankees v. Major League Baseball to Bush v. Gore, 1997–2000* (New York: Miramax, 2004), 382–384.

13. Tapper, *Down and Dirty*, 116–117.

14. "Judge Charles Burton Interview," 69.

15. Tapper, *Down and Dirty*, 121.

16. Ibid., 120–121; Toobin, *Too Close to Call*, 84–87; Washington Post, *Deadlock*, 89; "Judge Charles Burton Interview," 65.

17. Ibid.

18. Tapper, *Down and Dirty*, 121–122.

19. Ibid., 122–123; Toobin, *Too Close to Call*, 85–88; Boies, *Courting Justice*, 382–383.

20. Toobin, *Too Close to Call*, 89.

21. Ibid. See also Tapper, *Down and Dirty*, 126.

22. "Theresa LePore Interview," 82; Toobin, *Too Close to Call*, 90; Tapper, *Down and Dirty*, 128–131.

23. Van Natta and Bragg, "Scrutiny and Disagreements Accompany Hand Recount," A20.

24. "Theresa LePore Interview," 82; *Down and Dirty*, 130–131; *Too Close to Call*, 90–91; Washington Post, *Deadlock*, 88–89; David A. Kaplan, *The Accidental President: How 413 Lawyers, 9 Supreme Court Justices, and 5,963,110 Floridians Landed George W. Bush in the White House* (New York: William Morrow, 2001), 79–80. For a different read on the events of November 11, including an argument that all three board members did vote in favor of requesting an advisory opinion, see Bill Sammon, *At Any Cost: How Al Gore Tried*

to Steal the Election (Washington, DC: Regnery Publishing, 2001), 99–118. It should be noted that neither Theresa LePore's nor Judge Burton's recollections of these events as outlined in their 2001 interviews in Pleasants, *Hanging Chads*, supports this contrary reading of the facts.

25. Mitch Ceasar, "Some Things Are Not Meant to Be," in Robert P. Watson, ed., *Counting Votes: Lessons from the 2000 Presidential Election in Florida* (Gainesville: University Press of Florida, 2004), 34–35.

26. Tapper, *Down and Dirty*, 90–92, 163–164; Megan O'Matz and Robert Nolin, "Broward OKs Hand Recount in 3 Precincts," *South Florida Sun-Sentinel (SFSS)*, November 11, 2000, 28A; Sean Cavanagh and Robert Nolin, "Broward Panel Rejects Hand Tally of All Votes," *SFSS*, November 14, 2000, 22A.

27. Megan O'Matz and Sean Cavanagh, "Judge Lee Is Called a Stickler for the Law," *SFSS*, November 16, 2000, 14A.

28. L. Clayton Roberts to Al Cardenas, November 13, 2000 [reprinted in Joint Appendix, Motion for Writ of Certiorari, *Bush v. Palm Beach County Canvassing Board*, JA 52]. The memo to Cardenas was the first of a number of advisory opinions that Roberts issued. Soon after he received Cardenas's request, Roberts received another request for an advisory opinion from Judge Burton in Palm Beach County (Burton to Roberts, November 13, 2000 [Reprinted in Joint Appendix, Motion for Writ of Certiorari, *Bush v. Palm Beach County Canvassing Board*, JA47]). Roberts later would send out similar memoranda to the canvassing boards of Miami-Dade, Broward, and Volusia Counties.

29. Although Roberts as head of the Division of Elections had the power to issue advisory opinions, he was supposed to do so only in response to specific requests. And although political parties did have the right to request advisory opinions, such opinions were supposed to be limited to issues associated with primary elections or the layout of a ballot. Questions of this sort were the province of canvassing boards. And although it is true that soon after Roberts answered Cardenas's request, he received a similar request for an opinion from Judge Burton of the Palm Beach County Canvassing Board, Lee's copy of the answer was in response to Cardenas's request.

30. Tapper, *Down and Dirty*, 164; Robert Zelnick, *Winning Florida: How the Bush Team Fought the Battle* (Palo Alto, CA: Hoover Institution, 2001), 57.

31. Tapper, *Down and Dirty*, 132–134. See also David Barstow and Somini Sengupta, "How Local Personalities and Circumstances Are Shaping the Presidential Outcome," *NYT*, November 16, 2000, A27.

32. Anthony York, "The Volusia Triangle: Where Ballots Disappear, Partisans Scuffle and Election Officials Try to Put the Genie Back in the Bottle," *Salon.com*, November 11, 2000, http://archive.salon.com/politics/feature/2000/11/11/volusia/; "Florida Deadline Is Past, Ballots Still Being Counted," AP Wire, November 15, 2000; "The Fight Isn't Over Yet," *Court TV Online*, November 14, 2000, http://www.courttv.com/archive/national/decision_ 2000/111400-proposal_ap.html.

33. Tapper, *Down and Dirty*, 133–134.

34. Tapper, *Down and Dirty*, 136; Ellis Berger, "Miami-Dade Board to Rule on Recount of 10,750 Ballots," *SFSS*, November 14, 2000, 22A; 3, U.S.C. §5.

35. Berger, "Miami-Dade Board to Rule," 22A.

36. Ellis Berger and David Cazares, "Miami-Dade Decides Not to Expand Hand Recount," *SFSS*, November 15, 2000, 18A.

37. "Advisory Opinion 00-65," Office of the Florida Attorney General, November 14, 2000 (reprinted in Joint Appendix, Motion for Writ of Certiorari, *Bush v. Palm Beach*

County Canvassing Board, JA 40–46). (Citing the 1984 1st District Court of Appeals ruling in *Department of Professional Regulation, Board of Medical Examiners v. Durrani*, 455 So. 2d. 515.)

38. Ibid. Among the cases Butterworth cited were: *State ex rel. Smith v. Anderson*, 8 So. 1 (Fla. 1890); *Darby v. State*, 75 So. 411 (Fla. 1917); *State ex rel. Nuccio v. Williams*, 120 So. 310 (Fla. 1929); *Wiggins v. State ex rel. Drane*, 144 So. 62 (Fla. 1932); and *State ex rel. Carpenter v. Barber*, 198 So. 49 (Fla. 1940).

39. Ibid.

40. See, for example, *State ex rel. Smith v. Anderson*, 8 So. 1 (Fla. 1890); *Darby v. State*, 75 So. 411 (Fla. 1917); *State ex rel. Nuccio v. Williams*, 120 So. 310 (Fla. 1929); *Wiggins v. State ex rel. Drane*, 144 So. 62 (Fla. 1932); and *State ex rel. Carpenter v. Barber*, 198 So. 49 (Fla. 1940).

41. Zelnick, *Winning Florida*, 120–130; Tapper, *Down and Dirty*, 165–166. See also, Lucy Morgan, "Butterworth Opinion, Call Under Fire," *St. Petersburg Times (SPT)*, Nov 15, 2000, 7A and Brent Kallestad, "Attorney General Went against 1978 Standard to Avoid Election Advice," AP Wire, November 15, 2000.

42. "Advisory Opinion 00-65," Office of the Florida Attorney General, November 14, 2000.

43. "Statement of Katherine Harris, Secretary of State of Florida," November 13, 2000 (reprinted in Joint Appendix, Motion for Writ of Certiorari, *Bush v. Palm Beach County Canvassing Board*, JA 59–62).

44. Terri Sommers, "Decision Rests in a Twisting Legal Maze," *SFSS*, November 16, 2000, 1A; Mark Hollis and Linda Kleindienst, "Secretary of State Denies Hand Recount, Broward Goes Full Tilt with Retabulation," *SFSS*, November 16, 2000, 1A.

45. "Petition for a Writ of Mandamus," *Democratic Party of Florida, et al., v. Jane Carroll, et al.*, 17th Judicial Circuit Court of Florida, case no. 00019324 (07), November 14, 2000.

46. O'Matz and Cavanagh, "Judge Lee Is Called a Stickler for Law," *SFSS*, November 16, 2000, 14A. See also Jeff Shields and Brad Hahn, "Vote Counters Delay Another Hand Tally: While the Palm Beach County Board Decides to Way [*sic*] on State Supreme Court, Broward Gets Its Count Under Way," *SFSS*, November 16, 2000, 14A.

47. Tapper, *Down and Dirty*, 185. See also Dana Canedy, "A County Reconsiders a Hand Count," *NYT*, November 15, 2000, A22.

48. Toobin, *Too Close to Call*, 160–163.

49. Ibid., 162. See also Sean Cavanagh and Rafael Olmeda, "Broward's Counters to Forge on with Tally," *SFSS*, November 22, 2000, 12A.

50. *Fladell v. Palm Beach County Canvassing Board* (15th Circuit Court of Florida, CL 00-10965 AB).

51. Judge Miller's exact words were "If I find that the board isn't counting the pregnant chads and all the other stuff that's supposed to show . . . the intent of the voter, I will tell them to do it all again." Geraldine Baum, "Broward Recount Battle Marked by Drama, Comedy," *Los Angeles Times*, November 18, 2000, A16. See also Ronald Brownstein, "Democrats Pin Hopes on 'Voter Intent' Ruling Strategy," *Los Angeles Times*, November 20, 2000, A1; Howard Gillman, *The Votes That Counted: How the Court Decided the 2000 Presidential Election* (Chicago: University of Chicago Press, 2001), 53–54.

52. "Stay Order," *Palm Beach County Canvassing Board v. Harris*, case no. SC00-2346, November 17, 2000.

53. Jane Carroll later recanted her vote, arguing that she thought the vote was to keep

the current chad standard, not to change it. She would later express her opposition to wider standards in a separate brief filed with the state supreme court noting how she was "troubled by the conclusion reached by the County Attorney's Office." Sean Cavanagh et al., "Broward Panel Seeks to Count Dimpled Chad," *SFSS*, November 20, 2000, 1A.

54. Ibid.

55. Don Van Natta Jr., "Trying to Interpret a Ballot's Goosebumps," *NYT*, November 26, 2000, 38.

56. Sean Cavanagh, "Gore Picks Up 21 Votes in Broward County," *SFSS*, November 17, 2000, 10A.

57. Dion also noted that there was no partisan posturing on the board's part. They were just trying to follow the law with few guidelines as to the law's full requirements. Tapper, *Down and Dirty*, 224. Ed Pozzuoli disagreed, arguing to the press that "the Gore campaign now wants to lower the bar because it needs more votes." Mark Foley, a Republican congressman from Palm Beach Gardens, argued the decision reflected the chaos of the process. "It's just one more subjective standard," he said. "When is it going to stop?" David Able, "Board Changes Criteria for Determining Votes," *Boston Globe*, November 20, 2000.

58. Dana Canedy and David Gonzalez, "Broward Republicans Try to Stop the Music, but the Band Plays On," *NYT*, November 17, 2000, A29.

59. Toobin, *Too Close to Call*, 199.

60. Sean Cavanagh, et al., "Supervisor Resigns Post on Vote Board," *SFSS*, November 21, 2000, 13A; Toobin, *Too Close to Call*, 161–163; Tapper, *Down and Dirty*, 241–243.

61. *Palm Beach County Canvassing Board v. Harris*, case no. SC00-2346, November 21, 2000.

62. Tim Collie, "Palm Beach County Races to Finish Count," *SFSS*, November 26, 2000, 1A.

63. "The Florida Recount: Broward County Continues Manual Counts, Palm Beach Awaits State Supreme Court Decision before Proceeding," *CNN Transcript*, aired November 16, 2000, 2:06 p.m. EST, http://transcripts.cnn.com/TRANSCRIPTS/0011/16/bn.05.html.

64. Ibid.; *Too Close to Call*, 92; "Declaratory Order," *Florida Democratic Party v. Palm Beach County Canvassing Board*, case no. 00-11078 AH, 15th Judicial Circuit Court, November 15, 2000.

65. Terri Somers, "Decision Rests in a Twisting Legal Maze," *SFSS*, November 16, 2000, 1A.

66. Jeff Shields, "Demonstrations, Accusations and Chad: Palm Beach Canvassing Board Begins Its Recount after a Day of Protests and a New Ruling on Ballots," *SFSS*, November 17, 2000, 11A. See also Kevin Sack, "Key Recount Waits Again for Approval from Court," *NYT*, November 16, 2000, A31.

67. Jeff Shields, "Break Cuts Counting Time: Deadline Looms in West Palm," *SFSS*, November 26, 2000, 16A; Jeff Shields and Brad Hahn, "Palm Beach County Misses Deadline," *SFSS*, November 27, 1A; Don Van Natta Jr. and Rick Bragg, "Palm Beach Count Rejected by State," *NYT*, November 27, 2000, A1; Rick Bragg and Don Van Natta Jr., "Frustration in Aftermath of a Failed Recount," *NYT*, November 28, 2000, A26.

68. "Florida Deadline Is Past, Ballots Still Being Counted," AP Wire, November 15, 2000; "The Fight Isn't Over Yet," *Court TV Online*, November 14, 2000, http://www.courttv.com/archive/national/decision_2000/111400-proposal_ap.html; Tapper, *Down and Dirty*, 267–268. Lynne Rambo, "The Lawyers' Role in Selecting the President: A Complete Legal History," *Texas Wesleyan Law Review* 8 (Spring 2002): 169 note 339, 162.

69. Don Finefrock, "Dade Decides to Recount," *Miami Herald (MH)*, November 18, 2000, 1A; *Down and Dirty*, 200–202.

70. Ibid.

71. Ibid. See also Ellis Berger, "Board Reverses Decision, Orders Manual Recount," *SFSS*, November 18, 2000, 17A.

72. Tapper, *Down and Dirty*, 238–239; Don Finefrock, "Miami-Dade County Officials Ok Plan for Hand Recount," *MH*, November 19, 2000, 22A.

73. Don Finefrock, "Miami-Dade amid Protests, Gore Gains Some Ground, Both Candidates' Totals Grow as Big Manual Recount Begins," *MH*, November 21, 2000, 17A.

74. Don Finefrock, "Miami-Dade County Clashes during Recount Turn 'Sticky,' 'Rude,'" *MH*, November 22, 2000, 16A; *Down and Dirty*, 239.

75. Jacqueline Charles and Don Finefrock, "Democratic Leader Has Angry Encounter with Republicans," *MH*, November 23, 2000, 3C; *Down and Dirty*, 258–266.

76. Tapper, *Down and Dirty*, 260–263; Sammon, *At Any Cost*, 167–180.

77. Tapper, *Down and Dirty*, 260–276; Martin Merzer and Mark Silva, "A Stunning Reversal a Huge Blow to Gore: Dade Stops All Counting, Bush Takes Case to U.S. High Court," *MH*, November 23, 2000, 1A.

78. Ibid. See also Kaplan, *Accidental President*, 168–172. For a somewhat different read on the causes and impacts of these events, see Zelnick, *Winning Florida*, 62–68, and Sammon, *At Any Cost*, 167–180.

79. Paul Brinkley-Rogers, "Military Ballots' Rejected Votes Not Unusual," *MH*, November 21, 2000, 16A.

80. Paul Brinkley-Rogers and Tyler Bridges, "Ballot Rules Devastate Military Vote," *MH*, November 19, 2000, 1A; Richard Perez-Pena, "Floridians Abroad Are Counted, or Not, as Counties Interpret 'Rules' Differently," *NYT*, November 18, 2000, A11; Brinkley-Rogers, "Military Ballots' Rejected Votes Not Unusual," 16A.

81. Meg Laughlin, "Overseas Ballots: Military Vote Drive May Benefit Republicans," *MH*, November 17, 2000, 21A.

82. Richard Perez-Pena, "Absentee Ballots: G.O.P. and Democrats Trading Accusations on Military Votes," *NYT*, November 18, 2000, 1A.

83. Mark Hollis and William Gibson, "Final Tally on Hold: Bush Gains Overseas Votes amid Confusion," *MH*, November 18, 2000, 1A.

84. Paul Brinkley-Rogers et al., "Results: Bush Leading in Overseas Ballot Counts: Disputes over Votes' Validity Stall Election Tallies in Some Counties," *MH*, November 18, 2000, 28A.

85. Memo reprinted in "Remarks of Hon. Matt Salmon of Arizona," *Congressional Record*, December 6, 2000, E2137.

86. Brinkley-Rogers et al., "Results: Bush Leading in Overseas Ballot Counts," 28A; Washington Post, *Deadlock*, 130–131.

87. Tapper, *Down and Dirty*, 213, 217–219; Brinkley-Rogers, "Military Ballots' Rejected Votes Not Unusual," 16A. Zelnick, *Winning Florida*, 73–76, gives a different interpretation of the legal status of these ballots based on the Republican legal arguments before a number of state and federal courts on this subject.

88. Perez-Pena, "Absentee Ballots: G.O.P. and Democrats Trading Accusations," 1A.

89. Ibid. See also Tapper, *Down and Dirty*, 208–211; Martin Merzer, "Feud Heats Up: GOP Attacks Gore: Bush Margin Grows Slim in State Rises to 930 Votes," *MH*, November 19, 2000, 1A.

90. Richard Perez-Pena, "The Absentee Vote: Bush Files Suit to Restore Rejected Military Ballots," *NYT*, November 23, 2000, A36.

91. "Overseas Votes Counted for Bush Military Ballots Lent Crucial Support," *Florida Times-Union*, November 27, 2000, A9. The article goes on to note that "the absentee ballot issue was a loser for Democrats in more ways than one. Florida's military veteran population is second only to California's. 'Whoever is overly partisan and against counting military ballots will pay the political consequences,' said political scientist Susan MacManus of the University of South Florida." Political scientist Darrell West of Brown University agreed with this analysis, arguing that "this has been a public relations nightmare for Democrats. Just the symbolism of attempting to disbar the votes of active soldiers serving abroad is dreadful for the party."

92. Richard Perez-Pena, "Military Ballots Merit a Review, Lieberman Says," *NYT*, November 19, 2000, A1; Richard Perez-Pena, "Review Military Votes, Florida Attorney General Says," *NYT*, November 21, 2000, A18; Washington Post, *Deadlock*, 131–132.

93. Washington Post, *Deadlock*, 131–134. The Democrats called this vote windfall for Bush the "Thanksgiving stuffing." See also Ron Word, "Two Counties Give Bush Another 32 Votes," AP Wire, November 25, 2000; Lucy Morgan and Linda Gibson, "Bush Picks Up 45 Overseas Military Votes," *SPT*, November 26, 2000, 3A; "Florida Counties Holding Hearings to Decide Their Counts," AP Wire, November 24, 2000; Boies, *Courting Justice*, 387–398.

94. Boies, *Courting Justice*, 403.

95. George Bennet, "Deadline Missed, Recount Counts for Nothing," *Palm Beach Post*, November 27, 2000, 1A.

96. Tim Nickens et al., "Fight's Not Finished," *SPT*, November 26, 2000, 1A.

97. Linda Deutsch, "Lawyers Play Game of Political Chess as Deadline Nears," AP Wire, November 26, 2000.

98. Linda Deutsch, "Gore Places His Political Future in Hands of the Courts," AP Wire, November 27, 2000.

99. David Ballingrud et al., "Bush: I Win," *SPT*, November 27, 2000, 1A.

100. Linda Deutsch, "Bush Expands Florida Legal Team 'To Set the Record Straight'," AP Wire, November 27, 2000.

101. Terence Hunt, "Enter the Lawyers, in Courtrooms from Washington to Florida," AP Wire, November 28, 2000; Susan Milligan, "Gore Says Bush Is Stalling Process," *Boston Globe*, November 29, 2000.

4. The Battlefield of Litigation

1. See Marc Galanter, "Reading the Landscape of Disputes: What We Know and Don't Know (and Think We Know) about Our Allegedly Contentious and Litigious Society," *UCLA Law Review* 31 (1983): 4–70. See also Don Feder, "Lawyer-Slinging Culture," *Washington Times*, December 12, 2000, A16, which notes: "To say we're a litigious society is no less true for being clichéd. Every two seconds, a lawsuit is filed somewhere in America."

2. This included members of the current Supreme Court, whose understandings of federalism seemed to point away from a federal intervention in a wide range of circumstances, but most notably in electoral outcomes. See Jack M. Balkin, "*Bush v. Gore* and the Boundary between Law and Politics," *Yale Law Journal* 110 (June 2001): 1207–1458, which notes at pp. 1408–1409: "The same five conservative Justices who formed the majority in *Bush v. Gore* had been engaged, for over a decade, in a veritable revolution in constitutional doctrines concerning civil rights and federalism. In those decisions, the five conservatives

had been promoting a relatively consistent set of ideological positions like colorblindness, respect for state autonomy from federal interference, and protection of state governmental processes from federal supervision." See also Richard Brisbin Jr., "The Reconstruction of American Federalism? The Rehnquist Court and Federal-State Relations, 1991–1997," *Publius* 28 (Winter 1998): 189–215, and Harold Krent, "Judging Judging: The Problem of Second-Guessing State Judges' Interpretation of State Law in *Bush v. Gore*," *Florida State University Law Review* 29 (2001): 493–534.

3. *Colgrove v. Green*, 328 U.S. 549, 552 (1946).

4. Article II, Section 1.

5. Article I, Section 4.

6. 3 U.S.C. §5 (2000) provides: "If any State shall have provided, by laws enacted prior to the day fixed for the appointment of the electors, for its final determination of any controversy or contest concerning the appointment of all or any of the electors of such State, by judicial or other methods or procedures, and such determination shall have been made at least six days before the time fixed for the meeting of the electors, such determination. . . . shall be conclusive, and shall govern in the counting of the electoral votes as provided in the Constitution, and as hereinafter regulated, so far as the ascertainment of the electors appointed by such State is concerned."

7. On this subject, see the ruling of Judge Middlebrooks of the Southern District of Florida in *Seigel v. LePore*, 120 F. Supp. 2d 1041.

8. Washington Post, *Deadlock: The Inside Story of America's Closest Election* (PublicAffairs: New York: 2001), 101.

9. Todd S. Purdum, "Recount Fight Widens as Court Case Begins: Expanded Count Sought for Palm Beach Vote in Florida Standoff," *New York Time (NYT)*, November 13, 2000, A1.

10. See for example, "Second Amended Complaint," *Fladell v. Palm Beach County Canvassing Board*, CL 00-10965 AB, Circuit Court for the 15th Circuit Court of Florida. These cases were: *Fladell v. Palm Beach County Canvassing Board*, *Horowitz v. LePore* (15th Judicial Circuit, CL 00-10970 AG), *Elkin v. LePore* (Florida 15th Judicial Circuit, CL 00-10988 AE), *Rogers v. Election Canvassing Commission of Florida* (Florida 15th Judicial Circuit, CL 00-10992 AF), and *Gibbs v. Palm Beach County Canvassing Board* (Florida 15th Judicial Circuit, CL 00-110000 AH). They would be consolidated on November 13 into the case of *Fladell v. Palm Beach County Canvassing Board*. After this date, angry voters would file an additional ten complaints against the butterfly ballot with the Palm Beach County Circuit Courts. All were ultimately merged with *Fladell*. For a listing of all cases, see Robert Crown Law Library, Stanford Law School, "Election 2000," http://election2000.stanford.edu/.

11. In a tactical move to keep this matter out of the state courts, the Bush lawyers also asked for an order "consolidating or removing to this Court any and all actions filed across the State of Florida purporting to challenge the results of the November 7 statewide election." "Complaint for Declaratory and Injunctive Relief," *Siegel, et al. v. LePore, et al.*, case no. 00-9009 (U.S. District Court, SD of Florida). See also "Emergency Motion for Temporary Restraining Order and Preliminary Injunction and Supporting Memorandum of Law," *Siegel, et al. v. LePore, et al.*

12. "Opposition of the Florida Democratic Party to Plaintiffs' Emergency Motion for Temporary Restraining Order and Preliminary Injunction," *Siegel, et al., v. Lepore, et al.*

13. "Order on Plaintiffs' Emergency Motion for Temporary Restraining Order and Preliminary Injunction," *Siegel, et al., v. LePore, et al.*, 120 F. Supp. 2d 1041 (U.S. District Court, SD of Florida). The Bush team immediately appealed this ruling to the 11th Circuit

Court of Appeals asking for an immediate injunction halting the recount process. The appellate judges agreed with Judge Middlebrooks, however, and in a ruling handed down on November 17 denied the motion for an injunction on the ground that authority in these matters rested with the State of Florida and its courts. (This case was argued in conjunction with *Touchston v. McDermott*, 234 F.3d 1130, in which the 11th Circuit set out its reasons for denying the motion for an injunction.) A subsequent petition for certiorari to the U.S. Supreme Court was denied on November 24 (531 U.S. 1005). The 11th Circuit ruled on the substance of the Bush appeal on December 6—again ruling against Bush (234 F.3d 1163). The four judges in dissent, however, would set out arguments on equal protection and recounts that would be argued again by the Supreme Court in *Bush v. Gore*. See generally, Washington Post, *Deadlock*, 102–103; Abner Green, *Understanding the 2000 Election: A Guide to the Legal Battles That Decided the Presidency* (New York: New York University Press, 2001), 78–82.

14. R. W. Apple Jr., "Democrats Widen Attack—Recount Seems to Erode Bush's Edge," *NYT*, November 2000, A1.

15. Clayton Roberts to Judge Charles Burton, "Advisory Opinion DE 00-10," Florida Department of State, November 13, 2000 (reprinted in E. J. Dionne Jr. and William Kristol, eds., *Bush v. Gore: The Court Cases and the Commentary* [Washington, DC: Brookings Institution, 2001], 9–10).

16. See the appendix to this book, "Timeline of Events," for a listing of the leading cases in the postelection crisis, organized by the initial date of their filing with the state and federal courts.

17. For those wishing to view these cases in their chronological sequence, see generally Washington Post, *Deadlock*; Jack Tapper, *Down and Dirty: The Plot to Steal the Presidency* (Boston: Little, Brown, 2001); and Jeffrey Toobin, *Too Close to Call: The Thirty-Six-Day Battle to Decide the 2000 Election* (New York: Random House, 2001).

18. "Complaint," *Florida Democratic Party v. Palm Beach County Canvassing Board*, case no. CL 00-11078 AH, Circuit Court of the 15th Judicial Circuit of Florida, November 13, 2000; Jon Burstein, "Ballots Can't Be Tossed, Judge Says," *South Florida Sun-Sentinel*, November 16, 2000, 18A.

19. "Declaratory Order," *Florida Democratic Party v. Palm Beach County Canvassing Board*, November 15, 2000. The judge also noted from the bench that Katherine Harris's advisory opinion to halt manual recounts was improper. The board was "permitted" to count if it wished to. However, Labarga did note that he lacked jurisdiction to force Harris to accept the recounted ballots. "If she decides to accept them, fine," Labarga said. "If she doesn't, then you need to talk to her about it." Tapper, *Down and Dirty*, 177.

20. See "Order on Plaintiff's Emergency Motion to Clarify Declaratory Order of November 15, 2000," *Florida Democratic Party v. Palm Beach County Canvassing Board*, November 22, 2000, 2, for the specifics of the Plaintiff's "Motion to Clarify Declaratory Order of November 15, 2000." See generally Washington Post, *Deadlock*, 134.

21. Robert Zelnick, *Winning Florida: How the Bush Team Fought the Battle* (Palo Alto, CA: Hoover Institution), 71.

22. "Motion for Emergency Hearing," *Florida Democratic Party v. Palm Beach County Canvassing Board*, November 20, 2000. See also Zelnick, *Winning Florida*, 71.

23. "Order on Plaintiff's Emergency Motion to Clarify Declaratory Order of November 15, 2000," *Florida Democratic Party v. Palm Beach County Canvassing Board*, November 22, 2000, quoting from *Palm Beach County Canvassing Board v. Harris*, case no. SC00-2346, Florida Supreme Court, November 21, 2000. The last quote was drawn from a fairly long

quote by the Florida Supreme Court from the Illinois Supreme Court's ruling in *Pullen v. Mulligan*, 561 N. E. 2d, 585 (IL 1990).

24. "Order on Plaintiff's Emergency Motion to Clarify Declaratory Order of November 15, 2000," *Florida Democratic Party v. Palm Beach County Canvassing Board*. The first quote is taken from *Darby v. State ex rel. McCllough*, 75 So. 411 (FL 1917). The judge also cited *Delahunt v. Johnson*, 671 N. E. 2d 1241 (MA 1996) and *McCavitt v. Registrars of Voters of Brockston*, 434 N. E. 2d 620 (MA 1982) on this topic. See also Zelnick, *Winning Florida*, 71–72. Zelnick notes that Judge Roberts and the Palm Beach board read Judge Labarga's ruling as vindication of their two-corner standard and therefore did not change their determination of a valid ballot.

25. "Intervenor's Verified Motion for Disqualification and Memorandum of Law in Support Thereof," *Florida Democratic Party v. Broward County Canvassing Board*, case no. 00-019324, Circuit Court of the 17th Judicial Circuit of Florida, November 20, 2000, 7. See also generally "The Florida Recount: Broward County Judge Will Decide Whether to Allow Hand Recounts to Go Forward," *CNN Transcript*, airdate November 14, 2000, 11:38 a.m. EST, http://transcripts.cnn.com/TRANSCRIPTS/0011/14/bn.20.html.

26. "November 17, 2000 Hearing Transcript" and "Defendant's Brief on the Merits," both quoted in "Intervenor's Verified Motion for Disqualification and Memorandum of Law in Support Thereof," *Florida Democratic Party v. Broward County Canvassing Board*, November 20, 2000, 3–4. When George Bush's lawyers objected to the judge's ruling, Judge Miller's response was for the defendants to appeal. Ibid., 5. See also Thomas Tobin, "Broward Might Recount after All," *SPT*, November 15, 2000, which notes that Miller was a Republican.

27. Ironically, later recounts by media consortiums showed that it was only when one included the overvotes that Gore had any significant chance of gaining the votes he needed to win Florida. Martin Merzer et al., *The Miami Herald Report: Democracy Held Hostage* (New York: Saint Martin's, 2001), 188–198.

28. "Complaint," *Brown v. Duval County Canvassing Board*, case no. 00-2878, Circuit Court for the 2nd Circuit of Florida, December 5, 2000.

29. "Motion to Dismiss," *Brown v. Duval County Canvassing Board*, December 8, 2000.

30. "Order of Dismissal," *Brown v. Duval County Canvassing Board*, December 13, 2000.

31. In a November 20 motion, Republicans argued that Miller had prejudged matters and had deprived the Republican Party "the fair and impartial consideration to which every litigant is entitled." Justice demanded that they receive "nothing less than the cold neutrality of an impartial judge." This was especially called for given the national importance of the issues before the court. Yet they were not getting neutrality—hot or cold—in Judge Miller's courtroom. Rules were rules, and for a judge to order a county canvassing board to ignore the rules was clearly a case of partisanship trumping justice. Zelnick, *Winning Florida*, 60–62.

32. The decision to review only about 10,000 ballots in Miami-Dade County, for instance, sparked a loud and angry protest by about two dozen Republicans, who chanted "Voter fraud" and "the fix is in" outside the elections office. Ari Fleischer, a spokesperson for George W. Bush, argued that "This is an attempt by a board without a Republican to pull out the election for Al Gore. Al Gore controls the referees and the referees give Al Gore all the calls." Meanwhile, U.S. Rep. John Sweeney, a New York Republican and party observer of the recount process, complained that "This is an outrage. This is the most brazen attempt by the Gore campaign, the Democratic machine, and the thugs in that

building to hijack the American presidency." Brendan Ferrington, "Miami-Dade Limits Recount, Sparking GOP Protests," AP Wire, November 22, 2000.

33. *Bush v. Bay County Canvassing Board, et al.*, case no. 00-2799, Circuit Court for the 2nd Circuit of Florida. The counties named in this suit were Bay, Brevard, Clay, Collier, Duval, Escambia, Hillsborough, Leon, Manatee, Okaloosa, Orange, Pasco, Polk, and Santa Rosa.

34. "Complaint for Declaratory and Injunctive Relief," *Bush v. Bay County Canvassing Board, et al.*, November 24, 2000, 2–8.

35. *Boardman v. Esteva*, 323 So. 2d 259.

36. "Motion for Emergency Injunctive Relief and Memorandum in Support Thereof," *Bush v. Bay County Canvassing Board, et al.*, November 24, 2000, 3, 5–7.

37. "Complaint for Declaratory and Injunctive Relief," *Bush v. Bay County Canvassing Board, et al.*, November 24, 2000, 11.

38. Michael Cooper, "Lawyers for Bush Want a Judge to Reinstate Military Ballots That Were Disqualified," *NYT*, November 25, 2000, A13; Michael Cooper, "G.O.P. Drops a Suit: Tactics Shift on Military Ballots, with Eye on Specific Counties," *NYT*, November 26, 2000, 1A, 35A.

39. "Motion for Emergency Injunctive Relief and Memorandum in Support Thereof," *Bush v. Bay County Canvassing Board, et al.*, November 24, 2000.

40. Cooper, "G.O.P. Drops a Suit," 1A, 35A.

41. "Notice of Voluntary Dismissal," *Bush v. Bay County Canvassing Board, et al.*, November 25, 2000. The speculation as to the Republicans' motives for this tactical move comes from Ronald Labasky, an attorney for two of the defendant canvassing boards, who suggested that "any new lawsuits filed by the Bush camp may be an effort to find a more sympathetic judge." Cooper, "G.O.P. Drops a Suit," 35A.

42. These counties were Okaloosa, Walton, Hillsborough, Polk, Orange, Pasco, and Collier. Michael Cooper, "The Multipronged Strategy for Bush's Absentee Votes," *NYT*, November 27, 2000, A14; "Federal Judge to Hear Military Ballot Case," AP Wire, December 4, 2000.

43. "Complaint to Contest Election," *Harris v. Florida Elections Canvassing Commission*, CV00-2855, Circuit Court of the 2nd Judicial Circuit of Florida, December 1, 2000.

44. "Complaint," *Medina v. Florida Elections Commission* (CV00-2875), Circuit Court of the 2nd Judicial Circuit of Florida, December 5, 2000.

45. *Harris v. Florida Elections Canvassing Commission*, 122 F. Supp. 2d 1317 (ND of Florida, December 9, 2000). On appeal, the 11th Circuit Court of Appeals unanimously affirmed Judge Paul's judgment. "Turning to the merits, we see no reversible error in the district court's judgment," the three-judge panel ruled. "We note in passing that the district court's views are consistent with recent comments of Florida's highest court about the working of the absentee ballot law . . . [and] that to read Florida's law as Plaintiffs ask us to do would be a significant change in the actual election practices of Florida." A later petition to the Supreme Court to review the case was denied. *Harris v. Florida Elections Canvassing Commission*, 531 U.S. 1062, U.S. Supreme Court, January 5, 2001.

46. *Bush v. Hillsborough County Canvassing Board*, 123 F. Supp. 2d 1305, 1306, 1317. Judge Collier did order the counting of ballots denied "solely because the ballot envelope does not have an APO, FPO, or foreign postmark; or . . . because there is no record of an application for a state absentee ballot." These actions conflicted with federal law and hence were within her powers to correct. Ibid.

47. Stephen Hegarty, "Overseas Ballots Suddenly Crucial," *SPT*, November 9, 2000, 13A.

48. "Fladell Plaintiffs' Second Amended Complaint," *Fladell v. Palm Beach County Canvassing Board*, November 10, 2000.

49. "Order on Plaintiff's Complaint for Declaratory Judgment, Injunctive and Other Relief Arising from Plaintiff's Claims of Massive Voter Confusion Resulting from the Use of a 'Butterfly' Type Ballot during the Election Held on November 7, 2000," *Fladell v. Palm Beach County Canvassing Board*, November 20, 2000.

50. "Appellants'/Petitioners' Initial Brief," *Fladell v. Honorable Jorge Labarga, et al.*, case no. 00-4146, District Court of Appeals for the 4th District of Florida (undated, but likely filed on November 22 to 25, 2000).

51. *Fladell v. Labarga*, 775 So. 2d 987, November 27, 2000.

52. "Florida Supreme Court Scheduling Order," *Fladell v. Palm Beach County Canvassing Board, et al.*, case no. SC00-2373, Supreme Court of Florida, November 27, 2000.

53. *Fladell v. Palm Beach County Canvassing Board, et al.*, 772 So. 2d 1240, 1242.

54. Ibid.

55. "Bush Urges Voters to Cast Ballot for GOP Candidates in Mailing," AP Wire, October 11, 2000; Dara Kam, "Democrats Charge Bush with Misuse of State Seal," AP Wire, October 20, 2000.

56. "Democrat Sues Seminole County, Saying Poll Officials Favored GOP," AP Wire, November 17, 2000.

57. Ultimately, a federal judge overturned the election's results by throwing out all absentee ballots (arguing that it was impossible to determine how many absentee ballots were tainted). See, "Judge Orders New Miami Mayoral Election: Absentee-Ballot Fraud Voids Last November's Balloting," *CNN AllPolitics* (March 4, 1998), http://www.cnn.com/ALLPOLITICS/1998/03/04/miami.mayor/; "A Miami Voting Scandal," *CNN AllPolitics* (November 13, 1997), http://www.cnn.com/ALLPOLITICS/1998/03/04/miami.mayor/.

58. Mary Ellen Klas and Scott Hiaasen, "State Official Backs Seminole Ballots," *Palm Beach Post*, November 30, 2000, 1A; John Pacenti, "Fate of Absentee Ballots has Potential to Alter Election Outcome," Cox News Service, November 26, 2000.

59. Alicia Caldwell and Thomas Tobin, "Spotlight Grows on Ballot Flap in Seminole County," *SPT*, November 28, 2000, 9A; George Lardner Jr. and James Grimaldi, "Absentee Ballot Suit Worries Republicans," *Washington Post (WP)*, December 1, 2000, A25.

60. Jeffrey McMurray, "Democrats Allege Martin County Republicans Doctored Ballot Requests," AP Wire, December 1, 2000.

61. When state Democratic Party chair Bob Poe contacted Seminole County Supervisor Goard on October 30, he was told, as he recalled the conversation, to "go fly a kite." Lardner and Grimaldi, "Absentee Ballot Suit Worries Republicans," A25; Mike Schneider, "Republicans Protest as Lawyer Is Deposed over Seminole Case," AP Wire, December 2, 2000. Goard's lawyer, Terry Young, later noted, "Had the Democratic Party wanted to come in they could have come in, pulled up a chair and done the same thing." Caldwell and Tobin, "Spotlight Grows on Ballot Flap," 9A.

62. "It was totally improper," noted State Democratic Party chair Poe. "The Republican Party made a mistake. Rather than fix that mistake the right way, by having the ballot requests remailed, they took a shortcut. But there are consequences when you take illegal shortcuts." William March, "Court to Decide If Seminole County Absentee Ballots Were Tampered With," *Tampa Tribune*, November 26, 2000, 5.

63. Most of Gore's lawyers urged him to join this suit and, in essence, take it over. Gore's advisors in Washington disagreed. It was a classic case of legal thinking clashing

with political thinking. The politicians in Washington worried about the political fallout similar to that surrounding the overseas military absentee ballots—that Gore would seem inconsistent arguing for "counting every ballot" in South Florida but arguing against counting every ballot in Seminole County. More significant, Gore had real problems with disenfranchising thousands of voters who had done nothing wrong. In the overseas absentee ballot case, the voters had not followed the directions and thus submitted invalid ballots. Here, however, the ballots were valid, but it was the applications for these ballots that were in question. Combined with the potential for political fallout, Gore's Washington advisors decided to distance themselves from these proceedings. David Boies, *Courting Justice: From NY Yankees v. Major League Baseball to Bush v. Gore, 1997–2000* (New York: Miramax, 2004), 410–411; Washington Post, *Deadlock*, 160–161.

64. "Seminole Absentee Ballots Face Scrutiny," AP Wire, November 13, 2000; Mike Branom, "Judge Delays Hearing on Seminole County Absentee Ballots," AP Wire, November 18, 2000.

65. Mike Schneider, "Challenge to Seminole County Ballots Moved to Tallahassee," AP Wire, November 27, 2000; Caldwell and Tobin, "Spotlight Grows on Ballot Flap," 9A; Gary Kane, "Seminole Case Gets Down to the Law," Cox News Service, December 4, 2000; George Lardner, Jr., "Democrat Tests Seminole's Absentee Vote," *WP*, November 28, 2000, A13; William March, "Court to Decide if Seminole County Absentee Ballots Were Tampered With," *Tampa Tribune*, November 26, 2000, 5.

66. Schneider, "Challenge to Seminole County Ballots"; Pacenti, "Fate of Absentee Ballots."

67. "Complaint," *Jacobs v. The Seminole County Canvassing Board, et al.*, case no. 00-2816, Circuit Court for the 2nd Circuit of Florida, November 27, 2000, 7. Alicia Caldwell, "Rules Issue Could Change Election," *SPT*, December 4, 2000, 8A. The precedent of throwing out votes was the 1997 Miami mayoral election, where a federal judge finally threw out all the absentee ballots due to the high level of questionable ballots. Pacenti, "Fate of Absentee Ballots" (see also note 57 above). Other precedents included the 1975 Florida Supreme Court case of *Boardman v. Esteva*, wherein the court ruled that without a clear case of fraud, the voters' right to have their vote heard outweighed any technical violations of the law. Caldwell, "Rules Issue Could Change Election," 8A.

68. "Complaint," *Taylor v. The Martin County Canvassing Board, et al.*, case no. 00-2850, Circuit Court for the 2nd Circuit of Florida, December 1, 2000, 5–6.

69. A third absentee ballot case was also filed against Bay County on November 11 (*McCauley v. Bay County Canvassing Board*, case no. CV 00-2802). This complaint alleged that Republicans turned in "handfuls" and even in one case "a suitcase-full of absentee ballots" in defiance of Florida laws requiring that people can turn in only two absentee ballots beyond their own or that of a family member. Assigned to Circuit Judge L. Ralph Smith Jr. of the Second Circuit Court in Tallahassee, the case did not progress far and was ultimately dismissed with prejudice by the judge. "Order of Dismissal with Prejudice," *McCauley v. Bay County Canvassing Board*, December 7, 2000.

70. The Stanford Law School's "Election 2000" Web site (http://election2000.stanford .edu/#florida) provides copies of the many pleadings in both cases. The only cases with more pleadings than these two on the page are those associated with the two U.S. Supreme Court cases, *Gore v. Harris* and *Bush v. Gore*. On the refusal to dismiss, see Gary Kane, "Seminole County Ballot Suit Allowed," *Palm Beach Post*, December 6, 2000, 10A.

71. Mike Williams, "Long Day of Testimony in Absentee Vote Trial," Cox News Service, December 6, 2000; Larry Margasak, "Republican Elections Official Admits She Only

Helped Republicans," AP Wire, December 6, 2000; Jim Saunders, "Closing Arguments Set Today in Seminole Absentee Ballot Suit," *Florida Times-Union*, December 7, 2000, A7.

72. Mike Williams, "Tough Questions in Absentee Ballot Cases," Cox News Service, December 7, 2000; "Judge Sets High Standard of Proof for Gore Team in Absentee-Ballot Case," *Washington Times*, December 7, 2000, A12.

73. "Final Judgment for Defendants," *Taylor v. The Martin County Canvassing Board, et al.*, December 8, 2000; Vickie Chachere, "Florida Judges Throw Out Democratic Lawsuits," AP Wire, December 8, 2000; Noah Bierman and Sarah Eisenhauer, "Judges Refuse to Toss 25,000 Absentee Ballots," *Palm Beach Post*, December 9, 2000, 25A; Mike Williams, "Absentee Ballots: Finding No Fraud, Judges Refuse to Invalidate Votes," *Atlanta Journal and Constitution*, December 9, 2000, 11A.

74. "Final Order," *Jacobs v. Seminole County Canvassing Board, et al.*, December 8, 2000; Chachere, "Florida Judges Throw Out Democratic Lawsuits"; Bierman and Eisenhauer, "Judges Refuse to Toss 25,000 Absentee Ballots," 25A; Williams, "Absentee Ballots: Finding No Fraud," 11A.

75. "We especially note," wrote the justices, "that at the conclusion of its order, the trial court found that the Supervisor of Elections of Seminole County exercised faulty judgment in first rejecting completely the requests in question, and compounded the problem by allowing third parties to correct the omissions on the forms." *Jacobs v. Seminole County Canvassing Board, et al.*, no. SC00–2447, Supreme Court of Florida, December 12, 2000.

76. Ibid. A slightly different version of this opinion can be found at 773 So. 2d 519 (the Florida Supreme Court modified its initial ruling on December 21—the quotes above are taken from the initial opinion issued on December 12). The justices ruled the same way in *Taylor v. The Martin County Canvassing Board, et al.*, no. SC 00–2448, noting that their ruling in *Jacobs v. Seminole County Canvassing Board* was controlling in this case as well.

77. "Class Action Complaint," *NAACP et al., v. Harris, et al.*, case no. 01-CIV-120-GOLD, Southern District Court of Florida, January 10, 2002. See also Melanie Eversley, "Rights Groups File Lawsuit over Florida Election Practices," Cox News Service, January 10, 2001; August Gribbin and Jerry Seper, "Civil Rights Groups Sue Florida Officials; Say Blacks Hindered in Attempts to Vote," *Washington Times*, January 11, 2001, A1. A similar suit was filed in state court on January 9, 2001 (*Coyner v. Harris*). On February 6, 2001, the suit changed its name to *Payton v. Harris*. Neither suit seemed to have gone anywhere.

78. "NAACP Settles with the State of Florida and the Private Company Choicepoint, but Thousands of Voters Illegally Purged from the Rolls Still Can't Vote," *Democracy Now*, September 6, 2002, http://www.democracynow.org/article.pl?sid=03/04/07/036218; "Court Hears Motions on Florida Election Violations," Common Dreams Progressive Newswire, July 25, 2002; "Second Settlement of Voting Reform Lawsuit in Florida," *Jackson Advocate*, May 16, 2002; Gary Fineout, "Many Could Regain Voting Rights; A Lawsuit Settlement Calls for Officials to Double-Check Names of Purged Voters," *Lakeland Ledger*, September 4, 2002.

5. The Ticking of the Clock

1. "Statement of Katherine Harris, Secretary of State of Florida," November 13, 2000. See also, Todd S. Purdum and David Firestone, "Counting the Vote: The Overview; A Vote Deadline in Florida Is Set for Today," *New York Times (NYT)*, November 14, 2000, A1.

2. This latter message was communicated by Division of Elections director Clay Roberts when Palm Beach County Canvassing Board chair Charles Burton asked if it might

be possible to turn in a partial recount. Roberts's answer was no. Burton to Roberts, November 13, 2000, reprinted in Joint Appendix, Motion for Writ of Certiorari, *Bush v. Palm Beach County Canvassing Board*, case nos. 00-836 and 00-837, JA47.

3. L. Clayton Roberts to Al Cardenas, "Advisory Opinion DE 00-11," November 13, 2000, reprinted in Joint Appendix, Motion for Writ of Certiorari, *Bush v. Palm Beach County Canvassing Board*, JA 52. See also Robert Zelnick, *Winning Florida: How the Bush Team Fought the Battle* (Palo Alto, CA: Hoover Institution, 2001), 28; Steve Bickerstaff, "Post-Election Legal Strategy in Florida: The Anatomy of Defeat and Victory," *Loyola University of Chicago Law Journal* 34 (Fall 2002): 180–181; Jeffrey Toobin, *Too Close to Call: The Thirty-Six-Day Battle to Decide the 2000 Election* (New York: Random House, 2001), 71–76; Washington Post, *Deadlock: The Inside Story of America's Closest Election* (New York: PublicAffairs, 2001), 98–99.

4. "Advisory Opinion 00-65," Office of the Florida Attorney General, November 14, 2000, reprinted in Joint Appendix, Motion for Writ of Certiorari, *Bush v. Palm Beach County Canvassing Board*, JA 40–46.

5. *McDermott v. Harris*, case no. 00-2700, Circuit Court for the 2nd Judicial Circuit of Florida, November 13, 2000.

6. Purdum and Firestone, "Counting the Vote: The Overview," A1; See also "Motion to Intervene of the State Executive Committee of the Democratic Party," "Motion of George W. Bush to Intervene," "Motion of Al Gore to Intervene," *McDermott v. Harris*, November 13, 2000. The Broward board joined the suit two days later. "Motion to Intervene (Broward County)," ibid., November 16, 2000. Al Gore also filed a separate action for an injunction to force Harris to accept late amended returns. "Complaint for Injunctive and Declaratory Relief," *Gore v. Florida Election Canvassing Commission*, case no. 00-2717, Circuit Court for the 2nd Judicial Circuit of Florida, November 13, 2000.

7. Purdum and Firestone, "Counting the Vote: The Overview," A1. See also Jim Saunders and Randolph Pendleton, "Recount Given until 5 p.m. Florida Official Cites State Law; Decision Sets Off New Tussle," *Florida Times-Union*, November 14, 2000, A1.

8. Saunders and Pendleton, "Recount Given until 5 p.m.," A1; Alan Judd, "Ruling Today on Count Deadline," Cox News Service, November 13, 2000.

9. *Florida Statutes* (2000), Title IX, Sections 102.111–112.

10. Judd, "Ruling Today on Count Deadline."

11. "Statement of Katherine Harris, Secretary of State of Florida," November 13, 2000 (reprinted in Joint Appendix, Motion for Writ of Certiorari, *Bush v. Palm Beach County Canvassing Board*, JA 59–62).

12. Saunders and Pendleton, "Recount Given until 5 p.m.," A1.

13. Gary Fineout, "Bush, Gore Await Ruling; The Election May Hinge on a State Court Decision on Whether to Allow a Hand Count to Proceed," *Lakeland Ledger*, November 14, 2000, 1A.

14. Judd, "Ruling Today on Count Deadline."

15. Fineout, "Bush, Gore Await Ruling," 1A.

16. Saunders and Pendleton, "Recount Given Until 5 p.m.," A1.

17. Fineout, "Bush, Gore Await Ruling," 1A.

18. The exercise of discretion, the judge explained, "by its nature, contemplates a decision based upon a weighing and consideration of all attendant facts and circumstances." Did the returns arrive only minutes late? Was there a power outage that made the transmittal of the returns impossible? As related to this instance, significant questions included: "When was the request for a recount made? What reasons were given? When did the Canvassing

Board decide to do a manual recount? What was the basis for determination that such a recount was the appropriate action? How late were the results?" Before ruling out any amended returns, the "Secretary may, and should, consider all of the facts and circumstances," the judge concluded. "Order Granting in Part and Denying in Part Motion for Temporary Injunction," *McDermott v. Harris*, November 14, 2000.

19. "Order Granting in Part and Denying in Part Motion for Temporary Injunction," *McDermott v. Harris*, November 14, 2000. The Volusia County Board immediately appealed this ruling in the 1st District Court of Florida. "Notice of Appeal," *McDermott v. Harris*, November 14, 2000. The Democratic Party also joined in this appeal. Both cases would be joined with a Palm Beach County Canvassing Board case on the legitimacy of hand recounts by the Florida Supreme Court. "Stay Order," *Palm Beach County Canvassing Board v. Harris* (SC00-2346), *Volusia County Canvassing Board v. Harris* (SC00-2348), and *Florida Democratic Party v. Harris* (SC00-2349), Supreme Court of Florida, November 17, 2000.

20. Jackie Hallifax, "Judge Says 5 p.m. Vote Deadline Stands; Both Sides Hail Ruling," AP Wire, November 14, 2000.

21. Broward, Collier, Miami-Dade, and Palm Beach. (Volusia County had completed their recounts in time and were thus able to submit them by the 5:00 p.m. deadline on Tuesday.)

22. Robert Lee to Katherine Harris, "Request of Broward County Canvassing Board to Amend Certification of County Returns after November 14, 2000," November 15, 2000, reprinted in "Interveners' Supplemental Appendix 1," *Palm Beach County Canvassing Board v. Harris*, Supreme Court of Florida, November 16, 2000.

23. Jennifer Edwards to Katherine Harris, November 15, 2000, reprinted in "Interveners' Supplemental Appendix 1," *Palm Beach County Canvassing Board v. Harris*.

24. Miami-Dade Canvassing Board to Katherine Harris, November 15, 2000, reprinted in "Interveners' Supplemental Appendix 1," *Palm Beach County Canvassing Board v. Harris*.

25. Charles Burton to Katherine Harris, November 15, 2000, reprinted in "Interveners' Supplemental Appendix 2," *Palm Beach County Canvassing Board v. Harris*, Supreme Court of Florida, November 16, 2000.

26. "A Statement from the Secretary of State," November 15, 2000, reprinted in "Interveners' Supplemental Appendix 2," *Palm Beach County Canvassing Board v. Harris*. The Democrats anticipated this reaction from Harris. David Boies, *Courting Justice: From NY Yankees v. Major League Baseball to Bush v. Gore, 1997–2000* (New York: Miramax, 2004), 374.

27. See for example, Harris to Lawrence King, chair, Miami-Dade Canvassing Board, November 15, 2000, reprinted in "Interveners' Supplemental Appendix 3," *Palm Beach County Canvassing Board v. Harris*, Supreme Court of Florida, November 16, 2000.

28. "A Statement from the Secretary of State," November 15, 2000, reprinted in "Interveners' Supplemental Appendix 2," *Palm Beach County Canvassing Board v. Harris*.

29. Anne Gearan, "Democrats Arguing for Recounts in Federal, State Courts," AP Wire, November 16, 2000.

30. "Emergency Motion of Democratic Party of Florida and Vice President Al Gore to Compel Compliance with and for Enforcement of Injunction," *McDermott v. Harris*, November 16, 2000. David Boies and Dexter Douglass argued for a "hardball" approach in arguing this matter before Judge Lewis. They proposed calling Katherine Harris to the stand and grilling her on her ties to the Bush team to show how her actions were motivated largely by the goal of electing George W. Bush president. They would also have subpoenaed her records to prove the same points. The public relations–oriented among Gore's advisors

argued against this action. The Gore team's leadership felt that this was too confrontational and would hurt Gore politically. In the end, the public relations argument prevailed. Boies, *Courting Justice*, 378–379.

31. "Order Denying Emergency Motion to Compel Compliance with and for Enforcement of an Injunction," *McDermott v. Harris*, November 17, 2000.

32. The boards filed this "emergency petition for [an] extraordinary writ directed to state officers" under the Florida Supreme Court's original jurisdiction as set out by Article V, Section 3(h)(7), of the Florida constitution. Under these provisions, the Florida Supreme Court has original nonexclusive jurisdiction over such matters as habeas corpus, mandamus, quo warranto, and the Writ of Prohibition. "Nonexclusive" in this context means that these matters did not absolutely have to begin in the supreme court, but could be initiated there should the Court wish to take these matters up directly.

33. "Emergency Petition for Extraordinary Writ (Expedited Consideration Sought)," *Palm Beach County Canvassing Board v. Harris*, case no. SC00-2346, Supreme Court of Florida, November 14, 2000.

34. "Interim Order," *Palm Beach County Canvassing Board v. Katherine Harris and Bob Butterworth*, November 16, 2000.

35. "In order to maintain the status quo, the Court, on its own motion, enjoins the Respondent, Secretary of State and Respondent, the Elections Canvassing Commission, from certifying the results of the November 7, 2000, presidential election, until further order of this Court. It is NOT the intent of this Order to stop the counting and conveying to the Secretary of State the results of absentee ballots or any other ballots." "Stay Order," *Palm Beach County Canvassing Board v. Harris*, *Volusia County Canvassing Board v. Harris*, and *Florida Democratic Party v. Harris*, Supreme Court of Florida, November 17, 2000. Interestingly, on the same day, the U.S. 11th Circuit Court of Appeals sitting in Atlanta ruled against George W. Bush's motion for an injunction to halt recounts. Their reason was that the state proceedings were "not in any way inadequate to preserve for ultimate review in the United States Supreme Court any federal questions arising out of [the state court decisions]." *Touchston v. McDermott*, 234 F 3d 1130, 1133.

36. "Order Accepting Jurisdiction, Setting Oral Argument, and Setting Briefing Scheduling," *Palm Beach County Canvassing Board v. Harris*, *Volusia County Canvassing Board v. Harris*, and *Florida Democratic Party v. Harris*, Supreme Court of Florida, November 17, 2000.

37. On its face, "the statute [did] not include any words of limitation," noted the brief. Rather, "it provide[d] a remedy for *any* type of mistake made in tabulating ballots." This, in turn, was a reading that "comport[ed] with [both] common sense and Article VI Section 1 of the Florida Constitution." For "an accurate vote count is one of the essential foundations of democracy; it ensures that the peoples' expressed views are properly reflected in the outcome of elections." "Joint Brief of Petitioners/Appellants Al Gore, Jr. and Florida Democratic Party," *Palm Beach Canvassing Board v. Harris*, *Volusia County Canvassing Board v. Harris*, and *Florida Democratic Party v. Harris*, Supreme Court of Florida, November 18, 2000.

38. "Joint Brief of Petitioners/Appellants Al Gore, Jr. and Florida Democratic Party," *Palm Beach County Canvassing Board v. Harris*, *Volusia County Canvassing Board v. Harris*, and *Florida Democratic Party v. Harris*, Supreme Court of Florida, November 18, 2000. For a more detailed summary of the Gore brief, see Lynne Rambo, "The Lawyers' Role in Selecting the President: A Complete Legal History, " *Texas Wesleyan Law Review* 8 (Spring 2002): 175–176.

39. "Answer Brief of Petitioners/Appellants Al Gore, Jr. and Florida Democratic Party," *Palm Beach County Canvassing Board v. Harris, Volusia County Canvassing Board v. Harris,* and *Florida Democratic Party v. Harris,* Supreme Court of Florida, November 19, 2000. This brief was filed in response to George W. Bush's initial answer to Gore's initial brief on an issue raised by Broward County's initial brief.

40. "Answer Brief of Intervenor/Respondent George W. Bush," *Palm Beach Canvassing Board v. Harris, Volusia County Canvassing Board v. Harris,* and *Florida Democratic Party v. Harris,* Supreme Court of Florida, November 19, 2000, 6. For a more detailed summary of the Bush Brief, see Rambo, "Lawyers' Role in Selecting the President," 176–177.

41. "Answer Brief of Intervenor/Respondent George W. Bush," 6–7, 8–9.

42. Ibid., 18–19.

43. The primary law in question here was 3 U.S.C. §5—also known as the "safe harbor" provision. Passed in 1887 in response to the chaotic Hayes-Tilden election of 1876, this law was an attempt to provide a set of guidelines to assure no more Electoral College crises. In practical terms, this rule was meant to give states an incentive to (1) have in place a method for resolving election disputes and (2) apply them in a timely manner before they became a problem for Congress. In 2000, the safe harbor day was December 12. One key factor to 3 U.S.C. §5 was that the rules for settling electoral disputes had to be in place by Election Day. Any change in the rules postelection invalidated the process and left the state's electoral votes open to challenge in Congress. See generally Abner Green, *Understanding the 2000 Election: A Guide to the Legal Battles That Decided the Presidency* (New York: New York University Press, 2001), 86–89.

44. Ibid., 42–44.

45. Harris was also unhappy with the Republicans who "not to be outdone, [were] complaining about procedures for manual re-counting and the sanctity of the machine tabulation." "Answer Brief of the Secretary of State and the Elections Canvassing Commission," *Palm Beach County Canvassing Board v. Harris, Volusia County Canvassing Board v. Harris,* and *Florida Democratic Party v. Harris,* Supreme Court of Florida, November 19, 2000, 1–3.

46. "Initial Brief of the Attorney General," *Palm Beach County Canvassing Board v. Harris, Volusia County Canvassing Board v. Harris,* and *Florida Democratic Party v. Harris,* Supreme Court of Florida, November 18, 2000. See also "Reply Brief of the Attorney General," *Palm Beach County Canvassing Board v. Harris, Volusia County Canvassing Board v. Harris,* and *Florida Democratic Party v. Harris,* Supreme Court of Florida, November 19, 2000.

47. "Petitioner Broward County Canvassing Board's and Broward County Supervisor of Election's Initial Brief on the Merits," *Palm Beach County Canvassing Board v. Harris, Volusia County Canvassing Board v. Harris,* and *Florida Democratic Party v. Harris,* Supreme Court of Florida, November 18, 2000, 5. The Broward brief also requested from the justices "specific direction . . . as to the validity of the two-corner rule" for determining valid voter intent. Ibid., 8.

48. The courtroom was so cramped that the justices issued an order before the hearing setting limits on the number of media representatives allowed in the courtroom. See "Press Procedures for Oral Argument," *Palm Beach County Canvassing Board v. Harris, Volusia County Canvassing Board v. Harris,* and *Florida Democratic Party v. Harris,* Supreme Court of Florida, November 17, 2000.

49. Quoted in "Deadlines and 'Will of the Voters' Debated in Florida Supreme Court," *CNN Online,* November 20, 2000, http://archives.cnn.com/2000/ALLPOLITICS/stories/11/20/president.election/index.html.

50. The following is drawn from an unedited, unpaginated transcript of the Court proceedings held on November 20. *Palm Beach County Canvassing Board v. Harris, Volusia County Canvassing Board v. Harris,* and *Florida Democratic Party v. Harris,* Supreme Court of Florida, http://news.findlaw.com/cnn/docs/election2000/fsc1120transcript.html. For accuracy, the transcript was supplemented and revised by newspaper sources. Among the most useful journalistic accounts were: Charles Lane, "Analysis: Law; Familiar Principle Guides State Court," *Washington Post (WP),* November 22, 2000, A1; Bill Sammon, "Bush, Gore Camps Square Off in Florida Court; Wary Justices Eye Dec. 12 Deadline," *Washington Times,* November 21, 2000, A1; Charles Lane, "Analysis; Balancing Finality, Inclusion," *WP,* November 21, 2000, A1; Peter Slevin and Dan Balz, "Fla. High Court Considers Recounts; Justices Focus on Fairness and Calendar," *WP,* November 21, 2000, A1; Jo Becker, "'Results-Oriented' Court Gets Down to Business," *WP,* November 21, 2000, A16; Joe Follick, "High Court Drama," *Tampa Tribune,* November 21, 2000, 1; Jim Saunders, "Court Weighs Recount Arguments Complete, Nation Awaits Florida Justices' Ruling at Issue: Will Harris Be Forced to Accept Votes?," *Florida Times-Union,* November 21, 2000, A–1. See also, Rambo, "Lawyers' Role in Selecting the President," 183–194, for a more detailed description of the oral arguments before the Florida Supreme Court and Florida State University, *Florida Supreme Court Briefs and Opinions,* for a video feed of these proceedings, http://www.law.fsu.edu/library/flsupct/sc00-2346/sc00-2346.html.

51. State law allowed a losing candidate to challenge the election (102.168). Should there not be enough time for a challenge due to the extension of the contest deadline certification date (under 102.166), the result could prove to be a change in the rules in place under which the election was held. As such, this could be seen as a violation of the safe harbor requirements of 3 U.S.C. §5. See Green, *Understanding the 2000 Election,* 92.

52. This was, in fact, one of the Democrats' primary concerns—that once the vote was certified, the war on the public relations front would be lost. See Boies, *Courting Justice,* 382.

53. *Palm Beach County Canvassing Board v. Harris,* 772 So. 2d 1220, 1227–1228.

54. Ibid., 1228–1230.

55. Ibid., 1232–1236. See also Green, *Understanding the 2000 Election,* 53.

56. The "shall be ignored" section (102.111) was found near the end of a discussion that was mostly about the makeup and function of the state elections canvassing commission. The "may be ignored" section (102.112) was part of a statutory section titled "Deadline for submission of county returns to the Department of State; penalties." Not only did this section set out the deadline, but it set $200 per day personal penalties for county canvassing board members whose returns were late. The court argued that Section 102.112 was much more focused on the issue in contention and therefore should be seen as proof of the legislature's general intent in these matters and thus should be controlling. Section 102.111, in turn, was written into law in 1951, while Section 102.112 was adopted in 1989. Green, *Understanding the 2000 Election,* 51.

57. *Palm Beach County Canvassing Board v. Harris,* 772 So. 2d 1220, 1232–1236.

58. Ibid., 1236–1237.

59. Ibid., 1237–1239.

60. At this point, the Court noted how, in oral argument, they had "inquired as to whether the presidential candidates were interested in our consideration of a reopening of the opportunity to request recounts in any additional counties. Neither candidate requested such an opportunity."

61. The court then stated that this deadline would hold true, "provided that the office of the Secretary of State, Division of Elections is open in order to allow receipt thereof. If

the office is not open for this special purpose on Sunday, November 26, 2000, then any amended certifications shall be accepted until 9 a.m. on Monday, November 27, 2000." The court did not explain how it had arrived at the Sunday deadline.

62. *Palm Beach County Canvassing Board v. Harris*, 772 So. 2d 1220, 1240.

63. Dave Boyer and Audrey Hudson, "Reaction to Supreme Court Ruling Predictably Partisan," *Washington Times*, November 22, 2000, A12; David Ballingrud et al., "GOP Takes Loss Hard: Democrats Trade High-Fives," *St. Petersburg Times*, November 22, 2000, 7A.

64. *Pullen v. Milligan*, 561 N.E.2d 585, 611 (Ill. 1990).

65. Boyer and Hudson, "Reaction to Supreme Court Ruling Predictably Partisan," A12; Andrew Cain, "'Dimpled' Ballots Needed for Gore to Score Victory," *Washington Times*, November 22, 2000, A1. This failure on the part of the Florida Supreme Court would have significant ramifications in the case of *Bush v. Gore*.

66. David S. Broder and Matthew Vita, "Analysis: Politics; Bitter Struggle Is Certain to Escalate," *WP*, November 22, 2000, A1; "Text of Remarks by James A. Baker III of the Bush Campaign," *WP*, November 22, 2000, A17; Ballingrud et al., "GOP Takes Loss Hard; Democrats Trade High-Fives," 7A.

67. Broder and Vita, "Analysis: Politics; Bitter Struggle Is Certain to Escalate," A1; "GOP Vows to Battle Back; Democrats Hail Decision, but Still Face Sunday Deadline," *Atlanta Journal and Constitution*, November 22, 2000, A1; Linda Deutsch, "Bush Team Weighing 'Extraordinary' Response to Court Setback," AP Wire, November 22, 2000; Ken Herman, "Bush Believes Activist Judges Are Out to Get His Campaign," Cox News Service, November 22, 2000.

68. Jeffrey Toobin, *Too Close to Call: The Thirty-Six-Day Battle to Decide the 2000 Election* (New York: Random House, 2001), 42.

69. The Eleventh Circuit's rulings in *Touchston v. McDermott* and *Siegel v. Palm Beach County Canvassing Board*, though frustrating for their refusal to deal with the substance of Bush's equal protection arguments, did provide an additional opportunity to seek a Supreme Court review. Unfortunately for Bush, the Supreme Court was not yet willing to deal with the equal protection implications of the Florida recount and denied cert. in these matters. "Order Granting and Denying Cert," *Bush v. Palm Beach County Canvassing Board*, case nos. 00-836 and 00-837, U.S. Supreme Court, November 24, 2000.

70. Toobin, *Too Close to Call*, 182–184. A similar concern being debated within the Bush camp was the usefulness of a U.S. Supreme Court appeal. The numbers coming out of South Florida were not as bad as the Bush team originally had feared. They made it look as if Bush still would be ahead when the new certification deadline arrived. Bush lawyer Robert Zoellick, for instance, argued that there was nothing that the Florida Supreme Court could do that would undermine Bush's lead, so why appeal? This argument was strong enough that Zoellick and Baker (who supported the idea of appealing) wrote a memo for George W. Bush outlining the advantages and disadvantages of continuing the appeal. Among the arguments against appealing were: (1) "if we lose the case, the ruling could backfire on us by posing major political and/or legal impediments to any action by the Florida legislature to overturn Florida court decisions for Gore in the contest proceedings," and (2) "dropping the case would remove a Gore excuse for continuing to litigate and would reinforce a Bush call to rely on the numerous counts of the voting results rather than litigation." Arguments in favor of continuing the appeal included (1) "It would look bad to drop the case now. Furthermore, as long as the case is pending, the Florida Supreme Court is likely to be more careful in ruling on contest proceedings," and (2) "it makes more sense

to maintain the Supreme Court route if we are not absolutely determined to use the legislative route." In the end, Bush chose to continue the appeal. As Zoellick later suggested, "Bush and Cheney wanted legitimacy. They never felt they could get it from the legislature. So they stayed with the Court." Robert Zelnick, *Winning Florida: How the Bush Team Fought the Battle* (Palo Alto, CA: Hoover Institution, 2001), 82–84.

71. See generally text of 3 U.S.C. §5, note 45. See also Rambo, "Lawyers' Role in Selecting the President," 199–200; Stephen A. Siegel, "The Conscientious Congressman's Guide to the Electoral Count Act of 1887," *Florida Law Review* 56 (July 2004): 541–671.

72. Mary Ellen Klas and S. V. Date, "GOP Lawmakers: Florida Supreme Court 'Overstepped'," Cox News Service, November 22, 2000. See also Andrew Miga, "Analysis: High Court Decision Jolts Republicans into Launching an All-Out Presidential Offensive," *Boston Herald*, November 23, 2000, 004.

73. 3 U.S.C. §2.

74. *McPherson v. Blacker*, 146 U.S. 1 (October 17, 1892).

75. Their commission read in part: "To review all relevant federal and state law and the manner in which that law was applied at the state and local levels in the Presidential 2000 election. The select joint committee shall also review the responsibilities and options of the Florida Legislature with respect to final determination of the appointment of Florida's Presidential Electors." *Report and Recommendations: Select Joint Committee on the Manner of Appointment of Presidential Electors*, Florida Legislature, December 4, 2000, 2.

76. "Joint Proclamation," Florida Legislature, December 6, 2000. All of these votes were split along party lines. See generally Rambo, "Lawyers' Role in Selecting the President," 201.

77. Washington Post, *Deadlock*, 162–163; Toobin, *Too Close to Call*, 181, 184–185; Zelnick, *Winning Florida*, 82.

78. "Petition for a Writ of Certiorari," *Bush v. Palm Beach County Canvassing Board*, November 22, 2000, 1.

79. Ibid., i.

80. "Brief in Opposition," *Bush v. Palm Beach County Canvassing Board*, case nos. 00-836 and 00-837, Supreme Court of the United States, November 23, 2000.

81. "Order Granting and Denying Cert," *Bush v. Palm Beach County Canvassing Board*, November 24, 2000.

82. In support of this contention, the brief noted: "Under *any* permissible definition, . . . the Florida Supreme Court's decision in this case imposed new rules. There is simply *no* law enacted prior to Election Day that set forth the deadline of November 26 announced in the decision below or the virtually non-existent range of discretion within which the Secretary of State was allowed to operate. A legislative pronouncement that required (or authorized) late returns to be ignored was inverted into a requirement that late returns be accepted." "Brief for Petitioner," *Bush v. Palm Beach County Canvassing Board*, case nos. 00-836 and 00-837, November 28, 2000, 21 (note 5).

83. The brief also noted: "tellingly, even the Gore respondents do not dispute that a change in the law took place. They simply claim that the Florida Supreme Court's decision does not "'change the rules' *in any way that implicates federal law* [emphasis added—quoting from Gore's initial response to the petition for certiorari]." "Under 3 U.S.C. §5, however, *any* post-election change in the rules governing the appointment of presidential electors (much less the extensive revisions introduced by the Florida Supreme Court in this case) not only implicates federal law, it squarely ignores and overrides the federal requirements and standards enunciated in §5." Ibid., 27.

84. The brief therefore requested that "the state executive branch officials should be freed by this Court to carry out their duties without the unconstitutional interference of the state supreme court." Ibid., 13–14.

85. Ibid. See also generally "Reply Brief for Petitioner Bush," *Bush v. Palm Beach County Canvassing Board*, case nos. 00-836 and 00-837, November 30, 2000.

86. "Brief of Respondents, Al Gore Jr., and Florida Democratic Party," *Bush v. Palm Beach County Canvassing Board*, case nos. 00-836 and 00-837, November 28, 2000, 11–12. The brief later noted that "The act of interpreting and reconciling ambiguous or apparently conflicting statutory provisions is an exercise with which this Court is thoroughly familiar and has never been regarded as the 'making' of law exceeding the bounds of the judicial role." Further, it argued that "The Florida Supreme Court's interpretation of Florida's election law is no different from this Court's interpretation of many federal statutes, interpretations that have often become the target of the rejected criticism that the Court is 'making' law." Ibid., 16. Later still, it noted: "Indeed, the Florida legislature has itself plainly acquiesced in state judicial resolution of election disputes in presidential elections. In Section 102.171, it provided that the legislature, not the courts, should resolve disputes involving elections of state legislators. By contrast, it assigned to the courts the duty of resolving all other election disputes, including those arising in presidential elections. See Fla. Stat. §102.168(1)." Ibid., 20.

87. Ibid., 12.

88. Ibid., 12–13.

89. Ibid., 32, 35. As Gore's lawyers summarized the issue in a later reply brief, "allowing the legislature's manual recount provisions to be given effect is not like changing the rules after the game has been played. It is instead like using a more powerful photo-finish camera—indeed, one already mandated by the legislature—to determine the winner of the race more accurately." Quoted in Linda Greenhouse, "Contesting the Vote: The Supreme Court; While Justices May Not Settle the Dispute Yet, They Could Settle Key Questions," *NYT*, December 1, 2000, A30. See also generally "Supplemental Brief of Respondents Gore and the Florida Democratic Party," and "Reply Brief of Respondents Gore and the Florida Democratic Party," *Bush v. Palm Beach County Canvassing Board*, case nos. 00-836 and 00-837, November 39, 2000.

90. "Response of Harris, et al., to Petition for Writ of Certiorari," *Bush v. Palm Beach County Canvassing Board*, case nos. 00-836 and 00-837, November 24, 2000; "Brief of Respondent Butterworth," *Bush v. Palm Beach County Canvassing Board*, case nos. 00-836 and 00-837, November 28, 2000.

91. "Brief of American Civil Liberties Union" and "Brief of the American Civil Rights Union," *Bush v. Palm Beach County Canvassing Board*, case nos. 00-836 and 00-837, November 28, 2000.

92. See, for example, "Brief of Respondent Palm Beach County Canvassing Board," *Bush v. Palm Beach County Canvassing Board*, case nos. 00-836 and 00-837, November 28, 2000, and "Brief for the State of Alabama, the Attorney General of Alabama, and the Secretary of State of Alabama, as *Amici Curiae*, Supporting Reversal," *Bush v. Palm Beach County Canvassing Board*, case nos. 00-836 and 00-837, November 28, 2000.

93. "Brief of the Florida Senate and House of Representatives as *Amici Curiae* in Support of Neither Party," *Bush v. Palm Beach County Canvassing Board*, case nos. 00-836 and 00-837, November 27, 2000, 1–2, 8.

94. One key factor affecting court proceedings in these matters was the tight time frame in which all this litigation happened. Most of the briefs in *Bush v. Palm Beach County*

Canvassing Board arrived at the Supreme Court only three days before the oral argument. Collectively, these briefs added up to nearly 1,000 pages of text. Even with the help of their law clerks, this was still a lot of material for the justices to take in, understand, and respond to with thoughtful and reasoned questions. This issue is discussed in more detail in chapter 9, which analyzes the Supreme Court's *Bush v. Gore* ruling.

95. We must keep in mind that, by this date, the revised certification deadline was six days past. Bush already had been certified the winner in Florida and Gore had contested the election. In fact, on this day, Gore's lawyers were in the Florida Supreme Court seeking help in forcing the circuit court to count all of the disputed ballots—that court's decisions as to which would lead to the Supreme Court's ruling in *Bush v. Gore*. To stress a point made in chapter 3, these events were very compressed in time, and many litigations and actions were taking place simultaneously.

96. "Brief for Petitioner," *Bush v. Palm Beach County Canvassing Board*, case nos. 00-836 and 00-837, November 28, 2000, 27.

97. The following quotes are taken from a transcript of the proceedings published in the *NYT* on December 2, 2000, A12. A similar transcript is available at "FindLaw's Election 2000 Special Coverage," http://fll.findlaw.com/news.findlaw.com/cnn/docs/election2000/ussctranscript1201.pdf. Unless otherwise noted, all quotes are taken from the *NYT* transcript as checked for accuracy against the Findlaw transcript.

98. Or not, as the case might be. Scalia's reading that Article II placed state legislative action above the state constitution was plausible, but not the only possible reading. See generally discussion below. See also Green, *Understanding the 2000 Election*, 94–99.

99. *Bush v. Palm Beach County Canvassing Board*, 531 U.S. 70, 78.

100. This was a quote from *Minnesota v. National Tea Co.*, 309 U.S. 551, 555 (1940).

101. Specifically, the justices were "unclear as to the extent to which the Florida Supreme Court saw the Florida Constitution as circumscribing the legislature's authority under Art. II, §1, cl. 2" and how much "consideration the Florida Supreme Court accorded to 3 U.S.C. §5" in shaping their rulings. *Bush v. Palm Beach County Canvassing Board*, 531 U.S. 70, 78.

102. Zelnick, *Winning Florida*, 89, points out that the Court could rule this way in the interest of unity because the "price of unity was at this point cheap. . . . George W. Bush had already achieved certification and two of the three recount counties had failed to meet even the extended deadline."

103. *Palm Beach County Canvassing Board v. Harris*, 772 So. 2d 1273, 1289–1290.

104. Justice Sandra Day O'Connor was reportedly furious over the Florida Supreme Court's behavior in these matters. Her anger was so great that she even rebuked the Florida justices during oral argument in *Bush v. Gore*. Zelnick, *Winning Florida*, 91.

105. *Northern Securities Co. v. United States*, 193 U.S. 197, 400–401 (1904) (Holmes, J., dissenting).

106. See Larry Kramer, "The Supreme Court in Politics," in Jack Rakove, ed., *The Unfinished Election of 2000; Leading Scholars Examine America's Strangest Election* (New York: Basic Books, 2001), 115–117.

107. As Stanford law professor Pamela Karlan explains: "The Florida justices applied long-honored rules for interpreting competing laws. But . . . different judges take different approaches to interpreting laws, and there is a range of acceptable views. 'Some judges believe very much you just read the words of the statute, and that tells you everything you need to know.'" (For example, Supreme Court Justice Antonin Scalia.) "'Others say if a literal, wooden reading of statute doesn't get you to the meaning, you take a more-expansive view.'" (For example, the Florida Supreme Court.) "'This [ruling] fell in the boundaries,' she said.

'Was it the only approach to the question? No, but it was a reasonable one.'" "Judicial Activism Divides the Parties Once Again," *Florida Times-Union*, November 24, 2000, A-6.

6. Ballots before the Bench

1. These include, in no particular order of importance, the ongoing lawsuits over overseas military absentee ballots (still being argued at that time in multiple courts); improperly issued absentee ballots in Seminole and Martin Counties; the certification deadline case before the U.S. Supreme Court; and the soon-to-be-filed race-based vote dilution suits out of Duval County by the NAACP. Even the Palm Beach County butterfly ballot case was still active (though in its final stages). Meanwhile, George W. Bush's original suit before Judge Middlebrooks was still on appeal to the U.S. Court of Appeals for the Eleventh Circuit. To this list we can add the contest phase litigations. Any one of these lawsuits had the potential to end the election.

2. "Complaint to Contest Election," *Gore v. Harris*, case no. 00-2808, Circuit Court for the 2nd Judicial Circuit of Florida, November 27, 2000, 2–4.

3. Bush's defenders noted that this was the result of errors during the recount process, when some ballots were not counted. Contacted by the board for instructions, Katherine Harris's office told them just to send in the original ballot count. Robert Zelnick, *Winning Florida: How the Bush Team Fought the Battle* (Palo Alto, CA: Hoover Institution, 2001), 103.

4. "Complaint to Contest Election," *Gore v. Harris*, Circuit Court for the 2nd Judicial Circuit of Florida, November 27, 2000, 2–4.

5. Ibid., 8. The quote is from Dexter Filkins and Dana Canedy, "Counting the Vote: Miami-Dade County; Protest Influenced Miami-Dade's Decision to Stop Recount," *New York Times (NYT)*, November 24, 2000, A41.

6. "Complaint to Contest Election," *Gore v. Harris*, Circuit Court for the 2nd Judicial Circuit of Florida, November 27, 2000, 12. See also Zelnick, *Winning Florida*, 103.

7. The new board member in question was Marianne Marshall. The replaced board member was David Howard. The problem was that under Florida law no candidate who had had an opponent run against him or her in the election just passed could serve on a county canvassing board. *Florida Statutes* (2000), Title IX, Section 102.141. Marshall (argued the Gore complaint) had been in just such a challenged race; thus, a straight reading of the statute prohibited her from serving on the canvassing board. See "Complaint to Contest Election," *Gore v. Harris*, Circuit Court for the 2nd Judicial Circuit of Florida, November 27, 2000, 12. See also, Zelnick, *Winning Florida*, 103–104, for a differing view of Marshall's legitimacy.

8. "Complaint to Contest Election," *Gore v. Harris*, Circuit Court for the 2nd Judicial Circuit of Florida, November 27, 2000, 10–19.

9. Ibid., 19–22.

10. Mike Williams, "Gore Vows to Contest Miami Tally," *Atlanta Journal and Constitution*, November 24, 2000, 1A; "Certification Won't Be End in Florida Vote: Both Sides Could Challenge Election," Florida *Times-Union*, November 25, 2000, A-7. See also "Gore Plans to Contest Fla. County: Staff Says He Won't Concede Even If Bush Victory Declared," *Advocate* (Baton Rouge, Louisiana), November 24, 2000, 1A.

11. David Boies, *Courting Justice: From NY Yankees v. Major League Baseball to Bush v. Gore, 1997–2000* (New York: Miramax, 2004), 385.

12. Washington Post, *Deadlock: The Inside Story of America's Closest Election* (New York: PublicAffairs, 2001), 159–160.

13. Jeffrey Toobin, *Too Close to Call: The Thirty-Six-Day Battle to Decide the 2000 Election* (New York: Random House, 2001), 202; Washington Post, *Deadlock*, 165–166.

14. The gamble to extend the protest phase of the election had shrunk the period available for completing a protest. Even merely normal speed on the judge's part was dangerous. The judge needed to work fast lest the clock run out before the contest was heard, the ballots counted, and Gore had gained the necessary 538 votes. Anything less was a guaranteed loss for Gore.

15. Boies, *Courting Justice*, 412–413; Washington Post, *Deadlock*, 165–166; Zelnick, *Winning Florida*, 106, noted from a different perspective that "Sauls, in short, was about as good a selection to preside over the contest trial as the Bush team could have hoped for, and as tough as the Gore camp could have feared."

16. According to Toobin, *Too Close to Call*, 203, Douglass assumed that they would not draw Sauls as Sauls was currently hearing cases away from Tallahassee, riding circuit in the smaller counties that along with Leon County made up the 2nd Judicial Circuit Court. Beside which, he figured that they only had a one in five chance of getting Sauls under normal circumstances anyhow.

17. "Majority Want Gore to Concede," *Atlanta Journal and Constitution*, November 28, 2000, 1A; Sean Scully, "Democrats Throw Support behind Gore Challenges," *Washington Times*, November 28, 2000, A9; Susan Crabtree, "Impatience with Gore Growing," *Roll Call*, November 30, 2000; Joan McKinney, "GOP Representatives Urge Gore to Concede," *Advocate* (Baton Rouge, Louisiana), November 30, 2000, 7-A.

18. "Emergency Motion to Commence Counting of Votes in Miami Dade and Palm Beach Counties" and "Motion to Enter Expedited Scheduling Order," *Gore v. Harris*, Circuit Court for the 2nd Judicial Circuit of Florida, November 28, 2000. Quote in Toobin, *Too Close to Call*, 211. See also, Washington Post, *Deadlock*, 166–167; Boies, *Courting Justice*, 414–415. Boies and Douglass also filed a number of other motions to speed up the procedures. "Emergency Motion to Shorten Time and Request for an Emergency Hearing," *Gore v. Harris*, Circuit Court for the 2nd Judicial Circuit of Florida, November 27, 2000.

19. Washington Post, *Deadlock*, 168–169; Boies, *Courting Justice*, 415–417.

20. Washington Post, *Deadlock*, 167–168; Toobin, *Too Close to Call*, 212; Zelnick, *Winning Florida*, 108. See also, "Notice of Objection to Plaintiff's 'Expedited Trial Calendar,'" *Gore v. Harris*, Circuit Court for the 2nd Judicial Circuit of Florida, November 28, 2000; "[Defendant's] Witness List," *Gore v. Harris*, Circuit Court for the 2nd Judicial Circuit of Florida, November 30, 2000. Bush had also filed a motion to dismiss the case, arguing that Gore's contest motion was untimely and that by not naming all twenty-five Bush electors (now officially designated as electors following Harris's certification), Gore's motion was technically inadequate. "Motion and Memorandum in Support of Defendant George W. Bush and Dick Cheney's Motion to Dismiss for Lack of Subject Matter Jurisdiction, Failure to Name Indispensable Parties and Failure to State a Claim," *Gore v. Harris*, Circuit Court for the 2nd Judicial Circuit of Florida, November 30, 2000. On this motion, see also Lynne Rambo, "The Lawyers' Role in Selecting the President: A Complete Legal History," *Texas Wesleyan Law Review* 8 (Spring 2002): 219.

21. "Order Requiring the Delivery of Certain Ballots from Palm Beach and Miami Dade Counties," *Gore v. Harris*, Circuit Court for the 2nd Judicial Circuit of Florida, November 29, 2000; Washington Post, *Deadlock*, 168–169; Boies, *Courting Justice*, 415–417.

22. Boies, *Courting Justice*, 419.

23. Prior to this hearing, both sides filed motions with Judge Sauls and (on the Gore side) with the Florida Supreme Court. The Gore motions asked for the court to speed up

the proceedings while the Bush motions asked for more time. "Petition for Writ of Mandamus or Other Writ. Or, in the Alternative, Review of Trial Court Rulings. And Brief of Appellants," *Gore v. Harris*, case no. SC00-2385, Supreme Court of Florida, November 30, 2000. See also Roberto Suro, "Gore Asks Fla. High Court to Take Up Suit; Vice President Seeks to Speed Recount Appeal as Bush Expands Legal Attack," *Washington Post (WP)*, December 1, 2000, A18. "Order in Gore Petition," *Gore v. Harris*, Supreme Court of Florida, December 1, 2000. "Prehearing Brief on Issues to be Decided," *Gore v. Harris*, Circuit Court for the 2nd Judicial Circuit of Florida, December 1, 2000, 1–2. See also Toobin, *Too Close to Call*, 212–213.

24. Republicans, perhaps not realizing Boies's strategy of losing fast, were surprised at Boies's calling only two witnesses. One of their strongest worries was that Boies would petition the court to allow one of his experts to examine the disputed Miami-Dade ballots and then seek to bring this information into the record via that expert's testimony. Zelnick, *Winning Florida*, 107–108, 111–112.

25. Toobin, *Too Close to Call*, 216–217; Rambo, "Lawyers' Role in Selecting the President," 220–221. Zelnick, *Winning Florida*, 108–110, summarizes the testimony of Gore's expert witnesses in detail.

26. Zelnick, *Winning Florida*, 111–112.

27. Toobin, *Too Close to Call*, 120–122. Rambo, "Lawyers' Role in Selecting the President," 223–230. Zelnick, *Winning Florida*, 113–115, summarizes the testimony of Bush's expert witnesses in detail.

28. On redirect, however, Boies was able somewhat to save the day, when he had a Palm Beach Votomatic machine brought into the courtroom. In the process of setting it up, chads actually began to fall in large numbers from the compartment that held the separated chads—it was filled past overflow—thus proving part of Brace's earlier testimony. Rambo, "Lawyers' Role in Selecting the President," 222.

29. Toobin, *Too Close to Call*, 218–220; Zelnick, *Winning Florida*, 110–111.

30. Toobin, *Too Close to Call*, 221–222; Zelnick, *Winning Florida*, 115–116.

31. "Transcript of Judge Sauls' Ruling," *Gore v. Harris*, Circuit Court for the Second Judicial Circuit of Florida, December 4, 2000. See also Rambo, "Lawyers' Role in Selecting the President," 231–234, for a summary of Judge Sauls's ruling.

32. Indeed, continued the brief, "numerous Florida cases specifically state that the court's [sic] reviewed only the ballots contested by the plaintiff." "Brief for Appellants, or in the Alternative, Petition for Writ of Mandamus or Other Writs," *Gore v. Harris*, Supreme Court of Florida, December 6, 2000, 13, 23. (Given the shortness of time, this brief was not paginated. Page numbers in these notes are therefore derived by counting from the very first page to the last, including all cover/signature pages.)

33. True, the brief continued, "one ground for an election contest [was] an error or misconduct by members of the canvassing board, . . . [yet] the statute also authorize[d] a challenge based on '[r]eceipt of a number of illegal votes or rejection of a number of legal votes sufficient to change or place in doubt the result of the election,' §102.168(3)(c)." This provision, in turn, required "only proof that a potentially decisive number of valid votes were not counted, and focuses solely on the votes themselves; it neither call[ed] for 'review' of the Canvassing Board's decisions, nor suggest[ed] that the Board's decisions might be owed any deference." Hence, "without the citation of any case interpreting §102.168," and even though "§102.168 provide[d] for an original judicial proceeding to contest the rejection or receipt of particular ballots," the judge was refusing to count ballots that had "never been reviewed, and no 'discretion' as to what they mean ha[d] ever been exercised." "Brief

for Appellants, or in the Alternative, Petition for Writ of Mandamus or Other Writs," *Gore v. Harris*, Supreme Court of Florida, December 6, 2000, 13, 24.

34. Worse yet, the brief added, this "holding impose[d] a standard that actually [was] higher than plaintiffs' burden for prevailing on the merits." How could the plaintiff "be required to prove the entire case before the trial court examines what this Court [the Florida Supreme Court] ha[d] characterized as the 'best evidence' available?" It did not make sense. It also contradicted legal precedent. In past election contests, plaintiffs were "not required to prove their case before the evidence (i.e., the ballots) [were] considered. The ballots [*were*] the proof"—a point made most obvious in those cases in which the trial court reviewed the ballots, but later ruled against the plaintiff." "Brief for Appellants, or in the Alternative, Petition for Writ of Mandamus or Other Writs," *Gore v. Harris*, Supreme Court of Florida, December 6, 2000, 13–14, 27.

35. Ibid., 15, 28.

36. "Brief for Appellants, or in the Alternative, Petition for Writ of Mandamus or Other Writs," *Gore v. Harris*, Supreme Court of Florida, December 6, 2000, 31–32.

37. "Amended Brief of Appellees George W. Bush and Dick Cheney," *Gore v. Harris*, Supreme Court of Florida, December 6, 2000, 23–27.

38. *Florida Statutes* (2000), Title IX, Section 102.168.

39. On this point generally, see Rambo, "Lawyers' Role in Selecting the President," 271–272.

40. "Amended Brief of Appellees George W. Bush and Dick Cheney," *Gore v. Harris*, Supreme Court of Florida, December 6, 2000, 44–45.

41. On this point generally, see Rambo, "Lawyers' Role in Selecting the President," 271–272.

42. "Transcript of Judge Sauls's Ruling," *Gore v. Harris*, Circuit Court for the 2nd Judicial Circuit of Florida, December 4, 2000, 12.

43. Jackie Hallifax, "Justices Take Lead in Oral Arguments with Rapid-Fire Questions," AP Wire, December 7, 2000.

44. Lucy Morgan, "Justices Chastened but Full of Questions," *St. Petersburg Times*, December 8, 2000, 10A.

45. Appellate courts have a specific job. They do not rehear trials. They do not reexamine evidence or listen to witnesses. Their job is to ensure that the trial judge applied the law—both procedurally and substantively—correctly. Once the trial court has determined the facts of a case (the "who," "what," and "when" of the dispute), this fact pattern is held to be closed and set. All later decisions about the law are based on the fact pattern set at the trial level. Justice Shaw's question was rooted in this functional limitation.

46. "Unofficial Transcript," *Gore v. Harris*, Supreme Court of Florida, December 7, 2000, *Washington Post* OnPolitics Web site, http://www.washingtonpost.com/wsrv/on politics/elections/courttext120700.htm. As a Web document, this transcript is not paginated. A slightly different unofficial transcript can be found at "Arguments before the Florida Supreme Court on the Presidential Recount," *NYT*, December 8, 2000, A34–36. All quotes are taken from the *WP* transcript.

47. David R. Guarino, "Election 2000: Justices Get Straight to the Point," *Boston Herald*, December 8, 2000, 004.

48. Greg B. Smith, "Lawyers Clocked in Fight over Recount," *New York Daily News*, December 8, 2000, 2.

49. The justices in the majority were Anstead, Pariente, Lewis, and Quince. The chief justice, along with Justices Shaw and Harding, dissented.

50. *Gore v. Harris*, 772 So. 2d 1243, 1247–1248.

51. Ibid., 1253. The justices went on to explain: "We are dealing with the essence of the structure of our democratic society; with the interrelationship, within that framework, between the United States Constitution and the statutory scheme established pursuant to that authority by the Florida Legislature." In consequence of this fact, the "election should be determined by a careful examination of the votes of Florida's citizens and not by strategies extraneous to the voting process. This essential principle, that the outcome of elections be determined by the will of the voters, forms the foundation of the election code enacted by the Florida Legislature and has been consistently applied by this Court in resolving elections disputes." Ibid.

52. Ibid., 1255.

53. Ibid., 1243, 1254.

54. Ibid., 1255.

55. Ibid., 1256–1257. In defending this point, the majority not only pointed to past precedents of Florida law, but also noted, "Not surprisingly, other states also have recognized this principle." For example, they pointed to *Delahunt v. Johnston*, 423 Mass. 731, 671 N.E.2d 1241 (Mass. 1996) (holding that a vote should be counted as a legal vote if it properly indicates the voter's intent with reasonable certainty); *Duffy v. Mortenson*, 497 N.W.2d 437 (S.D. 1993) (applying the rule that every marking found where a vote should be should be treated as an intended vote in the absence of clear evidence to the clear contrary); and *Pullen v. Mulligan*, 138 Ill. 2d 21, 561 N.E.2d 585, 149 Ill. Dec. 215 (Ill. 1990) (holding that votes could be recounted by manual means to the extent that the voter's intent could be determined with reasonable certainty, despite the existence of a statute that provided that punch card ballots were to be recounted by automated tabulation equipment). Ibid.

56. *Gore v. Harris*, 772 So. 2d 1243, 1259.

57. Ibid., 1260–1262.

58. This reference was, in part, a direct response to the dissents. Responding to the two dissents in a footnote, the majority noted: "The dissents would have us throw up our hands and say that because of looming deadlines and practical difficulties we should give up any attempt to have the election of the presidential electors rest upon the vote of Florida citizens as mandated by the Legislature. While we agree that practical difficulties may well end up controlling the outcome of the election we vigorously disagree that we should therefore abandon our responsibility to resolve this election dispute under the rule of law. We can only do the best we can to carry out our sworn responsibilities to the justice system and its role in this process. We, and our dissenting colleagues, have simply done the best we can, and remain confident that others charged with similar heavy responsibilities will also do the best they can to fulfill their duties as they see them."

59. *Gore v. Harris*, 772 So. 2d 1243, 1262.

60. Ibid., 1262.

61. "Where a contestant alleges that the canvassing board has rejected a number of legal votes 'sufficient to change or place in doubt the result of the election' due to the board's decision to curtail or deny a manual recount," noted the justice, "the circuit judge should examine this issue *de novo* and not under an abuse of discretion standard." Ibid., 1271.

62. Ibid., 1270–1271.

63. "I read the statute as applying to *statewide results* in statewide elections," argued the justice. "Vice President Gore, as the unsuccessful candidate statewide, could contest the election results. However, [Gore] . . . had an obligation to show, by a preponderance of the evidence, that the outcome of the *statewide election* would likely be changed by the relief

they sought [emphasis added]." He failed. "It would be improper to permit Appellants to carry their burden in a statewide election by merely demonstrating that there were a sufficient number of no-votes that could have changed the returns in isolated counties. Recounting a subset of counties selected by the Appellants does not answer the ultimate question of whether a sufficient number of uncounted legal votes could be recovered from the statewide 'no-votes' to change the result of the statewide election. At most, such a procedure only demonstrates that the losing candidate would have had greater success in the subset of counties most favorable to that candidate." Ibid., 1271–1272.

64. "Even if such a recount were possible," the justice noted, "speed would come at the expense of accuracy, and it would be difficult to put any faith or credibility in a vote total achieved under such chaotic conditions." Ibid., 1272–1273.

65. Ibid., 1273.

66. Ibid., 1263.

67. "Judicial restraint in respect to elections is absolutely necessary because the health of our democracy depends on elections being decided by voters—not by judges. We must have the self-discipline not to become embroiled in political contests whenever a judicial majority subjectively concludes to do so because the majority perceives it is 'the right thing to do.' Elections involve the other branches of government. A lack of self-discipline in being involved in elections, especially by a court of last resort, always has the potential of leading to a crisis with the other branches of government and raises serious separation-of-powers concerns." Ibid., 1264–1265.

68. Ibid., 1264–1265.

69. Ibid., 1269–1270.

70. Washington Post, *Deadlock*, 202–203.

71. Boies, *Courting Justice*, 429–430; Toobin, *Too Close to Call*, 241–243. This had been the Catch–22 trap that the Supreme Court had avoided by not providing a closer definition of proof of a voter's intent. As David Boies noted in his autobiography, the Republican strategy was: "if no specific standard is set, complain about the absence of a single statewide standard; if a standard is set, complain that the courts have altered the rules after Election Day, forfeiting safe harbor protections and raising the specter that the court was not merely interpreting existing statutes but impermissibly writing rules itself." The result was a trap that the Florida courts would never quite get away from. Ibid. According to the *WP*, Beck knew that he was unlikely to win this fight before Judge Lewis. Rather, he was arguing to the few U.S. Supreme Court clerks—and hopefully justices—that might be watching the proceedings on television. His point was that "you must have a coherent standard that applies uniformly throughout the State of Florida." Given that there was unlikely to be much uniformity in the counting under Judge Lewis's intent standard order, this was proof of their ongoing argument that without set standards, vote counting by hand was a violation of the due process and equal protection clauses. Washington Post, *Deadlock*, 208–210.

72. Toobin, *Too Close to Call*, 242–243; Washington Post, *Deadlock*, 208–210; Boies, *Courting Justice*, 430–431.

73. Dexter Filkins and Dana Canedy, "U.S. Supreme Court's Ruling Stops Florida's Election Workers in Their Tracks," *NYT*, December 10, 2000, A43.

74. In Hillsborough County, for example, the canvassing board counted only "hanging chads," while in Pinellas County, the board counted some dimpled chads as long as they appeared in a pattern on the ballot; in some counties it took only a majority vote for a ballot

to be counted, while in others the affirmation of all three board members was necessary. Ibid. See also Rambo, "Lawyers' Role in Selecting the President," 291–292.

75. Rambo, "Lawyers' Role in Selecting the President," 291–292.

76. Dan Balz, "Divided U.S. Supreme Court Orders Freeze on Fla. Count; 5 Justices Grant Bush Stay; Hearing Set for Monday," *WP*, December 10, 2000, A1.

77. "Opposition of Respondent Albert Gore, Jr. to Emergency Motion for a Stay Pending Certiorari," *Bush v. Gore*, case no. 00 A 504, U.S. Supreme Court, December 8, 2000.

78. One of the grounds necessary for any stay to be ordered by the Supreme Court is, in fact, "a significant probability of reversal"—along with proof of immediate harm to the petitioner. Otherwise, the Court generally will not stay the actions of a lower court while hearing an appeal. Many, however, took Scalia's words to indicate that the minds of at least five of the justices already had been made up. At the least, legal scholars were surprised at the Court's stay ruling and Justice Scalia's statement. See Joe Battenfeld, "Presidential Race Courting Chaos," *Boston Herald*, December 10, 2000, 2 ("'It is quite surprising for the court to have issued the stay in the current time frame. . . . It's really not for the court to protect the Bush administration from political embarrassment.'"—quoting Gil Kujovich, Professor of Law, Vermont Law School).

79. "On Application for Stay," *Bush v. Gore*, 531 U. S. 1046. David Boies's immediate response to this argument was, "What possible irreparable harm could they be talking about?" Later, Boies questioned the stay's legitimacy in even stronger terms. Scalia, Boies noted, "doesn't want to have the legitimacy of [a potential Bush] presidency undercut by the fact that people will know there were more votes for Vice President Gore." Quoted in Howard Gillman, *The Votes That Counted: How the Court Decided the 2000 Presidential Election* (Chicago: University of Chicago Press, 2001), 126. See also generally Toobin, *Too Close to Call*, 248.

7. "A Florida Hurricane Heading to Washington"

1. *This Honorable Court: Part Two: Inside the Marble Temple*, PBS video, produced by WETA-TV (Washington, DC: Greater Washington Educational Telecommunications Association, May 1988).

2. Ted Olson, who argued both U.S. Supreme Court cases for George W. Bush, noted, "[T]he justices regard their responsibilities differently since theirs is the final court, with no further appeals possible. Since they carry the ultimate responsibility to determine what the law is and what the Constitution requires, they examine issues more broadly than other judges." Interview of Ted Olson by Ken Adelman, *Washingtonian*, February, 2001, 25.

3. "Usually one has months to prepare the briefs and weeks to get ready for oral argument. You read every relevant case, get familiar with all the statutes and their legislative history. We stage moot courts in our conference room with the lawyers familiar with the case pretending to be justices. They fling hard questions, and you go through your argument. I try to do that two or three times before each Supreme Court argument." Ibid., 25.

4. See Jeff Bleich, "Columns: Supreme Court Watch: Arguing before the Court," *San Francisco Attorney* 28 (February/March 2002): 16. See more generally John Flynn Rooney, "Lawyers Share Memories of Preparing for High Court," *Chicago Daily Law Bulletin*, February 23, 2004, 1, and Alexander Wohl, "Supreme Court/Litigation: Rehearsal Strategies," *American Bar Association Journal* 83 (September 1997): 56.

5. This work was on top of their usual crushing caseload duties. As Ted Olson notes,

the justices "had to read the two sets of petitions and briefs—which is a huge amount of work—on two cases in ten days. I heard that Justice Clarence Thomas commented to some students that he pulled his first all nighter since law school." Interview of Ted Olson by Ken Adelman, 25.

6. Kamen, "Challenge Like No Other: High-Stakes Case at 'Breakneck Speed,'" *Washington Post*, December 12, 2000, A34.

7. For a classic study of the Court's workings, including examples of how opinion writing can transform the outcome of a Supreme Court case, see Alexander M. Bickel, *The Unpublished Opinions of Mr. Justice Brandeis: The Supreme Court at Work* (Cambridge, MA: Belknap Press, 1957).

8. The justices in the majority, for instance, often have different reasons for their votes. The finished opinion, as a result, must account for all of these differing rationales lest the majority fall apart. Multiple drafts and edits are often required to get the wording just right so that each justice in the majority will sign the opinion. Then there are the potential dissents arising from the justices in the minority. A good majority opinion takes into account the views of the minority and attempts to counter the dissenters' arguments. This too can require multiple drafts. Even concurrences that agree with the results but differ in reasoning or remedy can demand another round of editing and revising. (In fact, threatening a concurrence or a dissent is one technique that justices often use to force the revision of an opinion to better reflect their own views.) See generally Michael Herz, "The Supreme Court in Real Time: Haste, Waste, and *Bush v. Gore*," *Akron Law Review* 35 (2002): 185–204.

9. Quoted in Hon. Abner Mikva, "The Scope of Equal Protection," *University of Chicago Legal Forum* (2002): 8.

10. Ted Olson notes how, when arguing before the Supreme Court, "you're not addressing one judge or even three, as happens in appeals courts. You have to factor in nine perspectives, which may differ markedly. It ends up almost like arguing before nine courts." Interview of Ted Olson by Ken Adelman, 25. See also comments of Burt Neubourn on *This Honorable Court: Part Two: Inside the Marble Temple*.

11. Martin Garbus, "We've Just Come through Best Lawyering of Our Lives," *New York Observer*, December 11, 2000, 6.

12. Elaine Sciolino, "For Supreme Court Hearing, Gore Picks Lawyer Handling Florida Case," *New York Times (NYT)*, December 11, 2000, A26. See also, David Boies, *Courting Justice: From NY Yankees v. Major League Baseball to Bush v. Gore, 1997–2000* (New York: Miramax, 2006), 436–439: "[O]ur only chance to win was to convince one of the five majority justices to break ranks. No one held out any hope of moving the three most committed Republicans on the Court—Rehnquist, Scalia, and Thomas. It had to be either O'Connor or Kennedy, and our best chance with them was to convince them that what the Florida courts were doing was merely implementing settled state law. The chance might not be a great one, but it was the only one we had, and I was in the best position to take it (438)."

13. Jake Tapper, "Boies v. Olson," *Salon.com*, November 19, 2000, http://archive.salon.com/politics/feature/2000/11/19/lawyers; "David Boies: Lawyer of the Year," *Time.com*, http://www.time.com/time/poy2000/runnersup.html.

14. Garbus, "We've Just Come through Best Lawyering of Our Lives," 6; Gary Kane, "Attorneys Battle for the Presidency," Cox News Service, December 6, 2000.

15. Tapper, "Boies v. Olson."

16. David Margolick, Evgenia Peretz, and Michael Shnayerson, "The Path to Florida," *Vanity Fair* (October 2004) (online version, available via Lexis/Nexis).

17. "Emergency Application for a Stay of Enforcement of the Judgment below Pending

the Filing and Disposition of a Petition for a Writ of Certiorari to the Supreme Court of Florida," *Bush v. Gore*, case no. 00-949, U.S. Supreme Court, December 8, 2000, 2.

18. "Brief for Petitioners," *Bush v. Gore*, December 9, 2000, 20.

19. Ibid., 16–17, 19–25.

20. The brief then argued, "Under the scheme devised by the court below, however, there literally is no point in the safeguards provided for such recounts at the protest stage. Indeed, there is no point in any candidate or canvassing board ever going through the protest process or in conducting a manual recount. To achieve the result reached by the court below, the legislature might as well have dispensed with the bulk of the election code and simply provided for the shipment of all ballots to the circuit court immediately following the certification of the election results. Indeed, if Florida law could plausibly be read in the manner announced by the court below, the court's own earlier efforts—merely two weeks ago—to extend the certification deadline so as to permit additional manual recounts are completely inexplicable." Ibid., 25.

21. Ibid., 21–28.

22. In arguing this point, Bush pointed directly to the *McPherson* precedents as discussed by the U.S. Supreme Court in *Bush v. Palm Beach County Canvassing Board*, (case nos. 00-836 and 00-837). Ibid., 29 (citing *McPherson v. Blacker*, 146 U.S. 1, 35 [1892]).

23. Ibid., 17, 28–33.

24. Ibid., 33–38.

25. See "Order Granting and Denying Cert," *Bush v. Palm Beach County Canvassing Board*, U.S. Supreme Court, November 24, 2000.

26. See *Siegel, et al., v. Lepore, et al.*, 120 F. Supp. 2d 1041 (U.S. District Court, SD of Florida); *Touchston v. McDermott*, 234 F.3d 1130 and 234 F.3d 1163 (11th Circuit Court of Appeals). *Siegel v. Lepore* was argued in conjunction with *Touchston v. McDermott*, which was where the circuit court set out its reasons for denying the motion for an injunction and later denying the appeal on the merits.

27. Under this plan, the Bush brief explained, residents of one county might have their votes counted if they had only indented their ballot, whereas in another county, such ballots would not be counted. "Indeed, the 'standards' used in . . . earlier manual recounts [such as Broward or Palm Beach Counties] . . . constituted equal protection violations, since, to the extent 'standards' existed at all, they varied widely from county to county, and even changed from day to day or hour to hour within a single Florida county." "Brief for Petitioners," *Bush v. Gore*, 40–42.

28. Ibid.

29. "With humans making subjective determinations about an absent voter's intent, without standards established by law," explained the brief, "there [was] a very substantial risk that the method for determining how to count a vote will be influenced, consciously or unconsciously, by individual desire for a particular result. That risk [was] heightened significantly here because of the irreversible damage done to the ballots during the recount processes and the clear errors that have occurred during the manual recounts." Ibid., 44–49.

30. Ibid., 49.

31. See generally "Brief of Respondent Albert Gore, Jr.," *Bush v. Gore*, December 9, 2000.

32. Ibid., 1–2.

33. The reference on the right to have one's votes be counted was to the Supreme Court's 1964 ruling in *Reynolds v. Sims*, 377 U.S. 533, 555, in which the Court held that "a consistent line of decisions by this Court in cases involving attempts to deny or restrict the

right of suffrage has made this indelibly clear. It has been repeatedly recognized that all qualified voters have a constitutionally protected right to vote, . . . and to have their votes counted." Further, "the right to vote freely for the candidate of one's choice is of the essence of a democratic society, and any restrictions on that right strike at the heart of representative government."

34. "Brief of Respondent Albert Gore, Jr.," *Bush v. Gore*, December 9, 2000, 1–2.

35. Ibid., 8–9, 13–14.

36. Ibid., 20.

37. Ibid., 15.

38. In reference to this point, the Gore brief referred the justices to *Leanard v. State*, 760 So. 2d 114, 118 (Fla. 2000) (Florida statutes are traditionally construed to preserve judicial review "rather than limiting the subject matter of the appellate courts.") The brief noted that this "[was] a principle with which the Florida Legislature [was] quite familiar." Ibid., 14.

39. Ibid., 13–14.

40. Ibid., 14–16, 21–25. As the brief noted, state constitutions "determined the very nature and composition of the state legislatures" on which Article II, clause 1 conferred power. Because state constitutions typically establish a legislature's quorum requirements, voting rules, and other qualifications and procedures, "any attempt to isolate one from the other would give rise to a host of unforeseen practical and legal problems." Ibid., 21.

41. Ibid., 26–31.

42. Besides which, the brief pointed out, the earlier ruling was issued by a district court, subordinate to the Florida Supreme Court. Hence, "even if that single decision were in point, the decision of the Florida Supreme Court—a superior tribunal—on an issue of statutory interpretation could hardly be deemed a sufficient change in the law that Congress would have intended the state's electors to lose their presumed validity." Ibid., 32.

43. Ibid., 33–41.

44. "Moreover," explained the brief, "with respect to the counting of punch card ballots, most States [did] not attempt specifically to define what particular appearance of the ballot [was] required before a vote [was] to be counted. Even those States that [did] have such standards usually ha[d] a 'catch-all' provision permitting the counting of any ballot that 'otherwise reflect[ed] the intent of the voter.'" In fact, even in those states that "adopted statutory guidelines to assist in ascertaining voter intent, the ultimate goal [was still] to determine how a voter intended to vote." Interestingly, among these states was George W. Bush's own Texas. "If the Florida standard [was] struck as unconstitutional, it [was] difficult to see how statutes such as the Texas election code could survive." Ibid., 43–47.

45. Ibid., 43–47.

46. At this point, Gore's brief pointed to Bush's arguments "that military absentee votes should be counted even if the ballots in question did not comply with various clear requirements of Florida statutory law." Ibid., 50.

47. Ibid., 47–50.

48. The official court transcript for the oral arguments in *Bush v. Gore* does not note the names of the justices asking questions. Unofficial transcripts from the *NYT* ("Contesting the Vote; Excerpts from Arguments before Supreme Court on the Florida Recount," December 12, 2000, A27) do provide this information. The following is taken from the *NYT* transcript as checked for accuracy against the official transcripts. As such, there is no pagination for quotes other than page 27 of section A of the *NYT* of December 12, 2000. Audiotaped copies of the oral arguments from C-Span can be found at the Legal Information

Institute's Web site, http://www.law.cornell.edu/background/election/.

49. "This is serious business," noted Justice Kennedy, "because it indicates how un-moored, untethered the Legislature is from the Constitution of its own state, and it makes every state law issue a federal question. Can you use this theory and say that it creates some sort of presumption of validity that allows us to see whether this—courts or the executive has gone too far? Is that what you're arguing?"

50. On Justice Breyer's actions and motivations, see Jeffrey Toobin, *Too Close to Call: The Thirty-Six-Day Battle to Decide the 2000 Election* (Random House: New York, 2001), 260–261; Washington Post, *Deadlock: The Inside Story of America's Closest Election* (New York: PublicAffairs, 2001), 222–223.

51. Linda Greenhouse, "Justices' Questions Underline Divide on the Whether Hand Recount Can Be Fair," *NYT*, December 12, 2000, A1.

52. Adding to the humor, after mixing up two justices' names, the clueless Klock said, "I will now give up." At that point, Justice Scalia, who often made a joke or two during oral arguments, deadpanned: "Mr. Klock, I'm Scalia."

53. "Nation Awaits Decision That Could Decide Election; Supreme Court Hears Arguments in Crucial Florida Recount Case," *Atlanta Journal and Constitution*, December 11, 2000, 1A; David E. Sanger, "On Their Biggest Day in Court, Rivals Remain True to Form," *NYT*, December 12, 2000, A25; Ron Fournier, "Gore's Last Stand? Court Loss Would Be 'End of the Road,' His Lawyers Say: Camps Enter Historic Court Battle Today," *Charleston Gazette* (West Virginia), December 11, 2000, 1A; David E. Sanger, "Bush's Aides Say an End Is in Sight," *NYT*, December 11, 2000, A1.

54. Andrew Miga, "U.S. Supremes Could Bring Speedy Reaction to Election Chaos; Nation Waits on Court's Last Word," *Boston Herald*, December 11, 2000, 001; Susan Milligan, "Gore's Chance on the Line Today: Court Risks Image, Scholars Say," *Boston Globe*, December 11, 2000, A1; Warren Richey, "A Final Decision at Hand . . . Maybe," *Christian Science Monitor*, December 11, 2000, 1.

8. Headfirst into the Political Thicket

1. David Bianculli, "Networks Fumble, Recover in Moment Worth the Wait," *New York Daily News*, December 13, 2000, 85; Howard Kurtz, "Instant Analysis—and Confusion; Sorting Out a Complicated Decision, Live and on Television," *Washington Post (WP)*, December 13, 2000, C1; Mike Allen and David Montgomery, "A Long Day of Waiting for Decision, Then Chaos; Candidates, Backers, News Media Scramble for Understanding," *WP*, December 13, 2000, A30; David Bianculli, "Matters of Great Wait: News Channels Keep Tuned to Supremes," *New York Daily News*, December 13, 2000, 85. See also Jeff Greenfield, *Oh, Waiter! One Order of Crow: Inside the Strangest Presidential Election Finish in American History* (New York: G. P. Putnam, 2001), 282–288; James Poniewozik, "Down by Law," *Time*, December 25, 2000, http://www.time.com/time/magazine/article/0,9171,998834-1,00.html.

2. Laura Krugman Ray, "The Road to *Bush v. Gore*: The History of the Supreme Court's Use of the *Per Curiam* Opinion," *Nebraska Law Review* 79 (2000): 517–576.

3. Ibid., 575. See also, David Margolick, Evgenia Peretz, and Michael Shnayerson, "The Path to Florida," *Vanity Fair* (October 2004) (online version, available via Lexus/Nexus); Jeffrey Toobin, *Too Close to Call: The Thirty-Six-Day Battle to Decide the 2000 Election* (New York: Random House, 2001), 264–265.

4. *Bush v. Gore*, 531 U.S. 103–104.

5. Of course, explained the per curiam, the state could, "after granting the franchise in the special context of Article II, . . . take back the power to appoint electors." But this was a matter not raised by this case. Ibid., 104.

6. Quoting from *Harper v. Virginia Bd. of Elections*, 383 U.S. 663, 665 (1966), the per curiam noted that "once the franchise is granted to the electorate, lines may not be drawn which are inconsistent with the Equal Protection Clause of the Fourteenth Amendment." Further, the opinion quoted from *Reynolds v. Sims* 377 U.S. 533, 555 (1964): "it must be remembered that 'the right of suffrage can be denied by a debasement or dilution of the weight of a citizen's vote just as effectively as by wholly prohibiting the free exercise of the franchise.'" Ibid., 105.

7. *Gore v. Harris*, 772 So. 2d. 1261–1262. The majority referenced this quote in their per curiam opinion. *Bush v. Gore*, 531 U.S. 120.

8. As to the jurisdictional issue, the per curiam held: "For purposes of resolving the equal protection challenge, it is not necessary to decide whether the Florida Supreme Court had the authority under the legislative scheme for resolving election disputes to define what a legal vote is and to mandate a manual recount implementing that definition." *Bush v. Gore*, 531 U.S. 105.

9. "The law does not refrain from searching for the intent of the actor in a multitude of circumstances; and in some cases the general command to ascertain intent is not susceptible to much further refinement. In this instance, however, the question is not whether to believe a witness but how to interpret the marks or holes or scratches on an inanimate object, a piece of cardboard or paper which, it is said, might not have registered as a vote during the machine count. The fact finder confronts a thing, not a person. The search for intent can [in this instance] be confined by specific rules designed to ensure uniform treatment." Unfortunately, "the want of those rules here has led to unequal evaluation of ballots in various respects." Ibid., 106.

10. Ibid., 106–107. The per curiam further explained: "An early case in our one person, one vote jurisprudence arose when a State accorded arbitrary and disparate treatment to voters in its different counties. *Gray v. Sanders*, 372 U.S. 368 (1963). The Court found a constitutional violation. We relied on these principles in the context of the Presidential selection process in *Moore v. Ogilvie*, 394 U.S. 814 (1969), where we invalidated a county-based procedure that diluted the influence of citizens in larger counties in the nominating process. There we observed that 'the idea that one group can be granted greater voting strength than another is hostile to the one man, one vote basis of our representative government.'" Ibid.

11. Ibid., 107–108. The opinion continued: "Indeed, it is respondent's submission that it would be consistent with the rules of the recount procedures to include whatever partial counts are done by the time of final certification, and we interpret the Florida Supreme Court's decision to permit this. . . . This accommodation no doubt results from the truncated contest period established by the Florida Supreme Court in *Bush I*, at respondents' own urging. The press of time does not diminish the constitutional concern. A desire for speed is not a general excuse for ignoring equal protection guarantees."

12. It was at this point that the Court noted, "Our consideration is limited to the present circumstances, for the problem of equal protection in election processes generally presents many complexities." This particular statement will be discussed in detail below.

13. Ibid., 109. This was not, however, to be taken as a general demand for uniformity in all cases. "The question before the Court is not whether local entities, in the exercise of their expertise, may develop different systems for implementing elections. Instead, we are

presented with a situation where a state court with the power to assure uniformity has ordered a statewide recount with minimal procedural safeguards."

14. Ibid., 105, 107, 109.

15. In addition, added the per curiam, "the Secretary of State has advised that the recount of only a portion of the ballots requires that the vote tabulation equipment be used to screen out undervotes, a function for which the machines were not designed. If a recount of overvotes were also required, perhaps even a second screening would be necessary. Use of the equipment for this purpose, and any new software developed for it, would have to be evaluated for accuracy by the Secretary of State, as required by Fla. Stat. §101.015 (2000)." Ibid., 110.

16. Ibid., 145, 135.

17. Ibid., 109.

18. Ibid., 111.

19. Ray, "Road to *Bush v. Gore*," 574–575.

20. Rehnquist opened his concurrence by stating, "We join the *per curiam* opinion. We write separately because we believe there are additional grounds that require us to reverse the Florida Supreme Court's decision." However, the wording of the concurrence and the general tenor of Rehnquist's and Scalia's questions in the oral argument imply that they viewed these arguments as strong ones, perhaps even stronger than the per curiam's. In fact, many have speculated that Rehnquist's concurrence was his original proposal for the Court's majority opinion, but that he could not generate enough support to offer it as such. *Bush v. Gore*, 531 U.S. 111–112. See generally Margolick, Peretz, and Shnayerson, "Path to Florida."

21. *Bush v. Gore*, 531 U.S. 112–115.

22. Ibid. The Chief Justice concluded this point by noting, somewhat combatively, "This inquiry does not imply a disrespect for state *courts* but rather a respect for the constitutionally prescribed role of state *legislatures*. To attach definitive weight to the pronouncement of a state court, when the very question at issue is whether the court has actually departed from the statutory meaning, would be to abdicate our responsibility to enforce the explicit requirements of Article II." Ibid., 115.

23. Ibid., 115–122.

24. Ibid., 153–156. Breyer was quoting from Alexander M. Bickel, *The Least Dangerous Branch: The Supreme Court at the Bar of Politics*, 2nd ed. (New Haven, CT: Yale University Press, 1986 [orig. ed. 1962]), 184.

25. Quoting from *United States v. Butler*, 297 U.S. 1, 79 (1936) (Stone, J., dissenting).

26. *Bush v. Gore*, 531 U.S. 105, 154, 157–158.

27. Ibid., 145–146.

28. Ibid., 146–147.

29. Ibid., 129.

30. Ibid., 130–133.

31. Ibid., 133–135.

32. Ibid., 123–124.

33. Ibid., 124–126.

34. Ibid., 126–127.

35. Ibid., 127–129.

36. Ibid., 135–141. At this point, Justice Ginsburg noted that "Rarely has this Court rejected outright an interpretation of state law by a state high court." She then went on to attack the chief justice's footnotes, which sought to deny this fact. In particular, she notes how

Fairfax's Devisee v. Hunter's Lessee, 7 Cranch 603 (1813), *NAACP v. Alabama ex rel. Patterson*, 357 U.S. 449 (1958), and *Bouie v. City of Columbia*, 378 U.S. 347 (1964), all cited by the chief justice, were "embedded in historical contexts hardly comparable to the situation here. . . . THE CHIEF JUSTICE's casual citation of these cases might lead one to believe they are part of a larger collection of cases in which we said that the Constitution impelled us to train a skeptical eye on a state court's portrayal of state law. But one would be hard pressed, I think, to find additional cases that fit the mold." Ibid., 139–140.

37. "Even in the rare case in which a State's 'manner' of making and construing laws might implicate a structural constraint," Justice Ginsburg added in a footnote, "Congress, not this Court, [was] likely the proper governmental entity to enforce that constraint." Ibid., 141.

38. Ibid., 141–143.

39. Ibid., 143–144. The usual practice is to begin or end a dissenting opinion with the phrase, "I respectfully dissent." A justice's omission of that adverb signals bitter and vehement disagreement beyond the usual.

40. David Boies, *Courting Justice: From NY Yankees v. Major League Baseball to Bush v. Gore, 1997–2000* (New York: Miramax, 2006), 448.

41. Ibid., 436.

42. Ibid., 448. Boies was, in fact, surprised and saddened by the Court's ruling that, given the shortness of time, "there was now no remedy for this 'unfortunate' forfeiture of the right of citizens to have their votes counted."

43. Ibid., 457.

44. Reports in the media also suggested that Scalia held nothing but disdain for the per curiam opinion's reasoning. The opinion's equal protection logic, according to Scalia, was mediocre and flaccid. "Like we used to say in Brooklyn," he supposedly told a colleague, "it's a piece of shit." Scalia, it should be noted, denied disparaging the majority opinion. On the other hand, he never publicly supported this logic post-decision, either. The quote is taken from Margolick, Peretz, and Shnayerson, "Path to Florida." This article, based on interviews with former Supreme Court law clerks, most from the chambers of the four liberal dissenting justices, proved highly controversial. Many questioned the accuracy of the reporting and attacked the ethics of the clerks who spoke to the reporters. For a critique of this article, see Tony Mauro, "High Court Clerks Bemoan '*Bush v. Gore*' Revelations," *Legal Times*, September 28, 2004, http://www.law.com/jsp/article.jsp?id=1095434485225.

45. Ibid.

9. A Self-Inflicted Wound?

1. On the Hayes-Tilden election in 1876, see Paul Leland Haworth, *The Hayes-Tilden Disputed Presidential Election of 1876* (New York: Russell & Russell, 1966 [orig. pub. 1906]); C. Vann Woodward, *Reunion and Reaction: The Compromise of 1877 and the End of Reconstruction* (New York: Oxford University Press, 1991 [orig. pub. 1956]); Lloyd Robinson, *The Stolen Election: Hayes versus Tilden—1876* (New York: Forge Books, 2001); Roy Morris Jr., *Fraud of the Century: Rutherford B. Hayes, Samuel Tilden, and the Stolen Election of 1876* (New York: Simon & Schuster; 2003); William H. Rehnquist, *Centennial Crisis: The Disputed Election of 1876* (New York: Knopf, 2004).

2. On this subject, see 3 U.S.C. §15.

3. This is why 3 U.S.C. §5 (the "safe harbor" provision) was so important in the Florida context. So long as the state got its vote certified and approved before the safe harbor dead-

line, Florida's certified choice was protected from these challenge provisions. Of course, there was nothing in the safe harbor provisions that required a state to take advantage of these protections, either. Chief Justice Rehnquist was simply wrong in arguing in his concurrence that the safe harbor provision created a hard and fast deadline.

4. 3 U.S.C. §15. See also Thomas H. Neale, *The Electoral College: How It Works in Contemporary Presidential Elections* (Washington, DC: Congressional Research Service, September 28, 2004), 7, http://fpc.state.gov/documents/organization/36762.pdf, and *The Short Guide to Counting Electoral Votes* (December 7, 2000), http://rpc.senate.gov/_files/120700Electoral.pdf.

5. On this point, see Elizabeth Garrett, "Leaving the Decision to Congress," in Cass R. Sunstein and Richard A. Epstein, eds., *The Vote: Bush, Gore and the Supreme Court* (Chicago: University of Chicago Press, 2001), 38–54.

6. See David A. Strauss, "*Bush v. Gore:* What Were They Thinking?" in Sunstein and Epstein, *The Vote*, 184–185.

7. Jack M. Balkin, "Supreme Court Compromises Its Legitimacy," *Boston Globe*, December 12, 2000 (online edition, http://graphics.boston.com/news/politics/campaign2000/news/Supreme_Court_compromises_its_legitimacy+.shtml); Neal Kumar Katyal, "Politics over Principle," *Washington Post (WP)*, December 14, 2000, A35; Ronald Dworkin, "A Badly Flawed Election," *New York Review of Books* (January 11, 2001): 53–54; Alan Dershowitz, *Supreme Injustice: How the High Court Hijacked Election 2000* (New York: Oxford University Press, 2001), 110. See also Ronald Brownstein, "For Every Cheer, There's a Jeer from the Other Camp," *Los Angeles Times*, December 10, 2000, A1; Robert G. Kaiser, "Slim Majority Raises Fear of Court Partisanship," *WP*, December 10, 2000, A32. For a detailed summary of the response to *Bush v. Gore* by legal academics and political pundits—pro and con—see Howard Gillman, *The Votes That Counted: How the Court Decided the 2000 Presidential Election* (Chicago: University of Chicago Press, 2001), 125–129, 151–163.

8. John O. McGinnis, "A Just and Wise Action," *New York Post*, December 14, 2000, 41; John C. Yoo, "In Defense of the Court's Legitimacy," in Sunstein and Epstein, *The Vote*, 240. Nelson Lund, professor of law at George Mason University School of Law, also contended that "*Bush v. Gore* was a straightforward and legally correct decision." Nelson Lund, "The Unbearable Rightness of *Bush v. Gore*," *Cardozo Law Review* 23 (March 2002): 1219–1279.

9. Both quoted in Gary Rosen, "Reconsidering '*Bush v. Gore*,'" *Ethnic News* 111 (June 2001): 35–41. See also Richard A. Epstein, "'In Such Manner as the Legislature Thereof May Direct': The Outcome in *Bush v. Gore* Defended," *University of Chicago Law Review* 68 (Summer 2001): 613–635, for a third defender of the chief justice's concurrence.

10. In conservative columnist Charles Krauthammer's colloquial observation, "Amid the chaos, somebody had to play Daddy. Its earlier admonition having been ignored, the Supreme Court eschewed subtlety and bluntly stopped the Florida Supreme Court in its tracks." Charles Krauthammer, "The Winner in *Bush v. Gore*?" *Time*, December 18, 2000, 104. Or, as the conservative pundit William Safire put it, "You cannot spit in the eye of the nation's highest court without suffering consequences." William Safire, "Biting the Ballot," *New York Times (NYT)*, December 11, 2000, A31. See also, William Safire, "Essay: The Coming Together," *NYT*, December 14, 2000, A39.

11. Richard Posner, *Breaking the Deadlock: The 2000 Election, The Constitution and the Courts* (Princeton: Princeton University Press, 2001), 175–178, concedes that a majority of Florida voters intended to support Al Gore rather than George W. Bush. In fact, Posner ad-

mits that, with better voting technology, Gore very likely would have been elected president. But none of this mattered, he insists. In particular, none of this excused the Florida Supreme Court's unconstitutional actions nor negated the necessity of the U.S. Supreme Court's intervention. In our representative democracy, Posner explains, with its inevitable concern for order and stability, an election is "a formal procedure, a statutory artifact," not "a public-opinion poll." Rather, what matters in elections is not some inchoate "general will," but votes—and what constitutes a vote is, by necessity, a matter to be determined by preestablished rules. By issuing its own rules *after the fact*, the Florida court did not perfect the democratic system, argues Posner, but rather undermined one of its fundamental tenets: that political succession take place according to procedures that were "fixed in advance, objective, administrable, and clear."

12. Posner notes that leaving the issue to Congress to settle was not an acceptable option because Congress was too political to handle the job adequately. "Eventually, with the nation's patience completely exhausted," Posner theorizes, either Bush or Gore would prevail in the House of Representatives and would have been named the winner. But his presidency "would have started behind the eight ball, with an irregular and disputed accession, an abbreviated term of office, and no transition." Ibid., 24, 123.

13. Larry D. Kramer, "No Surprise. It's an Activist Court," *NYT*, December 12, 2000, A23. This is a point made as well by Richard H. Pildes, "Democracy and Disorder," in Sunstein and Epstein, *The Vote*, 140–164.

14. Larry D. Kramer, "The Supreme Court in Politics," in Jack N. Rakove, *The Unfinished Election of 2000* (New York: Basic Books, 2001), 107, 152. A much darker variant of this argument exchanges "distrust of democracy" for "ego" in explaining the Court's actions. "Behind *Bush v. Gore*," argues Jamin B. Raskin, "lies a thick and unprincipled jurisprudence, hostile to popular democracy and protective of race privilege and corporate power." *Bush v. Gore* was not a constitutional aberration. Far from it. "Although no precise doctrinal foundation existed for what the conservative justices did," writes Raskin, "their unprincipled treatment of the issues is perfectly congruent with their reactionary approach to other key cases structuring political democracy." Jamin B. Raskin, *Overruling Democracy: The Supreme Court vs. the American People* (New York: Routledge, 2004), 3, 28.

15. On the justices as human actors facing difficult choices to which they responded on multiple levels, see generally Pildes, "Democracy and Disorder."

16. John Podhoretz, "Bush Still Wins: The Supreme Court Was Right," *New York Post*, April 6, 2001, 029.

17. This is in fact a point made strongly by then law professor and now federal circuit judge Michael McConnell, "Two-and-a-Half Cheers for *Bush v. Gore*," in Sunstein and Epstein, *The Vote*, 98–122.

18. Dan Keating of the *WP*, writing a summary of the Media Consortium Florida Ballot Project, puts it simply, "if all of the ballots were counted there were enough potential Al Gore votes to give him a victory, but any smaller subset of ballots would retain or even enlarge George W. Bush's margin." Dan Keating, "Democracy Counts: Media Consortium Florida Ballot Project" (paper prepared for presentation at the annual meeting of the American Political Science Association, Boston, August 2002), 7. Keating reports, in fact, that based on the consortium's findings, "Gore's name appeared on 80,772 of the overvotes compared to 40,073 for Bush, indicating that overvotes may have had the largest impact on Florida's election." Ibid.

19. Ibid., 8. The memo and interview was cited in Michael Isikoff, "The Final Word?"

Newsweek, Web exclusive article (November 19, 2001), http://www.newsweek.com/id/76207.

20. The largest single grouping of *undervotes* were the Palm Beach and the Miami-Dade County ballots. Both already were separated out and in Tallahassee, ready for immediate counting. The only remaining large group of undervotes that needed separating was in Duval County. The rest of the counties had a relatively small number of undervotes to examine.

21. Technically, the state might have had such time, as there was a precedent for just this delay. In 1960 Hawaii appointed two slates of electors and Congress chose to count the one appointed on January 4, 1961, well after the Title 3 deadlines. See William Josephson and Beverly J. Ross, "Repairing the Electoral College," *Journal of Legislation* 22 (1996): 166, note 154. However, as of December 11, everyone was still operating under the assumption that all recounts had to be completed by December 12 at the earliest and December 18 (the date for the Electoral College to meet) at the very latest.

22. *Report and Recommendations: Select Joint Committee on the Manner of Appointment of Presidential Electors*, Florida Legislature, December 4, 2000, 2.

23. "Joint Proclamation," Florida Legislature, December 6, 2000. All of these votes were split along party lines. See generally Lynne Rambo, "The Lawyers' Role in Selecting the President: A Complete Legal History," *Texas Wesleyan Law Review* 8 (Spring 2002): 201.

24. Jeff Glasser, "First the Courts, Then the Legislature," *U.S. News & World Report*, December 4, 2000, 44. See also, Hendrik Hertzberg, "All Perfectly Legal," *New Yorker*, December 11, 2000, http://www.newyorker.com/archive/2000/12/11/2000_12_11_041_TNY_LIBRY_000022267.

25. Stewart M. Powell and Mark Helm, "State Lawmakers Give Bush Insurance," *Times Union* (Albany, NY), December 7, 2000, A1.

26. Kenneth Lovett and Gregg Birnbaum, "Fla. Legislature to Pick Own Electors: GOP'ers Say It's Merely a Backup Plan," *New York Post*, December 7, 2000, 004. See also David Firestone, "Contesting the Vote: The Overview: With Court Set to Hear Appeal, Legislators Move on Electors," *NYT*, December 7, 2000, A1.

27. Peter Wallsten, "Fla. Legislature Ready to Save the Day for Bush," *Pittsburgh Post-Gazette*, December 9, 2000, A-8. See also, Dana Canedy and David Barstow, "Contesting the Vote: The Florida Legislature; Ruling Fuels G.O.P. Resolve to Appoint Electors and Democrats' Will to Fight," *NYT*, December 9, 2000, A14.

28. Dana Canedy, "Contesting the Vote: The Florida Legislature; House Adopts Bush Electors, but Act May Be Moot," *NYT*, December 13, 2000, A26. Only with Gore's concession speech did the Florida legislature halt its efforts to name pro-Bush electors. "Florida Legislature Ends Electors Bid," AP Wire, December 14, 2000.

29. In the House, 221 Republicans had a slim, yet effective majority over 212 Democrats and two independents (Bernard Sanders of Vermont and Virgil Goode of Virginia). In the Senate, the election resulted in a dead-even 50/50 split. This gave the Democrats a "nominal majority" in the Senate as Vice President Al Gore, as president of the Senate, would have cast tie-breaking votes—presumably in favor of his own slate of electors.

30. Keep in mind that the argument here is that the justices voted their partisan preferences, so having a 5–4 split on the court carry over to other voting options makes sense—if only for argument's sake.

31. 3 U.S.C. §15.

32. Mary Leonard and John Aloysius Farrell, "Path Packed with Constitutional Pitfalls," *Boston Globe*, December 9, 2000, A12, sets out the nightmare scenario of Jeb Bush

refusing to follow a court order to certify the Gore slate: "The Florida Legislature is expected to pass a resolution that names electors pledged to George W. Bush as the winners of the Nov. 8 election. But what if a subsequent court-ordered recount shows that Gore has won? The Florida courts would then be expected to order Governor Jeb Bush to certify his brother's defeat and award the state's 25 electoral votes and the presidency to the Democrats. Bush could refuse, said Michael Glennon, a constitutional law specialist from the University of California at Davis, and the state Supreme Court could then issue a writ of mandamus, ordering him to act at the cost of being held in contempt of court. 'Now we are getting into Saturday Night Massacre kind of stuff,' said Viet Dinh, a law professor at Georgetown University, referring to the constitutional crisis that occurred in the midst of the Watergate crisis. 'It's all confused.' A standoff between Jeb Bush and his own Supreme Court would probably end up in the federal courts, said Glennon, and ultimately in the US Supreme Court once again."

33. See Chief Justice William H. Rehnquist, "2003 Albritton Lecture: The Supreme Court and the Disputed Election of 1876," *Alabama Law Review* 55 (Spring 2004): 527–536; Haworth, *Hayes-Tilden Disputed Presidential Election of 1876*; Woodward, *Reunion and Reaction*; Robinson, *Stolen Election*; Morris Jr., *Fraud of the Century*; Rehnquist, *Centennial Crisis*.

34. *Short Guide to Counting Electoral Votes.*

35. Actually, following the 1876 model, the split would have been three Republicans to two Democrats. Such a split was not farfetched. In the history that actually happened efforts at a joint majority were attempted early on in the 107th Congress, in recognition of the Senate's 50/50 split—in this case with the Republicans holding the tie-breaking vote they got a 50.5 percent control. Before January 20, it was the Democrats that had the 50.5 percent control in committee seats. See Marilyn Rauber, "GOP Will Share Reins with Dems in Senate," *New York Post*, January 6, 2001, 007; Allison Stevens, "Snowe Ratios Idea Blasted," *The Hill*, January 3, 2001; "How to Run Divided Senate Still Undecided," *St. Petersburg Times (SPT)*, January 03, 2001, 3A; "Lott Says Managing Senate with 50–50 Split a Challenge, Not Problem," AP Wire, December 21, 2000.

36. Assuming that Congress followed the 1876 model, each house of Congress would have had five members on the commission, with an additional five coming from the Supreme Court. Membership on the commission, in turn, would have been organized by partisan affiliation. So, with the Republicans controlling both houses of Congress, they would have had ten votes for Bush plus whomever the five Justices voted for. Should the Senate have split 50/50, then a logical result would have given the Democrats two or three votes from the Senate. This again, would not have been enough to counteract the five Republican votes from the House, and presumably, the three to five Bush votes from the Supreme Court members. If the Senate had gone totally Democratic (an unlikely occurrence) then the breakdown of justices serving on the commission would have been key. Still, given the five-to-four split in the Court's ruling in *Bush v. Gore*, it is likely that at least three of the justices would have voted for Bush. On the 1876 Electoral Commission model, see Rehnquist, *Centennial Crisis*; Woodward, *Reunion and Reaction*.

37. The Papers of George Washington, *The Electoral Count for the Presidential Election of 1789*, http://gwpapers.virginia.edu/documents/presidential/electoral.html. See also Richard E. Berg-Andersson, "What Are They All Doing, Anyway? An Historical Analysis of the Electoral College," *The Green Papers*, September 17, 2000, http://www.thegreenpapers.com/Hx/ElectoralCollege.html.

38. Forrest Maltzman, Lee Sigelman, and Paul J. Wahlbeck, "Supreme Court Justices

Really Do Follow the Election Returns," *PS: Political Science and Politics* (October 2004): 839–842 (online at http://www.apsanet.org).

39. For two examples of vilifying literature on *Bush v. Gore*, see generally Vincent Bugliosi, *The Betrayal of America: How the Supreme Court Undermined the Constitution and Chose Our President* (New York: Nation Books, 2001), and Alan M. Dershowitz, *Supreme Injustice: How the High Court Hijacked Election 2000* (New York: Oxford University Press, 2002).

40. Ibid.

41. Writing in a different context, the late chief judge of the Fifth Circuit Court of Appeals, John R. Brown, noted, "Lifetime tenure insulates judges from anxiety over worldly cares for body and home and family. But it does not protect them from the unconscious urge for the approbation of their fellow men—and fellow men most often means those of like interest and backgrounds, business and professional experiences and predilections, and even prejudices." To this we can add, their political affiliations. John R. Brown, "Hail to the Chief: Hutcheson, the Judge," *Texas Law Review* 38 (December 1945): 45.

42. *This Honorable Court: Part Two: Inside the Marble Temple*, PBS video, produced by WETA-TV (Washington, DC. Greater Washington Educational Telecommunications Association, May 1988). Chief Justice Rehnquist and Justices O'Connor and Scalia were also present for this interview and all three agreed with Brennan's statement.

43. Linda Greenhouse, "Another Kind of Bitter Split," *NYT*, December 14, 2000, A1; Neil A. Lewis, "Justice Thomas Speaks Out on a Timely Topic, Several of Them, in Fact," *NYT*, December 14, 2000, A23; Greg B. Smith, "Court's Split Edict Comes under Fire," *New York Daily News*, December 14, 2000, 18. Reportedly, after hearing of Justice Thomas's comments, Chief Justice Rehnquist responded with the word "absolutely." Ibid.

44. Chief Justice Rehnquist, along with Justices O'Connor, Brennan, Scalia, and White discuss exactly this point in *This Honorable Court: Part Two: Inside the Marble Temple*.

45. Indeed, literally hundreds of law review articles, books and op-ed commentaries deal with this question, broadly defined. For examples, see the articles in Sunstein and Epstein, *The Vote*.

46. Note that this is not the same as saying that they were right (or wrong) in their reading of the other court's actions. Nor does it directly address the legitimacy (that is, constitutionality) of their specific constitutional reasoning. Rather, at issue here is the level of justification the justices had, or felt they had or should have had, for acting as they did.

47. For the rest of this chapter, we will use the terms "Florida justices" and "U.S. justices" to distinguish the two sets of judges.

48. *Gore v. Harris*, 772 So. 2d. 1256, 1261–1262.

49. *Bush v. Gore*, 531 U.S. 98, 105–106, 109.

50. Ibid., 112–115.

51. Ibid. at 114–115. The two cases cited were *NAACP v. Alabama ex rel. Patterson*, 357 U.S. 449 (1958) and *Bouie v. City of Columbia*, 378 U.S. 347 (1964). This argument is drawn from Gillman, *The Votes That Counted*, 144.

52. For a wider discussion of these points, see Charles L. Zelden, *Voting Rights on Trial* (ABC-CLIO: Santa Barbara, CA, 2002), chapter 4.

53. *Boardman v. Esteva*, 323 So. 2d 259 (1975); *Darby v. State*, 73 Fla. 922, 75 So. 411 (1917); *Beckstrom v. Volusia County Canvassing Bd.*, 707 So. 2d 720 (1998). Other relevant early cases include: *State ex rel. Peacock v. Latham*, 170 So. 819 (1940), 170 So. 309 (1936), 170 So. 472 (1936); *State ex rel. Nuccio v. Williams*, 97 Fla. 159, 120 So. 310 (1929).

54. *Florida Statutes* (2000), Title IX, Section 101.5614.

55. "Reply to Remand," *Palm Beach County Canvassing Board v. Harris*, case nos. SC00-2346, SC00-2348, and SC00-2349, Supreme Court of Florida, December 11, 2000, 10–11.

56. 510 U.S. 1141. For general discussions of Justice Scalia's judicial philosophy, see, Ralph A. Rossum, "Text and Tradition: The Originalist Jurisprudence of Antonin Scalia," in Earl M. Maltz, ed., *Rehnquist Justice: Understanding the Court Dynamic* (Lawrence: University Press of Kansas, 2003), 34–69; David M. Zlotnick, "Justice Scalia and His Critics: An Exploration of Scalia's Fidelity to His Constitutional Methodology," *Emory Law Journal* 48 (Fall 1999): 1377–1426; Autumn Fox and Stephen R. McAllister, "An Eagle Soaring: The Jurisprudence of Justice Antonin Scalia," *Campbell Law Review* 19 (Spring 1997): 223–309; Shawn Burton, "Comment: Justice Scalia's Methodological Approach to Judicial Decision-Making: Political Actor or Strategic Institutionalist?" *Toledo Law Review* 34 (Spring 2003): 575–609.

57. Antonin Scalia, "Originalism: The Lesser Evil," *University of Cincinnati Law Review* 57 (1989): 849–865 at 854, 863. See also Antonin Scalia, *A Matter of Interpretation: Federal Courts and the Law* (Princeton, NJ: Princeton University Press, 1997).

58. Antonin Scalia, "The Rule of Law as a Law of Rules," *University of Chicago Law Review* 56 (Fall 1989): 1175–1188. See also Fox and McAllister, "An Eagle Soaring," 226; Mark Tushnet, *A Court Divided: The Rehnquist Court and the Future of Constitutional Law* (New York: Norton, 2005), 152.

59. Scalia, "Rule of Law as a Law of Rules," 1179–1180.

60. The one exception to this was Chief Justice Wells.

61. "On Application for Stay," *Bush v. Gore*, case no. 00-949, December 9, 2000.

62. Christopher E. Smith, "Clarence Thomas: A Distinctive Justice," *Seaton Hall Law Review* 28 (1997): 1–28 at 9.

63. *Lewis v. Casey*, 116 S. Ct. 2174, 2188 (1996), Justice Thomas concurring.

64. Clarence Thomas, "Judging," *University of Kansas Law Review*, 45 (November 1996): 1–8 at 4.

65. Smith, "Clarence Thomas: A Distinctive Justice," 10.

66. See Mark A. Graber, "Clarence Thomas and the Perils of History," in Maltz, *Rehnquist Justice*, 70–102.

67. Thomas, "Judging," 4.

68. Graber, "Clarence Thomas and the Perils of History"; Smith, "Clarence Thomas: A Distinctive Justice," 10–12.

69. Thomas, "Judging," 6.

70. Keith E. Whittington, "William H. Rehnquist: Nixon's Strict Constructionist, Reagan's Chief Justice," in Maltz, *Rehnquist Justice*, 25–27.

71. Ibid. See also Mark Tushnet, "William Rehnquist as Historian," *Cornell Law Review* 91 (May 2006): 957–971.

72. William H. Rehnquist, "A Random Thought on the Segregation Cases," reprinted in *Nomination of William Hubbs Rehnquist: Hearings before the Senate Committee on the Judiciary*, 99th Congress, 2d session, 1986, 324–325. (Quoted in Whittington, "William H. Rehnquist," 4.)

73. "Editorial: Beyond the Election; Supreme Court Fault Lines," *NYT*, December 14, 2000, A38.

74. We discuss these points further on pages 223–232.

75. On Kennedy and O'Connor as swing votes, see Thomas M. Keck, *The Most Activist Supreme Court in History: The Road to Modern Judicial Conservatism* (Chicago: University of Chicago Press, 2004), 199–253.

76. Craig Joyce, "A Tribute to Justice Sandra Day O'Connor: Afterword: Lazy B and the Nation's Court: Pragmatism in Service of Principle," *Harvard Law Review* 119 (March 2006): 1257–1273.

77. Sandra Day O'Connor and H. Alan Day, *Lazy B: Growing Up on a Cattle Ranch in the American Southwest* (New York: Random House, 2003), 239–243.

78. Wilson Ray Huhn, "The Constitutional Jurisprudence of Sandra Day O'Connor: A Refusal to 'Foreclose the Unanticipated,'" *Akron Law Review* 39 (2006): 373–414.

79. Nancy Maveety, "Justice Sandra Day O'Connor: Accommodations and Conservatism," in Maltz, *Rehnquist Justice*, 103–139. See also, Tushnet, *A Court Divided*, 54.

80. Jan Crawford Greenburg, *Supreme Conflict: The Inside Story of the Struggle for Control of the United States Supreme Court* (New York: Penguin, 2007), 31–32.

81. Tushnet, *A Court Divided*, 156–159 (quote on 177–178).

82. Jeffery Rosen, "Supreme Leader: The Arrogance of Justice Anthony Kennedy," *New Republic* (June 18, 2007).

83. Tushnet, *A Court Divided*, 156–159; Earl M. Maltz, "Anthony Kennedy and the Jurisprudence of Respectable Conservatism," in Maltz, *Rehnquist Justice*, 140–156; Rosen, "Supreme Leader," presents a much darker version of this view of Justice Kennedy.

84. Greenburg, *Supreme Conflict*, 32.

85. Greenburg, *Supreme Conflict*, 177–178, notes the similarities between the two swing votes on the Rehnquist court. Greenburg also notes the difference between O'Connor and Kennedy. O'Connor "adopted malleable standards that she could manipulate in a future case to get a desired result" and "to walk away from positions she'd taken in earlier cases." Kennedy did neither—if only in his own mind. "I think I may adhere somewhat more closely to whatever standard I come up with," Kennedy noted in an interview with Greenburg. "I mean, if I say something, I want to stick with it." See also Rosen, "Supreme Leader," on Kennedy's decision-making style.

86. Joan Biskupic, "Election Still Splits Court Friction over Justices' Ruling on Ballot Count in Florida Continues to Cause Hard Feelings, Draw Angry Letters, Even Spark Talk of at Least One Imminent Retirement at High Court," *USA Today*, January 22, 2001, 1A; David Margolick, Evgenia Peretz, and Michael Shnayerson, "The Path to Florida," *Vanity Fair* (October 2004) (online version, available via Lexis/Nexis).

87. Mary Leonard, "Decision 2000/Judicial Roles; Souter, Breyer Pushed Search for Consensus," *Boston Globe*, December 14, 2000, A39.

88. Justice Kennedy, for his part, "scoffs at the suggestion he was on the fence." Indeed, in *Supreme Injustice*, 177, Greenburg quotes Justice Kennedy saying of Justice Souter: "I think with one more day, I might have persuaded him."

89. Margolick, Peretz, and Shnayerson, "Path to Florida." See also Leonard, "Decision 2000/Judicial Roles," A39.

90. Former deputy U.S. solicitor general Philip Lacovara, who convinced the Supreme Court to force then-president Richard M. Nixon to turn over his secret Oval Office tapes, notes: "Unanimity can be very important for public acceptance. This court's willingness to take this case, and decide it by a narrow margin, was quite a risky strategy, and it will probably cost the court a little bit of its public capital. . . ." Quoted in Maggie Mulvihill, "Supreme Court Hurt in Eyes of Scholars," *Boston Herald*, December 14, 2000, 006.

91. *Bush v. Gore*, 531 U. S. 98, 122.

92. For example, "Editorial: Be Thankful for a Political System That Is Working," *SPT*, November 23, 2000, 27A: "Thanksgiving is when we traditionally ponder the good things we have. It is not difficult to find events or things in our lives for which we can be very

thankful. . . . Something that does not normally come to mind immediately when we do our mental inventories of things we are thankful for is our unique, American political system. Even though the process looks messy and confused right now, please notice that there are no tanks rumbling down our streets or warplanes flying overhead. We can all discuss how anachronistic the Electoral College is, how unfair the ballot was in Palm Beach County, how half-witted the elderly voters are down there, how biased Katherine Harris is or how partisan the Florida Supreme Court's actions were. But there are no riots. And there is no violence. There is no power vacuum or constitutional crisis. We need not be concerned about some army general seizing control of the Capitol. Instead, we will watch football games all day and then sit down for our turkey dinners with our friends and our families. And we will let the 'system' work this out." See also Samuel Issacharoff, "Political Judgments," *University of Chicago Law Review* 86 (Summer 2001): 637–656, 637.

93. See the comment by Jonathan Schell, "Manufacturing a Crisis," *Nation*, December 11, 2000, http://www.thenation.com/doc/20001211/schell for a summary of "crisis" talk.

94. Joan Mckinney, "Members Fear Congress May be Drawn into 'Crisis,'" *Advocate* (Baton Rouge, Louisiana), November 23, 2000, 1-A.

95. Kenneth Lovett, "Joe Sees Crisis If Legislature Acts," *New York Post*, December 1, 2000, 006.

96. Quoted in Leonard and Farrell, "Next Move: Path Packed with Constitutional Pitfalls," A12.

97. Quoted in "'We're in a Constitutional Crisis': With Florida a Tossup and the Appearance That Al Gore Will Win the Popular Vote but Lose the Electoral Vote, Experts Square Off," *Salon.com*, November 8, 2000, http://archive.salon.com/politics/feature/2000/11/08/crisis/index.html.

98. Quoted in "Chief Justice Sees Constitutional Crisis in Florida Ruling," AP Wire, December 8, 2000.

99. "Text: Bush Campaign Adviser James A. Baker III," Friday, December 8, 2000, *The American Presidency Project*, http://www.presidency.ucsb.edu/showflorida2000.php?fileid=baker12–08.

100. Steve Dunleavy, "Florida Justice Isn't Just Blind, It's Deaf and Dumb," *New York Post*, December 9, 2000, 006.

101. Dwight Kiel, "Elections and Temperament: Rancor and Hyperbole after 32 Years of De-Alignment (Research Note)." *Florida Philosophical Review* 1 (Winter 2001): 72, http://www.cas.ucf.edu/philosophy/fpr/journals/volume1/issue2/Kielreview.html.

102. Jonah Goldberg, "This Is a Constitutional Crisis," *National Review Online*, December 11, 2000, http://article.nationalreview.com/?q=MGM3NTJjMWEzMjQ0MWYzZDIxZDA4ZjQ5NDA2NjUzZGQ=.

103. Schell summarized the postelection commentary on December 11, as follows: "The Democrats have hardly been pacifists in the struggle. Their record is barren of moves taken for any evident reason but winning the presidency. The language of Gore's spokesmen and lawyers has at times been intemperate, as when the lawyer Alan Dershowitz called Florida's Secretary of State Katherine Harris "a crook." Yet by far the most dangerous escalations have come from the Republican camp. During the first ten days of the crisis, the fight was kept within certain bounds on both sides. Then came the Florida Supreme Court's decision to order Harris to refrain from certifying the election until further instruction. The GOP responded with a torrent of unsubstantiated defamation of the Gore campaign and of the boards conducting the recount in Florida. House Republican whip and impeachment zealot Tom DeLay announced without evidence that the election was 'nothing less than a theft in

progress' in Florida. A new spokesman for the Bush campaign, Governor Marc Racicot of Montana, charged that Democratic supervisors, by disallowing absentee military ballots without postmarks by Election Day and with other deficiencies, 'have gone to war in my judgment against the men and women who serve in our armed forces,' and opined that 'when the American people learn about these things, they're going to ask themselves what in the name of God is going on here.' Governor William Janklow of South Dakota announced that the Democrats 'are going to steal the election.' And Bush's press secretary, Karen Hughes, accused the Gore campaign of 'reinventing and miscounting the true intentions of the voters.'" Schell, "Manufacturing a Crisis," *Nation*, December 11, 2000, http://www.thenation.com/doc/20001211/schell.

104. Margolick, Peretz, and Shnayerson, "Path to Florida."

105. Greenburg, *Supreme Conflict*, 31–32.

106. On the election of 1789, see Victoria Sutton, "Beyond Election 2000: Law and Policy in the New Millennium: Essay: The Electoral College—Now, More than Ever," *University of Florida Journal of Law and Public Policy* 13 (Fall 2001): 104.

107. On the election of 1800, see Joanne B. Freeman, "The Election of 1800: A Study in the Logic of Political Change," *Yale Law Journal* 109 (June 1999): 1989; Joanne B. Freeman, *Affairs of Honor: National Politics in the New Republic* (New Haven, CT: Yale University Press, 2001), chapter 5; R. B. Bernstein, *Thomas Jefferson* (New York: Oxford University Press, 2003), 128–134, and sources cited on pages 218–219; and Tadahisu Kuroda, *The Origins of the Twelfth Amendment: The Electoral College in the Early Republic, 1787–1804* (Westport, CT: Greenwood Press, 1994). Note that 2000 was the bicentennial of the 1800 election, and the specter of revisiting the crisis atmosphere of two centuries before haunted the nation in 2000.

108. See, e.g., Charles Sellers, *The Market Revolution: Jacksonian America, 1815–1846* (New York: Oxford University Press, 1991), 172–201.

109. Rehnquist, *Centennial Crisis*, 180. See also Morris, *Fraud of the Century*. The leading studies are Woodward, *Reunion and Reaction*, and Charles Fairman, *Five Justices and the Electoral Commission of 1877* (New York: Macmillan, 1987) [a supplement to Fairman's two-volume *Reconstruction and Reunion, 1864–88*, in which Fairman defends the integrity of the justices who served on the electoral commission]. Lizette Alvarez, "On Capitol Hill, Feelings of Finality and Disappointment and Sighs of Relief," *NYT*, December 13, 2000, 27, notes how for months after the election, Democrats called for "Tilden or blood," still unwilling to accept Tilden's defeat by what they deemed questionable means.

110. On Clinton's impeachment and trial, see Jeffrey Toobin, *A Vast Conspiracy: The Real Story of the Sex Scandal That Nearly Brought Down a President* (New York: Touchstone, 2000); Richard Posner, *An Affair of State: The Investigation, Impeachment, and Trial of President Clinton* (Cambridge, MA: Harvard University Press, 2000).

111. Ibid.

112. Alvarez, "On Capitol Hill, Feelings of Finality," 27.

113. Gerald Gunther, "A Risky Moment for the Court," *NYT*, December 1, 2000, A37.

114. Charles Lane, "Rehnquist: Court Can Prevent a Crisis; Chief Justice Cites 1876 Election Role," *WP*, January 19, 2001, A24.

115. Quoted in Lane, "Rehnquist: Court Can Prevent a Crisis," A24.

116. *Bush v. Gore*, 531 U.S. 98, 111.

117. Mark Sherman, "Justices Defend Florida Recount Decision," AP Wire, January 24, 2007.

118. Greenburg, *Supreme Conflict*, 31.

119. *Bush v. Gore*, 531 U.S. 98, 111.

120. Quoted in Greenburg, *Supreme Conflict*, 175.

121. Quoted in Greenhouse, "Another Kind of Bitter Split," A1. It should be noted that Sherry drew from all this the conclusion that "There is really very little way to reconcile this opinion other than that they wanted Bush to win."

122. On this point, see "Note: *Non Sub Homine?* A Survey and Analysis of the Legal Resolution of Election 2000," *Harvard Law Review* 114 (May 2001): 2187–2189, and Pamela S. Karlan, "The Evolution of the Newest Equal Protection from *Shaw v. Reno* to *Bush v. Gore*," *North Carolina Law Review* 79 (June 2001): 1360.

123. Cass R. Sunstein, "Order without Law," in Sunstein and Epstein, *The Vote*, 212.

124. Richard L. Hasen, "The Law of Presidential Elections: Issues in the Wake of Florida 2000: *Bush v. Gore* and the Future of Equal Protection Law in Elections," *Florida State University Law Review* 29 (2001): 386–391.

125. Pamela S. Karlan, "The Law of Presidential Elections: Issues in the Wake of Florida 2000: Unduly Partial: The Supreme Court and the Fourteenth Amendment in *Bush v. Gore*," *Florida State University Law Review* 29 (2001): 600–601.

126. Ibid., 601.

127. Law professor David Strauss, for instance, notes how the Court's use of equal protection presented a "plausible but potentially far-reaching principle: that at least where the right to vote is concerned, the states may not use discretionary standards if it is practicable to formulate rules that will limit discretion." Quoted in Hasen, "The Law of Presidential Elections," 399. See also Samuel Issacharoff, "The Court's Legacy for Voting Rights," *NYT*, December 14, 2000, A39: "The Supreme Court may have given us an advancement in voting rights doctrine. It has asserted a new constitutional requirement: To avoid disparate and unfair treatment of voters. And this obligation obviously cannot be limited to the recount process alone. . . . The court's new standard may create a more robust constitutional examination of voting practices."

128. For Marshall's views on elections and equal ballots see generally Charles L. Zelden, *The Battle for the Black Ballot: Smith v. Allwright and the Defeat of the Texas All-White Primary* (Lawrence: University Press of Kansas, 2004).

129. A third question on the reform potential of equal protection is also raised by these matters, namely the effectiveness of equal protection–based reforms in improving electoral administration. This topic will be raised in the Afterword once we have had a chance to discuss the events following *Bush v. Gore*.

130. As noted previously, they probably adopted this position after the Florida supreme court issued its reply to the remand in *Bush v. Palm Beach County Canvassing Board*, arguing that their actions were fully based on Florida statutes and not the Florida constitution. Joan Biskupic, "Election Still Splits Court Friction," 1A; Margolick, Peretz, and Shnayerson, "Path to Florida."

131. "Contesting the Vote: Excerpts from Arguments before Supreme Court on the Florida Recount," *NYT*, December 12, 2000, A27.

132. See, for example, Justice O'Connor's ruling in *Shaw v. Reno*, 509 U.S. 630, 641 (1993).

133. Linda Greenhouse, "O'Connor Held Balance of Power," *NYT*, July 2, 2005; "The O'Connor Court," *WP*, July 2, 2005, A28; Ramesh Ponnuru, "Sandra's Day: Why the Rehnquist Court Has Been the O'Connor Court, and How to Replace Her—Should It Come to That," *National Review*, June 30, 2003, http://findarticles.com/p/articles/mi_m1282/is_12_55/ai_103135850.

134. Mary Leonard, "Decision 2000/Judicial Roles," A39. On Justice Breyer's motivations, see Jeffrey Toobin, *Too Close to Call: The Thirty-Six-Day Battle to Decide the 2000 Election* (New York: Random House, 2001), 260–261; Washington Post, *Deadlock: The Inside Story of America's Closest Election* (New York: PublicAffairs, 2001), 222–223.

135. Stephen J. Breyer, *Active Liberty: Interpreting Our Democratic Constitution* (New York: Alfred A. Knopf, 2005), 131–132.

136. *Bush v. Gore*, 531 U.S. 98, 134.

137. The quote comes from David Margolick, Evgenia Peretz, and Michael Shnayerson, "Path to Florida."

138. Ibid.

139. Rosen, "Supreme Leader."

140. *Smith v. Allwright*, 321 U.S. 649 (1944), *Baker v. Carr*, 369 U.S. 186 (1962), *Reynolds v. Sims*, 377 U.S. 533 (1964).

10. The Unlearned Lessons of 2000

1. One irony of the Republicans' invoking of the concept of "moving on" is that in 1998 many Americans on the left who opposed the Republican-led effort to impeach President Bill Clinton formed an organization called MoveOn.org to lobby Congress and persuade the electorate that Congress should abandon the impeachment project and "move on."

2. "Bush's Inaugural Address: 'I Will Work to Build a Single Nation of Justice and Opportunity,'" *St. Petersburg Times (SPT)*, January 21, 2001, 10A.

3. E. J. Dionne Jr., "We'll Get Over It If You Get Off Your High Horse," *Washington Post (WP)*, January 28, 2001, B1; Brian Blomquist and Marilyn Rauber, "Lott Warns Dems Not to Pull Any Fast Ones," *New York Post*, January 4, 2001, 009; Mark Sherman, "Senate Republicans Unite behind Ashcroft," *Austin American-Statesman*, January 11, 2001, A1; Susan J. Barnard, "Country Will Recover from Election Problems," *Times Union* (Albany, NY), January 7, 2001, B4.

4. See Tom Murse, "Party-Line Response Here," *Lancaster New Era* (Lancaster, PA), December 13, 2000, A-16; Lee Hammel, "N.E. Congressmen Condemn Decision to Stop Recount," *Telegram & Gazette* (Massachusetts), December 12, 2000, A1; Jim Ross, "Democrats Smolder; GOP Breathes Relief," *SPT*, December 14, 2000, 1; Duane W. Gang and John Commins, "Area Republicans, Democrats Divided on Election's Outcome," *Chattanooga Times Free Press*, December 14, 2000, A9.

5. Daniel Schorr, "The Supreme Fix Was In," *Record* (Bergen County, NJ), December 17, 2000, 07.

6. Lizette Alvarez, "On Capitol Hill, Feelings of Finality and Disappointment and Sighs of Relief," *NYT*, December 14, 2000, A27; Susan Milligan, "Minority Party Urges Bush to Listen and Compromise," *Boston Globe*, December 15, 2000, A52. Sanford Levinson, "The Law of Politics: *Bush v. Gore* and the French Revolution: A Tentative List of Some Early Lessons," *Law and Contemporary Problems* 65 (Summer 2002): 7–37 at 36 provides an explanation: "Why is Bush the 'only President' we can even contemplate? The answer, I submit, is remarkably simple: Article II, section 1 provides that the President 'shall hold his Office during the Term of four Years.' Whatever our commitment to one or another theory of constitutional interpretation, whatever our sympathy toward deconstructionist or post-modernist approaches, all of us have been deeply socialized into an assumption that the person called President, whoever he may be, is entitled to remain in office unless events

meriting impeachment or disability under the Twenty-Fifth Amendment take place. Neither of these constitutional possibilities has the slightest application to the current situation."

7. James O. Goldsborough, "But the Institution Suffers a Self-Inflicted Wound," *San Diego Union-Tribune*, December 14, 2000, B-13; Robert J. Samuelson, "Self-Inflicted Wound," *WP*, December 12, 2000, A47; Leonard B. Rosenberg, "Unenviable Legacy?" *Record* (Bergen County, NJ), December 27, 2000, L6. An exception to this pattern was Jonathan Schonsheck, "Supreme Court Majority Erred: Rehnquist Should Resign," *Post-Standard* (Syracuse, NY), January 31, 2001, which, as the headline relates, called for Rehnquist's resignation.

8. David Cole, "The Liberal Legacy of *Bush v. Gore*," *Georgetown Law Review* 94 (2006): 1429–1430.

9. These same ABC News–*Washington Post* polls showed a markedly divided nation on the issue of Bush's legitimacy as president, with "approximately 40 percent maintain[ing] that he had not won the election fairly." The Gallup–CNN–*USA Today* polls showed "around 20 percent said he stole the election, about a third believed he won it on a technicality, and a near majority claimed he entered the White House 'fair and square.'" Karlyn Bowman, "Bush vs. Gore: How Much Did Americans Care?" *Roll Call*, November 15, 2001.

10. See Andrew Phillips, "Victory at Last," *Maclean's*, January 1, 2001, 108.

11. Briefly, in January 2001 a group of over 600 law professors, dubbing themselves Law Professors for the Rule of Law, launched a campaign to remind the electorate of the many flaws of the Supreme Court's decision in *Bush v. Gore*—flaws that not only eroded the Court's claims to be the nation's premier guardian of the rule of law but, they also insisted, undermined the legitimacy of the Bush administration. The fruits of this campaign were a full-page newspaper advertisement appearing in the *NYT* on January 13, 2001, and a short-lived website, http://www.the-rule-of-law.com. The organization dissolved when its members began to realize that there was no generally acceptable way to be at once law-abiding citizens and to reject the legitimacy of President Bush and those he would appoint to office. See generally Kathryn Abrams, "Extraordinary Measures: Protesting Rule-of-Law Violations after *Bush v. Gore*," *Law and Philosophy* 21, no. 2 (March 2002): 165–196.

12. On this point see generally, Michael J. Klarman, "*Bush v. Gore* through the Lens of Constitutional History," *California Law Review* 89 (December 2001): 1721–1765.

13. Kenneth T. Walsh et al., "A Tyranny of One," *U.S. News & World Report*, June 4, 2001, 17.

14. Carla Marinucci, "Fading Dreams or Comeback Hopes: The Vice President's Loyal Democratic Followers Ponder Two Paths for Al Gore's Future," *San Francisco Chronicle*, December 14, 2000, A14; Dan Freedman, "Democrats Look toward the Future," *Times Union* (Albany, NY), January 13, 2001, A4.

15. Paul Starr, "Failure to Convert," *American Prospect*, July 2, 2001–July 16, 2001, 48; George C. Edwards, "Strategic Choices and the Early Bush Legislative Agenda," *PS: Political Science and Politics* 35 (March 2002): 41–45.

16. Quoted in John Berlau, "Message Received," *Insight on the News*, November 26, 2002, 18.

17. Liz Marlantes, "How Anger over Florida Recount Still Roils Politics," *Christian Science Monitor*, September 18, 2003, 01.

18. See generally Richard L. Hasen, "The Untimely Death of *Bush v. Gore*," *Stanford Law Review* 60 (October 2007):1–44.

19. Democratic Investigative Staff, *How to Make over One Million Votes Disappear: Electoral Sleight of Hand in the 2000 Presidential Election* (House Committee on the Judiciary, August 20, 2001), provides a state-by-state listing of the electoral problems in 2000.

20. On this point generally, see Hasen, "Untimely Death of *Bush v. Gore*."

21. Hasen, "Untimely Death of *Bush v. Gore*" discusses the controversy over voter ID laws. Ibid., at 18–25. Electionline.org, "Election Reform Briefing: Securing the Vote," (Washington, DC: Election Reform Information Project, 2004) discusses the controversy over electronic voting.

22. "Executive Order Number 00-349," State of Florida, December 14, 2000. (Reprinted in *Revitalizing Democracy in Florida: The Governor's Select Task Force on Election Procedures, Standards and Technology*, March 1, 2001, 4–5.)

23. *Revitalizing Democracy in Florida.*

24. "Highlights of Florida's Election Reform Legislation," AP Wire, May 5, 2001; Jon Mills, "Reforms in Florida after the 2000 Presidential Election," *University of Florida Journal of Law and Public Policy* 13 (Fall 2001): 69–80.

25. Florida Election Reform Act of 2001 (S 1118), approved May 11, 2001; *Florida Statutes* (2002), Title IX (both available at http://www.leg.state.fl.us/statutes). See also "Highlights of Florida's Election Reform Legislation," AP Wire, May 5, 2001; Rachel La Corte, "Gov. Bush Signs Florida's Election Reform in West Palm Beach," AP Wire, May 9, 2001.

26. The only exceptions were Maryland and Georgia. In both states, "lawmakers enacted legislation this spring requiring the adoption of a uniform statewide voting system." Yet "neither state confronted problems with its election procedures anywhere near to the extent that Florida did." Still, "top election officials in both states saw the possibility of similar problems in the event of a close contest" and acted. *What's Changed, What Hasn't, and Why: Election Reform since November 2000* (Washington, DC: Election Reform Information Project, October 22, 2001), 9.

27. Oregon, for instance, "set aside $2 million earlier this year to establish a centralized voter database that would possibly reduce the likelihood of errors and a person voting more than once (H.B. 2002). However, a state board committee recommended in September that, due to the souring economic forecast for the state, the funding be withheld for now. That will prevent the implementation of a new system until at least the 2004 elections." Ibid., i, 8–12 (quotes on 8 and 11). See also National Conference of State Legislatures, "The States Tackle Election Reform," (March 24, 2003), http://www.ncsl.org/programs/legismgt/elect/taskfc/TackleElectRef.htm, which summarizes the data on state election reform in 2001 and 2002 and also includes a link to a database of state election reform legislation: http://www.ncsl.org/programs/legismgt/elect/elections.cfm. Other reasons for delay included legislators still awaiting the results of study groups or special task force studies; completed reports that recommended no changes be made; or, in some cases, simply the lack of political will to act. *What's Changed, What Hasn't, and Why*, 8–12.

28. *What's Changed, What Hasn't, and Why*, 8–10.

29. Ibid., 10–12; David Kimball and Martha Kropf, "Assessing Election Reform Four Years after Florida" (paper presented at the Annual Meeting of the Southern Political Science Association, New Orleans, January 2005), 2.

30. Princeton Survey Research Associates, *Ready for 2002, Forgetting 2000: Election Officials Oppose Federal Standards and See Only Minor Impact of Election 2000* (Election Reform Information Project, January 2002), 1–2, 11. Kimball and Kropf, "Assessing Election Reform Four Years after Florida," 1, estimate that "around 370 counties replaced older

voting technologies with optically scanned ballots or electronic voting machines in time for the 2002 election."

31. Indiana, for instance, spent $5 million to establish a statewide voter registration list maintained by the secretary of state and updated by county election officials through a secure Internet connection. Kansas, Iowa, and Oregon took similar steps (though Oregon's case, without a dedicated budget to fund the statewide database, resulted in no funding for Oregon's database as of 2002). Colorado lengthened the time for recounts from twenty-one to thirty days following an election and "stipulated that ballots must be recounted using the same procedures by which they were originally tallied." Arkansas allocated more money to train poll workers, whereas South Carolina turned to high school students as a source of extra poll workers. *What's Changed, What Hasn't, and Why*, 12.

32. *Ready for 2002, Forgetting 2000*, 9.

33. On the accuracy of these predictions, the actual problems experienced in the 2004 election, and the limits to reform prior to this election, see ElectionOnline.org, *Briefing: Election 2004* (Washington, DC: Election Reform Information Project, December 2004).

34. *Ready for 2002, Forgetting 2000*, 9–10.

35. Among the studies were: Caltech/MIT Voting Project, *Voting: What Is, What Could Be* (2001); National Commission on Election Reform, *To Assure Pride and Confidence in the Electoral Process* (2001); Survey Research Center and Institute of Governmental Studies, University of California, Berkeley, *Counting All the Votes: The Performance of Voting Technology in the United States* (2001).

36. Kevin Coleman and Eric Fisher, "Election Reform: Overview and Issues" (Washington, DC: Congressional Research Service Report, January 30, 2003): 6. See also *What's Changed, What Hasn't, and Why*, 20–24, for a complete breakdown and comparison of the leading six reform reports.

37. "Election Reform," *Hearings before the Committee on Rules and Administration, U.S. Senate, 107th Congress*, vols. 1–3 (Washington, DC: Government Printing Office, 2003).

38. This bill mirrored a similar measure sponsored by Representative John Conyers (D-IL) in the House, H.R. 1170. On the content of both bills see, USCCR, "Chapter 2: Federal Legislation Addressing Election Reform," *Election Reform: An Analysis of Proposals and the Commission's Recommendations for Improving America's Election System*, November 2001, http://www.usccr.gov/pubs/vote2000/elecref/ch2.htm.

39. *What's Changed, What Hasn't, and Why*, 3. See also Larry Lipman, "GOP Senators Skip Meeting, Vote on Reforming Elections," *Palm Beach Post*, August 3, 2001, 31.

40. See Alex Wayne, "Early Voting Critics Fear Fraud; Local and National Critics of Early Voting Say Guilford County Doesn't Have Enough Safeguards against Voter Fraud," *News & Record* (Greensboro, NC), October 28, 2000, A1; Michael O. Allen, "Dems Blast GOP over Ballot Watch," *New York Daily News*, November 5, 2000, 32; Juan Gonzalez, "If Contest Is Coercion, GOP Wins," *New York Daily News*, November 7, 2000, 30; Michael Rowett, "Huckabee: State Like a 'Banana Republic,'" *Arkansas Democrat-Gazette*, November 07, 2000, A1.

41. Quoted in, *What's Changed, What Hasn't, and Why*, 3, and Gabrielle B. Ruda, "Picture Perfect: A Critical Analysis of the Debate on the 2002 Help America Vote Act," *Fordham Urban Law Journal* 31 (November 2003): 236. See also Brandon Ferguson, "Bond, Brownback Address Regional Election Officials on Election Reform," AP Wire, December 10, 2001, wherein Bond notes, "Unless further safeguards are added to the bill to protect against voter fraud, the legislation is dead."

42. *What's Changed, What Hasn't, and Why*, 4. In 2002, Dodd stated his views on voter

fraud with even more candor: "While it's humorous to talk about dogs who voted, it's not funny to talk about people who showed up and didn't, and were denied to do so." Ruda, "Picture Perfect," 236–237.

43. "Election Reform," Hearings before the Committee on Rules and Administration, vol. 1, 116, 71.

44. On this point, see Hasen, "Untimely Death of *Bush v. Gore*," 18–25.

45. *What's Changed, What Hasn't, and Why*, 4.

46. See Ruda, "Picture Perfect," 246.

47. Amy Keller, "Electoral Reform Delayed until after Recess," *Hill*, July 26, 2001; Larry Lipman, "GOP Senators Skip Meeting, Vote on Reforming Elections," *Palm Beach Post*, August 3, 2001, 21A; Amy Keller, "Election Reform Efforts Expected to Move Forward," *Hill*, September 24, 2001; Larry Lipman, "Time Running Out for Congress to Enact Election Reform Legislation," Cox News Service, November 7, 2001; Amy Keller, "Ney, Hoyer Reach Election Reform Compromise," *Hill*, November 8, 2001; Noelle Straub, "Election Reform Talks Hit Snag," *Hill*, November 28, 2001; Edward Walsh, "Election Reform Bill Stalls over ID Debate; GOP Says Plan Hinders Anti-Fraud Effort," *WP*, February 28, 2002, A21; James Kuhnhenn, "Voter Registration Snag Delays Vote on Election Reform," *Charleston Gazette* (West Virginia), March 5, 2002, 6C; Stephen Dinan, "Cloture Vote Fails on Election Bill; Deal Seen as Near," *Washington Times*, March 5, 2002, A03; Edward Walsh, "Election Reform Passes in Senate; Bill Would Establish Federal Standards," *WP*, April 12, 2002, A1; Amy Keller, "New Life for Vote Reforms?" *Roll Call*, September 12, 2002; Amy Keller, "Members Demand Election Reform Deal," *Roll Call*, September 19, 2002; Larry Lipman, "Lawmakers Reach Election Reforms Deal," *Palm Beach Post*, October 5, 2002, 3A.

48. Help America Vote Act of 2002, 42 U.S.C.A. §§15301–15545; Edward Walsh, "House Approves Election Reform; $3.9 Billion Bill Aims to Overhaul Federal Voting System," *WP*, October 11, 2002, A35; Edward Walsh, "Election Reform Bill Is Passed by Senate; $3.86 Billion Allotted for Improvements," *WP*, October 17, 2002, A1; Janelle Carter, "Election Overhaul Bill Goes to White House," *Advocate* (Baton Rouge, Louisiana), October 17, 2002, 2A. For an overview of HAVA's assistance and requirements, see Leonard M. Shambon, "Implementing the Help America Vote Act," *Election Law Journal* 3 (September 2004): 424–443, and Martin J. Siegel, "Congressional Power over Presidential Elections: The Constitutionality of the Help America Vote Act under Article II, Section 1," *Vermont Law Review* 28 (Winter 2004): 373–422.

49. Daniel P. Tokaji, "Early Returns on Election Reform: Discretion, Disenfranchisement, and the Help America Vote Act," *George Washington Law Review* 73 (August 2005): 1207–1208.

50. Inadequate funding had proven to be a recurring problem with HAVA. See Press Release, "Chairman Feinstein Calls for Full Funding of Help America Vote Act in FY08 Budget," Feb. 27, 2007, http://www.votetrustusa.org/index.php?option=com_content&task=view&id=2295&Itemid=26.

51. Lida Rodriguez-Taseff, "Florida's Post 2000 Voting Systems Overhaul: The Road to Perdition," *John Marshall Journal of Computer and Information Law* 23 (Spring 2005): 499.

52. Ibid., 499–500.

53. Scott Wyman, "Broward Dives Right in on Cure for Election Miscues," *South Florida Sun-Sentinel (SFSS)*, September 21, 2002, 1A. See also Rafael A. Olmeda and Jeff Shields, "Missing Votes Add to Chaos: Accusations Swirl as Election Officials Wait 24

Hours for Some Precinct Results," *SFSS*, September 12, 2002, 1B; Brittany Wallman, Scott Wyman, and Buddy Nevins, "A State of Confusion. Some Precincts Opened Late. Others Closed Early. In Some Cases, Voter Rolls Were Missing. For Many Residents, Voting Was More of a Fight than a Right," *SFSS*, September 11, 2002, 1B.

54. Wyman, "Broward Dives Right in on Cure for Election Miscues," 1A.

55. Rodriguez-Taseff, "Florida's Post 2000 Voting Systems Overhaul," 500.

56. Brent Kallestad, "Vote Results Approved: Smoothly Run Election Is One for the Books," *SFSS*, November 18, 2002, 6B.

57. Ibid.

58. Kimball and Kropf, "Assessing Election Reform Four Years after Florida," 3.

59. Rodriguez-Taseff, "Florida's Post 2000 Voting Systems Overhaul," 503–505.

60. Mathew Haggman, "Elections 2004—When Did She Know?" *Daily Business Review*, June 2, 2004. Rodriguez-Taseff argues that this was a false statement on Hood's part, as members of her elections staff showed clear knowledge of this report prior to this date. Rodriguez-Taseff, "Florida's Post 2000 Voting Systems Overhaul," 505.

61. Rodriguez-Taseff, "Florida's Post 2000 Voting Systems Overhaul," 506. See also Mark Crispin Miller, *Fooled Again: How the Right Stole the 2004 Election and Why They'll Steal the Next One Too* (New York: Basic Books, 2005), 206–214.

62. The report also noted how "the protocols used when the voting terminals communicate with their home base, both to fetch election configuration information and to report final election results, do not use cryptographic techniques to authenticate either end of the connection nor do they check the integrity of the data in transit. Given that these voting terminals could potentially communicate over insecure phone lines or even wireless Internet connections, even unsophisticated attackers can perform untraceable 'man-in-the-middle' attacks." Tadayoshi Kohno, Adam Stubblefield, Aviel Rubin, and Dan S. Wallach, "Analysis of An Electronic Voting System" (February 27, 2004), unpublished manuscript, http://avirubin.com/vote.pdf. An earlier version of this paper appeared as *Johns Hopkins University Information Security Institute Technical Report* TR-2003-19, July 23, 2003.

63. Quoted in Kimball and Kropf, "Assessing Election Reform Four Years after Florida," 4. In an interesting (and troubling) turn, Kimball and Kropf's article provides a link to Diebold's Web site for a copy of this press release. Yet using this link takes one to the press release only to have it automatically redirect to Diebold's main homepage. A subsequent search using Diebold's own search engine did not turn up any mention of this press release.

64. Brigid Schulte, "Md. Voting System's Security Challenged Electronic Cheating Too Easy, Study Says," *WP*, July 25, 2003, B01. See also Scott Shane, "Scientists Say 'Nay' to Computerized Voting," *Baltimore Sun*, July 27, 2003, 1A.

65. Science Applications International Corporation (SAIC), "Risk Assessment Report: Diebold AccuVote-TS Voting System and Processes" (redacted), SAIC-6099-2003-261, September 2, 2003, http://www.elections.state.md.us/pdf/risk_assessment_report.pdf. See also Eric A. Fisher, "Election Reform and Electronic Voting Systems (DREs): Analysis of Security Issues," *CRS Report for Congress* (November 4, 2003), 9–10, http://www.epic.org/privacy/voting/crsreport.pdf.

66. Celeste Biever, "E-voting Given Go-Ahead Despite Flaws," *NewScientist.com News Service*, September 25, 2003, http://www.newscientist.com/article.ns?id=dn4205.

67. See generally John Schwartz, "Report Raises Electronic Vote Security Issues," *NYT*, September 25, 2003, A20; John Schwartz, "Ohio Study Finds Flaws in Electronic Voting," *NYT*, December 3, 2003, A24; "Reliable Voting," *Boston Globe*, December 27,

2003, A12; John Schwartz, "Test of Electronic Balloting System Finds Major Security Flaws," *NYT*, January 30, 2004, A20; John Schwartz, "Electronic Vote Faces Big Test of Its Security," *NYT*, February 28, 2004, A1.

68. Ronnie Dugger, "How They Could Steal the Election This Time," *Nation*, August 16, 2004, http://www.thenation.com/doc/20040816/dugger. "Hack the Vote: The Problem with Diebold Touch-Screen Voting Machines," *Pittsburgh Post-Gazette*, December 3, 2003, A27.

69. See also Christopher Keyes, "The Machine Age," *Texas Monthly*, March 2004, 50.

70. Lillie Coney, "E-Voting: A Tale of Lost Votes," *John Marshall Journal of Computer & Information Law* 23 (Spring 2005): 511: "Many state election administrators dismissed the concerns of the computer scientists as being the views of people who did not understand the election process. They contended the DRE voting systems were safe for voting because they met state election requirements." See also Robert Redding Jr., "Vote System Ready to Go," *Washington Times*, November 1, 2004, B01.

71. Quoted in C. B. Hanif, "Paper or Electrons?" *Palm Beach Post*, August 31, 2003, 1E.

72. Anne Marie Squeo, "Surprising Its Critics, Electronic Balloting Had Minimal Glitches," *Wall Street Journal*, November 4, 2004, B5. See also Brett Arends, "America Decides 2004: Vote or Diebold: Company Has Right 'Touch,'" *Boston Herald*, November 3, 2004, 24. Miller, *Fooled Again*, 186–187, argues that there were more machine breakdowns than the press reported. He also argues that most of these breakdowns were in primarily Democratic areas ("Throughout Bush Country, the Democrats were . . . plagued by statistically impossible bad luck").

73. For a short but informative summary of voting problems nationwide, see Andrew Gumbel, *Steal This Vote: Dirty Elections and the Rotten History of Democracy in America* (New York: Nation Books, 2005), 275–298.

74. Rachel La Corte, "Activists Concerned about Purged Voters," *Miami Herald (MH)*, July 13, 2004, 3B; Jim Defede, "Voter List Mess Shows Officials Can't Be Trusted," *MH*, July 11, 2004, 1B.

75. Erika Bolstad, Jason Grotto, and David Kidwell, "Thousands of Eligible Voters Are on Felon List," *MH*, July 2, 2004, 1A. See also Miller, *Fooled Again*, 213–224.

76. Quoted in Defede, "Voter List Mess Shows Officials Can't Be Trusted."

77. Bob Mahlburg, "Felon Voting Chaos Persists: State Trying to Ease Fears about Glitches," *SFSS*, July 7, 2004, 5B. Defede, "Voter List Mess Shows Officials Can't Be Trusted."

78. Under state law, "County election officials are required by state law to verify names of suspected felons, send registered letters notifying them they are being dropped from rolls and advertise names in a local paper if they don't respond." Mahlburg, "Felon Voting Chaos Persists."

79. Quoted in Miller, *Fooled Again*, 219; Bolstad, Grotto, and Kidwell, "Thousands of Eligible Voters Are on Felon List."

80. Erika Bolstad, "2 Hired to Check Felon Purge List," *MH*, June 25, 2004, 9B. Indian River County elections supervisor Kay Clem also was forced to hire a firm specializing in criminal checks after finding people without any criminal record listed as potential felons. Bob Mahlburg and John Kennedy, "Millions Spent on Felons List: Parties Split on Failed Vote Data," *SFSS*, July 14, 2004, 1B. For complaints made by civil liberty activists, see Miller, *Fooled Again*, 129–130.

81. Lesley Clark, "List Abandoned, but Doubts Linger," *MH*, July 11, 2004, 21A.

82. Rachel La Corte, "Activists Concerned about Purged Voters," *MH*, July 13, 2004,

3B. Before the 2000 presidential election, some counties had used the state list to purge felons, even after it was shown that the list was inaccurate. The fear was that the same thing would happen here. Bolstad, "2 Hired to Check Felon Purge List." See also Greg Palast, "Vanishing Votes," *Nation*, May 17, 2004, http://www.thenation.com/doc/20040517/palast. Part of the worry was based on the fact that a number of county elections supervisors had not yet managed to restore the "voting rights to some voters mistakenly purged in the last presidential election four years ago." Mahlburg, "Felon Voting Chaos Persists." See also Bolstad, Grotto, and Kidwell, "Thousands of Eligible Voters Are on Felon List."

83. Gary Fineout and Marc Caputo, "State Ceases Felon Voting Purge," *MH*, August 14, 2004, 6B; Donna E. Clark, "List Abandoned, but Doubts Linger," 21A. See Miller, *Fooled Again*, 221–222. Miller also describes Republican plans to intimidate minority voters on Election Day. Ibid., 222–224.

84. The editorial complained: "Bush, of course, knows that. By pretending differently, he simply shows his contempt for the whole process." Reprinted in "Governor Reveals Contempt for Civil Process," *SFSS*, August 1, 2004, 5H.

85. Miller, *Fooled Again*, 205–206; David Royse "Federal Judge: Provisional Ballots in Wrong Precinct Don't Count," AP Wire, October 21, 2004. See also "Two-Thirds of Florida's Provisional Ballots Rejected," AP Wire, January 3, 2005.

86. Fred Grimm, "Unchecked Box Another Excuse to Toss Voters," *MH*, October 7, 2004, 1B. Miller, *Fooled Again*, 203, quotes the *San Francisco Chronicle* (October 14, 2004) that "more than a third of the incomplete forms in Broward and Miami Dade counties came from African-American registrants, even though African Americans [made] up only 17 percent of the electorate in Broward and 20 percent in Miami Dade." Miller also notes that statewide there were "nearly three times the number of flagged [i.e. not processed] Democratic registration forms than Republican." Ibid.

87. For a detailed description of the many questionable election practices in Ohio, see *Preserving Democracy: What Went Wrong in Ohio* (House Judiciary Committee Democratic Staff, January 5, 2005), http://www.openvotingconsortium.org/files/Conyersreport.pdf.

88. One problem not directly attributed to Blackwell, but arguably encouraged by him, was that of voting list purges. Robert F. Kennedy Jr., "Was the 2004 Election Stolen?" *Rolling Stone*, June 1, 2006, http://www.rollingstone.com/news/story/10432334/was_the_2004_election_stolen, describes what happened: "Election officials in Cleveland, Cincinnati and Toledo" conducted "a massive purge of their voter rolls, summarily expunging the names of more than 300,000 voters who had failed to cast ballots in the previous two national elections. In Cleveland, which went five-to-one for Kerry, nearly one in four voters were wiped from the rolls between 2000 and 2004." Although many of the removed names "undoubtedly belonged to people who had moved or died, . . . thousands more were duly registered voters who were deprived of their constitutional right to vote—often without any notification—simply because they had decided not to go to the polls in prior elections." *Preserving Democracy: What Went Wrong in Ohio*, 67, 69, and 91, supports Kennedy's contentions. See also Fritz Wenzel, "Purging of Rolls, Confusion Anger Voters; 41% of Nov. 2 Provisional Ballots Axed in Lucas County," *Toledo Blade*, January 9, 2005.

89. William Hershey, "Suit Alleges Voter Impediments: Democrats Say Blackwell Trying to Limit Ballot Access," *Dayton Daily News*, September 28, 2004, B1. *Preserving Democracy: What Went Wrong in Ohio*, 36–39, covers this issue in detail.

90. The directive also required that when county boards received such underweight registration forms, that they should treat them as "an application for a new registration form" and mail out a new application to the voter. Secretary of State J. Kenneth Blackwell,

Directive no. 2004-31 (September 7, 2004). Quoted in *Preserving Democracy: What Went Wrong in Ohio*, 37.

91. Andrew Welsh-Huggins, "Some Election Boards Ignore New Order about Registration Paper," AP Wire, September 30, 2004.

92. Jim Bebbington, "Blackwell Rulings Rile Voting Advocates," *Dayton Daily News*, September 24, 2004, 1B.

93. Ibid.

94. Ibid.

95. Catherine Candisky, "Secretary of State Lifts Order on Voting Forms," *Columbus Dispatch*, September 30, 2004, 1C.

96. Candisky, "Secretary of State Lifts Order on Voting Forms."

97. "Playing with the Election Rules," *NYT*, September 30, 2004, A28.

98. *Preserving Democracy: What Went Wrong in Ohio*, 38.

99. Voting Rights Institute, *Democracy at Risk: The 2004 Election in Ohio* (Democratic National Committee, June 22, 2005), 170, http://a9.g.akamai.net/7/9/8082/v001/www.democrats.org/pdfs/ohvrireport/fullreport.pdf.

100. Quoted in Kennedy, "Was the 2004 Election Stolen?" Kennedy also references a report by "state inspectors who investigated the elections operation in Toledo [and] discovered 'areas of grave concern.' With less than a month before the election, Bernadette Noe," head of the county elections board and Toledo's Republican Party, "had yet to process 20,000 voter registration cards. Board officials arbitrarily decided that mail-in cards (mostly from the Republican suburbs) would be processed first, while registrations dropped off at the board's office (the fruit of intensive Democratic registration drives in the city) would be processed last. When a grass-roots group called Project Vote delivered a batch of nearly 10,000 cards just before the October 4th deadline, an elections official casually remarked, 'We may not get to them'. . . . The most troubling incident uncovered by the investigation," Kennedy notes, "was Noe's decision to allow Republican partisans behind the counter in the board of elections office to make photocopies of postcards sent to confirm voter registrations." In point of fact, "on their second day in the office, the operatives were caught by an elections official tampering with the documents." All told, the state "investigators slammed the elections board for 'a series of egregious blunders' that caused 'the destruction, mutilation and damage of public records.'" See also Norman Robbins, study leader, *Analyses of Voter Disqualification, Cuyahoga County, Ohio, November 2004* (Greater Cleveland Voter Registration Coalition, May 9, 2006), 1–2, http://download11.rbn.com/rstone/rstone/download/misc/AnalysesFullReport.pdf.

101. "Late Voter Registrations Could Cause Election Day Havoc," AP Wire, September 26, 2004.

102. Quoted in "Ohio Registration Gains Matter," *Dayton Daily News*, October 2, 2004, A8.

103. Walter R. Mebane, Jr., "Ohio 2004 Election: New Registrants, Provisional Ballots, Voting Machines, Turnout and Polls Open Elapsed Times in Franklin County Precincts," in Voting Rights Institute, *Democracy at Risk*, 146.

104. Ibid. See also Suzanne Hoholik and Mark Niquette, "Provisional Ballots: Election Directive Rattles Officials: What If Voters Get Unruly? Board Asks," *Columbus Dispatch*, October 7, 2004, 1A; William Hershey, "Blackwell's Directive Draws Rain of Ire," *Dayton Daily News*, October 10, 2004, B3; Mark Niquette, "Judge Blasts Blackwell: Secretary of State Faulted in Provisional-Ballot Case, Accused of Failing Ohio," *Columbus Dispatch*, October 21, 2004, 1A.

105. Hoholik and Niquette, "Provisional Ballots: Election Directive Rattles Officials"; Hershey, "Blackwell's Directive Draws Rain of Ire."

106. In essence, Blackwell's ruling replaced HAVA's "jurisdiction" (which could legitimately mean the county of residence) with the much narrower definition of a "precinct." On this point, see James Dao and Kate Zernike, "Judge Rules for Democrats in Dispute over Ohio Voting," *NYT*, October 15, 2004, A22.

107. Hershey, "Suit Alleges Voter Impediments." See also *Preserving Democracy: What Went Wrong in Ohio*, 5, 10, 12–13, 28, 30–41, 146.

108. Quoted in Hershey, "Suit Alleges Voter Impediments."

109. Gregory Korte and Jim Siegel, "Defiant Blackwell Rips Judge," *Cincinnati Enquirer*, October 22, 2004, 1A.

110. Mark Niquette, "Ohio Won't Count Ballots Cast at Incorrect Precincts," *Columbus Dispatch*, September 25, 2004, 1A.

111. Hershey, "Suit Alleges Voter Impediments."

112. Niquette, "Ohio Won't Count Ballots Cast at Incorrect Precincts."

113. Hoholik and Niquette, "Provisional Ballots: Election Directive Rattles Officials"; Hershey, "Suit Alleges Voter Impediments."

114. Hershey, "Blackwell's Directive Draws Rain of Ire."

115. Mark Niquette, "Suit Aimed at Ballot Rules: State Wrong about Provisionals, Democrats Say," *Columbus Dispatch*, September 28, 2004, 1C; Hershey, "Suit Alleges Voter Impediments."

116. *Sandusky County Democratic Party v. Blackwell*, 339 F. Supp. 2d 975, 996 (ND OH, 2004). See also Mark Niquette, "Provisional Balloting Broadened by Judge: Blackwell's Directive Determined to Be in Violation of Law," *Columbus Dispatch*, October 15, 2004, 1A; Niquette, "Judge Blasts Blackwell." For further proceedings on this matter, see *Sandusky County Democratic Party v. Blackwell*, 340 F. Supp. 2d 810; *Sandusky County Democratic Party v. Blackwell*, 361 F. Supp. 2d 688. At the same time that Judge Carr was ruling in this matter, he rejected a challenge brought by the League of Women Voters of Ohio and other groups against a state requirement that certain first-time voters must show identification at the polls. Mark Niquette, "Blackwell's Decision on Voter ID Is Upheld," *Columbus Dispatch*, October 21, 2004, 2A.

117. Niquette, "Provisional Balloting Broadened By Judge"; Joe Hallett and Mark Niquette, "Provisional Ballots: Blackwell Vows to Fight Ruling: Secretary of State Says He'll Appeal to High Court If Needed," *Columbus Dispatch*, October 16, 2004, 3B; James Dao and Kate Zernike, "Judge Rules for Democrats in Dispute over Ohio Voting," *NYT*, October 15, 2004, A22.

118. *Sandusky County Democratic Party v. Blackwell*, 387 F.3d 565.

119. Kennedy, "Was the 2004 Election Stolen?" text accompanying note 125. Kennedy goes on to remark on how, "to further compound their confusion, the new precinct lines were misidentified on the secretary of state's own Web site, which was months out of date on Election Day." The result would be that "many voters, out of habit, reported to polling locations that were no longer theirs. Some were mistakenly assured by poll workers on the grounds that they were entitled to cast a provisional ballot at that precinct. Instead, thanks to Blackwell's ruling, at least 10,000 provisional votes were tossed out after Election Day simply because citizens wound up in the wrong line." Ibid., text accompanying note 126.

120. Ford Fessenden, "A Big Increase of New Voters in Swing States," *NYT*, September 26, 2004.

121. Bob Fitrakis notes, as example, that "in Cincinnati, some 105,000 voters were moved

from active to inactive status within the last four years [by the Republican-dominated Hamilton County Board of Elections] for not voting in the last two federal elections." Bob Fitrakis, "None Dare Call It Voter Suppression," *FreePress.org*, November 7, 2004 (reprinted in Bob Fitrakis, Steve Rosenfeld, and Harvey Wasserman, eds., *Did George W. Bush Steal America's 2004 Election?: Essential Documents* [Columbus, OH: CICJ Books, 2005], 31).

122. *Preserving Democracy: What Went Wrong in Ohio*, 90. There is no evidence that Democratic county officials did the same to Republican voters, though the possibility of such actions exist.

123. Paul Farhi and Jo Becker, "Some Fear Ohio Will Be Florida of 2004," *WP*, October 26, 2004, A1.

124. On caging, see *Preserving Democracy: What Went Wrong in Ohio*, 40–43; Kennedy, "Was the 2004 Election Stolen?" notes 63–75.

125. Kennedy, "Was The 2004 Election Stolen?" text accompanying notes 64 and 65, explains that "during the summer of 2004, the GOP targeted minority voters in Ohio by zip code, sending registered letters to more than 200,000 newly registered voters in sixty-five counties." Kennedy's comments are based on court filings in "Order Granting Plaintiffs' Motion for a Temporary Restraining Order," *Miller v. Blackwell*, case no. C-1-04-735, October 26, 2004, U.S. District Court for the Southern District of Ohio.

126. One Republican operative, Mark Weaver, an attorney for the Ohio Republican Party, acknowledged the party's use of this technique. See Bill Sloat, "Judge Orders Halt to County Hearings Challenging Voters," *Cleveland Plain Dealer*, October 30, 2004, A1.

127. *Preserving Democracy: What Went Wrong in Ohio*, 40–43.

128. *Miller v. Blackwell*, 348 F. Supp. 2d 916, 921–922. See also *Preserving Democracy: What Went Wrong in Ohio*, 40–41; Andrew Welsh-Huggins, "GOP Asks Appeals Court to Allow Hearings on Challenged Voters," AP Wire, October 28, 2004; Mark Niquette, "Election Officials Happy Now That Provisional-Ballot Issue Is Put to Bed: Ohio GOP Withdraws Thousands of Challenges to New Registrants," *Columbus Dispatch*, October 25, 2004, 1A.

129. Tim Jones, "Court OK's GOP Bid to Challenge Voters," *Chicago Tribune*, November 2, 2004, C14.

130. *Preserving Democracy: What Went Wrong in Ohio*, 43–44. See also Donna Iacoboni, "Judge Cuts Number of Challengers at Polling Stations," *Cleveland Plain Dealer*, October 31, 2004, A1.

131. *Summit County Democratic Central and Executive Committee v. Blackwell*, 2004 U.S. Dist. LEXIS 22539, 24–25. (ND of Ohio, October 31, 2004.) See also Iacoboni, "Judge Cuts Number of Challengers at Polling Stations," for information on the state case and *Spencer v. Blackwell*, 2004 U.S. Dist. LEXIS 22062 (S.D. Ohio, 2004) for the second federal case.

132. At this point, the judges admitted, "The balance of harms in this case is close. If plaintiffs are correct in their view of the law, assuming they have standing because of the likelihood of significant delay, they will suffer irreparable harm. On the other hand, if the plaintiffs are not correct in their view of the law, the State will be irreparably injured in its ability to execute valid laws, which are presumed constitutional, for keeping ineligible voters from voting. In particular, the State's interest in not having its voting processes interfered with, assuming that such processes are legal and constitutional, is great. It is particularly harmful to such interests to have the rules changed at the last minute." *Summit County Democratic Central and Executive Committee v. Blackwell*, 388 F.3d 547, 550–551.

133. Ibid. The U.S. Supreme Court denied an application to vacate the 6th Circuit's

stays of the lower-court rulings. While troubled by the "undoubtedly serious" charges of voter intimidation, Justice John Paul Stevens did not feel that there was sufficient time before the election properly to review the filings and submissions. *Summit County Democratic Central and Executive Committee v. Heider,* 125 S. Ct. 305 (2004) (Stevens, J.). See also Adam Liptak, "Justice Lets Ohio Ruling on Monitors at Polls Stand," *NYT,* November 3, 2004, 6.

134. Bob Fitrakis, "None Dare Call It Voter Suppression," 28.

135. "Voting Issues Keep Courts Busy up to Last Minute," *Cleveland Plain Dealer,* November 3, 2004, S9.

136. Bob Fitrakis and Harvey Wasserman, "Hearings on Ohio Voting Put Election in Doubt," *FreePress.org,* November 11, 2004 (reprinted in Fitrakis, Rosenfeld, and Wasserman, *Did George W. Bush Steal America's 2004 Election?* 40).

137. Michael Powell and Peter Slevin, "Several Factors Contributed to 'Lost' Voters in Ohio," *WP,* December 15, 2004, A1.

138. "In Cuyahoga County, about 52% of this group of rejected provisional ballots were cast in the correct polling place, and, therefore, were due to poll worker failure to inform. Many of the remainder are likely due to registration errors on the part of the BOE or the voter, as explained above, and to occasional failures of the BOE website, which gave voters erroneous polling places." Norman Robbins, "Facts to Ponder about the 2004 General Election," (5-10-06 version), 2, http://www.clevelandvotes.org/news/reports/Facts_to_ Ponder.pdf. See also Spencer Overton, *Stealing Democracy: The New Politics of Voter Suppression* (New York: Norton, 2006), 46, who describes the experiences of Brandi Stenson, who along with her mother and brother stood in the wrong line in her polling place (which led her to the wrong precinct desk, located in the same building as the correct one, but without her name in the voting lists). "We were in the right building," Stenson noted. "We were in the wrong line." Rather than help Stenson find the right line, though, poll workers simply required her to vote provisionally. And since she voted provisionally in the wrong precinct, her votes were not counted. "I feel just like they didn't know what they were doing," Stenson said of the poll workers. "They wanted us to hurry up, because I was asking questions, my mom was asking questions. . . . They were trying to rush us out."

139. *Preserving Democracy: What Went Wrong in Ohio,* 68.

140. Robbins, *Analyses of Voter Disqualification, Cuyahoga County, Ohio, November 2004,* 1–2. In a related report, the NAACP reported that it had "receiv[ed] over 1,000 calls related to voter registration issues, generally from individuals who were not on the voter rolls even though they had voted in previous elections, individuals with questions on how to register, and individuals with concerns about not receiving a voter registration card." Quoted in *Preserving Democracy: What Went Wrong in Ohio,* 67.

141. Quoted in *Preserving Democracy: What Went Wrong in Ohio,* 69.

142. Fitrakis and Wasserman, "New Ohio Voter Transcripts Feed Floodtide of Doubt about Republican Election Manipulation," *FreePress.org,* November 11, 2004 (reprinted in Fitrakis, Rosenfeld, and Wasserman, *Did George W. Bush Steal America's 2004 Election?* 68–69).

143. Fitrakis, "None Dare Call It Voter Suppression," 30. See also Connie Mabin, "Some Cuyahoga County Absentee Ballot Voters Confused over Layout," AP Wire, October 20, 2004.

144. *Preserving Democracy: What Went Wrong in Ohio,* 65–67. See also "Elections Board Replaces Two Absentee Ballots That Omitted Kerry's Name," AP Wire, October 19, 2004; "Kerry's Name Omitted from Some Ballots," *Columbus Dispatch,* October 19, 2004, 2B;

"Oops: A Few Hamilton County Absentee Ballots Sent Out Without Kerry's Name," AP Wire, October 18, 2004.

145. Jon Craig, "New Ballot Machines No Longer in Play: Punch-Card System to Be Used in Most Counties for Election," *Columbus Dispatch*, July 17, 2004, 1C.

146. Fitrakis, "None Dare Call It Voter Suppression," 29.

147. Kennedy, "Was the 2004 Election Stolen?" text accompanying note 132.

148. Carolyn M. Sherman, "Slip-Sliding away in Columbus," *FreePress.org*, November 11, 2004 (reprinted in Fitrakis, Rosenfeld, and Wasserman, *Did George W. Bush Steal America's 2004 Election?*, 33–34); Fitrakis and Wasserman, "Hearings on Ohio Voting Put Election in Doubt," 39.

149. Powell and Slevin, "Several Factors Contributed to 'Lost' Voters in Ohio." Kennedy, "Was the 2004 Election Stolen?" text accompanying note 136, argues, "Long lines were not only foreseeable—they were actually created by GOP efforts. Republicans in the state legislature, citing new electronic voting machines that were supposed to speed voting, authorized local election boards to reduce the number of precincts across Ohio. In most cases, the new machines never materialized—but that didn't stop officials in twenty of the state's eighty-eight counties, all of them favorable to Democrats, from slashing the number of precincts by at least twenty percent." See also Overton, *Stealing Democracy*, 42–48.

150. James Dao, "Voting Problems in Ohio Spur Call for Overhaul," *NYT*, December 24, 2004, A1.

151. Powell and Slevin, "Several Factors Contributed to 'Lost' Voters in Ohio."

152. Bob Fitrakis, "How the Ohio Election Was Rigged for Bush," *FreePress.org*, November 22, 2004 (reprinted in Fitrakis, Rosenfeld, and Wasserman, *Did George W. Bush Steal America's 2004 Election?* 45–47); Bob Fitrakis and Harvey Wasserman, "How a Republican Election Supervisor Manipulated the Vote, in Black and White," *FreePress.org*, November 23, 2004 (reprinted in Fitrakis, Rosenfeld, and Wasserman, *Did George W. Bush Steal America's 2004 Election?* 48).

153. Voting Rights Institute, *Democracy at Risk*, 48.

154. *Preserving Democracy: What Went Wrong in Ohio*; Voting Rights Institute, *Democracy at Risk*; *Moss v. Bush*, case no. 02-2055, Supreme Court of Ohio. Final judgment in this case can be found at *Moss v. Bush*, 105 Ohio St. 3d 458.

155. John McCarthy, "Kerry Concedes after Long Ohio Night," AP Wire, November 3, 2004.

156. John McCarthy, "Candidates Differ on Issues, Unite on Recount," AP Wire, December 9, 2004; "Ohio's Election Recount Changes Some Vote Totals," AP Wire, December 17, 2004; Diane Suchetka, "Ohio Recount Narrows Bush's Margin of Victory," *Cleveland Plain Dealer*, December 29, 2004, B1.

157. The *WP* dismissed assertions of fraud as "conspiracy theories," while the *NYT* declared that "there is no evidence of vote theft or errors on a large scale." Manual Roig-Franzia and Dan Keating, "Latest Conspiracy Theory—Kerry Won—Hits the Ether," *WP*, November 11, 2004, A2; "Editorial: About Those Election Results," *NYT*, November 14, 2004, Section 4, p. 10. See also Miller, *Fooled Again*, 19–25, on the almost conspiracy of silence in the mainstream media over reports from liberal reporters such as Greg Palast.

158. Tom Beyerlein and Mara Lee, "Heavy Turnout Creates Lines, but Process Generally Smooth," *Dayton Daily News*, November 3, 2004, A1. See also Robert D. McFadden, "Voters Find Long Lines and Short Tempers, but Little Chaos at Polls," *NYT*, November 3, 2004, P4; Tom Beyerlein and Mara Lee, "Ohio Voting 'A Remarkable Exercise in Democracy,'" Cox New Service, November 3, 2004.

159. In the scholarly realm, felon voting was by far the hottest topic of discussion.

160. Brandon Keat, "Glitches Add Up for Electronic Vote Machines," *Pittsburgh Tribune Review*, April 21, 2005.

161. Bill Cotterell, "Equipment Test under Fire," *Tallahassee Democrat*, June 9, 2005; "Elections Supervisor: Some Diebold Voting Machines Can Be Hacked," AP Wire, December 15, 2005; "Voting Machines Won't Be Retested, State Officials Say," *MH* (Broward Edition), December 16, 2005; "Voting Machine Inventor Painfully Watching Florida Election," AP Wire, December 16, 2005.

162. David Ingram, "Voting Machines Reassessed: State Must Revamp Many of Them By '06," *Winston-Salem Journal*, June 24, 2005, B1; "Editorial: An Important Election Safeguard," *NYT*, June 10, 2005, A20.

163. Tom Stuckey, "Md. Gov. Doubts State's Election System," AP Wire, February 16, 2006. See also Ann E. Marimow, "Md. Official Resists Call to Change Voting System," *WP*, February 17, 2006.

164. Mark Niquette and Joe Hallett, "Voting Machines Risky, Study Concludes," *Columbus Dispatch*, August 16, 2006; Mark Niquette, "Voting Machines Pass Review: Study Showing Inaccuracies Was Flawed, Say Diebold, Cuyahoga County Board," *The Columbus Dispatch*, August 23, 2006, 3C. See also Joan Mazzolini, "10% of May Ballots Flawed: 'Serious Consequences,' Election Experts Say," *Cleveland Plain Dealer*, August 16, 2006.

165. Nancy L. Othón, "Officials Confident About Voting System Accuracy To Be Checked; Backups Ready If Necessary," *SFSS*, August 25, 2006, 8B; Ralph De La Cruz, "Commentary: E-Voting Without Any Paper Trail Doesn't Get My Vote," *SFSS*, July 2, 2006, 1D; Stephen L. Goldstein, "No 'Verify,' No Trust," *SFSS*, May 10, 2006, 23A; Marc Caputo and Gary Fineout, "New Tests Fuel Doubts About Vote Machines," *MH*, December 15, 2005. See also Mark Niquette and Joe Hallett, "Voting Machines Risky, Study Concludes," *The Columbus Dispatch*, August 16, 2006.

166. Todd Ruger, "Sarasota Elections Office Braces for 'Intense' Recount," Sarasota *Herald Tribune*, November 10, 2006; Tamara Lush, "How Do You Recount Electronic Votes?" *SPT*, November 10, 2006; Phil Davis, "Deja Vu: Another Florida Recount Likely," AP Wire, November 9, 2006. Among the system's reported problems were "proprietary software" and aging machines. "We know one machine completely taken out of service because it was not recording the vote when it was pressed by hand," reported Kindra Muntz of the Sarasota Alliance for Fair Elections. "They were told to use a stylus. Why should they use a stylus when it's supposed to be a touch-screen?" Other machines were simply temperamental, Muntz said. "There were some instances where people aren't pressing hard enough and some instances where people tried over and over again—three, four, five times." John Haughey, "Touch-Screen Debacle Proves Paper's Value," *Desoto Sun Herald*, November 10, 2006.

167. Jeremy Wallace, "Voting Machine Maker Warned of 'Issue,'" *Herald Tribune*, March 14, 2007; Christopher Drew, "Panel Cites Voter Error, Not Software, in Loss of Votes," *NYT*, February 24, 2007. The litigation in state court ended on November 28, 2007. However, as of the writing of this chapter, the political argument over this matter continues unresolved with the Congressional Accountability Office formally investigating the machines used in this election. In addition, Jennings' withdrawal of her suit did "not affect another challenge by 11 voters still pending in the same court." "FL13: Jennings Ends Lawsuit Over 2006 Loss," *Frontrunner*, November 29, 2007.

168. Anthony Man, "Touch-Screen Voting Machines on the Way Out?" *SFSS*, January

31, 2007; Abby Goodnough, "Florida to Shift Voting System with Paper Trail," *NYT*, February 2, 2007.

169. Abby Goodnough, "Florida Governor Is Hoping to Restore Felon Voting Rights," *NYT*, April 3, 2007; Farhad Manjoo, "What Was Charlie Crist Thinking? Why Did a Republican Governor Just Add Tens of Thousands of Democrats to the Voter Rolls in Florida?" *Salon.com*, April 6, 2007, http://www.salon.com/opinion/feature/2007/04/06/crist; Laleh Ispahani, Senior Policy Counsel, Racial Justice Program, National ACLU, and Muslima Lewis, Senior Staff Attorney and Director of Racial Justice and Voting Rights Projects, ACLU of Florida, "ACLU Background Memorandum: Florida Clemency Board Decision," April 6, 2007, http://electionlawblog.org/archives/ACLU %20Florida%20 Clemency%20Memo%204–6–07.pdf.

170. Marc Caputo, "Fla. Voting Machines Can Be Hacked," *MH*, July 31, 2007.

171. Richard Wolf, "States Work on Proposals to Make Voting Easier," *USA Today*, February 26, 2007; Mark Binker, "Legislature: House Tentatively Backs Voter Registration Change," *Greensboro News-Record*, March 28, 2007; "After Election Confusion, R.I. Lawmakers Unveil Reform Bill," AP Wire, February 22, 2007; Diana Bowley, "Compliance with Election Reforms on Track," *Bangor Daily News*, January 23, 2007, B8.

172. Kevin Yamamura, "Touch-Screen Voting Faces Fuzzy Future," *Sacramento Bee*, August 19, 2007, A1; Elizabeth Dwoskin, "Judge Gives New Jersey a Week to Fix Voting Machines," *NYT*, September 6, 2007, B3; Dan Goodin, "E-Voting Gets Bitch-Slapped in California," *The Register*, August 6, 2007, http://www.theregister.co.uk/2007/08/06/california_evoting_decertification/; Dan Goodin, "Surprise: Ohio's E-voting Machines Riddled with Critical Security Flaws," *The Register*, December 17, 2007, http://www.theregister.co.uk/2007/12/17/ohio_voting_machines_study/. A copy of the Ohio report can be found at: http://www.sos.state.oh.us/sos/info/everest.aspx; Joe Milicia, "Cuyahoga County hurriedly switching to new voting system," AP Wire, January 3, 2008; William Poundstone, "A Paper Trail for Voting Machines," *NYT*, January 7, 2008, 21; Clive Thompson, "Can You Count On These Machines?" *NYT*, January 6, 2008, Section 6, 40.

173. On this general point, see Sean Cockerham, "State Defends Voting Security: Polling Machines Leave Verified Paper Trail, Says Washington Elections Director," *News Tribune* (Tacoma, Washington), August 12, 2007.

174. According to the *MH*, the Republican drive to "attack" voter fraud had been ongoing since President Bush's first attorney general, John Ashcroft, launched his "Ballot Access and Voter Integrity Initiative" in 2001. As part of this effort, Justice Department political appointees pressured U.S. attorneys to prosecute voter-fraud cases, and the department's Civil Rights Division effectively rolled back policies to protect minority voting rights. According to Joseph Rich, who left his job as chief of the civil rights section in 2005, these events formed an unmistakable pattern: "As more information becomes available about the administration's priority on combating alleged, but not well substantiated, voter fraud, the more apparent it is that its actions concerning voter ID laws are part of a partisan strategy to suppress the votes of poor and minority citizens." Other areas of concern focused on the Bush administration's shift in enforcement priorities under the National Voter Registration Act, known as the "Motor Voter" law. "In the last six years, the number of voters registered at state government agencies that provide services to the poor and disabled has been cut in half, to one million." In fact, "instead of forcing lax agencies to increase registrations, the Justice Department sued at least six states and sent threatening enforcement letters to others requiring them to scour their election rolls for potentially ineligible voters."

Reviewing these actions, "Deputy Director Michael Slater of Project Vote, a national voter registration group, called this 'selective enforcement. . . . They've focused on purging of voters from registration rolls at the expense of enforcing provisions that encourage registration.'" Greg Gordon, "Voter Turnout Limits Said to Be White House Goal," *MH*, April 19, 2007. See also Richard Wolf, "Legal Voters Thrown off Rolls," *USA Today*, January 1, 2008, http://www.usatoday.com/news/politics/election2008/2008-01-01-voting-rolls_N .htm, for examples of how "Five years after passage of a federal law to create electronic registration databases to deter voter fraud, the new technology is posing hurdles that could disenfranchise thousands of legal voters."

175. "Requirements for Voter Identification," National Conference of State Legislatures, January 9, 2008, http://www.ncsl.org/programs/legismgt/elect/taskfc/voteridreq.htm.

176. Steve Bousquet, "Feds Approve State Election Law Changes," *SPT*, January 24, 2008, http://www.sptimes.com/2008/01/24/State/Feds_approve_state_el.shtml.

177. Eric Lipton and Ian Urbina, "In 5-Year Effort, Scant Evidence of Voter Fraud," *NYT*, April 12, 2007; Ian Urbina, "Panel Said to Alter Finding on Voter Fraud," *NYT*, April 10, 2007; Joel Bleifuss, "The Fraudulence of Voter Fraud: The Bush Administration Purged U.S. Attorneys for Failing to Prosecute Crimes That Didn't Occur," *In These Times*, April 18, 2007, http://www.inthesetimes.com/article/3135/. On the size of the voter fraud problem—or lack of one—see Lorraine C. Minnite, *The Politics of Voter Fraud* (Washington, D.C.: Project Vote, 2007); Justin Levitt, "The Truth About Voter Fraud" (Brennan Center for Justice: New York, 2007).

178. Amy Goldstein, "White House Cites Lax Voter-Fraud Investigations in U.S. Attorneys' Firings," *WP*, March 14, 2007, A6; Mark Follman, Alex Koppelman, and Jonathan Vanian, "How U.S. Attorneys Were Used to Spread Voter-Fraud Fears," *Salon.com*, March 22, 2007, http://www.salon.com/news/feature/2007/03/21/us_attorneys/.

179. *United States v. Missouri* (Case No. 05-4391-CV-C-NKL), U.S. District Court for the Western District of Missouri. At this court noted in its Final Judgment (April 13, 2007), 21–22: "It is also telling that the United States has not shown that any Missouri resident was denied his or her right to vote as a result of deficiencies alleged by the United States. Nor has the United States shown that any voter fraud has occurred. Increased voter participation and elimination of fraud were the primary goals of Congress when it mandated that the States make reasonable efforts to maintain accurate voter registration lists. The absence of evidence of fraud or voter suppression during the relevant time period weighs heavily in favor of a finding that the Defendants' efforts have been reasonable."

180. Adam Cohen, "A Woman Wrongly Convicted and a U.S. Attorney Who Kept His Job," *NYT*, April 16, 2007.

181. Overton, *Stealing Democracy*, 13–14.

Afterword: The Process Matters

1. Richard L. Hasen, "The Untimely Death of *Bush v. Gore*" (March 2007). Loyola-LA Legal Studies Paper No. 2007-21, http://ssrn.com/abstract=976701 and in *Stanford Law Review* 60 (October 2007): 1–44. On *Bush v. Gore* as a vehicle for reform, see Steven J. Mulroy, "Lemonade from Lemons: Can Advocates Convert *Bush v. Gore* into a Vehicle for Reform?" *Georgetown Journal on Poverty Law and Policy* 9 (Summer 2002): 357–377; Richard H. Pildes, "Foreword: The Constitutionalization of Democratic Politics," *Harvard Law Review* 118 (November 2004): 28–154; Daniel P. Tokaji, "First Amendment Equal Protection: In Discretion, Inequality, and Participation," *Michigan Law Review* 101 (June 2003): 2409–2524.

2. Responding in an online discussion of Hasen's article, Kerr asked, "When was the promise of election reform inspired by [Bush v. Gore] ever alive?" *Election Law Blog*, March 29, 2007, *http://electionlawblog.org/archives/2007_03.html.*

3. *Green v. County School Board of New Kent County*, 391 U.S. 430.

4. Gerald N. Rosenberg, *Hollow Hope: Can Courts Bring about Social Change?* (Chicago: University of Chicago Press, 1993); Michael J. Klarman, *From Jim Crow to Civil Rights: The Supreme Court and the Struggle for Racial Equality* (Oxford: Oxford University Press, 2004).

5. *Oregon v. Mitchell*, 400 U.S. 112 (1970). See generally Richard B. Bernstein, *Amending America: If We Love the Constitution So Much, Why Do We Keep Trying to Change It?* (New York: Times Books/Random House, 1993), 138–139.

6. Robert F. Kennedy Jr., "Was the 2004 Election Stolen?" *Rolling Stone*, June 1, 2006, http://www.rollingstone.com/news/story/10432334/was_the_2004_election_stolen. To be sure, electoral fraud and threats to the viability of democracy are not new. The United States has a long and colorful history of electoral manipulation, manipulated voters, and even fraud. Examples of disfranchisement, ballot box stuffing, and questionable election returns litter the historical landscape. Yet none of this history of failure changes the facts of, nor lessens the threats posed by, today's problems. Just because the inadequacies of our election systems have a long history is no justification for accepting such shortcomings. Nor is it grounds to ignore the current threats to our democratic institutions. On the history of electoral fraud and other problems with voting, see Tracy Campbell, *Deliver the Vote: A History of Election Fraud, an American Political Tradition—1742–2004* (New York: Carroll & Graf, 2006), and Andrew Gumbel, *Steal This Vote: Dirty Elections and the Rotten History of Democracy in America* (New York: Nation Books, 2005).

7. Charles S. Sydnor, *American Revolutionaries in the Making: Political Practices in Washington's Virginia* [originally published as *Gentleman Freeholders*] (Chapel Hill: University of North Carolina Press, 1952), 117–118.

8. See generally Michael Kammen, *A Machine That Would Go of Itself: The Constitution in American Culture* (New York: Alfred A. Knopf, 1986).

9. For an informed discussion of some the ways this more nationalized electoral system could be brought about, see Spencer Overton, *Stealing Democracy: The New Politics of Voter Suppression* (New York: Norton, 2006). For a more varied discussion of these prospects, see Ann N. Crigler, Marion R. Just, and Edward J. McCaffery, eds., *Rethinking the Vote: The Politics and Prospects of American Election Reform* (New York: Oxford University Press, 2004).

Appendix 2: A Note on Methodology

1. There have been a few exceptions to this pattern. One very useful example occurred in 1988 when a number of justices agreed to participate in a PBS documentary on the workings of the Supreme Court, *This Honorable Court: Part Two: Inside the Marble Temple*, PBS video, produced by WETA-TV (Washington, D.C.: Greater Washington Educational Telecommunications Association, May 1988). On the Rehnquist Court's publishing, see: William H. Rehnquist, *Centennial Crisis: The Disputed Election of 1876* (New York: Knopf, 2004); William H. Rehnquist, *The Supreme Court*, rev. ed. (New York: Vintage, 2001 [orig. pub., 1987]); William H. Rehnquist, *Grand Inquests: The Historic Impeachments of Samuel Chase and President Andrew Johnson* (New York: William Morrow, 1992); William H. Rehnquist, *All The Laws but One: Civil Liberties in Wartime* (New York: Knopf, 1998); Stephen

Breyer, *Active Liberty: Interpreting Our Democratic Constitution* (New York: Knopf, 2005); Sandra Day O'Connor, *The Majesty of the Law: Reflections of a Supreme Court Justice* (New York: Random House, 2003); Antonin Scalia, *A Matter of Interpretation: Federal Courts and the Law* (Princeton, NJ: Princeton University Press, 1997); Clarence Thomas, *My Grandfather's Son: A Memoir* (New York: Harper, 2007).

2. Exceptions to this pattern include Bob Woodward and Scott Armstrong, *The Brethren: Inside the Supreme Court* (New York: Simon and Schuster, 1979); Edward Lazarus, *Closed Chambers: The First Eyewitness Account of the Epic Struggles inside the Supreme Court* (New York: Times Books, 1998); David Margolick, Evgenia Peretz, and Michael Shnayerson, "The Path to Florida," *Vanity Fair* (October 2004). Online version available via Lexis/Nexis. More recent examples include: Jan Crawford Greenburg, *Supreme Conflict: The Inside Story of the Struggle for Control of the United States Supreme Court* (New York: Penguin, 2007); Jeffrey Toobin, *The Nine: Inside the Secret World of the Supreme Court* (New York: Doubleday, 2007); and Jeffrey Rosen, *The Supreme Court: The Personalities and Rivalries That Defined America*, (New York: Times Books, 2007).

3. When *The Brethren* came out, attorney John P. Frank, a former clerk to Justice Hugo L. Black, condemned the extent to which former Supreme Court law clerks had supplied so much of the behind-the-scenes fodder for Woodward and Armstrong's book. Prior to *The Brethren*, Frank asserted, "there have been no significant breaches of confidences by the young persons employed in that capacity for the 90 or so years since the custom originated. There have been anecdotes—I have published some myself and so have others—but none of these has gone to details of particular cases or to work habits and attitudes of justices as they relate to other justices." When *Closed Chambers* came out in 1998, Supreme Court journalist Tony Mauro announced that "Lazarus' book may be even more damaging than *The Brethren*." The *Economist* magazine went so far as to characterize the book as "an act of betrayal" and a "betrayal of trust" (all quotes taken from David J. Garrow, "'The Lowest Form of Animal Life'? Supreme Court Clerks and Supreme Court History," *Cornell Law Review* 84 [March 1999]: 855–894). As for the *Vanity Fair* article, see Tony Mauro, "High Court Clerks Bemoan '*Bush v. Gore*' Revelations," *Legal Times*, September 28, 2004, http://www.law.com/jsp/article.jsp?id=1095434485225; Scott Ballenger et al., Letter to the Editor, "High Court Clerks and Appellate Lawyers Decry Vanity Fair Article," *Legal Times*, September 27, 2004, 61. The letter to the *Legal Times* was signed by ninety-six people, most of whom formerly clerked for conservative Supreme Court justices; Charles Lane, "In Court Clerks Breach, a Provocative Precedent," *Washington Post*, October 17, 2004, D1.

4. Laura Kalman, "The Power of Biography," *Law and Social Inquiry* 23 (Spring 1998): 493–495.

5. On a positive note, Rehnquist was known for preferring that all communications on a case be in writing. This bodes well for their usefulness to researchers when they open sometime in the future. On Rehnquist's preferences, see Greenburg, *Supreme Conflict*, 15.

6. On the potential pitfalls in using judicial papers, see Kalman, "The Power of Biography," 495–497.

7. The best source of public records on all the postelection litigation are the libraries of Stanford University, http://election2000.stanford.edu/, University of Michigan, http://www.lib.umich.edu/govdocs/elec2000.html#voteequip, and Florida State University, http://www.law.fsu.edu/library/flsupct/sc00-2346/sc00-2346.html and http://www.law.fsu.edu/library/election/index.html, each of which host and maintain collections of most of the public documents filed in the many litigations spawned by the 2000 postelection crisis. Other useful archives are provided by the Legal Information Institute at Cornell

University, http://www.law.cornell.edu/background/election/, Findlaw.com, http://news.findlaw.com/legalnews/us/election/election2000.html, and JURIST Legal News and Research at the University of Pittsburgh's School of Law, http://jurist.law.pitt.edu/election2000.htm.

8. For example, David Boies, *Courting Justice: From NY Yankees v. Major League Baseball to Bush v. Gore, 1997–2000* (New York: Miramax, 2006), W. Dexter Douglass, "A Look Back—One Lawyer's View," *Florida Journal of Law and Public Policy* 13 (Fall 2001): 15–21, and Robert Zelnick, *Winning Florida: How the Bush Team Fought the Battle* (Palo Alto, CA: Hoover Institution, 2001).

9. For example, Margolick, Peretz, and Shnayerson, "Path to Florida."

10. Comments from the justices can be found in a wide range of sources. The most available are recent histories of the Court, such as Jeffrey Toobin, *The Nine*, and Greenburg, *Supreme Conflict*.

11. The number of books in this category are too numerous to list. For a few good examples of the insights that can be gained from an experienced court watcher, see Jeffrey Toobin, *Too Close to Call: The Thirty-Six-Day Battle to Decide the 2000 Election* (New York: Random House, 2001); Richard A. Posner, *Breaking the Deadlock: The 2000 Election, the Constitution, and the Courts* (Princeton, NJ: Princeton University Press, 2001); Howard Gillman, *The Votes That Counted: How the Court Decided the 2000 Presidential Election* (Chicago: University of Chicago Press, 2001); and Bruce Ackerman, ed., *"Bush v. Gore": The Question of Legitimacy* (New Haven, CT: Yale University Press, 2002).

12. There is also the expectation that sooner or later the necessary manuscript sources will open to scholars and we can evaluate in greater detail the course of events.

13. In doing this, I am seeking to abide by historian Laura Kalman's stricture for historians to "give the public a sense of what historians do" when taking on controversial subjects and—as in this case—drawing on limited resources in making an argument or explaining an event. See Laura Kalman, "The (Un?) Bearable Liteness of E-Mail: Historians, Impeachment and *Bush v. Gore*," *Theoretical Inquiries in Law* 4 (July 2003): 579–620.